The Quality of Freedom

Khodorkovsky, Putin, and the Yukos Affair

RICHARD SAKWA

OXFORD

UNIVERSITY PRESS

OXFORD

UNIVERSITY PRESS

Great Clarendon Street, Oxford ox2 6DP

Oxford University Press is a department of the University of Oxford.
It furthers the University's objective of excellence in research, scholarship,
and education by publishing worldwide in

Oxford New York

Auckland Cape Town Dar es Salaam Hong Kong Karachi
Kuala Lumpur Madrid Melbourne Mexico City Nairobi
New Delhi Shanghai Taipei Toronto

With offices in

Argentina Austria Brazil Chile Czech Republic France Greece
Guatemala Hungary Italy Japan Poland Portugal Singapore
South Korea Switzerland Thailand Turkey Ukraine Vietnam

Oxford is a registered trade mark of Oxford University Press
in the UK and in certain other countries

Published in the United States
by Oxford University Press Inc., New York

British Library Cataloguing in Publication Data

Data available

Library of Congress Cataloging in Publication Data

Data available

Typeset by SPI Publisher Services, Pondicherry, India
Printed in Great Britain
on acid-free paper by
CPI Antony Rowe, Chippenham, Wiltshire

ISBN 978–0–19–921157–9

1 3 5 7 9 10 8 6 4 2

Contents

List of Tables   ix
Acknowledgements   x
Preface   xii

1. Introduction: Freedom and Property   1
   Logics of modernity   2
   Dimensions of freedom   5
   Power, property, and the market   14
     A new dual state   14
     Freedom and property   16
     The cultural revolution of property   20
   Varieties of capitalism   24
     Embedding capitalism and development   24
     Liberalism and freedom   27

2. The Birth and Transformation of Yukos   30
   Khodorkovsky: From Komsomol activist to oligarch   31
     Background   31
     Menatep: From banking to industry   33
     Establishment and privatization of Yukos   40
   Yukos: Consolidation and crisis   45
     Consolidation and development   46
     The oligarchs are born   52
     Merger mania   56
     The 1998 partial default   59
     The loser takes the fall   61
   Yukos transformed   62
     A revolution in production   63
     Corporate transformations   67
     Personal issues   70

3. The State and the Oligarchs   74
   Pluralist state to regime consolidation   75
   Putin's policy of 'equidistance'   78
     Muddy waters   79
     Business and state in the new dispensation   84
     Between assaults   86
   From equidistance to subordination   88
     'The State and the Oligarchs'   89
     The revenge of the state   92
     An interaction model   94

Models of the Yukos affair   95
  The ideology of statism   96
  The political theory   99
  The factional theory   101

4. Why Yukos?   108
  A state within a state   108
  Independent political entrepreneurship   112
    Khodorkovsky's defection   113
    Party politics   115
    The reorganization of power   118
    Foreign policy aspects   121
  Yukos in society   123
    Open Russia   123
    Philanthropy and patriotism   126
  Questions of economic policy   128
    Merger of Yukos and Sibneft   129
    Policy conflicts: Pipelines and markets   133
    Rosneft, Gunvor, and the emergence of an anti-Yukos
    'politburo'   139
  Personal aspects   142
    Face to face: 19 February 2003   142
    Personal relations   144

5. The Assault Against Yukos   148
  The assault begins   148
    First arrests   149
    Khodorkovsky's response   151
    Khodorkovsky's arrest   157
    First reactions   158
    Political fallout   161
  Murky matters   164
    Paris and beyond   165
    Avisma, Valmet, and shell companies   168
  The attack on Yukos   170
    Yukos after Khodorkovsky   171
    Tax matters   178
    The 'scam of the year': The sale of Yuganskneftegaz (YNG)   184

6. Khodorkovsky Goes to Jail   188
  Yukos investigated   188
    Pre-trial detention   189
    The case against Khodorkovsky and his associates   193
  Criminal charges   194
    The Apatit case   195
    Pichugin: The Tambov cases and Valentina Korneeva   196

Petukhov and the Nefteyugansk case 199
The East Petroleum case (Yevgeny Rybin) 203
The Mitra and Lesnoi case 204
Khodorkovsky's trial 206
'Basmanny justice' 207
Reaction to the trial and verdict 213
Appeals 218
In the penal colony 222
The Krasnokamensk prison colony: From Rokossovsky
to Khodorkovsky 223
Life as a prisoner 226

7. There Will Be Blood 231
The broader assault 231
The Temerko case 232
The Bakhmina case 234
Vasily Aleksanyan 235
Other cases 237
The end of Yukos 239
Bankruptcy 240
Twisting the knife 245
Civil proceedings 246
The attack continues 248
Further charges 249
International appeals and rulings 254
Problems of state and law 257
International commentary 257
Law and power 262

8. From Oligarch to 'Dissident' 264
Business and the state 265
The crisis of Russian liberalism 268
Features of the crisis 269
Khodorkovsky as political philosopher and commentator 274
Property and freedom 278
Prison and the world: Property and freedom 278
First interview from jail 280
Freedom the Russian way 282
The left turn 284
'Freedom does not bring happiness' 285
Realism or fatalism 287
Another left turn 290
Civil society and development 291
Left Turn 2 293
The world in 2020 296

Freedom, the market, and sovereign democracy   297
    The ambiguities of Russian liberalism   298
    Commentator on Russian politics   300

9. Propaganda and Public Opinion   304
    The struggle for hearts and minds   305
        Media and propaganda   305
        Public relations   308
        Media and martyrdom   311
        Public opinion   312
    Russia's image and foreign policy   314
        Yukos and orange technologies   314
        In the international arena   318

10. Political and Moral Economy   322
    Building national champions   322
        Rosneft and the turn to statism   323
        Gazprom and planned merger with Rosneft   326
        Rosneft goes global   329
        The state and the energy sector   332
    The energy sector and Russia's economy   333
        The economic consequences of the Yukos affair   334
        The dual economy   338
        Continuing consolidation   340
    A new model of political economy   344
        Deprivatization   344
        Towards a new embedded capitalism   348
        Meta-corruption, or an economy of rents   351
        A moral economy   353

11. Polity and Power   357
    Political consequences   358
        Resources and power: The oil curse?   358
        The political system and civil society   365
        The debate on freedom in the wake of Khodorkovsky's arrest   369
    An 'energy superpower'   370
        Energy imperialism?   371
        Resource nationalism   376

12. Conclusion: A Question of Interpretation?   380
    The Yukos case: Right and wrong?   380
    Class and state power   387
    Fate and freedom   392

Bibliography   397
Index   411

List of Tables

2.1. The growth of Yukos   50

2.2. Yukos oil production, 1998–2005   64

5.1. Yukos capitalization   172

5.2. The official income tax rate and actual taxation of selected
    companies (in %)   180

5.3. Budget revenues from the oil and gas sector   182

Acknowledgements

The debts, both intellectual and personal, incurred in a work of this nature are numerous. In working on this book I have been endlessly surprised by the depth of knowledge and thoughtfulness of people on the subject, and their willingness to share their expertise and opinions with me. Although the topic lends itself to polarized views, and indeed there has been no shortage of these, there have also been a rather large number of people who have tried to take a balanced view of the issue. Particularly helpful to me in the development of the book have been the following: Sarah Carey, an independent director of Yukos from 2001 to 2004, chair of the board of the Eurasia Foundation; Irina Demchenko, director of RIA Novosti in London; Thomas Graham, senior director at Kissinger Associates Inc., senior director for Russia on the US National Security Council in 2004–7; Andy Kuchins, the head of Russian and Eurasian programmes at the Center for Strategic and International Studies in Washington, DC; Boris Mezhuev, an independent scholar in Moscow now affiliated with the Foundation for Effective Politics; Vladimir Milov, the head of the Institute of Energy Policy in Moscow; Nikolai Petrov, at the Carnegie Moscow Center; Efim Iosifovich Pivovar, Rector of the Russian State Humanities University (RGGU); William E. Pomeranz, deputy director of the Kennan Institute of the Woodrow Wilson International Center for Scholars; Blair Ruble, Director of the Kennan Institute; Olga Sidorovich, Director of the Institute of Law and Public Policy in Moscow; Dimitri Simes, Director of the Nixon Center; Konstantin Simonov, head of the National Energy Security Foundation in Moscow; and Angela Stent, Director of the Center for Eurasian, Russian and East European Studies at Georgetown University.

I have had so many conversations on the topic that it is almost impossible to recognize all, but I am particularly grateful for talks with, and for the help provided by, Robert Amsterdam, Birgit Bauers, Bruce Bean, Timothy Colton, Anand Doobay, Alexander Doroshenko, Charles Grant, Philip Hanson, Stephen Holmes, Martin Hope, Andrei Kolesnikov, John Laughland, Sergei Markov, Vitaly Merkushev, Leonid Mlechin, Tom Remington, Simon Pirani, Peter Rutland, Peter Solomon, Alexei Venediktov, and Irina Yasina. I would also like to thank Derek Averre, John Barber, Philip Boobbyer, Bill Bowring, Yitzhak Brudny, Julian Cooper, Peter Duncan, Clifford Gaddy, Axel Kaehne, Leonid Ionin, Luke March, Boris Guseletov, Lena Guseletova, Bobo Lo, Neil Robinson, Kasim Sadikeglu, Jonathan Stern, Joan Urban, David White, Stephen White, and Andrei Zagorsky for rich and varied discussions on Yukos and allied issues. There were also numerous interviews with people who have not been willing to go on the record, although they have provided me with much detailed and general background information. I have used most of this material as general briefing and to inform my assessment. The faults, of course, remain my own.

It is my great pleasure to acknowledge the support of British Academy Small Research Grant SG-47170, 'The Yukos Affair and the Development of Russian Energy Policy'. I am particularly pleased to acknowledge the support of the Kennan Institute of the Woodrow Wilson International Center for Scholars, Washington, D.C., which provided a stimulating environment to work on this project while undertaking a Short-Term Fellowship there in November 2007. The award of an Honorary Senior Research Fellowship at the Centre for Russian and East European Studies allowed me access to the rich materials held at the University of Birmingham, for which I am most grateful. I am also grateful for the secretarial and other assistance of Gemma Chapman, Nicola Cooper, Ann Hadaway, and Suzanne Robinson, together with the constant support of Jean Hudson, in the Department of Politics and International Relations at the University of Kent. Above all, I would like to thank Dominic Byatt at OUP for his patience and support for this project.

Preface

In a dawn raid on his plane in Novosibirsk on 25 October 2003 Mikhail Khodor-kovsky, the head of the Yukos oil company, was arrested. This event has spawned a mountain of literature and provoked a debate that shows little sign of abating. By that time Khodorkovsky had become one of the world's richest and most powerful men, while Yukos had been transformed from a ramshackle conglomeration of Soviet production, refining, and distribution units into a vertically integrated oil company that was set to go global. It was Russia's second largest producer, and if the plans to merge with Sibneft had been completed, it would have become the country's biggest oil company, with up to 40 per cent of its stock ready to be sold to an American company. On all counts, this looked like a success story for Russia, but it was precisely at this moment that the authorities struck. After a long period of detention, in May 2005 Khodorkovsky was sentenced to nine years in jail (reduced to eight on appeal) and the Yukos oil company was broken up, its name erased from share registers, and its cheery yellow and green strip, once so common in petrol stations across Russia, has disappeared.

The purpose of this book is to explain why all of this occurred. It will provide some theoretical discussion as well as detailed analysis of the rise and fall of Yukos. It will also examine the relationship between the state and big business during Russia's traumatic shift from the Soviet planned economy to the market system. Since 1985 Russia has been engaged in one of the most grandiose acts of political and economic reconstitution undertaken by any nation in history. Mikhail Gorbachev's 'perestroika' (restructuring) tried to remake the Union of Soviet Socialist Republics (USSR) into a democratic socialist state, but the more successful his reforms, the less was left of the system that he tried to save. In the end, by December 1991 even the country disintegrated into fifteen separate republics. The outcome and consequences for the nation and its people were revolutionary in all fundamental respects.

The revolution continues, and it is in this context that we shall examine the Yukos affair. A revolution has its own laws and dynamics, its victims and its idealism, its heroes and villains, and these were vividly in evidence in Russia's new era of transformation. With President Boris Yeltsin at its head between 1991 and 1999, Russia became a capitalist democracy, but it did so in a revolutionary way—that is, law, constitutionality, and the regular operation of institutions were subordinated to the imperative of change. However, this was a hybrid revolution, since part of the transformation was designed precisely to create the conditions where extraordinary politics no longer needed to apply, and where law and insti-tutions would be able to operate autonomously. The whole process of change in Russia, in its extraordinary depth and intensity while appealing to principles of normality and regularity, was intensely contradictory and gave rise, as we shall see, to a distinctive type of dual state. Freedom would be granted to the nation, but this freedom could only be exercised within the constraints of the logic of the transformative process itself.

Vladimir Putin's assumption of the presidency in 2000 represented a new phase of Russia's hybrid revolution, when contradiction itself became a mode of governance. Every act and institution was imbued with a double valance. The phrase 'dictatorship of law', with which Putin launched his leadership, effectively reveals the use to which he would put contradiction as a governing instrument. His eight-year presidency was committed to restoring the privileges of the state against the declared willfulness of 'oligarchs', the conventional name for the small group of super-rich individuals who profited from the revolutionary change in property ownership in the 1990s (and we shall use the term purely in that conventional sense), as well as regional leaders and other political and social actors. Putin's regime, however, was unwilling to subordinate itself to the constraints of the constitutional state or the supervision of popular representative institutions, notably parties and parliament, and thus it stood outside of the process which it declared to be its goal. Revolutionary expediency once again came into contradiction with the revolution's attempt to transform Russia into a law-based democratic capitalist state.

It is in the forks of this contradiction that the Yukos affair developed, and in which Khodorkovsky was brought low. Khodorkovsky himself was no stranger to the contradictory essence of Russia's latest revolution, and thus he was both Putin's antagonist and at the same time a protagonist of the contradiction that Putin's regime reflected. We should be wary, therefore, of unduly romanticizing Khodorkovsky's resistance to the consolidation of Putin's statism and model of political economy, although giving due weight to dignity and courage in adversity; or indeed, of aligning with the Putinite view that this 'over-mighty subject' embodied a threat to the government's ability to forge policies and strategies that represented the interests of the many and not the few. We should also distinguish between the attack on Khodorkovsky personally and the assault against the Yukos oil company, although in practice the two campaigns are almost inseparable. The reason for this fusion is that the logic of the two campaigns had a common source: to remove a challenge to the regime's putative prerogatives in the political sphere; and to assert those same prerogatives in economic life. It is not entirely clear whether the attack on Yukos was a consequence of the personal attack on Khodorkovsky, or vice versa; whether Khodorkovsky's persecution was a by-product of the state's attack on Yukos as it (or some faction within the regime) attempted to achieve a partial redistribution of the property settlement of the 1990s.

The attack on Khodorkovsky, according to Brzezinski, had 'far-reaching systemic consequences. It wedded political power with financial wealth, setting Russia on the way to state capitalism. The other oligarchs, intimidated like the *boyars* before them, bowed to power but were then allowed to share their wealth with power. Oligarchic sycophancy became the norm.'[1] There is much truth in this, although the contradictory nature of the system is obscured in such a

---

[1] Zbigniew Brzezinski, 'Putin's Choice', *The Washington Quarterly*, Vol. 31, No. 2, Spring 2008, p. 99.

one-dimensional presentation. The Yukos affair did have systemic consequences: the other oligarchs were certainly cowed while the regime emerged with no serious competitors, but while statism was reinforced, it would be an exaggeration to talk of the creation of state capitalism. There were a range of short-term consequences, including a dip in inward investment, a rise in capital flight, and some disruption in oil output, but these soon recovered. The most important long-term outcome was the consolidation of a *dirigiste* political economy, in contrast to the neo-liberalism of the 1990s, in which the state asserted its assumed right to oversee the national economy. This was a state-directed economic strategy that fell short of state capitalism, and even more state corporatism, and certainly lacked central planning. *Dirigisme* in the economy was accompanied by regime consolidation at the political level, although this was not full-blown authoritarianism but heavy-handed political management. State capitalism was not introduced, but a rather more interventionist state created state corporations in what it considered strategic sectors of the economy as part of a state-directed modernization strategy. A dual economy emerged to accompany the dual state.

Two key issues emerge, and will be at the centre of this study. The first is the relationship between agency (in this case Khodorkovsky and Yukos on the one hand, and Putin and the regime on the other) and structure (Russia's transformation into a capitalist democracy on the one hand, and Russia's apparent systemic proclivity for statist authoritarianism on the other). Two agents and two structures came into collision. Thus the work will engage in an act of historical reconstruction, tracing the story of Khodorkovsky's emergence during perestroika as one of the country's leading entrepreneurs, the development of Yukos in the Yeltsin years into one of the country's most predatory and dynamic oil majors, the transformation of the company into a modern corporation in the early Putin period, and then the epochal confrontation between business and state that culminated in Khodorkovsky's arrest and imprisonment, accompanied by the destruction of the Yukos company. Like Henry II, Putin turned on 'this troublesome priest', and the confrontation between the state and temporal power that led to the murder of Thomas Becket on 29 December 1170 reappeared in a new guise as a struggle between political and economic power. Equally, as the eccentric study of the Plantagenets by John Harvey demonstrates, in Becket's behaviour as Archbishop of Canterbury 'there is a sad atmosphere of cant'.[2] This did not prevent Becket becoming a saint, and while an equally strong strain of cant can be found in Khodorkovsky's utterances, his status as a political victim of the Russian regime is no less evident. The causes and consequences of this extraordinary confrontation between the two great forces of modernity, the state and the market and their associated conceptions of freedom, will be at the centre of this analysis. As always, events in Russia act as a mirror to the age, laying bare the sinews of ambition and purpose. This is a classical 'modern' story, with larger-than-life characters engaged

---

[2] John Harvey, *The Plantagenets* (London, Fontana/Collins, [1948] 1967), p. 45.

in struggles for wealth and power, and can be understood in classical modernist terms through detailed analysis of sources, speeches, and acts.

The second theme is rather less susceptible to such methods, although it is no less a modernist aspiration—the struggle for freedom. However, freedom in the abstract is almost meaningless. Freedom is always embedded in a specific set of social relations, and it is in the terrain of the proper limits and scope for freedom that the most important tracts in Western political philosophy have been concerned. We certainly do not intend to reprise these debates in detail in this work, but neither can any study of the Yukos affair avoid referring to them. It is not just that this conflict between economic and political power raises many of the questions whose apparent resolution in Marxian socialism had given birth to the Soviet Union in the first place, but also that the transcendence of communism raised no fewer questions of theory and practice. The Yukos affair can be viewed as little more than a tawdry conflict between self-aggrandizing individuals and elite groups, and while this was certainly part of the story, to limit ourselves to this would be to miss its profound implications; instead, we need to understand the complex dynamics of Russia's hybrid revolution, and also deal with larger questions about post-communist transformations as a whole.

The Yukos affair can be examined through three sets of issues: the philosophical, developmental, and moral/civic. In philosophical terms, the Yukos affair raises fundamental questions about the embeddedness of freedom in a set of liberal human and property rights, the presumption of collective privileges, the challenge of mutuality and collective responsibility, and the ability of the state to act as the embodiment of the public good. What good is freedom, the right to vote and freedom of movement, as many in post-communist Russia would ask (along with Amartya Sen in his disquisitions on developing societies), if a people does not have equal and free access to health, education, and other welfare benefits? The second set develops this question and focuses on classical issues of models of modernization. More specifically, how could property acquired in a 'revolutionary' way in the 1990s be made legitimate, and what is the most appropriate model of economic and social progress in a country that had already twice pursued different models of development (the Tsarist and the Soviet). On a more specific level (our third set), the Yukos affair, for participants and observers alike, raised fundamental questions of individual moral responsibility and conscience, as well as problems of civic engagement.

What does 'civility' mean when faced not only with an aggressive state that suffocated independent civic initiatives, but also by a no less aggressive invasion of private and public space by the values of the market, unchecked by the values of the epoch of high liberalism that reserves even within civil society a sphere of civil activity relatively free from the commercialization that is characteristic of the market. The loss of earlier bonds of mutuality and the relatively simple moral decisional universe of the late Soviet years gave rise to a simplified dissident mentality that coloured much of the discussion of the Yukos affair, accompanied by a no less simplified popular narrative about the 'good old days' of the Soviet era and the injustices of the 1990s. The official narrative raised the 1990s to quasi-mythical status, as a decade of corruption, theft, decline, state disintegration, and humiliation in world politics. On this basis the Putin regime advanced a mix of 'reactionary' and 'remedial' policies: reactionary, as a counteraction to the 1990s, but by the same token perpetuating some of the arbitrariness of that period, though from the opposite end of the spectrum; and remedial, since the fundamental principles of the market and political order created in the 1990s were not challenged but some of its alleged excesses were to be treated. However, as the Yukos affair developed the regime moved beyond reactionary and remedial actions and, buoyed by rising energy rents, began to develop a transformative agenda.

Myths serve as shorthand to represent political truths, a 'fiction that gives us the facts' in Sally Vickers' pithy phrase, and for the Putin regime the chaos of the 1990s became almost a foundation myth against which it built a counter-narrative of economic stability, state restoration, sovereign democracy, and the assertion of the country's interests in world politics. Those who threatened this myth of restoration, like Khodorkovsky, came to be seen as a threat to the maintenance of stability and effective governance. Countering this, Khodorkovsky ever more energetically propounded his own narrative of events: the independent businessman who by the use of entrepreneurial flair and civic engagement would free Russia from baneful statism, corruption, and heavy-handed political control, and allow the country to flourish in partnership with the West. Thus a number of competing narratives competed and interacted with each other.

This is the story of Khodorkovsky's rise and fall, as well as that of his company, Yukos, combined with elements of the larger story of the development of the Russian oil industry and energy policy from the 1990s, as well as the development of democracy, the polity, and the market as a whole. There will inevitably be elements of neo-Kremlinology, the attempt to ascertain what really was going on within the corridors of power, but this will be based less on speculation than on empirical study of the dynamics of factional conflict. The study is not only about Khodorkovsky, but also about those who write about him. There are numerous competing narratives: Khodorkovsky as hero who built up one of Russia's most successful companies, who was brought down in his prime since his success threatened the prerogatives of a narrow political elite and the bureaucracy; as a speculator who levered his Communist Youth League (Komsomol) and political connections to become one of Russia's powerful oligarchs, and who treated politicians and the state as just one more commodity, and who used all his efforts to avoid paying taxes while the mass of the people sank into poverty; or the tale of a Soviet individual who through luck and skill built up a successful company no different from a dozen others, was brought low by political enemies, but who in jail found himself and became the conscience of the nation. As Panyushkin writes in his book on Khodorkovsky's time in prison: 'Khodorkovsky is like a forum in which we, people living in Russia, argue about what we are. Half assert that we are a great nation. The other half affirm that we are slaves without rights. The choice is yours.'[3] He goes on to say: '[T]he Khodorkovsky affair is not about how they jailed an oligarch, or about how unfair are the Russian courts. It is about how someone in Russia can become free. And what happens to them when they do.'[4] It is also, we may add, about recognizing the limits of that freedom.

Canterbury, July 2008

---

[3] Valerii Panyushkin, *Mikhail Khodorkovskii: Uznik tishini. Istoriya pro to, kak cheloveku v Rossii stat' svobodnym i chto emu za eto budet* (Moscow, Sekret Firmy, 2006), frontispiece.

[4] Ibid, p. 7.

1

Introduction: Freedom and Property

> In the early 1990s our people were paupers—and it's ridiculous to say they
> were free. When you have a car to ride in and things to buy—that's freedom.
>
> Vladislav Surkov[1]

In a lavishly illustrated analysis of the development of the Russian oil industry,
sponsored by Yukos, Mikhail Khodorkovsky praised the historical achievements
of Russian business, and in particular the oil industry. In his Foreword he wrote:

> Russia ended its twentieth century with a collapse, and this led many Russians to lose faith
> in their country, in their own abilities. The rethinking of the Russian past was inevitable
> after the era of Soviet historiography, but this has also been disappointing. The achieve-
> ments in which many generations took pride turned out to be propagandistic myths.
> However, a new unbiased approach to the history of our motherland reveals hundreds of
> glorious episodes in its past, which the Soviet period denigrated for political reasons.

The oil industry in Khodorkovsky's view was one of these 'glorious episodes'.
He stressed that in the early twentieth century it developed largely through the
application of private capital, while 'the interference of the state provided only
short-term benefits and usually provoked long-term problems'. He praised the
largely forgotten heroes of the development of the oil industry in the Soviet period.
The book, now sponsored by Yukos, brings together evidence of three centuries
of development, which gives the country its current pre-eminent position in the
field.[2] The story of Yukos illustrates some of these themes: the heroic struggle to
force oil from the ground and to get it to markets through the unsung labour of
the prospectors, engineers, and oil workers; the tension between state intervention
and private capital; and the role of the larger-than-life entrepreneurs, of whom
Khodorkovsky was only one of a long line. His words also had a prophetic ring in
that the struggle over the interpretation of events had been characteristic in both
the imperial and Soviet periods, and continues in contemporary discussions of the
Yukos affair.

---

[1] Quoted by Neil Buckley, 'From Shock Therapy to Consumer Cure: Russia's Middle Class Starts
Spending', *Financial Times*, 31 October 2006.

[2] *Russkaya neft' o kotoroi my tak malo znaem* (Moscow, Neftyanaya kompaniya Yukos and izdatel'stvo 'Olimp-Biznes', 2003), p. 5.

LOGICS OF MODERNITY

The Yukos oil company was established in the early 1990s, and within a decade it had grown to become one of the world's major players. By the end of its first decade the company improved its corporate governance, rejecting some of the worst predatory and ruthless aspects of the 1990s, so that by 2003 it had become a model for the development of modern Russian corporate capitalism. However, in that year the government launched a sustained assault against some of the company's leading executives and associates, and by October of that year Khodorkovsky himself was in jail. The charges against him and his colleagues focused on tax avoidance and fraud, but as we shall see, numerous other factors were involved, including Khodorkovsky's alleged political ambitions. At issue fundamentally was the question raised by Khodorkovsky in his Foreword cited above: the appropriate relationship between the state and private capital, and who would determine key issues of economic policy and strategic development. Two logics of modernity collided, each coherent and valid in its own terms, and gave rise to what we shall call the Yukos affair.

The Yukos affair exercised a profound influence on Russian politics in the early part of the twenty-first century, but it also raised universal issues about the role of the state in developmental agendas, the quality of political relationships, and, indeed, about the very category of 'freedom'. Our concern in addressing the problem of freedom in contemporary society is not so much philosophical but 'spiritual', in the original sense of the term as dealing with conscience, responsibility, and obligations towards the broader community. While 'freedom' may well have come to Russia in the 1990s following the collapse of communism, the unaccustomed conditions meant that the necessary framework of constraints, limits, and mutual responsibilities was lacking. Society had lost its moral compass, and thus individuals and the state as a whole were deprived of the usual signifiers that convey the moral code of a society down the generations.

It was in this world that a group of individuals were able to exploit their skills and connections, and to establish the basis for a capitalist democracy characterized by the mega-wealth of a few and the immiseration of the many. Russia endured what Milton Friedman called 'shock therapy', but tempered economically by entrenched and new interests that exploited the weakened state to their own advantage. A plutocratic social order was created in which the political and economic elites converged (although they did not merge), and wealth was concentrated in the hands of a few. From a Marxist viewpoint this was once again a period of 'primitive accumulation', although building on two earlier industrialization campaigns in the late tsarist and early Soviet periods, and accompanied therefore less by 'extra-economic coercion' than by 'intra-economic' violence. Accompanied by the rhetoric of neo-liberal globalization, a man-made disaster was inflicted upon the nation that was exploited by economic entrepreneurs, notably the so-called oligarchs, and their Western allies.[3] This was Schumpeterian

---

[3] Cf. Naomi Klein, *The Shock Doctrine: The Rise of Disaster Capitalism* (London and New York, Allen Lane, 2007), who writes about the early 1990s and the launching of 'shock therapy': 'many of

'creative destruction' on a grand scale.[4] Russia swiftly became one of the most unequal societies in the world, and one in which a select group was able to forge mutually beneficial ties between the political and economic levels. However, in these years the foundations of Russian capitalism were established, and the basis laid for the economic boom that began in 1999 and lasted throughout the years of Vladimir Putin's presidency (2000–08), fuelled by high energy prices. Yukos thrived in the environment of the 1990s, where connections with power were one of the most important business assets and the courts were used to ensure the necessary outcomes. With Putin's ascent to power, however, a new model of state–business relations was imposed, dubbed the policy of 'equidistance': no business tycoon would be allowed to have a privileged relationship with the state, and they would all be held equally at arm's length. Within the state, however, a group of economic entrepreneurs emerged with their own agendas.

The new system worked well enough in the first years of Putin's leadership. Some of the more egregiously political of the so-called oligarchs were humbled, notably Vladimir Gusinsky and Boris Berezovsky, and both ended up in exile. The business community as a whole was not unhappy to see them go, since their flamboyant model of capitalism tended to discredit the capitalist system as a whole. The Yukos company continued to thrive, and moved towards the Western model of corporate governance. By early 2003 there were plans to merge with the Sibneft oil company, which would have created a major world energy company. At the same time, Yukos took on an ever more political role, and Khodorkovsky increasingly made little secret of his political ambitions. The details of this period will be discussed later, including the many reasons for the estrangement between the regime and Yukos, and personally between Putin and Khodorkovsky.

The Yukos affair revealed the clash between the logic of two different spheres. While Khodorkovsky represented the claim that the business world had the right to engage in political life to shape conditions suitable for its own purposes, Putin insisted that the state had the right to pre-eminence not only in the political sphere, but also over the broad directions of economic policy. Indeed, Putin went further in insisting that the state had the right to a dominant voice in detailed issues, including the direction of pipelines and access to resources and markets. Above all, the model of politics that Putin operated meant that the regime claimed a specific tutelary right over the management of the political system. For Putin, democracy was less a set of institutions but, to paraphrase Michael Mann, 'an ideology of equality, one that legitimates itself through a claim to represent the people and aims at a popular redistribution of social power'.[5] Equally, Amitai

Washington's power brokers were still fighting a Cold War. They saw Russia's economic collapse as geopolitical victory, the decisive one that ensured U.S. supremacy', p. 250.

[4] Joseph A. Schumpeter, *Capitalism, Socialism and Democracy*, fifth edition (London, George Allen & Unwin, 1976).

[5] The paraphrase is by Dylan Riley, 'Democracy's Graveyards?', *New Left Review*, No. 48, November–December 2007, pp. 125–36, at p. 125, reviewing Michael Mann, *The Dark Side of Democracy: Explaining Ethnic Cleansing* (Cambridge, Cambridge University Press, 2005).

Etzioni argues that security is the prerequisite for the development of democratic institutions, and not the other way round, as the occupying forces understood in Germany and Japan after the Second World War, but not in Iraq in 2003[6]—a sentiment that fully accords with Putin's views. As far as Putin was concerned, politics was far too important to be left to the free play of political forces, and thus the regime had not only the right but also the duty to manage day-to-day political matters. The free play of market forces came up against the concept of *dirigisme* in economic and political life, accompanied by a redistribution of power away from independent economic actors (notably the oligarchs) to the bureaucracy: not quite a 'popular redistribution of social power' in Mann's sense but a corrective to previous policies that was certainly popular. Although communism had collapsed a decade and half earlier, and with it belief in total state-sponsored modernization, the struggle between free market principles and the idea that the state has a higher responsibility to its citizens had certainly not died.

As we shall see, the Yukos affair has a resonance in debates and renewed leftist political programmes in Latin America, in particular in the Venezuela of Hugo Chávez and the Bolivia of Evo Morales. The hegemony of neo-liberalism was challenged on both theoretical and empirical grounds, and above all in the political sphere. How can we speak of freedom when there is gross inequality and the aggregative role of the state is undermined by particularistic interests?[7] The Yukos affair thus raises questions about the neo-liberal project; but it also poses the problem more broadly about the transferability of Western-style liberalism and its universality. At the same time, the Yukos affair took place against the background of President George W. Bush's enhanced rhetoric for a 'freedom' agenda. The National Security Strategy signed by Bush on 21 September 2002 returned to the theme advanced by Woodrow Wilson nearly a century earlier, that America's historical mission was freedom: 'We created this nation to make people free, and we, from the point of view of conception and purpose, are not limited to America, and now we are making people free. If we do not do this then the whole glory of America will evaporate, and its power dissolve.' The extract was quoted in a book edited by Khodorkovsky (which we discuss in Chapter 8), and commented on as follows: 'These codes of power hardly fit into the political semantics of modernity.'[8]

<hr/>

[6] Amitai Etzioni, *Security First: For a Muscular, Moral Foreign Policy* (New Haven, CT, Yale University Press, 2007).

[7] Cf. Ernest Gellner and Cesar Cansino (eds.), *Liberalism in Modern Times: Essays in Honour of José G. Merquior* (Budapest, Central European University Press, 1996).

[8] Aleksandr Neklessa, 'Bitva za novuyu zemlyu: Prishestvie postsovremennogo mira', in M. B. Khodorkovskii (ed.), *Mir v 2020 godu* (Moscow, Algoritm, 2007), pp. 60–141, at p. 88. Thomas Carothers comments on this as follows: 'The Bush line on a "global freedom agenda" unfortunately caused people all over the world to distrust and dismiss democracy promotion as a rhetorical cover for the projection of U.S. power, a projection they believe often contravenes democracy and employs objectionable methods'; 'Is a League of Democracies a Good Idea?', Carnegie Endowment for International Peace, *Policy Brief*, May 2008, p. 6.

DIMENSIONS OF FREEDOM

The Yukos affair represented a clash between various concepts of freedom, including the personal and the political. The struggle between economic and political power, between individual self-affirmation and representations of the collective interest, took place in the broader context of a narrative of 'transitional' politics in which a categorical view of democratization as the highest public good was challenged by the regime's view that sovereign development was a higher value. While not denying democracy as its fundamental legitimating ideology, it was ranked alongside other public goods, above all, security, stability, and welfare. Putin's 'reactionary-remedial' approach was part of a meta-transition from the perceived disintegration and disorder of the previous decade (a new Time of Troubles, *smutnogo vremeni*) to state stabilization and development, to which standard Western definitions of 'transition' as the move from authoritarianism to democracy were subordinated.

Maurice Cranston notes that while freedom has a positive connotation in the Anglo-Saxon world, deprived of its context it is one of the vaguest concepts in political philosophy:

The word 'freedom'—like its synonym 'liberty'—has a strong laudatory emotive meaning for English-speaking people, whether in political or more general use. But what of its descriptive meaning? That we have seen must vary with the context. In itself, the word 'freedom' cannot be said to have more than a *partial* descriptive meaning. For the word to be understood the listener must...understand what any particular freedom is freedom from or freedom for.[9]

In the Yukos affair we are faced with different understandings of freedom. These are denoted by separate words in the Russian language, and each raises aspects of interest to us. The classic Russian word for freedom or liberty is *svoboda*, defined by Dahl in his dictionary as 'the ability to act as one wishes, the absence of restrictions, slavery or subordination to the will of another'.[10] This is the primordial political sense of freedom, characterized above all by the absence of undue restraint by coercive power, accompanied by the ability to make pertinent life choices. Khodorkovsky would implicitly claim that he was exercising his inalienable right to *svoboda*. However, the logic of Putin's action suggests that this was not at all the way that he would define Khodorkovsky's exercise of freedom, and instead suggested he was engaging in *proizvol*, a type of wilful and arbitrary practice that lacks a sense of duty or mutual obligation. There is also a third way in which freedom can be translated from the Russian; *volya*, literally meaning will or volition, hence *svobodnaya volya* means free will, but there is also the meaning of freedom and liberty. The populist movement of the 1870s, *Narodnaya Volya*, which in 1874 and 1875 descended upon a rather bewildered peasantry, is usually translated as 'People's Will', but it also has some of the other connotations.

---

[9] Maurice Cranston, *Freedom*, third edition (London, Longmans, Green & Co., 1967), p. 15.

[10] Vladimir Dal', *Tolkovyi slovar' zhivogo velikorusskogo yazyka*, Vol. 4 (Moscow, Russkii Yazyk, [1882] 1980), p. 151.

There is thus considerable controversy over how best, from a literal perspective, to understand the concept of 'freedom' in the Russian context. The richness of the vocabulary, which makes the work of translation so difficult, indicates the complexity with which the substance of the idea of freedom is appreciated in Russian social life.

The concept of freedom is undoubtedly a contested concept, and the Yukos affair brought various formulations sharply into focus. Putin's administration ever more demonstratively rejected the 'philosophical imperialism' of decontextualized approaches to freedom, which prioritized democracy over public order issues, security, and development, and rejected attempts by hegemonic systems to impose a way of life that had taken centuries to develop in certain countries on other societies within an accelerated time frame. As far as Putin was concerned, this would represent depriving a society of its freedom to choose its developmental path. The ahistorical notion of democracy removed it from its roots as a way of managing intra-elite and societal conflicts and gave it an absolutism that ignored historical processes of rule setting. However, in rejecting the tutelary authority of the international democratization regime, the administration enhanced its own tutelary powers over society, and thereby limited the freedom of its own citizens to express themselves politically or for social forces to interact in a liberal pluralist manner.

The Yukos affair stands at the vortex of fundamentally different appreciations of the relationship between the right of citizens to develop political forms of representation, and the demand by modern states that in certain fundamental respects people are subjects, to be subordinated to the military and developmental projects of the government. We thus have conflicting demands, which in an unformed system such as Russia's in the post-communist era could take particularly sharp forms. The tensions between citizenship and subjecthood, between political and economic representations of selfhood, are by the same token rendered more transparent. Although much of Russian politics at this time was deeply opaque, the philosophical issues could not be more transparent, although that certainly does not render them any simpler or amenable to facile resolution. Let us now posit four representations of freedom, as they manifested themselves in the Yukos affair. We make no claims for philosophical profundity, but argue that without an understanding of the conflict between conceptual orientations, the Yukos affair is reduced to little more than a banal conflict over property and power. It certainly was this, but it also reveals the conflict between deeper ideological and theoretical tendencies in Russian life in the early post-communist period.

1. Active citizenship and liberalism

We can characterize the first as a model of active citizenship within the framework of a liberal society. Khodorkovsky in effect claimed his right as a citizen to become involved in political life on his terms, without deferring to the existing power system. He carved out a vision of what an oppositional political figure could look like and how such a figure should act. By the time of his arrest in 2003

Khodorkovsky forcefully asserted his claim to exercise his political rights and personal freedoms in the public domain. For him, freedom increasingly meant 'expression of individuality, or self-expression'.[11] For Khodorkovsky, freedom increasingly became interpreted as the absence of impediments, a classically liberal approach that helped align his aspirations with the dominant values in the Euro-Atlantic political community, but which are not the values predominant in Russia. Khodorkovsky repudiated the stoicism that is characteristic of Russian political subjectivity, and which as we shall see was accentuated (particularly in the business class) as a result of the Yukos affair, and insisted that indifference was not a political category that he could accept. Instead in a number of ways, including the creation of the Open Russia Foundation, Khodorkovsky sought to shape the political environment.

Differences between liberal and radical ideas of freedom are conventionally reduced to the tension between 'positive' and 'negative' freedom.[12] T. H. Green had already developed the notion of positive freedom as being more than the absence of restraint or encumbrance but the 'capacity to do or enjoy something that is worth doing or enjoying'.[13] This precisely describes Khodorkovsky's approach: the fall of Soviet power removed the constraints on economic and civic life, but it would take boldness and courage to actualize the new potential, and Khodorkovsky demonstrated both. What he did lack, however, was an inner restraint. Although he may have lacked self-awareness, he was nevertheless always an acute observer of changing social and political realities.

For radicals, without mechanisms to ensure that the conditions of freedom are equal for all, freedom becomes ' "merely negative", freedom from some constraint which is irrelevant in the absence of the enabling conditions'.[14] The partisans of negative freedom stress that the absence of coercion, however exercised, is rather more than 'mere'; and provides the framework for self-affirmation in personal and economic life. As Berlin recognizes, to live in a political community entails the exercise of constraints, and therefore we encounter 'the central question of politics—the question of obedience and coercion'; why someone should obey anyone else, and the conditions and limits of that obedience.[15] Berlin cites Benjamin Constant's concerns, in the shadow of the French revolution and its Rousseauan extension of state interference in every aspect of a citizen's life, that the transfer of 'sovereignty' from a monarch to popular government makes little difference to the individual crushed by despotic power in whatever forms it comes, including the rule of oppressive laws.

---

[11] Christian Bay, *The Structure of Freedom* (Stanford,CA, Stanford University Press, 1958), p. 15.

[12] For the classic statement, see Isaiah Berlin, 'Two Concepts of Liberty', in his *Four Essays on Liberty* (Oxford, Oxford University Press, 1969), chapter 3, pp. 118–72.

[13] From the review of Ben Wempe, *T. H. Green's Theory of Positive Freedom: From Metaphysics to Political Theory* (Imprint Academic, 2006), *The Times Higher Educational Supplement*, 20 October 2006, p. 28.

[14] Stanley I. Benn, *A Theory of Freedom* (Cambridge, Cambridge University Press, 1988), p. 139.

[15] Berlin, 'Two Concepts of Liberty', p. 121.

For Boris Kapustin the tension between 'freedom from the state' and 'freedom through the state' is central, and is a theme that is at the centre of debates in the 2000s. In 1999 he noted:

We have acquired freedom from the state to some extent (from the pressure of official ideology and censorship, from the arbitrary rule of an only employer represented by the state, from the 'vigilant eye' of the political police). We have not acquired the rights and freedoms that can exist only under the state protection and due to its creative activity: the right to be free of crime, to live in a healthy environment, and the right of access to minimally acceptable 'social boons' of national health service, education, and social security. Liberal freedoms, unlike individual and group arbitrariness, cannot be achieved in the context of a decayed, corrupt, and technically impotent state.... Liberal freedoms cannot be achieved through separating the state from society.[16]

Kapustin insisted that if the Russian liberals were truly dedicated to freedom they would do more than condemn the communist past and the Communists of the time, organized in the Communist Party of the Russian Federation (CPRF), but would devise a critique of the 'pseudo-liberal' regime in power, which had separated itself from society and 'was privatised by the clans embodying the unity of power and property'. For him liberalism represented an 'eternal dissatisfaction with what has been achieved and a clear understanding that freedom is not a fact but rather a new possibility of human existence to which their active will is directed'. Liberalism was a process, and the establishment of the basic institutions of representative democracy in Russia in the early 1990s was far from denoting the triumph of liberalism. Thus the ideology of the end of history, propounded by Francis Fukuyama and others, meaning the 'final' triumph of liberalism, was for Kapustin 'an ideology of its death as the force of spirit and freedom'.[17] For Kapustin the core of liberalism is a response to the problem of human existence in modernity, arguing that the foundation of social order and communal existence is individual freedom, defined as the right (i.e. the ability and possibility) of a person to act at their own discretion.[18] The institutional forms that this could take, however, were stymied in Russia, and no way was found to combine 'the maximisation of private benefit' with 'a system of universal usefulness' without recourse to 'authoritarian-despotic methods'.[19] The contradiction between individual benefit and public good had come to crisis point by the time Putin came to power, and ultimately once again the problem was forcefully resolved.

2. Constrained citizenship and paternalism

The second model of freedom can be defined in terms of constrained citizenship and an ideology of paternalism. If the first model draws more on John Locke, then the second tends towards Thomas Hobbes. Freedom for liberals is

---

[16] Boris Kapustin, ' "Freedom from the State" and "Freedom Through the State" ', *Social Sciences*, No. 3, 1 July 1999.

[17] Loc. cit.

[18] B. G. Kapustin, 'Tri rassuzhdeniya o liberalizme i liberalizmakh', *Polis*, No. 3, 1994, pp. 13–26.

[19] B. G. Kapustin, 'Nachalo rossiiskogo liberalizma kak problema politicheskoi filosofii', *Polis*, No. 5, 1994, p. 30.

a condition of self-determination and draws on Kantian notions of autonomy and that the human being is an end in itself. This was the spirit of the great anti-revolutions in 1989–91 that transcended communism, not by engaging in a counter-revolution that would have perpetuated the logic of coercion of the communist order from the opposite perspective, but an 'anti-revolution' that repudiated the very principles on which the communist order had been built.[20] The Yukos affair indicated the restoration of an anti-Kantian perspective which once again subordinated the individual to meta-political imperatives, in this case the reassertion of state power and control over the disposition of property and the parameters of economic life.

The tension between freedom and justice was seldom as sharply posed as in post-communist Russia, and is a theme that Khodorkovsky took up in his various missives from prison (see Chapter 8). Democracy, of course, is 'a constantly and painfully calculated combination of freedom and justice, the opposites manifested in dialectical unity'; but in the Russian context of managed democracy in the 2000s, the symbols and substance of both freedom and justice were appropriated into a discourse of state reconstitution. For the Putinites, the reassertion of the presumed prerogatives of the state was the only road to freedom and justice, whereas the liberals lamented their inability to 'make the breaking up of the state monopoly on power irreversible',[21] an extraordinary ambition in any circumstance. Discussion in the late perestroika period onwards, according to a recent study, 'extolled the virtues of liberalism, which invariably proved to be, upon closer examination, a copy of crisis-stricken Western democracy', and '[a] confusion of liberalism and democracy made it possible to sidestep the issue of the class nature of democracy and the socioeconomic and political structures of liberalism taking shape within it'. But the worst of it was as follows: 'It was assumed that the reforms had to be carried out by the state, which at the same time had to withdraw from the market. At that time this patent nonsense did not strike the eye, because the public consciousness functioned in the logic of elementary abstractions.'[22] Quite apart from the contradictory nature of the reforms, their sheer scope set the stage for the Yukos affair later. This was, as Colton notes, 'the largest divestiture of state resources *anywhere* (italics in original) in history'.[23]

Putin's political philosophy drew its provenance from Boris Chicherin, one of the intellectual inspirations for the 1993 constitution that Putin so resolutely refused to change. In an article published in 1862, Chicherin argued that '[t]he essence of defensive (*okhranitel'nogo*) liberalism is the combination of the principle of freedom with the principle of power and law: in political life its slogan

---

[20] Richard Sakwa, 'The Age of Paradox: The Anti-revolutionary Revolutions of 1989–91', in Moira Donald and Tim Rees (eds), *Reinterpreting Revolution in Twentieth-Century Europe* (London, Macmillan, 2001), pp. 159–76.

[21] Vadim Dubnov, 'The Folly of the Right', *New Times*, No. 11, 30 November 2005, p. 31.

[22] Lyudmila Evstigneeva and Ruben Evstigneev, 'Ot uskoreniya k uskoreniyu: Razmyshleniya nad itogami dvadtsatiletiya', *Obshchestvennye nauki i sovremennost'*, No. 3, 2005, p. 26.

[23] Timothy J. Colton, *Yeltsin: A Life* (New York, Basic Books, 2008), p. 233.

is liberal measures and strong power'.[24] For Putin, political freedom was something to be exercised in the passive voice, combined with restraint and regulation. Freedom in the absence of regulation in the 1990s, in his view, became licence (*proizvol*). At the heart of Putin's idea of freedom in the context of his reactionary-remedial thinking were the ideas of constraints, limits, and obligations, and in particular, deference to the existing political authorities. This trait was certainly much in evidence in his own political biography, where his strong relationships with superiors translated into a distinctive cult of loyalty and personal subordination. At the same time, Putin's practice of inner restraint was reflected in a broader appreciation of the constraints perceived necessary for societal cohesion, combined with a developmental perspective.[25] However, in pursuing the Yukos case Putin did not make the populist argument that the extreme of wealth was antithetical to the development of a free society. This would have been a classically neo-Soviet approach, and it was vigorously advanced by the CPRF, and was one even shared by Thomas Jefferson, who feared the inequality that would accompany the rise of manufacturing,[26] but Putin, who remained at heart a convinced economic liberal (while modifying some of the perceived excesses of neo-liberalism), seldom condemned the oligarchs on social grounds. He remained loyal to the Yeltsin view, as the latter put it in a speech to the US Congress on 17 June 1992, that '[f]reedom and communism are incompatible'.[27]

Instead, Putin stressed state autonomy and socially contextualized freedom. In his 'Russia at the Turn of the Millennium' open letter on the eve of taking over the reins of power he insisted that Russia had turned its back on communism because of its lack of freedom: 'The main thing is that Soviet power did not make the country prosperous, the society dynamic, or the people free.... We spent seven decades heading away from the main highway of civilisation towards a dead end.'[28] In his Federal Assembly address on 25 April 2005 he was unequivocal: 'We are a major European nation, we have always been an integral part of Europe and share all its values and the ideals of freedom and democracy. But we will carry out this process ourselves, taking into account all our specific characteristics, and do not intend to report to anyone on the progress we make.'[29] This reflected Alexander Solzhenitsyn's thinking, who insisted that 'the realisation of freedoms should not threaten the existence of the motherland or offend against people's religious feelings or ethnic sentiments', and that sacred things are values on a par with 'human rights'.[30]

[24] B. N. Chicherin, 'Razlichnye vidy liberalizma', in I. E. Diskin (ed.), *Revolyutsiya protiv svobody: Diskussiya o reformakh Aleksandra II i sud'be gosudarstva* (Moscow, Evropa, 2007), p. 102.

[25] Cf. Amartya Sen, *Development as Freedom* (New York, Random House, 1999).

[26] John Dewey, *Freedom and Culture* (New York, Capricorn Books, 1939), p. 8.

[27] Colton, *Yeltsin*, p. 267.

[28] Putin, 'Russia at the Turn of the Millennium', in Richard Sakwa, *Putin: Russia's Choice*, second edition (London and New York, Routledge, 2008), p. 320, revised translation.

[29] http://www.kremlin.ru/text/appears/2005/04/87049.shtml; *Rossiiskaya gazeta*, 25 April 2005.

[30] Interview with Vitalii Tret'yakov, 'Aleksandr Solzhenitsyn: "Sberezhenie naroda—vysshaya izo vsekh nashikh gosudarstevennykh zadach" ', *Moskovskie novosti*, No. 15, 28 April 2006, p. 1.

The notion of 'managed democracy' from 2005 gave way to the idea of 'sovereign democracy', assuming a paternalist model of political engagement. As Stanley Benn notes: 'To protest against paternalism is not therefore necessarily to claim that the subjects are being treated contrary to their best interests, but that they are deprived of their right to decide for themselves what their interests are, and how best they would be served.'[31] Khodorkovsky was alive to the element of moral conflict in the case, and in his various publications from jail he reflected on the problem of how to legitimize a property settlement that not only had negative social consequences, in that it swiftly reduced Russia to the level of America in terms of inequality, but also posed grave ethical issues: property that had been created by the Soviet people was transferred at a huge discount to a small group of people well placed to lever access to power into property. Stephen Fortescue may well be right to argue that the key thing is what the new property owners did with their new assets, and in most cases, and certainly in the case of Khodorkovsky, they created new value in the form of modern corporations and thus generated wealth that in the form of taxation was in part returned to the people.[32] However, the 'original sin' of the 1990s settlement is a stain that even Khodorkovsky admitted could not be removed so easily.

3. *Dignity and duty: liberalism and* sobornost'

There is yet a third sphere in which the tension between different concepts of freedom operated, at what may be called the existential level. We shall have more to say about Khodorkovsky's personal relations with his entourage and others in his rise to the Olympus of business life, yet here we can note that once it became clear that he had provoked the regime's ire, Khodorkovsky conducted himself as an individual in an impressive way. Not only did he continue to exercise his rights as a citizen, notably in a number of missives and commentaries on contemporary Russian life that we shall examine later, but also in his role as defendant in a trial that was clearly shaped by the preferences of the political authorities, and then later as a political prisoner (possibly even as a 'prisoner of conscience' to use the old dissident term of the Soviet era), Khodorkovsky revealed personal qualities that reflected his vision of inner freedom. As for Putin, the Yukos affair revealed his highly disciplined sense of duty, probably genuinely believing that the trial had to go ahead for the good of the country, although he personally had reservations about what was being done in the name of the state that he so dearly loved. Part of freedom as far as Putin is concerned is to give up freedom in the name of a higher duty. This strain in Putin's personality probably owes as much to his Orthodox beliefs as they do to Soviet upbringing. Putin's reluctant assumption of the presidency itself in the last days of 1999 is testimony to his highly developed sense of duty, since there is little evidence that it was a post to which he aspired with the passion characteristic of most leaders.

[31] Benn, *A Theory of Freedom*, p. 11.
[32] Stephen Fortescue, *Russia's Oil Barons and Metal Magnates: Oligarchs and State in Transition* (Basingstoke, Palgrave Macmillan, 2006), chapter 4.

The distinction can be characterized as one between a liberal conception of freedom, where society is intended to facilitate human self-expression, and the Orthodox concept of *sobornost'*, where individual freedom should develop the potential of the community. Developed in particular by Alexei Khomyakov, *sobornost'* was the free communion of an association of believers, and thus excluded the notion of a contract and inverted the liberal relationship between the individual and society. Contract belongs to the sphere of human relations, and one does not bargain with God. The spiritual 'vertical' is then reflected in a 'power vertical' in the relationship between the sovereign and the subject. Like liberalism, Russian Orthodoxy is characterized by a permanent attempt to combine unity and diversity, but the search is ultimately transcended in a higher communion with God in which the legal constitution of the individual and community is subordinated to a spiritual communion. Thus the idea that the relationship is based on a covenant, by contracting parties as it were, is denigrated; and for many this is a source of the 'legal nihilism' that has characterized so much of Russian political life.

In this light, the Yukos affair can be seen to be a modern representation of the Orthodox struggle for unity and diversity, testing the limits of individual freedom and collective responsibility. The tension between these various sets of binary values, Yuri Lotman argued, is characteristic of Russian culture. He identifies a number of polar opposites, including charity versus justice, love versus the law, personal morality versus state law, and holiness versus politics.[33] The tension between these is a universal theme, yet in Russia, Lotman argues, they take the form of a binary opposition: it is one or the other; politics or *pravda* (truth), you cannot have both. The only way forward, according to Lotman, is to adopt an explicitly *evolutionary* consciousness, transcending these stark antinomies to find some sort of synthesis.[34] The *leitmotif* of Putin's leadership was precisely the repudiation of revolution,[35] yet the Yukos affair showed how deeply culturally ingrained was the polarizing dynamic. Putin himself drew back from adopting one pole or another, and hence the characteristically indeterminate nature of his position; but Khodorkovsky was less afraid of employing axiological categories, and sought to portray his struggle as one of the free citizen against the despotic state. However, in his various epistles it is clear that he, too, was looking for an evolutionary position and in this, both he and Putin found common cause. As typical products of the late Soviet era, the two shared a profoundly anti-revolutionary mentality (that is, opposed to the very logic of revolution)[36] but found themselves caught up in a profoundly revolutionary historical process—the establishment of the foundations of post-communist Russian statehood and economy.

---

[33] Yuri Lotman, *Kultura i vzryv*, cited by Tim McDaniel, *The Agony of the Russian Idea* (Princeton, NJ, Princeton University Press, 1996), p. 17.

[34] Loc cit.   [35] Sakwa, *Putin*, chapter 2.

[36] Cf. Richard Sakwa, 'From Revolution To *Krizis*: The Transcending Revolutions of 1989–91', *Comparative Politics*, Vol. 38, No. 4, July 2006, pp. 459–78.

4. *Self-affirmation and political liberation*

On a fourth and final level we can raise broader issues about the quality of freedom in post-communist societies, and thus about the nature of freedom more broadly in contemporary society. Putin and Khodorkovsky became locked into a single community of fate, a type of mutual dependency that tested them both. It may seem not paradoxical but absurd to suggest that a man sentenced to 8 years in a labour camp, and enduring long days of deprivation, humiliation, and the most direct loss of freedom, could exercise such power over a man at the pinnacle of the political tree, the presidency of one of the world's great powers. Yet we have seen this type of relationship before, and Nelson Mandela's 'long walk to freedom' from incarceration for nearly a lifetime in Robbin Island ended with him becoming president of South Africa.[37] Deprived of formal freedom, Mandela retained the autonomy of moral choice that is the essence of existential freedom. While the analogy between Mandela and Khodorkovsky should not be taken too far, since the circumstances could hardly be more different, there are undoubtedly aspects worthy of comparison.

At the same time, it should be stressed that Putin's Russia was not an authoritarian system of the traditional South American type, with the effective disenfranchisement of a significant body of the citizenry. Putin was clearly the advocate of a modernizing and developmental agenda, and sought Russia's integration into the existing international system. His own agenda threatened to be derailed by the Yukos affair, and certainly damaged him in the eyes of international public opinion. Putin perceived the challenge from Yukos and from Khodorkovsky personally as endangering his plans for the autonomous modernization of Russia. His vision was based on traditional Russian notions of the strong state leading the modernization agenda but combined with a distinctive view of freedom, a view shared by a large proportion of the Russian people.[38] Khodorkovsky, by contrast, represented the spontaneous action of market forces, barely constrained by the political level and certainly contemptuous of the attempt to limit these forces by the state.

The Yukos affair thus raises fundamental questions about Russia's post-communist trajectory, the nature of political community, the quality of public authority, the nature of Russian capitalism, the strategy pursued by Putin's administration and also by the existential confrontation between two personalities, each of whom in their own way believed they were pursuing the path of freedom most appropriate for the good of Russia. Only history would tell whose definition was the most viable. In this struggle, the man in the Kremlin and the man in the labour camp were even; and it is not difficult to envisage circumstances where their roles could be reversed.

---

[37] Nelson Mandela, *A Long Walk to Freedom: The Autobiography of Nelson Mandela* (London, Abacus, 1995).

[38] Richard Rose, William Mishler, and Neil Munro, *Russia Transformed: Developing Popular Support for a New Regime* (Cambridge, Cambridge University Press, 2006), in particular chapter 4, which finds strong support for 'freedom', 'Russia one and indivisible', and 'Christianity', while the idea of socialism left people cold.

POWER, PROPERTY, AND THE MARKET

The nature of the anti-revolutions of 1989–91 that transcended the communist order of the time remains contested. At least two elements were involved. The first represented the fulfilment of an eighteenth-century agenda of human rights and individual freedom. The second, however, both undercut and reinforced this liberal tendency. This was the economic revolution that represented, on the one hand, the commodification of labour power and the disempowerment of the various agencies that in one way or another had represented a distinctive vision of working-class engagement in Soviet-type socialism, while at the same time, liberating the society as a whole from an economically incompetent system that in many ways imposed archaic forms of subordination and dominance.

A new dual state

Ernst Fraenkel described how in Nazi Germany the prerogative state acted as a separate law system of its own, although the formal constitutional state was not dismantled. Two parallel systems of law operated, where the 'normative state' operated according to sanctioned principles of rationality and impartial legal norms, while the 'prerogative state', governed by the party, exercised 'unlimited arbitrariness and violence unchecked by any legal guarantees'.[39] The normative state continued to regulate market relations and private matters, but the Nazi regime used the powers of the prerogative state to destroy its enemies and to eliminate threats. As time passed the prerogative state encroached evermore on the impartial rules of the normative state.[40] The contradictions between the two systems grew ever sharper as the prerogative state evermore undermined the rule of law and stifled civic activity. The idea of a dual state has been applied to the Soviet Union, where Lenin was quite explicit that 'law is politics', and where 'revolutionary legality' could not be subordinated to the normal constraints of law and constitutionalism.[41] Gordon Smith notes that '[t]he legal system in the USSR under Stalin clearly resembled Fraenkel's "dual state"'.[42] Laws were to be observed unless 'revolutionary expediency' decreed otherwise. As Shuman notes, '[t]here were to be rules for stability', but, quoting Rheinstein, 'they could at any time be swept away by the royal prerogative'.[43]

---

[39] Ernst Fraenkel, *The Dual State: A Contribution to the Theory of Dictatorship*, translated from the German by E. A. Shils, in collaboration with Edith Lowenstein and Klaus Knorr (New York, Oxford University Press, 1941; reprinted by The Lawbook Exchange, Ltd, 2006), p. xiii.

[40] Fraenkel, *The Dual State*, pp. 241–4.

[41] The concept of the dual state was applied to Soviet Russia in 1951 by Rheinstein (no first name given), see the untitled 'Brief Reviews' by S. I. Shuman of V. I. Lenin, P. I. Stuchka, M. A. Reisner, E. B. Pashukanis, J. V. Stalin, A. Y. Vyshinsky, P. Yudin, S. A. Golunskii, M. S. Strogovich, and I. P. Trainin, *Soviet Legal Philosophy* (Cambridge, MA, Harvard University Press, 1951), *Michigan Law Review*, Vol. 50, No. 6, April 1952, pp. 956–60, at p. 957, n. 8.

[42] Gordon B. Smith, *Reforming the Russian Legal System* (Cambridge, Cambridge University Press, 1996), p. 34.

[43] Shuman, 'Brief Reviews', p. 957.

Robert Amsterdam, international defence council for Mikhail Khodorkovsky, has drawn attention to the parallels with post-communist Russia. His analysis contains many fruitful insights on the way that the rule of law was subverted in the Yukos case. Amsterdam notes that '[t]he prerogative state accepted that the courts were necessary to assure entrepreneurial liberty, the sanctity of contracts, private property rights and competition, but this did not mean that the courts or the law were inviolable'.[44] For Fraenkel, the destruction of legal independence was the central feature of the prerogative state.[45] As Knoops and Amsterdam put it, 'the concept of the Dual State implies that, despite the normative value and safeguards of certain legal mechanisms in terms of checks and balances, the entire legal system can become or de facto function as an instrument at the disposal of the political authorities'.[46] They draw attention to the procedural and human rights violations attending Khodorkovsky's prosecution and that of his colleagues, and 'the total lack of independence of the Russian judicial authorities handling the case, the ransacking and seizure of documents from the offices of one of Khodorkovsky's lawyers in violation of attorney–client privilege, and the restriction of the access of the accused to legal counsel'.[47] At the heart of the defence case is the argument that the elimination of Yukos destroyed a competitor to state-owned energy companies and a rival in the political arena: 'Both the criminal and the tax proceedings were clearly politically motivated, since only Khodorkovsky and Yukos were singled out by the authorities for the alleged offenses, which involved common industry practices under the legal regime existing at the time.'[48] As a result, Philip Hanson talks of a 'dual economy' emerging following the Yukos affair, whereby sectors in which the state wishes to exert more control (above all energy) are subject to prerogative interference, whereas the bulk of the economy is governed by the normal instruments of constitutional law.[49]

There are undoubtedly elements of dualism in the post-communist Russian political and economic system. However, while the distinction between the normative and the prerogative state is undoubtedly fruitful, this model suggests a rather too stark binary model, and one in which the prerogative state operates as a unitary actor with a conscious design to assert its powers with no regard to the norms espoused by the constitutional state. This would be an inappropriate model for Russia. Instead, we have a system torn between the declared intention to abide by the constitution and the development of a range of para-constitutional practices that does not repudiate the constitutional state but subverts it to achieve certain immediate political goals. The fundamental legitimacy of the system is

[44] Robert R. Amsterdam, *The Dual State Takes Hold in Russia*, mimeo, Royal Institute for International Affairs, 7 February 2008, p. 2.

[45] Fraenkel, *The Dual State*, p. 24.

[46] Geert-Jan Alexander Knoops and Robert R. Amsterdam, 'The Duality of State Cooperation Within International and National Criminal Cases', *Fordham International Law Journal*, Vol. 30, 2007, p. 263.

[47] Knoops and Amsterdam, 'The Duality of State Cooperation', pp. 289–90.   [48] Ibid., p. 290.

[49] Philip Hanson, 'The Russian Economic Puzzle: Going Forwards, Backwards or Sideways?', *International Affairs*, Vol. 83, No. 5, September–October 2007, pp. 869–89.

founded on the principles installed by the constitution, but political practices
diverge when the regime's interests are threatened. Thus, rather than suggesting a
fully fledged dual system, we argue that Russian politics is characterized precisely
by the tension between the two levels: the normative state retains priority and is
the source of systemic legitimacy, but the administration (the regime) develops
a range of para-constitutional practices to achieve its goals without denying the
priority of the normative state. In other words, we do not have a prerogative state
but a regime which operates at the interstices of the potential prerogative state and
the nascent elements of a normative state.[50]

The regime is the site of numerous factional conflicts, and is thus far from being
a unitary actor. As we shall see, the Yukos affair developed in a situation of rampant intra-elite conflict, and was advanced by one faction against those of a more
liberal disposition, who sought to prevent the use of judicial measures against an
independent entrepreneur. Rather than the Yukos affair demonstrating that Russia
was returning once again to a mono-centric system, the Yukos affair showed just
how fragmented the new Russian state order was. Although the presidency is at
the heart of the political system, and enjoys enormous powers according to the
1993 constitution, it acts within a framework not only of constitutional limitations but also of para-political practices. While the political parties, representative
system, and public politics of the normative state were relatively weak, the para-
constitutional system allowed the development of a second political order, a para-
political sphere populated by factions and informal practices.

The Yukos affair is thus characterized by a dualism. On the one hand, the regime
claimed that it was pursuing quite legitimate tax recovery and the prosecution of
real crimes, but on the other hand, it was quite clear that elements of prerogative
law were operating, stimulated in part by the interaction of certain factions and
the judiciary, accompanied by the intervention of powerful economic interests.
The Yukos affair helped strengthen the development of para-constitutionalism
and para-politics, but at the same time exposed them as never before and thereby
helped mobilize resistance to the emergence of a more powerful prerogative state.
Thus the argument that 'the abuses of the Prerogative State are masked by the
order and progress of the Normative State',[51] while accurate to a point, occludes
perhaps the more important phenomenon: the struggle between two legal orders
and various definitions of freedom in conditions of uncertainty.

Freedom and property

The official attitude to private property in Russia changed radically twice in the
twentieth century. After October 1917 property became delegitimized, and was
considered not a sphere in which freedom could be exercised but as the root of
exploitation and subjugation. However, in the final Soviet years the distinction

---

[50] See my *Crisis of Russian Democracy: Factionalism and the Medvedev Succession* (in preparation),
chapter 1, for more development of the argument.
[51] Knoops and Amsterdam, 'The Duality of State Cooperation', p. 295.

between ownership and possession became increasingly more pertinent. Although legal title to significant property was prohibited, access to goods and the possession of property gave rise to a type of Soviet bourgeoisie. Although private property was strictly limited, personal property became more extensive. After 1991 official attitudes to property changed cardinally once again, but the tension between ownership and possession, private and personal property, continued in new forms.

While the liberal reformers of the 1990s loudly proclaimed the onset of a new era of democracy, they focused on creating the economic foundations of the new order.[52] Zweynart has demonstrated how in the period between 1987 and 1991 Soviet economic ideology was repudiated and replaced with liberal ideas borrowed from the West, a process that in his view represented a Kuhnian paradigm shift.[53] In a later article, however, he noted how even the Soviet reception of Western economic ideas was tempered by cultural traditions, a modification that was accentuated later: 'Between 1992 and 2002, most Russian economists distanced themselves from the liberal enthusiasm of 1990 and returned to the paths prescribed by the intellectual and cultural traditions of their country'—traditions that in his view reach back far beyond the 70 years of state socialism.[54] Like Procaccia (see below), Zweynart looks to the patristic legacy of Russian Orthodox Christianity, characterized in his view by holistic ideas, which contrasted the unity of belief and thought in contrast to Western rationalist fragmentation, and anthropocentric beliefs in the need to develop the whole human personality, and thus feared social differentiation and the division of labour.

The echoes with the Marxian concerns about alienation and separation of humanity from its 'species being' are obvious, and were noted among others by Nikolai Berdyaev.[55] This holistic-anthropocentric approach sustained a hostile attitude to capitalism among Russian intellectuals, but it was certainly not absent in the West itself, as Karl Polanyi noted in his discussion of the separation of the state and economy.[56] As in the West, there were plenty of critics of the integralist approach to social development, notably Peter Struve and other 'Legal Marxists' in the late nineteenth century. Today reformers like Yegor Gaidar accept a culturalist approach and argue that Russia has an 'Eastern' society (cast aside from a Western pattern of development by the Mongol invasions) in which 'requisitions, seizures of property, loss of social status or title might be the lot of even the wealthiest property owners in a despotic regime, should they fail to cultivate their

[52] Yegor Gaidar, *State and Evolution: Russia's Search for a Free Market* (Seattle, WA, University of Washington Press, 2003).

[53] Joachim Zweynart, 'Economic Ideas and Institutional Change: Evidence from Soviet Economic Debates 1987–1991', *Europe–Asia Studies*, Vol. 58, No. 2, March 2007, pp. 169–92.

[54] Joachim Zweynart, 'Conflicting Patterns of Thought in the Russian Debate on Transition: 1992–2002', *Europe–Asia Studies*, Vol. 59, No. 1, January 2007, pp. 47–69, at p. 48.

[55] Nikolai Berdyaev, *Istoki i smysl russkogo kommunizma* (Paris, YMCA-Press, 1955; reprinted Moscow, Nauka, 1990).

[56] Karl Polanyi, *The Great Transformation: The Political and Economic Origins of Our Time*, Foreword by Joseph E. Stiglitz, Introduction by Fred Block (Boston, MA, Beacon Press, 2001 [first published 1944]).

government connections'.[57] The characteristic feature of the 'Eastern' society, as Khodorkovsky was to discover, was the instability of property rights; rendered in Gaidar's words, 'a function of political authority'.[58] Culturalist interpretations of Russian development, clearly, are far from hegemonic, yet paternalistic approaches drawing on the holistic-anthropocentric tradition do have a profound resonance today, and in part explain Putin's phenomenal popularity throughout his two terms as president.

The political framework of the new order is defined by the constitution adopted in December 1993, a document which reflects the aspirations of the period as well as the contradictions and conflicts that attended the birth of the present constitutional order. Russia's constitution is quite explicitly a liberal document. Article 2 proclaims: 'The individual and their rights and freedoms are the supreme value. Recognition, observance and protection of human and civil rights and freedoms is the obligation of the state.' Article 8.2 asserts that '[i]n the Russian Federation private, state, municipal, and other forms of property enjoy equal recognition and protection', while Article 35 is even more explicit:

1. The right of private ownership is protected by law.

2. Each person is entitled to own property and to possess, utilize, and dispose of it both individually and together with others.

3. No one may be deprived of his property except by court decision. The compulsory expropriation of property for state requirements may be carried out only if full compensation is paid in advance.

The right to private property is thus enshrined in several instances, yet Khodorkovsky's property rights were violated. The Yukos affair raised the question about who is the ultimate owner of private property, and the limits to ownership power. Although the legal and constitutional framework had changed, remnants of the old Soviet mentality remained, where possession could be enjoyed by grace of the authorities but not in normal circumstances be converted into inalienable property. Khodorkovsky sought precisely to effect this conversion, but he was brought up sharply, and his property was effectively confiscated. A new model of political economy then developed, in which business owners were to show loyalty to the state, and in which the state developed a range of state corporations that inhabited a strange para-statal no-man's-land between state and private property.

The reconstruction of a neo-patrimonial order inevitably brings us back to Pipes's argument that this traditionally was the defining feature of the country: 'From the time I interested myself seriously in Russia, I became aware that one of the fundamental differences between her history and that of the other European countries lay in the weak development of property.'[59] In his view, property 'provides the key to the emergence of the political-legal institutions that guarantee liberty'.[60] He defined patrimonial governance as 'a system which recognised no

[57] Gaidar, *State and Evolution*, p. 5.   [58] Gaidar, *State and Evolution*, p. 53.
[59] Richard Pipes, *Property and Freedom* (New York, Alfred A. Knopf, 1999), p. xi.
[60] Ibid., p. xii.

distinction between sovereignty and property, allowing the tsar to act as both the ruler and the owner of his realm'.[61] For Pipes, property, defined as possession backed with the force of law, gives rise to freedom, while its absence encourages arbitrary authority. Mancur Olson draws attention to the ancient Roman distinction between *possessio* and *dominium* when applied to property rights:

> Though individuals may have possessions without government, the way a dog possesses a bone, there is no private property without government. Property is a socially protected claim on an asset—a bundle of rights enforceable in courts backed by the coercive power of government.[62]

Pipes identified four types of freedom: political freedom, above all the right to choose those who rule; legal freedom, 'the right in relation with other individuals and the state to be judged by third parties in accord with the law'; economic freedom, 'the right freely to use and dispose of one's assets'; and personal rights, the ability to live as one chooses as long as it does not infringe on the rights of others.[63] He was inclined towards Locke's view that property predates sovereignty: 'The state of nature was not, as Hobbes thought, a ferocious jungle, but a happy condition of freedom and equality.'[64] He did not accept that patrimonialism was in some way a genetic feature of Russian development, since in Novgorod a different pattern had emerged. Instead, he traced its roots in the liquidation of private property in the Grand Duchy of Moscow, which came to conquer the rest of the country and imposed its system of rule where sovereignty and ownership were fused, where 'the monarch not only ruled the realm and its inhabitants, but literally owned them'.[65]

Yuri Pivovarov notes that the Russian revolution was diametrically opposed to the idea of private property. If the French revolution had conclusively affirmed the principle of private property in the *Code Civil*, the Bolshevik revolution was designed to put an end to it. He quotes Leo Tolstoy to the effect that the idea that 'property is theft' would exist as long as Russian popular power (*rod lyudskoi*) existed.[66] To this day Russian views on the legitimacy of private property are highly ambivalent. The Putin regime, by undermining popular power, was able to affirm the rights of private property, but as Khodorkovsky was to discover, in a constrained and selective manner. 'The Bolshevik revolution', Pivovarov argues, 'continues'.[67] In his various letters from prison, Khodorkovsky stressed that the fundamental challenge for the Russian polity was to legitimize the property settlement of the 1990s, and by the same token to ensure the legal sanctity of private property.

These concerns are reflected in a recent study by Procaccia, who takes up Pivovarov's theme that Russian culture determines economic behaviour. He asks why Russia has not been able to become a 'normal' Western-style market economy,

---

[61] Ibid., p. xiii.

[62] Mancur Olson, 'Why the Transition from Communism is so Difficult', *Eastern Economic Journal*, Vol. 21, No. 4, 1995, pp. 437–61, at p. 458.

[63] Pipes, *Property and Freedom*, p. xvi.   [64] Ibid., p. 35.   [65] Ibid., p. 160.

[66] Yu. P. Pivovarov, 'Istoki i smysl russkoi revolyutsii', *Polis*, No. 5, 2007, p. 45.   [67] Ibid., p. 55.

noting that corporations have not been able to adapt to Western standards of behaviour and that private contracts are rarely observed. The answer lies less in the standard issues associated with the economic transition from a planned to a market economy, but the cultural infrastructure that gave rise to contract and the corporation in the West lacks grounding in Russia. The notion of 'contract' has not taken root since it affirms the right of the individual to enter into agreements with others that are enforceable by law, whereas in Russia the culture is more anonymous, as demonstrated by the art of iconography which rejects individualism. The Western freedom to enter into contract is more than a legal or economic act but denotes a specific definition of a rational and autonomous notion of self, able to define one's own goals and needs. This is the basis of Western liberalism, but Russia, he argues, took a very different path, emphasizing (as we saw above) spiritual and cultural values. Thus when capitalism was restored in the 1990s it lacked the cultural basis to become a contractual and corporate nation. This cultural gulf between Russia and the West is far deeper than the mere seventy-four years of the communist experiment, and the 'transition' by the same token in Russia is of a very different quality than in most other post-communist countries. The introduction of corporate and contract-based market relations would be as much a cultural revolution as an economic transformation.[68] This interpretation helps explain the theoretical basis for the emergence of the dual state.

The cultural revolution of property

If this was not enough, there is another, no less intractable, problem. Contrary to much of the accepted wisdom that the 1990s, however crudely, represented a transition to the market, Andrew Barnes argues that the political economy of the period can be best understood as a struggle over property. The main actors were not only the infamous oligarchs but also officialdom at the central and regional levels, and the struggles did not stop with privatization but continued once property was in private hands. The goal was not simply to accrue the wealth that came with property, but ownership was a way of buttressing institutional and personal status. The model he presents is of a constantly shifting terrain, where property rights remain fluid and fungible, and where powerful political actors conduct their struggles and property as not much more than a proxy for status.[69] The struggles were determined less by ideological commitments or preferences, for or against 'the market', but were rational responses to conditions of uncertainty. The argument can be extended into the 2000s, although the struggle for property took on new forms. In his first years, Putin damped down the internecine struggles between oligarchs and sought to provide institutional mechanisms for the transition to a more secure environment for ownership. However, the fire was

[68] Uriel Procaccia, *Russian Culture, Property Rights and the Market Economy* (Cambridge, Cambridge University Press, 2007).
[69] Andrew Barnes, *Owning Russia: The Struggle over Factories, Farms and Power* (Ithaca, NY, Cornell University Press, 2006).

not extinguished, and once the assault against Khodorkovsky began in 2003 it quickly took the form of an assault against his company, and in the end Yukos was bankrupted and dismembered. The primary actors now, however, were no longer private entrepreneurs but state officialdom, exacerbating the factional struggles within the regime.

In his remarkable study of what he called *The Great Transformation*, which from the late eighteenth century transformed labour, land, and money into commodities, Polanyi examined the relationship between economy and society. He argues that 'the idea of a self-adjusting market implied a stark utopia. Such an institution could not exist for any length of time without annihilating the human and natural substance of society'.[70] In discussing the origins of the Great War he argues that 'the origins of the cataclysm lay in the utopian endeavour of economic liberalism to set up a self-regulating market system'.[71] In a paragraph with striking relevance to the transformation of Russia in the 1990s he notes: 'Nowhere has liberal philosophy failed so conspicuously as in its understanding of the problem of change. Fired by an emotional faith in spontaneity, the common-sense attitude toward change was discarded in favour of a mystical readiness to accept the social consequences of economic improvement, whatever they might be.'[72] The principles of what he considered to be 'traditional statesmanship' were undermined by a 'crude utilitarianism' that rendered the elite in the 1990s, as it had done in the earlier period, 'blind to the role of the government in economic life'.[73]

Stiglitz makes the connection with Russia explicit: 'We recognize that the manner in which and the speed with which reforms were put into place in Russia eroded social relations, destroyed social capital, and led to the creation and perhaps the dominance of the Russian Mafia.'[74] The communist experiment was now followed by another one, the attempt to impose a self-regulating market 'before *government* had had a chance to put into place the necessary legal and institutional infrastructure'.[75] Throughout history, according to Polanyi, the economy had always been embedded in society, with economic relations subordinated to perceived social needs. In the early nineteenth century this was repudiated in favour of a liberal belief in spontaneously generating and self-regulating markets. Polanyi's key argument, however, is that the aspiration to create a self-regulating market creates a counter-movement in which peoples resist, what he calls the 'double movement': the principle of market liberalism is countered by 'the principle of self-protection', which once again begins to embed the economy within a framework that allows society itself to survive.[76] Polanyi likens the process to a giant elastic band: pulled too far in one direction, society resists and pulls strongly in the opposite direction.[77] No image is more apt to describe the Putinite counter-movement to what were perceived to be the excesses of the 1990s.

---

[70] Polanyi, *The Great* Transformation, p. 3.   [71] Ibid., p. 31.   [72] Ibid., p. 35.
[73] Ibid., p. 39.
[74] Joseph E. Stiglitz, 'Foreword', in Polanyi, *The Great Transformation*, pp. x–xi.
[75] Ibid, p. xii.   [76] Polanyi, *The Great Transformation*, p. 138.   [77] Ibid., p. 240.

Excessive laissez-faire generates a counter-movement towards greater state regulation. Thus it is not surprising that the Putin elite praised Franklin D. Roosevelt's New Deal, another case of the elastic band pulling against the orthodoxies of an earlier period. The theoretical richness and political realism of Polanyi's thinking have prompted a number of works to apply Polanyian insights to the post-communist transitions.[78] Woodruff takes issue with Polanyi's, and Gaidar's, 'assumption of a straightforward identity of society and state through the nexus of the monetary system',[79] but discounting this assumption, Woodruff talks of Russia between 1992 and 1994 enduring a 'triple movement': price liberalization; a counter-move towards non-monetary exchange (barter) to keep enterprises afloat; and the endorsement of barter by the state to allow the economy to survive.[80] Woodruff questions the view that sees the emergence of barter and monetary substitutes as a recrudescence of feudalism, since although the national market might have been fragmented in the 1990s the whole industrial system was predicated to be part of a national economy and not as a series of sub-national markets.[81]

The analogy with feudalism, so common in discussions of post-communist Russian politics, refers then less to the nature of the economic order than to the quality of social relations. Hence Yulia Latynina could argue that by the late 1990s 'slaveowners were replaced by proprietors', oligarchs who no longer counted their wealth in terms of 'guns and businessmen under their thumb, but by stock portfolios and profit margins'. However, the whole process has moved into reverse and '[p]rivate ownership is once more giving way to feudal ownership', and '[w]hen an oligarch resists this process ... [h]is property is taken away and handed over to the bureaucrats, as in the case of Yukos'.[82]

The 'varieties of capitalism' approach examines, as we shall see, various ways in which markets are embedded in different capitalist societies.[83] However, in his final chapters Polanyi is well aware that when the elastic band is pulling with equal strength in both directions, society can enter into crisis; and pseudo-solutions of the fascist sort emerge, promising to overcome political and economic stalemate. The separation of government from business, achieved in 1694 'in an exemplary fashion in the character of an independent Bank of England',[84] also separated business from government. In America 'private property was given the highest

[78] For an early collection, see Christopher Bryant and Edmund Mokrzycki (eds.), *The New Great Transformation?* (London, Routledge, 1994); see also Maurice Glasman, *Unnecessary Suffering: Managing Market Utopia* (London, Verso, 1996). For a broad philosophical overview, see John Gray, *False Dawn: The Delusions of Global Capitalism* (London, Granta Books, 1998).

[79] David Woodruff, *Money Unmade: Barter and the Fate of Russian Capitalism* (Ithaca, NY, Cornell University Press, 1999), p. 115, who also adopts a broadly Polanyian perspective.

[80] Ibid., pp. 115–16.   [81] Ibid., pp. 206–7.

[82] Yulia Latynina, 'Goodbye Oligarchs, Hello Feudal Capitalism', *Moscow Times*, 8 December 2004, p. 10.

[83] For a good overview, see Rogers Hollingworth and Robert Boyer (eds.), *Contemporary Capitalism: The Embeddedness of Institutions* (Cambridge, Cambridge University Press, 1997). See also Martin Myant and David Lane (eds.), *Varieties of Capitalism in Post-Communist Countries* (Basingstoke, Palgrave Macmillan, 2006).

[84] Polanyi, *The Great Transformation*, p. 233.

conceivable protection', but as a consequence, '[i]n spite of universal suffrage, American voters were powerless against owners'.[85] Not surprisingly, for liberals popular democracy was perceived as a danger to capitalism since they feared that it would act as too powerful a force pulling in one direction.

Socialism in Polanyi's view promised to bring market forces back under the control of society: 'Socialism is, essentially, the tendency inherent in an industrial civilization to transcend the self-regulating market by consciously subordinating it to a democratic society.'[86] There was a double tendency deeply embedded in Polanyi's own work, in that he was well aware of the dangers of both laissez-faire and excessive embeddedness; his long disquisition of the Speenhamland system established in 1795 is testimony to that. In the final chapter he contrasts the striving in society for regulation with the danger to freedom that this entails— especially with the example of the Soviet Union before him. The market, he insists, 'has been the outcome of a conscious and often violent intervention on the part of government which imposed the market organization on society for noneconomic ends'.[87] Socialism promised to restore the primacy of society over the economic system. However, the problem of freedom becomes central, at the institutional level as well as at the moral or religious level. At the institutional level a balance has to be drawn between achieving the desired end and diminished freedoms.

But, as Polanyi argues:

On the more fundamental level the very possibility of freedom is in doubt. It appears that the means of maintaining freedom are themselves adulterating and destroying it. The key to the problem of freedom in our age must be sought on this latter plane. Institutions are embodiments of human meaning and purpose. We cannot achieve the freedom we seek, unless we comprehend the true significance of freedom in a complex society.[88]

Moves towards integration and planning in society should be accompanied by 'the strengthening of the rights of the individual in society',[89] but liberals insist that '[t]he freedom that regulation creates is denounced as unfreedom', and Polanyi bitterly notes that '[w]ith the liberal the idea of freedom thus degenerates into a mere advocacy of free enterprise'.[90] Writing at the time of crisis, Polanyi warns that either one should remain loyal to 'the illusionary idea of freedom and deny the reality of society', or 'accept that reality and reject the idea of freedom': the first was the liberal path; the second the fascist one.

Inescapably we reach the conclusion that the very possibility of freedom is in question. If regulation is the only means of spreading and strengthening freedom in a complex society, and yet to make use of this means is contrary to freedom per se, then such a society cannot be free.[91]

The abandonment of 'market utopia' restored the reality of society, but accompanied by a dividing line between liberalism on the one side, and fascism and communism on the other—with the difference between the latter being not primarily

---

[85] Ibid., p. 234.　　[86] Ibid., p. 242.　　[87] Ibid., p. 258.　　[88] Ibid., p. 262.
[89] Ibid., p. 264.　　[90] Ibid., p. 265.　　[91] Ibid., p. 267.

economic: 'It is moral and religious.'[92] Polanyi's rather pessimistic conclusion was prompted by the great crisis of the first half of the twentieth century, but the attempt to naturalize the neo-liberal agenda in the rhetoric of globalization after the fall of communism has provoked no less a crisis. Early twenty-first century financial turbulence is a symptom of the crisis.

VARIETIES OF CAPITALISM

The debate about varieties of capitalism continues, and different visions of what a capitalist democracy should look like in Russia lie at the heart of the Yukos affair. The usual distinction is between *liberal* market economies, where the state takes the back seat in economic management, and *coordinated* market economies, where the state is far more active, a type of the social market economies widespread in Western Continental Europe. The Yukos affair in effect represented a shift from the first to the second, with the additional intensification of political management as well.

Embedding capitalism and development

The roots of the Putinite reaction draw deeply on Russian political traditions and the preferences of a significant part of the elite. For many, however, the Putinite micro-management of political and economic processes represented little more than the imposition of a new despotism and a reversion to classic stereotypes of Russian political behaviour, a theme to which we shall return. The high level of popular support for this new type of 'enlightened despotism' was demonstrated by the consistently high popularity ratings for Putin right up to the end of his presidency. Many observers concluded that by their own free will Russians are willing to give up their hard-won freedoms. Shocked, humiliated, and impoverished by the rapacious oligarchs in the 1990s, the Russian people in the 2000s, it is argued, embrace enlightened despotism as the salvation of the viability of the state and as a way of constraining the willfulness of the entrepreneurial class.[93] In other words, although pulling the elastic the other way (notably in the Yukos affair) while at the same time remaining committed to neo-liberal market solutions, Putin's Russia was not able to transcend the crisis but remained trapped between the dangers of economistic liberalism and the threat of proto-fascism. Neither was able to provide an effective framework for social freedom.

We should be beware of ascribing automaticity to a Polanyian reaction against a particularly aggressive form of neo-liberal disembedding process. Developments in post-communist Russia reflected deep political cultural predispositions, but

[92] Polanyi, *The Great Transformation*, p. 267.

[93] For an examination of the tension between freedom and security, see Richard Rose and Neil Munro, *Elections without Order: Russia's Challenge to Vladimir Putin* (Cambridge, Cambridge University Press, 2002).

no less did they reflect the profound social and economic realities of a society transforming itself. If Russian exceptionalism exists, it reflects only a national response to universal challenges. The starting point of the debate over different 'models of capitalism' is that 'national societies differ importantly with respect to how they organize their economies, and indeed the extent to which they do so'. While some societies allow market forces extensive leeway, 'in others markets are more socially or institutionally embedded':

[A]n economy is socially embedded insofar as the transactions by which it is made up either are also supposed to serve other than economic purposes (in other words, are constrained by non-economic objectives such as social cohesion or national defense) or are supported by non-economic social ties (that is, are facilitated by particularistic relations such as tribalism or paternalism or by enforceable social obligations that engender trust among economic actors).[94]

Germany and Japan, in different ways, developed embedded capitalist economies, a tradition that from the late nineteenth century developed in authoritarian forms, but in the post-war era were combined with democracy. Thus the common contrast today between liberal and authoritarian capitalism rather simplifies matters.[95] Non-liberal discourse had a long history in Germany, and focused on ways in which capitalism could be embedded as Germany industrialized. From the 1870s this took an increasingly conservative inflexion, and 'became associated with an extreme ethos of public responsibility between the state and organized social groups, ultimately giving rise to the specifically corporate organizational form of German embedded capitalism'. In Japan this developed in a different way: 'Japanese anti-liberalism based itself mostly on a segmentalist pattern of social organization in which the large enterprise was reconstituted as a social community, as opposed to German-style solidarism of nationwide bodies of functional representation.'[96] Later both were able to absorb liberal and even socialist traditions. In all of this, governing elites were crucial, presided over by a powerful state bureaucracy without the sanction of democratic legitimacy.[97] The objectives in both Germany and Japan, and later South Korea, were similar—national development.

Post-communist Russia differs in three crucial respects from this developmental model. First, the country is already a relatively advanced industrial society, and thus the problem of development is very different from the other countries, and the adoption of elements of the 'embedded' model could be seen as anachronistic,

---

[94] Wolfgang Streeck, 'Introduction', in Wolfgang Streeck and Kozo Yamamura (eds.), *The Origins of Nonliberal Capitalism: Germany and Japan in Comparison* (Ithaca, NY, Cornell University Press, 2001), pp. 1–38, at p. 2.

[95] Azar Gat, 'The Return of the Authoritarian Great Powers', *Foreign Affairs*, Vol. 86, No. 4, July–August 2007, pp. 56–69.

[96] Gerhard Lembuch, 'The Institutional Embedding of Market Economies: The German "Model" and its Impact on Japan', in Streeck and Yamamura (eds.), *The Origins of Nonliberal Capitalism*, chapter 2, p. 10.

[97] Cf. Philip Menow, 'Welfare State Building and Coordinated Capitalism in Japan and Germany', in Streeck and Yamamura (eds.), *The Origins of Nonliberal Capitalism*, chapter 3, pp. 94–121.

and in danger of returning Russia to an outmoded economic model. Second, the development of the Russian business class, the bourgeoisie in its narrow technical meaning, combined both organic and voluntaristic principles: the old Soviet managers organically transformed themselves into capitalist directors, while a whole new business group was created by state sponsorship, notably the Komsomol entrepreneurs of whom Khodorkovsky was the most vivid example. Russia began to build 'capitalism without capitalists', and thus the mediating role of the state remained endemic, even at the times of its greatest weakness in the 1990s.[98] The business class developed as an agent of modernization to rival the state itself, but there was always a counter-tendency, with deep roots in the Soviet modernization experience, that considered the state as the primary developmental agent. Third, Russia's bureaucratic elites are constrained (although not always governed) by the democratic and ownership principles that lie at the heart of Russia's new constitutional order. The tension between developmental and democratic impulses is in part the source of the most profound contradictions in the development of the post-communist Russian polity, and herein lie the origins of the dual state.

There are also profound similarities with earlier developmental models. As Streeck notes, long before 'globalisation', liberalism was the baseline against which embedded forms of capitalism sought to develop.[99] It remains the baseline, and even the German 'social market economy' is forced to adapt to neo-liberal agendas, and there are fundamental questions whether the German model of embedded capitalism itself can survive.[100] In that context, although Putin reasserted the assumed prerogatives of the state over the business class, there were major limits to his 're-embedment' project. Although his regime advanced a more 'social' face than its predecessor, it remained firmly within the neo-liberal intellectual framework and made no corporatist deals with any significant section of society. It did, however, develop a range of para-statal corporations, a process that accelerated as a result of the Yukos affair.

The liberal reformers of the 1990s sought precisely to 'disembed' the economy, with Gaidar arguing that the transformation was purely 'a matter of socio-economic structure',[101] where changes in the ownership structure and the creation of competitive markets would wrench Russia from its Eastern trajectory towards Western modernity. At the same time, the new business class, notably the oligarchs, were considered the subjects of the modernization process. The paradox of this economistic approach is that the liberal reformers necessarily were forced to rely on the state to push through their agenda and at the same time were not overly concerned by the pretensions of the oligarchs, and thus the whole process was accompanied by a reckless 'institutional nihilism' that gravely weakened the

[98] G. Eyal, Ivan Szelenyi, and E. Townsley, *Making Capitalism Without Capitalists* (London, Verso, 1998).

[99] Streeck, 'Introduction', p. 32.

[100] See Wolfgang Streeck, 'German Capitalism: Does it Exist? Can it Survive?', in Colin Crouch and Wolfgang Streeck (eds.), *Political Economy of Modern Capitalism: Mapping Convergence and Diversity* (London, Sage Publications, 1997), chapter 2, pp. 33–54.

[101] Gaidar, *State and Evolution*, p. 107.

quality of governance as a whole. Even in the 1990s a classically liberal macro-economic policy was accompanied by some non-liberal features at the micro-management level. State capacity was required to achieve a distinct type of residual embeddedness, and thus as the state strengthened in the 2000s, the greater was the shift towards this form of capitalism. It was based neither on Japanese-style enterprise solidarity nor on German-model national institutions. Instead, it was the state itself that was the arbiter and manager of the non-economic imperatives. It did so against the trend in free market liberal capitalism that has developed since the 1970s, but the new embeddedness was at most partial and remained highly political. No major interest groups in society, and certainly not the trade unions and the working class as a whole, were incorporated and thus empowered, and instead the process took firmly *dirigiste* forms.

As with a number of other resource-based economies, a new era in global capitalism emerged in which the problem of embeddedness once again become central. Various forms of capitalism emerged that were labelled 'authoritarian', but the notion of some form of embedded capitalism may be a more appropriate analytical framework.[102] However, in the post-socialist and post-modernization era it is unclear how an economy can become embedded; and thus the tension between embedment projects and wilful political intervention becomes stark. Streeck notes that Polanyi's *Great Transformation* had highlighted increased economic and social regulation, conducted by a more interventionist nation state 'in what by the nineteenth century had already become an international free market economy'.[103] Russia is undergoing a classically liberal economic revolution, combined in a highly contradictory manner with the attempt to restore and recreate elements of embeddedness. Part of the agenda is the great transformation in reverse. Today we have something which

> would seem to amount not just to another wave of economic liberalization, but to a perhaps permanent dismantling of collective capacity to resist liberalization or bind it with a non-liberal institutional context. States embedded in markets, however important they may continue to be for the well-being of their citizens, are something other than than markets embedded in states.[104]

Liberalism and freedom

The Yukos affair was a paradigm of the struggle to achieve liberalism in Russia as a whole. Clearly, freedom is a fundamental dimension of liberalism, together with a range of other values, notably private property, market forces, the rule of

---

[102] Zweynart notes the focus of contemporary Russian institutional economics on the interplay between formal and informal institutions, stressing the importance of traditional behavioural and cultural patterns; in contrast to the view of neoclassical economists, such as Vladimir Mau, who refused to engage with the issue since it could not be 'verified empirically', Zweynart, 'Conflicting Patterns of Thought in the Russian Debate on Transition', pp. 61–2.

[103] Streeck, 'Introduction', p. 37.   [104] Ibid., p. 38.

law, political liberty, and some form of accountability. However, freedom cannot be reduced to liberalism: and the fundamental debate in post-communist Russia is the degree to which freedom can be found in other forms. For example, Akhiezer's analysis of civilization as a category of modernity suggests that freedom can take non-liberal forms.[105] Liberalism is a peculiarly Western form of civilizational expression. Alexander Yakovlev, one of those who fought for the radicalization of perestroika, insisted that Russia could be considered a democratic society only when the state based its actions on legality and the government enjoyed adequate legitimacy.[106] However, Yakovlev well understood that the country's history and culture gave rise to 'a baffling resistance of Russia to the principles of legality and legitimacy of political institutions'.[107] As far as Boris Kapustin is concerned, a distinctly Russian approach to the understanding of liberalism must be sought.[108] The key element in bringing about a new social order is human agency and not the ineluctable operation of sociological laws or the imperative working out of a philosophical idea.[109]

This stricture applies equally to political culture interpretations of the Yukos affair. Much commentary suggested that the government's attack on the company reflected a millennium of arbitrary state power. Hedlund provides a powerful expression of cultural interpretations, arguing that the 'Muscovite model' was reproduced in post-communist Russia, 'where both privatisation and fiscal policy became vehicles for traditional Muscovite rent-granting. Those who succeeded in pleasing the tsar would be granted fattening *kormlenie* in the form of tacit rights to loot oil companies.'[110] In his view, 'through the Yukos affair Putin's Kremlin has made a public mockery of the very notion of the sanctity of property rights, and thus again made clear to would-be entrepreneurs that playing path dependent games for influence and patronage is vastly more important than running businesses according to the rules of modern business schools'.[111] Even the head of the Russian Constitutional Court, Valeri Zor'kin, was susceptible to such arguments: 'Let us speak frankly: our society is ill. We have come from a thousand-years-long slavery and despotism of the authorities when every official was a slave to the superior officials and a despot to the subordinates.'[112] From a different

---

[105] Discussed by Axel Kaehne, *Political and Social Thought in Post-Communist Russia* (London and New York, Routledge, 2007), p. 39.

[106] Alexander Yakovlev, *Striving for Law in a Lawless Land: Memoirs of a Russian Reformer* (Armonk and London, M. E. Sharpe, 1996).

[107] Kaehne, *Political and Social Thought in Post-Communist Russia*, p. 17.

[108] Kapustin, 'Liberal'naya ideya v Rossii'.

[109] Kapustin, 'Freedom from the State'; Kaehne, *Political and Social Thought in Post-Communist Russia*, p. 107.

[110] Stefan Hedlund, 'Vladimir the Great, Grand Prince of Muscovy: Resurrecting the Russian Service State', *Europe–Asia Studies*, Vol. 58, No. 5, July 2006, p. 795.

[111] Ibid, p. 798. For a development of the idea of path dependency, see Stefan Hedlund, *Russia's 'Market' Economy: A Bad Case of Predatory Capitalism* (London, UCL Press, 1999), chapter 8, pp. 268–305.

[112] Vitalii Tseplyaev, 'V. Zor'kin: Pochemu vlast' tak tsinichna?' *Argumenty i fakty*, No. 25, 21 June 2006, p. 3.

perspective Bessonova argues that Russia throughout the ages can be described as an 'economy of distribution' (*razdatochnaya ekonomika*), and thus undermines the development of a normal market economy. The distribution economy is deeply rooted in Russian culture, and serves by turns developmental and power consolidation purposes.[113] The Yukos affair certainly was a grand exercise in redistribution, but then so was the liberal programme of the 1990s, as was the whole Soviet era.

[113] O. E. Bessonova, *Razdatochnyaya ekonomika Rossii: Evolyutsiya cherez transformatsiyu* (Moscow, Rosspen, 2006).

2

The Birth and Transformation of Yukos

You can describe that period any way you like, and you can assess the work of the first president of Russia any way you like. But one thing is beyond any doubt: it was precisely during that period, when Boris Yeltsin was in charge of Russia, that the people of our country, the citizens of Russia, gained the main thing for the sake of which all these transformations were taking place—freedom. This is the huge historic contribution of Boris Yeltsin.

Vladimir Putin[1]

The controversy over the Russian 1990s continues. This was the decade in which the foundations of Russian capitalism were established, and a new dynamic Russia was born, but it was also the era when the political ideals of 'August 1991', the aspiration to create a democratic, constitutional, and law-based state, were subverted, and a class of super-rich individuals (the 'oligarchs') emerged combining economic, media, and political power while a large proportion of the population sank into poverty. Nevertheless, the sinews of a market economy were established, and only a month after the partial default of August 1998 strong economic growth was resumed that continued for the next decade. From a trough of only $10 a barrel of oil in 1998, the price began an upward trajectory against which background economic and political elites struggled to control this 'black gold'. Economic growth was accompanied by a boom in the energy sector, with Russia by 2002 becoming the world's second largest exporter of oil and oil products (after Saudi Arabia). Khodorkovsky's Yukos company exploited the new opportunities to the full, but ultimately fell foul of the state. The 1990s were to cast a long shadow over the succeeding decade, and helped ensure that the desire for order was combined with the demand for strong state. It was this state which under Putin moved to curb the power of the social forces unleashed in the 1990s.

---

[1] Annual press conference for international journalists, 31 January 2006, http://president.kremlin. ru/text/appears/2006/02/101129.shtml. These sentiments were repeated by Putin in his eulogy at the memorial banquet in the Kremlin following Yeltsin's funeral on 25 April 2007: 'It is the rare person who is given the destiny to become free himself and at the same time to carry millions along behind him, and to inspire truly historical changes in his homeland and transform the world', Colton, *Yeltsin*, pp. 447–8.

KHODORKOVSKY: FROM KOMSOMOL ACTIVIST TO OLIGARCH

By the time of his arrest in 2003 Khodorkovsky was top of the Forbes Russia list with $3.7 billion,[2] but the publication of details of the ownership structure of Yukos in June 2002 allowed calculations that in fact Khodorkovsky's share in the company came to $7.7 billion.[3] For many he represented the exemplary 'oligarch', the colloquial term for the economic magnates who made their fortunes during the period of anarchic privatization (known in Russian as *prikhvatizatsiya*, 'piratization') in the 1990s.[4] In contrast to the 'grey privatization' typical in Central Europe, where relatively few insiders managed to leverage political influence for property, the process in Russia can be labelled 'black privatization', and it was to cast a long shadow over the succeeding decade. The new Russian oligarchs fell into three main social categories: 'former factory managers, former members of the communist-era *nomenklatura* (the office-holding class), and those who prior to 1987 were on the margin of Soviet society'.[5] Khodorkovsky if anything fell into the latter category, categorized by Goldman as 'the upstart oligarchs'.[6] His story has been told in a popular novel describing the rise of an outsider oligarch who tried to transform himself into a political leader, which appears a lightly fictionalized version of Khodorkovsky's story and that of the country, in which Putin appears as himself to rebuff the attempt of money to buy power.[7]

Background

Mikhail Khodorkovsky was born in Moscow to a Jewish-Russian family of modest means on 26 June 1963. Like Putin, he spent his first years in a cramped communal apartment, in this case two rooms on Prospekt Mira in north Moscow, and his family only moved into a separate flat in 1971 (it would be another six years before Putin's family received a flat of their own). His parents were typical Moscow technical intelligentsia. His father, Boris Moiseevich, and his mother, Marina Filippovna, were both chemical engineers and spent their working lives at the 'Kalibr' factory turning out precise measuring equipment. In seventh class (aged 13) the young Mikhail took extra lessons in maths in the evenings, and for two summers from the age of 15 he refused to go to Pioneer camp, 'saying he was tired of the

---

[2] 'Kratkii kurs istorii milliarderov', *Izvestiya*, 1 March 2003, p. 2.

[3] Valerii Butaev, 'Khodorkovskii priznalsya v $7 mlrd. s kopeikami', *Komsomol'skaya Pravda*, 22 June 2006, p. 3.

[4] For an outstanding analysis of the way that the oligarchs made their fortunes, including a detailed study of Mikhail Khodorkovsky's rise (pp. 100–26), see David E. Hoffman, *The Oligarchs: Wealth and Power in the New Russia* (New York, PublicAffairs, 2002).

[5] Marshall I. Goldman, *The Piratization of Russia: Russian Reform Goes Awry* (London and New York, Routledge, 2003), p. 103.

[6] Ibid., chapter 7, pp. 123–55.

[7] Marina Yudenich, *Neft'* (Moscow, Popularnaya literatura, 2007).

childish games there', and instead worked in a local bread factory.[8] Like another of the leading oligarchs Roman Abramovich, he started earning extra income from an early age. After the bakers he worked as a carpenter in his local housing cooperative, and then for four years headed a building brigade (the *shabashniki*), including work in Moldova and on BAM, the Baikal–Amur Mainline railway to the north of the Transiberian line.

Khodorkovsky's favourite subject was chemistry, and he changed specialist schools three times until he found one with what he considered the appropriate level of expertise.[9] In 1981 he entered the renowned Mendeleev Institute of Chemical Engineering (MKhTI im. Mendeleeva), graduating in 1986. In his military training at the institute he became a specialist in explosives. He was a model Soviet citizen, and rose to become deputy head of the Komsomol (Communist Youth League, VLKSM) organization in his institute, was elected a member of the Sverdlovsk Komsomol district committee, and then became deputy head of the Frunze district Komsomol committee, at which time he joined the Communist Party of the Soviet Union (CPSU). It was in this district that all the top members of the VLKSM Central Committee were registered, providing many contacts that came in useful later. He was responsible for expelling the then wife of Gleb Pavlovsky, who later became the Kremlin's favourite spin doctor, from the Komsomol when her husband was arrested for 'dissident' activities in the early 1980s.[10] Pavlovsky did not bear a grudge and later opposed Khodorkovsky's arrest.

Party membership did not help him when it came to entering postgraduate studies or in job allocation (*raspredelenie*) after graduating. He was considered too much of a risk-taker to be allowed into graduate school, with a particular liking for explosive substances. He wrote his final year dissertation under the supervision of Alexander Fogel'zang, who considered Khodorkovsky unsuited for research work in experimental chemistry. The Rector Gennady Yagodin is alleged to have stated: 'If the Jew Fogel'zang doesn't accept the Jew Khodorkovsky, then so be it.'[11] The Jewish factor, however, may have played a part since in the late Soviet years an unofficial 'numerus clausus' operated based on the notorious 'fifth point' in the Soviet passport stating nationality. The system applied a perverse type of 'affirmative action' to reduce the assumed disproportionate number of Jews in leading professions. As one of the best students in his class, Khodorkovsky had first choice of jobs on offer, and he chose to go to a 'postbox' ('pochtovyi yashchik'), a closed defence-related enterprise, but because of 'point 5' he was advised to go to an open establishment.[12] Failing to enter graduate school or to be appointed to his chosen post, Khodorkovsky instead turned his energies to business.

---

[8] Mumin Shakirov, 'Khodorkovsky's Parents Worry and Remember', *Moscow Times*, 2 June 2008.

[9] Inna Luk'yanova, 'Chelovek s rublem', *Profil'*, No. 43, 23 November 1998.

[10] Author's interview with Gleb Pavlovsky, Russia House, 28 January 2008.

[11] Larisa Kallioma, 'U Mishi ruki ne ottuda rastut, emu nel'zya exsperimental'noi khimiei', *Izvestiya*, 6 June 2005, p. 3.

[12] Luk'yanova, 'Chelovek s rublem'.

Menatep: From banking to industry

Khodorkovsky graduated just at the time when opportunities dramatically expanded as a result of Gorbachev's perestroika. On 25 July 1986 the CPSU Central Committee adopted rules to govern the development of scientific-technical creative centres for youth (Tsentry nauchno-tekhnicheskogo tvorchestva molodezhi, NTTMs) an idea proposed by the Central Committee of the VLKSM, with further regulations adopted on 28 January 1987 and on 11 and 13 March.[13] The green light was given for the massive development of a 'Komsomol economy' that provided the seedbed for a post-communist entrepreneurial class, acting as privileged auxiliaries to the formal economy. The sponsor of this Chinese-style Party capitalism was Yegor Ligachev, but the initiative turned out very different to what he had anticipated. Youth entrepreneurship quickly turned into a massive money laundering exercise.

With twelve partners from the Mendeleev Institute, in December 1986 Khodorkovsky opened a private café, traded new technologies to Soviet enterprises, imported computers, and sold Polish, Armenian, and French cognac. In 1987 legislation was adopted that allowed the creation of private commercial banks. In that year, with a group of colleagues, he created an NTTM under the Frunze Komsomol district committee, taking on the post of deputy with Sergei Monakhov, the head of the Frunze Komsomol organization, as leader. The cooperative was intended to introduce scientific innovation into production, although basically what they did was buy and sell computers and make a lot of money. A lucrative contract with the High Temperatures Institute of the Academy of Sciences provided an early boost to fuel further development. With a delay of sixty years they took up Nikolai Bukharin's slogan of the New Economic Policy (NEP) years in the 1920s: 'Enrichessez-vous.' By December 1987 over sixty city and districts NTTMs had been established, and soon after their rights were extended. By spring 1990 there were about 600 NTTMs and over 17,000 youth, student, and academic cooperatives sponsored by the Komsomol, employing about a million people.[14] Attempts to rein in the Komsomol economy by that time were futile. Up to the August 1991 coup Khodorkovsky considered himself 'a loyal Communist Party member',[15] and if the Soviet order had not dissolved he would no doubt have been at the head of Chinese-style capitalism within a socialist framework.

Soon after launching himself into business Khodorkovsky in 1987 was joined by Leonid Nevzlin, who answered an advertisement for young entrepreneurial staff. Born on 21 September 1959, Nevzlin in 1981 graduated from the Gubkin Moscow Institute of the Petrochemical and Gas Industries, and later graduated from the Moscow Plekhanov Institute of Economics with a higher degree in management and marketing, and at that time was working as a programmer in

[13] Ol'ga Kryshtanovkaya, *Anatomiya rossiiskoi elity* (Moscow, Zakharov, 2005), pp. 296–7.

[14] Ibid., p. 299.

[15] Rose Brady, *Kapitalizm: Russia's Struggle to Free its Economy* (New Haven, CT, Yale University Press, 1999), p. 55.

'Zarubezhgeologiya'. Nevzlin ably fulfilled all of Khodorkovsky's tasks and quickly rose to become his deputy. The team was also joined by Vladimir Dubov, the son of the bread magnate Matvei Dubov, and by Monakhov's wife, Tatyana Anisimova. Another of Khodorkovsky's associates in this early period was Vladislav Surkov, who later under Putin and Dmitry Medvedev worked as a deputy head of the presidential administration.[16] By the end of 1987 Khodorkovsky was working full-time as director of a network of NTTMs, employing 5,000 people on various research contracts. From the first Khodorkovsky, known at the time as 'Khaider', took a hefty personal share of the profits, normally a quarter and occasionally up to a half.[17]

In August 1988 the Commercial Innovation Bank for Scientific and Technical Progress (AKIB), chaired by Khodorkovsky up to 1990, was co-founded by Zhilsotsbank and the State Committee for Science and Technology, operating as a cooperative based on NTTM principles in partnership with the Moscow Soviet. It was within this framework that the interbank organization 'Menatep' (Mezhotraslevye i nauchno-tekhnicheskie programmy, from whence the name 'Menatep') was developed with some twenty separate enterprises. At this time the Centre for Inter-Sectoral Scientific-Technical Programmes (Tsentr mezhotraslevykh nauchno-tekhnicheskikh program) was created. Khodorkovsky used his leadership of the Scientific and Youth Union to merge the various organizations into the trading company, which on 29 December 1988 was registered as a bank and formally took on the name of Menatep in May 1990 when it was reregistered, and in December of that year was one of the first companies in Russia to issue what at the time passed for shares.

Bank Menatep had a starting capital of only R5 million ($8 million), a very low figure for the time, and persistent rumours suggest that some of the bank's early funds were provided by the Komsomol Central Committee, and even from the CPSU itself.[18] Khodorkovsky admitted later that he relied on protection from the state committee on science and technology to ward off challenges from the police and security services. The company's development from 1989 was greatly helped by Khodorkovsky's Komsomol colleague, Alexei Golubovich, whose parents held top positions in the Soviet State Bank and thus allowed one of its subsidiaries, the Frunze district branch of Zhilsotsbank, to help Menatep, as well as through the elite connections of the parents of his associate, Vladimir Dubov, which gave Khodorkovsky access to political figures all the way up to Gorbachev.[19] These political links allowed Menatep to handle the accounts of the Chernobyl disaster committee (nuclear reactor No. 4 at Chernobyl in Ukraine had exploded on

---

[16] Kryshtanovkaya, *Anatomiya rossiiskoi elity*, p. 303.

[17] Vladimir Perekrest, 'Za chto sidit Mikhail Khodorkovskii', Part 1, *Izvestiya*, 17 May 2006; http://www.izvestia.ru/investigation/article3092856/index.html.

[18] Goldman, *The Piratization of Russia*, p. 147.

[19] This information surfaced following the search of the basement of Media-Most's security department in 2000 in which a database was found with telephone transcripts, Rimma Akhmirova, *Ya sidel s khodorkovskim: Dokumental'nye khroniki* (Moscow, Sobesednik, 2005), p. 133; see also V. M. Kartashov, *Who Is Mr. Hodorkovsky?* (Rostov-na-Donu, Feniks, 2007), pp. 83–4.

25 April 1986), up to 60 per cent of which are alleged to have disappeared. At the same time Khodorkovsky continued his studies, and in 1988 graduated as a specialist in finances (*finansist*) from the Plekhanov Economics Institute. Only later, in January 1990, was the bank joined by Platon Lebedev, who would go on to become its head. Lebedev was also a graduate of the Plekhanov Institute who had then been employed as a planner in Zarubezhgeologiya (where Nevzlin had also worked), before demonstrating that he was a financier of genius.

Menatep soon overtook most of its competitors. There were a number of reasons for this. First, the bank's area of specialization, foreign trade, was one where capital accumulation grew the fastest. Second, the bank was particularly active in the foreign currency market, and Menatep was one of the first private banks to receive a licence to deal in this. Foreign currency operations were handled by Menatep SA, established in late 1989 for this purpose, which had subsidiaries in Gibralter (which from 1997 became Group Menatep Ltd, later GML) and Budapest. Third, and certainly far from least, if state enterprises diverted virtual rouble resources (*beznalichnye*) through the accounts of NTTMs they could receive in exchange real money. In effect, this was a licence to print money as state companies used the bank to convert nominal rouble accounts into currency. The golden days of this particular scheme did not last long, once everyone jumped on the bandwagon, but Khodorkovsky had plenty of other schemes to keep him busy. Fourth, the company was also active in domestic trade, including computers from France and Napoleon cognac. Fifth, the bank from 1990 took in money from the population (some R2.5 million), who heeded the warnings broadcast in Menatep advertising campaigns about the danger that inflation would take away their life savings. Very few ever saw returns from the allegedly high dividend earning vouchers (*veksely*) that they bought, and most lost the capital they invested. Menatep now became a household name, with a reputation not much better than Sergei Mavrodi's MMM pyramid scheme.[20] Finally, and perhaps most crucially, the company enjoyed strong links with the government. On one occasion in its early days Menatep took a $1 million state loan, sold it at commercial rates and returned the loan in roubles, and made a handsome profit of R9 million on the deal.[21] Menatep took the lead in acting on behalf of the state to conduct transactions, acting as a delegated authority. By 1991 Menatep was one of the first banks licensed to service trade with Ukraine and Belarus.[22] There are also rumours that the bank played a part in handling the possibly mythical Communist 'party gold' transactions in the final period of Soviet power.[23] There were persistent rumours that Menatep had been founded on 'Party money', and by the time of

[20] For details of the scheme, see Sergei Mavrodi, *Vsya pravda o 'MMM': Istoriya pervoi piramidy. Tyuremnye dnevniki* (Moscow, RIPOL klassik, 2007).

[21] Kryshtanovkaya, *Anatomiya rossiiskoi elity*, p. 305.

[22] Valery Kryukov and Arild Moe, 'Banks and the Financial Sector', in David Lane (ed.), *The Political Economy of Russian Oil* (Lanham, MD, Rowman & Littlefield, 1999), chapter 2, pp. 47–74, at p. 52.

[23] Kirill Venediktov, 'Roman s neft'yu: Zek i gubernator', *Smysl'*, No. 1 (20), January 2008, pp. 28–9, at p. 28. This activity was handled by N. Kruchina, head of administration of the CC CPSU, who committed suicide soon after the August 1991 coup.

the August 1991 coup the CPSU Central Committee had created over a hundred banks and commercial structures, many of them headed by active or reserve KGB officers.[24]

Like many banks of the time, Menatep (like Inkombank, Al'fa-Bank and others, most of which also had their roots in the Komsomol) was sponsored by a business group, and they in turn provided the flexibility and resources for trading and manufacturing groups to expand. With the fall of communism and the coming to power of Yeltsin in Russia in 1991, Menatep's fortunes soared.[25] Khodorkovsky's trading operations included international commodity shipments, notably a major oil-for-sugar deal with Cuba, and he also dealt with the notorious trader Marc Rich. His offshore operations antedated the fall of communism by a year. Above all, Bank Menatep was authorized to handle the funds of the finance ministry, the state taxation service, and (with Most-Bank headed by Vladimir Gusinsky, who was also head of the banking consortium handling Moscow's budget) the city of Moscow. Menatep handled the funding of a number of federal programmes: in addition to managing the cash for the Chernobyl cleanup it was later involved in the reconstruction of Chechnya, in the course of which some $4.4 billion disappeared.[26]

Khodorkovsky remained chair of Menatep's board of directors to April 1996, at which point Lebedev took over operational control. In 1991 Khodorkovsky acted as an adviser to the Russian prime minister Ivan Silaev, which gave him access to privileged information. He was one of those defending the White House, the seat of the Russian government, during the attempted coup of August 1991, although he went more out of loyalty to his chief than out of ideological conviction.[27] In 1992, Khodorkovsky became head of the investment fund for the fuel-energy industry with the status of deputy minister of fuel and energy of the Russian Federation, responsible for private investment. At this time Surkov, head of advertising for Menatep, was also an adviser on public relations to the Russian government.[28] Surkov devised Menatep's first campaigns and made Khodorkovsky famous.[29] Following the creation of Rosvooruzhenie, the arms export monopoly, by presidential decree on 18 November 1993 Menatep handled its foreign currency accounts. In 1993 Khodorkovsky headed both the management and the board

---

[24] Kartashov, *Who Is Mr. Hodorkovsky?*, pp. 105, 114–15. One of them, the Vserossiiskii Birzhevoi Bank, funded Boris Yeltsin's presidential campaign in June 1991, and thus already he was becoming financially independent of the democratic movement that brought him to power. Similarly, the head of the bank, A. Konanykhin, received privileges in turn and free access to the Kremlin once Yeltsin moved in there in late December 1991, making him Russia's richest man, and establishing a pattern of state–business relations that would prove fateful for Yeltsin's presidency.

[25] For an account of this early period, see Paul Klebnikov, 'The Oligarch Who Came in From the Cold', *Forbes*, 18 March 2002; http://www.forbes.com/forbes/2002/0318/110_print.html.

[26] David Satter, *Darkness at Dawn: The Rise of the Russian Criminal State* (New Haven, CT, Yale University Press, 2003), pp. 272–3, n. 5; for further details of these alleged machinations, see Matt Bivens and Jonas Bernstein, 'The Russia You Never Met', *Demokratizatsiya: The Journal of Post-Soviet Democratization*, Vol. 6, No. 4, Fall 1998, pp. 613–47.

[27] Panyushkin, *Mikhail Khodorkovskii*, p. 63.

[28] Kartashov, *Who Is Mr. Hodorkovsky?*, p. 85.   [29] Hoffman, *The Oligarchs*, pp. 122–3.

of directors of Menatep. In March 1993 he was appointed deputy to the fuel and energy minister, Yuri Shafranik, as well as acting as an adviser on finances to Prime Minister Chernomyrdin. In a meeting in the Kremlin at that time he called on business to go into industry, since it was shameful to make money out of trade.[30] In 1994 he joined the council of authorized banks under the Moscow mayor's office, and at the same time worked as the deputy head of the Russian government's Council for Industrial Policy and Entrepreneurship, and up to 1996 was part of a government group designed to improve wage payments. Menatep was the only bank mentioned by name in a 1994 CIA report warning that 'the majority of Russian banks are controlled by the dreaded Mafia'.[31]

In 1992 Menatep shifted its focus from purely financial activities to create Rosprom, a holding company to manage its industrial interests. Khodorkovsky became chair of the board of directors of the reformed Rosprom, which was registered as a stock company on 1 September 1995. In the early 1990s, Menatep was flooded with more money than it knew how to handle, and thus in 1994/5 Menatep was an active player in investment auctions, winning controlling shares in a number of companies. In his characteristic manner Khodorkovsky thought in grandiose terms, and as good as his word, used some of this money to create a major industrial empire. He bought up any available company, including the Apatit mineral fertilizer company in Murmansk region that was later to play such a fateful role in the Yukos affair, as well as the Uralelektromed' copper plant, the Sredneuralsky and Kirovogradsky copper works, the Volga pipe plant, Russia's largest producer of titanium AO Avisma, as well as textile, wood, and food plants, including the Ust-Ilimskii wood-processing plant.[32] By March 1996, through Rosprom, Menatap had controlling shares in twenty-nine industrial enterprises and major holdings in another fifty.[33]

Most of these companies were bought in investment auctions, in which money had to be found after purchase. Of course, most of the new owners did not fulfil their promises, Khodorkovsky among them. In the case of the Apatit plant, the company was bought cheaply, through Menatep's 'AOZT Volna' subsidiary, but the condition of the purchase was to invest in the company. Fearing that the old Apatit management would simply steal the money or misuse it, Menatep took over the management of the company, paid the wages, optimized taxes and invested in infrastructure, or so Menatep argued. These indirect investments were the basis for the judicial resolution of charges that Menatep had made the requisite

[30] Perekrest, 'Za chto sidit Mikhail Khodorkovskii', Part 1.

[31] Marshall I. Goldman, *Oilopoly: Putin, Power, and the Rise of the New Russia* (Oxford, Oneworld Publications, 2008), p. 109. There were also persistent reports about Menatep's links with organized crime, notably in laundering the funds of the Ingush mafia. Khodorkovsky immediately sought to bring the CIA on-side, and organized a major event for them and influential Americans at the Russian embassy in Washington, the first major case of his independent foreign policy entrepreneurship. Kartashov, *Who Is Mr. Hodorkovsky?*, p. 101.

[32] http://www.alexey-pichugin.ru/index.php?id=251.

[33] Natal'ya Gotova, 'Mikhail Khodorkovskii ukhodit v promyshlennost'', *Segodnya*, 29 March 1996.

investment in Apatit, until the case was reopened on political grounds.[34] Later the company was returned to the state, as was the Volzhsky Pipe Factory for similar reasons.

Menatep was the most prominent of all the new banks and from the first had a distinctive approach to business. It devoted considerable efforts to public relations, including the regional press. The company did not hesitate to exploit its links with the authorities. As Surkov put it at the time, the company planned to forge a 'clan' with its major clients, including regular contacts and the creation of a special department in Menatep to lobby the interests of its clients in state structures.[35] It was in this context that Lebedev first used the term 'oligarch' to describe the new elite when on 11 November 1992 Menatep announced the creation of a special department 'to provide banking services for the financial-industrial oligarchy'.[36] In other words, Menatep was willing to extend its usual manner of working, where business and the state were entwined, to its clients. Menatep created one of the most powerful lobbying structures in post-communist Russia. The relationship was largely one-way, with Menatep shaping government policy, while the state had few levers to exert influence in the other direction. Lobbying power was the great strength of the company in the early days, but it also later proved its downfall once the regime changed and the company was unable to change its attitude to government.

This activity was overseen by Nevzlin and Dubov, enjoying particularly close relations with Boris Fëdorov, minister of finance until January 1994, although close relations continued thereafter. The 'merger' of state and business was evident when in October 1994 Konstantin Kagalovsky was appointed deputy head of Menatep's board of directors. From November 1991 Kagalovsky had negotiated on behalf of the Russian government with international financial institutions, and from October 1992 until he joined Menatep he was Russia's nominated IMF director. Khodorkovsky enjoyed good relations with the former acting prime minister Yegor Gaidar, and was one of the main financial sponsors of his party, Russia's Choice, in the December 1993 elections.[37] Early evidence of the tension between Nevzlin's more neo-liberal views and those of Khodorkovsky, who according to John Lloyd 'was a supporter of a strong, centrist government and a powerful state in partnership with the financial sector', was already apparent.[38] These elections, taking place in the shadow of the bloodshed of October 1993 (when Khodorkovsky unequivocally supported Yeltsin in his confrontation with parliament), proved a disappointment for organized liberalism, and thereafter all parties declined as instruments of political intermediation as the regime increasingly relied directly on the support of big business and the security apparatus.

[34] Panyushkin, *Mikhail Khodorkovskii*, pp. 63–5, 213–17.

[35] *Kommersant*, 13 October 1992; Kartashov, *Who Is Mr. Hodorkovsky?*, pp. 86–7.

[36] Kartashov, *Who Is Mr. Hodorkovsky?*, p. 196.

[37] Ibid., p. 88. The Media-Most group headed by Gusinsky also supported Gaidar, but his main party-building effort went into supporting the social liberal Yabloko party headed by Grigory Yavlinsky.

[38] John Lloyd, *Rebirth of a Nation: An Anatomy of Russia* (London, Michael Joseph, 1998), p. 306.

Gustafson is sceptical about the 'myth of the all-powerful Russian banks', but concedes that banking power was strongly in evidence in the case of Yukos and Sidanko.[39] Professional oilmen in these companies gave way to the rule of financiers with no experience in the industry. In Menatep no single shareholder owned more than 5 per cent of stock, with more than twenty organizations, including the oil trader Nafta-Moskva, among its main early shareholders. With the abolition of state financing for capital investment in the oil industry in 1993/4, accompanied by the conversion of state oil enterprises into joint-stock companies and their subsequent privatization, the opportunities for Moscow banks expanded, at the expense of the smaller regional banks. It was at this time that holding companies such as Lukoil, Yukos, and Surgutneftegaz were established (see below), requiring strong financial organizations to manage their financial affairs. The initial partner for Yukos was Promradtekhbank, which had helped manage the company from its inception in 1992. However, as the drive to convert ramshackle holding companies into vertically integrated operations began, Promradtekhbank lacked the size or skills and was marginalized, and in the end became the depository for Yukos shares.

Although later Yukos would fall victim to a faction of the *siloviki* (officials with a security background or orientation), the company was no stranger to the security establishment, having become one of the largest employers of ex-KGB officials.[40] In the 1990s most companies employed former security officials, usually organized as an 'analytical department'.[41] Like all other companies of the time, Menatep proved an attractive soft-landing for unemployed KGB officers, employing some 230 people in its security service in the early 1990s. One of these was Victor Ivanenko, for a brief period the head of the KGB's successor agency. Another was former KGB general Alexei Kondaurov, who joined Menatep in 1994 as the deputy head of security and then he led the analytical office in Rosprom before in 1997 moving over full-time to head the analytical office in Yukos and becoming an adviser to Khodorkovsky.[42] He collected data (some would say *kompromat*) on the company's opponents. He was elected a Communist deputy in 1999, and remained in parliament until December 2007. Both Ivanenko and Kondaurov, subordinates to Khodorkovsky, outranked Putin, who had risen no higher than lieutenant-colonel in the service.

The Menatep headquarters in Kolpachnyi Pereulok, a neo-Gothic edifice with turrets and crenellations built by Baron von Knoppe in the late nineteenth century,

[39] Thane Gustafson, *Capitalism Russian-Style* (Cambridge, Cambridge University Press, 1999), p. 89.

[40] Arkady Ostrovsky, 'Putin Oversees Rise of Security Apparatus', *Financial Times*, 31 October 2003.

[41] Paul Klebnikov, *Godfather of the Kremlin: Boris Berezovsky and the Looting of Russia* (New York, Harcourt, 2000); we shall be citing the Russian version, Pavel Khlebnikov, *Krestnyi otets Kremlya Boris Berezovskii, ili Istoriya razgrableniya Rossii* (Moscow, Detektiv-Press, 2001), p. 6. The security service of Vladimir Gusinsky's Most group numbered over a thousand, with its largest part headed by the former KGB colonel-general Filipp Bobkov, a former deputy head of the KGB, ibid., p. 151.

[42] Interview with Anthony Latta, 'Khodorkovsky, Menatep and Yukos', *Moscow News*, 24 March 2004, p. 1.

had formerly hosted the city and regional Komsomol committees, and its transfer to private entrepreneurs symbolized the new era. The huge cars of Menatep
officials blocked the pavements, forcing pedestrians (the 'little people' in Leona
Helmsley's vivid phrase), to navigate between moving traffic. There was a new
power in the land, and it was not bashful in announcing its presence.

Establishment and privatization of Yukos

Already by the late Brezhnev years, oil and gas exports had become the main
source of foreign currency for the Soviet Union, which was used to import
machine tools and consumer goods.[43] Soviet oil production peaked in 1987 at
625.5 million tonnes (12.6 million barrels a day, henceforth mbd), of which
570 million (11.4 mbd) were pumped by Russia alone, but by 1992 Saudi
Arabia overtook Russia to become the world's largest oil producer. Soviet oil
production began to fall in November 1988, with a precipitous collapse of
54 million tonnes in 1991 alone, and by 1998 Russian output had fallen to only
53 per cent (303 million tonnes, 6.1 mbd) of its peak a decade earlier.[44] Thereafter
oil production began to rise, with a rapid acceleration in the early 2000s to reach
480.5 million tonnes (9.8 mbd) in 2006 and once again overtook Saudi Arabia in
output terms in 2007.[45] By the late 1990s, the energy complex had become one of
the key sectors of the Russian economy, accounting 'for 25 per cent of industrial
output, 38 per cent of the federal budget revenues, and more than 50 per cent of
the overall value of exports'.[46] The oil industry alone in 1998 provided 22 per cent
of the budget at all levels, up from 6 per cent in 1994.[47]

In the early 1990s the integrated Soviet oil industry was broken up, but the gas
industry was kept as a single unit. The old gas ministry was transformed into a
hybrid state *kontsern*, Gazprom, in August 1989 under its former minister and
now CEO, Viktor Chernomyrdin, who went on to become prime minister from
December 1992 to March 1998. Gazprom would become Russia's largest corporation, owning more than a fifth of the world's gas deposits.[48] If the Komsomol
economy was one source of the new elite, another was former state managers ('red
directors') who took charge of whole branches of the economy. They thrived by
exploiting the grey area between state and private interests. Chernomyrdin's successor at the head of Gazprom was his deputy, Rem Vyakhirev, who in November

[43] See Thane Gustafson, *Crisis Amid Plenty: The Politics of Soviet Energy under Brezhnev and Gorbachev* (Princeton, NJ, Princeton University Press, 1989).

[44] Goldman, *Oilopoly*, p. 36; Russian figures modified by Anders Åslund, 'Russia's Energy Policy: A Framing Comment', *Eurasian Geography and Economics*, Vol. 47, No. 3, 2006, p. 323.

[45] Goldman, *Oilopoly*, p. 37.

[46] David Lane, 'Introduction', in David Lane (ed.), *The Political Economy of Russian Oil* (Lanham, MD, Rowman & Littlefield, 1999), p. 2.

[47] *Izvestiya*, 12 January 1999, p. 2.

[48] See Jonathan P. Stern, *The Future of Russian Gas and Gazprom* (Oxford, Oxford University Press for the Oxford Institute for Energy Studies, 2005).

1992 was authorized by Yeltsin to change the company from a wholly state-owned joint stock company into a private one, and in February its stock went on the market, leaving only 38 per cent in state hands by the time Putin came to power in 2000.[49] Vyakhirev allowed various entities of the company to be hived off to insiders, including the distribution company Itera, based in Jacksonville, Florida. The main companies dealing with the transport of oil and oil products, Transneft and Transneftprodukt, also remained in state hands, as did the coal industry (Rosugol') and the electricity industry, which became RAO UES (Russian Stock Company United Energy Systems, Edinye Energosistemy, henceforth UES) until broken up and privatized from 1 July 2008. UES from March 1998 was headed by Anatoly Chubais, the architect of privatization and one of the few former academics to make a successful career in politics and state management.

Prior to 1992 the Russian oil industry was organized in thirty-two production associations and twenty-nine refineries.[50] From that year the sector was broken up into a number of what were intended to become vertically integrated companies on the Western model, as well as being regionally concentrated. In September 1991 the property of the fuel and energy ministry was transformed into a joint stock company Rosneftegaz, which by presidential decree No. 1403 of 17 November 1992 simply became Rosneft, and the same decree opened the way for the privatization of the industry, effectively hiving off companies from Rosneft. The ministry was no longer allowed to manage companies. Rosneft had always been intended to be a major state-owned player, and its leadership never quite got over losing valuable assets, and later took its revenge.[51] Thus Russia set out on a different path to the oil producing states of the Middle East, Mexico, and Norway, where monopolistic state-owned companies predominate. Vagit Alekperov, as acting minister of the petroleum industry, already in November 1991 had bundled together the Langepaz, Urengoi, and Kogalym oilfields into a single concern called LUKoil (hereafter Lukoil)[52] and placed himself at its head.[53] This was a classic case of 'nomenklatura privatization', and it would be repeated later with Surgutneftegaz.

The detailed plan for the industry as a whole was devised by Shafranik, the minister of fuel and energy between 1993 and 1996. Seven pyramid structures were created, which bundled controlling stakes of a larger number of producing

[49] See Mikhail Zygar and Valeri Panyushkin, *Gazprom: Novoe russkoe oruzhie* (Moscow, Zakharov, 2008).

[50] Nina Poussenkova, *From Rigs to Riches: Oilmen Vs. Financiers in the Russian Oil Sector* (Rice University, TX, The James A. Baker III Institute for Public Policy, October 2004), p. 1.

[51] See Nina Poussenkova, 'Rosneft' kak zerkalo russkoi evolyutsii', *Pro et Contra*, Vol. 10, Nos. 2–3, March–June 2006, pp. 91–104.

[52] Some companies at various points presented their name in part or in full in upper case. Thus in the 1990s it would be technically correct to write of YuKOS, LUKoil (to this day) and ONAKO. For the sake of consistency and aesthetic simplicity I shall use lower case throughout for all companies.

[53] Lukoil also had four refineries in Perm, Volgograd, Ufa, as well as the Mazeikiu plant in Lithuania, Konstantin Simonov, *Russkaya neft': Poslednii peredel* (Moscow, Eksmo Algoritm, 2005), p. 10.

companies into oil holding companies combining production, refining, and distribution capacities: Lukoil, Sidanko, Sibneft, Rosneft, Tyumen Oil Company (TNK), Yukos and the Eastern Oil Company (VNK, which had a controlling stake in Tomskneft and the Achinsk refinery, and a 20 per cent stake in the Tomsk petrochemical plant). Domestic oil prices were allowed to rise ever-closer to world levels, and in March 1995 the system of state export quotas was abolished. By 1998 the break-up of the Russian oil industry had been largely achieved, with a deregulated sector dominated by a dozen more or less vertically integrated companies.[54] One of these was Yukos.

The Yukos oil company was created in April 1993 as a result of the merger of two state-owned companies, the West Siberian oil producer Yuganskneftegaz (henceforth YNG) based in the Khanty-Mansi autonomous *okrug* (district) of Tyumen region, and the Volga-based refining company Kuibyshevnefteorgsintez. The former contributed the 'Yu' and the latter the 'kos' to Yukos. The company included the upstream producer Samaraneftegaz (SNG), three refineries in Samara *oblast'* (region), eight oil distribution networks, and various geological and technical service agencies.[55] The company was formally registered on 12 May 1993 within the framework of the government decree of 15 April 1993. The company was Russia's second largest oil producer, and in terms of reserves in first place. The company's general director was Sergei Muravlenko, a professional *'neftyanik'* ('oilnik') who had worked as a director with YNG. In its early days Yukos was notorious for its lack of internal cohesion. In particular, from the first the relationship between Yukos and its main production subsidiary, YNG, was antagonistic. The pyramid structure is an open invitation for the holding company to exploit subsidiaries in which they have no real stake. YNG itself became a joint-stock company and created its own bank, Tokobank, which went on to become a major national bank. Although Muravlenko had come from YNG this did not prevent major conflicts between the two organizations. YNG resisted attempts of the parent company to consolidate the enterprise. As so often, Khodorkovsky used his government contacts to resolve the problem, in this case through Vladimir Lopukhin, who had been minister of fuel and energy in Gaidar's government in 1991/2. Khodorkovsky, at the head of Menatep, acted as an adviser to Lopukhin, and devised the first investment programme of the ministry. Lopukhin had then become head of the Russian subsidiary of the French bank, Lazard Frères, which acted as a consultant to Yukos. Khodorkovsky, Muravlenko, and Lopukhin worked closely after 1992, and once Lopukhin lost his post with Lazard Frères, Menatep was ready to step in and work with Muravlenko to transform Yukos into a consolidated company.[56]

---

[54] Lukoil, Yukos, Surgutneftegaz, Sidanko, Slavneft, Rosneft, Sibneft, Tyumenskaya Neftyanaya Kompaniya (TNK), Vostochnaya Neftyanaya Kompaniya (VNK), Onako, Komitek, and Tatneft. David Lane and Iskander Seifulmulukov, 'Structure and Ownership', in Lane (ed.), *The Political Economy of Russian Oil*, p. 19. Onako was taken over by TNK in 2000, and Slavneft by Sibneft in 2002.

[55] The three oil refineries (NPZ) were Kuibyshev, Syzran, and Novokuibyshev.

[56] Kryukov and Moe, 'Banks and the Financial Sector', p. 57.

Khodorkovsky established close relations with Chernomyrdin once he was appointed deputy prime minister responsible for the fuel and energy complex on 30 May 1992,[57] and these served him well during Chernomyrdin's premiership when he turned a blind eye to abuses in the privatization process. In the first stage of privatization from August 1992 vouchers were distributed free of charge to Russian citizens, but the majority soon accumulated in the hands of a few companies. Every single investment company created to manage citizen stock portfolios failed, leading to widespread anger and disillusionment with the whole process. From 1 July 1994 privatization vouchers were no longer valid, and cash auctions became the main instrument for privatization. The state kept a large stake in some of the oil companies for the first three years, owning 45 per cent of the stock of Lukoil, Yukos, and Surgutneftegaz, while 40 per cent was sold for investment tenders by banks and other investors, and the rest were to be acquired by voucher-holders. Foreign investors could hold no more than a 15 per cent stake, a ceiling that was later lifted.[58] The problem of legitimizing the privatization process of the 1990s was one of the central political preoccupations of the 2000s and its architect, Chubais, became one of the most reviled figures in Russian politics, as he admitted in a later interview.[59]

The 1992 privatization programme for the oil industry stipulated that the state would initially retain a controlling interest. The general rule was that 38 per cent of ordinary shares (51 per cent of voting shares) were to be retained by the state for three years. With most oil companies established in spring 1993, this period would run out in early 1996. Although it could easily have been extended by parliament, the pressing financial needs of the state, with the budget deficit by 1995 reaching 10 per cent of GDP, led to the disbursement of the state's share. Seizing the opportunity, a number of leading banks offered credit to the government on security of government shares in privatized enterprises. The idea was given public expression on behalf of a consortium of commercial banks by Vladimir Potanin, head of Oneksimbank, at a cabinet meeting on 30 March 1995, which Khodorkovsky also attended as well as Alexander Smolensky from the Stolichnyi Bank.[60] Potanin alone spoke, and the plan was adopted by the deputy premiers Chubais and Oleg Soskovets, as well as the prime minister, Chernomyrdin.[61] The scheme was formalized by a presidential decree of 31 August 1995, allowing investors to take over a share of trust stakes for a set period in exchange for extending credit to the government. The allocation of shares would take place through auctions, from which foreigners were excluded. Investment tender competitions in state-owned oil companies would also take place, so

[57] Kartashov, *Who Is Mr. Hodorkovsky?*, pp. 86, 124.
[58] Lane and Seifulmulukov, 'Structure and Ownership', p. 25.
[59] Spiegal-Gespräch, 'Alles andere als optimal', *Der Spiegel*, No. 39, 24 September 2007, pp. 78–82.
[60] For a general analysis of the loans-for-shares scheme, see Duncan Allan, 'Banks and the Loans-for-Shares Auctions', in David Lane (ed.), *Russian Banking: Evolution, Problems and Prospects* (Cheltenham, Edward Elgar, 2002), pp. 137–59.
[61] Khlebnikov, *Krestnyi otets Kremlya Boris Berezovskii*, p. 199.

the winner would pay for shares and also commit to investment in the relevant company.[62]

By September 1995 a list of forty-four companies was drawn up by the State Property Committee (Goskomimushchestvo, GKI, headed by Chubais) of which twenty-nine were selected to be auctioned in the first wave, including Norilsk Nickel (51 per cent of its shares), Lukoil (5 per cent), Yukos (45 per cent), Surgut-neftegaz (40 per cent), Sidanko (51 per cent), Sibneft (51 per cent), and a little later a quarter of Svyazinvest.[63] Already by late 1995 the first loans-for-shares and investment auctions were held, accompanied by accusations that the auctions had been rigged, but the results were nevertheless approved by Chubais' ally, Alfred Kokh, now at the head of GKI, and stand to this day. While Lukoil management was able to keep control of most of its assets, and there remains a mystery about the beneficiaries of the privatization of Surgutneftegaz,[64] Yukos fell prey to the Menatep bank group. Menatep was put in charge of processing the bids for the Yukos auction, and it was represented in the auction on 8 December 1995 by the two permitted bids (the main one was the Laguna company, especially created for the purpose since Yukos could not represent itself),[65] while a third, which offered more money than Khodorkovsky's team, not surprisingly, was disqualified on technical grounds.[66] Menatep thus gained 45 per cent of state stock in the loans-for-shares auction for $159 million, $9 million above the starting price. The associated investment tender in December 1995 saw a further 33 per cent of Yukos stock going to Menatep for $150 million, with the bank pledged to invest a further $300 million over the next three years. The bottom line was that Khodorkovsky and his partners paid a total of $350 million upfront for control of 78 per cent of Yukos stock, suggesting that the total value of the company was $450 million, although at the same time they were taking on some $3 billion of debt. With later share emissions that further diluted the state's holding, by autumn 1996 Menatep owned 90 per cent of Yukos stock. When the shares began trading in 1997, Yukos's

---

[62] Kryukov and Moe, 'Banks and the Financial Sector', p. 62.

[63] Kryshtanovkaya, *Anatomiya rossiiskoi elity*, p. 326.

[64] At the privatization auction of Surgutneftegaz in 1995 a 62 per cent stake was purchased by a pension fund that was in reality a Surgutneftegaz subsidiary, so the company became owned by a subunit. The fate of this 62 per cent stake is unknown, and it remains unclear about who owns it despite the efforts of the minority shareholders owning the other 38 per cent to find out. When the largest foreign investment fund in Russia, Hermitage Capital (one of the minority shareholders), started its own investigation in 2004, its head, Bill Browder, in November 2005 was banned from Russia and various tax proceedings have been started against the company. The CEO of Surgutneftegaz from the first was the Kremlin loyalist Vladimir Bogdanov, who headed what became the company from the mid-1980s.

[65] The hitherto unknown company was registered in Taldom in Moscow region, and the whole process was conducted in a manner prefiguring the role that the unknown Baikal Finance Group would play in December 2004 in allowing Rosneft to buy Yukos's main production field, Yuganskneftegaz. The state had now learnt to play by the same rules as the oligarchs.

[66] The third bid represented a consortium of Al'fa bank, Inkombank, and Rossiiskii Kredit, and was rejected for 'the absence of properly filled out banking documents', Satter, *Darkness at Dawn*, p. 108; Khlebnikov, *Krestnyi otets Kremlya Boris Berezovskii*, p. 203; Panyushkin, *Mikhail Khodorkovskii*, pp. 72–3.

market capitalization was $9 billion, and reached some $15 billion by early 2002. In 1996, however, Khodorkovsky was still joking that the winners of the shares-for-loans auction were 'a collection of bankrupts', although he personally was not doing so badly.[67]

It was at this time that Norilsk Nickel fell into Potanin's hands as a result of the loans-for-shares scheme. The winners were exclusively new banks. As a study of the affair in 1999 notes: 'The development of close relationships with the state remains an important business strategy in Russia.'[68] This was never truer than with Boris Berezovsky, who was able to acquire Sibneft, belatedly created in August 1995 at his behest through his Logovaz-United Bank allied with Stolichnyi Bank Sberezhenii (SBS). The SBS bank in effect acted as the executive agency for Berezovsky, even though it formally was responsible for organizing the auction of Sibneft shares.[69]

In the case of Yukos, Menatep had established a close relationship with the company, so it was already an insider at the time of the auctions. Unlike some other oil companies, Menatep then played a major part in the further development of the oil company.[70] For this it used Rosprom, effectively a financial-industrial group (FIG), but one created from below that already by late 1994 was one of the biggest with about sixty companies within its portfolio.[71] FIGs were formally established by the law of 27 October 1995 as a way of bringing together financial and industrial organizations, and were to be officially registered as a specific form of organization, although there were many unregistered ones.[72] Whatever the legal form, Khodorkovsky would go on to play a large part in shaping the Russian oil industry, and his personal leadership would be crucial in the development of Yukos, based to a large degree on personal connections, powerful public relations, and willingness to innovate.

YUKOS: CONSOLIDATION AND CRISIS

If the first stage in Yukos's development was assembling the company and giving it a rudimentary corporate structure, the second was privatization of its stock, the bulk of which went to Menatep, then the third stage was transforming ownership into control. The methods used to achieve this reflected the harshest period of

---

[67] Khlebnikov, *Krestnyi otets Kremlya Boris Berezovskii*, p. 262.

[68] Kryukov and Moe, 'Banks and the Financial Sector', p. 63.

[69] Menatep at this time helped Berezovsky acquire Sibneft, and in turn the latter's financial structures helped Menatep win Yukos, a system of mutual guarantees, Khlebnikov, *Krestnyi otets Kremlya Boris Berezovskii*, p. 201.

[70] Valery Kryukov and Arild Moe, *The Changing Role of Banks in the Russian Oil Sector* (London, RIIA, 1998).

[71] Kryshtanovkaya, *Anatomiya rossiiskoi elity*, p. 325.

[72] Juliet Johnson, 'Russia's Emerging Financial-Industrial Groups', *Post-Soviet Affairs*, Vol. 13, No. 4, 1997, pp. 333–65.

'robber baron' capitalism in Russia. A whole range of 'informal corporate governance practices' were applied, including share dilution, asset stripping, transfer pricing, undermining shareholder voting rights and forced bankruptcies. As Adachi notes, these practices 'performed important functions in relation to the conversion of post-Soviet former state enterprises into functional firms, able to perform as business units in a market economy'.[73] Yukos became notorious for the vigorous application of these methods, but out of it emerged a competitive vertically integrated company.

Consolidation and development

Having taken over Yukos, the first wholly private Russian oil company, the immediate task for Menatep-Rosprom was to consolidate responsibility. At a meeting of Yukos's board of directors in April 1996, Menatep representatives took over some leading roles in the company, with Khodorkovsky becoming first vice president with responsibility for planning (including oil refining, petrochemicals, and sales) while at the same time remaining the head of Rosprom and Menatep.[74] Yukos, like most of the major business structures of the period, was built around a core team that changed little over the years. By mid-1996 over a hundred Menatep people had moved over to work in Yukos. In February 1997, Khodorkovsky took over as head of the joint board of the Rosprom-Yukos company, and from March 1998 headed Yukos-Moskva. From 1998 all upstream operations were managed by the Yukos-EP division, downstream activities by Yukos-RM, with Yukos-Moskva in charge of planning and strategy. The old oil company (NK Yukos) would become no more than a holding company.

Second, ownership was consolidated. In May 1996, a cash auction sold 7.96 per cent of Yukos's charter capital, of which 7.06 per cent was acquired by Menatep. Thus by early 1997, over 85 per cent of Yukos stock was controlled by the Rosprom-Menatep group (40 per cent of the charter fund belonged to the group, while 45 per cent was mortgaged to it).[75] The share owned by the state was rapidly diluted, down from 45 per cent to 38.57 per cent of Yukos's charter fund in 1996. At that time Menatep owned 51.5 per cent of Yukos's charter capital and, in addition, a depository package of 33.3 per cent of shares.[76] An investment auction announced in November 1996 saw a Menatep-affiliated company (Monblan, fulfilling the role played by Laguna earlier) win at just above the starting price of

[73] Yuko Adachi, 'The Ambiguous Effects of Russian Corporate Governance Abuses of the 1990s', *Post-Soviet Affairs*, Vol. 22, No. 1, January–March 2006, p. 67.

[74] In addition, in 1996 Khodorkovsky joined the consultative council on banking attached to the Russian government, and was a member of the commission responsible for conducting investment auctions in the RF Ministry of the Economy. From November 1998 to October 1999 Khodorkovsky was a member of the Collegium of the RF Ministry of Fuel and Energy.

[75] Lane and Seifulmulukov, 'Structure and Ownership', p. 30.

[76] Lane and Seifulmulukov, 'Structure and Ownership', p. 31; Kryukov and Moe, 'Banks and the Financial Sector', p. 64.

$160 million, and as a result 94 per cent of Yukos shares were held either directly or indirectly by Menatep. By 1998 Menatep had taken over most of the rest of the government's stock, and thus gained full control of the company.

The third step was to tighten control over its subsidiaries, and to centralize operations and management flows. By 1997 Yukos consisted of 20 subsidiaries. The most important by far was YNG in West Siberia, a relatively new field developed from the 1970s producing some 70 per cent of Yukos output. Oil production by YNG had fallen from 1.4 million bpd in 1987 to 0.5 million bpd in 1995, and most drilling by that time had stopped for lack of funds.[77] Next in importance were the older fields owned by Samaraneftegaz. Oil production in the Samara region began in 1936, and despite the province's maturity, in 2006 still produced 9.4 million tonnes. The subsidiaries had been privatized as distinct business entities, and this two-tier structure encouraged them to fight to retain their business autonomy.[78] The abolition of the joint-stock status in the case of YNG was a long and painful process and engendered a hostility that lasted to Yukos's demise. External managers were appointed to affiliate companies, and no longer chosen by shareholder meetings of the subsidiaries. The outside share-holders in these subsidiary companies were squeezed out, often by insalubrious means, including moving shareholders' meetings to remote locations at short notice.[79]

Above all, Yukos pioneered the use of transfer pricing, whereby the Moscow headquarters bought oil from its production subsidiaries at enormous discounts (in 2000 it paid $1.50 a barrel, a fifth of the domestic price and a twentieth of world levels) and then resold it, allowing wealth to be concentrated in the holding company, undermining minority shareholders and avoiding taxes. The exploitative relationship between Yukos and its subsidiaries has been described as follows:

Yukos owned several operating subsidiaries, each of which had large minority interests. Yukos purchased oil from these subsidiaries at even lower prices [than the reported $8.60], averaging $7.50 per barrel—low enough so that these subsidiaries, with combined pretax profits of around $1 billion before Yukos acquired control, were soon reporting minimal profits or outright losses, and defaulting on their tax payments. Yukos had bled them of whatever cash they had.[80]

---

[77] Poussenkova, *From Rigs to Riches*, p. 22.

[78] Nat Moser and Peter Oppenheimer, 'The Oil Industry: Structural Transformation and Corporate Governance', in Brigitte Granville and Peter Oppenheimer (eds.), *Russia's Post-Communist Economy* (New York, Oxford University Press, 2001).

[79] Edward Lucas, *The New Cold War: How the Kremlin Menaces both Russia and the West* (London, Bloomsbury, 2008), p. 62.

[80] Bernard Black, Reinier Kraakman, and Anna Tarassavo, 'Russian Privatization and Corporate Governance: What Went Wrong?', *Stanford Law Review*, Vol. 52, 2000, p. 1769. It may be noted that Sibneft under Berezovsky was even more ruthless. Its main production asset was Noyabrskneftegaz, which in 1996 earned $600 million, but after Berezovsky got to work it technically earned $0 in 1997, with the $600 million turning up as Sibneft profit, ibid., p. 1772.

The sale of oil to Yukos without the approval of the subsidiaries' minority share-holders violated company law, but nothing was done despite attempts by the Russian Securities Commission to investigate the matter.

In the wake of the 1998 crisis, Yukos defaulted on its loan payments (above all for the purchase by Menatep of 54 per cent of VNK in 1997, funded by foreign loans secured against future oil exports) and thus 30 per cent of its shares were seized by Western companies. Yukos imposed a punitive package of measures on its major subsidiaries—notably Yuganskneftegaz, Tomskneft, and Samaraneftegaz: a massive new share issue through obscure offshore companies that valued the companies at less than 10 per cent of their real worth, and even this was paid for through promissory notes issued by other dubious Yukos subsidiaries, with the net effect that control was transferred from Yukos to the offshore companies; ridiculously low prices for output, at around $1.30 per barrel in 1999 prices; and shareholder approval for the transfer of assets to yet other obscure offshore companies. Owning only 51 per cent of the subsidiaries, Khodorkovsky took the bold step of getting a compliant judge to declare that the minority shareholders were acting in concert, in violation of the antimonopoly law, and thus they were disqualified from voting. When they turned up at the meeting armed guards prevented them from entering, whereas Yukos shares were counted since they were considered disinterested. Yukos's remaining shares were then transferred to various offshore companies.[81]

Yukos was accused of value extraction as early as 1996, allowing companies to report minimal profits or even losses, and thus avoid paying taxes. A critical report in the *Stanford Law Review* summed up one of the alleged scams:

For 1996, Yukos's financial statements show revenue of $8.60 per barrel of oil—about $4 per barrel less than it should have been. Khodorkovski [*sic*] skimmed over 30 cents per dollar of revenue while stiffing his workers on wages, defaulting on tax payments, destroying the value of minority shares in Yukos and its production subsidiaries, and *not* reinvesting in Yukos's oil fields.[82]

Given the uncertainties of the period, some of this may have been rational behaviour, and it was certainly not unique to Yukos, but it laid down a seedbed of distrust and hostility that would flourish later. As the report notes:

It's doubtful that running Yukos honestly could have earned Khodorkovski a fraction of what he earned by skimming revenue, let alone offshore and tax-free. He made a rational, privately value-maximizing choice. Even if running Yukos honestly was the best long-run strategy, Khodorkovski might have preferred present profit over future uncertainty. Besides, skimming was a business that he knew, while oil production was a tough business that he might fail in.[83]

The fourth step was the restructuring of the financial management of the company. The prominent role of banks in the late 1990s was not unique to Yukos, with Al'fa Bank enjoying a 40 per cent stake in TNK (which had been carved out of

---

[81] Black, 'Russian Privatization and Corporate Governance', pp. 1770–1.
[82] Ibid., pp. 1736–7.   [83] Ibid., p. 1737.

Rosneft in 1995),[84] Oneksimbank, 85 per cent of Sidanco, and SBS/Berezovsky, 99 per cent of Sibneft, acting through numerous intermediaries. The privatization of Sibneft represented the turning point when the state lost strategic control over the oil industry. Yukos now became the main focus of the work of Menatep and Rosprom, with 70 per cent of the assets of Menatep tied up in the oil company, while Yukos represented over 80 per cent of Rosprom's turnover. Rosprom, based in Mosalsk, was little more than a smoke screen with no shares of its own but through which complex financial operations were conducted. Khodorkovsky himself left the chairmanship of the bank's board to head the Rosprom company, established to manage its industrial assets, including Yukos. 'Bankers', as Simonov notes, 'definitively became resource managers (*syrevikov*)'.[85]

The turnover of Yukos at that time was $5 billion, whereas Rosprom's was less than $1 billion, so it was understandable that there had been a mass exodus of managers from Rosprom-Menatep to Yukos. In his first press conference as head of Rosprom on 12 April 1996 Khodorkovsky spoke of Rosprom's assets, numbering thirty companies at the time, and its investments in sixty others. He disclosed that the company did not consider itself obliged to fulfil investment conditions in taking over companies,[86] an approach that would be the hook on which he would be convicted later. In 1997 Khodorkovsky became head of the Yukos board, and he went on to transform the company into one of Russia's leading corporations. In 1998 the management structure of Rosprom was changed, becoming a holding company in which banking became one stream of activity alongside its oil and other interests. Instead of Menatep controlling Rosprom, the relationship was in effect reversed. A new structure was created to manage its oil interests, Yukos-Moskva, which as noted was headed by Khodorkovsky and the entire management team of Rosprom moved over. Menatep had facilitated the transfer of Yukos ownership into new hands but did not become the direct owner, although its difficulties after the 1998 financial crisis affected Yukos. By 1998 Menatep's shares in Yukos had been mortgaged to Western banks as collateral for its various debts.

The fifth strategy was the disbursement of social welfare, housing, and other responsibilities from the company to local authorities. Most of them were in no position to finance these activities, provoking massive resentment against the company. The number of staff employed by the three main subsidiaries (YNG, SNG, and Tomskneft) by 1999 fell threefold, from 76,000 to 25,000.[87] By 2004 the total number of staff directly employed by the company had fallen to some 110,000, although this was still high in international terms.

The sixth step was the acquisition of other companies, now focused on the energy sector, a process that only stopped when Yukos itself came under attack

---

[84] Details in Simonov, *Russkaya neft'*, pp. 13–14.   [85] Ibid., p. 17.

[86] Rustam Narzikulov, 'Chto zabyl i chto pomnit Khodorkovskii', *Nezavisimaya gazeta*, 13 April 1996.

[87] Pavel Danilin, Natal'ya Kryshtal' and Dmitrii Polyakov, *Vragi Putina* (Moscow, Evropa, 2007), p. 165.

The Quality of Freedom

Table 2.1. The growth of Yukos

1993	1996	2004
Upstream: Yuganskneftegaz *Downstream:* Kuibyshevnefteorgsyntez Syzran refinery Novokuibyshev refinery	*Upstream:* Yuganskneftegaz Samaraneftegaz *Downstream:* Kuibyshevnefteorgsyntez Syzran refinery Novokuibyshev refinery	*Upstream:* Yuganskneftegaz Samaraneftegaz Tomskneft Vostsibneftegaz Artikgaz Urengoil *Downstream:* Kuibyshevnefteorgsyntez Syzran refinery Novokuibyshev refinery Achinsk refinery Strezhevoi refinery Angarsk petrochemical company Mazeikiu Nafta

Source: Nina Poussenkova, *From Rigs to Riches: Oilmen vs. Financiers in the Russian Oil Sector* (Rice University, TX, The James A. Baker III Institute for Public Policy, October 2004), pp. 45–6, modified.

(see Table 2.1). In 1997 Yukos took control of VNK and Sakhaneftegaz, in 2000 it took over the East Siberian Oil and Gas Company, in 2001 the Angarsk Petrochemical Company, and in 2002 Artikgaz, Rospan, and Urengoil.[88] Yukos's aggressive acquisition strategy was in part responsible for its downfall, provoking ill-tempered exchanges with Putin in early 2003 when Yukos failed to win control of Severnaya Neft, an asset that both Yukos and Sibneft coveted but which in the event was won by Rosneft. We shall return to these acquisitions later. Yukos also engaged in other struggles with the state-owned enterprise. There was a particularly sharp dispute with Rosneft over control of the Vankorskoe oil and gas field (Yeniseineftegaz), the company at the heart of the Vladimir Temerko case later. Rosneft did not have it all its own way, and in November 2002 Sibneft and TNK beat Rosneft to win the state's 75 per cent stake in Slavneft. Yukos, which had decided not to participate in the contest, supported Sibneft's bid with a loan.

The early period in Yukos activities is thick with reports of alleged malpractices (more on this in Chapter 5), notably Menatep's use of the shell company Monblan, headed by the Menatep executive Kagalovsky, to complete the purchase of Yukos. Kagalovsky was one of Khodorkovsky's closest long-term associates, who following his stint during 1992–5 as Russia's representative to the IMF, during 1994–8 served as first deputy at Bank Menatep, and between 1996 and 2001 was

---

[88] Wojciech Konończuk, *The 'Yukos Affair', its Motives and Implications*, CES Studies, No. 25, Centre for Eastern Studies, Warsaw, August 2006, p. 35.

on the Yukos board of directors. Later Kagalovsky and his wife Natasha Gurfinkel-Kagalovsky would figure in the Bank of New York (BONY) money laundering case, and in 2003 he appeared on the Yabloko party list for the Duma elections. At a time when capital flight was running at between $10 and $15 billion a year, BONY from 1999 was accused of laundering some of these funds. The case rumbled on and came to involve Semën Mogilevich, an alleged mafia figure, wanted by the FBI, who was finally arrested in Moscow in late January 2008 on the eve of the presidential election of that year. BONY was also accused of being involved in the diversion of some of the $24 billion granted by the IMF in July 1998 as part of an emergency financial stabilization package, a case that provoked the resignation of the IMF's head on 14 February 2000.

By 1999 Yukos was Russia's largest oil company in terms of total recoverable reserves, with 85 per cent in YNG and 15 per cent in SNG.[89] YNG was the largest oil production field in Russia, but with about half of its 350 fields in the region at the stage of declining extraction returns (emptied up to 60–70 per cent), and the various difficulties saw output of oil and gas condensate declining from 71 million tonnes in 1986 to 27 million tonnes in 1995. Financial performance was also disastrous in these years, with YNG deeply indebted to the government and owing large wage arrears to its workers, caused largely by consumer payment arrears. The agricultural sector and regional governments took extended credits, with little prospect of repayment. Yukos shared these problems with other companies, but Yukos's financial performance was worse than most because of poor management and loose control over its subsidiaries. The best-managed company by far was Surgutneftegaz, which in the mid-1990s had no debts to the government, no wage arrears to its workforce, and regularly paid dividends to shareholders and its taxes on time.

Just weeks before the August 1998 default the first deputy prime minister Boris Nemtsov, with the government desperate for funds, set a two-week deadline for the oil companies to clear their debts. Even with low oil prices, energy export duties made up a very large proportion of government revenues. In the first quarter of 1998 these fell by 25 per cent as world oil prices declined to a trough of $10 per barrel. From 1999 oil prices began an upward trajectory that saw prices peak at $167 a barrel in September 2008. With the government drive to collect back taxes in 1998, Yukos and other companies planned major job cuts. Yukos targeted administrative posts, as well as cutting social spending on housing, hospitals, and welfare programmes in its production areas.[90] Given that many were in effect 'company towns', the effect was devastating, and as we shall see in later chapters, provoked considerable tensions, leading even to accusations of the murder of the mayor of Nefteyugansk.

---

[89] David Lane and Iskander Seifulmulukov, 'Company Profiles: LUKoil, YuKOS, Surgutnefteftgaz, Sidanko', in Lane (ed.), *The Political Economy of Russian Oil*, Part 1 Appendix, pp. 111–24, p. 114.

[90] Peter Glatter, 'Federalization, Fragmentation, and the West Siberian Oil and Gas Province', in Lane (ed.), *The Political Economy of Russian Oil*, chapter 6, pp. 143–60, at p. 156.

The oligarchs are born

The optimism of the perestroika years gave way to the terrible conflict between the president and parliament in the 'phoney democracy' period from 1992, which in October 1993 led to a violent confrontation. Between 1994 and 1998 Russia entered a third phase, in which democratic idealists were eclipsed, and in their place a new business class consolidated its power. A recent study makes clear the link between the Soviet era and the creation of the new elite:

Citizens and comrades who had learnt how to live in Soviet conditions, rationing the distribution of deficit social goods, 'Komsomol entrepreneurs' of the Mikhail Khodorkovsky type, represented a clearly defined strata, who with the onset of perestroika significantly influenced the country's development. It is precisely from this social layer that state activists of the Yeltsin intake were recruited.[91]

In his study of the oligarchs Fortescue categorizes Khodorkovsky as a *nomenklaturshchik* even though he was far from being a leading member of the Soviet ruling class, but he was an active Komsomol official.[92]

Khodorkovsky took a systematic approach to his relations with the authorities. We have noted how in the early 1990s Khodorkovsky acted as an adviser to the prime minister, and served as a deputy to the RF minister of fuel and energy, in which capacity he met Boris Berezovsky and they forged a firm and long-standing business partnership.[93] He was part of the official delegation that accompanied Yeltsin on his visit to Spain in 1994. By 1996 Khodorkovsky admitted the need for state patronage, noting that 'big business cannot exist without the state'.[94] Khodorkovsky had particularly good relations with Yevgeny Primakov, foreign minister from January 1994 to September 1999 and then prime minister until May 1999. Despite the wide gulf in their ages, both shared a Soviet mentality, and the relationship shielded Khodorkovsky from investigation during Primakov's premiership.

Khodorkovsky was at the World Economic Forum in Davos (2–5 February 1996) where he overheard the conversation in which the international financier George Soros warned Berezovsky that if the Communists came to power in Russia the liberal economy and democracy would be destroyed, and Berezovsky himself destroyed.[95] The latter soon joined with his arch-enemy Gusinsky to save

---

[91] Evgenii Andryushchenko, 'Za klanom klan?', *Literaturnaya gazeta*, No. 2 (6154), 23–9 January 2008, p. 3.

[92] Stephen Fortescue, *Russia's Oil Barons and Metal Magnates: Oligarchs and State in Transition* (Basingstoke, Palgrave Macmillan, 2006), p. 27.

[93] Khlebnikov, *Krestnyi otets Kremlya Boris Berezovskii*, p. 77. In 1992–3 it was Bank Menatep that serviced Berezovsky's first ventures into oil, timber, and aluminium exports, ibid, p. 210. In mid-1995 Menatep acted as a guarantor and creditor to Berezovsky's Avtovaz at a time of difficulty for the latter, ibid, p. 175.

[94] Allan, 'Banks and the Loans-for-Shares Auctions', p. 155.

[95] Panyushkin, *Mikhail Khodorkovskii*, pp. 69–70.

Yeltsin.[96] Presidential elections were due in June, and it was clear that Yeltsin's re-election campaign was floundering. At the time, Yeltsin enjoyed a popularity rating of 4 per cent, while Gennady Zyuganov, at the head of the CPRF, had a rating of 35 per cent. About a fortnight after the Davos meeting Khodorkovsky was one of the group of business and media leaders who went to see Yeltsin and offered not only money but also experienced political strategists.[97] After a characteristically long pause by Yeltsin, Khodorkovsky wondered whether 'the tsar was thinking about whether to send us all to the execution block'.[98] An 'analytical group' was created and Chubais was brought in to mastermind Yeltsin's re-election.[99]

Uncertain of the outcome of the forthcoming elections, in the notorious 'Appeal of the Thirteen' of April 1996 a group of top oligarchs urged Yeltsin to come to terms with his main challenger, Zyuganov.[100] Khodorkovsky was one of the initiators of the letter together with Berezovsky, and urged that the election should be postponed to save the country from catastrophic divisions:

Society is divided. The split is widening disastrously day by day. The rift that divides us into reds and whites, ours and theirs, runs through Russia's heart.... At this crucial hour, we entrepreneurs of Russia, propose to intellectuals, military personnel and representatives of executive and legislative branches of government, law-enforcement agencies and news media, to all those in whose hands real power is concentrated today and on whom Russia's fate depends, that they pool their efforts in searching for a political compromise that can prevent acute conflicts that threaten Russia's basic interests and its very existence as a state.[101]

Whoever won the election, the letter argued, would implement policies 'categorically rejected by a large part of society', and the 'mutual repulsion of political forces was so great' that it could lead to 'civil war and the break-up of Russia'. The letter warned that for many 'the word "democracy" has become all but synonymous with an anti-state attitude. The practice of spitting on Russia's history and the things it holds sacred and of trampling on the Soviet period of Russia's history must be rejected and stopped', while 'we cannot allow the great ideas of freedom, civic spirit, justice, law and truth—the main elements of true people's rule—to be discredited'.[102] The letter ended with both a warning and an appeal:

[96] For a vivid description of Berezovsky's conflict with Gusinsky in 1994–5, and their alliance in 1996–7 on the basis of common support for Yeltsin's re-election, see Aleksandr Korzhakov, *Boris Yeltsin: Ot rassveta do zakata* (Moscow, Interbuk, 1997).

[97] The others were Boris Berezovsky, Vladimir Gusinsky, Vladimir Potanin, and Mikhail Fridman, and the meeting was called at their request. Boris Yeltsin, *Midnight Diaries* (London, Weidenfeld & Nicolson, 2000), pp. 20–1.

[98] Colton, *Yeltsin*, p. 355.

[99] Marina Shakina, 'Biznesmeny vykhodyat iz-za kulis', *Nezavisimaya gazeta*, 27 April 1996.

[100] 'Get Out of the Impasse', *Current Digest of the Post-Soviet Press*, Vol. XLVIII, No. 17, 22 May 1996, pp. 1–3; from 'Vyiti iz tupika!', *Kommersant*, 27 April 1996, p. 1. The letter, published on that day in all the major papers, was signed by Khodorkovsky, Nevzlin, and Muravlenko from Mentaep-Yukos as well as Berezovsky, Gusinsky, Potanin, Smolensky, Fridman, and five others.

[101] 'Get Out of the Impasse', p. 1.   [102] Loc. cit.

Those who encroach on the Russian state system by putting their stakes on ideological revanchism and social confrontation must understand that our country's entrepreneurs have the necessary resources and will to influence both politicians who are too unprincipled and politicians who are too uncompromising. Russia must enter the 21st century as a flourishing, great power. This is our duty to our forefathers and our descendants.[103]

Although not spelled out, the implication of the letter was that the elections should be postponed, since the choice appeared to be either elections or civil war, or some compromise reached. The plan was defined by Khodorkovsky later; for Zyuganov to become prime minister with extended powers, while Yeltsin would remain president as the 'guarantee of democratic freedoms and human rights'.[104] Already at this point the oligarchs were not too concerned about democratic niceties, and although their suggestion was rejected and the elections went ahead, the letter demonstrated just how confident the oligarchs had become. In the event, the oligarchs pledged their support for Yeltsin, and made unquantifiable sums available to his campaign.

It was in these presidential elections that the oligarchs first made their political mark, and this was then repeated in a different way in 1999/2000. In the first instance the group of 'seven bankers' (*semibankirshchina*) predominated, and in the second, through 'family' groups. While the 'bureaucratic' component of Yeltsin's power system favoured a postponement of the election,[105] the 'oligarchic' leg in alliance with reformists such as Chubais resolved on a frontal attack on the Communist opposition, in which perhaps a billion dollars were spent. The consequences were not long in coming. As Pavel Khlebnikov notes: 'Entering into politics, he [Berezovsky] outdid everyone even here. Having privatised a vast swathe of Russian industry, Berezovsky now privatised the state.'[106] As Berezovsky put it in the notorious interview in which he claimed that the seven had been responsible for Yeltsin's re-election and controlled 50 per cent of the Russian economy: 'We hired Chubais and invested huge sums of money to ensure Yeltsin's election. Now we have the right to occupy government posts and enjoy the fruits of our victory.'[107] Their grip on the media was no less tight, controlling 70 per cent of the Moscow press and radio and 80 per cent of national television.[108]

No less humiliating for the authorities was an interview with *Nezavisimaya gazeta* in which Khodorkovsky made no bones about the relationship between politics and business: 'Politics is the most lucrative field of business in Russia. And it will be that way forever. We draw lots in order to pick out a person from

    [103] 'Get out of the Impasse', p. 3.

    [104] Discussed in Mikhail Khodorkovskii, *Levyi povorot* 2 (Moscow, Galleya-Print, 2006), p. 5.

    [105] Aleksandr Korzhakov, *Boris El'tsin: Ot rassveta do zakata—Posleslovie* (Moscow, Detektiv Press, 2004), pp. 482–3.

    [106] Khlebnikov, *Krestnyi otets Kremlya Boris Berezovskii*, p. 10.

    [107] The seven bankers were Boris Berezovsky, Vladimir Potanin, Mikhail Khodorkovsky, Vladimir Gusinsky, Alexander Smolensky, Mikhail Fridman, and Pyotr Aven. Chrystia Freeland, John Thornhill, and Andrew Gowers, 'Moscow's Group of Seven', *Financial Times*, 1 November 1997.

    [108] Goldman, *The Piratization of Russia*, p. 2.

our milieu for work in power.'[109] Vladimir Potanin, head of Oneksimbank, had indeed been delegated by the oligarchs in the wake of Yeltsin's re-election to enter the government, working as first deputy prime minister in charge of the economy from August 1996 until March 1997, and Berezovsky was deputy head of the Security Council from October 1996 until sacked on 4 November 1997. Oligarchs now firmly entered the lists as the most influential politicians in the country, with Berezovsky between 1997 and 2000 consistently ranking as the top oligarch and in 1998 and 2000 listed as the fourth most influential person in the country, although Khodorkovsky of all the major oligarchs ranked lowest, in those years placed only twenty-fifth and sixtieth, respectively.[110]

According to Satter, '[b]y 1997 a ruling criminal business oligarchy was in place. A small group of bankers and business men, all of them previously unknown but with close connections to both gangsters and government officials, had gained control of the majority of the Russian economy.' They included Berezovsky, the head of the Logovaz car dealership; Potanin, the head of Oneximbank; Gusinsky, the head of the Most Bank; and 'Mikhail Khodorkovsky, the head of the Menatep Bank'.[111] The shares-for-loans scheme had endowed a small group with such an enormous concentration of economic power that they soon flexed their political muscles, provoking their critics to suggest that only authoritarian methods would be enough to stop them.[112]

Thomas Graham, who worked for part of the 1990s at the US embassy in Moscow, characterizes the period as follows:

Under President Yeltsin, Russia suffered a socio-economic and political collapse unprecedented for a major power not defeated in a major war. Between 1990–1998, the economy plunged by 40%. The state was dysfunctional, with significant parts privatized by corrupt oligarchs and with regional barons asserting their independence. Russia was humiliated as its finances were run out of Washington by the International Monetary Fund, and outside powers shamelessly interfered in Russia's domestic affairs in support of Yeltsin. Many Russians thought their country was on the path to becoming a failed state; many Westerners were contemplating a world without Russia.[113]

During the 1996 presidential campaign the oligarchs had used Yeltsin's need for support to gain further inroads into the state, but it would be going too far to talk of 'state capture'. Berezovsky's boast that the 'seven bankers' had won Yeltsin's re-election for him, and that they controlled much of the Russian economy, and by implication the whole system, was fanciful. Large parts of Russian life remained beyond their purview—the military, the agricultural sector, regional leaderships (notably Moscow mayor Yuri Luzhkov and the president of Tatarstan, Mintimir Shaimiev), and ultimately the ministerial bureaucracy. While they could be bought individually, as a class they resented the interference of business leaders

---

[109] Cited by Andrei Piontovsky, 'Modern-Day Rasputin', *Moscow Times*, 12 November 1997.
[110] Kryshtanovkaya, *Anatomiya rossiiskoi elity*, p. 330.
[111] Satter, *Darkness at Dawn*, p. 54.
[112] Fortescue, *Russia's Oil Barons and Metal Magnates*, p. 59.
[113] Thomas Graham, 'A Modernizing Tsar', *Wall Street Journal Europe*, 22 January 2008.

in administration. It was this resilient strand of state autonomy that Putin would later tap to reassert the power of the regime against big business.

With Nevzlin, one of his closest associates, Khodorkovsky wrote a book about the development of post-communist Russian business, and in a Gordon Gekko-like manner praised the virtues of money-making, describing their goal as to become billionaires. The 1990s were Russia's 1980s, when for the elite a 'loadsa-money' mentality predominated. The book makes thoroughly unpleasant reading at times as the two sought to emboss greed with the patina of virtue.[114] The pair was typical of many Russians of the time, who adopted a brash neo-liberalism that exalted market relations at the cost of everything else. They were good students of Milton Friedman, who had argued that freedom was inextricable from capitalism.[115] This included a personal vendetta against Pioneer camps, a number of which Khodorkovsky bought and then closed, depriving city children of access to fresh air, and a contemptuous attitude to free medical care, and indeed to the whole Soviet infrastructure of free services.[116] By the end of the decade this provoked a reaction. Even before the economic crisis of 1998 the era of triumphant neo-liberalism was coming to an end and the ideology of 'the consolidation of the state' was becoming manifest.[117]

Merger mania

Faced by ever-sharpening budgetary deficits, the government looked for ways of raising revenues. The shares-for-loans and other auctions had raised little money, and in general the state had in financial terms gained minimally out of the whole privatization process. Casting around for sources of revenue, the government planned to sell one of the last major oil companies it still owned, Rosneft, but on far more competitive terms than earlier disbursements. The cap on foreign-owned shares in the company was lifted in July 1997, ensuring that any sale would involve far greater sums than paid for oil companies earlier. Already the tender for a 40 per cent stake in TNK in July 1997 raised $820 million from Al'fa Bank, far more than the bid minimum.

The effect of insider dealing was apparent in July 1997 in the sale of the telecommunications giant Svyazinvest to Potanin, in government at this time, leading to an outcry by other oligarchs.[118] Berezovsky and Gusinsky unleashed their respective television channels to launch a frenzied media campaign to force

[114] Mikhail Khodorkovskii and Leonid Nevzlin, *Chelovek s rublëm* (Moscow, Menatep-Inform, 1992).

[115] Milton Friedman, *Capitalism and Freedom* (Chicago, IL, University of Chicago Press, 1962).

[116] Danilin et al., *Vragi Putina*, p. 164.

[117] Sergei Vasilyev, 'Liberalism is a Synonym of Order', *New Times*, No. 4, 1 April 1998. Vasilyev had formerly been part of Gaidar's team, and at the time was first deputy chief of staff of the Russian government. His article refuted the idea that liberalism had to be synonymous with disorder. The fact that he felt the need to do this was necessary was symptomatic of the problem.

[118] For a vivid description of the 'soap opera' attending the sale of 25 per cent plus one share of Svyazinvest on 25 July 2007, see Goldman, *The Piratization of Russia*, pp. 1–11.

the government to review the outcome of the tender.[119] It is from this period that the model of political-business clan conflict emerged.[120] Oligarch feuding became so intense that on 15 September 1997 Yeltsin called the six leading bankers together to establish some rules of the game,[121] although with little effect. The attempt by the government of 'young reformers' led by Sergei Kirienko from March 1998 to bring some order into the country's finances and thus to avert a default were sabotaged by the oligarchs. Berezovsky allegedly incited miners to strike and financed them when they blocked railway lines.[122] When Kirienko tried to raise oil taxes, Nevzlin, with Khodorkovsky sitting next to him, warned that '[i]f Yeltsin does not come to a deal with us in a friendly way, we will have him out in two moves', and noted that if Yeltsin insisted on trying to squeeze higher taxes, for the oligarchs 'it would be cheaper to buy the Communists and finance street demonstrations, and by the autumn Yeltsin would be out of the Kremlin'.[123] In 2003 it appeared that Khodorkovsky and his associates returned to the idea of 'buying the Communists', but Putin proved a much harder nut to crack.

The desperate need for capital against the background of low energy prices led to a number of strategic alliances and mergers, resulting in the creation of BPAmoco in December 1998 (reverting to the name BP in 2002), ExxonMobil, ChevronTexaco, and the merger of Total, PetroFina, and Elf in 1999/2000. Not all deals worked out, with that between British Petroleum and Sidanco announced in November 1997 later turning very sour, while Gazprom and Shell declared a joint interest in the privatization of Rosneft which came to nothing. The government planned to sell a controlling 75 per cent stake in Rosneft, setting a minimum price of $2.1 billion with a further obligation for major investment Yukos did however acquire a controlling stake of 53.8 per cent of VNK in early December 1997 for $800 million, but with the price of oil falling Yukos was forced to retire debts and pay off foreign creditors, placing even more pressure on its ability to pay local taxes. It was against this background that the company faced a major conflict with the mayor of Nefteyugansk, the hometown of its major producer, YNG (Chapter 5).

Rosneft had been the last of the state-owned oil companies to be slated for full-scale privatization. A quarter of its stock was offered to present and former employees, and another 25 per cent was to be offered for investors. The final tender for 75 per cent of the company's shares was set for May 1998, with a

[119] The struggle is vividly described by Elena Tregubova, *Baiki kremlevskogo diggera* (Moscow, Ad Marginem, 2003), pp. 63–70.

[120] A. Makarkin, *Politiko-ekonomicheskie klany sovremennoi Rossii* (Moscow, Tsentr politicheskikh tekhnologii, 2003), p. 6.

[121] In attendance were Fridman from Al'fa Bank, Alexander Smolensky from SBS-AGRO, Khodorkovsky from Rosprom (this is how he is listed in Yeltsin's memoirs), Gusinsky from Most-Bank, Vladimir Vinogradov from Inkombank, and Potanin from Oneksimbank, Yeltsin, *Midnight Diaries*, p. 96.

[122] Dmitrii Yur'ev, *rezhim putina: Postdemokratiya* (Moscow, Evropa, 2005), p. 104, n.

[123] Tregubova, *Baiki kremlevskogo diggera*, p. 76.

minimum price of $2.1 billion. The successful bidder was to invest at least $400 million in the next three years.[124] Just a few days after acquiring VNK, Yukos and Sibneft forged a strategic alliance to bid for Rosneft.[125] Having agreed to work together on the Rosneft bid, the next logical step was the consolidation of Menatep's oil interests with Sibneft, and on 19 January 1998 a protocol of understanding was signed to merge Yukos and Sibneft, announced at a grand press conference that day with prime minister Chernomyrdin in attendance as well as the minister of fuel and energy, Kirienko. The plan was to create a new company called Yuksi, with 60 per cent of the shares belonging to Yukos and 40 per cent to Sibneft shareholders. Berezovsky wanted to get rid of Sibneft since '[t]he oil business, with its long-term plans and gigantic investments was alien to Berezovsky's nature'.[126] The merger would also have brought together an anti-Chubais coalition of oligarchs (Berezovsky, Gusinsky, Smolensky, and Khodorkovsky), since at this time Chubais had begun to talk of 'people's capitalism' and threatened oligarch hegemony. The new company would have been bigger than Lukoil, with the head of the latter, Alekperov, in May 1998 announcing a plan to take over Sidanco.

None of these plans came to fruition. The Yuksi deal fell apart in May 1998 because of 'the fall in oil prices, financial uncertainty, and forceful government demands for the payment of tax arrears',[127] which exacerbated tensions between the two companies. There was disagreement over how Sibneft's debts to the state would be handled; Yukos had no such debts, but it was financially stretched after the purchase of VNK. In addition, Berezovsky's partner, Roman Abramovich, began to demand a higher price, and in the end in July 1998 the merger was officially called off. At the same time, the sale of Rosneft was postponed 'because Potanin and his arch rival Boris Berezovsky were at odds over who would get it, and no one wanted another disruptive oligarch brawl after the Svyazinvest debacle'.[128] Rosneft at the time was headed by Sibneft's nominee Yuri Bespalov, and he started transferring shares to Sibneft. However, in the end the government aborted the privatization of Rosneft since, in a period of capital deficit, it did not receive a single bid at the required level. This was to have momentous consequences since Rosneft was the last remaining state oil company, together with the much smaller Zarubezhneft.[129] Bespalov was forced to leave and in October 1998 he was replaced by Sergei Bogdanchikov, who would play a fateful role in Yukos's destruction. Khodorkovsky on behalf of Yuksi withdrew from the Rosneft auction, considering the price too high, as did all the other potential bidders. The value

[124] Lane and Seifulmulukov, 'Structure and Ownership', p. 35.
[125] 'Menatep sozdast al'yans s "Sibneftyu" dlya pokupki aktsii "Rosnefti"', *Segodnya*, 17 December 1997.
[126] Khlebnikov, *Krestnyi otets Kremlya Boris Berezovskii*, p. 273.
[127] Lane and Seifulmulukov, 'Structure and Ownership', p. 32.
[128] Matthew Brzezinski, *Casino Moscow: A Tale of Greed and Adventure on Capitalism's Wildest Frontier* (New York, Free Press, 2001), p. 197.
[129] Three-quarters of Rosneft shares were held by state-owned Rosneftegaz, and 9.44 per cent by the 'RN-Razvitie' subsidiary.

of the rouble was falling, oil prices were declining, and international financial markets were in turmoil. It was a close call. Instead of Yukos taking over Rosneft, in the end it was Rosneft that acted as the instrument for Yukos's destruction.

The 1998 partial default

By late 1997 Russia's foreign debt reached $123.5 billion and its domestic debt, mainly in treasury bills, reached $95 billion. Debt servicing alone swallowed 5 per cent of GDP, with over a quarter of budget spending not backed by revenues. Faced with mounting budget shortfalls, exacerbated by falling energy prices, the government tried to cover its debts by issuing stocks (GKOs) at ever-higher interest rates. The whole system collapsed on 17 August 1998, when the government declared a moratorium on debt repayments, and companies were forced to default on foreign loans. The financial crisis inflicted a severe blow on Russian investors, and signalled that the golden age of oligarchic capitalism in Russia had come to an end. Companies dependent on the financial sector suffered most, including Gusinsky's Most Group, Potanin's Oneksimbank, while Smolensky's SBS-Agro and Vladimir Vinogradov's Inkombank were ruined. Bank Menatep-Moscow, with 70 per cent of its assets in state securities on the eve of the default, later lost its banking licence. It transferred what was left to its sister bank, Menatep-St Petersburg in a 'bridge' operation that undermined the ability of creditors to gain redress. Menatep-Moscow filed for bankruptcy in 1999 but its temporary manager, Alexei Karamanov, alleged that assets had been hidden in foreign accounts and that Menatep officials had been less than forthcoming about its resources. Materials relating to the company were 'accidentally' lost when a truck transporting 607 boxes of its documents plunged off a bridge into the Dubna river on 24 May 1999.

The bank still faced a $250 million claim from its creditors, including some foreign banks, which had lent Menatep $266 million, secured by a 32 per cent stake in Yukos. Lebedev, the director of Group Menatep, and Khodorkovsky tried to convince them to accept a three-year repayment plan, secured against oil exports rather than Yukos shares. The largest creditors, Daiwa Bank, West Merchant Bank (a subsidiary of Westdeutsche Landesbank) and Standard Bank of South Africa, refused, and took over the collateral, representing 29 per cent of Yukos shares. Their main concern was to cover their losses, but in mid-1999 the two companies precipitously sold their stake, reputedly receiving only half the amount of their loan, scared into dumping their shares by Khodorkovsky's threat of a share offering in Yukos that would have diluted their holdings to insignificance. At the same time Yukos was selling some of its prime assets to offshore companies (presumably linked to the Yukos management), and it appeared to be in danger of becoming little more than a shell company.

The aim according to Yukos's defenders was to fight off the maverick American investor, Kenneth Dart, the heir to the Styrofoam fortune and the leading private investor in Yukos, with some $2 billion committed by 1998 in various affiliated oil-producing companies including YNG, SNG, and Tomskneft.[130] More broadly, Khodorkovsky sought to win undivided control over Yukos' assets by issuing millions of shares and moving the real assets abroad, leaving minority shareholders with little more than empty shells.[131] Once the foreign companies were off the scene, Khodorkovsky and his associates repurchased most of the stock, the share offering was cancelled, and the assets that had been moved offshore were returned to Yukos in Russia.[132] These machinations, and there were many more, gave the company a particularly unsavoury reputation, and it was only in 2003 that Yukos dared to go back to Western capital markets.

Entrepreneurs who focused on natural resource extraction were better placed than banks to weather the storm, including Rem Vyakhirev of Gazprom (the company at the time provided a quarter of all Russia's taxes) and Vagit Alekperov of Lukoil (also a major contributor to the budget), or with diversified interests such as Khodorkovsky's Menatep and Berezovsky of Logovaz. For companies less exposed to the short-term securities market the crisis provided an opportunity to expand, notably Moscow's Al'fa Bank, long close to Yeltsin's administration, which was authorized to service the St Petersburg budget. The government declared that it would save some banks, among which Menatep figured (although it had few depositors and no regional network), now taking advantage of its network of supporters in the corridors of power. The Most Group was also to be saved because of its extensive media network, which would be needed in the hard battles that would attend the succession in 1999–2000. Although the crisis shook up Russian capitalism, it did not change the rules of the game: 'Much of politics is informal, authority is personalized, institutions are weak, the distinction between public and private is blurred, and money is the currency of political power.'[133] It was at this time that Khodorkovsky underwent some sort of 'internal revolution of values',[134] whose end result was the various missives from prison (see Chapter 8). He later wrote that from the default he learned that 'not only laws but also ethics are important': 'I decided that I must not only repay all debts, but also do something so people lived better', and production stopped being my main aim and 'I understood, that I would have to leave business', and that I would have to spend more time on public affairs.[135]

On the morrow of the default on 19 August, Moscow mayor Luzhkov announced the end of an era: 'Ladies and gentlemen', he declared, 'the experiment is over'.[136] Luzhkov's announcement was premature, but he was right in so far as

---

[130] The struggle with Dart focused in particular on his ownership of the Acirota company, which owned 13 per cent of Tomskneft, technically an affiliate of VNK, Panyushkin, *Mikhail Khodorkovskii*, pp. 120–1; see also Fortescue, *Russia's Oil Barons and Metal Magnates*, p. 63.

[131] Hoffman, *The Oligarchs*, pp. 448–52.

[132] Klebnikov, 'The Oligarch Who Came in From the Cold'.

[133] Donald N. Jensen, 'Rumors of Oligarch's Demise Greatly Exaggerated', RFE/RL, *Newsline*, 7 December 1998.

[134] Panyushkin, *Mikhail Khodorkovskii*, p. 96.

[135] The letter was written from pre-trial detention after October 2003 to Panyushkin, *Mikhail Khodorkovskii*, p. 110.

[136] Brzezinski, *Casino Moscow*, p. 308.

the nature of Russian capitalism changed after 1998, as did the economic conditions. The 1998 default marked the shift from financial to industrial capitalism, and the emphasis moved from speculation to production. Like all other export-oriented Russian companies, Yukos benefited from the fivefold devaluation of the rouble following the partial default, since oil was priced in dollars. The company sharply increased production and export volumes, drawing on Western expertise to exploit 'easy oil', output from wells that had been poorly tapped in the Soviet period (see below). Its stock value rose sharply, and the sector's disposable revenues began an upward trajectory that were to fund Putin's state-building projects, although Yukos in the end became a victim of that process.

The loser takes the fall

Yukos was particularly active in placing state officials on its payroll, and according to some tried to buy executive officials 'wholesale' to ensure that policy outcome was in its favour. Yukos, MDM, and Russian Aluminium were considered the most aggressive in this respect in the second half of the 1990s. According to one anonymous insider, '[t]heir lobbying knew no bounds'.[137] There were also persistent rumours about criminal connections. The interior minister, Anatoly Kulikov, in February 1996 warned of growing ties between criminal groups and the oil business, and he mentioned Yukos, along with Rosneft and Lukoil.[138] Khodorkovsky was the only oligarch taken by prime minister Primakov on his visit to Malaysia in November 1998. Despite his good relations with Primakov, when the prime minister in October 1998 announced that the country's budgetary problems would be solved at the expense of energy producers and exporters, Khodorkovsky took the lead in criticizing the measure and stated that he would be aggressive in the defence of industry. He noted that the industrialists' failure to defend their position earlier in the year, when they had warned against lifting all restrictions on foreigners participating in the GKO market and had called for a rouble devaluation in connection with the fall in the price of oil, had led to disaster. He now warned that any increase in energy taxes would not lead to greater receipts since 'we simply won't pay them'. He warned that if the view of the industrialists was once again ignored he would leave the economic and political scene, since he did not want 'to participate in a situation which I do not control'.[139] The appointment of the former Yukos employee, Victor Kalyuzhny as energy and fuel minister in 1999 was considered to be a result of Khodorkovsky's lobbying, as was his subsequent dismissal in 2000 when he incurred Khodorkovsky's displeasure.

Yukos was well known for its aggressive stance in dealing with subordinate companies and other enterprises. Khodorkovsky's struggle with Amoco (later merged with British Petroleum) over ownership of the giant Priobskoe oil field in the West

---

[137] *Newsweek Russia*, No. 20, 29 May–4 June 2006.
[138] 'Lukoil: Politika i biznes', *Izvestiya*, 15 May 1997.
[139] Elena Kryazheva, 'Agressivnye eksportery', *Nezavisimaya gazeta*, 3 October 1998.

Siberian Khanti-Mansi autonomous district revealed his tough approach. Amoco had been developing the field in partnership with the Yukos subsidiary YNG, but in 1998, just at the moment when full-scale production began to tap into the estimated 3.5 billion barrels of oil that lie beneath this bleak tundra region, Amoco was levered out, losing the $300 million it had invested in the project. Having gained full control of Yukos in 1997, Khodorkovsky discovered that the company was under no legal obligation to continue to work with Amoco.[140] Another victim of Khodorkovsky's tough approach was Dart, whose stock in late 1998 was diluted, using rising oil revenues, leading to Dart losing up to half of his investment, although in 1999 a settlement was achieved.

Yukos thus ended the 1990s with arguably the worst reputation of all. The liberal paper *Novaya gazeta* in 1999 ran a story called 'Chronicle of an Ideal Crime', arguing that the privatization of the oil industry had turned into the 'theft of the century', and noted that if most of the newborn oil magnates at least tried to keep up the appearance of honesty, there were some who did not even do this. 'The list of open cynics in the domestic oil market is led by Mikhail Khodorkovsky, a chemical engineer by training and a financial alchemist by nature. It was he who achieved in the oil sector what criminals throughout the ages have called an "ideal crime".' The report noted that what he had done with Yukos and VNK in just two to three years 'is unprecedented in the history of oil piracy'. The report stressed: 'The main thing is that he is now closer than any other oil oligarch to achieve his cherished and genius plan to deprive the country of an enormous part of its oil resources.'[141] Coming from a paper that would later be Khodorkovsky's staunchest defender, this was strong stuff. Equally ironic, when Khodorkovsky took the paper to court, it was none other than the Basmanny court, whose name would later become a synonym for the subordination of law to power, that on 3 October 2000 found in his favour, declaring that the article had 'defamed his honour, dignity and business reputation'.[142]

YUKOS TRANSFORMED

In the early 2000s big business began to transform itself from morally dubious 'oligarch capitalism' into respectable national capital. Although Joel Hellman had argued that the initial winners of economic liberalization would block further reforms, the oligarchs had already begun to change themselves before the state-bureaucratic apparatus moved against them.[143] As world oil prices and exports rose, Khodorkovsky in October 1999 announced an ambitious investment

[140] Klebnikov, 'The Oligarch Who Came in From the Cold'.

[141] Aleksei Osipov, 'Khodorkovskii i "Yukos": Khronika "ideal'nogo prestupleniya" ', *Novaya gazeta*, 4 October 1999.

[142] 'Oproverzhenie', *Novaya gazeta*, 9 November 2000.

[143] Joel S. Hellman, 'Winners take All: The Politics of Partial Reform in Postcommunist Transitions', *World Politics*, Vol. 50, No. 2, January 1998, pp. 203–34.

programme.[144] In the early 2000s most major Russian oil companies launched a transparency drive, with the notable exception of Surgutneftegaz.[145] Khodorkovsky was in the vanguard of this transformation, changing Yukos from one of the most ruthless and predatory companies to a symbol of a more open and transparently managed enterprise. It adopted Western accounting standards and issued clear financial accounts every three months, and in 2002 Menatep published a list of its main shareholders. Pumping 2 per cent of global oil output, Yukos took advantage of the rise in energy prices, tripling in just two years to reach $33 per barrel by 2000. Khodorkovsky was one of the most successful oligarchs to shift from finance to industrial capital, a process hastened by the 1998 financial collapse, although the financial side of his activities represented by Menatep remained strong. As one of Russia's best performing companies, Yukos gained significant sympathy in the West in its later struggle with the Kremlin, and it made the assault against the company appear all the more irrational and politically motivated. The problem was that Khodorkovsky had forgotten his own insight. In an interview in the late 1990s he announced that if the prime minister asked him to resign as head of his bank, he would do so without hesitation: 'That's how Russia is organized. The state is always the dominant force in the economy.'[146]

A revolution in production

Having wrested full control of its subsidiaries, Khodorkovsky hired Western companies on a fee basis to help bring the Priobskoe and other fields into full production. In 1999 Yukos produced 44.5 million tonnes/year (895,000 bpd) of crude, rising to a peak of 85.6 million tonnes/year (1.7 million bpd) in 2004 (see Table 2.2). Up to 1999 traditional methods predominated, with ever more drilling, an unwillingness selectively to improve well production, and the failure to invest in new technologies and equipment. With mounting debts and wage arrears, Khodorkovsky was one of the first of Russia's new generation of oilniks to understand that things had to change. The new approach was charted by two expatriate American engineers. Joe Mach was already a well-known petroleum engineer with an instinct for production enhancement, having worked thirty years with Gulf Oil and the Franco-American oilfield services giant Schlumberger when he joined Yukos in December 1998 as vice president for production. He had worked for Schlumberger in Russia for some years, so was familiar with the technical problems of the region. In January 1999 Mach called on the services of

---

[144] In 1999 Yukos invested R1.7 billion, but planned to increase this to R11 billion in 2000, of which R8.35 billion would go directly into raising output, Tat'yana Lysova, 'Kuda devat' den'gi', *Vedemosti*, 25 October 1999.

[145] Surgut covered its ownership structure in a complicated cross-holding scheme, and in 2003 stopped publishing GAAP-compliant financial reports, Catherine Belton and Neil Buckley, 'On the Offensive: How Gunvor Rose to the Top of Russian Oil Trading', *Financial Times*, 14 May 2008.

[146] Chrystia Freeland, *Sale of the Century: Russia's Wild Ride from Communism to Capitalism* (New York, Crown Business, 2000), p. 157.

Table 2.2. Yukos oil production, 1998–2005

	1998	1999	2000	2001	2002	2003	2004	2005
Overall oil production (million tonnes) of which:	44.6	44.5	49.6	58.2	69.7	80.7	85.7	24.5
Yuganskneftegaz	25.7	26.2	30.2	36.2	42.9	49.7	51.8	n.a.
Samaraneftegaz	8.2	7.2	7.9	9.5	11.0	12.3	12.4	9.6
Tomskneft	10.5	10.3	11.0	11.7	14.4	16.1	17.5	13.1

Note: Yukos exports in 2002 were 24.4 million tonnes (35 per cent of production) and in 2003 26.8 million tonnes (33 per cent), Poussenkova, *From Rigs to Riches*, p. 47.

Source: Matthew J. Sagers, 'The Regional Dimension of Russian Oil Production: Is a Sustained Recovery in Prospect?' *Eurasian Geography and Economics*, Vol. 47, No. 5, 2006, p. 512.

another brilliant petroleum engineer Don Wolcott, who had worked among others with ARCO in Alaska and with Schlumberger. At that time Yukos had some 14,000 active oil wells producing an average of 58 barrels (8 tonnes) a day, and about 4,700 injection wells inserting an average of 200 barrels of water per day. These figures are comparable to American ones, but with an average fluid level of 1,310 feet for the typical 8,200-feet deep well, and with pumps set at the too-shallow depth of 3,940 feet, the wells were manifestly under-producing at less than 10 per cent of potential. The key issue after thirteen years of production decline was not so much damaged wells and reservoirs but poor production and water-flood technical management.[147]

There was much discussion at this time whether Russia was a mature province that had reached its production peak in the late 1980s, caused in particular by bad well intervention ('workover') and drilling techniques, which damaged wells and worsened reservoir damage because of 'over-production'. Mach and Wolcott recommended that instead of drilling some 1,000 wells a year Yukos should focus on production enhancement of existing wells. To counter the output fall of 250,000 barrels per day in the 1990s, the company had drilled 1,600 new wells, an expensive and counter-productive strategy, so Khodorkovsky readily accepted the proposal. In addition, a whole new generation of petroleum engineers was trained in Tomsk at Yukos's expense, which went on to transform production techniques in the Russian oil industry.[148] Schlumberger in particular applied its expertise to the harsh Russian conditions, as did the Anglo-Norwegian company Kvaerner.[149] Instead of using the old Soviet water pumping system, which is

[147] Michael J. Economides and Donna Marie D'Aleo, 'Yukos: Turning Round a Supertanker', *Transitions Online*, 10 April 2008, www.tol.ca; in *Johnson's Russia List* (hereafter *JRL*), No. 75, 2008, item 35. A more developed version can be found at Michael J. Economides and Donna Marie D'Aleo, *From Soviet to Putin and Back: The Dominance of Energy in Today's Russia* (London, Energy Tribune Publishing, 2008).

[148] Economides and D'Aleo, 'Yukos'.

[149] In September 2001 cash-rich Yukos bought a 12.1 per cent stake in Kvaerner, and the next month offered to buy another 12.9 per cent. It was not clear what Yukos planned to do with its stake. John Helmer, 'Oil Giant Yukos Tackles Norse Saga', *The Russia Journal*, 19 October 2001.

extremely wasteful, Schlumberger pioneered the application of hydraulic frac-
turing techniques (hydrofracking, which ironically had been pioneered in Russia
but that had then been abandoned), which are used to this day. The company
developed a range of advanced seismic monitoring equipment to provide 3D
representations of geologic data and software that allows more accurate real-
time measurement of oil, gas, and water flows. Improved reservoir management,
including the extensive use of principle-pattern management technology that
divided its reservoirs into tens of thousands of basic cells allowed recovery rates
to improve.[150]

The results were little short of spectacular. The long-term decline in production
between 1988 and 1999 was dramatically reversed, and in the next four years
output rose by some 20 per cent annually. Output of the Priobskoe field alone
rose from 40 million barrels in 2001, to 90 million in 2002 and 129 million
in 2003, while total Yukos output rose from 890,000 bpd in 1999 to almost
1.8 million bpd in 2004, accompanied by dramatic falls in production costs.[151]
From producing only 60 per cent of Lukoil's output in early 2000, Yukos rivalled
Lukoil in 2002 to become Russia's best performing oil company in terms of output.
However, there remain big questions whether the company was effective in terms
of asset management, and instead only lifted bypassed oil, the so-called brownfield
reserves.[152] Surgutneftegaz was the leader in terms of what is called in the business
'extensions and discoveries', followed by Lukoil, 'whereas Yukos and Sibneft stand
out by virtue of very low levels of exploration drilling in proportion to their crude
oil production'.[153] The company focused on maximizing reserve potential, and
operated its fields at close to saturation pressure.[154] If that was all that Yukos
was good at, then, Gaddy notes, with the task completed it was rational for
the Kremlin to remove it from the scene to allow companies more focused on
exploration and development to develop the resource base to take its place.[155]
However, Yukos had plans of its own, and was now positioned to become an oil

---

[150] Seth Lubove, 'Do Oil and Data Mix?', 18 March 2003, http://www.forbes.com/forbes/2002/
0318/076_2.html.

[151] Economides and D'Aleo note that this was achieved even though the active well count was
reduced from 14,000 wells in 1999 to 8,000 by 2003, while recovery increased from 33 per cent to
42 per cent and the proportion of water in the total liquids produced fell from 77 per cent to 69 per
cent, 'Yukos'.

[152] For a discussion of Yukos as a 'financier-controlled' company focused on maximizing current
output by lifting the oil left over from the 1992–9 years with little 'new' oil, as opposed to a more
paternalistic insider-controlled company such as Surgutneftegaz and Lukoil with long-term investment
strategies, see Clifford G. Gaddy, 'Perspectives on the Potential of Russian Oil', *Eurasian Geography and
Economics*, Vol. 45, No. 5, 2004, pp. 349–50.

[153] Valery Kryukov and Arild Moe, 'Russia's Oil Industry: Risk Aversion in a Risk-Prone Environment', *Eurasian Geography and Economics*, Vol. 48, No. 3, 2007, p. 348.

[154] Poussenkova, *From Rigs to Riches*, p. 22.

[155] Gaddy, 'Perspectives on the Potential of Russian Oil', p. 350. The lack of investment in new
fields may have been a function of insecure property rights, but this then becomes a chicken and egg
argument: lack of confidence in the long-term inhibits investment, which precisely provokes the attack
which prompted the lack of investment in new fields in the first place.

major and to compete with well-established global companies like BP, Shell, and ExxonMobil.

Yukos became ever more ambitious, buoyed by an increase of profits by 154 per cent over the previous year in 2000 to reach $3.3 billion, with total output up 11 per cent year on year. Debt was reduced to $370 million while cash reserves rose sixfold to $2.8 billion.[156] With proven reserves of 12 billion barrels of oil equivalent, by 2002 Yukos was up with the top companies in the world, although its earnings of $3.7 billion on revenues of $7.3 billion in 2001 rendered it no more than middling in financial terms. Nevertheless, it had an ambitious international strategy, including the purchase of refineries and service stations in Europe and sought to take the lead (as we shall see) in a plan to build a $1.7 billion pipeline to pump West Siberian oil to China. Yukos bought a 22 per cent stake in the Kvaerner company in November 2001, an oil field in Kazakhstan, 49 per cent of Slovakia's oil pipeline network (Transpetrol, a 515 km part of the Druzhba main crude export pipeline from Russia to Western Europe) in December 2001, and a 27 per cent stake in the Mazeikiu Nafta refinery in Lithuania in June 2001 (increased to 53 per cent a year later) from the American firm Williams International and the Lithuanian government, which had jointly owned the plant since 1999.[157] Yukos also moved into the gas sector, and used a levered bankruptcy to gain control of Rospan, which had 555 million cubic metres of gas reserves, for $121 million although its market value was at least $9 billion. The company also bought a 68 per cent stake in Artikgaz, with proven reserves of some 200 billion cubic metres, for $190 million. Yukos also moved into the electricity generating business, buying a number of regional power stations.[158] By 2002 Yukos accounted for 17 per cent of Russian oil production, increasing output by 35 per cent in the previous two years to 1.2 million barrels a day, with output rising by 19.3 per cent in 2002 alone. In that year its crude oil exports jumped by 31.1 per cent.[159] In 2003 Yukos (even without Sibneft) jockeyed with Lukoil to be recognized as the country's largest oil company. In that year alone its output rose by 11 per cent. Its downstream operations also developed, refining 280 million barrels of oil in 2003. The yellow and green Yukos badge became a familiar sight at petrol stations across much of Russia. The company invested large sums in modernizing its filling stations, which it recouped by charging higher prices than its competitors, but in return consumers had modern facilities and high-quality fuel. Of the seventeen people on the Forbes list of the world's richest people for 2003, six were associated with Yukos or Group Menatep. The transformation of the company was accompanied by Khodorkovsky's reinvention of himself as an enlightened capitalist.

---

[156] Patrick Gill, 'Yukos Buys Nafta Stake, Posts Results', *The Russia Journal*, 22 June 2001.

[157] In April 2002 Yukos signed an equity-for-crude deal with Williams International that gave the former a major stake in the refinery, 'Yukos Signs Final Deal on Mazheikiu', *Moscow Times*, 12 April 2002, p. 5.

[158] Andrew Barnes, 'Russia's New Business Groups and State Power', *Post-Soviet Affairs*, Vol. 19, No. 2, 2003, p. 164.

[159] *Moscow Times*, 4 March 2003, p. 5.

Corporate transformations

Khodorkovsky managed not only to survive the shipwreck of the Russian economy of August 1998 but also Putin's early attack on the most egregiously political of the oligarchs. Of the seven 'boyars' originally listed by Berezovsky in 1996, only four were still active in Russia in 2001: Mikhail Fridman, Vladimir Potanin, Petr Aven, and Khodorkovsky. In 2000, Yukos returned to the Moscow stock market, from which it had been delisted a year earlier for regulatory offences. At a Russian investment conference in London in June 2000 Khodorkovsky insisted that Yukos had put its poor corporate governance record behind it, and sought to issue internationally traded shares. He dismissed Berezovsky's claims that Russian oligarchs exercised significant political influence: 'If we had just 10 per cent of the political influence that Berezovsky claims, we would never have allowed the government to impose the unbearable tax burden on business that it has.' He was open about his lobbying activities in parliament and the press, which was later to provoke his downfall: 'I don't really see the difference, politically, between Yukos and General Motors. Both have about 2 per cent of [their country's] GDP. Both lobby in parliament for their interests. Both propagandise in the press.' Khodorkovsky stressed the need to reduce the tax burden on business, arguing that 'As long as the tax regime is unjust, I will try to find a way round it', and he agreed with Putin's moves to reduce the powers of Russia's regional leaders.[160]

Years of poor corporate governance meant that Yukos stock was traded at a considerable discount.[161] With little faith in his stock, whose value since 1998 had fallen dramatically, Khodorkovsky had little choice but to try to recapitalize his company. Market and structural reforms had changed the business climate, and instead of levering governmental contacts, siphoning budget funds, or transferring resources offshore, in conditions of reduced macroeconomic risk and fewer fears of a revision of earlier privatization, there were now powerful incentives to shift to value creation and market competition. Improved corporate governance would also facilitate access to foreign capital markets.[162] Already by late 1999 Sibneft under Abramovich, who controlled 40 per cent of the stock, had introduced international accounting standards, a corporate governance charter, and non-executives on its board,[163] and the danger now was that Yukos would fall behind its competitors. The premium was now on qualified corporate managers and less on a powerful oligarch with political access. In those terms, Yukos's transformation was only partial: it became more transparent and better managed, but it remained ultimately an oligarch-led structure, with all of the willfulness that that entailed. At the same time, the company had ruthlessly driven forward vertical integration, in part as a defence mechanism to avert takeovers by creditors along the production

---

[160] Simon Pirani, 'Oligarch? No, I'm Just an Oil Magnate', *The Observer*, 4 June 2000.

[161] Igor Semenenko, 'Yukos Disburses $100M Dividend', *Moscow Times*, 23 January 2001.

[162] For a statement of this view, see Alexander Kim, 'More Important Than the Oil Price', *Moscow Times*, 54 February 2002, p. 10.

[163] Andrew Jack, 'Phantom of the Kremlin Appears', *Financial Times*, 5 November 1999.

chain, which reduced the 'virtual economy' syndrome of inflated value added at each stage,[164] since ultimately there was only one responsible accounting centre. Yukos became a classic example of what Andrew Barnes calls a 'deep business group'.[165]

In 2001, the company hired the American public relations company APCO Worldwide, and Khodorkovsky presented himself as the defender of shareholder and investor rights. The company also made amends for some of its earlier actions, repaying some of the creditors on whose loans Menatep had defaulted. The head of APCO, Margery Kraus, joined Group Menatep's advisory board. An extraordinary shareholders' meeting on 28 March 2000 agreed to give Yukos-Moskva full operational control of what by then had become the country's second largest oil company, and thus stripped NK Yukos of its remaining managerial powers. Yukos-Moskva had since 1998 been in effective control, and the move was announced as part of an attempt to provide greater transparency to the company's management structure. As noted, the company consisted of Yukos-Moskva, which carried out management functions, combined with the upstream unit Yukos EP and the downstream operator Yukos RM. NK Yukos had no management functions but it remained the 100 per cent owner of Yukos-Moskva. All shares in subsidiaries had been consolidated into shares in the parent company.[166] Yukos shares by 2001 traded in London, and other financial markets. Despite the greater transparency, it remained unclear why Yukos-Moskva needed to be kept as the management company.

By 2002 one-third of the Yukos board of directors were foreigners, with the five coming from Europe and the United States. The Washington lawyer, Sarah Carey, a graduate of Harvard Law School and a specialist in Russian business, served as an independent non-executive board member from 2000 to 2004. She was joined by Michel Soublin, an accountant with Schlumberger, Raj Kumar Gupta, a former vice president of Phillips Petroleum, Bernard Loze from France, and Jacques Kosciusko-Morizet, a former vice president of Le Crédit Lyonnais. At this time the former British foreign minister Lord David Owen was appointed chair of Yukos International. Yukos entered into numerous deals with Western companies on the basis of equality, refusing to accept asymmetrical terms because of the harsher conditions of doing business in Russia.[167] Long-standing disputes with companies such as ING Barings and Le Crédit Lyonnais were resolved, and Khodorkovsky also offered to compromise with Kenneth Dart and called off the propaganda campaign that Yukos had long been waging against him.[168]

---

[164] Cf. Clifford G. Gaddy and Barry W. Ickes, 'Russia's Virtual Economy', *Foreign Affairs*, Vol. 77, No. 5, September–October 1998, pp. 53–67.

[165] Barnes, 'Russia's New Business Groups and State Power'.

[166] Andrew McChesney, 'Yukos Reshuffles in the Name of Transparency', *Moscow Times*, 29 March 2000, p. 11.

[167] Natalia Gevorkyan interview with Khodorkovsky, June 2002, 'Mikhail Khodorkovskii: Rokefelleru bylo namnogo tyazhelee', *Kommersant*, 1 June 2005.

[168] Goldman, *The Piratization of Russia*, p. 149.

An American, Bruce K. Misamore, who had previously worked for Marathon Oil and PennzEnergy, was hired as chief financial officer in February 2001. By 2002 Yukos had published three years of accounts meeting American Generally Accepted Accounting Principles (GAAP) standards, paid out regular dividends on common stock (rising from $300 million in 2000, $500 million in 2001 to $2 billion in the first nine months of 2003),[169] and introduced the rule that any new stock issue had to be approved by 75 per cent of shareholders. The company's accounts were audited by PricewaterhouseCoopers (PwC), one of the world's 'big four' auditors created in 1998 out of the merger of Price Waterhouse and Coopers Lybrand, who later changed their minds on the accuracy of the company's accounts for this time.

By May 1999, 31.9 per cent of Yukos stock was foreign-owned.[170] In connection with plans to gain American Depository Receipt (ADR) third-level listing on the New York Stock Exchange, which demands a lot of information about a company's ownership structure, in July 2002 the company for the first time published details of its share capital. Group Menatep (a separate legal entity from Bank Menatep) controlled 61 per cent of Yukos, while 22 per cent was free-floating and 10 per cent was owned by the veteran pension trust. Group Menatep—later called simply GML—was based in Gibralter and was run reportedly from little more than a post office box, but was nevertheless the main holding company for Yukos. The main owners of Group Menatep were Khodorkovsky and five other shareholders, with Khodorkovsky personally holding 9.5 per cent of Menatep stock valued at some $7.7 billion.[171] In terms of ownership of Yukos stock, Khodorkovsky's share was 5.8 per cent.[172] Market capitalization rose from $300 million in 1999 to $20 billion in 2002, by which time it had $3.4 billion in cash reserves and just $96 million of debt.[173] The company shifted from the maximization of cash revenues to long-term asset maximization. In 2000 alone Yukos paid $1.9 billion in taxes.[174]

The legacy of the past could not be shaken off so easily, however, and as late as January 2002 the Audit Chamber claimed that Yukos had been asset-stripping VNK.[175] When threatened with a lawsuit by the minority investor Birkenholz in 1999, 37 per cent of Tomskneft shares were transferred from VNK to four offshore

---

[169] Poussenkova, *From Rigs to Riches*, p. 29. Most of these generous dividends went to a small group of top managers who owned 61% of stock, with a relatively small free-float stake.

[170] Kryukov and Moe, 'Banks and the Financial Sector', p. 72.

[171] The main shareholders in Group Menatep were Khodorkovsky (9.5 per cent), Leonid Nevzlin (8 per cent), Platon Lebedev (7 per cent), Vladimir Dubov (7 per cent), Mikhail Brudno (7 per cent), and Vasily Shakhnovsky (4.5 per cent), Kononczuk, *The 'Yukos Affair'*, p. 55, n. 8; http://www.alexey-pichugin.ru/index.php?id=251.

[172] Nevzlin's share came to 4.9 per cent, Shakhnovskii 4.3 per cent, Brudno 4.3 per cent, Lebedev 4.3 per cent, Dubov 4.3 per cent and others 2.75 per cent, Valerii Butaev, 'Khodorkovskii priznalsya v $7 mlrd. s kopeikami', *Komsomol'skaya Pravda*, 22 June 2006, p. 3.

[173] Simon Pirani, 'The Ohio Drawl that Speaks for Russia's No. 2 Oil Company', *Financial News*, December 2002; http://quintissential.org.uk/SimonPrirani/misamore-fndec02.htm.

[174] Lucas, *New Cold War*, p. 63.

[175] Anna Raff, ' "Impartial" Western Triad Probes Yukos', *Moscow Times*, 21 January 2002, p. 9.

companies, allegedly with the approval of the state nominee on VNK's board, although the government was never satisfied with this explanation.[176] VNK was reduced to little more than a shell company. When the state planned to auction its residual 36.8 per cent state in VNK for an estimated $225 million on 14 February 2002, Khodorkovsky warned any potential purchaser that they would acquire a 'bitter pill'. In 2001, the heads of the 'club of 4' (Yukos, Lukoil, TNK, and Sibneft) created an informal cartel to regulate conflicts in the oil sector, and it had given Yukos the green light to buy the state's share of VNK, but at its first major test this collapsed.[177] Yukos faced stiff competition from TNK, with whom relations had broken down because of a conflict over the acquisition of the gas company Rospan. Both offered over $400, but in the end the sale of VNK was postponed because of doubts over the actual assets available and the matter was referred to the prime minister, Mikhail Kasyanov. Disappointed about his failure to incorporate VNK fully into Yukos, Khodorkovsky threatened, irrespective of the outcome, to direct all of VNK's profits into philanthropy.[178] The struggle over VNK threatened to undermine all the work that Yukos had done to launder its image.

The company from the first had its own ideas on important policy issues. Russia in 2002 came under intense pressure from the Organisation of Petroleum Exporting Countries (OPEC) to cut oil production to push up the price of oil to around $30, but Khodorkovsky led the struggle against this, even though some other Russian oil majors were more amenable. Yukos (and Sibneft) opposed the Russian government's decision to cut crude oil exports by 150,000 bpd in the first quarter of 2002, the lowest option on the table.[179] In the end, Khodorkovsky's voice was the loudest in the Kremlin, and Russia did not substantively align itself with the producers' cartel.[180] The planned merger in 2003 with the Sibneft company, run by Abramovich, would have created one of the world's largest oil majors. At its peak Yukos was estimated to be worth $40 billion. It was at this point that the company was struck down.

Personal issues

Khodorkovsky was just 19 when he married his first wife, Elena Dobrovolskaya. She was also a member of the Mendeleev Institute's Komsomol committee. They had a son, Pavel, in June 1985, who later studied in a Swiss boarding school and then went to university in the United States. In 1987, Khodorkovsky found someone else, but he supported his former wife to set up her own travel business (called

[176] Aleksandr Tutushkin, 'Khodorkovskii sderzhal slovo', *Vedemosti*, 27 April 2001.

[177] Oleg Chernitskii, 'Yukos vstal na dyby', *Vremya novostei*, 7 February 2002, p. 7; a good overview of the VNK saga is provided by Anna Raff, 'Anatomy of an Oil Company Sell-Off', *Moscow Times*, 30 May 2002, p. 1.

[178] Mariya Ignatova, 'Tak ne dostavaisya ty nikomu', *Izvestiya*, 7 February 2002, p. 6.

[179] John Helmer, 'Government, Producers Reach Oil Export Compromise', *The Russia Journal*, 7 December 2001.

[180] Klebnikov, 'The Oligarch Who Came in From the Cold'.

'Ledi-Viktoriya') after they divorced. His second wife, Inna Valentinovna, joined the evening department of the Mendeleev Institute in 1986, and was then employed as a laboratory assistant before working in the Institute's Komsomol organization, where she met Khodorkovsky, and later she joined the currency operations department of Menatep. They were not married when their daughter Anastasia was born in 1991, but the wedding took place soon after, and in 1999 they had twin sons, Ilya and Gleb. Inna did not complete her studies and gave up paid work to devote herself to the family.

By 2002, aged only 38, Khodorkovsky was ranked number 101 (the highest of Russia's seven billionaires) of the world's rich with a net worth of $3.7 billion.[181] By 2003 Forbes estimated that his personal wealth had risen to $8 billion, making him Russia's richest person and twenty-sixth in the global rankings. Khodorkovsky 'used to personify the predatory Russian oligarch', but his own image had been burnished along with that of his company.[182] Khodorkovsky liked to describe himself as three generations of Rockefellers rolled into one: robber baron, respected business leader, and philanthropist. Khodorkovsky set up home in the elite exurb of Zhukovka, about an hour's drive west from Moscow city centre and once the home of Soviet generals and top Party officials. A number of his associates and Yukos executives also built houses in a closely guarded compound set among pine trees and gently rolling hills. According to Klebnikov, 'the compound itself bears a resemblance to a prison camp. It is surrounded by high walls, with powerful lights every 30 paces. Guards with machine guns patrol the perimeter.'[183]

The transformation of Yukos in the new millennium was accompanied by a physical transformation in Khodorkovsky himself. If up to the end of the 1990s he had a rather Soviet look about him, with heavily rimmed glasses, a rather thickset body, a moustache, and rather ill-kempt hair, in the 2000s he had a makeover, with shorter hair, the moustache was gone, his glasses changed to a rather Lennon-like rimless look, and he looked fitter.[184] He also joined the international jet set lifestyle, with fancy yachts and Saville Row suits. How far his thinking had changed is not clear. Addressing a meeting of the American Chamber of Commerce in Moscow in May 2001 Khodorkovsky patiently explained to his American guests why Russian business leaders dealt so brutally with shareholder rights: 'It's the mentality. Twenty years ago, under Soviet power, to be honest meant to die of hunger, and in some regions this mentality continues.'[185] This was probably not a message that the Americans wished to hear.

---

[181] The others were Roman Abramovich at number 127, Mikhail Fridman at 191, Vladimir Potanin at 234, Vladimir Bogdanov at 277, Vagit Alekperov at 327, and Oleg Deripaska at 413, 'Who Owns Russia?', 18 March 2002; http://www.forbes.com/forbes/2002/0318/110tab.html.

[182] Serge Schmemann, 'In Going Legit, Some Russian Tycoons Resort to Honesty', *New York Times*, 12 January 2003.

[183] Klebnikov, 'The Oligarch Who Came in From the Cold'.

[184] Panyushkin, *Mikhail Khodorkovskii*, p. 149.

[185] Oleg Chernitskii, 'Eshche odin chestnyi oligarkh', *Vremya novostei*, 16 May 2001, p. 4.

Khodorkovsky had long been a member of the Rand US–Russia Business Leader Forum, an invitation-only organization with which the veteran Sovietologist Jeremy Azrael was closely involved. The body meets twice a year, once in Russia and then in America, and was designed to socialize Russian CEOs in the ways of Western business, including acclimatizing them to the notion of corporate social responsibility (CSR) while improving their image and influence in America and over civil society. Khodorkovsky was one of the original members from the early 1990s, along with Gusinsky, while on the American side members included Donald Rumsfield and Kenneth Lay, who was later to achieve notoriety as the head of Enron. It was in this forum that Khodorkovsky got to know Bruce Jackson, formerly of Lockheed Martin and something of an intellectual entrepreneur who virulenty advocated Nato enlargement. Jackson had a live interest in post-Soviet matters, being married to a Belarusian, and had close ties to the Democrats as well as the Republicans. As we shall see, the Yukos case in part represented a battle of the lobbies, notably in trying to exercise influence over the US administration. Khodorkovsky was also a member of the US–Russia Business Council, for which members have to pay a hefty annual subscription. It was headed by Gene Wilson, with whom Khodorkovsky maintained strong personal relations.

Khodorkovsky also joined the Carlyle Group, the world's largest private equity firm specializing in military-industrial investments enjoying close ties with the Pentagon and, it almost goes without saying, the Bush (father and son) White House. Other members included James Baker, the former American secretary of state, the former defence secretaries William Perry and Frank Carlucci, the former British prime minister John Major, as well as a number of other prominent figures. In the new world of the 'war on terror' after 11 September 2001 the Group levered its contacts to shape the security agenda of the new era. Group Menatep was also able to lever these contacts into support for Yukos once the assault on the company began in 2003. Earlier that year Menatep had created an international advisory board, whose functions are unclear in business terms but were obviously directed towards the creation of an international lobbying network on behalf of Yukos. One of the advisory board members was Stuart Eizenstat, who had worked in the US treasury under President Bill Clinton, who was also an adviser to APCO and whose law company in October 2003 agreed to work with Kissinger/McLarty Associates: Mack McLarty had been chief of staff under Clinton and was a member of the Carlyle Group. In spring 2002 Menatep announced that it would invest $50 million in the Carlyle Group. Following Khodorkovsky's arrest Eizenstat, who had also formerly served as American ambassador to the European Union, sprang to his defence.[186]

Khodorkovsky had risen from a poor boy growing up in the suburbs of Moscow to international financier and global capitalist. His rise coincided with the fall of communism and the disintegration not only of the Soviet state but also of the

---

[186] Judy Sarasohn, 'Russia's Jailed Titans Have Washington Ally', *Washington Post*, 25 December 2003.

civilization with which it was associated. Khodorkovsky in many ways was an exemplary model of the Soviet citizen, active in its Komsomol youth organization, but also reflected the other side of Soviet citizenship: the ability to dissimulate and to break rules to survive. Opportunities could not have been grander from the early 1990s as the Soviet economic order was destroyed and whole industries came on to the market at discounted prices. The state retreated into an enclave based on the Kremlin, while the country fell prey to criminal-economic entrepreneurs. With the rule of law in abeyance, the distinction between criminal and legitimate business activity was blurred. A powerful new force emerged in Russia, the super-wealthy oligarchs, who were even prepared to dictate to the state. The economy was disembedded from a society, half of whose members fell into poverty. The transformation of Yukos in the early 2000s was accompanied by growing geopolitical ambitions of its leadership. Conflict with a resurgent Russian state was inevitable; the only unclear issue was the form that this struggle would take.

3

The State and the Oligarchs

> If the choice is between freedom and the idea of the state, then we will all renounce personal freedom. To hell with that freedom.
>
> Aleksandr Prokhanov[1]

Putin's statism was imbued with paradoxes and contradictions. Although Putin stressed the universal applicability of law, yet in certain individual cases and in dealing with the insurgency in Chechnya and with the 'over-mighty subject' Khodorkovsky, human rights and the rule of law were subordinated to the state's goals. In talking of law Putin was inclined to favour the rights of the state against those of individuals and social organizations in general. Putin's statism was no doubt in part generated by considerations of power consolidation, but it was also prompted by a deeply held belief in the moral privileges of the state as the champion of the common good. In his 8 July 2000 state-of-the-nation speech he argued that 'an era is beginning in Russia where the authorities are gaining the moral right to demand that established state norms should be observed' and that 'strict observance of laws must become a need for all people in Russia by their own choice'.[2] He insisted that the close relationship between big business and government should be broken. In an interview soon after he insisted that he sought to put an end to the situation in which Russians appeared to have become subjects of different regions rather than citizens of a single country.[3] Oligarchs and regional barons were the two categories that he clearly had in his sights. The Russian state had fallen victim to the very reforms which it had sponsored, and now the state fought back. The power of individual oligarchs was not consolidated in the form of class power, and thus they proved defenceless when the government turned to the attack.

---

[1] Aleksandr Prokhanov, 'Propadi ona propadom, eta svoboda!', *Komsomol'skaya pravda*, 3 September 1991, p. 4.

[2] 'Vystuplenie pri predstavlenii ezhegodnogo Poslaniya Prezidenta Rossiiskoi Federatsii Federal'nomu Sobraniyu Rossiiskoi Federatsii', http://www.president.kremlin.ru/events/42.html.

[3] 'Vladimir Putin—"Rossiya ne dol'zhna byt' i ne budet politseiskom gosudarstvom": Prezident Rossii dal intervyu "Izvestiyam"', *Izvestiya*, 14 July 2000, p. 1.

PLURALIST STATE TO REGIME CONSOLIDATION

The struggle over the distribution and management of former state property lies at the root of the Yukos affair and much of contemporary Russian politics. Kimmage labels the view that a new set of rules for financial-industrial actors was established in Putin's early period as the 'political' theory: 'So long as the oligarchs stayed out of politics, the state would let sleep the unquiet ghosts of privatisation past.'[4] As we shall see, there is also the 'factional' theory of the Yukos affair, in which elite groups (above all a section of the *siloviki*), who had been marginalized in the 1990s, now sought not only to reassert their place in Russian politics but also to get a share of assets hitherto monopolized by the oligarchs. A third family of interpretations focus on the ideology of statism, the political economy issue in which the regime adopted a new developmental strategy accompanied by a rebalancing of relations between the state and the market. We will examine the various models later in this chapter, but here consider some broad theoretical issues about the relationship between business and the state.

Lucan Way argues that from 1996 Yeltsin turned to the oligarchs as a form of surrogate organizational capacity, given the weakness of the state and the party system, revealed harshly in the 1995/6 electoral cycle. While personal loyalty (*lichnaya predannost'*) remained one of his key managerial principles, he sought to find a way to manage the regions, parliament, and the electoral process, and he found the solution in 'organizational outsourcing': 'In essence Yeltsin "rented" organizational capacity from various outside formal and informal groups—oligarch networks, regional government and political parties—who provided support at key moments.'[5] He also stiffened their resolve by inducting personnel from the security services into regime administration, a process that was well advanced before Putin assumed the presidency. However, the system proved tenuous, and both the oligarch and regional groups defected as the succession approached in 1998/9. The Yeltsinite political bargain, as Way notes, trading 'autonomy for political support', facilitated defection, as with the Luzhkov–Primakov alliance with leading governors in 1999 in the form of the Fatherland-All Russia alliance (OVR).[6] In his comparative analysis of the Yukos affair and the break-up of John Rockefeller's Standard Oil, which at its height controlled 90 per cent of the American oil market, Volkov notes that early capitalism 'is a socio-historical formation in which actors are stronger than institutions',[7] and this was certainly the case in post-communist Russia.

[4] Daniel Kimmage, 'Putin's Restoration: Consolidation or Clan Rivalries?', in Geir Flikke (ed.), *The Uncertainties of Putin's Democracy* (Oslo, NUPI, 2004), p. 135.

[5] Lucan A. Way, *Pigs, Wolves and the Evolution of Post-Soviet Competitive Authoritarianism, 1991–2005*, Center on Democracy, Development, and The Rule of Law, Stanford University, working paper, No. 62, June 2006, p. 29.

[6] Ibid., p. 31.

[7] Vadim Volkov, ' "Delo Standard Oil" i "delo Yukosa" ', *Pro et Contra*, Vol. 9, No. 2, September–October 2005, p. 67.

Makarenko notes:

Under Putin these [political-financial] groups have been built into the system of power as influential, but peripheral elements. However their influence on the taking of important state decisions (above all, in the realm of personnel appointments and concrete economic policy decisions) remains very high. In so far as this influence is not balanced by the adequate development and strengthening of formal democratic institutions, the threat of the 'oligarchisation of power' remains.[8]

It was this threat that was highlighted in 2003 and which provided the rationale for the assault of the most active of the remaining oligarchs, Khodorkovsky.

Zudin dismisses the idea that a coherent oligarchy came to dominate politics in the mid-1990s, and instead convincingly describes a situation in which there was 'oligarchs without oligarchy'. When the magnates did act collectively, it was more a sign of weakness rather than strength.[9] For Zudin the key process was the re-establishment of hierarchy. In the 1990s the development of business elites forcefully created a type of political polycentrism, moderating the super-presidential system while not developing into a fully fledged alternative order, since the business elite lacked internal hierarchy, and instead the system was characterized by a symbiotic relationship between the state and business. The 1998 default and Putin's accession opened a new era with the recreation of a monocentric system and hierarchy. Putin's policy of distancing business leaders was accompanied by the removal of political instruments from the hands of the oligarchs, notably control over the mass media (which affected Gusinsky and Berezovsky particularly severely). In the first phase the new model included the institutionalization of business–state relations through the creation of a government council for entrepreneurship and regular meeting with the Russian Union of Industrialists and Entrepreneurs (RUIE), which itself was transformed into a more effective peak organization; corporatization, through an enhanced role for business associations, with the administration sponsoring the development of 'Delovaya Rossiya' (Business Russia), OPOR (Ob"edinenie predprinimatel'skikh obshchestv Rossii, United Entrepreneurial Societies of Russia) and the Trade-Industrial Council (Torgovo-promyshlennaya palata, TPP), and the formation of a 'consultative regime', through regular meetings between state and business leaders.

The Yukos affair represented a conflict between two modernizing agents, the state and big business. As a result of the affair, however, the latter was seriously weakened as a collective actor and the major independent force in Russian politics was thrown out of the game, allowing the state to become the dominant player. The initiative passed to companies closely linked to the state, notably Gazprom and Rosneft, accompanied by the establishment of a firm hierarchy known as the

---

[8] Boris Makarenko, 'Demokraticheskii transit v Rossii', *Mirovaya ekonomika i mezhdunarodnye otnosheniya*, No. 11, 2004, p. 56.

[9] Aleksei Yu. Zudin, 'Oligarchy as a Political Problem of Russian Postcommunism', *Russian Social Science Review*, Vol. 41, No. 6, November–December 2000, pp. 6–7.

'vertical of power'.[10] Khodorkovsky by 2003 sought to move beyond the consultative regime, and his various initiatives effectively meant that Yukos became a distinctive type of party substitute, a mega-party acting as a type of state within the state striving to dominate political parties, parliament, and the public sphere, and this Putin and his associates found intolerable.

Peter Rutland examines a number of models of the political economy of the oil industry, and more broadly of the whole system, as it emerged in the 1990s.[11] The Kuwaitization model, in which Russia plays to its comparative advantage and becomes a natural resource exporter of oil and gas but also of metals and other primary goods, he considers too simplistic, and one which would render Russia passive victim of international market forces. No Russian leader would accept this, or survive long if they did. At the same time, this model suggests the pre-eminence of the natural resource lobby in domestic and foreign policy. The liberalization model was pursued by Gaidar from late 1991, and was designed to unleash market forces while reducing the role of the state. Although encountering enormous opposition in parliament and society, the fundamentals of a neo-liberal approach were pushed through, including the break up of the integrated Soviet oil industry and the lifting of export quotas, but opponents pointed to the lack of investment, wages, and tax arrears. To counter this, the liberal model provided the framework for the rationalization of the new companies, and ensured that no single lobby was able to capture the state. The liberal economic model is accompanied by a pluralistic model of domestic politics.

The third approach suggests that things are basically very simple: 'the triumph of rent-seeking over profit seeking', allowing a small group to exploit their monopolistic position.[12] There were elements of this, notably with Berezovsky's Sibneft, but history was to show that as soon as circumstances allowed, the new owners in the energy sector were ready to invest and to transform their companies into classical profit-seeking corporations. The 'Russian bear' model focuses on the use of energy and other economic weapons to pursue its foreign policy objectives, what would later take the name of the 'energy superpower' strategy (Chapter 11). The fifth approach is the pluralism model, suggesting that no single group is able to dominate the policy process. Indeed, Rutland argues that in certain respects the lack of a single defining perspective, with incoherent and conflicting goals pursued by all sorts of policy entrepreneurs meant that the country suffered from 'pluralism run amok, where the "decision-making process" seems to be invented for each decision'.[13] Rutland notes that there were limits to this reckless pluralism, and the government retained a hold, however tenuous, on the decision-making process, and the appropriate ministries and bureaucracies were engaged in developing more or less coherent policies. The imposition of order in the state was Putin's priority when he came to power in 2000, and within three years the

---

[10] Aleksei Zudin, 'Gosudarstvo i biznes v Rossii: evolyutsiya modeli vzaimootnoshenii', Neprikosnovennyi zapas: Debaty o politike i kul'ture, http://www.nz-online.ru/print.phtml?aid=80018067.

[11] Rutland, 'Oil, Politics, and Foreign Policy', in Lane (ed.), *The Political Economy of Russian Oil*, Chapter 7, pp. 163–88, at pp. 179–83.

[12] Ibid., p. 181.   [13] Ibid., p. 182.

pluralist model had given way to state consolidation and the reassertion of government prerogatives, but this was accompanied by the intensification of factional
conflict as the pluralism chased out of society was internalized within the regime.
Pluralism gave way to policy fragmentation, and the struggle between these groups
in the end decided the fate of Yukos.

From the very first Putin adopted the opposite strategy to that of Yeltsin, and
instead of outsourcing political capacity, he sought to concentrate the sources of
administrative power in the regime's hands. His first priority was the imposition
of the 'power vertical' on regional leaders, the assertion of state authority in the
energy sector, accompanied soon afterwards by the development of a dominant
ruling party in the form of United Russia. Surkov, now in the presidential administration, was responsible for domestic policy, and sponsored the development
of United Russia, and in general oversaw the domestic political scene. He can
be characterized as a 'democratic statist', and thus stood outside the '*siloviki*'
even though he spent his military service with the GRU (military intelligence)
during 1983–5. Using this party, Putin was able to exercise the latent powers of
the executive more effectively than Yeltsin, especially over the legislature. One
by one, autonomous actors with independent sources of political power were
suborned or co-opted, as with Luzhkov in Moscow. The aim was not simply
personal aggrandizement since Putin's political consolidation was designed to
create a more effective developmental state, although it also had collateral benefits
for the regime. This applies equally when he turned his attention to one of the
major sources of independent power, the world of big business.

PUTIN'S POLICY OF 'EQUIDISTANCE'

In his first year in power Putin returned to the problem of the relationship between
the oligarchs and the state on many occasions. In the run-up to the 26 March 2000
presidential election, Putin asked: 'What then should be the relationship with the
so-called oligarchs? The same as with anyone else. The same as with the owner of
a small bakery or a shoe repair shop.'[14] In a later interview, asked what would be
the future for the oligarchs, Putin answered that if one meant 'those people who
fuse, or help the fusion of power and capital, there will be no oligarchs of this
kind as a class'.[15] This was a clear allusion to Stalin's threat in 1929 to 'liquidate
the kulaks as a class'. In an interview later that year Putin noted: 'In our country
representatives of big business who try to influence political decision making while
remaining in the shadows have been regarded as oligarchs. There must be no such
group of people.' He defended the need for big business, but absolutely refused to

[14] Vladimir Putin, 'Otkrytoe pis'mo Vladimira Putina k Rossiiskim izbiratelyam', *Izvestiya*, 25
February 2000, p. 5; www.putin2000.ru/07/05.html.
[15] Interview with Radio Mayak, 18 March 2000, in BBC Summary of World Broadcasts, SU/3793
B/3; also cited by Hoffman, *The Oligarchs*, p. 475.

allow them a privileged political role: 'I cannot imagine people anywhere near me who try to exert influence from the shadows.'[16] In a crucial meeting with business representatives on 28 July 2000, he formalized the principle of 'equidistance' (*rav-noudalennost'*) in relations between the state and oligarch groups: 'We will prevent anyone attaching themselves to political authority and using it for their own goals. No clan, no oligarch should come close to regional or federal authorities—they should be kept equally distanced from politics.' At that meeting he noted the 'highly politicised' actions of law enforcement agencies against certain oligarchs, but noted that 'you yourselves to a significant degree formed this state through the political and quasi-political structures that you control'.[17] The basic deal was a 'pragmatic exchange of political restraint for secure property rights', and as Tompson notes, the meeting has assumed the character of a 'foundational political myth', even though the basic framework had been shaped by a whole series of actions since Putin's assumption of power.[18] We shall examine these first before looking at the 28 July meeting and its consequences.

Muddy waters

Putin feared that the consolidation of oligarch power would render Russia a 'domain democracy', where certain groups (such as the military or entrepreneurs) can exercise veto powers by taking 'certain political domains out of the hands of democratically representatives'.[19] The plutocratic social order of the 1990s was repudiated, although the scope for enrichment by individual oligarchs remained within the framework of a new set of conventions. Putin imposed an informal 'social contract' on big business: as long as the oligarchs paid their taxes and stayed out of politics, they would be left to get on with their affairs. The state would deal with oligarchs on the basis of 'equidistance', ending the phenomenon of court oligarchs inhabiting the corridors of power and using state power to advance their business interests. The new policy of equidistance was imposed by making an example of two of the most egregiously political of the oligarchs. Berezovsky, at the head of a major media and energy holding company, was forced into exile, together with Gusinsky, the founder of the NTV television channel, part of the Media-Most banking and media empire that owned a string of newspapers. By the same token, the Putin administration was able to impose a degree of uniformity on the main electronic mass media.

---

[16] 'Vladimir Putin: Pozitivnye tendentsii est'', no poka eto tol'ko tendentsii. Prezident Rossii v intervyu ORT, RTR i Nezavisimoi gazete podvodit itogi 2000 goda', *Nezavisimaya gazeta*, 26 December 2000, p. 1.

[17] 'Vstupitel'noe slovo na vstreche s rukovoditelyami krupneishikh rossiiskikh kompanii i bankov', 28 July 2000, http://www.kremlin.ru/appears/2000/07/28/0000_type63376_28808.shtml.

[18] William Tompson, 'Putting Yukos in Perspective', *Post-Soviet Affairs*, Vol. 21, No. 2, April–June 2005, p. 168.

[19] Wolfgang Merkel, 'Embedded and Defective Democracies', *Democratisation*, Vol. 11, No. 5, December 2004, p. 49.

Even before he assumed the presidency Putin began the struggle to reassert the state's authority in the energy sector. In late October 1999 Putin, as prime minister, signed a decree according to which energy magnates could no longer be voting participants in the fuel and energy ministry.[20] The likes of Vyakhirev (Gazprom), Chubais (UES), and Alekperov (Lukoil) were thus excluded from direct participation in formulating policies of the ministry that provided Russia's single largest source of revenue. The debate in 1999 over the 2000 budget demonstrated the power of the oil lobby and just how entwined politics and oil had become in the country. Already the struggle to oust Vyakhirev from Gazprom had begun, to ensure that the Kremlin could directly control the revenues from the energy giant as well as to isolate Gusinsky, with whom Vyakhirev had forged a close relationship. Gazprom funded Gusinsky's heavily indebted NTV to the tune of some half a billion dollars. Chubais's attempts to oust Bogdanchikov and place someone more amenable at the head of Rosneft, however, were blocked. Khodorkovsky met Putin twice before his formal election in March 2000 to discuss energy issues, and formed a favourable impression but noted that Putin was 'more of a politician than an economist'. He hoped that the new administration would put an end to talk of a group of well-connected oligarchs running the Kremlin: 'I hope the legends about the oligarchs will die along with the changing of presidents', and he warned that '[a]nyone who calls him [Berezovsky] an entrepreneur is mistaken'. He declared that the influence of American companies lobbying in Washington was much greater than anything seen in Moscow: 'We are like children in comparison.'[21] This was an imbalance that he sought to rectify to his cost.

The first to feel the cold wind, however, was Gusinsky, and the attack on him prefigured that on Khodorkovsky later. The Media-Most offices were raided on 11 May 2000, and on 13 June Gusinsky was arrested and held in custody for four days. Putin was in Spain at this time and appeared bewildered by what was happening at home. The tax affairs of a number of other companies became the objects of scrutiny in July, including Gazprom, Norilsk Nickel, Lukoil, and the biggest car manufacturer, Avtovaz. Norilsk Nickel had fallen into Potanin's possession (through his holding company Interros) as a result of the his shares-for-loans plan of 1995/6, and now the authorities called for the repayment of $140 million in compensation for his alleged underpayment when the plant had been privatized in an auction that he helped organize. The inclusion of Avtovaz in the list indicated the renewal of the investigations into the affairs of Berezovsky, who had made his first millions by association with the hugely loss-making car company through his car dealership business, Logovaz. Berezovsky's interests had by now diversified to include Aeroflot, Sibneft, and the media (including a 49 per cent stake in the main TV station, ORT).[22] As Berezovsky put it in June 2000, the

---

[20] *Izvestiya*, 31 October 1999.

[21] Brian Killen, 'Interview: Russian Oil Baron Impressed by Putin', *JRL*, No. 4085, 2 February 2000, item 7.

[22] All this is described well by Klebnikov, *Godfather of the Kremlin*.

way that business had been conducted in the last decade meant that no one 'could survive a serious government effort to find something to charge them with'.[23]

In July 2000 Putin criticized 'people who feel comfortable in conditions of disorder, catching fish in muddy waters and wanting to keep things as they are'. Yeltsin himself had occasionally talked in these terms, and as prime minister Primakov had launched an investigation against some business leaders, notably Berezovsky and Smolensky. In April 1999, Berezovsky had been charged with 'illegal business activity', but these charges were dropped in November (when Putin was already prime minister) because of a lack of evidence linking him to the Aeroflot case. The investigation into Berezovsky's activities when Aeroflot's cash flow fell into his hands, passing through a Swiss intermediary, had been conducted by Yuri Skuratov when he was prosecutor general, but Skuratov was dismissed from his post in Yeltsin's last year.[24] Berezovsky used his businesses as cash milch cows, running down their capitalization for immediate benefit. Berezovsky had acquired Sibneft in 1995 at a deep discount, and although it produced 40 per cent as much oil as Surgutneftegaz, the market capitalization of the latter (one of the best-managed oil majors in Russia) was eleven times higher. Berezovsky, as Khodorkovsky well understood, was always more interested in politics than business. Primakov's efforts to investigate Berezovsky and others in fact provoked the oligarchs to close ranks against him, and he was dismissed as premier on 12 May 1999. A few days later Berezovsky's nominees were settling into ministerial posts, notably Nikolai Aksënenko, encouraging the notion of 'family' power, a union of oligarchs and Yeltsin's entourage.

Even at the time the process by which the attack against leading business was conducted was condemned as 'absolutely illiterate'. The letter by the deputy prosecutor, Yuri Biryukov, of 7 July 2000 calling for Potanin to reimburse what the state had lost through his 'criminal actions', and accusing him of having acted 'in conspiracy' with Kokh (the former head of the State Property Committee), lacked evidence and rather pre-empted a judicial process that could have proved them.[25] This was a style of behaviour that typified the Yukos affair. Already in 2000 the attack on such a range of disparate figures conducted in such an unprofessional manner aroused considerable speculation about the motives: 'What is the driving force of this open aggressive behaviour by the executive authorities against big Russian business?'[26] A number of options were suggested, ranging from the attempt to impose the 'dictatorship of law', a campaign that would reach out to other businesses (Sibneft and Yukos were named); to the simple attempt by the regime to gain financial resources for its political line—but why open up a second front at a time when Putin was locked in struggle with governors to change the

[23] Cited in Dale R. Herspring and Jacob Kipp, 'Understanding the Elusive Mr. Putin', *Problems of Post-Communism*, Vol. 48, No. 5, September/October 2001, p. 9.

[24] For his analysis of the anti-oligarch investigations and his scandalous dismissal, see Yurii Skuratov, *Variant drakona* (Moscow, Detektiv Press, 2000).

[25] Natal'ya Arkhangel'skaya et al., 'Provokatsiya', *Ekspert*, No. 27, 17 July 2000, in *Ekspert: Luchshie materialy*, No. 2, 2007, pp. 14–16.

[26] Arkhangel'skaya et al., 'Provokatsiya', p. 15.

federal system? The third explanation was that despite Putin's promise during the presidential election campaign earlier that year that '[w]e will not allow the results of privatisation to be reviewed', his hand was forced by factional struggles in the Kremlin.

Berezovsky's rather inglorious political career in Russia was now fast coming to an end. In the December 1999 parliamentary elections he won a seat from the single-member constituency in the North Caucasian republic of Karachaevo-Cherkessia, and thus gained immunity from prosecution. On 17 July 2000 he announced that he planned to resign his Duma seat in protest at the 'authoritarian' trends in Putin's government,[27] arguing that he did not want 'to take part in the destruction of Russia and the establishment of the authoritarian regime'.[28] He described the guarantee of immunity as worthless, which in his case it probably was since most deputies would have been only too glad to strip him of his immunity and see him in court.[29] His official letter of resignation was submitted on 19 July and highlighted three issues: the attempt to rein in regional leaders; the criminal cases opened against a number of businessmen; and the lack of attention devoted by Moscow to the problems in Karachaevo-Cherkessia. He called for an amnesty for all past economic crimes, and denounced the anti-corruption drive as 'an orchestrated campaign, directed at destroying major independent businesses'.[30] He noted that '[e]veryone who hasn't been asleep for the past 10 years has willingly or unwillingly broken the law'.[31] In November 2000 he went into 'exile' in London and focused on plotting Putin's overthrow.

Gusinsky joined Berezovsky in his condemnation of Putin's government. He asserted that the anti-oligarch campaign signalled the end of the democratic freedoms that Russia had enjoyed in the 1990s. As he put it: 'In Russia there used to be a police regime. It disappeared temporarily and now it is being rebuilt'.[32] Gazprom had provided considerable financial backing for NTV, and many considered that this was the real reason for the firm coming under investigation.[33] Indeed, it was documentation dealing with the company's links with Media-Most that were seized when its headquarters were raided on 11 May 2000. Similarly, Alekperov, head of Lukoil, was associated with a number of television stations and held a joint stake with Potanin in the liberal daily *Izvestiya*. At the same time, some of the other oligarchs, notably Abramovich, not only avoided scrutiny but, with his aluminium associate Oleg Deripaska, was able during Putin's rise to power to amass an empire that brought 70 per cent of Russia's aluminium industry under their control. In

---

[27] *The Guardian*, 18 July 2000, p. 12.   [28] *Financial Times*, 18 July 2000.

[29] Andrei Kamakin, 'Boris Berezovskii sdaet immunitet: I perekhodit v neprimirimuyu oppozitsiyu', *Segodnya*, 18 July 2000, p. 1.

[30] *The Guardian*, 18 July 2000, p. 12.

[31] Sarah Karush, 'Berezovsky Says He's Quitting the Duma', *Moscow Times*, 18 July 2000, p. 1.

[32] Amelia Gentleman, 'Putin Picks off Opponents who Matter Most', *The Guardian*, 14 July 2000, p. 20.

[33] For a good study of the background to these events, see Laura Belin, 'The Russian Media in the 1990s', in Rick Fawn and Stephen White (eds.), *Russia After Communism* (London, Frank Cass, 2002), pp. 139–60.

2000, Abramovich levered out the arch-manipulator Berezovsky from his share of Sibneft, allegedly threatening to destroy the company unless Berezovsky sold out at a discount.

The methods used against Gusinsky and Berezovsky were similar to those used at first against Yukos in 2003, including various public signals and the use of heavy-handed searches and attempts at resolving the issues through informal mechanisms. After having signed a document in July 2001 transferring his property to the state in exchange for an end to the case, Gusinsky later claimed that he had been blackmailed into signing by the press minister Mikhail Lesin and other officials. The mixture of political motives and straightforward commercial issues was also to be repeated later. However, in the end Gusinsky lost his economic assets but kept his freedom, although in exile, while Berezovsky fled once it became clear that Primakov's attempts to put him on trial would be continued by Putin. The close involvement of the state in all the attacks is another common feature, although sometimes disguised in the form of tax, criminal or debt cases accompanied by the exercise of crude coercive instruments. The differences between the cases are also significant, with NTV facing major solvency questions, whereas Yukos in economic terms in 2003 was enjoying a period of unprecedented growth.

Seventeen leading businessmen, including Vyakhirev and Alekperov, wrote a collective letter to the Prosecutor General protesting against the arrest of Gusinsky and warning that democracy was in danger. They noted that Gusinsky's arrest sent a negative signal to the business community in Russia and abroad. Putin was prepared to engage with these concerns, and a round table was arranged with some of the leading oligarchs. He also met in January 2001 with leading editors, and in the course of the five-hour meeting repeatedly stressed that he would not infringe freedom of speech, but that in his view (in the words of one of those present) 'Berezovsky and Gusinsky do not have even a tangential relationship with freedom of speech.... One should not, the president insisted, confuse freedom of speech with the use of the mass media for the pursuit of selfish mercenary purposes.'[34] The dilemma was neatly captured by Dmitry Furman:

In the abstract, Mr Putin's campaign against the illegal activities of various oligarchs and their apparently illegal influence is completely acceptable and essential for the democratic development of Russia.... But the struggle is taking place in the context of an undemocratic, authoritarian regime. The logic of this campaign seems to be an attempt to liquidise [*sic*] any political or economic power that asserts its independence from the Kremlin.[35]

Putin himself put a very different slant on events. In his interview with *Izvestiya* on 14 July 2000 he defended actions by the tax police and the federal Prosecutor General's office against companies like Media-Most, Avtovaz, Lukoil, and Potanin's Interros. He insisted that 'the state has the right to expect entrepreneurs to observe the rules of the game', and he insisted that the state 'would act more

[34] Valerii Fadeev, 'Gazety i den'gi', *Ekspert*, No. 3, 22 January 2001, in *Ekspert: Luchshie materialy*, No. 2, 2007, p. 24.

[35] Amelia Gentleman, 'Putin Picks off Opponents who Matter Most', *The Guardian*, 14 July 2000, p. 20.

vigorously toward the environment in which business operates. I am referring first and foremost to the tax sphere and the restoration of order in the economy.'[36] Putin insisted that all the oligarchs would be kept at equal arm's length from the government.

Business and state in the new dispensation

Not since the Bolshevik revolution of 1917 had Russia seen an autonomous bourgeoisie, and Soviet prejudices against their independent class power remained strong, as did the view that they had no right to have direct political access to government. Twenty-one top figures of Russia's business elite met with the president on 28 July 2000 to lay down the ground rules of relations between the government and business. This was not the first meeting between the business elite and the Kremlin, and under Yeltsin four had been held. We have mentioned the 15 September 1997 meeting, held in the wake of the Svyazinvest privatization scandal, when the top oligarchs had been invited to meet Yeltsin to lay down the rules of engagement.[37] Not much had come of the initiative, and the Kremlin now sought to ensure that the business leaders did not gain the impression that they were equal political interlocutors with the elected presidency.

The aim of the July 2000 meeting was to establish a level economic playing field in which the role of the state as referee would be enhanced and respected. The attendees were an eclectic group, but equally notable were the absentees.[38] The agenda was set by Nemtsov, the leader of the liberal Union of Right Forces (SPS) Duma faction. He insisted that '[t]he business and power should not attack or blackmail each other, they should be partners working towards the economic recovery of Russia'.[39] The business leaders presented a three-point declaration to the government: first, for the Kremlin to declare a moratorium on any investigations into the legitimacy of privatization over the past decade and not to initiate

---

[36] *Izvestiya*, 14 July 2000.   [37] Colton, *Yeltsin*, p. 405.

[38] Among those attending were Vagit Alekperov, head of Lukoil, at the time being investigated for alleged large-scale tax evasion; Vladimir Potanin, head of the Interros financial-industrial group, whom prosecutors accused of conspiring to defraud the state of $140 million in connection with the 1995 privatization of Norilsk Nickel; Rem Vyakhirev, head of Gazprom, Russia's natural gas monopoly, whose offices were raided in connection with the criminal case against Media-Most chief Vladimir Gusinsky; Al'fa Group co-founder Mikhail Fridman; Russian Aluminium co-founder Oleg Deripaska; Yevgeny Shvidler, the president of the Sibneft oil company; and United Energy Systems (UES) chief Anatoly Chubais, whose company, state auditors charged, may have been partially sold to foreigners in violation of Russian law. Leading absentees were Media-Most's Gusinsky; Berezovsky, the archetypal insider who at this time declared himself in 'constructive opposition' before later that year moving into 'unconstructive' opposition; Roman Abramovich, formally a State Duma deputy but the brains behind Sibneft and Oleg Deripaska's partner in Russian Aluminium; and Moscow banker Alexander Mamut, who was close to Abramovich and who remains a key Kremlin insider, Jamestown Foundation, *Monitor*, 27 July 2000. Although Berezovsky was not physically present, his interests were considered to be represented by Shvidler and Deripaska, representing companies partially owned by Berezovsky, Gregory Feifer, 'Oligarchs Hope for Agreement with Putin', *The St Petersburg Times*, 28 July 2000, p. 3.

[39] Arkady Ostrovsky, 'Oligarchs to Seek Peace Deal with Putin', *Financial Times*, 24 July 2000.

any redistribution of former state property; second, the business community must undertake to play by the rules, pay taxes, and scrupulously obey the law; third, the government must rid itself of corrupt bureaucrats, while business tycoons for their part must undertake not to use government institutions or bribe state officials to fight their competitors.[40] The link between power and property was hardly challenged by such an extra-constitutional 'pact', which in any case left out some of the key players.

The 'new deal' did not contract big business to keep out of politics, but warned them not to use political instruments in their own struggles or against the state. Many went on to pursue political careers, notably Abramovich as governor of Chukotka. In addition, Putin made clear that he would prefer a more institution-alized forum to manage relations with big business, and after the meeting most leading oligarchs joined the RUIE, which had hitherto been not much more than a club of 'red directors' and middle-ranking industrial managers. It was led by the veteran survivor of Soviet and Russian politics, Arkady Vol'sky, who had served as an aide to both Yuri Andropov and Mikhail Gorbachev in the 1980s. The RUIE now acted as the collective voice of big business, lobbying its interests while at the same time constraining its membership. Putin addressed the group on an annual basis.

As long as Putin's anti-oligarch campaign was conducted by the presidency there could be legitimate questions about its political selectivity. Instead of using the courts, he relied on strong-arm tactics led by the MVD, the FSB, and the Prosecutor General. Only when the anti-corruption campaign was conducted by a demonstrably free and independent judiciary would fears that it was designed to further political ends be allayed. There were signs of this in the enhanced role played by the Audit Chamber, an independent body authorized to monitor the use of federal budget funds and headed by the former prime minister and one time head of the FSB, Stepashin. In July 2000 the Audit Chamber began to investigate the 51 per cent state-owned UES, the electricity monopoly, and alleged that in the period when UES was partially privatized between 1992 and 1998 shares had been improperly sold to foreigners (who were allowed no more than a 25 per cent stake in the company) and that it was part of the general attempt to defend the interests of minority shareholders.[41]

An essential aspect of the new social contract was the emphasis on 'social responsibility' of big business. While Putin persecuted the oligarchs on a selec-tive and partial basis, with the others he struck a new bargain: invest your ill-gotten gains in the manufacturing ('real') part of the Russian economy or else face the consequences. A notable example of this business–state alliance was the involvement of Deripaska's Russian Aluminium company in the purchase and subsequent restructuring of the Gorky Automotive Works (GAZ) in Nizhny Novgorod. Putin thereby hoped to see filched assets return from offshore haunts

---

[40] The points were outlined by Nemtsov, in Arkady Ostrovsky, 'Oligarchs to Seek Peace Deal with Putin', *Financial Times*, 24 July 2000.

[41] 'Auditors Target UES Shares in Foreign Hands', *Moscow Times*, 14 July 2000.

and invested to revive the economy. Companies forged in the corrupt world of the epoch of 'piratization' were encouraged to become good capitalists based on transparent accounting standards and responsibility to shareholders (including minority ones) and legally accountable directors. However, the involvement of the state distorted the economic playing field, since as the Yukos affair developed the state sought to identify 'national champions' and to intervene actively in the management of economic life. While Putin's policy was logical from a short-term perspective, this model of economic development effectively represented meta-corruption, the state-sanctioned distortion of the economic sphere. Renewed state activism provoked much speculation that the Russian economy was moving towards the South Korean *chaebol* model or the Japanese *keiretsu* system. As the East Asian financial crises of 1997/8 demonstrated, however, 'croney capitalism', whether of the East Asian type or the Russian system of dirigiste capitalism, was prone to instability and crises.

The reaction of big business to the new conventions was far from complaisant. As Kononczuk notes, 'the oligarchs' political activity during 2000–2003 did not so much decrease as transform in nature'.[42] Big business shifted the focus of its lobbying activity from the presidential administration to parliament and regional governments. In the State Duma the 'Russian Energy' cross-party bloc, with several dozen deputies, represented the interests of the energy lobby. A group sponsored by Yukos but also including Lukoil, TNK, and Surgutneftegaz was coordinated by Vladimir Dubov, a Menatep shareholder who had been elected on what became the United Russia ticket. Dubov took over as head of the Duma's tax committee and actively worked to shape a fiscal regime favourable to the big oil companies (details of this in the next chapter).[43] In the regions the oil majors backed their candidates in gubernatorial elections and sought to shape elections to regional legislatures.

Between assaults

With the most egregiously political of the oligarchs out of the way, a period of quiet ensued in relations between the state and big business and the regime focused on other concerns, notably reforming the party system. It also enjoyed the dramatic rise in oil income, growing from $14 billion in 1999 to $140 billion in 2005/06, allowing it to pay off early the bulk of its debts to the London and Paris Clubs and, later, to squirrel revenue away into a Stabilization Fund, created on 1 January 2004. However, habits of the 1990s had certainly not disappeared. The sale of Slavneft in late 2002 was accompanied by traditional claims of insider dealing and favouritism. The old director, Mikhail Gutseriev, had been ousted in May 2002 in a boardroom coup instigated by the prime minister, Kasyanov, and

---

[42] Kononczuk, *The 'Yukos Affair'*, p. 38.

[43] There was a division of labour in the group, with each company responsible for 'its' party: Lukoil worked with the Party of Russian Regions; TNK with the Union of Right Forces; and Yukos with Yabloko, Kononczuk, *The 'Yukos Affair'*, p. 56, n. 32.

replaced by a former Sibneft official Yuri Sukhanov. Sibneft then proceeded to buy up shares in alliance with TNK. The ugly scenes in May 2002, when the Slavneft offices in the centre of Moscow were seized by private security guards in an attempt to restore Gutseriev to power, were reminiscent of Yeltsin's 'wild East' days of the 1990s, especially when Kasyanov sent in the police to evict the intruders. In October Kasyanov hastily pushed through the privatization of Slavneft, with all 75 per cent of the state's stake sold as a single block with a reserve price of $1.3 billion (later raised to $1.7 billion). In the days preceding the auction (set for 19 December) the competitors, Lukoil and Surgutneftegaz, were encouraged to withdraw their bids while the Chinese National Petroleum Company (CNPC) was barred on a technicality. Sibneft and TNK went on to win the auction as the sole joint bidders for $1.86 billion.[44] The case recalled the insider dealings of the Yeltsin years, above all the loans-for-shares scandals.

Barnes argues that contrary to the view that after the earlier privatizations the new private owners would favour the rule of law to allow them to invest in production, in fact 'leading economic actors there are still engaged in a complex struggle for property that transcends simple processes of privatization or consolidation and shows no sign of abating'.[45] Although investment rates rose after 2000, they remained very low, and Russia's main business lobby, the RUIE, remodelled after 2000 at Putin's instigation, was certainly far from constituted as an independent collective voice able to ensure the impartial exercise of the rule of law. Instead of creating a new body, business magnates entered the RUIE en masse in autumn 2000, and eclipsed the old guard of Soviet industrial directors, much to Volsky's displeasure.[46] The RUIE now became known as 'the oligarchs' trade union'.[47] Writing on the eve of the Yukos affair, Barnes notes that 'economic groups in Russia are still strong enough to manipulate governmental decisions to their advantage, use selective legal enforcement in pursuit of assets, or simply ignore laws when it suits them'.[48] Big business had modified its approach, but it was still not clear what would be the limits of acceptable behaviour. The Yukos affair would provide the answer.

The 1998 crash had reduced the role of banking conglomerates, as with Menatep St Petersburg, which no longer owned major industrial assets, but now companies struggled between themselves to take over assets, using a range of dubious methods, including forced bankruptcies and the like. In Chapter 2 we noted Yukos's aggressive acquisition strategy in the early 2000s, which confirms Barnes's argument about the way that these companies were no longer tied to banks but sought to become ever deeper and wider, although few at the time were successful in becoming both. The struggle for property continued, and no post-transition period of consolidation had arrived. Tensions between statist and market-driven

---

[44] *Moscow Times*, 6 March 2003, p. 5.

[45] Andrew Barnes, 'Russia's New Business Groups and State Power', *Post-Soviet Affairs*, Vol. 19, No. 2, 2003, p. 155.

[46] Konstantin Smirnov, 'Vol'skomu volya', *Kommersant-Vlast'*, 3 October 2005, pp. 38–42, at p. 42.

[47] Kryshtanovkaya, *Anatomiya rossiiskoi elity*, p. 361.

[48] Barnes, 'Russia's New Business Groups and State Power', pp. 155–6.

energy policy came to a head in 2003, as did the contradiction between companies going international or transnational. The prime example of the latter was the $6.7 billion deal completed in August 2003 when BP joined forces with Renova Group, Al'fa Group, Access Industries, and Interros to create BP-TNK, with shares split equally between the British company and its Russian partners. When in the same year Khodorkovsky sought to protect his assets by transnationalizing the company by selling a large stake of Yukos to a foreign company, the government stepped in.

The Yukos affair signalled that the state had now become an active player, and the drive to reduce the proportion of economic assets owned by the state was reversed. In his annual address to the Federal Assembly on 16 May 2003 Putin advanced the ambitious plan to double Russian GDP in the space of a decade. This would require annual growth in excess of 7 per cent, and although widely ridiculed at the time as a throwback to the exhortatory style of Soviet central planning, the target was basically met by the end of the decade. The goal was accomplished by the development of para-statal economic corporations to provide a developmental impetus in selected areas. More immediately, the speech warned that 'monopolists are suffocating the competitive part of our economy'. It signalled a new activism by the state in economic life, to which the Yukos company fell victim.

FROM EQUIDISTANCE TO SUBORDINATION

The defeat of Berezovsky and Gusinsky in 2001 left no substantial opposition in society. From the summer of 2003, however, a new type of opposition emerged from within the system itself, intending to modify the administration's policies. The intra-systemic opposition sought to achieve a redistribution of property, a change of elites at the national and regional level, and the development of a new state ideology that would allow the 'new oligarchy' to consolidate power. A new breed of Kremlin 'oligarchs' had already subordinated the representatives of the state and quasi-state corporations, and now they sought to discipline the independent oligarchs at the head of Russia's big business. Pavlovsky stressed that if these new oligarchs won, then Putin's position would be immeasurably weakened and he would become their hostage. He looked to support from medium business, alarmed by the beginning of the Yukos case, but in this he was disappointed.[49] Although the new intra-systemic opposition, the group that I shall call the 'politburo' (see below), had no independent legitimacy and relied on Putin, it was able to push through its agenda. In part this was possible because of the weakening of the outer bulwarks of the new property order, 'the liberal parties, the liberal press and the liberal bureaucracy'.[50] Ultimately the development of the

[49] Gleb Pavlovsky, 'Brat—3', *Ekspert*, No. 32, 1 September 2003, in *Ekspert: Luchshie materialy*, No. 2, 2007, pp. 63–7, at p. 63.

[50] Pavlovsky, 'Brat—3', p. 66.

case depended on Putin's personal preferences, and his decision to subordinate the business community in the run-up to the December 2003 election.

'The State and the Oligarchs'

The opposition to Putin's path came not from the right (the liberals) but from the securitized left. The 'left revanche' against the privatization of the 1990s was sustained by the incomplete revolution in Russia's transition from the Soviet system to the new order. The semi-Soviet Russian ruling elite had developed considerably since 1991, and were well aware of the global context in which they operated, yet when faced by threats they reverted to the stock administrative responses of their predecessors. In part this was because the Russian system had developed as a peculiar amalgam of a modern constitutional state (the 'stationary bandit' described by Mancur Olson), and a semi-autonomous administrative regime (the 'roving bandits').[51] The Yukos case exposed the fault lines in this construction, as well as the multiple identities of the regime itself. The Yukos affair was not a Stalinist-type operation planned in advance and implemented methodically, but was provoked by a set of actions and reactions without a single common cause. Different factions within the regime had different agendas, but gradually an 'affair' (*delo*) took shape embedded within a narrative that also evolved as the case advanced.

One of the key bodies shaping this evolving narrative was the Council of National Strategy (Sovet po natsional'noi strategii, SNS), founded in 2002 by Stanislav Belkovsky (the adopted son of a KGB colonel-general) and Iosif Diskin.[52] First available from 26 May but formally published on 4 June 2003, the SNS issued a report called 'The State and the Oligarchs', which signalled the beginning of the political assault on Yukos.[53] The SNS had already issued two reports which had raised similar concerns. The first was discussed by the SNS board on 4 October 2002 and was called 'The Great Game in Russia'.[54] The report examined the key groups in Russian politics and how they affected the decision-making process. It argued that since 1995 Russia had been pursuing the path of 'oligarchical modernization', and as the economic power of the oligarchs increased, so too did their political influence:

[51] Mancur Olson, *Power and Prosperity: Outgrowing Communist and Capitalist Dictatorships* (Oxford, Oxford University Press, 2000). The Yukos affair suggests that the shift from roving to stationary bandits, which for Olson signalled the beginning of civilization, good government, and ultimately democracy, is incomplete in Russia.

[52] The SNS included twenty-three experts across the political spectrum, a number of whom disagreed with the findings of the report and resigned (see below), Vladimir Pribylovsky, 'What's The Scandal About?', *Moscow Times*, 11 June 2003, p. 8.

[53] The full version of 'Gosudarstvo i oligarkhiya' is available (accessed 7 November 2007) at http://www.strategeia.ru/news_453.html. An abbreviated version was republished as 'Gosudarstvo i oligarkhiya', *Zavtra*, 27 June 2003, p. 3.

[54] 'Bol'shaya igra v Rossii', http://www.strategeia.ru/news_451.html.

As a result the 'oligarchs' are turning into a 'super-elite', concentrating political and economic influence, limited today by only one barrier—the prohibition on direct conflict with the president as a person. In this sense the federal government is not an independent subject. It de facto fulfils the function of executive committee for oligarch affairs (an instrument to balance oligarchic interests).

On 1 January 2003 a further report was issued, 'Risks and Threats Facing Russia in 2003', that continued the theme, warning that Russia was losing influence in the world and that business groupings were eclipsing the autonomy of political actors.[55] The ruling layer, consisting in the report's view of 'oligarchs' and their political structures, were willing to trade Russia's influence as a regional power and as a partial continuer of Soviet global status in return for the legitimation of the capital that they gained in the 1990s. Only the United States, as the world's remaining superpower, could provide this external legitimation, while at home Putin's 'stable and popular regime' guaranteed the existing economic order.

A few months later, however, the Council argued in 'The State and the Oligarchs' that the oligarchs had moved on to the offensive, looking to usurp the domestic regime while consolidating their external legitimacy. The importance of this report for the later development of the case can hardly be overstated, and signalled that the Yukos affair was framed as a way of resisting the encroachments of big business on the prerogatives of the state. Having completed the privatization of the economy, the report argued, the oligarchs were now privatizing politics. The report warned of the dangers of 'a creeping oligarchical coup' whereby the country's system of governance would be changed to ensure 'the union of super-big business and executive power'. Khodorkovsky was named ten times in the report and Yukos twenty-five times, with Roman Abramovich coming in second with nine and twenty-two mentions for Sibneft. In the end, however, only the former was singled out for attack.

The oligarch system, the report argued, had been created outside market mechanisms, where wealth had effectively been handed over by the presidency, and Yukos was given as the example:

The controlling packet of shares in NK Yukos (78%) was bought in a loans-for-shares auction by the Menatep group, controlled by M. Khodorkovsky and his partners, in 1995 for $350mn. Already by 1997, soon after Yukos shares became publicly available, the corporation's market capitalisation reached $9bn. Recently (before the announcement of the merger with Sibneft) Yukos's capitalisation approached $15bn.

By noting the massive increase in the company's value already by 1997, the authors were stressing that this had come before the new Yukos management had been able to do much in the way of adding value to the company. The presidency was the major obstacle to oligarch plans; hence, they favoured a shift to a more parliamentary system, with Khodorkovsky named as the main proponent of rebalancing

---

[55] 'Riski i ugrozy dlya Rossii v 2003 godu', http://www.strategeia.ru/news_452.html.

the constitution and probably the main beneficiary if he were to become prime minister:

According to the plans of a key member of the ruling class, as early as 2004 a new government may be formed under the control of and accountable to parliament. The front-runner to be prime minister of such a government, formed under a new constitution, is considered to be Mikhail Khodorkovsky.

The report stressed the 'anti-national' character of the oligarch system. Its property tended to be registered abroad, often in offshore companies. This was not just for tax-minimization and cash flow purposes, but because 'in the collective understanding of the oligarchs foreign property in Russia is defended substantially more than domestic'. Thus the oligarchs were 'drawing on the resources of foreign states to guarantee their interests in Russia's political-economic space'. They also noted that most oligarchs kept their families abroad (although this did not, significantly, apply to Khodorkovsky). The document identified what it called 'oligarchic autism', the inability to recognize that the interests of the mass of the people should be taken into account in governmental policy, or indeed that anything that took place outside the oligarch's narrow world had any strategic or even tactical significance. In sum, in the report's view, the 'capitulationist state, wreathed in liberal rhetoric, today does not even fulfil the role of "nightwatchman", but opens the path for strengthening the power and influence of the oligarchs'. The idea of 'equal distance', the report insisted, acted as little more than a cover for the consolidation of oligarch power.

Although Putin may have reversed the process of state capture by leading oligarchs in 2000, the report warned that they were now attempting to subvert the state by stealthier means—an 'oligarch's coup'. Economic magnates had privatized the economy, and they sought to privatize the political system by winning a Duma majority sympathetic to the economic class. If they pushed through constitutional changes making the government responsible to the parliamentary majority, then in the authors' view, the seizure of power would be complete. The president would have a far more limited role. To achieve their goals parties would have to be brought under oligarch control, and to this end Yukos stepped up its political contributions. The report identified Khodorkovsky as the chief ideologue of the strategy, supported by some other oligarchs including Abramovich, Oleg Deripaska (head of the Base Element holding group), and Mikhail Fridman (chair of Al'fa Group and of the board of TNK-BP). By 2004 a new government under the control of parliament could be created, with Khodorkovsky the leading contender for the post of premier.

The report was presented to Putin by Igor Sechin, deputy head of the presidential administration and a key representative of the *siloviki*, and Viktor Ivanov, also a key member of the presidential staff, although it is not clear whether they played any part in its preparation. The report can be considered the political manifesto of the *siloviki*, the security officials who made up an important constituency in Putin's power base. A small group of them came together to form what I shall call the 'politburo', since in their behaviour and views they hark back to the Soviet era. The 'politburo' faction was the driving force behind the Yukos affair, pushing Putin further than his own inclinations may have taken him.[56] Andrew Wilson speaks of the Yukos affair as an act of grand dramaturgy designed to reshape the orientations of the political system,[57] but this view is mistaken. Putin's administration did not enter into this unholy struggle with clear intentions, let alone a grand design, but stumbled from event to event, torn by the factional fights that were characteristic of his presidency. More than that, issues of fundamental political and economic consequence were being resolved, and thus there was nothing 'virtual' about the enormous stakes in play or the methods employed.

The revenge of the state

The 1998 financial crisis signalled the end of a distinctive period. Rutland argues that 'the demise of oligarchic capitalism was due to deep contradictions in the model, and not merely to contingent factors such as Yeltsin's incompetence or the August 1998 crash'. He singles out two main contradictions: 'First, the oligarchs were parasitic on the Russian state.' They not only drained the exchequer of financial resources but they also undermined the working of state institutions. 'Second, the oligarchs were deeply divided among themselves.'[58] We have noted the intense conflict over the Svyazinvest privatization in 1997, and even the instinct of self-preservation could not prevent the feuding continuing, despite Yeltsin's attempts to arbitrate some sort of truce. The competitive nature of oligarch power almost by definition precluded collective action, even in self-defence. By the early 2000s a third contradiction was becoming increasingly evident, the challenge to the autonomy of state power itself. The Putinite 'social contract' of 2000 to 2003 was inherently unstable, if only because none of the fundamental issues had been resolved. Not only was the balance of power between the oligarchs and the bureaucracy in contention, but the struggle for the moral high ground remained in play. Khodorkovsky may have tried to win plaudits by adopting Western accounting standards and the like, but the manifestly instrumental way in which he did this, accompanied by a campaign of self-promotion, could not but antagonize the authorities as well as other business-people.

[56] There is much circumstantial and some direct evidence that Putin was not the initiator of the assault against Yukos, but was convinced by others that it was necessary. Eberhard Schneider, for example, drawing on sources in the Kremlin close to Voloshin and Kasyanov, is unequivocal about Putin's initial secondary role, Eberhard Schneider, 'The Russian Federal Security Service under President Putin', in Stephen White (ed.), *Politics and the Ruling Group in Putin's Russia* (London, Palgrave Macmillan, 2008), pp. 49–52.

[57] 'The anti-oligarch "dramaturgiya" proved to be the perfect virtual object, an enormously powerful lodestone realigning all parts of the political system.' According to Wilson, Putin used Khodorkovsky's arrest to stamp his authority on the elite, Wilson, *Virtual Politics*.

[58] Peter Rutland, 'Business and Civil Society in Russia', in Alfred B. Evans Jr., Laura A. Henry, and Lisa McIntosh Sundstrom (eds.), *Russian Civil Society: A Critical Assessment* (Armonk, NY, M. E. Sharpe, 2005), p. 78.

The assault against the oligarchs as a class was renewed in the run-up to the December 2003 parliamentary elections and the March 2004 presidential campaign. The Duma campaign was characterized by an anti-business edge, with almost all political parties stressing populist oligarch-bashing. Sergei Glaz'ev, one of the leaders of the Kremlin-sponsored Rodina party, a left-populist project party designed to draw votes away from the Communists, called for the introduction of a 'resource tax', a punitive and retrospective levy on big business intended to recuperate some of the losses endured by the state in the loans-for-shares auctions and other privatizations. Already from March 2003 the mass electronic media were dominated by the question of how to make the oligarchs pay for the sins of the 1990s.[59]

It was the assault against Yukos that signalled the Kremlin's determination to restore its authority in the country, but it was part of a broader assault. On 19 June 2003 one of Yukos's senior security officials, Alexei Pichugin, was arrested and later charged with organizing up to five contract killings, and on 26 June the General Prosecutor's Office (GPO) conducted a search of Yukos's Moscow headquarters. On 2 July the head of the Menatep international finance group (Yukos's main shareholder), Platon Lebedev, was arrested in connection with $280 million worth of share acquisitions in 1994, in the country's largest phosphate company, Apatit, as well as with tax evasion by Menatep subsidiaries in the Tomsk region. The fundamental charge against him was of large-scale fraud. Nevzlin and Khodorkovsky were questioned as witnesses in the Lebedev case. Months of pressure culminated in Khodorkovsky's arrest on 25 October. We shall return to these events later. At the same time various threats were made against other oligarchs. A long-running case against Oleg Deripaska at the head of Russian Aluminium (Rusal) was resurrected, while the Kremlin made clear to Abramovich, at the head of Sibneft, that his extravagant purchase of the Chelsea Football Club in London was frowned upon. The planned merger between Yukos and Sibneft to create one of the world's largest oil companies was suspended. Even the ultra-Kremlin loyalist Potanin, at the head of Interros (the owner of Norilsk Nickel) was not immune to pressure when it became clear that he was looking for ways to transfer some of his assets abroad.

The 'social contract' between business and the Kremlin was being redrafted. It was no longer enough for big business to stay out of politics: in the circumstances of a revived state the economic sphere was to be reshaped by the authorities, and the oligarchs were to understand that their historic role as independent creators of capitalism was over. A new model of political economy was to emerge in which the very notion of 'oligarch' was to become anachronistic. Putin's attempts to restructure Russian political economy signalled a sea change in the legal environment. Oligarchs like Berezovsky had long warned of the danger from the left, epitomized above all by the return to power of the Communists, but Khodorkovsky now found himself outflanked on the right, by the presidency in alliance with the security establishment. However, pervading the apparent anti-oligarch campaign there

---

[59] Kryshtanovkaya, *Anatomiya rossiiskoi elity*, p. 363.

hung the suspicion that one set of tycoons was using the law and the presidency against another set, and thus to corner the market. In particular, Abramovich, who in early 2000 had participated in the creation of a holding that controlled most of Russia's aluminium production, was known to covet Norilsk Nickel. Abramovich had made his fortune when he had teamed up with Berezovsky in 1995 to acquire Sibneft in one of the most notorious shares-for-loans deals, and in 2000 Berezovsky sold his stake to Abramovich before fleeing to London. Other oligarchs, notably Fridman at the head of TNK and Deripaska at the head of a rambling metals conglomerate, Basic Element, turned over a new leaf and gradually brought their companies up to international levels of corporate governance. They willingly accepted the new rules of the game and thus went on to become key figures in the new era. Although Khodorkovsky had improved the management of Yukos, he was not someone who would share the benefits of the new order.

An interaction model

At the heart of Putin's thinking was a narrative about the 1990s, which we earlier characterized as reactionary-remedial. Russian discourse is reminiscent of British post-1945 evaluations of the 'hungry 1930s', accompanied by the cry of 'never again', which formed the basis for the creation of the welfare state. For many, however, the 1930s were a golden age, witnessing for example the extensive development of light industries in West London. Similarly, while the 1990s in Russia saw massive inequality develop and a class of business magnates emerge, it was also the decade when capitalism in the main was built. Putin returned frequently to the idea that in the 1990s business had accrued powers that were not legitimate, and had thus encroached upon the prerogatives of the state. This is certainly part of the picture, but does not by any means cover the complexity of the relationship. A survey conducted by Timothy Frye of 500 company managers in late 2000 suggested a system of mutual 'exchange' between businesses and the state.[60] This would suggest that the 'state capture' model is at best a simplification, a view confirmed by the increased numbers of actions taken against companies by state administrative agencies from the late 1990s in arbitration courts. The 'state', of course, is an abstraction, and there is no doubt that certain business leaders were able to exert a direct influence on certain policies in certain institutions. Although Berezovsky's influence on the Kremlin leadership was not as great as he liked to think, the ability of big business, and Yukos in particular, to shape and block legislation is a classic case of overweening business power.

The 'exchange' model is a fruitful one at the level of the individual company, but at the macro level can be complemented by an 'interaction' model of business and state. As the state began to reassert its presumed prerogatives in the late 1990s, notably during Primakov's premiership and even more under Putin, the business

---

[60] Timothy Frye, 'Capture or Exchange? Business Lobbying in Russia', *Europe–Asia Studies*, Vol. 54, No. 7, November 2002, pp. 1017–36.

community responded by adopting a number of defensive strategies. One of these was consolidation, creating larger conglomerations that could by their sheer size deter encroachments by the state. The property rights of businesses could be buttressed by seeking foreign partners and selling packets of shares to external stakeholders (the transationalization strategy). However, even this could be at best a temporary balance, given the persistent distrust between the state and business. Certain issues remained unresolved, above all the distribution of the mineral rents and production sharing agreements (PSAs). The showdown came over legislation governing taxation of natural resources. On this issue, Yukos was prepared openly to challenge government plans to increase taxation and to review agreements. As we shall see, this involved trying to win a group of supportive deputies from across the political spectrum in the December 2003 parliamentary elections, blocking of legislation on PSAs, and merging with another company (Sibneft) and selling shares to a foreign company. In response the government launched a selective attack against Yukos which did not, however, signal that at last the economy would be differentiated from politics.

MODELS OF THE YUKOS AFFAIR

Putin did not at first set out to subordinate the business elite, since his concern in the early period was to create an attractive environment for Western investment and to reverse capital flight.[61] However, the pressure to return to the question by 2003 had become overwhelming, entailing a revision of the fundamental relationship between the state and big business. The methods Putin used to pursue this undermined his aims. Attacks against certain oligarchs were not able to eliminate the regime's dependence on business interests or the close relationship between some of them and Kremlin insiders. The main charge against Putin was the selective nature of the campaign, provoking the suspicion that it was directed not so much against corruption as against his critics and opponents, and above all those who threatened his political pre-eminence. Equally, some of his favoured companies, notably Rosneft, Gazprom, and Gunvor (see below) profited incommensurately.

While the attack was undoubtedly selective, it was far from arbitrary. Putin targeted those who had flaunted their closeness to power in the most provocative manner, or had allegedly abused their dominance of the media. Putin was setting the rules of the political game, and in attacking a few oligarchs he was disciplining the rest. There was an implicit threat: toe the line if you wish to keep the assets 'gained' in the 1990s.[62] By 2003 this was no longer enough, and commentators

---

[61] Zudin argues that from the first Putin set out to subordinate the oligarchs to the state, but this is probably an exaggeration. Aleksei Zudin, 'Neokorporativizism v Rossii', *Pro et Contra*, Vol. 6, No. 4, 2001, pp. 171–98.

[62] For an analysis of this, see A. A. Mukhin, *Novye pravila igry dlya bol'shogo biznesa, prodiktovannye logikoi pravleniya V. V. Putina* (Moscow, Tsentr politicheskoi informatsii, 2002).

such as Lilia Shevtsova saw the renewed assault against the oligarchs as part of the revenge of the bureaucracy and so-called power structures to establish a corporatist system. As far as she was concerned 'the oligarchy is a myth. Bureaucracy continues to be the dominant force within the Russian system of governance, as it has been through the ages.'[63] Volkov sees the Yukos case 'as the strengthened state terminating the implicit and informal contract it had with the oligarchs, and proceeding to create an alternative system or relations with business in which formal rules will have more weight'.[64] We will now return to our three main models of the Yukos affair—the ideological (statist), the political, and the factional.

The ideology of statism

It is easy to reduce the Yukos affair to little more than a conflict over power and property, and these issues were far from negligible. However, there was also an important ideological current at work, which while not consolidated and torn by contradictions, nevertheless helped frame the terms of debate. The assertion of state control over natural resources is well developed in international practice. Already in 1917 the Mexican constitution entrenched the principle of state ownership of energy resources, and it was on this basis that President Lázaro Cárdenas nationalized the petroleum industry on 18 March 1938, to wild popular acclaim. United on little else, Shiite and Sunni scholars agree that minerals belong to the 'community', and the attempt to privatize the Iraqi oil industry in the wake of the 2003 Anglo-American invasion provoked an upsurge of attacks on the energy infrastructure. Article 109 of the Iraqi constitution adopted by referendum in October 2005 is unequivocal that hydrocarbons are 'national Iraqi property' and would thus remain in the public sector.[65] Equally, in Kazakhstan concern over delays, environmental issues, and escalating costs in developing the huge Kashagan offshore Caspian oil field, with reserves of at least 35 billion barrels, led to attempts to re-negotiate the terms of the deal with lead investor, the Italian company ENI.[66] Resource nationalism under Putin, therefore, fits firmly into a larger international pattern; and at the same time can be seen in Polanyian terms as the elastic band, stretched too far in one direction, rebounding.

Already in an interview in January 1997 Surkov, at the time a member of Menatep Bank's board of directors, enunciated a thoroughly statist perspective. Asked about the chances of economic growth, he insisted that 'if genuine state management of the economy does not appear, there will be no economic

---

[63] Lilia Shevtsova, 'Whither Putin After the Yukos Affair?', *The Moscow Times*, 27 August 2003, p. 7.

[64] Vadim Volkov, 'The Yukos Affair: Terminating the Implicit Contract', *PONARS Policy Memo*, No. 307, November 2003, p. 2.

[65] Dilip Hiro, *Blood of the Earth: The Global Battle for Vanishing Oil Resources* (London, Politico's, 2008), pp. 144–8, 345.

[66] Birgit Bauers, 'Kazakhstan's Economic Challenges: How to Manage the Oil Boom?', *Transition Studies Review*, Vol. 14, No. 1, 2007, pp. 188–94.

growth'.[67] He noted that Menatep was an investment bank, and argued that its strategy was less to do with financial speculation than with providing productive investment capital, above all in the oil, chemical, and light industries: 'We are a bank that is tied to production, with the growth of the economy, the state, and in that sense, we are a "state" bank.'[68] He insisted that, as in war, national priorities should be established, and then it was a matter of will to see them implemented.[69] Later Menatep was to join the speculative frenzy in high-yielding government bonds (GKOs) that culminated in the financial crash of August 1998, but the spirit of Surkov's thinking was unmistakable. It would lead him to become one of the most eloquent defenders of Putin's consolidation of the state and the leading advocate of 'sovereign democracy'.

As for Putin's own views, they were given considered expression in his doctoral (*kandidat*) dissertation, *Strategic Planning for the Renewal of the Minerals and Raw Materials Base in the Leningrad Region in the Context of the Transition to a Market Economy*, awarded by the St Petersburg Mining Institute in June 1997. Putin's dissertation drew on an earlier work by King and Cleland, whose main argument was that 'true strategic planning has to take into account unforeseen changes',[70] so it was far from being a simple paean to statism. The inspiration for Putin's thesis work came from the Rector of the Institute, Vladimir Litvinenko, in office since 1994 and who had long argued for greater state control over Russia's natural resources so that the country could control its own fate and exert its full weight in world affairs. As he put it later: 'There was a time when the most important resource was salt. Then it was metal of any kind, then later it became gold. . . . In the specific circumstances the world finds itself in today, the most important resources are hydrocarbons . . . They're the main instrument in our hands—particularly in Putin's—and our strongest argument in geopolitics.'[71] A year after Putin completed his thesis, Sechin was also awarded his doctorate (*kandidat*) from the same institute.

In 1998 Putin wrote an article, published the following year, summarizing and extending his views on Russia's economic development. He argued that Russia would have to grow at twice the rate of the West to reduce 'Russia's lag behind the developed countries in terms of GDP per capita'. The basis for such growth would be the 'extraction, processing and exploitation of mineral raw material resources' above all oil and gas, of which Russia had abundant reserves. To achieve this Russia would have to create vertically integrated financial-industrial corporations 'capable of competing on equal terms with western multinational corporations'. The Soviet legacy meant that it was unlikely that Russia would be able to create

---

[67] 'Gosudarstvo, kapital, volya', in Vladislav Surkov, *Teksty 97–07* (Moscow, Evropa, 2008), pp. 185–90, at p. 185

[68] Ibid., p. 186.   [69] Ibid., p. 190.

[70] William King and David Cleland, *Strategic Planning and Policy* (New York, Nostrand Reinhold, 1978); summary by Clifford G. Gaddy and Andrew C. Kuchins, 'Putin's Plan', *The Washington Quarterly*, Vol. 31, No. 2, Spring 2008, p. 119.

[71] Stephen Boykewich, 'The Man With the Plan for Russia Inc.', *Moscow Times*, 6 June 2006, p. 1; Thierry Wolton, *Le KGB au pouvoir: Le système poutine* (Paris, Buchet-Chastel, 2008), p. 194.

competitive companies without state support. The state would also be required to defend the 'interests of society as a whole' and to act as the arbiter between competing economic interests and to obstruct the 'monopolistic behaviour' that would otherwise predominate and which 'inhibits innovation'. Left to themselves, according to Putin, private businesses would not innovate.[72] This view provides some theoretical basis for the later assault against Yukos.[73] Market mechanisms would be used, but they would be constrained by strategic guidance by the state. As Putin put it: 'The state must regulate the extractive complex using purely market methods, and in this regard the state must assist the development of processing industries based on the extractive complex.'[74]

While state dominance of the energy sector may have some rationale, especially in circumstances of high demand and the commensurate high prices, this model was hardly likely to be effective in the manufacturing and service sectors. The article reflected a distrust of private enterprise, but at the same time Putin was unequivocal about the need for free market capitalism to develop in Russia. As in the political sphere, this was a model for modernization from above. Putin's character was as full of contradictions as his policies, and hence the various factions reflected a facet of his political personality. Ultimately there was a common thread to his actions—the attempt to modernize Russia, but to do that in a Russian way. The priority was sovereignty, security, and development. His programme can be seen as one of national democracy, where the democratic imperative is tempered by the government's perception of national developmental and security concerns. Putin's ideology combined liberal principles in the economy, statism in domestic policy, and great power nationalism (*derzhavnost'*) in foreign policy.

The views of the 'democratic statist' group of the Surkov type overlapped in part with those of the politburo, but were certainly not the same, and their personal relations were not always warm. The democratic statists criticized the liberal reliance on the unfettered role of market forces, but favoured the development of a constrained form of market capitalism. Their views reflected classic *dirigiste* positions when it came to economic development, which were implemented in the early years of the French Fifth Republic, and complemented Putin's own emergence as a Gaullist figure: aligned with the West but seeking national autonomy in policy-making and an independent voice in international affairs. The new *dirigisme* lacked central planning, and thus what was lost in coherence was gained in consensus, allowing even liberals in government (such as finance minister Alexei Kudrin) to share the approach. The leverage gained by restoring elements of state control to the energy sector, the country's single most important industry, was intended to achieve sustainable growth from a

[72] Harley Balzer, 'Vladimir Putin's Academic Writings and Russian Natural Resource Policy', *Problems of Post-Communism*, Vol. 53, No. 1, January–February 2006, pp. 48–54, with Putin's article 'Mineral Natural Resources in the Strategy for Development of the Russian Economy', at pp. 49–54.

[73] Harley Balzer, 'The Putin Thesis and Russian Energy Policy', *Post-Soviet Affairs*, Vol. 21, No. 3, 2005, pp. 210–25.

[74] Putin, 'Mineral Natural Resources in the Strategy for Development of the Russian Economy', p. 50.

more competitive industrial base. This in part helps explain the muted response of liberals to the Yukos affair, quite apart from intimidation by representatives of the politburo. As for the liberal parties, they failed to enunciate a clear strategy of national development, and when it came to the Yukos case were concerned not to be seen to identify too closely with the fallen oligarch. They were unable to mount a critique of the dangers of bureaucratic capitalism and the cronyism with which it is usually accompanied.

The political theory

We saw above how in his early years in office Putin had tamed the most aggressively political of the oligarchs, but on a number of counts the new policy of equidistance was unstable. The precarious balance in relations between big business and the government was untenable. In a perceptive analysis William Tompson, senior analyst at the OECD, examines the relationship between Putin and the 'oligarchs' through the prism of a 'two-sided commitment problem'. He argues that for a number of structural reasons no stable accommodation between Putin and the oligarchs was possible: both sides had incentives to defect from any arrangement at the earliest opportunity. Even if they had wanted to stick to the terms of a deal, they would not have been able to; and even if a bargain was struck in good faith, neither side could convince the other of the firmness of its resolve. Underlying the whole problem is the lack of institutions strong enough to ensure that the state obeys its own rules. Within this framework Tompson examines the whole trajectory of the relationship between the government and big business in the Putin years, culminating in the Yukos affair. The case for Tompson acts as a torch, throwing light on a whole range of problems in Russian polity, above all the weakness of the rule of law.[75] The state was unable 'to make a credible commitment to respect property rights and limit itself to rule-governed behavior'; and at the same time the business community was unable 'to act collectively to restrain state power'.[76] As Tompson notes: 'Many of the charges involved were probably true, but there was no doubt that Yukos was the victim of politically motivated and highly selective law enforcement.'[77]

The push to reassert state direction in the economy was in historical terms understandable. However, there was, as a recent study argues, a 'civilized' way of doing so and an 'uncivilized' one. In the general economy civilized methods predominated, but in the energy sector rather more robust methods gained prominence, reflecting the emergence of the dual state. The civilized approach focuses on the consolidation of state shares in one holding company and then extending the state's stake by market methods, with legal restrictions if necessary

[75] William Tompson, 'Putin and the "Oligarchs": A Two-sided Commitment Problem', in Alex Pravda (ed.), *Leading Russia: Putin in Perspective* (Oxford, Oxford University Press, 2005), pp. 179–202.

[76] Tompson, 'Putting Yukos in Perspective', p. 178.

[77] Tompson, 'Putin and the "Oligarchs"', p. 192.

on the role of outside (including foreign) shareholders. The Yukos case was an exemplary case of the other approach:

The uncivilized method of increasing state control over strategically important enterprises is based on manipulated allegations of legal wrongdoings (especially concerning tax, safety and environmental regulations), which lead to pressure in the form of bad publicity, office searches and the confiscation of company documents, frozen bank accounts, hefty fines and the arrest of senior managers.[78]

The Putin style of governance was a mix of formal and informal practices, and thus the mix of 'civilized' and 'uncivilized' methods was characteristic of his regime. If the first aspect of the informal social contract after 2000 was remedial, to remove undue influence by a small number of 'court' oligarchs', the second aspect was more broad-ranging and constraining, and became part of the system of governance. Ledeneva puts it well: 'Reserving informal leverage against oligarchs in order to make them stay in line is an effective tool and an essential feature of political power in Russia.'[79] She suggests that informal arrangements were the preferred tool of the authorities so that they were not in turn constrained by more transparent arrangements, and that clear rules would 'liberate' the oligarchs, and deprive the state of informal means of control. This implies that more transparent and formal arrangements were an option, and this is far from clear. As for the Yukos case, Ledeneva notes:

A variety of interpretations exist, including blaming the authorities for the selective use of law and those blaming Khodorkovskii for his arrogance, notoriety, and political ambitions. What most of these interpretations have in common, however, is that Khodorkovskii violated the unwritten rules announced in June 2000 [*sic*] at the meeting between Putin and the oligarchs, who were told to stay out of politics. Instead, Khodorkovskii was financing oppositional parties (including both liberal and Communist parties) and civil society, buying too much influence in the State Duma, and declaring his participation in the 2008 presidential election.... Importantly, Khodorkovskii's case points to the gap between formally claimed principles and informal agreements yet again, and gives ground to Western lawyers familiar with Soviet courts to suggest that nothing much has changed in Russia after all.[80]

Khodorkovsky violated the informal conventions established since 2000, but he also infringed the formal institutional framework. No governing regime would have been happy to see the pillars of authority, such as the Duma, the political parties, and regional leaderships, succumbing to the influence of a powerful society-based political entrepreneur. As for his 'political ambitions', already in 1994 Yeltsin had reacted vigorously when warned of Gusinsky's alleged 'political ambitions' (in this case, by Gusinsky's political enemy of the time, Berezovsky), provoking the

---

[78] Julia Kusznir and Heiko Pleines, 'The Russian Oil Industry between Foreign Investment and Domestic Interests', in Robert Orttung et al. (eds.), *Russia's Energy Sector between Politics and Business*, Working Papers of the Research Centre for East European Studies, Bremen, No. 92, 2008, p. 33.

[79] Alena V. Ledeneva, *How Russia Really Works: The Informal Practices that Shaped Post-Soviet Politics and Business* (Ithaca, NY, and London, Cornell University Press, 2006), p. 194.

[80] Loc. cit.

2 December 1994 assault against Gusinsky's headquarters by a unit of Korzhakov's Presidential Security Service, and the dismissal of Boris Gromov, who Gusinsky had allegedly wanted appointed minister of defence instead of Pavel Grachev.[81] Already by the time of the Svyazinvest scandal in 1997 Yeltsin had come to the conclusion that the oligarchs had to be limited, noting in his memoirs (drafted by Valentin Yumashev) that 'the time had come when the oligarch's influence upon politics, the government, and society was harmful to the country.... [O]ur greatest threat came from the people with big money, who gobbled each other up and thus toppled the entire political edifice we had built with such difficulty.'[82] Putin behaved in much the same way that Yeltsin would have done when faced by an apparent political challenge. The overall result of Putin's assault against the oligarchs was decline in their role as autonomous political actors accompanied by changes in their operational methods, but they remained central to Russian development and played a prominent role in Russia's international economic activity.[83]

The factional theory

We discussed Putin's policy of equidistance earlier, but there is another aspect that has perhaps not been stressed enough—his policy of what may be called 'internal equidistance'—that is, preventing any one of the various factions in Russian politics from becoming dominant within the regime. As I have argued elsewhere, the word 'regime' (rather than government or administration) is used to describe the Russian power system because it is inadequately constrained by the constitutional state from above and lacks effective accountability to the institutions of mass representation from below (parliament, political parties, civil society generally).[84] Within the regime politico-bureaucratic factions struggled for mastery, and power became the key to property.

The Yukos affair threw the spotlight on Putin's political style and on the groups able to seize the policy agenda, and indeed on the tensions in the whole Putinist 'project'. The timing of the case was not accidental, coming when energy prices were rising to their historically second highest point (in relative terms). The government was showered with the accompanying bonanza, thus intensifying competition over the appropriation and application of these resources. These two factors—the struggle against the 'over-mighty' oligarch and competition over control of rents—exacerbated fissures inherent in the political system and intensified

[81] Khlebnikov, *Krestnyi otets Kremlya Boris Berezovskii*, pp. 156–7.
[82] Yeltsin, *Midnight Diaries*, p. 94.
[83] For an informative and balanced study, see Peter Duncan, *'Oligarchs', Business and Russian Foreign Policy: From El'tsin to Putin* (UCL SSEES, Centre for the Study of Economic and Social Change in Europe, October 2007), Economics Working Paper No. 83.
[84] Richard Sakwa, 'The Regime System in Russia', *Contemporary Politics*, Vol. 3, No. 1, 1997, pp. 7–25; *Russian Politics and Society*, fourth edition (London and New York, Routledge, 2008), pp. 466–70; *Putin: Russia's Choice*, second edition (London and New York, Routledge, 2008), chapter 5, which contains some material on Putin's anti-oligarch campaign on which this chapter draws.

the struggles at the heart of Russian politics. It would be misleading, however, to describe these as battles between 'clans', since that would suggest a permanence and depth to the various groups that are probably exaggerated. Instead, we argue that a model focused on 'factionalism' is more appropriate. The corollary of this is that the Yukos affair in the end did not mark a transformation of the regime—that is, the triumph of one faction over all others—but the temporary dominance of one faction in one sphere of policy, with Putin throughout concerned to ensure factional balance.

Already on 9 July 2003, in response to 'The State and Oligarchs' report and the various arrests, Vol'sky on behalf of the RUIE, in a letter given to Putin, explicitly named the *siloviki* and their allies as responsible for discord with big business. The RUIE called on the president to deal with the matter and to stop the campaign that had been 'launched by forces who feel threatened by stability'.[85] The report from the first was considered the ideological preparation for an attack against big business. This was certainly the view of some liberal former SNS members, who in August 2003 accused Belkovsky and Diskin of acting on behalf of one of the Kremlin factions to provide ideological cover for their actions: 'Our bureaucracy', they insisted, 'cannot tolerate clean and legal business'.[86] Gleb Pavlovsky, one of the Kremlin's favourite spin doctors, released his own analysis in September 2003 arguing that the *siloviki* faction was trying to destroy the 'family' group of old Yeltsinites, and noted that a new centre of influence had been established. This consisted of a group comprising Sergei Pugachëv, the founder and main share-holder of Mezhprombank, together with Sechin and Ivanov. Lieutenant general Viktor Ivanov had trained with Putin at the KGB school, and then from 1994 to 1998 he had headed the administrative affairs department of the St Petersburg mayor's office, at a time when Putin was first deputy mayor from April 1994 to June 1996. On Putin's appointment to head the FSB in 1998, Ivanov joined him as head of the department managing FSB property, and from April 1999 until January 2000 he was deputy head of the FSB. Following that he became deputy head of the presidential administration, responsible for personnel matters. The economic base of the group was the relatively modest Rosneft and Mezhprombank, which they hoped to enlarge at the expense of family affiliated businesses. The group sought to reconfigure Russia's political and economic life to their advantage and to make themselves the president's only support (which would in effect make him their hostage).

In Pavlovsky's view, the group wanted to see the creation of powerful business groups aligned with the Kremlin, and to create powerful state monopolies in the energy sector. Big business would be subordinated to the regime, but Pavlovsky argued against the redistribution of property and warned that the destruction of the oligarch system would allow the emergence of a new class of

---

[85] N. Vardul, 'Sem del s pravom perepiski', *Kommersant-Vlast'*, 28 July–3 August 2003.

[86] Boris Makarenko, Mark Urnov and Liliya Shevtsova, 'My ne sdaem imena v arendu', *Moskovskie novosti*, No. 30, 5–11 August 2003, p. 6.

'oligarchs in khaki' who would use the state to their advantage.[87] Even as the Yukos affair gathered pace it managed to divide the administration, with Kasyanov and Alexander Voloshin, at the head of the presidential administration since 19 March 1999, defending Khodorkovsky against those intent on pressing the case forward. Khodorkovsky's arrest was dubbed by one commentator as 'Putin's October', representing the 'ascendancy of the *siloviki*'.[88]

A study at this time argued that the pressure on Khodorkovsky 'reflects a shifting balance of power in the Kremlin, where players who have emerged during Vladimir Putin's presidency are asserting themselves to challenge well-established alliances between the old guard, leading financial-industrial groups, and political parties ahead of the elections'. Yukos had traditionally relied on what became known as the family to gain leverage in the corridors of power as well as on mayor Luzhkov's Moscow group, 'sometimes playing these clans off each other to remain relatively independent'. Khodorkovsky recognized this in an interview in Krasnoyarsk: 'My opinion is that what we are seeing here is the beginning of a fight for power between various branches of the sphere around Vladimir Vladimirovich.'[89] As the influence of the Moscow clans waned, the power of the 'politburo' waxed and rendered Yukos vulnerable to attack. Although Abramovich had traditionally been part of the Moscow group, he was able to shift his position in line with the prevailing wind, and in the end was insulated from attack because of his close relationship with Putin.

The remnants of the 'family', the Yeltsin era officials and business people, were oriented towards a laissez-faire economic policy and a minimal role for the state. The presidential administration in the 1990s facilitated the rise of the oligarchs, a union reinforced in the heat of Yeltsin's re-election campaign in 1996, and although shaken at the time of the financial collapse in 1998 the link continued into Putin's presidency. According to Volkov, the presidential administration acted as 'the protection agency for the oligarchs and the oligarch's business interests', and in turn the oligarchs provided taxes and informal rents 'for the reproduction of the dominant political position of the presidential administration'.[90] Simonov suggests describing the 'family' as an 'old Muscovite' nomenklatura-political grouping: 'old' because it represented a system with its roots in the 1990s that was eclipsed in the Putin years; and 'Muscovite' because it represented an alternative to the St Petersburgers (the 'Pitertsy') so prominent under Putin.[91] The key figures here are Voloshin, who resigned as head of the presidential administration on 30 October 2003 in protest at Khodorkovsky's arrest, and Kasyanov, prime minister until he was dismissed in February 2004. Voloshin invited Surkov to the Kremlin

[87] Gleb Pavlovskii, 'Koridory vlasti: Mochit' nel'zya zamalchivat', and the title of his analytical note of 2 September is 'O negativnykh posledstviyakh "letnego nastupleniya" oppozitsionnogo kursa prezidenta RF menshinstva', *Novaya gazeta*, No. 67, 11 September 2003, pp. 2–4; Konończuk, *The 'Yukos Affair'*, pp. 40, 43.

[88] Adrian Karatnycky, 'Putin's October Revolution', *National Review*, 8 December 2003.

[89] Simon Saradzhyan and Valeria Korchagina, 'A Family Squabble for Oil, Power', *Moscow Times*, 8 July 2003.

[90] Volkov, 'The Yukos Affair', p. 3.   [91] Simonov, *Russkaya neft'*, p. 21.

in spring 1999 as his assistant, and in August as his deputy. Surkov's advancement may well have been sponsored by his former colleague at Menatep, and then Al'fa Bank, Alexander Adamov, who had studied with Voloshin in the early 1970s at the Moscow Institute of Railway Engineering.[92] Voloshin guaranteed Khodorkovsky's inviolability, and when this failed, he resigned.

The Yukos case became an instrument in the factional struggles in the Kremlin, with a particular section intent on using the case to assert their authority and to build a property empire of their own.[93] There is no consensus on the breakdown of factional conflict in the Kremlin. Our categorization is based primarily on policy orientation, rather than place of origin or professional background. Both these factors are important, since clearly Putin's colleagues from St Petersburg (the Pitertsy) are one of the most recognizable groups in his administration, while those with a background in the security services are also an identifiable group. As he consolidated power Putin became ever more exasperated with the old Muscovites, and advanced ever more resolutely the 'new Petersburgers'.[94] St Petersburg was the cradle of a new political class that in Putin's mind represented an alternative to the Moscow elite, which in his view had brought the country to its knees in the 1990s. This new elite demonstrated ever greater political and economic ambition, which would be fateful for the oil industry.

Putin's team of associates from St Petersburg and from his time in the KGB was one of the most enduring groups during his presidency, and cut across not only factional allegiances but also intersected with economic interests. His Petersburg associates included Alexei Miller, Gazprom's chief executive, who worked with Putin in the St Petersburg mayor's office in the 1990s. So, too, did Dmitry Medvedev, who combined his work in the presidential administration and later as first deputy prime minister with chairing Gazprom, and Igor Sechin, the president's deputy chief of staff as well as Rosneft chairman. Vladimir Yakunin, from 2005 chief executive of Russian Railways, also worked with Putin in the same period. Alexei Kudrin, later minister of finances, was one of those from St Petersburg who helped Putin make the move from the second city to the capital. This network represented an important source of 'political capital' that Putin could rely on to ensure his own power.

The Pitertsy, however, were divided between a liberal and a *silovik* wing. The liberals, such as Sergei Ignat'ev at the head of the Central Bank, agreed with the old Muscovites on a number of points, above all on stable property rights and the need to get Russia off the oil hook by increasing taxation on the sector to allow investment in manufacturing industry. They believed that liberalization would render the energy sector more competitive, including possibly opening up the distribution network for private pipelines and throwing both Gazprom and

---

[92] Makarkin, *Politiko-ekonomicheskie klany sovremennoi Rossii*, p. 22.

[93] Pavel K. Baev, 'Putin's Team in Disarray over Oil Money', The Jamestown Foundation, *Eurasia Daily Monitor*, Vol. 2, No. 55, 21 March 2005.

[94] Simonov, *Russkaya neft'*, p. 23.

the electricity monopoly, UES, to market forces. The Petersburg *siloviki*, on the other hand, favoured a stronger role for the state in general and in the oil sector in particular.

Contrary to much commentary, Putin's KGB past did not automatically make him leader of a newly militant security apparatus thirsting for revenge. However, the *siloviki* viewpoint was an important one, reinforcing Putin's statist orientation. The *siloviki* stressed the need to restore the coherence of the state and had strong views about how the economy should be run. They were particularly concerned to ensure the consolidation of their power and the perpetuation of their rule even after Putin left the presidency (the two terms allowed by the constitution ended in 2008). Numerous studies have noted the increased role of the *siloviki* under Putin, with federal and regional elite structures gaining an increased security component.[95] While the concept of a cohesive 'militocracy' is exaggerated, the general view that the state should take the priority over the anarchy of the market in strategic economic issues and over the unpredictability of the democratic representation of civil society in politics was something close to Putin's heart.

By all accounts the attack on Yukos was orchestrated by Sechin. Born in Leningrad on 7 September 1960, he studied foreign languages in Leningrad State University (Putin's alma mater) during 1977–84. He then worked as a military translator in Mozambique and some other countries (a typical cover for security work) before joining the directorate for foreign economic ties in the Leningrad City Soviet, and between 1991 and 1996 he worked as head of office in the Committee for Foreign Economic Ties, headed by Putin, at the St Petersburg city council. Like Putin, from 1996 he worked in the presidential and governmental apparatus in Moscow, running Putin's office in 1998 when he was first deputy head of the presidential administration, and from November to December 1998 he headed the secretariat in Putin's prime ministerial office. He was appointed deputy head of the presidential administration on 31 December 1999, the day that Putin became acting president. From 2001 he was responsible for Putin's timetable and 'Sechin controlled all the paper flow that reached Putin' and loyalty was considered his main asset.[96] He was also in charge of dealing with business conflicts, although formally he had no official business role until 2004. He joined the board of Rosneft on 25 June 2004 and became chairman of the board a month later on 27 July. That appointment had been prepared carefully, with at least six months of meetings with senior managers in Rosneft.

Sechin, considered the *éminence grise* behind the Yukos case, clearly pressed for the complete liquidation of Yukos and for the continuation of the campaign against Yeltsin-era oligarchs. By the time he joined Rosneft Sechin was already notorious as the key player in deposing Rem Vyakhirev as the head of Gazprom,

---

[95] On the size and role of the *siloviki* in Putin's administration, see Olga Kryshtanovkaya and Stephen White, 'Putin's Militocracy', *Post-Soviet Affairs*, Vol. 19, No. 4, October–December 2003, pp. 289–306; and for updated figures, Ol'ga Kryshtanovkaya and Stephen White, 'Inside the Putin Court: A Research Note', *Europe-Asia Studies*, Vol. 57, No. 7, November 2005, pp. 1065–75.

[96] Peter Baker and Susan Glasser, *Kremlin Rising: Vladimir Putin's Russia and the End of Revolution*, revised edn (New York and London, Scribner, 2007), p. 271.

and in organizing Khodorkovsky's arrest and pushing forward the 'Yukos affair'.[97] One of the main detectives working on the Yukos case, General Salavat K. Karimov, is alleged to have reported to Sechin twice a week on progress on the case. The hard line politburo group in the Yukos case included another former KGB officer Viktor Ivanov, also a deputy head of the presidential administration, the head of the Federal Security Service (FSB) Nikolai Patrushev, and Yuri Zaostrovtsev, head of the FSB's economic crimes department, and Prosecutor General (until June 2006) Vladimir Ustinov. There were close family ties between two of these, with Ustinov's son Dmitry married to Sechin's daughter Inga, suggesting that factional links were at the margins becoming clan-type relations. According to one report, this group was 'pushing for a hard line toward Yukos as part of a wider plan to "reshape the market and also strengthen state control, along with their own influence"'.[98] We use the term 'politburo' both as a handy label and an indication of the Soviet-style thinking behind their actions.

The *siloviki* were able to take over supervision of the energy sector, and thus preserved the integrity of Rosneft and Gazprom as state companies, and gradually brought Lukoil and Surgutneftegaz within their orbit. The Soviet-style leadership of these companies was attuned to the new spirit coming from the Kremlin, and adjusted its behaviour accordingly.[99] The electricity sector under Chubais, however, continued its march towards privatization, a classic instance of Putinite balancing. The ambitions of the politburo moved beyond companies in state hands and those close to them, and they looked to extend their power over companies that remained resolutely independent, notably Yukos, TNK, and Sibneft. TNK saved itself (at least for a time) by an alliance with a foreign company (BP), while in 2003 Sibneft and Yukos planned to merge and then to take the TNK path of transnationalization. It was at this point that the politburo struck, realizing that transnationalization was an effective block on deprivatization. They forced a demerger of Yukos-Sibneft, blocked the sale of shares in the joint company to a foreign corporation, and ultimately destroyed Yukos. Sibneft in the end was peacefully absorbed by Gazprom.

Khodorkovsky's arrest signalled the weakening of the old Muscovites, but the position of the economic liberals remained strong. In the sphere of macroeconomic policy the liberal team remained intact, notably Kudrin as finance minister and German Gref at the head of the Ministry of Economic Development and Trade. As we shall see, these people were deeply pained by the Yukos affair, but in the main kept their counsel and by quiet means sought to mitigate the worst effects of the case. The notable exception to the policy of behind the scenes resistance was Andrei Illarionov, Putin's never less than outspoken economic adviser between 2000 and his resignation on 27 December 2005. We shall hear much

---

[97] Dmitrii Butrin, Petr Netreba and Denis Rebrov, 'Svet v kontse skvazhiny', *Kommersant*, 13 May 2008.

[98] Charles Gurin, 'Top Kremlin Official Becomes Rosneft's Board Chairman', *Eurasia Daily Monitor*, Vol. 1, Issue 61, 28 July 2004. He quotes Elena Dikun, '"Delo Yukosa" v sude kreml'—Yukos neokonchennaya voina', *Moskovskie novosti*, No. 18, 21 May 2004, p. 4.

[99] Simonov, *Russkaya neft'*, p. 27.

from Illarionov in due course. In the immediate term, Voloshin's resignation allowed Medvedev to take over as chief of staff, and thus strengthened the liberal component of the regime.

Although the factional tendencies identified above existed and contributed to policy debates during Putin's presidency, his leadership was not factionalized. No distinctive faction was able to dominate his leadership, nor was his leadership shaped by the struggle between factions, although aspects of policy (e.g. in the energy and shipping sphere), was shaped by factional preferences. The concept of faction represents less stable and cohesive groups, but is more of a metaphor for different trends within the regime. Putin certainly listened to the various views, but in the end his policy preferences tended to predominate. It would be misleading to suggest that his presidency was characterized by a great divide between *siloviki* and liberals, or that the Yukos affair emerged out of this struggle. As we have seen, there were plenty of *siloviki* in the employ of business magnates. Yet particular factions were able to advance their views, and in our case the 'politburo' faction drove through the destruction of Yukos.

Putin's regime was certainly oriented towards the retention and perpetuation of power, but at the same time it had a clear ideological orientation towards a state-shaped developmental agenda. This strategy got bogged down in the middle part of his presidency by the struggle over ownership questions, and in particular the belief that the 'oligarchs' represented a threat to the achievement of his goals, and thus there was the need to reassert state prerogatives in the sphere of political economy and economic policy-making. This took the form of the Yukos affair, which deflected attention away from Putin's reformist agenda and exacerbated divisions within the administration. With the taming of the 'over-mighty subjects' the Kremlin went on the offensive, not only to ensure its own prerogatives in economic policy and political life, but also to forge a new model of political economy where the state's preferences predominated. The Yukos affair represented a major disciplinary act not only ensuring the business leaders stayed out of politics, but also brought the state back into the heart of business life. This was achieved not by re-nationalization but through 'deprivatization'. Economic policy was no longer to be a matter left to autonomous economic agents but would be coordinated with the state.

4

Why Yukos?

And thus these sixty thousand inhabitants for generations have read and heard about truth (*pravda*), about mercy and freedom, and all of them to their dying day lie from morning to night, torture one another and fear freedom and hate it like an enemy.

Anton Chekhov[1]

The arrest of Mikhail Khodorkovsky on 25 October 2003, following months of pressure against the Yukos company, on charges of tax evasion and irregularities during the privatization process from 1994, was a clear indication that a new model of state–economy relations was emerging. The arrest signalled the breakdown of the policy of 'equidistance' proclaimed by Putin on assuming the presidency in 2000, in which the so-called oligarchs would no longer have privileged access to political power. It also signalled an attempt by the so-called *siloviki* to break the hold that the 'old Muscovites', and their associated ideas and elites, still had on government. Kononczuk quite rightly notes that analysis of the Yukos affair is complicated by 'the overlap of its numerous plots and aspects', and its 'multidimensionality and ambiguity makes it difficult to restrict oneself to one particular interpretation or one decisive cause'.[2] A mix of objective issues, notably the prospective sale of a large part of the company to a foreign corporation; subjective factors, above all Yukos's involvement in politics and civic affairs; and personal issues, with Khodorkovsky emerging as an independent politician, combined to provoke the attack. With the eclipse of Berezovsky and Gusinsky and the political self-restraint exercised by the other magnates, Khodorkovsky emerged as the leader not only of the nascent bourgeoisie but also of a quasi-political movement.

A STATE WITHIN A STATE

As the state strengthened in the early 2000s, so too did the counter-state in the form of Yukos. State consolidation took the form of bureaucratic aggregation on the basis of a technocratic policy agenda accompanied by factional

[1] Anton Chekhov, 'Moya zhizn': Rasskaz provintsiala', *Izbrannye sochineniya*, Vol. 2 (Moscow, Khudozhestvennya literatura, 1979), p. 199.

[2] Kononczuk, *The 'Yukos Affair'*, p. 34.

conflict.[3] Andrei Piontovsky asks the question: why was Khodorkovsky singled out, and not Deripaska or Chubais? He, like them, was a child of the original sin of the merger of power and money, and like the others he was appointed as one of the super-rich. However, '[u]nlike the others, he has recently tried to draw a line under his past and to play the game according to different rules. He has rendered his company transparent, openly pays his taxes, and engages in social projects. That is, he has let it be understood that he no longer wanted to be dependent on the authorities. This could not please either the bureaucracy or the siloviki, who are the armed wing of the bureaucracy.'[4] He went on to argue, echoing Khodorkovsky's own sentiments, that in ten years he had travelled the path that took American businesspeople three generations. He notes the paradox that '[t]he former oligarch Khodorkovsky is fighting today against oligarchical capitalism'.

This was a rather sanguine view of the transformation. Khodorkovsky's activities ever more assumed the expansive characteristics of an empire, generating its own rules and moving into ever-new spheres of social, political, and economic life; and which appeared to accept national and international law on its own terms and only when it suited the company's purposes. In their landmark study of the 'shadow' economy in Russia, Klyamkin and Timofeev argue that 'the Russian system of shadow relations is nothing other than a privatised state, developing as an all-encompassing *para-state*, [italics in original] which at the same time falls well within the conceptual framework of the "shadow economy"'.[5] In other words, the widespread development of informal relations and survival strategies bypassing formal social and constitutional institutional structures generated a type of alternative state, with codes of meaning and political practices of its own.

The complex of social relations that we call Yukos generated an extraordinarily concentrated form of para-state. Just like the state itself, the company began to generate a distinctive type of 'administrative resource' of its own, developing its own policies on a number of important issues and pursued them with a single-minded determination that was characteristic of all Khodorkovsky's endeavours. Indeed, on a number of occasions (as in his relations with the town of Nefteyugansk), 'Khodorkovsky ignored budgetary and regional politics, and subordinated the state to himself on the grounds that the state was corrupted and he, Khodorkovsky, was more effective than the state'.[6] Khodorkovsky also did not hesitate to advance his views on the Russian tax system.[7] Like Putin, but from the opposite end of the state–society spectrum, Khodorkovsky refused to be constrained by existing institutions, and found para-constitutional solutions

---

[3] See Andrei Yakovlev, 'The Evolution of Business–State Interaction in Russia: From State Capture to Business Capture?', *Europe-Asia Studies*, Vol. 58, No. 7, November 2006, pp. 1033–56.

[4] Andrei Piontovskii, 'Luchshe nachat' s yuridicheskikh garanti', *Ekspert*, No. 33, 8 September 2003, in *Ekspert: Luchshie materialy*, No. 2, 2007, p. 73.

[5] Igor' Klyamkin and Lev Timofeev, *Tenevaya Rossiya: Ekonomiko-sotsiologicheskoe issledovanie* (Moscow, RGGU, 2000), p. 12.

[6] Panyushkin, *Mikhail Khodorkovskii*, p. 81.   [7] Ibid., p. 91.

to practical problems. The company became a type of 'corporate state', acting as a miniature state-like entity and pursuing its own interests in a hierarchical state-like manner while enlisting horizontal networks against Putin's regime. The administration, in turn, feared that the merger of vertical and horizontal axes of power would in due course threaten the autonomy of the state itself.

Although the company proclaimed its transparency, only 18 per cent of its shares were traded publicly and the rest were held by insiders, mostly top managers, who were thus linked in a powerful community of fate. A distinctive Yukos spirit was generated within the company, and this affected its relations with the external world and its employees. Even after Alexei Gulubovich, in the mid-1990s the head of Menatep's investment operations and later the director of Yukos's strategic planning and corporate finances, left the company in 2001, he continued to attend investor meetings of Menatep 'so that I was not suspected of disloyalty'.[8] Yuliya Latynina notes this characteristic of the 'Khodorkovsky clan': 'In the team no one ever betrayed another', but outsiders were considered expendable.[9] Unlike the Luzhkov clan, where family relations became important, Khodorkovsky's group was based on an abstract loyalty to 'the firm'; although taking deeply personalized forms of obeisance to the company's leaders and in particular to the charismatic *vozhd'* (Führer or leader), Khodorkovsky himself. Access to the body of the leader became increasingly limited to a small band of loyalists.[10] A cult of personality in one company developed.

Like other corporations Yukos ran an extensive security service, which engaged in analysis as well as providing coercive power when required, work overseen by Nevzlin. As Olga Kostina, who worked with Nevzlin recalls, when a Yukos employee bought an apartment, it was not unusual for a security operative to check its dimensions and to ask about the source of funding, concerned whether any Yukos secrets had been sold. Nevzlin in her view had great faith in the special services, and she argued that he believed in the power of fear to manage people. She left the company to work in the Moscow mayor's office, but even there Nevzlin called frequently to find out what she was doing, and when she answered that she no longer worked for him, he responded: 'No, you are mistaken. You will always work for me.'[11] In November 1998 a bomb exploded outside her door, for which as we shall see (Chapter 5) Alexei Pichugin was charged in his first trial.

Unlike many businesses in the 1990s, which achieved certain limited ends (usually the capture of cash flows) and then moved on, a feature which in particular characterized Berezovsky's business style, Khodorkovsky's empire took

---

[8] Vladimir Perekrest, 'Za chto sidit Mikhail Khodorkovskii', Part 2, *Izvestiya*, 18 May 2006; http://www.izvestia.ru/investigation/article3092896/index.html.

[9] Yuliya Latynina, 'Imperiya khodorkovskogo: Kuda ubegayut neftedollary', *Sovershenno sekretno*, August 1999; quoted by Leonid Kosals, 'Klanovyi kapitalizm v Rossii', Part 1, *Neprikosnovennyi zapas: Debaty o politike i kul'ture*, http://www.nz-online.ru/print.phtml?aid=80019312.

[10] Reported by Shakhnovsky, Elena Tokareva, *Kto podstavil khodorskovskogo* (Moscow, Yauza, 2006), p. 143.

[11] Perekrest, 'Za chto sidit Mikhail Khodorkovskii', Part 2.

on increasingly stable forms.[12] Indeed, its vaunting ambitions in the early 2000s and the proliferation of social and political initiatives meant that the company began to traverse the path taken by the modern state itself from roaming to stationary bandit (Chapter 3); in other words, to take on state-like characteristics. The company in the early 2000s negotiated with China as if it was a sovereign state, and in his various dealings with foreign powers 'Khodorkovsky was acting like a king, not a subject'.[13] Another account puts it as follows: 'He [Khodorkovsky] even started appearing in foreign capitals—often acting more like a head of state than like an oil magnate.'[14] Between 1989 and 1991 the main opposition to Gorbachev's regime at the head of the Soviet state was not political parties but the embryonic Russian state; and in the period of phoney democracy between 1992 and 1993 parliament as an institution challenged Yeltsin's presidency; and both crises had erupted into violence and catastrophic breakdown, and a similar logic was at work here. Both earlier crises reflected the inability of political parties to mediate political conflicts or of civil society as a whole to temper them. State-like formations substitute for underdeveloped political parties and operate according to a zero-sum exclusive logic. Khodorkovsky's expanding empire began to claim a society-forming capacity, and at that point became a direct threat to Putin's regime at the head of the Russian state.

Elena Tokareva, the head of the *Stringer* journal and website established in 2000 specializing in political information, argues: 'From 2002 the Yukos corporation entered the political phase of its development and its main efforts were no longer directed even to producing oil but focused on buying power in the country as a whole, and whole regions.' As we shall see, Yukos launched a whole range of political projects which, in Tokareva's view, provoked the state's response, and the tax question was no more than a blind to avoid talking about political issues.[15] Menatep-Yukos had always been able to avoid responsibility for its actions, but this era was coming to an end—but consumed by hubris, the company's leaders ignored the warning signs.

The fundamental question facing any analysis of the Yukos affair is the degree to which it acted as a criminal enterprise (particularly in the 1990s), or whether indeed the attack by the state was motivated by political concerns. Of course, these two versions are not mutually exclusive. In his characteristically ironic manner, Khodorkovsky is alleged to have commented more than once that he could not respect a state that had not yet put him in jail.[16] If this is true, then Putin in the end decided to teach Khodorkovsky to respect the state. By the same token, the destruction of Yukos damaged society-forming processes as well as the independence of the rule of law and the integrity of the state itself. Khodorkovsky and

[12] Kosals, 'Klanovyi kapitalizm v Rossii', Part 2, http://www.nz-online.ru/print.phtml?aid=80022545.
[13] Goldman, *Oilopoly*, p. 112.
[14] Michael Specter, 'Kremlin, Inc.: Why are Vladimir Putin's Opponents Dying?', *The New Yorker*, 29 January 2007, p. 58
[15] Tokareva, *Kto podstavil khodorskovskogo*, p. 129.
[16] Perekrest, 'Za chto sidit Mikhail Khodorkovskii', Part 2.

Yukos, as we shall see below, sponsored the development of civil society and public politics, but it did so in a state-like manner, a contradiction which lies at the heart of the whole Yukos affair. On the other side, the state in the Yukos affair acted like business corporations had done earlier in their struggle for property, including the instrumental use of law and the application of coercive power. In mimicking the para-state behaviour of the shadow economy, the constitutional state itself began to take on para-statal characteristics, another contradiction that inhibited the development of a classic rule of law state. As for the economy, the anarcho-oligarchy of the 1990s by the late Putin presidency gave way to a bureaucratic oligarchical system characterized by the creation of state corporations and an internally differentiated oligarchy. Conflict between business and the state gave way to a dangerous merger of the state and business.

One aspect of this was the commercialization of services that were intended to operate for the public good, which manifests itself in what can be called *venal corruption*. More broadly, when the logic of one sphere (in our case, the market), invades another sphere, in this case the service and public goods providing offices of the state, we are dealing with something far more profound, and we call this *meta-corruption*. The systemic breakdown of the boundary between the state and the market in the Yeltsin era continued in an inverted form into the Putin period. The Yukos affair represented an attempt to put an end to one type of meta-corruption but it gave rise to another type.

INDEPENDENT POLITICAL ENTREPRENEURSHIP

In the conditions of the 1990s it was impossible for big business not to be involved in politics, and this gave rise to what Hale calls 'politicized financial-industrial groups' (PFIGs) at both the national and regional levels.[17] As we have seen, this was Khodorkovsky's special forte, with close links between Menatep-Yukos managers and government officials from the very beginning. The Menatep-Yukos PFIG made a notable intervention during Yeltsin's re-election campaign in 1996, and by the early 2000s this had turned into a systemic challenge. The relationship between state and business was extraordinarily fungible. A notable case was Surkov, who between 1992 and 1997 was on the board of directors of Menatep and worked briefly with Al'fa-Group in 1998/9 before entering the presidential administration. A vice president of Yukos between 1994 and 1998, Sergei Generalov, served as fuel and energy minister between May 1998 and May 1999 and he went on to become an SPS deputy in the Third Duma.[18]

---

[17] Henry E. Hale, *Why Not Parties in Russia? Democracy, Federalism and the State* (Cambridge, Cambridge University Press, 2006), pp. 163–95.

[18] For the increased proportion of business representatives in government, see Ol'ga Kryshtanovkaya and Stephen White, 'The Rise of the Russian Business Elite', *Communist and Post-Communist Studies*, Vol. 38, No. 3, September 2005, pp. 293–307.

Khodorkovsky's defection

Although Khodorkovsky personally was sceptical, others in Yukos forged close ties with Luzhkov and Primakov, and Yukos supported Primakov when he became prime minister in September 1998. Khodorkovsky was ambivalent about the creation of Luzhkov's Fatherland (Otechestvo) party in January 1999, a core element of what became Fatherland–All Russia (OVR), combining Moscow capitalism with regional leaders, which aspired to storm the Kremlin in the 1999/2000 electoral cycle. In the event, they were outwitted by the Kremlin insiders, which saw Berezovsky and Putin temporarily allied to ensure a smooth succession and the creation of a pro-presidential block of deputies in the form of Unity (later United Russia) in the Duma. Khodorkovsky kept his options open in this campaign and did not align himself with the old Muscovites or any other faction, although he made no secret that he provided personal funds in support of the liberal Yabloko party, headed by Grigory Yavlinsky, in the December 1999 parliamentary election.[19]

In December 2001, Khodorkovsky recounted how at the request of the RUIE, on whose bureau he had been since October 2000, he was preparing a report for the president on the bureaucratic burden on business, 'created above all by the law and order agencies'. Khodorkovsky warned that a major company could become the object of attention, and thereby 'lose millions of dollars of potential investment for the country'.[20] In response, it appears that Yukos was delegated by an informal business trade union (above all representing a cartel of oil companies) to advance their interests in parliament, a mission that Khodorkovsky rather foolishly took on.[21]

Oligarch intervention at the highest level of power, above all in the presidential administration and cabinet of ministers, now gave way to lobbying and formal representation in legislative bodies. In the December 1999 elections Khodorkovsky not only supported Yabloko but also made funds available for the SPS, headed collectively by Nemtsov, Irina Khakamada, and Chubais, the movement 'Golos Rossii', and in a less open manner 'Unity', as well as the CPRF.[22] The billionaire Vladimir Dubov, a Yukos executive owning a large block of the company's shares, was elected to the Third Duma in 1999 on the OVR list, which was later subsumed into United Russia, and became head of the tax committee. Business leaders also took up gubernatorial posts. In April 2001, Yukos deputy managing director Boris Zolotarëv was elected governor of the Evenk autonomous okrug, while in September 2002, the director of Norilsk Nickel, Alexander Khloponin, was elected governor of Krasnoyarsk krai.

---

[19] 'Khodorkovskii podderzhivaet "Yabloko"', *Novye izvestiya*, 11 November 1999.

[20] Reported in 'Deistvuyushchie litsa: interv'yu—Mikhail Khodorkovskii', *Vedemosti*, 4 August 2005, p. A5.

[21] Author's interview with Alexei Venediktov, Moscow, 19 June 2008.

[22] Vladimir Perekrest, 'Za chto sidit Mikhail Khodorkovskii', Part 3, *Izvestiya*, 7 June 2006; http://www.izvestia.ru/investigation/article3093561/index.html.

By 2003 it was clear that Khodorkovsky was no longer willing to abide by the informal rules of the game. Putin was informed that 226 deputies in the Third Duma (1999–2003) owed allegiance to Yukos,[23] a simple majority of the total of 450, although this figure is probably exaggerated and the real figure was closer to a hundred.[24] This was a Duma in which the word 'lobbying' barely describes the ability of interested parties to shape preferences, with activists running about with packets of money on the eve of important votes. The budget committee in the Third Duma, chaired by Alexander Zhukov (although not, it is always stressed, because of him) had 'practically turned into a structural sub-unit of Yukos'.[25] A particularly sharp bone of contention was the government's attempts to modify the December 1995 production-sharing agreements (PSA) law, whereas Khodorkovsky was deeply opposed to the whole principle of PSAs since he considered them a form of unfair competition by giving preferences to foreign investors, a view to which Putin's government came round once Khodorkovsky was safely in jail.[26] Of the 21 PSA projects originally mooted in 1994/5, only three were signed: Sakhalin-1 led by what became ExxonMobil in 1999, Sakhalin-2 headed by Shell, and Total's project in Siberia (the Kharyaga field in Timan-Pechora) before the scheme was abolished in late 2003.

Various pieces of legislation were shaped according to Yukos's preferences, including revisions to the PSA law, the indexation of the natural resource tax, access to pipelines, crude and oil products export taxes, and petrol distribution.[27] In the debate on amendments to the PSA law on 14 May 2003 Khodorkovsky spoke by mobile phone to his partisans with points to be made.[28] The Kremlin was clearly angered in June 2003 by its inability to introduce a new unified petroleum tax as a result of vigorous lobbying by affected energy companies. Two attempts to raise excise taxes on oil companies were blocked, and it is estimated that the government may have lost up to $2 billion in revenue from Yukos alone because of the favourable tax regime. Khodorkovsky is alleged to have warned the trade and development minister German Gref: 'If you push through these oil taxes, I'll have you fired.'[29] Yukos was also able to mould legislation in its favour, notably the modifications to the tax code that left in a clause allowing exemptions on profit tax in agreements between regional governments and businesses. Chukotka, Kalmykia, and Mordovia signed such agreements with Yukos and other companies, saving them over $1.5 billion a year.[30] Andrew Jack reports that a senior

[23] Perekrest, 'Za chto sidit Mikhail Khodorkovskii'.

[24] Vyacheslav Kostikov, 'I viden uroven' g-na', *Argumenty i fakty*, No. 25, 2006, p. 8.

[25] Natal'ya Arkhangel'skaya, 'Dumskaya monopol'ka', *Ekspert*, No. 3, 26 January 2004, in *Ekspert: Luchshie materialy*, No. 2, 2007, pp. 89–91, at p. 90.

[26] PSAs allowed foreign partners to receive 90% of the oil and gas until they had recouped their investments, paying only a small royalty fee to the Russian government.

[27] Danilin et al., *Vragi Putina*, pp.171–4 provides a table with details.

[28] Simonov, *Russkaya neft'*, p. 101. The deputy in question was Sergei Shtogrin, Danilin et al., *Vragi Putina*, p. 183.

[29] Marshall Goldman interview with Bernard Gwertzman, 2 June 2005, http://www.cfr.org/publication/8155/goldman.html.

[30] Vadim Visloguzov, 'Deputat barrelya', *Kommersant-Vlast'*, 8–14 December 2003.

Yukos executive warned that if the company did not get its way with a new law 'we will start a war against the government'; and Khodorkovsky himself is alleged to have boasted: 'With money, you can ultimately buy anything.'[31] Following Khodorkovsky's arrest the government wasted no time in abolishing 'onshore offshore' tax havens on 18 November 2003, and closed oil tax loopholes at this time.

From the Kremlin's perspective it appeared that Khodorkovsky was working to ensure that he had a group of loyal deputies in the Duma that could if necessary block legislative initiatives that ran counter to the interests of Yukos, and thus against the interests of the magnate class as a whole. While other companies also engaged in lobbying, Yukos's activity was more than just about blocking or individual pieces of legislation but represented a broader attempt to shape the whole energy legislative agenda. Ivan Grachev, a Duma deputy and the leader of the Party for the Development of Entrepreneurship, was unequivocal: 'Yukos was chosen [for attack] out of political considerations. Its level of activity in the present [Third] Duma, above all in the budget committee, is incomparable with the activity of all other companies.' He noted that Yukos effectively enjoyed a blocking majority in the finance committee, and 'one cannot deny that they abused the position', with their behaviour raising questions not only among committee members but also in the business community. This explains why, in his view, the attack on Yukos aroused such a weak reaction among both businesspeople and politicians. The attack was provoked, in his view, because 'Khodorkovsky openly declared his intention of continuing the practice and even to develop it by winning a blocking vote, no longer in a single committee but in the whole Duma'. Grachev stressed that Yukos deputies, including Dubov (the chair of the tax committee), worked within the law, 'but extremely aggressively'. In his view the company was trying to create a system that would uniquely serve its interests, often against the interests of the business community as a whole, as with the planned profit tax.[32]

Party politics

Business support for political parties was nothing new, but in the run-up to the 7 December 2003 parliamentary elections it became controversial, and on this issue Yukos became particularly exposed. This was the year of Yukos, with the company seldom out of the news on a whole range of issues. The 'controlled chaos' sponsored by Khodorkovsky was countered by what would become the ideology of 'sovereign democracy'.[33] The fears of the exponents of 'managed democracy' appear to have been confirmed by Khodorkovsky's behaviour in the run-up to

[31] Andrew Jack, *Inside Putin's Russia* (London, Granta Books, 2004), p. 310.

[32] *Ekspert*, No. 41, 3 November 2003, in *Ekspert: Luchshie materialy*, No. 2, 2007, p. 79.

[33] The term 'controlled chaos' was apparently used by Khodorkovsky to describe the best environment for the development of big business. Perekrest, 'Za chto sidit Mikhail Khodorkovskii', Part 3.

the Duma elections. If Khodorkovsky controlled some 100 deputies in the Third Duma, he apparently had ambitions to extend his hold in the Fourth. The Yukos candidate list according to Mikhail Grishankov, the head of the Duma's anti-corruption committee, ran to over 200 names.[34]

With the disappearance of Gusinsky, previously Yabloko's other main sponsor, the party became more dependent on Khodorkovsky. Already in January 2003 Khodorkovsky exerted considerable effort to unite the two main liberal parties, Yabloko and SPS, but to no avail.[35] Khodorkovsky was wise enough to understand that unless they campaigned together they would hang separately.[36] As in 1999, Khodorkovsky made no secret of his 'investment' in various parties.[37] On 7 April 2003 Khodorkovsky announced: 'My political sympathies lie with SPS and Yabloko and I am willing to provide personal funds to finance them', and noted that a minority shareholder and former manager of Yukos (he did not give the name but it was probably Vasily Shakhnovsky) would provide personal support for the CPRF.[38] Yavlinsky admitted that Yukos contributed 'several million dollars' for the campaign in 2003.[39] Khodorkovsky repeatedly stressed that the money did not come directly from Yukos.[40] The party lists showed that Yukos hoped to enter about thirty to forty deputies 'to form their own faction by the name of Yabloko'.[41] As Yabloko's main sponsor, Yukos nominees occupied prominent positions on its party list.[42] Alexander Osovtsov, director of the Open Russia Foundation, Yukos executive Konstantin Kagalovsky, and Galina Antonova, head of strategic planning in Yukos, ran on the Yabloko list.[43] Yukos was also active in funding a corps of single-mandate deputies.

Six top Yukos executives ran in the 2003 State Duma elections. At least five Yukos associates were on the CPRF party list, notably the Yukos shareholder and chair of the Yukos supervisory board, Sergei Muravlenko, and Alexei Kondaurov.[44] Kondaurov had run in 1999 but had been too far down the list (number four in the Far East) to make it into the Duma, but in 2003 he was placed in thirteenth spot and remained in parliament until December 2007. He was one of the key figures running the CPRF's Duma campaign in 2003 and acted as the link with Yukos. He had also tried to close down a special issue of *Stringer*, the investigative journal edited by Tokareva, which was critical of Yukos.[45] According to Boris Kagarlitsky,

[34] Perekrest, 'Za chto sidit Mikhail Khodorkovskii', Part 3.

[35] Panyushkin, *Mikhail Khodorkovskii*, p. 185.

[36] For a detailed study of the issue, see David White, *The Russian Democratic Party Yabloko* (Aldershot, Ashgate, 2006).

[37] Valery Vyzhutovich, 'Tycoon Puts His Cards on the Table', *Moscow News*, 16 April 2003, p. 3.

[38] Kseniya Veretennikova, 'I pravym i levym', *Vremya novostei*, 8 April 2003, p. 4.

[39] David Nowak, 'This Economist Keeps on Swinging', *Moscow Times*, 5 October 2007, p. 1.

[40] Maksim Mironov, ' "Yukos" partiyam ne platit', *Trud*, 23 July 2003, p. 2.

[41] 'Yabloko List', *Moscow Times*, 5 December 2003.

[42] Vladimir Gel'man, 'Political Opposition in Russia: A Dying Species?', *Post-Soviet Affairs*, Vol. 23, No. 3, 2005, p. 240.

[43] Visloguzov, 'Deputat barelya'; Simonov, *Russkaya neft*', p. 102.

[44] Francesca Mereu, 'Capitalists Signing up as Communists', *Moscow Times*, 2 December 2003, p. 1.

[45] Tokareva, *Kto podstavil khodorskovskogo*, p. 136.

Yukos 'bought 13 places on the CPRF's list of candidates for its own people, at a cost of $12 million'.[46] Viktor Kazakov, a former director of Yukos-EP, was one of the few Yukos people to run on the UR list.

Yukos was not the only oil company fighting for a presence in parliament, but it was unusual for the balance of its nominees to be in oppositional groupings. There is much speculation that Khodorkovsky resisted 'invitations' to provide support for Kremlin-backed United Russia. This is levied as a type of 'loyalty tax', and Khodorkovsky's repeated refusals singled him out from other oligarchs. State-friendly Lukoil, for example, had five people on the United Russia list, and TNK also had five with UR and two running with the Communists; whereas with Yukos the proportion was reversed, with five on the CPRF list and only two with UR. As one study puts it, 'Yukos's enormous wealth could be converted into real power by recruiting parliamentarians and creating its own caucus in the Duma'. The aim, the authorities alleged, was 'to privatise parliament and the government'.[47]

The entry of Yukos as a major political player was perceived by the Kremlin as a threat to its political prerogatives. At a meeting on 26 April 2003, when Putin approved the merger of Yukos and Sibneft (see below), Putin asked Khodorkovsky for Yukos to stay out of politics and not to finance the opposition. Khodorkovsky answered that it was not Yukos that was providing finance but he was doing so out of his own pocket, something which any citizen had the right to do. Putin appeared to agree with this view, but asked that Yukos not finance the Communists. Again, Khodorkovsky answered that it was not Yukos that was funding the CPRF but certain Yukos shareholders, again from personal resources. Khodorkovsky left the meeting with a good impression of Putin although he was worried since 'the president was suspiciously benevolent'.[48] In the event, reports came to Putin that Khodorkovsky had met with the communist leader, Zyuganov, and offered his support. Called in by Putin to explain himself, Khodorkovsky denied it. Baker and Glasser recount the story as follows: ' "Putin was furious", a well-connected government official said, "because he already had the minutes from the conversation between Khodorkovsky and Zyuganov, and the minutes came not from the FSB...but from the Communist Party staff. And when someone lies to the president, it makes it personal".' When Kasyanov and Voloshin tried to intervene on Khodorkovsky's behalf, arguing that Voloshin had authorized the financing, Putin responded negatively: 'That's Khodorkovsky. It's his game. He wants to buy parliament. I can't allow this.'[49]

From the Kremlin's perspective, the promiscuous breadth of Khodorkovsky's support for political parties represented an attempt to buy influence in the new Duma, ensuring that legislation was passed in Yukos's interests while blocking threats. To the end Khodorkovsky asserted his right to participate in politics,

---

[46] Reported by Boris Kagarlitsky, presenting his report 'Storm warning: Corruption in Russia's Political Parties', *Rossiiskie vesti*, No. 13, 6 April 2006.

[47] Benediktov, 'Roman s neft'yu', p. 29.   [48] Panyushkin, *Mikhail Khodorkovskii*, p. 187.

[49] Baker and Glasser, *Kremlin Rising*, p. 283.

although he agreed that corporations had no such right. However, speaking in September 2003 he insisted that 'the heads of corporations have the right to lobby their economic interests and should be able to do this openly'. He warned that the events around Yukos could have negative consequences: 'The conflict is between autonomous citizens, giving birth to civil society in the country, and law enforcement organs, who consider that they have the right to dictate to citizens how they should live, and who believe that force is law.' He did not believe that a wholesale redistribution of property would take place. In his view: 'Civil society in Russia will be built only when every group can advance its view publicly and in detail.'[50]

The attack on Yukos weakened Yabloko's prospects: 'Not only was Yabloko's primary source of funding disrupted, but the arrest also called attention to the fact that the "anti-oligarch" Yabloko had in fact been financed by the largest of the oligarchs.'[51] The same applies to the CPRF, which was forced to explain placing millionaires on its list and accepting money from big business while condemning oligarch power.[52] Soon after Khodorkovsky's arrest one of his partners, Dubov, was dropped from United Russia's electoral list, reinforcing the open break between the Yukos company and anything to do with the presidential administration. In the event, three Yukos people were elected to the Fourth Duma on the CPRF list: Alexei Kondaurov, Sergei Muravlenko, and Yuly Kvitsinky, a former deputy foreign minister and former ambassador to Norway. However, the failure of Yabloko and SPS to cross what was then a 5 per cent representation threshold meant that this tranche of Yukos candidates would not serve as deputies. The initiative passed to the government, which with the arrest of Khodorkovsky and his associates could demonstrate its anti-oligarch credentials. If the goal of the Yukos affair was to reduce the company's influence on the electoral process and in parliament, then this was now achieved, but the pressure on the company did not stop. Political concerns were just one element in precipitating the affair.

The reorganization of power

Khodorkovsky did not limit his opinions to economic matters, and in early 2003, on behalf of the RUIE, he put forward ideas for the reorganization of government and administrative reform, suggesting a much slimmed-down 'mini-government' comprising only 12 policy ministers responsible for managing the needs of the private sector.[53] This was similar to the administrative reform proposed by Dmitry Kozak and implemented, although not very effectively, in 2004.

---

[50] Anna Skornyakova, 'Mikhail Khodorkovskii prodolshit lichno zanimat'sya politikoi', *Nezavisimaya gazeta*, 1 September 2003, p. 4.
[51] Hale, *Why Not Parties in Russia?*, p. 62.   [52] Ibid., p. 66.
[53] *Novaya gazeta*, No. 1, 12 January 2006.

The political background to the case lies in debate about transforming Russia into a parliamentary republic. Much commentary at the time suggested that Putin was preparing a shift of power from the presidency to a parliamentary cabinet-based government headed by a more powerful prime minister. At this time Khodorkovsky also advocated Russia's transformation into a parliamentary republic.[54] According to Nevzlin: 'I learned from Khodorkovsky himself that he informed the president of this concept. Putin heard him out and that was that.'[55] The move to a more controllable parliamentary system would be a way of reducing political risks for the business community. There had long been rumours that Surkov was working on plans to enhance the responsibilities of the parliamentary majority. In his annual address to the Federal Assembly on 16 May 2003 Putin warned against parliamentary populism in the forthcoming Duma elections, while welcoming them as a new stage in the development of the country's multi-party system. Most significantly, he looked forward to a 'professional and efficient government relying on the parliamentary majority' being formed after the elections.[56]

Thus Putin at first was inclined to agree with the idea of a government responsible to the parliamentary majority, hence reference to the idea in his speech, and we know that a decree had been drafted to start the process. Reports even suggested that an announcement to that effect had already been prepared, but in the event was never delivered.[57] The move was suddenly stopped in its tracks, and Putin only returned to the issue to condemn the idea as premature.[58] The reason for the volte-face remains intriguing, but one can assume that opponents of the idea had warned Putin that the government-forming role of the Duma could be exploited by unfriendly forces. It was at this time that the Kremlin

[54] Yulia Latynina, 'What Really Happened to Medvedev', *Moscow Times*, 23 November 2005. In April 2003 the report commissioned indirectly through the Foundation for the Development of Parliamentarianism by Open Russia to the Systems Analysis Research Foundation, called 'An Investigation in Constitutional-Legal Problems of State Development, Improving the Constitutional Foundations of the Russian Federation', argued that a shift to a government of the parliamentary majority would not require changes to the constitution but the adoption of a straightforward federal constitutional law. Vladimir Perekrest, 'Za chto sidit Mikhail Khodorkovskii', Part 5, *Izvestiya*, 19 June 2006; http://www.izvestia.ru/investigation/article3093655/index.html.
[55] Andrei Panov and Aleksandr Bekker, 'Rossiya bez tsarya', *Vedemosti*, 1 February 2005.
[56] http://www.president.kremlin.ru/text/appears/2003/05/44623.shtml; BBC Monitoring, 16 May 2003.
[57] Andrei Kolesnikov, 'Vladimir Putin pozvolil sebe svobodu slov', *Kommersant*, 1 February 2006, p. 2.
[58] In his press conference on 31 January 2006 Putin strongly refuted the idea of the government being formed by the parliamentary majority: 'As for a party-based government, everything is possible in the future, but I am against introducing such a practice in today's political environment in Russia. I am deeply convinced that in the post-Soviet area, while we have a developing economy, a statehood that is being consolidated and are finally determining the principles of federalism, we need strong presidential power ... so far, we have not yet developed stable national political parties. How under such conditions can we talk about a party-based government?' 'Stenogramma press-konferentsii dlya rossiiskikh i inostrannykh zhurnalistov', http://president.kremlin.ru/text/appears/2006/01/100848.shtml.

became concerned about Khodorkovsky's putative prime ministerial ambitions, and it is quite possible that these fears prevented Putin taking this step. Khodorkovsky characteristically took what was probably a good idea but then forced it to extremes, arguing that the powers of the presidency should be drastically reduced to little more than 'supreme arbitrator'.[59] Advocacy of a parliamentary republic was undoubtedly a key factor in tilting Putin towards allowing the attack on Yukos.

The broader context was the problem of the succession. Limited to two successive terms as president, Putin would have to leave office in 2008. This would leave the presidency vacant, and Khodorkovsky was much touted as a possible successor to Putin. No other oligarch was considered in this light, and thus from the start of 'operation successor 2' (the first was in 1999) Khodorkovsky emerged as a potential rival to the existing Kremlin elite. According to Golubovich, discussions within Yukos began in 2001 about advancing Khodorkovsky to a high political position.[60] Khodorkovsky ever more frequently spoke of handing over management of Yukos to others. On 3 April 2003 he announced that he intended to resign as head of the Yukos board in 2007, a post that he had held since 1998, and that he did not wish to do so after his forty-fifth birthday.[61] In an interview with *Der Spiegel* later that month Khodorkovsky declared that he intended to retire as chair of the Yukos board of directors on his forty-fifth birthday in 2008: 'When I'm 45 I no longer want to be a business manager. I may well go into politics.'[62] This was interpreted by some as a declaration that he planned to run for the presidency in 2008, when, as it happened, he would be 45. Thus the conflict between Putin and Yukos was in part a putative struggle for the presidency.

Khodorkovsky was not the only one of the Yukos team with an interest in politics. Nevzlin had been on the federal list of the 'Preobrazhenie' electoral bloc in 1993, and in the 1990s was active in various lobbying groups for entrepreneurs. In 1998 he worked as the first deputy head of the ITAR-TASS information agency while retaining his senior posts with Rosprom and Menatep, before in October 1998 becoming first deputy head of Yukos, and from 1999 taking up the same post with Yukos-Moskva. In 2001, after Gusinsky went into exile, he took over as president of the Russian Jewish Congress before becoming the representative for the Republic of Mordovia in the Federation Council, a post he occupied from November 2001 to March 2003. In the upper chamber he became deputy head of the foreign affairs committee. In March 2003 he moved to become deputy head of Khodorkovsky's Open Russia Foundation (a post he held until January 2004), and at the same time between June and November 2003 he acted as Rector of the Russian State Humanities University (RGGU, see below).

The political theory has two broad aspects: the first focuses on the relationship between the state and the oligarchs in broad terms; while the second examines

[59] Panov and Bekker, 'Rossiya bez tsarya'.

[60] Perekrest, 'Za chto sidit Mikhail Khodorkovskii', Part 5, *Izvestiya*, 19 June 2006.

[61] Yuliya Bushueva and Elizaveta Osetinskaya, 'Khodorkovskii otmeril sebe srok', *Vedemosti*, 4 April 2003; also in *Finans*, 14 April 2003.

[62] K. Mattkhoiz, 'Neftyanoi korol' Khodorkovskii', *Der Spiegel*, 24 April 2003; at http://www.inosmi.ru/translation/179334.html.

detailed issues of Khodorkovsky's political actions in 2003. Although the scale and tone of Khodorkovsky's actions may have been distinctive, most of what he did was not unique to him. As Liliya Shevtsova notes: 'Khodorkovskiy [*sic*] was not punished for supporting Yabloko, the Union of Right Forces or the Communists, nor for the merger with Sibneft—all of this had been approved by Putin himself. Besides, Khodorkovskiy is not alone in supporting opposition candidates for the next Duma, nor is he alone in pursuing an aggressive business strategy (for a real predator, take a look at Oleg Deripaska).'[63] This is not quite the case, since as Baker and Glasser note, Khodorkovsky was going beyond anything attempted before: 'He was talking about virtually privatizing the two market-oriented parties, Yabloko and the Union of Right Forces, as well as placing sizeable numbers of legislators in the Communist party and Putin's own newly renamed United Russia party.'[64] The political theory on its own does not explain the assault on Yukos, but it certainly plays its part.

Foreign policy aspects

We saw in Chapter 2 how Khodorkovsky had become enmeshed in some peak American organizations. It was well known that Khodorkovsky had good relations with numerous American politicians;[65] and this was one of the reasons for his sense of invulnerability in 2003 as his arrest approached (Chapter 5). In turn, Khodorkovsky became 'the oil industry's most pro-United States advocate.'[66] In a number of spheres Khodorkovsky began to advance a parallel foreign policy.

In particular, with 17 per cent of Russian oil production at his disposal in 2003, Khodorkovsky rejected the pleas of OPEC to allow the price of oil to rise, although other Russian companies such as Lukoil were in favour, while the government temporized (Chapter 2). One of the most insistent explanations for the attack on Yukos is that the company, and Khodorkovsky personally, strongly backed the war in Iraq in 2003. We know that Voloshin, at the time head of the presidential administration, played a significant role in trying to drum up support for the war. The coincidence of views encouraged Voloshin to provide political cover for Khodorkovsky and his activities at this time. Khodorkovsky's logic in supporting the war was simple: he anticipated a long period in which Iraqi oil supplies would be disrupted (which in the event proved the case), thus pushing up the price; although publicly Khodorkovsky favoured a period of lower but stable oil prices. Khodorkovsky was not alone in supporting the war. The liberals were also in favour, although for different reasons—the overthrow of a vicious dictator and the restoration of freedom to the Iraqi people. While the business logic for

---

[63] Liliya Shevtsova, 'Whither Putin After the Yukos Affair?' *Moscow Times*, 27 August 2003, p. 7.

[64] Baker and Glasser, *Kremlin Rising*, p. 281.

[65] Nick Paton Walsh, 'Moscow Court Says Tycoon Must Stay in Jail', *The Guardian*, 16 January 2004.

[66] Caroline McGregor, 'Powell Frets Over State of Democracy', *Moscow Times*, 27 January 2004.

Yukos may have been impeccable, it terms of larger politics it was completely
misjudged. Putin on this issue refused to allow Russia to become a pawn in the
intrigues of others. On the one hand, he was pushed by Washington to join the
assault; while on the other, Germany, and even more France, tried to bring Russia
in as part of 'old Europe'. Their resistance to the neo-conservative attempt to
remould the Middle East, and with it the shape of world politics, by sanctioning an
attack against a sovereign state without due cause was a principle close to Putin's
heart; but while he endorsed their arguments, he feared that Russia would end
up trapped if he became part of an informal anti-American alliance over this
issue.

Caught in a delicate web of power politics, the last thing Putin needed was
an independent foreign policy entrepreneur forcing his hand. Russia was often
accused of speaking with multiple voices on foreign policy issues, but under Putin,
for good or ill, order in this sphere was imposed. Russian foreign policy became
far more single-minded, yet Iraq proved to be a great test, and not only for Russia.
Certainly, Putin feared being pushed into a war that he considered technically
complicated and politically wrong, but there were also more immediate concerns.
On the eve of war in early 2003 the Americans refused to recognize Russian
economic interests in Iraq, and in particular its claim to the giant West Qurna
oil field. In 1979 alone Soviet engineers had sunk 300 wells in preparation to start
pumping, but the war with Iran halted the start of production. A PSA with Lukoil
in the mid-1990s gave the company a 50 per cent stake, the Iraqi state a quarter,
and two other Russian government agencies the other quarter, intended to repay
Iraq's $8 billion Cold War debt incurred when the country had been a Soviet
client state.[67] None of these interests were recognized by the Anglo-American war
coalition.[68]

The link between Khodorkovsky and the neo-conservatives was far from
abstract. He contributed funds to support their activities, and enjoyed supportive
relations with the unreconstructed cold warrior Richard Perle. Yukos in America
became part of the pro-war coalition, which included ExxonMobil, *The Washington Post* and *The Wall Street Journal*. Yukos and Khodorkovsky tried to shape the
foreign policy agenda in other spheres as well. His support for an oil pipeline to
Daqing in Manchuria had enormous implications for Russian policy in the Far
East, as did his plans for an independent pipeline to Murmansk (see below). Even
more ambitious was the purported suggestion made by Nevzlin in a meeting with
the American secretary of state that if Khodorkovsky came to power he would
push for Russian nuclear disarmament.[69]

---

[67] Michael Wines, 'Coddling Iraq a $40Bln Gamble', *Moscow Times*, 4 February 2002, p. 9.

[68] Not long before his overthrow Saddam Hussein had repudiated the interests of Russian companies, since Russia had supported Western sanctions, but it appears odd that the Americans were so
punctilious in following Hussein on this subject while repudiating his views in all others.

[69] The conversation was reported by Stanislav Belkovsky, in Perekrest, 'Za chto sidit Mikhail
Khodorkovskii', Part 5, *Izvestiya*, 19 June 2006; also mentioned by Tokareva, *Kto podstavil
khodorskovskogo*, p. 133. Neither gives the date.

YUKOS IN SOCIETY

From the early 2000s Yukos developed a broad range of activities in society, and took the well-worn path trodden by major oligarchs earlier and entered the media market. Khodorkovsky appeared ever-less interested in business and turned his talents to other spheres, including politics. Khodorkovsky was one of the few of the new generation of super-rich businesspeople whose concern for Russia's long-term future led to major investments in Russian education, culture, and research, combined with attempts to improve the governance of his own corporation. All of this was cut short by the assault against his company and his person.

Open Russia

In 2001 Yukos provided nearly one-third of the $150 million donated for charitable purposes by Russian businesses, including funds for 1,000 scholarships and $743,000 to repair flood damage in Lensk.[70] However, in January 2002 the government removed tax breaks for donations, which stalled the shift towards corporate philanthropy. This did not stop Khodorkovsky, and in December 2001 he established the Open Russia Foundation, modelled on George Soros's Open Society Institute (OSI), to support civil society development in Russia. Open Russia addressed social welfare, public health, cultural and civic education, and other issues, including working with partner bodies, community development, and support for small businesses. Its programmes in education and internet development continued work started by OSI. His aim, as Khodorkovsky often put it, was to help create a 'normal country';[71] but it also helped him change his image from robber baron to international philanthropist. Within months Open Russia had opened branches in fifty Russian regions, and began to fill the ideological vacuum that Putin's technocratic style of governance encouraged. Open Russia was the first public association to sign an agreement with the culture ministry, and in May 2002 a memorandum of understanding was signed for joint work on developing and modernizing the network of village libraries in some selected regions.[72] In 2003 the budget for Yukos's philanthropical work was $45 million.[73]

The management board on 14 March 2002 noted: 'The target audience are youths between 12 and 18, whose world views are just forming. The aim is to create a positive informational field around Open Russia and its leadership.'[74]

---

[70] Irina Sandul, 'Corporate Russia Reaches into its Pockets', *The Russia Journal*, 19 July 2002.

[71] Panyushkin, *Mikhail Khodorkovskii*, p. 146.

[72] Mikhail Vasil'ev, 'Khodorkovskii znaet, kak proiti v biblioteku', *Rossiiskaya gazeta*, 28 May 2002, p. 3.

[73] Sarah L. Henderson, *Building Democracy in Contemporary Russia: Western Support for Grassroots Organizations* (Ithaca and London, Cornell University Press, 2003), p. 52.

[74] Vladimir Perekrest, 'Za chto sidit Mikhail Khodorkovskii', Part 4, *Izvestiya*, 18 June 2006.

This meant in effect the creation of a political party in the form of a philan-thropic organization, and Open Russia never made a secret about its support for 'democratic parties'. Open Russia was managed by Irina Yasina from its inception, and the former American secretary of state Henry Kissinger was appointed to its management board, along with senator Bill Bradley and the director of the Hermitage, Mikhail Piotrovsky. Its mission statement declared that '[t]he founders of the Open Russia Foundation believe that openness is the first principle of substantial and mutually enriching communication between the peoples of Russia and the West'.[75] Its fundamental aim was to cultivate a new generation who could participate in business and politics with the confidence to act as equals. For this purpose Khodorkovsky sponsored 'schools for public policy', which developed into a network of over fifty organizations and which advanced the principles of civic education, something that was at the core of the work of Open Russia. It also sponsored a 'Club of Regional Journalists', the members of which, among other things, met annually as a group. Addressing the second such convocation in April 2003, with 120 journalists from fifty-three regions in attendance, Khodorkovsky argued that the CPRF was the only party worthy of the name, and noted that the Iraq war would have negative consequences for Russia, but he stressed that oil comprised only 15 per cent of the country's GDP.[76] The Club continued to work even after the demise of Yukos, now sponsored by George Soros and USAID.[77]

A body with a similar name was established in Britain in December 2001 under the patronage of Lord Jacob Rothschild, with a much narrower remit to award grants to academic institutions and other NGOs. Separate from this, in 2001 Khodorkovsky created an endowment for Hill Scholarships, a scheme for Russian 'Rhodes' scholars to study at Oxford. The UK-based Khodorkovsky Foundation supported a range of philanthropic activities in Russia, including the Korallovo orphanage and lycée in Odintsovo district, located 60 kilometres from Moscow in an old country estate, for 150 children run by Khodorkovsky's parents. Khodorkovsky established the institution in 1994, and it took children from some of Russia's worst tragedies, including the Dubrovnik 'Nord-Ost' theatre and the Beslan school sieges. Interestingly, until about 2005 a picture of Putin and Khodorkovsky embracing hung in the lobby of the orphanage as a reminder of the time when the two enjoyed good relations. On the last day of Khodorkovsky's trial in May 2005 a group of twenty-five senior children attended the court. The Foundation also supported Elena Nemirovskaya's Moscow School of Political Studies, providing summer schools for young officials and politicians. Speaking to a seminar of the School on 26 July 2003 Khodorkovsky noted that the developing conflict was 'between business and authoritarianism', and he insisted, 'I will never surrender. If I do, they will go for others', and in discussing the media he extolled

[75] http://openrussiafoundation.com/About_the_Foundation.asp; the site is no longer available.
[76] 'Den'gi: S kem delit den'gi M. Khodokovskii?', *Argumenty i fakty*, No. 16, 16 April 2003, p. 9.
[77] Author's interview with Irina Yasina, 18 June 2008, Moscow.

the 'civic courage' of journalists, a term that he used frequently at this time.[78] The Foundation sponsored the Russian Booker literary prize until 2006.

Open Russia sponsored an innovative Institute for Applied International Relations (IAIR), intended to advance a liberal perspective on Russian foreign policy. It was headed by Vadim Razumovsky, a career diplomat who left the service in the early 1990s to go into business, and later joined Menatep and then the Yukos team. He became a founding board member of Open Russia and in that capacity was responsible for setting up IAIR and became its director. He was ably assisted by the deputy director, Andrei Zagorsky, an independent policy analyst who has been long affiliated with the Moscow State Institute for International Relations (MGIMO). The IAIR conducted a series of conferences and workshops, launched a series of policy-relevant research and dialogue projects, and also issued three series of publications (IAIR monographs, studies, and policy papers), and provided training programmes in applied political studies, including providing stipends for Ph.D. students with appropriate research and dialogue projects.

Critics suggested that Open Russia usurped state functions and opposed, as Valeri Fadeev, the editor of the *Ekspert* weekly, put it, 'the main trend in the country's development—gaining autonomy, sovereignty and a new identity'. In Fadeev's view, Russia could not become just another Poland or Czech Republic: that would be to misunderstand 'the mission and meaning of Russia's existence'.[79] The similarity in the name of Khodorkovsky's Foundation and George Soros's Open Society Institute is no coincidence, and both came under pressure. Masquerading as an NGO, Open Russia came to be seen as a type of proto-party.[80] As a network structure it would have been able to mobilize an anti-Putin movement, and thus even before the Orange revolution in Ukraine in late 2004 the authorities became alarmed. They had been no less concerned with the work of OSI in Russia and had placed pressure on that organization. Soros himself insisted that Khodorkovsky 'acted within the constraints of the law in supporting political parties. I am doing the same in the United States.'[81] However, while Khodorkovsky's philanthropic and educational work was both needed and legitimate, he portrayed his activities as representing an epochal transformation of Russia and played up the public relations side for all it was worth, which would have annoyed the most benign of governments.[82]

---

[78] Notes by Charles Grant, head of the Centre for European Reform, to whom I am most grateful.

[79] Perekrest, 'Za chto sidit Mikhail Khodorkovskii', Part 4.

[80] Tokareva, *Kto podstavil khodorskovskogo*, p. 133 argues that Khodorkovsky borrowed the idea of a 'network movement' from George Soros, with the similarity in name to the latter's Open Society Institute a nod of acknowledgement.

[81] Interview with Yevgeny Kiselev, 'I'm Doing the Same in the U.S.', *Moscow News*, 5 November 2003, p. 1.

[82] Alfa Bank was also active on the charitable front, supporting a number of orphanages as well as helping the 75 children of crew members of the Kursk submarine, sunk in the Barents Sea in August 2000, but few heard of this activity.

Philanthropy and patriotism

Khodorkovsky supported a range of NGOs, philanthropic and educational activity, and he was particularly assiduous in cultivating his image in America as he sought to build support in the West. He made a number of donations in the United States to burnish his image as an enlightened capitalist. In November 2001 he donated $1 million to the Library of Congress, an event organized in part by APCO. Khodorkovsky forged close links with influential policy institutions in Washington, DC, by giving generous grants to the Carnegie Endowment for International Peace, the American Enterprise Institute (AEI) and other non-profit-making institutions, although the Brookings Institution refused his offer of support.[83] His $500,000 grant to the Carnegie Moscow Center was openly declared and represented a legitimate attempt by Carnegie to find sources of support in the Russian business community, but some of the other recipients (notably AEI) were rather less transparent. In 2002, Khodorkovsky contributed $100,000 for first lady Laura Bush's favourite venture, the National Book Festival. Khodorkovsky's largesse was not confined to foreign beneficiaries, and he contributed to a number of civic projects for the development of Khanty-Mansiisk, the capital of the Khanty-Mansi oil-producing region, including an impressive art gallery stocked with nineteenth- and twentieth-century masters as well as some remarkable modernist European art. Khodorkovsky helped fund Alexander Yakovlev's book on the Gulag.[84]

One of the more audacious projects undertaken by Khodorkovsky and his associates was the election of Nevzlin as rector of the Russian State Humanities University (RGGU) on 17 June 2003. Long led by Yuri Afanas'ev, one of the radical democrats who helped Yeltsin come to power, in the wake of the fall of the communist system in 1991 the university took over the premises of the former Higher Party School (VPSh). It is not clear what motivated Afanas'ev now to develop the link with Yukos, although the university was promised undisclosed support, rumoured to be $100 million over ten years.[85] In the event, even though an office was prepared to his specifications, Nevzlin barely entered the building. On 14 November 2003, the minister of education, Vladimir Filippov, personally tried to convince RGGU's Educational Council (*Uchënyi sovet*) to dismiss Nevzlin, but the professors, in a rare act of courage, refused. Although the academics had not been keen to see Nevzlin, a man with no scholarly reputation, take up the post, once installed, it became a matter of principle to defend him. Nevzlin himself resigned as rector on 17 November 2003 to avoid damaging the university and fled to Israel. The university had by then received $5 million, which was used for some infrastructural developments but above all to enhance staff salaries, which as a result became the highest in Russia. The underlying logic of the association with

[83] Timothy O'Brien, 'How Russian Oil Tycoon Courted Friends in US', *New York Times*, 5 November 2003.

[84] Published in English as Alexander M.Yakovlev, *A Century of Violence in Soviet Russia* (New Haven, CT, Yale University Press, 2004).

[85] *Moscow Times*, 18 November 2003, p. 3.

RGGU appears to have been to achieve a reputational laundering that may have allowed Nevzlin and his associates an enhanced role in public and political life. The Yukos leadership had a 'business plan for Russia':

> They attacked corruption, they were removing one of the biggest oil companies from state control, they funded the opposition, they were educating a new generation of free citizens, and they were developing humanities education. Just a little bit more and Russia would move out of president Putin's personal control, and would become a western country.[86]

The ambivalent relationship between the company and a region can be illustrated by the case of Tomsk. The company's headquarters were directly opposite the regional administration's office, symbolizing the contrasting realities of economic and political power, and the green and yellow Yukos flag proudly asserted the company's autonomy. There are persistent allegations that Yukos failed to invest in the oilfields in the region, and instead extracted in a manner that did not secure the long-term viability of the field. Attempts by local scholars to write a history of the oil industry in the region were not supported.[87] However, the regional branch of Open Russia was extremely active and funded a number of projects. The company also gave extensive support to the Polytechnical Institute, supporting the development of specialists in the petroleum industry. The company also invested in the local television company, ensuring favourable coverage when Khodorkovsky visited the region about once every two months. Relations with the Khanty-Mansi region were no less ambivalent. Vladimir Karasëv, the deputy head of the regional government, noted:

> There was no such thing as the Khodorkovsky era here. Yukos was simply one of the vertically integrated companies—not the best, in some respects the worst. These people [the Yukos management] did not understand that one cannot endlessly extract profits. They understood too late that one should also invest in people. They had more accidents than anyone. Other companies built social infrastructure here from the very beginning. Yukos did finally understand all this and changed its mentality, but it was too late.[88]

Given more time it is possible that Yukos could have rehabilitated its reputation and gone on to become one of Russia's great companies and a major sponsor of impartial philanthropy, but for this a lower profile would have been required. Instead Khodorkovsky conducted his good works in a classically Soviet campaigning spirit, and the respect that he won with the one hand was lost with the other.

Although the policy of 'equidistance' may have remained in operation, a number of Russian oligarchs appeared to have forgotten the other part of the new social contract—investment in the domestic economy and society, on the Kremlin's terms. The purchase of Chelsea FC in 2003 by Abramovich attracted

---

[86] Panyushkin, *Mikhail Khodorkovskii*, p. 166.

[87] The group was led by Sergei Miroshnikov, a professor at Tomsk State University and later the chairman of the International Cooperation Committee of the Tomsk regional administration. Author's interview, Salzburg, 8 July 2005.

[88] 'Valdai: Participant Quotes', *Russia Profile*, Vol. 3, No. 8, October 2006, p. 46.

much negative comment, and was contrasted with the purchase for the nation of Fabergé eggs by Viktor Vekselberg.[89] Capital flight remained high, suggesting that the new business elite had little confidence in the country, while the purchase of extravagant properties abroad reinforced this impression. The support given to Western educational and cultural institutions aroused particular ire. Potanin provided generous funds to the Guggenheim Museum in New York, while Fridman gave a large donation to the Jewish Museum there. In 2003, moreover, Yukos planned to distribute some $3 billion in dividends, more than four times as much as the previous year, and thus would have meant fewer resources to invest in the business. In the context in which Western support for oligarchic capitalism in Russia was increasingly perceived to be the final stage of the Cold War, Khodorkovsky was fast running out of friends in the country.

QUESTIONS OF ECONOMIC POLICY

After an initial period of relative liberalism, from 2003 there was a clear 'turn to statism' in energy and other policies.[90] By taking action against Khodorkovsky the Kremlin was not only reasserting control over economic policy, but warning others not to challenge the Kremlin's prerogatives in this area. The case reflects the powerful current of dissatisfaction with the privatizations of the 1990s. Like most other Russian corporations, the Yukos empire emerged from the 'wild East' 'grabitizations' (or 'piratizations') of the Yeltsin era, with Yukos assets purchased for around one-thirtieth of their later market value.[91] While the Kremlin insisted that it was not engaging in a general rollback of the results of the earlier privatization, it did seek to strengthen the position of state-owned assets in Russia's new marketplace. This was made explicit in the energy strategy adopted by the government on 28 August 2003, which outlined the tasks through to 2020 and, while predicated on the use of market mechanisms, stressed the strategic importance of managing energy resources. The first sentence argued: 'Russia possesses great energy resources and a powerful fuel and energy complex that provide the basis of economic development and are the instrument for carrying out domestic and foreign policy.' The next sentence made the point explicit: 'The country's

---

[89] Later this became almost a 'voluntary-compulsory' tax on doing business safely in Russia, as when metals magnate Alisher Usmanov in October 2007 donated the collection of Russian art that had belonged to the cellist and conductor Mstislav Rostropovich to the Konstantinovsky Palace in St Petersburg. He had bought the collection for $72 million, but noted: 'Everything that I have, I am ready to give to Russia, if it is needed, since I am a citizen of Russia and am proud of that.' 'Another Billionaire Ready to Give Everything to the State', RFE/RL, *Newsline*, 2 October 2007, http://rferl.org/newsline/2007/10/021007.asp#archive.

[90] Philip Hanson, 'The Turn to Statism in Russian Economic Policy', *The International Spectator*, Vol. 42, No. 1, March 2007, pp. 29–42.

[91] David M. Woodruff, *Khodorkovsky's Gamble: From Business to Politics in the YUKOS Conflict*, PONARS Policy Memo 308, November 2003, p. 2.

role in world energy markets to a large extent defines its geopolitical standing.'[92] The core of the strategy, devised by the energy minister Igor Yusufov, was to increase oil production, and thus the political importance of the sector could only grow.[93] Alexander Temerko, then a Yukos vice president, noted that on reading the strategy 'we knew they'd go after some company' to give the state leverage over the whole sector.[94] At that time partially or largely foreign-owned companies were producing a quarter of Russia's oil.[95] At this time companies such as Norilsk Nickel also came under pressure, but after the payment of a symbolic 'windfall' levy the tax hounds were called off. When it came to Yukos, however, far more than money was at stake and no amount of Danegeld could save Khodorkovsky.

Merger of Yukos and Sibneft

On the eve of the war in early 2003 there were fears that oil prices would collapse (once the full potential of Iraqi reserves were released onto the market), pushing some of Russia's indebted oil companies, together with the Russian banking system, into insolvency. This is one reason why Putin gave the go-ahead for the sale in February 2003 by Victor Vekselberg (Access/Renova), Mikhail Fridman (Al'fa Group), and Len Blavatnik of half of TNK to BP to create Russia's third largest oil company, and one in which a foreign company was a major strategic investor.[96] The deal was finally signed on 26 June in London in the presence of Tony Blair and Putin. Just a few months later the situation had changed; with Iraqi oil supplies in jeopardy it was clear that the price would stay high.

It was against this background that the merger of Yukos and Sibneft was announced on 22 April 2003. The deal would have created Russia's biggest and the world's fourth largest oil company in terms of production, pumping 2.3 million barrels of crude a day and it would have been the world's second in terms of reserves at 19.5 billion barrels. In an interview on 16 June 2003 Khodorkovsky explained the various benefits that the merger would bring the country.[97] The new company would control 35 per cent of oil refining and 39 per cent of petrol production through its six major refineries in Russia (Omsk, Achinsk, Angarsk, and the three in Samara region, as well as Mazeikiu Nafta in Lithuania), and Russia's largest distribution network with 2,500 petrol stations.[98] YukosSibneft would have dominated 'big oil' in East Siberia and the Far East. With a relatively low capitalization of only $35 billion, the stock of the joint company could only

[92] *Energitecheskaya strategiya Rossii na period do 2020 goda*, 28 August 2003, www.minprom.gov.ru/docs/strateg/1.
[93] Simonov, *Russkaya neft'*, p. 35.
[94] Miriam Elder, 'How the State Got a Grip on Energy', *Moscow Times*, 14 March 2008, p. 1.
[95] Goldman, *Oilopoly*, p. 113. [96] Fortescue, *Russia's Oil Barons*, pp. 126, 141–2.
[97] Tat'yana Lysova, 'Deistvuyushchie litsa: interv'yu—Mikhail Khodorkovskii, predsedatel' pravleniya NK "Yukos" ', *Vedemosti*, 16 June 2003.
[98] Poussenkova, *From Rigs to Riches*, p. 36.

go up. Yukos received a 92 per cent stake in Sibneft in exchange for 26 per cent of Yukos shares and $3 billion in cash—effectively representing a friendly Yukos takeover of Sibneft, with 55 per cent of the new company controlled by Menatep. The merger was completed on paper by 3 October 2003, and the physical merger was due to be completed by 1 January 2004.

Abramovich at this time was disbursing his assets, selling his stake in Sibneft to Khodorkovsky for $3 billion, and soon after announced his intention to sell his stake in Basic Element (Russian Aluminium) for much the same amount. The apparent sell-out by oligarchs and their attempt to distance themselves from Russia in the end influenced the Kremlin's view of the merger. Abramovich's motive in suggesting the merger also remains unclear. After all, when in 1997/8 there had been discussions to create Yuksi, the deal was opposed by Abramovich, and he did not enjoy warm relations with Khodorkovsky. According to Nevzlin, Abramovich had set a trap for Khodorkovsky. With the merger complete, Abramovich allegedly planned to use a shareholders' meeting to take over the company, and then present it to the Kremlin.[99] There is some circumstantial evidence for Nevzlin's view, since following Khodorkovsky's arrest Abramovich sought to take over the merged conglomerate. When he was rebuffed by the new team he called off the merger, and left Khodorkovsky and the demerged Yukos to its fate. In September 2005 he sold Sibneft to Gazprom. Abramovich's shrewd relationship with the authorities comes out clearly in a perceptive biography. Managing his companies was left to others: 'It is the task of squaring the authorities that requires Abramovich's particular form of genius', whereas Berezovsky, Gusinsky and Khodorkovsky 'allowed their egos to cloud their judgement'.[100] Khodorkovsky refused to be a divisional manager of Russia Inc., and he paid the price.

At first the merger appears to have been condoned by the Kremlin. Khodorkovsky met Putin on 26 April 2003 and explained the terms, and Putin gave the go-ahead.[101] The merger was approved by the Anti-Monopoly Committee on 14 August 2003. Just a fortnight later, on 28 August, a consortium of Western banks led by Société Générale agreed a $1 billion loan to Yukos at the best rates ever offered to a Russian company. It looked as if the early stage of the Yukos affair (the arrests of Pichugin and Lebedev) was no more than a passing storm in a teacup. However, powerful wheels had already been set in motion. Fears that the Yukos-Sibneft company, which was due to come into operation on 1 January 2004, would create a giant beyond the Kremlin's ability to influence tilted the balance of Kremlin opinion against the merger. The new company would have challenged the state's claimed prerogatives over energy and broader security questions; and the attack on Yukos was the outcome.

The Kremlin's alarm was increased by Khodorkovsky's plan to sell a 25 per cent stake, and possibly even 40 per cent, of the new super-company to

---

[99] Wolton, *Le KGB au pouvoir*, pp. 186–7.

[100] Dominic Midgley and Chris Hutchins, *Abramovich: The Billionaire from Nowhere* (London, Harper Collins, 2005), p. 9.

[101] Panyushkin, *Mikhail Khodorkovskii*, p. 186.

ChevronTexaco, ExxonMobil or some other company (Khodorkovsky was sending out mixed signals). The discussions, led by Khodorkovsky and Abramovich,
started in spring 2003, and even the most liberal of Russian commentators noted:
'Obviously, this sale is not in Russia's interests.'[102] As was seen later with the
attempt by Sinopec to buy America's Unocal in June 2005 or the sale of American
ports to Dubai, such large deals in what are considered strategic sectors are blocked
by national governments. As Ajay Goyal puts it:

By July [2003], even Putin comprehended that Russia's place in the world would become
threatened by a sale of Yukos to an American company. Worse, Kremlin officials warned
the boss, if Yukos were allowed to proceed, the sell-out would become a stampede, an even
greater flight of capital than Russia's vulnerable economy had suffered to date, as every one
of the oligarchs offloaded the country's largest, most important natural assets to foreign
buyers.[103]

Khodorkovsky had also at some point met with American vice president Dick
Cheney, and discussed the sale, which would have made him independent of the
Kremlin, backed not only by foreign oil but also by a foreign power. Meeting
with Lee Raymond, the head of ExxonMobil at the World Economic Forum in
Moscow on 1 October, the American company offered $25 billion for 25 per cent
of Yukos-Sibneft. Khodorkovsky planned to retain 30 per cent of the capital of the
merged company, which according to Western law represents a blocking minority.
By 3 October Khodorkovsky could announce that the Yukos-Sibneft merger was
substantially complete, but he dismissed rumours of plans to sell a 25 per cent
stake to ExxonMobil.[104]

In an interview with the *New York Times* on 6 October 2003 Putin seemed
to take a relaxed approach to sale of a quarter and even 40 per cent, suggesting
that the Yukos sale could go ahead 'if preliminary discussions take place with the
Russian government'.[105] Appropriate consultation with the Russian government
however did not take place, and it appears that Putin twice told Khodorkovsky
that he disapproved of the planned sale.[106] On 7 October, however, the Russian
press reported that the government saw 'no legal objections to the deal'. Tem-
porizing by the Russian leadership over the issue may well have been provoked
by anticipation of President Bush's visit to Putin's dacha in Sochi on 14 October.
Bush, with his close links to the Texas oil industry, was lobbying hard for the sale
to go ahead. His mother and former First Lady, Barbara Bush, had close links
with Texaco, the company had been one of the main sponsors of Bush's election
campaign in 2000, and Condoleezza Rice up to early 2001 had been on the board
of ChevronTexaco. As far as the American leadership was concerned this was

---

[102] Tat'yana Gurova and Aleksandr Privalov, 'My teryaem ego!' *Ekspert*, No. 41, 3 November 2003,
in *Ekspert: Luchshie materialy*, No. 2, 2007, pp. 78–85, at p. 80.

[103] Ajay Goyal, 'Analysis: Sale of a State', *The Russia Journal*, 31 October 2003, pp. 10–13, at p. 10.

[104] *Itar-Tass Weekly News*, 3 October 2003.

[105] *Itar-Tass Weekly News*, 6 October 2003; Denis Rebrov, 'Ne dozhdetes', *Vremya novostei*, 7 October
2003, p. 2.

[106] Valeria Korchagina, ''93 Tender Won by Exxon Annulled', *Moscow Times*, 30 January 2004.

the favoured company, whereas ExxonMobil was considered more sympathetic to the Democrats. It appears that Khodorkovsky demanded the release of Platon Lebedev (arrested on 2 July) as the price for selling to ChevronTexaco, but Putin declared that if he conceded this he would stop being president; and it was at this point that Khodorkovsky activated negotiations with ExxonMobil.[107] Such a sale would have set Putin against Bush, and this was something that Putin sought to avoid at all costs. At that point Putin took the 'politburo' off the leash.[108]

Having given its public blessing for the sale to go ahead, yet considering the sale against the national interest and in danger of souring relations with the Americans, the Russian leadership appeared to have boxed itself in. The attack on Yukos and its leadership was one way of breaking out of the impasse. In due course, and after considerable delay and controversy, a law regulating foreign investment in 'strategic companies', requiring all large deals between Russian and foreign companies to be approved by the Russian government, was drafted;[109] and a law on investment in strategic sectors was adopted in Putin's last days as president (see Chapter 10). In 2003, however, there was a danger that the sale could be achieved by Menatep, located offshore, hence possibly the firmness with which the attack was launched.[110] Fear that the oligarch was undermining Russia's national interests, and subordinating Russian budget revenues to the whims of Texan boardrooms, set alarm bells ringing throughout the Kremlin. Khodorkovsky did not listen, and paid the penalty.

The Russian government, after several missteps, came to the view that while it favoured the globalization of the Russian economy, with Russian companies entering world capital markets and buying up foreign companies, and certainly encouraged FDI in Russia itself, it was wary of the transnationalization of strategic Russian industries. The tie-in of BP and TNK was a classic case of transnationalism, with TNK firmly locked into the strategic thinking of the British company. The creation of TNK-BP, according to one expert, 'gave Britain a powerful instrument for lobbying its interests in Russia'.[111] However, the model did not catch on, and the attempt by Yukos to transnationalize itself by bringing in a large-scale American partner was stopped. As we shall see, Gazprom was encouraged to go global, but its shares could only be traded freely on the international market after the state had gained a majority interest (51 per cent) and Gazprom's core interests in Russia were protected. Very few companies, even Gazprom, met the

---

[107] 'Exxon in Talks over $25bn Deal with Yukos', *Financial Times*, 3 October 2003, reporting that ExxonMobil was considering the purchase of 40 per cent, and possibly over 50 per cent, of YukosSibneft.

[108] Author's interview with Iosif Diskin, Moscow, 4 March 2008.

[109] Maria Levitov, 'Ministry Drafts Criteria for Strategic Companies', *Moscow Times*, 30 January 2006.

[110] Gurova and Privalov, 'My teryaem ego!' pp. 80–1.

[111] Nelli Sharushkina, head of the Moscow branch of the Energy Intelligence Group, quoted by Lyudmila Romanova and Andrei Bobrov, ' "Yukossibneft" snova prodaetsya', *Gazeta*, 16 September 2003, p. 8.

criteria of transnationalism.[112] Talks on the sale of Yukos to a foreign company were suspended in the wake of Khodorkovsky's arrest and never restarted.[113]

Policy conflicts: Pipelines and markets

Pipeline networks today create the sinews of geopolitical order, establishing new diplomatic realities that once built endure for generations, bringing together some countries and regions while marginalizing others.[114] Energy supplies and pipeline politics have become a central issue in Russian–EU relations, and play a critical role in the international relations of the CIS: 'Cheap and abundant energy supplies were like a bonding agent that kept the Soviet Union together; energy supplies and interdependence have also been central to the processes of both separation from the center and reintegration in the former USSR.'[115] Russia sought to reduce transit dependence on third countries, an aim which continued with the building of North Stream in the Baltic, or to diversify export routes, as with the building of South Stream across the bed of the Black Sea and across the Balkans to Austria. Pipeline politics have therefore become a matter of the highest state interest, and thus when Yukos began to define its own policy in this area, the Russian government was alarmed.

To accompany the rise in its output, Yukos began to look for new markets and new export routes. The first sale of 250,000 tonnes of Russian crude to Exxon in Houston, Texas, in June 2002, which sought to test the American market, however, turned into a scandal. The oil services company Dardana went to court to seize the shipment as part payment for the compensation that it had been awarded by the International Arbitration Court in Stockholm over Yukos's failure to pay a $17 million debt incurred by YNG before 1995 to the service company PetroAlliance.[116] Despite endless discussions, no reliable, cost-effective, or viable Russian supply line to the United States has been established. With Yukos's demise plans were put on hold, to the point that two years later Putin recognized that '[o]nly a small part of Russian energy resources reaches the US market.'[117] With talk of a new 'Cold War' and the distrust engendered by the Yukos affair, no American company was selected to develop the Shtokman gas field, and instead the Norwegian StatoilHydro and the French Total were chosen.

[112] Christopher Kenneth, 'Russian Corporations Eye Global Markets', *The Russian Journal*, 14 February 2003, pp. 6–7.

[113] 'Talks on Yukos-Exxon-Chevron Merger Suspended', *Itar-Tass Weekly News*, 27 October 2003.

[114] Rafael Kandiyoti, *Pipelines: Flowing Oil and Crude Politics* (London, I. B. Tauris, 2008).

[115] Margarita Balmaceda, *Energy Dependency, Politics and Corruption in the Former Soviet Union: Russia's Power, Oligarchs' Profits and Ukraine's Missing Energy Policy, 1995–2006* (London, Routledge, 2008), p. 1.

[116] Svetlana Novolodskaya, Yuliya Bushueva, 'Syupriz dlya "Yukosa" ', *Vedemosti*, 22 July 2002; Anna Raff, 'US Delivery Lands in Texas Court', *Moscow Times*, 22 July 2002.

[117] 'Putin meets with Leaders of US Oil and Gas Industry', *Itar-Tass Weekly News*, 17 September 2005.

Russia's oil exports are controlled by Transneft, the state-owned monopoly, regulated by a complex system of access quotas. It operates 48,610 kilometres of pipeline, including the 4,000 kilometre-long Druzhba-1 line that funnels some 1.2 million barrels of oil a day from the West Siberian fields to the West, 336 pumping stations and 849 reservoirs to store oil. For most of the 1990s the network had stagnated, but with the appointment of Semën Vainshtok in late 1999 the infrastructure was much enhanced. It was able to complete a number of strategic projects, including the Baltic Pipeline System, as well as the Sukhodolnaya-Rodionovsk line which redirected flows to Novorossiisk without transiting Ukraine.[118] Transneft enjoyed profits of over $5 billion in 2004. Its monopoly remains an irritant for oil companies and they used their lobbyists in the State Duma to challenge this. The *siloviki*, on the other hand, defended the state monopoly, realizing that any compromise would dilute their power. In short, energy export routes are a matter of the highest strategic concern to the Kremlin, and Khodorkovsky's challenge was not taken lightly.

In May 2001 Rem Vyakhirov was replaced by Alexei Miller, sponsored by the Petersburg *siloviki* as part of their replacement of the old Muscovite elite, leaving Khodorkovsky even more exposed. The state at that time had a 39 per cent stake in Gazprom, a company that enjoys a 20 per cent share in the world gas market and owns about 60 per cent of Russia's known gas reserves. Khodorkovsky questioned Gazprom's effective monopoly over the production and export of gas, and thus he created yet another enemy. Yukos already produced gas for certain markets, and Khodorkovsky claimed that Yukos could produce gas more economically than Gazprom. This was probably true, since Gazprom is not known for its efficiency. Yukos had ambitious schemes to develop its gas interests, planning by 2005 to produce 15 bcm and by 2015, 50 bcm, and to achieve this in mid-2002 had acquired the Siberian gas-producing companies Artikgas and Urengoil. Yukos explored the possibility of building a pipeline to Murmansk on the Barents Sea, where its gas could be liquified and exported to European and other markets, above all to the United States. Yukos would have thus bypassed the Gazprom pipeline system and become a competitor in world markets.

More realistically, in November 2002 four Russian companies (Yukos, Lukoil, TNK, and Sibneft) formed a consortium to build a $3.5 billion oil pipeline from Western Siberia to Murmansk, with a planned annual capacity of around 100 million tonnes, to open in 2007. The line would have bypassed the Transneft system and opened up world markets (above all America) to exports. It takes nine days for a tanker to travel from Murmansk to America, whereas it takes thirty-two days from the Gulf. In January 2003, however, Kasyanov warned that Russian law made no provision for private pipelines, a statement that may well have been prompted by Putin, and urged the companies to invest in a state-owned pipeline to Murmansk in return for preferential rates. Khodorkovsky reacted sharply, noting: 'According to existing law, there are no reasons why private pipelines cannot

---

[118] Todd Prince, 'Pipeline Monopoly a Power in Its Own right', *Moscow Times*, 25 June 2002, p. 14.

exist.'[119] Under pressure from the oil oligarchs, to whom he had traditionally been considered close, Kasyanov later modified his position and suggested that the state had no objections to the private pipeline. Control over access to oil pipelines was one of the few remaining instruments of state management of the oil industry, and was not something that it would casually relinquish. Quite apart from the issue of control, there is the question of whether there is enough oil in Western Siberia to warrant a pipeline to the North, and it is a project that has not advanced since the demise of Yukos.

A further issue that divided Yukos from the Kremlin was the plan to build a 2,400 km oil pipeline from Angarsk to Daqing in Manchuria, the centre of China's oil refining industry. Up to 1993 China had been self-sufficient in oil, but with annual economic growth rates averaging 8–10 per cent oil imports had increased by 22 per cent per annum, hence the search for reliable energy sources dominated China's foreign policy. Already in March 2000 Yukos announced plans to build a $1.7 billion pipeline to China, although at that time the route had not been decided, but the aim was to shift Yukos's oil exports to China, which reached 1 million tonnes in 2000, from rail to pipe.[120] The plan was devised against the background of the development of intensified energy cooperation between Russia and China, although the relationship was torn between 'strategic partnership' and 'mutual distrust'.[121] As far back as 1994 plans had first been advanced for an oil pipeline linking Eastern Siberia with China, and in 2002 the Chinese leader Jiang Zemin and Putin signed an outline agreement. However, environmental concerns about the route of the pipeline, passing close to the earthquake-prone northern shore of Lake Baikal, as well as the rebuff CNPC had received in 2002 when it tried to buy Slavneft, as well as complaints by deputies in parliament that Russian assets would be sold into foreign ownership, provoked Chinese concerns about the level of Russian commitment to the plans. The Japanese proposal announced by prime minister Koizumi in January 2003 that it would help fund an alternative pipeline to the Pacific coast (from Angarsk to Nakhodka on the Sea of Japan), and Russian delays in making clear what its strategy would be, intensified Chinese concerns.[122] When Hu Jintao took over as Chinese leader in autumn 2002, he tried to revive the energy relationship, and his first foreign visit as leader was to Moscow in May 2003.[123] However, this was on the eve of the attack on Yukos, and pipeline policy for a time became entwined with the domestic political struggle.

[119] Konończuk, The 'Yukos Affair', p. 55, n. 15.

[120] Andrew McChesney, 'Oil Pipeline to China on Track', *Moscow Times*, 29 March 2000, p. 11.

[121] Shoichi Itoh, 'Sino-Russian Energy Relations: The Dilemma of Strategic Partnership and Mutual Distrust', in Hiroshi Kimura (ed.), *Russia's Shift Toward Asia* (Tokyo, The Sasakawa Peace Foundation, 2007), chapter 4, pp. 63–77.

[122] The paper by Shoichi Itoh follows every twist and turn of the discussions, 'The Pacific Pipeline at a Crossroads: Dream Project or Pipe Dream?', Research Division, ERINA, working paper, 2007. See also E. Chau, 'Rossiiskie truboprovody: Nazad v budushchee?', *Pro et Contra*, No. 3, 2004, pp. 164–73.

[123] Peter Ferdinand, 'Sunset, Sunrise: China and Russia Construct a New Relationship', *International Affairs*, Vol. 83, No. 5, 2007, p. 848.

In summer 2002 Khodorkovsky reiterated his commitment to building the privately owned Angarsk–Daqing pipeline to cater for China's fast-growing energy needs.[124] The pipeline would have broken Transneft's effective monopoly on oil transport, and thus removed one of the last instruments whereby the state could control the company. Panyushkin argues that the Daqing pipeline plan may well have been the key factor in the whole Yukos affair: 'Perhaps in years to come, when Khodorkovsky and Putin and Bush will be long forgotten, books will be written and films made about the Daqing pipeline, as the last serious intrigue of the end of the oil century.'[125] With the pipeline Khodorkovsky would have moved out of the ambit of Russia into the world elite, and Yukos would have been part of the global geopolitical game. China would free itself from dependence on Middle East oil, controlled by America, and Yukos (and even more so when merged with Sibneft and ExxonMobil or ChevronTexaco) would have gained almost state-like powers to regulate relations between countries. America, not surprisingly, was less than happy to see an energy alliance between Russia and China, and this may have been a factor in its muted response to Khodorkovsky's arrest. Such an alliance may well develop, but forged at the interstate level and not by a policy entrepreneur of the likes of Khodorkovsky.

The struggle over the two routes took on a factional form, with the *siloviki* favouring the Pacific route, while Kasyanov preferred the Chinese option.[126] Khodorkovsky's ambitions were opposed not only by Transneft but also by the Kremlin, which was engaged in a delicate balancing act between Japan and China. The head of Transneft, Vainshtok, was the major proponent of the alternative pipeline to the Pacific port of Nakhodka, although he conceded that there was not enough oil to fill both. The Far Eastern option, with a pipeline from Tayshet tracking to the north of Lake Baikal to the Pacific near Nakhodka, offered Russia broader markets, whereas the Daqing line potentially rendered Russia hostage to the Chinese market. Japan's position appeared the stronger, with a pipeline to the Pacific serving a variety of markets and thus giving Russia greater leverage over prices than would be allowed by a monopsonic market. What applies to gas is also relevant for oil: 'As Russia learned from its experience with the "Blue Steam" pipeline connecting Russia with Turkey, a single buyer is in a relatively strong bargaining position to demand lower prices once the pipeline is built or else it refuses to buy the gas.'[127] In November 2002, Putin, at a meeting of the Security Council, also initially favoured the Pacific route and appeared to put a stop to the Yukos plan.[128] A month later this was openly challenged by Khodorkovsky, declaring that a pipeline would be built to Daqing by 2005. A further declaration in February 2003 has been described as 'pure blackmail': he warned that if the pipeline took the Nakhodka route, Yukos would refuse to supply it with oil.[129]

[124] Simonov, *Russkaya neft'*, pp. 60–4.   [125] Panyushkin, *Mikhail Khodorkovskii*, p. 155.
[126] Simonov, *Russkaya neft'*, p. 256.
[127] Tatiana Mitrova, 'Gazprom's Perspectives on International Markets', *Russian Analytical Digest*, No. 41, 20 May 2008, p. 5.
[128] *Izvestiya*, 12 September 2002.   [129] Kononćzuk, *The 'Yukos Affair'*, p. 37.

In that month, as we shall see below, the Chinese pipeline plan rubbed salt in the wound of the estrangement between Putin and Khodorkovsky.

Yukos also encountered difficulties in negotiations with the Chinese, since they refused to pay more than $12 a barrel, half the world rate at the time. Despite this, in spring 2003, at a time when the Kremlin was veering towards Japan, Khodorkovsky once again declared that Yukos would not export its West Siberian oil to the Pacific.[130] On 28 May 2003 Yukos finally signed a $2.5 billion agreement with China to build the Angarsk–Daqing line, despite the government leaning towards Japan at the time, accompanied by a twenty-year oil delivery contract to deliver 20 million tonnes of oil annually by 2005 and 30 million by 2010.[131] Since it costs three times as much to transport oil by rail than pipeline, Yukos's efforts to shift to the latter are understandable. However, to the end Khodorkovsky insisted that there simply was not enough oil in the region to supply both the Pacific and Chinese pipelines, and that forecasts of 80 million tonnes could be achieved at the earliest by 2020.[132] By autumn 2003 the Yukos oil pipeline project was losing momentum, and when Kasyanov visited China in September the only outcome was an agreement to raise rail deliveries of Yukos oil to China to 10 million tonnes per year by 2005. With the arrests of Lebedev and Khodordovsky two champions of the Chinese vector of Russian energy policy were lost, and in particular proponents of the Daqing pipeline, tilting arguments further towards Japan. With the veto removed, Yukos's West Siberian oil was now available to go East. The Kremlin continued to vacillate, but retained its commitment to build the Far Eastern line. The government at last on 30 December 2004 backed the Transneft plan to build an $18bn East Siberian–Pacific Ocean (ESPO) pipeline to the Far East, but with a branch from Skovorodino to Daqing. The Kremlin was still hedging its bets, but Japan's reluctance to commit resources to a pipeline whose initial priority destination remained unclear tilted the balance towards China. Khodorkovsky was right to argue that the Chinese branch line would bring more immediate benefits, especially since doubts remain over the feasibility of the Nakhodka line, but in the long term the Pacific line made strategic sense.[133]

In late 2004 China advanced a $6 billion loan to Russia's Foreign Economic Bank (Vneshekonbank) that was used by Rosneft to purchase Yukos's main production asset, Yuganskneftegaz. Rosneft agreed to supply China with 48.4 million tonnes of oil by 2010 for an advance payment of $6 billion, a delivery price of $18 a barrel (well below the going rate). Chinese help in dismembering Yukos no doubt helped tilt the balance towards China. Although on

---

[130] *Izvestiya*, 3 June 2003.

[131] The deal was given the green light by Putin and Chinese president Hu Jintao at a meeting in Moscow on 24 May, Valeria Korchagina and Simon Saradzhyan, 'Putin, Hu Sign Off on Oil Pipeline', *Moscow Times*, 28 May 2003, p. 1.

[132] Khodorkovsky made these comments in early September 2003 to the managers of the Angarsk petrochemical plant, Sergei Kez, 'Neft', Datsin i Yukos', *Nezavisimaya gazeta*, 8 September 2003, p. 4.

[133] For a detailed analysis of the options, see Leszek Buszynski, 'Oil and Territory in Putin's Relations with China and Japan', *The Pacific Review*, Vol. 19, 2006, pp. 287–303.

31 December 2004 the Russian government announced that the pipeline would
go to Perevoznaya Bay near Nakhodka, by April 2005 Chinese negotiators convinced Moscow that the first stage of the pipeline should go to Daqing. That
has remained the position ever since, with a Pacific 'second stage' dependent
on finding enough oil in Eastern Siberia to fill it. At a meeting in the Kremlin
with the Valdai Forum foreign experts on 5 September 2005 Putin confirmed that
the Chinese pipeline option was now favoured to be built first.[134] In 2006 Putin
insisted that the ESPO pipeline should be routed far to the north of Baikal to
avoid a potentially disastrous oil spill polluting the lake. There remain doubts
whether there is sufficient capacity in the Eastern Siberian oilfields to support
what had now become the 2,694 kilometre-long pipeline to the Pacific.[135] These
are issues of great strategic concern for the Kremlin, and the attempt by Yukos to
make policy in this area represented for the administration a threat of the highest
order.

The plan to build a pipeline to Murmansk bypassing the Gazprom system ended
in failure, and now the decision in favour of the Pacific route allowed Transneft to
maintain its monopoly over pipeline routes. Together, Transneft and Gazprom
dominate Far Eastern oil and gas projects. It is clear, as one analyst puts it, that
economic and financial issues have 'taken a back seat in project decisions'. Fradkov in April 2004 announced that the government would not allow any private
pipelines to be built, and Putin insisted that new pipelines would remain state
property and private players, foreign or domestic, would not be allowed entry
into the transportation of oil or natural gas.[136] In a meeting with EU leaders in
Sochi in May 2006 he declared that this was the 'holy of holies', and the Russian
government would not sign up to the Transport Protocol of the Energy Charter
Treaty since that would mean renouncing control. The grandiose plans for closer
Russian–American energy cooperation, outlined by Khodorkovsky and high offi-
cials from both countries at the second Russian–American Energy Summit in
St Petersburg in September 2003, also fell victim to the oligarch's disgrace.[137]
Instead America, Europe, and China entered into a period of competition with
Russia over energy resources and distribution, undermining the energy security
of all.

---

[134] Personal notes.

[135] Rosneft promised to supply 25 million tonnes of crude for ESPO in 2009 from its Vankor
field, with 2 million tonnes from Rosneft/TNK-BP's Verkhnechonsk field, and 2 million tonnes from
Surgutneftegaz's Talakan field. The total capacity of the pipeline was 56 million tonnes of crude once it
came into full operation soon after 2010, which probably exceeded the ability of the Eastern Siberian
fields to supply, and some would probably have to be diverted from Western Siberia, Sergei Blagov,
'Russia Pushes Oil Companies to Find More Oil in Eastern Siberia', *Eurasia Daily Monitor*, Vol. 4, No.
199, 26 October 2007.

[136] *Russia Profile*, 29 November 2004.

[137] The meeting was attended by Donald Evans, the US energy secretary, "as well as the Russian
energy minister" Igor' Yusufov. Lyudmila Romanova, 'Dialog: Mikhail Khodorkovskii: "To, chto ya
vam khochu skazat", ya vse ravno ne skazhu', *Gazeta*, 23 September 2003, p. 9.

Rosneft, Gunvor, and the emergence of an anti-Yukos 'politburo'

We have mentioned Rosneft a few times, and it is worth now examining the company in a little more detail because of its central role in the assault against Yukos. As we have seen (Chapter 2), Rosneft was the legatee of the old state oil monopoly, and it was reformed in its present status in 1995. The company has a special place in the development of the Russian state and political economy. At the time of the Yukos affair the state still owned 100 per cent of its capitalization, although 49 per cent of shares were later sold off, including through an IPO on the London Stock exchange.

Bogdanchikov's appointment as chief executive in 1998 allowed Rosneft to develop by demonstrating, as one study of state-business relations in Russia put it, 'emphatic loyalty to the regime, that it has no ambitions to be independent in political matters, and indeed, does not strive to exercise political influence'.[138] Bogdanchikov had previously worked for five years as head of one of Rosneft's major subsidiaries, Sakhalinmorneftegaz, and he brought his former colleagues from the Far East to run the company. Unlike Yukos or TNK, Rosneft did not bring in any foreign directors.[139] Rosneft had just survived being taken over by Sibneft and Yukos, and Bogdanchikov now fought ferociously to defend the company's independence and interests. He was supported by Primakov, prime minister between September 1998 and May 1999, who ensured that Purneftegaz, producing at the time 70 per cent of Rosneft's output, remained with the company, and also blocked Rosneft's privatization. With the change of presidency Putin became Bogdanchikov's new patron, and helped him transform Rosneft into a major energy company. Bogdanchikov enjoyed direct access to Putin, and was favoured by him since he was not one of the oligarchs and had no political ambitions.[140] Bogdanchikov later enjoyed the support of Sechin, who supported his ambition to turn Rosneft into a world-class oil major.

As noted, an informal 'politburo' took shape ranged against Yukos. Its key members were Sechin himself, and his sub-faction included FSB deputy director Alexander Bortnikov, whom Sechin sponsored in 2004 to head the FSB's Economic Security Department, Putin's aide Viktor Ivanov, Vladimir Ustinov at the head of the GPO, and deputy prosecutor general Yuri Biryukov, as well Gennady Timchenko, one of the key partners in the oil trader Gunvor.[141] On the eve of his arrest Khodorkovsky launched an unprecedented personal attack against the GPO,

[138] A. A. Mukhin, *Novye pravila igry dlya bol'shego biznesa, prodiktovannye logikoi pravleniya V. V. Putina* (Moscow, Tsentr politicheskoi informatsii, 2002), p. 252.

[139] Makarkin, *Politiko-ekonomicheskie klany sovremennoi Rossii*, p. 99.   [140] Ibid., p. 100.

[141] Bortnikov's appointment to head the FSB on 11 May 2008 was variously seen as a victory for Medvedev or a confirmation of Putin's continued control over the security agency. As for Ustinov, his role is unequivocal: 'Ustinov was a key figure in the legal onslaught against Yukos and its former CEO, Mikhail Khodorkovsky. He also led other politically tinged legal campaigns during his six-year tenure as prosecutor general under Putin.' Nabi Abdullaev and Miriam Elder, 'Putin Appears to be the Big Winner', *Moscow Times*, 13 May 2008.

noting that Biryukov had spoken of 'a war between the procuracy and the Yukos oil company', and he called his opponents 'werewolves in uniforms' ('oborotnyami v pogonakh') who break the law to 'discredit their uniforms'. Khodorkovsky insisted that his company was not in conflict with the state but with 'unscrupulous officials'.[142] In their behaviour and views the 'politburo' harked back to the Soviet era, although now operating in conditions of market capitalism. The appointment of Sechin to chair the board at Rosneft in August 2004 confirmed the interlocking nature of interests.

A key player in what was becoming an anti-Yukos coalition was Timchenko, who controlled not only the Swiss-based Gunvor International, but also other oil traders: Russia's Transoil, Estonia's Tarcona, and Finland's International Petroleum Products (IPP), and dozens of other companies and offshore firms, with his transactions protected not only by Estonian bureaucrats but also by Russia's *siloviki*. During 1987–9 Timchenko and associates established a foreign trade venture under the name of Kinex, as the external trading arm of the Kirishinefteorgsintez refinery in the town of Kirishi in Leningrad region, which belonged to what became Surgutneftegaz.[143] The company established close links with the St Petersburg mayor's office, and in particular with Putin (at the head of the foreign economic relations office in the city from June 1991) and Sechin. With regions given the power to issue export licences for material resources, Timchenko and his colleagues met Putin in June 1991 to discuss exports, and thereafter Timchenko and Putin met regularly. Timchenko was the beneficiary of a large export quota of fuel oil to be exchanged for food at a time of hardship in St Petersburg. The associated scandal, in which Putin was alleged to have transferred quotas to obscure intermediaries, was investigated by Marina Sal'e and Yuri Gladkov for the St Petersburg city soviet, and the report resurfaced into the public domain on the eve of the 2 December 2007 parliamentary elections.[144] In 1998 Timchenko established contact with the new CEO of Rosneft, Bogdanchikov, and some Rosneft oil was sent to the Kirishi refinery. Thereafter an ever-increasing volume of Rosneft oil was exported through Timchenko's companies. He also maintained close links with Surgutneftegaz, headed by Bogdanov, a classic Soviet-era *neftyanik* loyal to Putin and the Kremlin.

As Putin rose up the political pole, so Timchenko's empire grew. In 1999 he was allowed to trade a proportion of Surgutneftegaz's crude output, which until then had gone through the central national trader, Nafta-Moskva. This crude was traded through Kinex and a new company called Gunvor Energy, established in

---

[142] Interview published in *Novaya gazeta*, 20 October 2003; Vitalii Ivanov, 'Pereshli na lichnosti', *Vedemosti*, 21 October 2003.

[143] For a good discussion of early relations and the development of Surgutneftegaz, see Mariya Ignatova, 'Surgutskii pas'yans: Glava "Surgutneftegaz" Vladimir Bogdanov otdal posrednikam $1 mlrd. Zato sokhranil vlast' nad kompaniei stoimost'yu $27 mlrd.', *Forbes*, Aprel' 2004.

[144] 'Doklad Mariny Sal'e i Yuriya Gladkova o deyatel'nosti V. V. Putina na postu glavy komiteta po vneshnim svyazyam merii Sankt-Peterburga', copyright 'Okalman', 28 November 2007, available at http://www.compromat.ru/main/putin/saliedokl.htm.

spring 1999.[145] On Putin's assumption of the presidency in 2000, Timchenko had a hand in some key appointments, notably when together with Sechin on 6 May 2000 they imposed Dmitry Skarga at the head of Sovcomflot, against the wishes of the transport minister, Sergei Frank, a decision that they would come to rue. Timchenko also supported the appointment of Ryazanov as a member of the Gazprom board, who later went on to become the head of Gazpromneft (formerly Sibneft). Timchenko increasingly relied on his association with Putin and Sechin, and began to shed his old comrades. In autumn 2002 he established Gunvor International without any of his former colleagues and shifted all the business from Gunvor Energy. He established Clearlake as the shipping arm of Gunvor International, and Gunvor-Clearlake became the largest charterer at the new port of Primorsk, opened in 2001 by Putin. It is rumoured that the residual Gunvor Energy was used to ship Iraqi crude as part of the abuse of the 'oil for food' programme with Saddam Hussein's Iraq. Timchenko and Gunvor were named as financiers in the programme by the Paul Volcker committee of the UN, which looked into the matter. Timchenko's offshore companies registered in Cyprus were associated with the main Russian company working in Iraq at that time, Zarubezhneft.[146] Timchenko played a key part in the destruction of Yukos, and in particular the sale of Yuganskneftegaz in December 2004, and his company certainly benefited from the elimination of a rival.

Åslund notes that in February 2004 the presidential candidate and speaker of the First Duma, Ivan Rybkin, had named three people as Putin's financial intermediaries, including Timchenko. Rybkin argued that Timchenko had taken over from Roman Abramovich as the Kremlin's banker in the 2003/04 electoral cycle. By late 2007 the Gunvor oil trading company apparently had a net worth of $20 billion, and acted as the trading company for four Russian oil companies.[147] Gunvor handled a third of Russia's seaborne oil exports (some 60 million tonnes a year) on behalf of Surgutneftegaz, Gazpromneft (the former Sibneft), TNK-BP, and Rosneft.[148] Earlier Yukos had traded through its own Swiss subsidiary Petroval, but with bankruptcy its main assets were transferred to Rosneft, and its foreign trading activities to Gunvor. On the back of Rosneft's acquisition of the main Yukos assets, the Swiss-based Gunvor Group became one of the world's largest oil traders, posting profits of $8 billion on turnover of $43 billion in 2007.[149]

---

[145] The partners in the new venture were Timchenko, Yevgeny Malov, Andrei Katkov, Audu Lucas, Yuri Nikitin, Torbjohn Tornqvist, and two silent partners whose shares were held by Timchenko (allegedly Putin and Sechin).

[146] Roman Shleinov, 'Sem'ya-2: Kto unasledoval chernoe zoloto', *Novaya gazeta*, 14 November 2005.

[147] Anders Åslund, 'Unmasking President Putin's Grandiose Myth', *Moscow Times*, 28 November 2007, p. 9.

[148] Elena Vrantseva, Igor' Prokop'ev and Andrei Demenkov, 'Komu kto povezet', *Russkii Newsweek*, 15 January 2007; *Le Monde*, 10 July 2007.

[149] For more details, see Catherine Belton and Neil Buckley, 'On the Offensive: How Gunvor Rose to the Top of Russian Oil Trading', *Financial Times*, 14 May 2008.

The turn to statism in 2003 was accompanied by the establishment of national 'energy champions', and while there was much hesitation over the form that this would take, one thing was clear—the independent Yukos oil company stood in the way of achieving the Kremlin's strategic goals. The tangled world of oil acquisitions and struggle for assets need not detain us. It should be noted, however, that the courts are routinely used by one side or the other in the struggles of the energy majors, and by the government.

PERSONAL ASPECTS

The case against Yukos has a grimly personal element directed against Khodorkovsky as a business leader and as an individual. In the 1990s Khodorkovsky amassed a vast fortune and paid little tax, but as a *Financial Times* leader puts it, 'so did other oligarchs'.[150] The point in this case, the paper went on, is that 'Mr Khodorkovsky was chosen because he was the richest and politically the most outspoken. That decision was arbitrary and immoral.' The personal aspects of the case are well brought out by Andrew Jack, the *Financial Times* correspondent in Moscow, who describes in detail the strained relations between Yukos and the government, and in particular Khodorkovsky's refusal to subordinate himself to Putin.[151] A recent tendentious study argues that Khodorkovsky was always motivated by envy, and considered it unfair that Putin, who had never risen higher than a lieutenant-colonel in the KGB, 'was occupying a post higher than that of a marshal'.[152]

Face to face: 19 February 2003

Yukos engaged in a number of struggles with state-owned enterprises. There had been a particularly sharp dispute with Rosneft over control of the Vankorskoe oil and gas field (Yeniseineftegaz). Tensions came to a head when Rosneft gained control of a small oil company (Severnaya Neft, headed by the insider Andrei Vavilov, a former deputy finance minister and a senator in the Federation Council), an asset that both Yukos and Sibneft tried to win. The price paid by Rosneft appears excessive ($600 million instead of its estimated top value of around $300 million), with the surplus then allegedly spread between Vavilov, Bogdanchikov, and government officials as a bribe, and possibly used to fund Putin's re-election campaign. This particular case was to have an affect wholly disproportionate to its importance.

At a fateful meeting of business leaders with Putin on 19 February 2003 Khodorkovsky was the second main speaker, after Alexei Mordashov of Severstal

[150] 'Settle Yukos: Still Time for the Kremlin to Limit Economic Damage', *Financial Times*, 8 November 2004.
[151] Jack, *Inside Putin's Russia*, pp. 306–13.   [152] Danilin et al., *Vragi Putina*, p. 158.

had reported on administrative obstacles on small and medium businesses. This was the fifth such meeting since Putin had come to power. The first, on 28 July 2000, as we have seen, set the rules of the game, and the next three—on 31 May 2001 focusing on legal, pension, administrative, and tax reforms and Russia's entry into the WTO; on 6 June 2001 on the motor industry; and on 23 May 2002 on accelerating economic growth—were all low key. If not for later events, the fifth meeting, whose theme was administrative reform, would also have been unremarkable.[153] In his opening remarks Putin noted that the struggle against corruption was essential, but not through coercive means but to ensure that rules were easier to obey than to avoid.[154]

Khodorkovsky's speech on behalf of the RUIE was called 'Corruption in Russia: A Brake on Economic Growth'. It should have been delivered by the head of Al'fa Bank, Fridman, but two days before the meeting he had refused to take on the role. When asked later why he had done so, Khodorkovsky replied: 'Buiinykh malo' ('There are not enough rebellious spirits').[155] It is clear from the video of the meeting that Khodorkovsky was extremely nervous, pale, and with a broken voice. He provided some opinion polling data and other statistics, including the assertion that corruption had reached $30 billion a year, a quarter of the state budget, and that according to the Indem Foundation 72 per cent of Russians feared going to court since the bribes were too high. He noted that even children had been corrupted, detailing the pressure on places in institutes training low-paid tax inspectors and other civil servants, and suggested that some arithmetic other than wages entered their calculations—obviously the bribes that they would be able to receive on graduating.[156] As Khodorkovsky went on Putin's expression became ever harder, and at this comment he exclaimed that it was wrong to presume guilt like this.

This was not enough to stop Khodorkovsky, and he urged that corruption should be made a shameful phenomenon. He then cited the example of Rosneft's takeover of Severnaya Neft, and openly challenged Putin over the acquisition, demanding that Gref (who at the time was chair of Rosneft's board) explain how Rosneft had won control of the firm. If in the 1990s the state had sold its companies too cheaply, in the 2000s it was paying too much to buy them back. Khodorkovsky admitted that business had in part been responsible for corruption in the 1990s, but it was now time to stamp it out from whatever source. In effect Khodorkovsky was saying that those around the table, including the president, were guilty of corruption.[157] Putin in a steely voice noted that Rosneft 'is a state

[153] For a vivid account, see Andrei Kolesnikov, *Vladimir Putin: Ravnoudalenie oligarkhov* (Moscow, Eksmo, 2005), pp. 17–21.

[154] http://www.kremlin.ru/text/appears/2003/02/29787.shtml.

[155] Elena Dikun, 'Delo Yukosa' v sude kreml': Yukos neokonchennaya voina', *Moskovskie novosti*, No. 18, 21 May 2004, p. 4.

[156] Mikhail Khodorkovskii, 'Korruptsiya v Rossii—tormoz ekonomicheskogo rosta', Powerpoint presentation, http://www.khodorkovsky.ru/faq/2636.html, in section 'Voprosy i otvety: Za chto on sidit'.

[157] Panyushkin, *Mikhail Khodorkovskii*, pp. 158–62.

company and needs to increase its insufficient reserves', whereas companies like Yukos had 'super-reserves' anyway.[158] The question was: how did it get them? Putin then paused, allowing the threat to sink in, and then added that Yukos had some tax problems which it had to sort out, and think why they arose in the first place.

According to Victor Gerashchenko, who would go on to head the Yukos board, that was not the end of the meeting. Khodorkovsky spoke again and appealed to Putin for his approval to lay the oil pipeline to China, the plan we discussed above. According to Gerashchenko Putin unequivocally said 'no'; there was a project to build a line to Nakhodka, 'and that was the plan that would be implemented'. Khodorkovsky continued to object, insisting that his pipeline would use private capital and not state funds, but Putin was adamant. Still Khodorkovsky refused to remain silent, and to the astonishment of those present he declared: 'Vladimir Vladimirovich, you do not understand the importance of establishing relations with China', and sat down. 'After this meeting', according to Gerashchenko, 'Khodorkovsky was told unequivocally to leave Russia. He would not budge an inch: what did I say that was wrong? He demanded.'[159]

Those present at the meeting later reported that the exchange had been marked by a high degree of personal animosity. Nevzlin even alleges that as a result of the meeting Sechin and Viktor Ivanov were instructed by Putin to begin gathering evidence against Yukos, and that Biryukov was placed in charge of the Yukos case, with Zaostrovtsev, head of the economic security department at the FSB, given the equivalent job. They then began investigating various murder and assault cases, and tried to link them to Yukos managers.[160] Khodorkovsky himself realized that Yukos faced difficult times, and soon after warned a meeting of Yukos department heads that the company would be attacked, and those who were not ready should leave.

Personal relations

Personal relations between Putin and Khodorkovsky were for the most part proper, but as 2003 advanced they became increasingly strained. A trivial but perhaps psychologically important point about the 19 February 2003 meeting is that Khodorkovsky attended in his trademark rollneck sweater, whereas Putin is a stickler for formality on these occasions.[161] Khodorkovsky's informality was seen by the presidential administration as a sign of his arrogance and almost open contempt not only for the president but also for the dignity of the office and the state that he represented. The political was becoming personal. As a later commentary put it,

[158] Goldman, *Oilopoly*, p. 114.
[159] Victor Gerashchenko, 'I Encountered Total Disregard for the Law', *Novaya gazeta*, 10 July 2008, translated at http://www.khodorkovsky.info/timeline/136489.html.
[160] Valerii G. Shiryaev, *Sud mesti: pervaya zhertva dela Yukosa* (Moscow, OGI, 2006), p. 17.
[161] Kryshtanovkaya, *Anatomiya rossiiskoi elity*, p. 366.

[T]here is Vladimir Putin's personal animosity towards Khodorkovsky. There was a time when the owner of the most successful business venture in Russia tried to talk to the president in the manner he would with owners of the businesses that caught his fancy. Putin took offence, and as far as Putin is concerned, offending the president is no better than offending the state itself. From Putin's point of view, Khodorkovsky posed a threat to the very foundations of Russian statehood and, what was worse, had the capacity to turn this threat into reality.[162]

Despite his great intelligence (or perhaps because of it), Khodorkovsky had a certain *hauteur* in his relations with Putin, and underestimated the latter's determination and qualities as a statesman. Among his friends he referred to Putin dismissively as 'lieutenant Vova' (in this context, a denigratory diminutive of Vladimir the mid-ranking secret policeman). As far as Khodorkovsky was concerned, he had hired former security officials like Putin by the dozen to work in Yukos. He was used to dealing with them as subordinates, and this attitude spilled over into his relations with the president.[163] In a meeting with Putin in early 2003 (it is not clear when precisely), Khodorkovsky took a call on his mobile phone, and continued to talk as if the president of Russia did not exist.[164]

As for Putin's motivations, as he frequently stated, he had been trained to keep his feelings under control. Although he condemned the excesses of the 1990s, he made no attempt to challenge globally the property settlement of that era. In his book of interviews published in 2000 he categorically rejected the idea of a new redistribution of property, although he accepted a role for 'state property on a limited scale'.[165] As Belkovsky notes, the roots of the contemporary Russian political system lie in the attack on the White House in October 1993, and then the presidential election of 1996: 'Oligarchs like Berezovsky, Gusinsky, Abramovich and Khodorkovsky came to power, who then divided Soviet property among themselves.' Rather than opposing this, Belkovsky argues:

Putin did not fight for power. He was placed in his present position by precisely these people. Berezovsky, Abramovich and others made him president to fulfil one task—to guarantee the inviolability of the results of privatisation, to permit the conversion of the privatised enterprises into 'cash flow', as well as to legalise its capital in Russia and abroad.[166]

These comments, however, were made in 2007, when Belkovsky had been disappointed that Putin did not press the attack against the 1990s property settlement further. The Yukos affair remained by and large an isolated event and did not signal a new property revolution. Putin's first public comment on the

---

[162] Dmitry Kamyshev, *Kommersant-Vlast'*, No. 20 (623), May 2005.

[163] Author's interview with Dimitri K. Simes, Director of the Nixon Center, 8 November 2007.

[164] Reported by Blair Ruble, who was at the meeting.

[165] Vladimir Putin, *First Person: An Astonishingly Frank Self-Portrait by Russia's President Vladimir Putin*, with Nataliya Gevorkyan, Natalya Timakova, and Andrei Kolesnikov, translated by Catherine A. Fitzpatrick (London, Hutchinson, 2000), p. 179.

[166] ' "Man sollte die active Rolle Putins nicht überschätzen": Der russische Politologe Belkowski sieht wirtschaftliche Kräfte am Werk im Kreml und prophezeit den Niedergang Russlands', *Die Welt*, 12 November 2007.

Yukos arrests came in his 20 September 2003 meeting with American journalists, when he portrayed the affair as a purely legal matter with criminal overtones; the latter no doubt a reference to the Pichugin case. The *New York Times* quoted him as saying 'Nobody can be free from complying with the laws', and he noted that the investigation was examining 'assassinations or murders in the merger of companies'.[167]

At a conference devoted to problems of liberalism in Russia, Yevgeny Yasin argued that 'Khodorkovsky is a very complex individual. He became a symbol of the most difficult period of contemporary Russian history. In his time he became the richest person, using those methods of enrichment that were current at the time of the establishment of Russian capitalism.' Instead of a system based on contract, prerogative power returned accompanied by the instrumental use of law, but he noted that struggle between 'the authorities and business, between the presidential administration and the oligarchs' had been inevitable since at least 1997. Nevertheless, in Yasin's view the Yukos affair represented a major defeat for Putin, since his declared aim of establishing a democratic rule of law state was undermined. With the Yukos affair the development of independent democratic institutions were stymied. At the same conference Alexander Auzan argued that 'Khodorkovsky is a national problem', reflecting society's reluctance to accept large-scale private property, and thus Khodorkovsky became the scapegoat for pathological privatization, for big capital's attempts to shape the political sphere, and for society's acceptance of the development of a monopolistic form of capitalism after 2003. Khodorkovsky's rehabilitation would signal the restoration of the rule of law and 'of the institutions of Russian statehood'.[168]

Khodorkovsky became the most intransigent exponent of the view that the economy should be disembedded from social control, and in particular from state supervision. He was pushing the Polanyian elastic band far to the side of the view that economic life should enjoy an autonomous existence, and indeed, should shape the socio-political sphere. Kimmage puts this well:

Once upon a time, a Russian oil company called Yukos and a man named Mikhail Khodorkovsky embodied a dream—that the free market, perhaps more than any other force, could and would complete Russia's transformation from a struggling post-communist question mark into an economically prosperous democracy ruled by reasonable laws and anchored in the institution of private property.[169]

The partisans of this view, Kimmage notes, were always more numerous in the West than in Russia. The transformation of Yukos appeared to demonstrate the redemptive power of transparent corporate governance, international accountants, and investment in social projects. Khodorkovsky himself had also

---

[167] Cited by Kimmage, 'Putin's Restoration', p. 131. The official record of the meeting at Novo-Ogarëvo makes no mention of Yukos, http://www.kremlin.ru/text/appears/2003/09/52624.shtml.

[168] *Khodorkovskikh chtenii*, Konferentsii 'Rossiiskie al'ternativy', 10 July 2007, http://www.polit.ru/dossie/2007/10/05/conf.html.

[169] Kimmage, 'Putin's Restoration', p. 129.

undergone a transformation: 'With an almost messianic fervor, he had adopted his new cause to the point where he seemed to be waging a quest for martyrdom. No longer the young man who would give up his bank if the government asked, Khodorkovsky had turned into a quixotic crusader almost eager for prison.'[170]

Ajay Goyal takes an uncompromising view, dismissing the claims by Western editorials that the arrest of Yukos officials represented an attack against 'democracy' and 'freedom':

What had actually happened was that Khodorkovsky had broken an honor agreement he and other oligarchs had reached with Putin in 2001—if they stayed out of politics and did not do anything against the national interest, he would let sleeping dogs lie and keep them out of prison. The oligarchs were given a conditional amnesty in 2001—the terms of which were almost too kind and favourable to them and which Khodorkovsky was breaking in a fit of arrogance.[171]

Khodorkovsky took himself very seriously, but it appeared that his judgement was ever more distorted by a refusal to recognize that the dynamics of politics had changed since the 1990s. Khodorkovsky's thinking was characterized by an increasingly pronounced self-denial and inability to understand the real dynamics of Russian politics and his own role in it. This took place just at the time, in 2002/03, when he was becoming an open politician. He had a strong sense of his role in Russia, and although he undertook perfectly realistic analysis, he also had a very dangerous and very large blind spot when it came to understanding the very different but no less legitimate logic represented by Putin and his regime.

---

[170] Baker and Glasser, *Kremlin Rising*, p. 286.
[171] Ajay Goyal, 'Analysis: Sale of a State', *The Russia Journal*, 31 October 2003, pp. 10–13, at p. 10.

5

The Assault Against Yukos

Gas has become more dangerous than communism.

Mirek Topolánek[1]

The political model suggests that the assault against Yukos and Khodorkovsky was prompted by his various political interventions; whereas the factional model suggests that the security-oriented bloc in the Kremlin launched the attack to allow a redistribution of power and property. Behind both lies the idea of statism, the *dirigiste* view that the state, within the framework of market economics, had the duty to ensure the strategic development of the country. As we saw in the previous chapter, Khodorkovsky engaged in numerous activities, each one of which may be considered legitimate but the attempt to pursue them all at the same time was not only over-ambitious but ill-judged. By the time he agreed to leave Yukos to experienced managers to focus on his own matters, it was too late. The destruction of Yukos and the independent power of big business opened the door to the partial triumph of the *siloviki*, until they in turn degenerated into factional conflict as the Putin succession approached.

THE ASSAULT BEGINS

According to Belkovsky, the Yukos case had nothing to do with ideology but was a purely business matter in the context where 'Russian power was never the outcome of elite consensus'.[2] Belkovsky argued that Putin conducted politics in the form of 'wars', with the second Chechen war from 1999, the triumph of United Russia and his re-election in the elections of 2003/04, and the Yukos affair as a whole.[3] The Yukos 'war' now began in earnest, and with it 'the Putin administration crossed a threshold'.[4] The assault against the oligarchs may have been intended to destroy them 'as a class', but it took the form of an attack against individuals.

---

[1] Czech prime minister Mirek Topolánek, cited by G. P. Armstrong, *Russian Federation/CIS Weekly Sitrep'*, 26 October 2006.
[2] Stanislav Belkovskii and Vladimir Golyshev, *Biznes vladimira putina* (Ekaterinburg, Ul'tra. Kul'tura, 2006), p. 42.
[3] Ibid., p. 41.   [4] Colton, *Yeltsin*, p. 442.

First arrests

It is unclear when we can say that the Yukos case formally began.[5] The signal that Yukos had been singled out as a matter of especial concern was the question raised by the Duma backbencher Vladimir Yudin on 6 June 2003 about Yukos's privatization of the Apatit plant.[6] In early 2003 Sechin had already arranged for three Duma deputies to write a letter requesting an investigation into Khodorkovsky's acquisition of shares in Apatit, the case that was to lead to his conviction.[7] His associates, however, were targeted first, possibly as warning shots. On 19 June 2003 the head of the fourth department in the economic security service of Yukos, Alexei Pichugin, a former KGB officer, was arrested and accused of organizing two murders and two attempted murders, allegedly on the orders of Nevzlin, thus setting in train the attack on the company. In July 2004 Nevzlin, who by then faced tax evasion and misappropriation charges, was accused of being the mastermind behind the murder of Olga and Sergei Gorin, the attempted murder of the Moscow government's PR director Olga Kostina and of Rosprom managing director Sergei Kolesov in 1998.

On 26 June 2003 the GPO conducted a search of the company's Moscow headquarters. On 2 July the head of the Menatep international financial association (Yukos's main shareholder), Platon Lebedev, was arrested in connection with the alleged fraudulent acquisition of a 20 per cent stake, worth $280 million, in 1994 in Apatit. The charges against him were of large-scale fraud and tax evasion. On the same day the GPO issued an international search for Ramil Burganov, the head of VNK. On 4 July Nevzlin and Khodorkovsky were questioned as witnesses in the Lebedev case, with the investigator focusing on Apatit.[8] In an interview with a regional TV station three days later Khodorkovsky argued that the attack on Yukos was the outcome of a struggle among Kremlin factions for power before the presidential elections.[9]

In the wake of Lebedev's arrest the RUIE met on 9 July and agreed to appeal directly to Putin to warn against a wholesale review of past privatizations, but no public statement was issued.[10] On 8 July Kasyanov declared that the arrest of people charged with economic crimes was excessive, but pressure continued throughout the summer. On 9 July Duma deputy Mikhail Bugera (the deputy

---

[5] The first of the Yukos-related cases could be the embezzlement charges laid in January 2002 against Ramil Burganov, a former Yukos executive and general director of VNK, Daniel Kimmage, 'Table, Chair, Yukos', RFE/RL, *Newsline*, 14 July 2003. Since Yukos only completed the purchase of VNK in 2002, it is unlikely to have had any political significance, although Burganov in 2003 was once again targeted.

[6] Dmitrii Kamyshev, 'I. o. tsarya', *Kommersant-Vlast'*, No. 44, 12 November 2007, pp. 15–18, at p. 16.

[7] Personal information from Dmitry Skarga, at the time head of Sovkomflot.

[8] Vladimir Demchenko, 'Dorogie svideteli: Mikhail Khodorkovskii i leonid Nevzlin doprosheny i opushcheny', *Izvestiya*, 5 July 2003, p. 1.

[9] Hanson, 'The Turn to Statism in Russian Economic Policy', p. 36.

[10] Valeria Korchagina and Caroline McGregor, 'Oligarchs to Appeal to Putin on Yukos', *Moscow Times*, 10 July 2003, p. 1.

head of the Russian Regions caucus) called on the GPO to investigate tax offences by Yukos, claiming that the company had paid only R90 million ($3.3 million) in taxes in 2002, a figure completely at variance with Yukos's GAAP results, which showed it paid $445 million, and the company asserted that it paid a total of $3.4 billion (on tax matters, see below).[11] On 14 July Putin declared that economic crimes should not be fought by the use of 'the prison cell', but he condemned businesspeople who sought to defend their interests through excessive parliamentary lobbying. Already on 18 July the GPO declared that it was investigating seven criminal cases connected with Yukos, and on 23 July Lebedev was charged with tax avoidance, above all through the use of promissory notes (*vekselya*). The interweaving of attacks on personnel associated with Khodorkovsky and later on his own person and the issue of possible tax evasion by the company as a whole demonstrates how difficult it is to separate the two processes. From Lebedev's arrest to his own and beyond, Khodorkovsky tried to calm investors by asserting that the attack was restricted to certain Yukos shareholders and not aimed at the company itself, but this argument looked ever-less credible.

On 3 October heavy-handed searches were conducted of the company's business centre in Zhukovka (where several prominent Menatep shareholders lived) and the Korallovo orphanage financed by Yukos. Although the search provoked harsh criticism, with Khodorkovsky calling the raids 'an attempt to intimidate us', it appears that a computer server of Bank Menatep was found, with material relating to the documents lost in the truck that mysteriously fell off a bridge in May 1999.[12] On that day the offices of Vladimir Dubov, a Yukos shareholder with a 4.2 per cent stake in the company and a Duma deputy for United Russia, were searched. Dubov did not even wait for his term as deputy to expire but as soon as he heard of Khodorkovsky's arrest he fled to Israel, thus greatly weakening Yukos's position in parliament. On 9 October 2003 Yukos-Moskva's chief executive with a 4.2 per cent stake in the company and former Moscow deputy mayor, Vasily Shakhnovsky, was arrested and on 17 October charged with fraud and tax evasion. In November his selection as senator representing the Evenk autonomous *okrug* legislature was annulled by the Krasnoyarsk *krai* Supreme Court. A search of the Yukos-related public relations company ASK on 23 October netted a haul of $700,000 in cash as well as five computer servers. The company also handled Yabloko's election account, and as a result the party was dealt a severe blow from which it never recovered.[13] At this stage the attack was not limited to Yukos, with Sibneft (effectively merged with Yukos) in mid-October charged with evading taxes to the tune of $332 million. The date 29 December 2003 would prove fateful for Yukos. On that day it received notice of a full tax review, and it was accused of illegally exploiting tax advantages and minimizing taxes through the use of shell companies.

[11]   Korchagina and McGregor, 'Oligarchs to Appeal'.
[12]   Ivan Sas, 'Khodorkovskii uezhaet', *Nezavisimaya gazeta*, 7 October 2003, p. 1.
[13]   Catherine Belton and Alex Nicholson, 'Probe of Yukos Hits Yabloko', *St Petersburg Times*, 24 October 2003.

As the December 2003 parliamentary and the March 2004 presidential elections approached, the government launched an assault against corruption in state bodies, in particular against bribery and extortion by police and other security officials (the 'werewolves in uniform' campaign). On 23 June 2003 some forty simultaneous raids were conducted, leading to the arrest of about fifteen suspects including seven MVD colonels, an FSB officer, and the head of the emergency ministries security directorate, lieutenant-general Vladimir Ganeev. The arrests were given prominent media coverage, with the MVD officials charged with running a protection racket with the proceeds laundered through a veterans association charity. At the same time, the Russian government had been pressed by Western powers to crack down on corruption, with one author in particular noting the continuing 'operative links' between organized crime and the new oligarchs.[14] However, when the assault against the most egregiously outspoken of the oligarchs began, the response in the West was less than enthusiastic—with some justification. The attempt to deal with genuine problems was bound up with political issues.

Kasyanov on several occasions noted that it was inappropriate for arrests to take place if the key issue was the investigation of taxes, while the presidential adviser on the economy, Andrei Illarionov, was loud in his denunciation.[15] Even the pro-Kremlin head of the Effective Politics Foundation, Gleb Pavlovsky, argued that the arrests threatened all property owners in Russia, including those with privatized apartments. All this had little effect, and the case ground on relentlessly. The Petersburg 'politburo' was intent on destroying the power and privileges of the old Moscow elite, and the protests of the latter appeared only to spur them on.

Khodorkovsky's response

Khodorkovsky's response to the arrest of Yukos officials was complex. On the evening of Lebedev's arrest Khodorkovsky met with Kasyanov, and the latter apparently passed on a message from Putin that Khodorkovsky had no need to worry; Lebedev's arrest apparently had not been a 'political order' but reflected conflicts between oligarchs.[16] Khodorkovsky's immediate reaction was to threaten the government, a week after Lebedev's, that he could deprive Russia of oil and heating.[17] This tactic only reinforced the administration's fear that Khodorkovsky represented a threat to the hard-won stability. His second response was to separate the attack on him personally from the work of the oil company. Addressing the managers of the Angarsk petrochemical plant in early September 2003, Khodorkovsky stressed that his message to the Yukos board was as follows: 'I am pleased that our security agencies and the political forces that can influence them have enough sense to realise that their political-bureaucratic games should

[14] Louise L. Shelley, 'Crime and Corruption: Enduring Problems of Post-Soviet Development', *Demokratizatsiya*, Vol. 11, No. 1, winter 2003, pp. 110–14.

[15] Simonov, *Russkaya neft'*, p. 87.   [16] Panyushkin, *Mikhail Khodorkovskii*, p. 177.

[17] Ajay Goyal, 'Analysis: Sale of a State', *The Russia Journal*, 31 October 2003, pp. 10–13, at p. 10.

not affect the production of Russia's largest company.'[18] He was to be disappointed in the 'good sense' of his opponents.

His third strategy sought to consolidate Western opinion, above all that of influential policy-makers and the media, behind Yukos, and thus as it were establish a defensive shield around the company that the Kremlin would breach at its own cost. The idea was to raise the penalty threshold of any action against Yukos and its associates. For this Menatep hired various PR agencies, above all in Washington DC, to mould public opinion on the Yukos case (see Chapter 9). He travelled ceaselessly to mobilize opinion behind him, including seventeen trips abroad between Lebedev's arrest and his own, adopting the mantle of 'defiant democrat'.[19] His fourth response was a more personal one. At a press conference on 6 October 2003, Khodorkovsky condemned the aggressive tactics of the prosecutor's office, and declared: 'If their intention is to get me to leave the country or put me in jail, then they should put me in jail. I'm not going to be a political exile.'[20] He had no intention of becoming another Berezovsky or Gusinsky, railing impotently against Putin's regime from exile.

Khodorkovsky had long tried to mobilize international opinion behind him. Already in early 2001 he tried to 'find friends' in America, and sought a meeting with the newly elected George Bush. Following background checks on dubious issues in his business past, this was refused.[21] Nevertheless, Khodorkovsky as we have seen established close relations with many influential figures in the American elite. Already in July 2002 Khodorkovsky was greatly encouraged by a meeting he had with Dick Cheney at Jackson Hall in Wyoming, and he now intensified the American leg of his strategy, including a visit to Sun Valley, Idaho, in July 2003, where he met senior American business and government officials. His daughter at this time was placed in a summer camp in America, while on 16 July Khodorkovsky returned to Moscow.[22] A week earlier he had met Dick Cheney to discuss ExxonMobil's plan to buy a large stake in Yukos. Khodorkovsky visited America repeatedly in the summer and autumn of 2003 to advance the third strategy by visiting major think tanks and lobbying bodies. Vol'sky noted that the authorities could misinterpret his American visits, but as usual Khodorkovsky pursued a resolutely independent (some would say provocative) course.[23] Speaking to journalists in Berlin in August 2005 Khodorkovsky warned that people in the president's circle were trying to get their hands on business, and that if it were allowed to continue, the country would set on the Latin American path of development.[24]

[18] Sergei Kez, 'Neft', Datsin i Yukos', *Nezavisimaya gazeta*, 8 September 2003, p. 4.

[19] Baker and Glasser, *Kremlin Rising*, p. 289.   [20] Kimmage, 'Putin's Restoration', p. 132.

[21] *New York Times*, 5 November 2001.

[22] Svetlana Smetanina, 'Krome nekrupnykh politicheskikh intrig, vse ostal'noe v strane razvivaetsya normal'no', *Gazeta*, 17 July 2003, p. 7.

[23] Loc. cit.

[24] Evgeniya Obukhova, '"Lyudi iz okruzheniya prezidenta" boryutsya s biznesom', *Nezavisimaya gazeta*, 13 August 2003, p. 3.

On 9 October 2003, just a fortnight before his arrest, he gave the keynote address to the US–Russia Business Council in Washington, noting that Yukos had become the largest company in Russia in terms of capitalization, and the world's fourth largest oil company following the merger with Sibneft in August. A mere ten years ago, he stressed, it would have been unthinkable for a Russian oil company to have a foreign chief financial officer, whereas Yukos had appointed the American, Bruce Misamore, to that post. The company also now applied GAAP, quarterly reporting, had appointed independent directors, and held international audits. Because of the shortfalls of the tax system companies had earlier opted for PSAs, whereas now the likes of BP and ExxonMobil demonstrated that substantive investments could take place under the national tax regime. He noted that the question of property rights had now been largely settled in Russia, and few serious politicians questioned the status of private property, although he noted that individual rights still had a long way to go to catch up with modern standards. He illustrated this argument with the case against his colleague, Lebedev, who had been held in jail for three months on flimsy evidence. Presciently, he argued: 'There is no independent judiciary in Russia, and law-enforcement agencies use Soviet-style methods that are not appropriate for a modern, civilized country.'[25] He was well aware that the political situation remained open: 'In the next four years, the country must decide what direction its development will take, and resolve what kind of model will be followed in Russia: whether it will be authoritarian; follow a Mexico-style path; or a more modern, civilized model.'[26]

In a speech to the Carnegie Endowment for International Peace in Washington on the same day, 9 October, Khodorkovsky defended his company's right to engage in public activity and he raised some wider issues:

Indeed, we, along with our business colleagues, together defend our interests before the parliament. We do this in public, we do this openly, and we feel this is a perfectly normal thing to do....But the company does not take part in political battles. We don't, as a company, support individual deputies in the parliament. We don't support political parties. As a company we don't take any part in any election, and this is natural. At the same time, neither the shareholders of the company nor I personally have ever renounced our civil rights as citizens. Some of the employees support some political parties, others support other political parties....And that's normal.

Russia has made its choice in the question between private ownership and state ownership of property, and the choice was private property. This choice has already been made....The question right now is a much more difficult choice. Are we going to become a democratic Russia for the first time in our thousand-year history, or are we going to continue along our thousand-year path of authoritarianism? This is not a simple choice. But

---

[25] Mikhail B. Khodorkovsky, 'Keynote Address', *Russian Business Watch*, Vol. 11, No. 3, Fall 2003, p. 2.

[26] Ibid., p. 3.

modern civilization gives Russia no hope of becoming a modern society in the economic sense without becoming the same in the democratic sense.[27]

Khodorkovsky associated his personal fate with the future of open democratic politics and private property in Russia. Whether such an association is warranted is a question that lies at the crux of evaluations of the Yukos case.

Those who heard him speak report that Khodorkovsky was full of confidence, and gave little indication that he feared imminent arrest.[28] His sense of invulnerability was inspired by a number of factors: his belief that his ties with the West were such that the Russian government would fear to touch him, and that his plans to tie up with one of the US oil majors would give him some protection. Khodorkovsky's foreign interlocutors added to his self-confidence. The American vice president, Dick Cheney, was sympathetic to Khodorkovsky's cause, as were a number of leading politicians, including Tom Lantos, the Democratic Congressional representative from California's thirteenth district. Khodorkovsky had attended Lantos's seventy-fifth birthday celebrations in Budapest in February 2003, and he later urged Khodorkovsky to stay in the West. Bruce Jackson, the president of the Project on Transitional Democracies since 2002 and an influential figure in Washington, especially on foreign policy issues (he had strongly advocated the war on Iraq), vigorously supported Khodorkovsky. They informed him that at the Camp David summit on 27 September 2003 Bush had raised his case with Putin, and in the context of such high level representations Khodorkovsky was led to believe that the Russian authorities would hardly risk jeopardizing the relationship with the United States by arresting him. However, not only was Khodorkovsky misinformed, and his fate had not been raised at Camp David, but some of the Texan oil people with whom Bush associated had been at the sharp end of Yukos's tough business practices (in Chapter 2 we saw, for example, how Amoco had lost its stake in YNG in 1998). In addition, Western oil companies were upset at Yukos's opposition to PSAs and whispered unpleasant words about the company to Bush.[29]

The National Security Adviser at the time, Condoleezza Rice, on whom Bush relied on for much of his information about Russia, took an anti-oligarch stance. As a specialist in Russian affairs she had watched the oligarch antics in the 1990s in horror. The summit in any case had been designed to re-launch what had become a rather flagging 'strategic partnership', forged after the events of 9/11, and the affairs of one individual hardly rated as the priority in that context. As Bush stressed:

President Putin and I talked about expanding our cooperation in Iraq and Afghanistan. The President and I agree that America, Russia and the entire world will benefit from the advance of stability and freedom in these nations, because free and stable nations do not

---

[27] *Constitutional and Due Process Violations in the Khodorkovsky/Yukos Case*, a white paper prepared by defence lawyers on behalf of Mikhail Khodorkovsky, Platon Lebedev, Alexei Pichugin (Moscow, n.d.), compiled by Robert Amsterdam and Charles Krause, p. 24.

[28] Author's interviews with participants. However, according to Goldman (*Oilopoly*, p. 115), on 11 October he met with his lawyers to discuss actions in case of his arrest.

[29] Author's interview with Dimitri K. Simes, 8 November 2007.

breed ideologies of murder or threaten people of other lands.... Old suspicions are giving way to new understanding and respect. Our goal is to bring the U.S.–Russian relationship to a new level of partnership.[30]

Khodorkovsky and Yukos, therefore, lacked the kind of Western support on which their supporters counted.[31] However, the Russo-American relationship continued to stagnate, in part because of the fallout of the Yukos affair, although Bush personally remained loyal to the sentiments he expressed at the press conference: 'Plus, I like him [Putin], he's a good fellow to spend quality time with.'[32] Despite the strong personal relationship that survived to the end of both their respective presidencies, Yukos joined Chechnya as an issue that poisoned Russia's relations with Western powers.

Khodorkovsky also tried to rally domestic resistance to the imminent attack, the fourth prong of his survival strategy. He assumed that he had adequate protection (a *krysha*, or 'roof') in the form of Voloshin at the head of the presidential administration and Kasyanov at the head of the government. Meeting with Western journalists on 29 July 2003 Voloshin stressed that Putin had not had advance notification of the various Yukos searches and arrests of that month, and would not be able to influence the course of the investigation.[33] Kasyanov's response to Lebedev's arrest was to warn of 'civil war', although it is not clear who would be fighting whom, and he probably meant that an attack on Yukos could provoke another bout of inter-oligarch infighting that had marked the late 1990s, notably at the time of the Svyazinvest privatization in summer 1997.[34] Voloshin himself at this time was convinced that Khodorkovsky would not be arrested.

Medvedev apparently joined with half a dozen like-minded Kremlin officials and tried to prevent the arrest.[35] Putin, however, always feared being manipulated by his entourage and thus was deeply suspicious of the initiative. When Medvedev approached Putin on behalf of the group to request an end to the Yukos affair, Putin is alleged to have exclaimed: 'This is a conspiracy.'[36] The liberals, however, were far from united. Kudrin on the whole supported the attack on Yukos, declaring that its 'tax transgressions must be punished', noting that it was not the only oil company in this category but it was in his view the worst.[37] Kudrin

---

[30] 'President Bush Meets with Russian President Putin at Camp David', Office of the Press Secretary, 27 September 2007, http://www.whitehouse.gov/news/releases/2003/09/20030927–2.html.

[31] Putin early on formed a very poor opinion of Tony Blair, considering him a sanctimonious lightweight, and despite various jaunts together his negative view only strengthened, and thus Blair was unlikely to be of any use to Khodorkovsky.

[32] 'President Bush Meets with Russian President Putin at Camp David'.

[33] The journalists were from the *Wall Street Journal* and the *Financial Times*, Kimmage, 'Putin's Restoration', p. 131.

[34] Goyal, 'Analysis: Sale of a State', p. 10.

[35] Evgeniya Pis'mennaya, 'Medved' s chelovecheskim litsom', *Russkii Newsweek*, No. 51, 17–23 December 2007, http://www.runewsweek.ru/theme/print.php?tid=147&rid = 2267.

[36] Pavel Sedakov, Mikhail Fishman and Konstantin Gaaze, 'Putin: Ostavil ten' v istorii', *Russkii Newsweek*, No. 20, 12–18 May 2008, http://www.runewsweek.ru/theme/print.php?tid=165&rid = 2533.

[37] Simonov, *Russkaya neft'*, p. 48.

was particularly incensed by his inability to close down the three 'onshore offshores', Mordovia (actively used by Yukos), Chukotka, and Kalmykia. Even Medvedev, although opposed to the attack on Yukos, shared the *silovik* diagnosis that Russia was fighting for its survival as a state, and hence the premium was on the unity of the elite.[38] The paradox of Putin's position is that he feared being manipulated, yet a section of his entourage in this case exaggerated Khodorkovsky's misdemeanours, while Khodorkovsky did nothing to allay these fears.

In one of his last press conferences before the arrest Khodorkovsky revealed that he had organized a collective letter to Putin from the RUIE, not so much talking about a non-aggression pact but trying to inform Putin about the lawlessness of the judiciary and the threat that this posed to economic growth. He insisted that Yukos had not manifested any political ambitions, but that its leaders had exercised their civic rights. All businesses lobbied their interests, he insisted, but Yukos in parliament was the first to do this openly. If it came to a choice between property and civic rights, Khodorkovsky declared, he would choose rights, 'since without them it would be impossible to keep property'.[39] To rally resistance among regional elites and *obshchestvennost'* (the public sphere) Khodorkovsky undertook an extraordinary tour of the provinces, visiting Orël, Belgorod, Lipetsk, Tambov, Voronezh, Saransk, Samara, Saratov, and Nizhny Novgorod, and then he was due to visit Irkutsk, Angarsk, and Tomsk. He never made it to the last three.

Throughout Khodorkovsky pursued a strategy of personal resistance. He made clear that he would not take the Berezovsky or Gusinsky path and go into exile. Although Khodorkovsky visited the United States numerous times after the pressure on Yukos had begun, he was clear that he would return to confront whatever fate the Kremlin had in store for him. Indeed, for his October visit to Washington he travelled with his family, and thus they could have stayed together in exile. He was strongly urged by Nevzlin and others at this time to take this step. Among other things, Nevzlin considered that this would be a way of saving the company. The symptoms of political schizophrenia in Khodorkovsky thus became more pronounced. The tension between his powerful intellect and his political ambitions became ever-sharper. On the one hand, he fully appreciated the gravity of his situation and he was able in a purely intellectual manner to analyse the situation perfectly well; while on the other he appeared simply unable to appreciate the resolution and viewpoint of his opponents, and thus he fundamentally misunderstood what was going on. He was playing one game, while Sechin and other hardliners were playing another, while Putin as usual temporized, but once he made up his mind he acted decisively. With thirty to forty deputies already considered to be aligned with Yukos, and with the goal in the December 2003 to raise this to over 100 (effectively, a blocking minority) irrespective of whether they were

---

[38] Interview in *Ekspert*, 4 April 2005, p. 72.

[39] Tat'yana Vitebskaya, Vladimir Demchenko, Mariya Ignatova, Susanna Oganezova, Natal'ya Pashkalova, 'Mikhail Khodorkovskii, president kompaniya "Yukos": "Eto—poslednii boi" ', *Izvestiya*, 27 October 2003, p. 1.

liberals or communists, and with clearly expressed political ambitions for 2008, Khodorkovsky represented a real political challenge to the regime. His actions also made the other oligarchs nervous. Thus Khodorkovsky was cast to his fate.

Khodorkovsky's arrest

In the months preceding his arrest Khodorkovsky had not only made several programmatic speeches in Europe and America, but he had also toured Russia's regions meeting governors and giving a number of university lectures. In a press conference on 23 October in Saratov Khodorkovsky was open about the 'ordered subtext to these actions', referring to the pressure on his colleagues. Speaking to students in Samara on the theme of 'Oil, Society and the Development of the Russian Economy', he condemned Putin's calls to double Russian GDP in a decade as unrealizable and a dead end, and that the only way to escape from the 'energy vicious circle' was to invest in the talented minority, the intellectual elite of the country.[40] On the eve of his arrest Khodorkovsky addressed a civic forum of business and government leaders in Nizhny Novgorod which, paradoxically, discussed the legal framework for a new social contract between the state and big business.[41] Right to the end Khodorkovsky did not in his heart believe that he would be arrested, although intellectually he was well aware of the possibility. When Irina Yasina, head of Open Russia, warned him that he would be arrested, Khodorkovsky responded: 'They won't jail me. After all, they are not enemies of their own country.'[42] Eric Kraus, chief analyst at Sovlink, saw things rather differently: 'There is no rational reason for why he [Khodorkovsky] did not back down. Khodorkovsky has foreign support and a good security service. Putin has a nuclear arsenal. In a collision course, Khodorkovsky was always going to come out the loser.'[43]

Khodorkovsky was arrested on 25 October in a dawn raid on his chartered TU-134 plane at Tolmachevo airport in Novosibirsk. He had made a refuelling stop there on his journey from Nizhny Novgorod to Irkutsk, where he was due to deliver a lecture on civil society to the local Open Russia-supported school for public politics and then to go on to inspect the Yukos oil refinery in Angarsk. At 5 a.m. the plane was stormed by some 20 black-uniformed members of the FSB's anti-terror Al'fa unit, and all those on board, including flight attendants, were forced on the floor.[44] Khodorkovsky was reputed to travel with armed guards, which may explain the excessive use of force. Other FSB units also made

[40] Svetlana Bocharova and Andrei Bondarenko, 'Khodorkovskii na Volge', *Nezavisimaya gazeta*, 24 October 2003, p. 4.

[41] Kononczuk, *The 'Yukos Affair'*, p. 57, n. 52.

[42] This was repeated to me on several occasions by people who met with Khodorkovsky at this time, including Irina Yasina; Panyushkin, *Mikhail Khodorkovskii*, p. 162.

[43] Catherine Belton, 'Khodorkovsky Arrested on 7 Charges', *Moscow Times*, 27 October 2003, p. 1.

[44] Tat'yana Gurova and Aleksandr Privalov, 'My teryaem ego!', *Ekspert*, No. 41, 3 November 2003, in *Ekspert: Luchshie materialy*, No. 2, 2007, pp. 78–85, at p. 78.

heavy-handed interventions at his daughter's school. According to Belkovsky, the arrest was carried out in what was deepest night in Moscow to force Putin to accept a fait accompli. According to this account, Putin had not been able to make up his mind, and now Sechin seized the initiative to place Putin in a position where he had to accept the facts on the ground.[45] If he had ordered Khodorkovsky's release he would look weak and an instrument in the hands of others, but to accept the arrest and all that it entailed brought him into the *silovik* camp on this issue, and set Russia and his presidency on a new path. A more credible version is that two days before the arrest the prosecutor general, Vladimir Ustinov, came to Putin with a folder outlining Khodorkovsky's alleged crimes. On reading the material Putin declared: 'Let the law do its work', and the machine was thus set in motion.[46]

Khodorkovsky was arrested on the charge of not having complied with a subpoena to act as a witness in the Lebedev case. Khodorkovsky's lawyers had made it clear that he would not be able to appear in court on the set date because he was away on his regional trip. Russian law states that enforcement procedures are applied only when there is evidence of the wilful or malicious evasion of appearing as a witness. The use of FSB forces was inappropriate in the given circumstances. A number of procedural rules were violated, including the fact that the arrest of a witness took place on a holiday, and that he was taken under armed escort to Moscow, which is not the usual way to behave with a witness. Later that day he was already being questioned by the GPO investigator Salavat Karimov, who would figure in many Yukos cases. That evening judges in the Basmanny court denied bail and sanctioned his imprisonment for two months up to 30 December, later extended for another three months and similar periods thereafter up to the end of his trial. Khodorkovsky considered this was a way of preventing him dealing with the attack on Yukos.[47] The broader case against him involved seven charges, including personal income tax evasion, avoiding corporate taxes, falsifying documents, and theft (see Chapter 6). On 30 October the GPO froze 44 per cent of Yukos shares (valued at around $15 billion) belonging to various offshore Menatep affiliates, ostensibly to prevent them being transferred.[48]

First reactions

Khodorkovsky's arrest shocked the Russian and international business and political communities, but the reaction was remarkably restrained. Khodorkovsky as we have seen had been a long-time member of the Rand US–Russia Business Leader Forum, and he was due to attend a session on his return from Siberia.

---

[45] Author's interview with Stanislav Belkovsky, Moscow, 3 March 2008.
[46] Author's interview with Andrei Kolesnikov, Moscow, 19 June 2008.
[47] Vladimir Fedosenko, 'Mikhail Khodorkovskii ostaetsya za reshetkoi', *Rossiiskaya gazeta*, 2 December 2004, p. 2.
[48] Soon afterwards 4.5 per cent were unfrozen, leaving 39.5 per cent sequestered.

Members had already gathered in Moscow when news came through of his deten-tion in Novosibirsk.[49] Various oligarchs such as Fridman were in attendance, but they issued little more than a symbolic note of protest. Medvedev, however, was quite open about his opposition to the arrest. Voloshin and Kasyanov, as well as Medvedev, were not opposed to subordinating Yukos to the state, but they all opposed criminalizing the affair and arresting Khodorkovsky.[50]

On the day of the arrest the RUIE met with two other business organizations (Delovaya Rossiya and OPOR) and signed a common declaration drafted by Chubais and some others, meeting in the Balchug hotel: '[T]he escalation of actions by the authorities and law enforcement agencies against Russian busi-ness has severely damaged the atmosphere in society. Trust of business in the authorities has been undermined', and stressed that society would only be calmed by 'a clear and unambiguous statement' by President Putin.[51] Although Chubais criticized Khodorkovsky's behaviour, he categorically opposed his arrest, fearing among other things that it would damage the investment climate in Russia. How-ever, Chubais later tempered his condemnation, fearing (correctly as it turned out) that outspoken defence of the oligarch would have a negative effect on the vote for SPS in the forthcoming parliamentary elections. In an interview that evening he categorized Khodorkovsky's arrest as a 'mistake by the authorities', and went on to stress that 'a mistake by the authorities in response to mistakes by business is much graver'.[52]

Vol'sky twice spoke to Putin about Khodorkovsky's arrest and resolutely left Khodorkovsky's name on the list of members of the RUIE's bureau. Most of the rest remained silent.[53] In the aftermath of the arrest the RUIE board met twice to discuss the case, and although initially it planned to protest, its response remained low-key. Only six of the twenty-seven members of the RUIE board spoke against Khodorkovsky's arrest, and the rest accepted that the business community had to shoulder its share of the blame. Not a single leading magnate stood up publicly to defend Khodorkovsky, including the architect of privatization, Chubais. Igor Yurgens, the deputy head of the RUIE, noted how the case undermined the trust of business in the security services, that 'the selective application of law leads to it being undermined', and that the case strengthened the drift to a 'unipolar political model in which 'parties and governors are totally dependent on the Kremlin'.[54] The RUIE was as divided as its membership. A survey of the heads of eighty-three companies conducted by the business journal *Kompaniya* in the early stages of the Yukos affair found that they were split over whether it threatened private property, but an absolute majority did not think that the case would

---

[49] Author's interview with Angela Stent, Director of the Center for Eurasian, Russian, and East European Studies at Georgetown University, 29 November 2007, who was present at the meeting.

[50] Author's interview with Alexei Vendediktov, Moscow, 19 June 2008.

[51] Gurova and Privalov, 'My teryaem ego!', p. 78; Kryshtanovkaya, *Anatomiya rossiiskoi elity*, p. 364.

[52] Andrei Kolesnikov, *Anatolii Chubais: Biografiya* (Moscow, AST Moskva, 2008) p. 204.

[53] Ibid.

[54] *Ekspert*, No. 41, 3 November 2003, in *Ekspert: Luchshie materialy*, No. 2, 2007, p. 78.

affect their business or their relations with state agencies.[55] Many business leaders agreed with the regime that Khodorkovsky had defected from the unwritten conventions of political behaviour and had reneged on the unwritten rules of the game.

Putin on 27 October responded to the calls of business organizations and politicians to comment on the Yukos affair. His response was irrevocable, insisting that there would be 'no meetings or deals over the work of the law enforcement agencies', and if the courts held Khodorkovsky, they must have a case, and argued that all were equal before the law, including 'a big businessman, irrespective of how many billions he had in his personal or corporate accounts'. However, he acknowledged the concerns of the business community, remembering how in the Soviet period specific cases turned into general campaigns. The charges laid against Khodorkovsky could have been preferred against any number of tycoons of the era, and the analogy was drawn with the trial against the alleged 'Industrial Party' in 1929 that signalled the beginning of the era of Stalinist repression.[56] However, Putin insisted that 'in connection with the case under discussion there would be no generalisation, analogies, precedents, in particular associated with the results of privatisation', but warned against 'speculation and hysterics' and forbade the government to 'get involved in this discussion'.[57] Putin affirmed that the fundamental principles of the 'equidistance' period would not be repudiated: the privatizations of the 1990s would not be revised as long as business continued to pay informal rents to the regime, supported its socio-economic projects and kept out of politics. The inadequacies of the equidistance model were also perpetuated, notably the failure to institutionalize stable business–politics relations, the continued prevalence of informal rules, and the Byzantine struggle of factions for power and property.

At an extended meeting with 800 RUIE business leaders on 14 November 2003, Putin was greeted by extended applause, rather surprisingly in the light of recent events. In his final address Putin noted that 'it is sometimes hard to tell where business ends and the state begins; and where the state ends and business begins', and condemned the use of security agencies in business conflicts; noting that in connection with a 'specific case' (obviously Yukos was meant) 'one must apply a certain legal culture and not drift into extra-procedural decisions'.[58] Delegates carefully avoided the Yukos question, but Putin raised the issue himself, which was awarded an ovation. In comments that are not repeated in the official text, he asserted that the Yukos case was an isolated event and that there would be no return to the past, but that the law must be upheld.[59] He insisted that Russian business 'must develop a new system of social guarantees for the population in accordance with the new demands of the time'.[60] Business responded to the

---

[55] Cited by Volkov, 'The Yukos Affair', p. 5.   [56] Gurova and Privalov, 'My teryaem ego!', p. 79.

[57] Statement to the Cabinet, http://www.kremlin.ru/text/appears/2003/10/54587.shtml.

[58] http://www.kremlin.ru/text/appears/2003/11/55586.shtml.

[59] Kolesnikov, *Vladimir Putin: Ravnoudalenie oligarkhov*, pp. 130–1.

[60] Rutland, 'Business and Civil Society in Russia', p. 86; from Interfax, 14 November 2003, www.interfax-news.com.

calls and supported the government's various programmes, including support for service personnel wounded in Chechnya. The RUIE bureau meeting soon after, with no discussion, appointed Victor Vekselberg to replace Khodorkovsky at the head of its committee for international cooperation, but Khodorkovsky formally remained a member of the bureau.[61]

When asked on television in July 2004 who he thought was behind the attack on Yukos, Vol'sky refused to answer: 'I am very scared to name names now', he said. 'I am simply scared. I have six grandchildren, after all, and I want them to live.'[62] When thirty-three business representatives (including twenty-two from RUIE) met with Putin on 1 July 2004, they agreed in advance not to raise the Yukos question. Potanin, who has a long history of working closely with the Kremlin, was apparently the key figure in ensuring that the RUIE did not make much of the Khodorkovsky case. Potanin was instrumental in ensuring that Alexander Shokhin, Surkov's favoured candidate, in October 2005 replaced Vol'sky, who had been a critic of Khodorkovsky's arrest. Nevzlin's hopes that Yukos could use Surkov's old links with the company to help Khodorkovsky proved illusory.[63] Surkov by 2003 had become a completely loyal member of Putin's team. Surkov kept a discreet silence over his relations with Khodorkovsky, and he was certainly no friend of Yukos in the presidential administration.

Political fallout

In a rather disturbing echo of Stalinist practices, some fifty writers, scientists, cosmonauts, and artists issued a public letter in which they called for an exemplary sentence to be imposed on the fallen oligarch.[64] Abramovich as we shall see sought to take advantage of Khodorkovsky's position to take over the new Yukos-Sibneft company. The opposition parties restricted themselves to critical declarations, and even Yabloko and SPS, those most affected by Khodorkovsky's arrest, refused to take protest to the streets. Even the Yukos management was at a loss to think of an effective response.

Those who revealed themselves not to be entirely loyal became political casualties of the Yukos affair. Just five days after Khodorkovsky's arrest Voloshin resigned as head of the presidential administration, the most immediate political casualty of the shifting balance of power in the Kremlin. Voloshin's departure on 30 October represented a defeat for the old Yeltsin style of political management.

[61] 'Eks-glava Yukosa fakticheskii vyveden iz sostava byuro RSPP', *Gazeta*, 17 November 2005, p. 2.

[62] Peter Baker, 'Putin Finding Power in the Pump', *Washington Post*, 11 August 2004, p. A01; Philip Hanson and Elizabeth Teague, 'Big Business and the State in Russia', *Europe-Asia Studies*, Vol. 57, No. 5, July 2005, p. 664.

[63] Tokareva, *Kto podstavil khodorskovskogo*, p. 226.

[64] The effect of the letter, authored by talk show host Alexander Gordon, was minimal and was largely derided in the media, for example Yulia Latynina, 'Ideology is For Intellectuals', *Moscow Times*, 8 February 2006, who notes: 'The Kremlin doesn't need guidance from intellectuals, because it has no interest in ideology. What the Kremlin needs is publicity. An ideology implies a clear and consistent system of values. The Kremlin wants to leave itself plenty of room to maneuver.'

In a late July 2003 meeting with journalists Voloshin, as noted, conceded that the case represented a political campaign against Yukos, but insisted that Putin had not known about it in advance.[65] Following Voloshin's resignation it appears that Putin threw his weight behind the continued attack on Yukos and Khodorkovsky personally. Sechin's role in all of this appears consistent: the political attack on Yukos allowed him to expand his economic fiefdom; and the development of Rosneft at Yukos's expense allowed the state to pursue a number of strategic priorities, which we shall explore later. However, Voloshin's replacement as head of the presidential administration was not a *silovik* but the St Petersburg lawyer Dmitry Medvedev, and the economic liberals in the government remained in their posts. In addition, Voloshin remained chair of the board of directors of RAO UES, and thus the electricity monopoly remained a bastion of liberals to balance the *silovik* stronghold in Rosneft. Gazprom was torn between the two, and Medvedev engaged in an intense struggle to prevent a *silovik* takeover of the gas corporation, for which he called on the Petersburg liberals for help.[66] One manifestation of this struggle was the conflict over merger with Rosneft (Chapter 10).

Some leading politicians, even at the highest level, were demoted when they criticized the affair. Kasyanov had called the arrest of Lebedev 'excessive', and argued that the situation surrounding Yukos had a deleterious effect on Russia's image and alarmed potential investors. In late 2003 he again expressed concern about the freezing of Yukos shares. The 'politburo' had long agitated for his dismissal, as one of the few independent figures in the regime ready to question Putin's judgement, as over the handling of the Dubrovka theatre siege in October 2002. Kasyanov was summarily dismissed on 24 February 2004, a fortnight before the presidential elections.[67] There are rumours that he was sacked because of his attempt to get involved in the distribution of Yukos assets.[68] In May 2005 he argued: 'This trial is a farce. The Khodorkovsky case has brought Russia to a turning point, while the verdict could mean that the point of no return will be passed.'[69]

Kasyanov's replacement, Mikhail Fradkov, was a compromise figure in the factional struggle in Putin's entourage but he was clearly affiliated with the hardliners. In the cabinet reshuffle the Yukos-friendly energy minister Igor Yusufov left his post, and the ministry itself was merged with industry under a new minister, Victor Khristenko, who had no close relationship with Yukos. The new federal energy agency in the new ministry was headed by Sergei Oganesyan, who had previously worked as a vice president in Rosneft. Thus Yukos was systematically deprived of administrative cover. It also lost political cover with the failure of the two main liberal parties, Yabloko and the SPS, to pass the 5 per cent representation threshold, and thus the Fourth Duma (2003–07) lacked a liberal caucus. The

[65] Woodruff, *Khodorkovsky's Gamble*, p. 4.   [66] Simonov, *Russkaya neft'*, pp. 175–6.

[67] 'Illarionov Says Yukos Affair is Political', *Eurasia Daily Monitor*, Vol. 1, No. 126, 12 November 2004.

[68] Andrei Gromov, Tat'yana Gurova, Oleg Kashin, and Maksim Rubchenko, 'Ne po tsarskoi vole', *Ekspert*, No. 44, 21 November 2005, in *Ekspert: Luchshie materialy*, No. 2, 2007, pp. 114–18, at p. 114.

[69] Valeriya Korchagina, 'Kasyanov Steps Up Criticism of Putin', *Moscow Times*, 20 May 2005, p. 3.

'liberal debacle', as Vladmir Ryzhkov termed it, provoked one of Khodorkovsky's most interesting commentaries on contemporary Russian politics, 'The Crisis of Russian Liberalism' (see Chapter 8). It is still not clear why the liberals did not make more of the obvious issue that the procuracy was being used for blatant political goals.

The response of the liberal parties was remarkably mute. This paralysis of the liberal spirit may well have been provoked in part by fear, but probably more importantly was the lack of conviction that the property acquired in the 1990s was legitimate and that its new owners had acted wisely as its custodian. The liberal parties hesitated to claim credit for the growing economic success of the country. Yabloko of course could not do so, since it had criticized every step of the way in the 1990s, while SPS was dogged by its negative features. As a powerful commentary put it at the time: 'If a single leading party seriously depended on the views of its electorate, it would be banging every available bell over the Yukos case: it's not every day that there is such an opportunity to outline one's views and the interests of one's electorate—and this just before an election.'[70]

Politicians in this election, however, were banging a very different bell. There was much talk at the time of the big energy companies having to pay a 'resource rent' ('prirodnaya renta'), effectively something akin to New Labour's 'windfall tax' imposed on companies on coming to power in 1997. The liberals estimated that this could bring in about $3 billion, while Glaz'ev talked of up to $40 billion. There was no agreement among political leaders on the issue, and in response, as one commentator put it: 'Not receiving a reply from the elites, the president will have to seek and find an answer himself, thus demonstrating the superfluity of the elite.'[71] As the interviewer put it to the then head of the presidential administration, Medvedev, 'there are practically no parties actively defending freedom, private life and the associated property rights, and thus the presidential administration actively participated in structuring political space in Russia'. Medvedev conceded that '[t]he absence of a normal rightist ideology gives rise to substitutes and prejudices'.[72] He went on to argue that '[t]raditional state capitalism is a dead-end path for economic development', but he did recognize that 'state companies have far from exhausted their potential'.[73] As chair of the board at Gazprom, he was in a position to know.

The 2003 election took place in the shadow of the 'redistribution of natural rent'. Voters were faced with a clear choice between supporting the assault against the oligarchs and voting against the authorities. In the event, in giving such strong support to the pro-presidential party, the Yukos case was given some sort of popular legitimacy. As the journalist Sonin notes:

---

[70] Tat'yana Gurova, Aleksandr Privalov, and Valerii Fadeev, 'Nasha malen'kaya svoboda', *Ekspert*, No. 33, 8 September 2003, in *Ekspert: Luchshie materialy*, No. 2, 2007, pp. 68–75, at p. 73.

[71] Valerii Fadeev, 'Opasnost' prostoty', *Ekspert*, No. 1, 12 January 2004, in *Ekspert: Luchshie materialy*, No. 2, 2007, pp. 86–8, at p. 87.

[72] Interviewed by Valerii Fadeev, 'Sokhranit' effektivnoe gosudarstvo v sushchestvuyushchikh granitsakh', *Ekspert*, No. 13, 4 April 2005, in *Ekspert: Luchshie materialy*, No. 2, 2007, pp. 100–5, at p. 100.

[73] Ibid., p. 104.

It is entirely possible that Khodorkovsky might be a free man today and Sibneft might still be in private hands if United Russia had garnered only 25 percent of the vote instead of the 40 percent that it actually polled in 2003 and the Union of Right Forces and Yabloko had ended up with some of the Duma seats that went to Rodina. The Putin administration can be accused of many sins, but there is no denying that its actions and policies have more closely reflected the public mood than did President Boris Yeltsin's elitist, more progressive government.[74]

In the presidential election of March 2004 Irina Khakamada's candidature, on behalf of the rump liberals, was supported by Khodorkovsky's former deputy Nevzlin. Her provocative statements concerning the Dubrovka siege, when a group of Chechens took hostage over a thousand members of the audience watching the popular Nord-Ost musical, much weakened her appeal, and clearly enraged Putin—as most issues associated with Chechnya tended to do. Nevzlin's involvement in the campaign only intensified the administration's animus against Yukos. The division between Khodorkovsky and his former colleague, Nevzlin, became apparent at this time. It was soon after this that Khodorkovsky changed his tactics and issued his first major letter from prison, 'The Crisis of Russian Liberalism', which we shall discuss in Chapter 8.

In his address to the Federal Assembly on 26 May 2004 Putin revealed the emergence of a gulf between words and deeds, suggesting that instead of a dialogue between the leader and the people the discussion was beginning to take the form of a monologue. His comments about non-governmental organizations that are 'fed by an alien hand' harked back to the Soviet era.[75] The speech was imbued with a paternalistic and bureaucratic approach to the problem of managing society, rather than reflecting a confident and pluralistic democratic community of equal citizens. Equally, the tone of Western commentators concerning Russia became more harshly reminiscent of Cold War times. An 'Open Letter to the Heads of State and Government of the European Union and NATO' by some fifty public figures, published on 28 September 2004, castigated political developments under Putin and in particular the attack on Yukos.[76]

MURKY MATTERS

Defenders of the Yukos leadership make the quite justifiable claim that in its rise to prominence and then in its business practices they did nothing that other companies were not doing, and in some cases (as with tax minimization schemes) probably less than some, notably Sibneft. Some of their tax and other financial

[74] Konstantin Sonin, 'Election Still waiting for the Big Question', *Moscow Times*, 11 September 2007, p. 10.
[75] Vladimir Putin, 'Poslanie Federal'nomu Sobraniyu Rossiiskoi Federatsii', *Rossiiskaya gazeta*, 27 May 2004.
[76] For an accusation that the letter was inspired by people funded by Khodorkovsky, see Eric Kraus, 'Return to Sender', *Moscow Times*, 6 October 2004.

machinations, moreover, were legal at the time. This is undoubtedly true, but the Yukos defence is undermined by something that is hard to define but which from early on was a recognizable 'Yukosian' spirit or style. This was also the case, in a different way, with everything associated with Berezovsky, described so well by Pavel Khlebnikov (in English Klebnikov), although the latter's views were contested in various court cases by Berezovsky. The Yukos defence is rather weakened by the distinctive energy with which it invested its activities. The Russian government's attack on Yukos, portrayed by Yukos defenders as political, was in part an assault against the murky world of financial manipulations.

Paris and beyond

This was notably the case in the development of myriad offshore companies. The exposure by the Paris-based former Yukos associate Elena Collongues-Popova of the way that taxes were avoided by these companies took the lid of what turned out to be some quite extraordinary activity.[77] Her first husband was a KGB colonel, and after the marriage broke up she moved to France, where she gained French citizenship. She worked for Alexei Golubovich (then financial director of Yukos) between 1996 and 2000 and admitted to placing over a billion dollars transferred by Golubovich from Moscow into some thirty offshore accounts. When she began to have problems with French tax officials, she argued that she had been acting on behalf of Menatep in transferring Yukos shares abroad to avoid creditors and to obscure Yukos ownership. The French tax police found that she had been moving large money transfers between offshore accounts owned by Golubovich, who was also the director of the Swiss-based Menatep SA. Collongues-Popova claimed that she used offshore companies to achieve 'back-to-back' sales of Rosprom-held shares, in which shares would be transferred to an offshore company which represented a real buyer when in fact they were selling to themselves, which would then be rolled into a final buyer, and thus taxes would be evaded.[78]

The police raided her apartment in October 1998 when looking for evidence in connection with the BONY scandal. Police seized thousands of documents filed in boxes at her home relating to Menatep, Rosprom, Yukos, and Avisma. She was ordered to pay back taxes of $15 million, a sum including a $1 million fine she received in a criminal trial in Paris where she was sentenced to a year in jail, suspended if she paid the fine. She was particularly incensed because it appeared that Yukos in 1999 and 2000 tried to disown her and refused to help. In a bizarre twist to the story, she alleges that Golubovich forged her signature to transfer shares from shell companies back to Menatep, as part of the operation to clean up Yukos's financial operations. In other words, documents were forged as part of Yukos's reinvention as a more transparent company. When Collongues-Popova tried to take over a Swiss account opened by her for Golubovich in her name, he

[77] Jeanne Whalen, 'A Jilted Banker's View of Khodorkovsky's Empire', *Wall Street Journal*, 2 January 2004.
[78] Lucy Komisar, 'Menatep Paper Trail', *The Russia Journal*, 5 November 2003.

objected and he and his wife started a bitter legal battle. Collongues-Popova later offered evidence in the Yukos case, but although offered immunity she refused to return to Russia to give evidence in person.

There is also a connection between the Yukos affair and the Alexander Litvinenko case. Litvinenko was a former FSB officer who had been associated with Berezovsky since 1994 and fled to London in November 2000 to join Berezovsky in campaigning against Putin's regime. He was apparently poisoned with polonium-210 on 1 November 2006 and died on 23 November. Soon after Litvinenko's death, the *Observer* ran a story about Yulia Svetlichnaya, in which she describes her meeting with Litvinenko. She described him as an eccentric, governed by wild fantasies of being some sort of Chechen warrior, extravagant claims, and prone to indulge in blackmail. She accused him of possessing documents that he planned to use to blackmail leading Russians politicians and businesspeople.[79] In his last investigation Litvinenko claimed to have discovered a plan by the FSB to claw back millions from oligarchs who had gone into exile, most of whom had worked for Yukos. He claimed to have a list detailing the amounts to be taken from each of the targets, and that teams of Russian agents were scouring foreign countries in search of them. He visited some of the victims to warn them of alleged Russian plans to intimidate them and their families to extort money. Litvinenko, typically, stated that he was too scared to commit the details of the alleged plot to paper, and insisted on telling those involved in person. Litvinenko secretly flew to Israel a fortnight before his poisoning to meet Nevzlin, who was top of the alleged hit list. Nevzlin later argued that the Litvinenko investigation 'shed light on most significant aspects of the Yukos affair', and asserted that Litvinenko's poking about in the Yukos affair was the reason that his enemies in the Kremlin had him silenced.[80] Nevzlin apparently passed the dossier to Scotland Yard, although since Litvinenko had not written down the material, it is unclear what was in the file. The GPO later suggested that Nevzlin himself may have been behind Litvinenko's murder.[81]

By then Stephen Curtis had died in a helicopter crash not far from Bournemouth on 4 March 2004, a fortnight after he had gone to Scotland Yard saying that he had received death threats and that he feared that Moscow had sent a hit team to assassinate him. He chaired a company funded by Russian oligarchs (including Nevzlin), ISC Global, whose last project had been to discredit Putin and those around him, allegedly with the help of British security officials.[82] Curtis's

[79] Mark Townsend, Jamie Doward and Tom Parfitt, 'The Litvinenko Affair', *The Observer*, 3 December 2006, p. 2. The propaganda war over Litvinenko's death is a fascinating story in itself, with a particularly distorting role played by the Murdoch press and the Berezovsky and Bell-Pottinger PR machine, but that is not our concern here.

[80] Daniel McGregory and Tony Halpin, 'Spies Sent "To Seize Cash from Yukos Exiles"', *The Times*, 9 December 2006.

[81] Sam Jones, 'Kremlin Claims Ex-Yukos Chief Ordered Murder of Litvinenko', *The Guardian*, 28 December 2006, p. 16.

[82] Reported in *The Sunday Times*, 14 May 2006, in Catherine Belton, 'Menatep Boss Tried to Smear Putin', *Moscow Times*, 15 May 2006, p. 5.

law company had represented Berezovsky in the British courts in the latter's libel case against an article by Pavel Khlebnikov in *Forbes* magazine on 30 December 1996 describing him as 'the godfather of the Kremlin'. The case began in 1997 and dragged on for six years, in which time Khlebnikov published a book of the same title, detailing Berezovsky's alleged criminal activities. In 2003, the court ruled in Berezovsky's favour, although not with great enthusiasm.

Litvinenko's motives for getting involved in the Yukos affair are unclear. Svetlichnaya claims that Litvinenko had confided to her his plans to blackmail some of those on the FSB target list. She claimed to have received over 100 emails from him in the days before his poisoning.[83] Svetlichnaya's account was attacked in the press, and indeed she had been disingenuous in describing her role. She claimed to be writing a book about Chechnya, as well as being a student at the University of Westminster, but it turned out that she worked as communications director at 'Russkie Investory' (Russian Investors), a brokerage company established in 1994 and run by none other than Golubovich.[84] Golubovich himself had been placed under house arrest in Italy on 10 May 2006 because of suspected embezzlement and fraud and then extradited to Russia, where he became an adviser to the FSB and was placed in a witness protection programme. Thus Golubovich saved his skin by co-operating, a model the authorities encouraged others to follow. When refused, as in the case of Svetlana Bakhmina, the authorities were implacable in their pursuit of 'justice'.

Litvinenko had tried to draw Collongues-Popova for information about bribes and the offshore banking links associated with Yukos's former oil refinery Maziekiu Nafta in Lithuania. More to the point, Litvinenko appears to have been collecting information on Golubovich, on whom Collongues-Popova had no shortage of material. Litvinenko's associate Yevgeny Limarev (the person who had warned Mario Scaramello—a consultant to the Mitrokhin commission investigating Russian intelligence activity in Italy—about an alleged Russian plot to murder him, along with Litvinenko and Limarev himself) travelled to Paris to meet Collongues-Popova and her partner, the businessperson who had also worked with Golubovich, Roger Kinsbourg. At the time when Litvinenko was flying to Israel with a dossier on the Yukos affair one of Yukos's founders, Yuri Golubev, was found dead in his London flat.[85] Litvinenko had also apparently provided information that in May 2004 led to the arrest of nine alleged criminals, including the Yukos lawyer Alexander Gofstein.[86] There is thus a link between Litvinenko's death and the Yukos affair, but the precise details remain unknown.

[83] McGregory and Halpin, 'Spies Sent "To Seize Cash from Yukos Exiles"'.

[84] Hilde Harbo, 'Odd Links in Litvinenko Smear', *Aftenposten*, 6 December 2006; http://www.aftenposten.no/english/world/article1559336.ece.

[85] Lucy Komisar, 'The Strange Case of Dirt-Peddler De-Luxe and "Dubious Julia"', 17 January 2007, http://www.thecopydude.com/?p=131.

[86] Lucy Komisar, 'Poisoned Russian Linked to Investigation of Possibly Bribes by Ex-Yukos Official', The Komisar Scoop, 27 December 2006, http://thekomisarscoop.com/2006/12/27/poisoned-russian-linked-to-investigation-of-possible-bribes-by-ex-yukos-official.

The Maziekiu scandal involved Lithuania's former prime minister, Algirdas Brazauskas. Built to run on Russian crude, when the refinery was privatized in 1999 the Lithuanian government tried to find a non-Russian partner to reduce dependence (even though reliant on Russian oil), and sold a strategic stake to the American company, Williams International. However, this company fell into financial difficulties and sold its stake to Yukos; and Yukos lodged its majority share in the refinery with its Dutch subsidiary Yukos International Ltd. In his meetings with Collongues-Popova and Kinsbourg, Limarev was looking for evidence of corruption in the Russian government, and also details of the relationship between Golubovich and Brazauskas, above all any details of bribes. Kristina, Brazauskas's wife, was a close friend of Olga Mirimskaya, Golubovich's wife, who conducted extensive banking operations in the Baltic republics. Golubovich came into conflict with his former Yukos colleagues, notably Nevzlin and Brudno, over control of Maziekiu, as well as over his share of Yukos assets in Holland, Switzerland, and the Czech Republic. In an interview in December 2005 Golubovich claimed that his Menatep assets were being taken from him by his former associates, and in 2006 he was forced to sell his shares in the company.[87]

Avisma, Valmet, and shell companies

The review of the privatization of the Apatit fertilizer company in 1994 was the starting signal for the Yukos affair, but a number of other cases are also relevant. Menatep's interest in Avisma, the giant titanium company, has not been raised directly in any of the Yukos trials, yet looms large in the story. Menatep in a 1995 auction won a majority share in Avisma, and its financial flows had allegedly been diverted to Switzerland, in a manner reminiscent of the way that Berezovsky had been accused of siphoning Aeroflot's cash flow through his Swiss company Andava. The case also involved the billionaire Kenneth Dart and two other American citizens, who on 17 September 1997 bought over $85 million of Avisma stocks from Yukos, and in part payment transferred $74 million to Bank Leu to accounts managed by Collongues-Popova. Dart, a scion of the founder of the Dart Container Corporation, was himself no stranger to aggressive tax minimization strategies, and had apparently taken Irish citizenship to escape the clutches of the IRS. The USAID associate Jonathan Hay was also involved through his affiliation with US-based Dart Management, and in that capacity was appointed to the board of Avisma. Hay also provoked considerable controversy over his involvement with an American-sponsored aid programme to Russia, and was later sued by the US government. In a legal claim against Menatep, Dart accused the Irish-based TMC Trading International of controlling the sale of Avisma's produce and excluding the Dart minority interest from a share in the profits. This was a classic case in which an offshore or Swiss company was designated 'nominee' owner in official papers, and the identity of the real or 'beneficial' owner was obscured.

[87] Komisar, 'Poisoned Russian Linked to Investigation'.

TMC was by all accounts little more than a shell company. It shared offices in Dublin with Valmet, its alleged creator. Valmet's main activity indeed was the creation of offshore companies to the order of clients, and thus was the mother of all shell companies and did a brisk business with Khodorkovsky and his associates. The list of offshore companies owned by Khodorkovsky and his associates runs into the many dozens, possibly hundreds, employing the usual gamut of techniques, including creating networks in a series of three with similar names, a process called layering or laddering. The Houston-based energy supplier Enron was another company which took full advantage of corporate secrecy rules, with 780 shell companies in Grand Cayman alone and another 80 in the Turks & Caicos islands, which under its chief executive Kenneth Lay allowed the company to deceive investors, regulators, and the American tax authorities until the whole edifice came crashing down in late 2001. By 2003 over 50 per cent of Yukos shares were reputedly owned by wholly owned Menatep subsidiaries called Yukos Universal, based in the Isle of Man, and Hulley Enterprise Ltd, domiciled in Cyprus. Khodorkovsky apparently controlled Group Menatep through a small direct investment and a larger share held in a 'special trust'. The corporate structure of Yukos-Menatep was allegedly designed by the Clifford Chance law firm and the Swiss bank UBS.[88] The well-known financial adviser Peter Bond was one of the key operators of Valmet, which also had offices in the Isle of Man and Bermuda. He was accused of running the Avisma scheme on behalf of Bank Menatep; but in typical Yukosian manner, Menatep was itself one of the owners of Valmet's holding company, the Bermuda-based Valmet Group, a nice case of laddering by the mother of all ladders.

Even in the era of rampant neo-liberalism a limit had been reached. Two former bankers, André Strebel, a Swiss citizen and Ernest Backes of Luxembourg, on 26 November 2003 filed charges with the Swiss attorney general against Khodorkovsky, Lebedev, and Golubovich, accusing them of fraud, asset-stripping, and supporting a criminal organization. Backes was the co-author (with the French journalist Denis Robert) of the book *Revelation$*, which exposed the double bookkeeping and other alleged nefarious activities of the financial clearing house, Clearstream (formed in 1999 out of the merger of Cedel and the compensation company of the Deutsche Bourse). Menatep opened a non-published Cedel account in May 1997, and also made a number of cash transactions, a further breach of the rules; and there was also heavy traffic between Menatep and BONY, much involving Natasha Gurfinkel-Kagalovsky, the wife of the Menatep vice president who was head of the department dealing with Russia, a post she had to leave in 1999 when the American government began to investigate money-laundering issues. Strebel and Backes called on the Swiss authorities to investigate the activities of the Swiss offices of Menatep SA, Menatap Finances SA, Valmet (in liquidation at the time) and Bank Leu associated with alleged fraud against

[88] *Time* (Europe), November 2003; cited by Stephanie Ayres, 'Yukos: A Big Oil Company's Fate at Stake in Billion-Dollar Russian Tax Roulette', Part I, 'Yukos, Apatit, and Avisma', *Financial Crime News*, October 2005, p. 2, http://home.att.net/~fcwriter/features26.htm.

Avisma and money laundering by Menatep. The suit claimed that since its creation 'the Bank Menatep SA has been mixed with the affairs of members of the Russian oligarchy and criminal organizations, such as Mikhail Khodorkovsky and Alexander Konanykhine. It is also related to another mafia figure, Semyon Mogilevich, called the godfather of organized crime in Russia'.[89] The two claimed that tens of millions of dollars had been diverted away from Avisma through transfer pricing schemes in which titanium was sold cheaply to the shell company TMC, and then sold at market prices abroad.

This is the classic way of avoiding taxes and cheating minority shareholders. The complaint cited the evidence of Collongues-Popova that in 1998 up to $300 million was transferred from various companies by Golubovich to Bank Leu and other Swiss accounts. Strebel argued that the suit was filed in the belief that '[t]his activity by Lebedev and Khodorkovsky must be stopped': 'There are thousands of Lebedevs and Khodorkovskys. If we stop them, maybe the other 900 Khodorkovskys will think a little about it. If we don't start with one or two or three, there is no reason to do anything.' As for why Khodorkovsky was singled out, Strebel responded: 'Because he is one of the significant examples of this criminal activity, because he was able to make $8 billion in three years. He was the perfect example.'[90] Khodorkovsky may well have been an egregious example of the way that offshore tax havens facilitated dubious operations, but as a recent work by Misha Glenny argues, they also allowed the anarchic development of transnational crime and encouraged the degeneration of international finance capitalism into little more than organized banditry.[91] The crash of 2008 was Enron writ large.

THE ATTACK ON YUKOS

We will discuss the judicial trials against Khodorkovsky and his associates in Chapter 6, but at this point we will return to the fate of the company. The attack on the man and the assault on the company are analytically distinct, although overlapped almost from the first. However, what began as isolated incidents against Yukos, by mid-2004 turned into a sustained assault that in the end brought the company to its knees. To insulate the company, Khodorkovsky quickly divested himself of direct responsibility. On his arrest Alexander Temerko took over as head of the board of directors in Moscow, charged with the Herculean task of leading Yukos's defence against the assault by state officials. In the spring of 2004 Khodorkovsky formally lost control over the company, and in January 2005 responsibility for Menatep, still one of the main shareholders in Yukos, was transferred to Nevzlin. However, without a recognized and authoritative leader at its head who could fight

---

[89] Lucy Komisar, 'Criminal Complaint Filed Against Khodorkovsky, Lebedev, and Golubovich in Switzerland', *The Russia Journal*, 28 November 2003.

[90] Komisar, 'Criminal Complaint Filed Against Khodorkovsky'.

[91] Misha Glenny, *McMafia: Crime Without Frontiers* (London, The Bodley Head, 2008).

for the company in Russia's tribal politics, the company was effectively defenceless. Khodorkovsky himself was transformed, as he put it in his letter 'Property and Freedom' (see Chapter 8), from one of the richest businessmen in the world into a 'member of the middle class', a 'straightforward citizen'.

Yukos after Khodorkovsky

The attack on Khodorkovsky personally and the assault against the Yukos oil company are distinct processes, yet in practice after his arrest they are almost impossible to separate. The struggle against Khodorkovsky boiled down to the challenge posed by an over-mighty subject, but even before his arrest in October 2003 investigation into the tax affairs of Yukos had begun. Punitive tax claims were imposed soon after, with the tax ministry in December claiming that Yukos between 1998 and 2003 had underpaid its taxes by some $5 billion through tax breaks for investments in the regions and through transfer pricing. Nevertheless, the evidence suggests that the government did not set out with the intention of destroying the company.[92] Shareholders certainly believed this, and the stock price rallied in April 2004 before beginning the long but irregular decline into worthlessness (see Table 5.1 for total capitalization). At the end of February 2003 the RTS share price was $10.93, reaching a historic peak of $15.92 on 16 October 2003 before falling to $9.51 on 10 December and then rising to just below the earlier peak to $15.54 on 12 April 2004. The price then fell to $6.20 on 16 June but rallied to $9.25 when on 17 June Putin in Tashkent declared that the government was not interested in Yukos's bankruptcy, although he stressed that the company's fate would be decided by the courts. This spurred the biggest stock market rally since he had come to power, with Yukos shares alone rising by an astonishing 34.2 per cent.[93] This encouraged Yukos to propose yet another plan to pay off what was then a $3.4 billion tax demand, including a staged buyout of the Menatep stake, although not all in Yukos supported the proposal. This deal, like all others, was rejected by the government. A month later the announcement on 20 July of the sale of Yuganskneftegaz, Yukos's main production unit, as payment for the tax bill drove down the share price, from which it never recovered. The share price was $0.21 on 6 November 2007 when trading in Yukos stopped.[94]

---

[92] Hanson cites an anonymous source that when in pre-trial detention Khodorkovsky had been offered a deal whereby all charges would be dropped if he surrendered his assets, but the offer had been refused since Khodorkovsky believed that the authorities would not dare to honour its promise since it would be so damaging to the country's business reputation, Philip Hanson, 'The Russian Economic Puzzle: Going Forwards, Backwards or Sideways?', *International Affairs*, Vol. 83, No. 5, September–October 2007, p. 880, n. 24. Khodorkovsky was probably right, and in addition the details of to whom the company would be transferred and how remained unclear.

[93] Simonov, *Russkaya neft'*, p. 107; Catherine Belton, 'Putin Tip Powers Yukos Recovery', *Moscow Times*, 18 June 2004, p. 1.

[94] All share prices from 'Chto dostalos' ot Yukosa', *Kommersant-Vlast'*, No. 45, 19 November 2007, pp. 40–1.

Table 5.1. Yukos capitalization

Date	Ordinary shares (million USD)
December 2000	3,796.6
December 2001	10,636.9
December 2002	19,711.1
June 2003	29,688.6
August 2003	32,954.9
September 2003	33,481.9
November 2003	30,954.5
December 2003	27,752.2
February 2004	32,148.7
March 2004	36,933.5
May 2004	26,816.2
June 2004	18,268.5

Source: Nina Poussenkova, *From Rigs to Riches: Oilmen Vs. Financiers in the Russian Oil Sector* (Rice University, TX, The James A. Baker III Institute for Public Policy, October 2004), p. 49.

According to Eric Kraus, Sovlink's chief equity strategist: 'It looks like Menatep is trying to bring down everything with it, while the government appears to be willing to inflict as much damage as need be.' Caught in the crossfire, international investors were the main victims.[95] The reaction of Menatep stockholders and Yukos management in the wake of Khodorkovsky's arrest encouraged those in the regime favouring a hard line.[96] The method chosen was a review of the company's tax affairs, with accounts that had long been signed off reopened, as well as a half-hearted attempt to withdraw licences from the company on environmental grounds.[97] As each push against Yukos encountered relatively little and always confused resistance, the attack was intensified.

In the wake of Khodorkovsky's arrest the management system of Yukos was restructured. On 28 October 2003, three days after his arrest, it became known that Khodorkovsky would not be on the joint Yukos–Sibneft board, although it was claimed that this had been the plan from the start. Operational management passed to a reprofiled Yukos board headed by Temerko; the brief was to fight the various tax liabilities, and to try to save the company. On 3 November Khodorkovsky resigned from the directorship of Yukos, arguing that he wished to prevent the 'Khodorkovsky affair' becoming the 'Yukos affair', and announced that he would focus on his work as head of Open

---

[95] Catherine Belton, 'Investors Caught in Yukos Crossfire', *Moscow Times*, 22 July 2004, p. 1.

[96] Interview with senior Yukos official who prefers to remain anonymous.

[97] The idea had been mooted by Vitalii Artyukhov as one of his last acts as natural resources minister before his dismissal in March 2004, Miriam Elder, 'The Mysterious Influence of Inspector Mitvol', *Moscow Times*, 12 December 2006. Oleg Mitvol, deputy to the new minister, Yuri Trutnev, led the way in using environmental concerns to review the ownership structure of projects in Sakhalin and elsewhere.

Russia,[98] not something that the authorities were pleased to hear. Khodorkovsky's shares in Yukos were frozen by the prosecutor general to prevent their sale, although Nevzlin on 12 January 2005 received Khodorkovsky's 60 per cent share in Group Menatep, which controlled the company.[99] Khodorkovsky's offer to hand over his share of Yukos to pay the tax bill was ignored, since that would mean lifting the freeze on Menatep's majority stake in Yukos. Despite Khodorkovsky's renewed offer in July 2004 of surrendering his 59.5 per cent share in Menatep, finance minister Kudrin argued that time had run out on restructuring what had now become an $8 billion tax bill for the year 2000 alone.[100] The result was the forced sale of Yukos's main asset, YNG, in December 2004. Khodorkovsky argued that 'with the sale of YNG I am freed of all responsibility for what is left of the business and the group's finances in general. That's it. Period. I see my future, as I did earlier, in public affairs to build civil society in Russia.'[101] By removing Khodorkovsky from operational management, the company hoped that the Kremlin's hostility would be mitigated, but it had no discernible effect.

This strategy was accompanied by bringing in new people with a record of working successfully with the Kremlin. One of these was the Russian-born American citizen Simon Kukes, an experienced oil manager who had previously been CEO at TNK.[102] However, Abramovich wanted to see Yevgeny Shvidler, head of Sibneft, appointed to replace Khodorkovsky, and this would have made sense in the context of the merger plans. Abramovich hoped to use the 19 per cent of the joint company owned by minority shareholders to lever himself into control of the company, since the courts had frozen Khodorkovsky's 44 per cent share, but the plan failed since Khodorkovsky preferred to see the merger deal fail than give in to Abramovich's pressure. Disappointed, on 26 November Abramovich pulled the plug, leading to a protracted and messy demerger process. By the end of December a deal was reached whereby Yukos received $3 billion back and 26 per cent its shares in exchange for 92 per cent of Sibneft shares.[103] Abramovich once again, as he had done at the time when Berezovsky had come under attack, understood the realities of the power system and acted accordingly, a trick that Khodorkovsky never quite grasped. In return, Abramovich's expatriation of shares

---

[98] Ivan Gordeev, Nikolai Gorelov and Viktor Paukov, 'Po sobstvennomu zhelaniyu: Mikhail Khodorkovskii ushel iz yukosa', *Vremya novostei*, 4 November 2003, p. 1.

[99] Even before his arrest Khodorkovsky had transferred his Yukos shares to a trust fund under Menatep, registered in the British Virgin Islands, but it was clear that Khodorkovsky was still in control, since his offer to pay Yukos's tax obligations would have had to come from somewhere. Oksana Shevel'kova and Nikolai Makeev, 'Kontsy v vodu: Khodorkovskii Menatep ne otdal', *Gazeta*, 13 January 2005, p. 7.

[100] Catherine Belton, 'Yukos Owner Renews Offer', *Moscow Times*, 13 July 2004, p. 1.

[101] Fedor Chaika, ' "Ya izbavlen ot otvetstvennosti za ostavshiisya biznes": Mikhail Khodorkovskii podaril "Yukos" Leonidu Nevzlinu', *Izvestiya*, 13 January 2005, p. 1.

[102] Duma deputy Vladimir Yudin, whose complaint had earlier signalled the beginning of the Yukos affair, now submitted a further appeal against Kukes, alleging a range of illegal activities at TNK including money laundering, bribery, blackmail, and tax evasion. Catherine Belton, '$5Bln Tax Charge Hangs Over Yukos', *Moscow Times*, 3 December 2003, p. 1.

[103] Simonov, *Russkaya neft'*, p. 98.

and capital abroad, as well as what had become in Russia the scandalous purchase of Chelsea FC, was forgiven.

In the wake of Khodorkovsky's arrest the former Conoco executive Steven Theede, who had joined Yukos in August 2003 as chief operating officer, took over as head of Yukos-Moskva on Shakhnovsky's resignation to take up his post as senator from Evenkia. When he had been Conoco vice president Theede in 2001 had clashed with Khodorkovsky over PSAs, which as we have seen Khodorkovsky considered gave foreign companies an unfair advantage, but he was now effectively head of the company that he had once fought. Bruce Misamore remained Yukos's financial director. On 14 November Stephen Curtis, the British lawyer we have encountered earlier, took over Lebedev's post as managing director of Group Menatep, and thereafter the management of Yukos and Menatep diverged. Curtis took over where Lebedev had left off, devising a complex network of accounts for Yukos executives that stretched across various tax havens from Mauritius to the Dutch Antilles. Another appointment at this time was Victor Gerashchenko, who had been removed as head of the Central Bank of Russia (CBR) in March 2002, where he had been accused of abusing his powers. Gerashchenko had been responsible for the financial crash on 'black Tuesday' in 1994, and as head of the CBR had awarded himself generous bonuses. In the last days of 2003 Gerashchenko was nominated by the Rodina bloc's supreme council as its official candidate in the March 2004 presidential elections, but to his great relief he was denied registration by the CEC.[104] Instead he withdrew from the race, and on 24 June 2004 he took on the no less challenging role as chairman of the board of directors at Yukos. Gerashchenko in 2004 acted as the spearhead of Yukos shareholders for a dialogue with the government. These appointments, while logical in themselves, narrowed the opportunity to open effective negotiating channels with the Kremlin, and probably sealed the fate of the company. Already by the end of 2003, as noted, the value of Yukos shares had fallen by 40 per cent of their peak on the eve of Khodorkovsky's arrest, although the company remained largely intact.

This changed with an arbitration court decision in Yakutiya on 11 December 2003 to strip Yukos of the licence to develop the central block in the giant Talakan oil and gas field in East Siberia. The tender for Talakan had been won by Sakhaneftegaz in March 2001 for $501 million, and in 2002 this company was swallowed up by Yukos; but having failed to pay the tender price, it was only granted a temporary operating licence which expired on 10 October 2003. The energy ministry then on 30 October granted Surgutneftegaz, which had come a distant second in the 2001 tender, with a $61-million bid, a one-year temporary licence, but argued that as the earlier runner-up it should be granted long-term (twenty-five years) operating rights. It was with this claim that the Yakut arbitration court agreed on 11 December.[105] In a further blow a fortnight later on

---

[104] He had been nominated only by the Party of Russian Regions, and not by the bloc as a whole, and hence needed to collect more signatures to support his candidature. Alexei Titkov, *'Party Number Four'—Rodina: Whence and Why?* (Moscow, Panorama Centre, 2006), p. 19.

[105] Kimmage, 'Putin's Restoration', pp. 133–4; Simonov, *Russkaya neft'*, p. 182.

29 December the tax ministry declared that Yukos had underpaid its 2000 tax bill by R98 billion ($3.5 billion) from minimizing VAT and earnings, and the use of regions with favourable tax regimes (*zakrytye administrativno-territorial'nye obrazovaniya*, ZATO). A pattern was thus set for repeated waves of tax demands, which typically exceeded the net profits of the company in a given year. In 2000 Yukos had declared a net profit of $3.1 billion, just below the tax claim. With the writing on the wall, on 10 December 2004 three foreign members of the Yukos board, Sarah Carey, Raj Kumar Gupta, and Jacques Kosciusko-Morizet, resigned.

The London-based office of Menatep under Curtis had its own chequered history. Curtis was accused in an American lawsuit of provoking a collapse in the Yukos share price, allegedly as a result of a complex tax evasion scheme.[106] Curtis was a master at creating offshore shell companies and had earlier established a number of offshore accounts for Yukos. Curtis was known for his privacy, yet became increasingly concerned that he was under surveillance. The causes of his helicopter crash in March 2004 on his way home to his Dorset castle remain a mystery; and the solution to that particular riddle may well have gone to the grave with him. As noted, not long before his death he had been in contact with Litvinenko, which makes the matter even more impenetrable. His wife reported that Curtis received threatening letters and had informed relatives that if anything 'untoward' happened to him '[i]t will not be an accident'.[107] Reports suggest that he was on his way to meet a British intelligence agent to discuss information about Yukos and Menatep. While working as an accountant and consultant for Khodorkovsky Curtis created ISC Global, whose premises (in the same building as Berezovsky's office) were searched as part of the polonium trail following Litvinenko's death in November 2006.[108]

Yukos's response to the state's attack was hampered by competing views on the appropriate tactics. One group was convinced that the Soviet experience taught that those who repent were not forgiven but destroyed, which would lead to the destruction not only of the company but of all big business in Russia, which in their view would be expropriated. The 'party of war' within Yukos, led in the first instance by Nevzlin, hoped that Western pressure would force the government to relent. The argument against entering into negotiations with the regime appeared to be reinforced by the lack of governmental response to Khodorkovsky's emollient letter 'The Crisis of Russian Liberalism' of March 2004 (Chapter 8). Instead, the procuracy intensified its investigations in Tomsk, Samara, and other regions where Yukos worked. The change of government effectively stopped Kukes's negotiations, since not a single minister with whom he had been discussing Yukos's fate entered the new government formed by Fradkov in March 2004. As a sign of how desperate they had become, Lord David Owen, who had been chairman of

---

[106] On Curtis, see Michael Gillard and Jonathan Calvert, 'British Lawyer Hatched Putin Smears', *The Sunday Times*, 14 May 2006, p. 5.

[107] McGregory and Halpin, 'Spies Sent "To Seize Cash from Yukos Exiles"'.

[108] Ian Cobain and Tom Parfitt, 'Moscow Frustrates Yard's Poison Death Inquiry', *The Guardian*, 6 December 2006, p. 4.

Yukos's international arm in London for two years, was drafted in to give advice on how the group could stave off bankruptcy. In November 2004 Misamore was summoned by prosecutors for questioning, but, fearing for his personal safety, instead of returning from a business trip abroad decided to stay away, although he denied any wrongdoing: 'Any attacks on me would be political.'[109] By late 2004 all six members of Yukos's senior management team had left Moscow.

The 'party of peace' in Yukos was led by Shakhnovsky. He set a personal example by compromising, and in return for confessing his guilt was amnestied. The moderates sought to mobilize leading politicians to temper the government's behaviour. Following Lebedev's arrest the softliners asked Yeltsin to intervene, and he had then telephoned Putin. Similarly, the former chief of staff Yumashev, his successor Voloshin, and Kasyanov were all mobilized to support Yukos, but with little effect. The peaceniks then hoped that Gerashchenko's appointment to chair the Yukos board would convince the authorities that Yukos no longer represented a threat. They anticipated that such an authoritative figure would force the Kremlin to take Yukos seriously; and indeed, shortly before his formal appointment he was invited to the Kremlin to meet the chief of staff, Medvedev.[110]

Views within the Kremlin were no less divided. The hardliners (the 'polit-buro' faction) included Vladimir Ustinov, Nikolai Patrushev, Igor Sechin, and Viktor Ivanov, who favoured strengthening state control over the market, above all to favour businesses close to their *silovik* views. These included Sergei Bog-danchikov's Rosneft, as well as the Akron chemical company headed by Vyacheslav Kantor. Kantor had allegedly been feeding analytical notes to the Kremlin warning about an anti-state conspiracy by Khodorkovsky and his company, adding in particular that during his various visits to America in 2003 Khodorkovsky had consciously tried to undermine the president. If the *siloviki* could take over Yukos they would win enormous financial resources for their projects, and indeed, for their personal plans. For them Gerashchenko was a malleable figure, who could play the role that Kokh did in transferring NTV into state hands early on in Putin's presidency. However, Yukos was in a different league to Gusinsky's Media-Most, being fully integrated into the global economy and responsible for one-fifth of the shares on Russia's stock market.

The moderates in the Kremlin included Surkov, Medvedev, and Dmitry Kozak. They opposed limiting the role of the market, fearing that the attack on Yukos would damage the business environment while strengthening the hand of the *siloviki*. The liberals hoped to save Yukos, possibly joined with Sibneft, but under new management of the sort that now led Gazprom and UES. They considered Gerashchenko someone with whom a deal could be made. The rest of the business community would have been satisfied with such an outcome, since Khodorkovsky had never been a popular figure among the business elite. He had never hidden his political ambitions, and spoke with foreign leaders as an equal and represented

---

[109] Valeria Korchagina, 'Yukos Exodus May Hit Output', *Moscow Times*, 26 November 2004, p. 7.

[110] Elena Dikun, ' "Delo Yukosa" v sude kreml': Yukos neokonchennaya voina', *Moskovskie novosti*, No. 18, 21 May 2004, p. 4.

himself as the vanguard and leader of the Russian business class. That is why they showed little 'class solidarity' when Khodorkovsky was arrested, and indeed many breathed a sigh of relief, not least because the blow had fallen on someone else.[111] Many had assumed that the authorities would first attack Oleg Deripaska, one of the leading 'family' members (he was married to Yumashev's daughter) who was also the most aggressive and with little traction in the West. However, the aluminium titan was able to mobilize his connections and fulfilled the Kremlin's tasks, notably through financing Rodina and the LDPR in the December 2003 elections, and he not only survived but prospered in the Putin years.

On 9 July 2004 the bailiffs moved in on the oil company after the authorities refused to give Yukos an extension on paying its $3.4 billion tax bill. Up to that point Sechin's plan had been one among many promoted by the various factions, but from this point Sechin, who took over as head of the Rosneft board on 27 July, had the upper hand. One report stated: 'Sechin has been drawing up the strategy for months.... The research has all been done. The paperwork and the planning are now all in place. It is only waiting for the president's order for it to be enacted.'[112] The 'politburo' came to see anyone who opposed their plans as 'dissidents'. Although they did not dare to label top political leaders with this tag, they did manage to block the advancement of dissident sympathizers like Kozak, and in his case Sechin was even able to send him into 'internal exile' as presidential envoy to the Southern Federal District in the wake of the Beslan crisis in September 2004. For lower-level officials they were less merciful.

Dmitry Skarga, at the head of Sovkomflot since 6 May 2000, came to be considered a 'dissident' when he refused the illegal demand made in May 2004 by his former sponsor, Sechin, to arrest Yukos oil carried on Sovkomflot vessels. At this time Yukos was doing all it could to pay off the tax claims, and the only way it could do this was to maintain exports. Thus Sechin in particular sought to throttle Yukos's financial flows and thus its ability to avoid bankruptcy. Since Sovkomflot was not owed any money by Yukos, any attempt to arrest its shipboard property would be patently illegal.[113] Skarga refused an instruction from Sechin in August 2003 to raise finance to support deputies, by offering them a contract with the company that would then be terminated if they were elected in the December elections, but would entitle them to substantial compensation. Skarga was also diffident about arranging for Sovkomflot to run the 57-metre yacht *The Olympia*, which Putin had apparently received in May 2002 in Sochi from Abramovich (state officials of course are not allowed to receive personal gifts), and suggested that it should be sold.[114] On 8 April 2004 Kozak told Skarga that Putin had read the note

---

[111] Loc. cit.

[112] Simon Bell and Sylvia Pfeifer, 'Kremlin Prepares to Seize Yukos's Oil', *Daily Telegraph*, 10 July 2004.

[113] It appears that Sechin also tried to impound Yukos oil in Transneft pipelines, for which there is no provision in the Russian Tax Code, Bell and Pfeifer, 'Kremlin Prepares to Seize Yukos's Oil'.

[114] Dar'ya Pyl'nova and Dmitrii Shkylev, 'Stoimost' prezidentskoi yakhty "Olimpiya" porydka 50 mln dollarov', *Novaya gazeta*, 30 May 2005; Larisa Kaftan, 'U prezidenta v Sochi poyavilas' novaya yakhta "Olimpiya" ', *Komsomolskaya Pravda*, 28 August 2002.

and then immediately shredded it. Skarga also opposed the merger of Sovkomflot (with fifty-six vessels) and Novoship, based in Novorossiisk with fifty-five vessels, preferring rather to see an IPO by Sovkomflot and a diversity of competing shipping companies in Russia rather than a state-owned super-fleet that would have less resistance to external shocks, such as an environmental disaster caused by one of their ships. Skarga was summarily dismissed from his post at the head of Sovkomflot on 7 October 2004, when he still had a year to run on his contract. Thus the term 'dissident' once again entered circulation among Russia's political elite, signifying now the refusal to be subordinated to Kremlin factions and to maintain some sort of critical independence. Khodorkovsky was an exemplary instance of such a dissident.

Tax matters

In March 2003 Putin undertook a reorganization of the security agencies. The major change was the creation of the Federal Anti-Narcotics Agency (Gosnarkokontrol', FSKN), headed by Viktor Cherkesov, the former presidential envoy to the Northwestern region. Cherkesov was a close Putin ally having worked with him in St Petersburg in the 1980s, and in the 1990s headed the FSB in St Petersburg when Putin was deputy mayor. The FKSN was concerned with far more than narcotics, having absorbed the 40,000 employees of the powerful Tax Police. The FSKN appeared to have less to do with controlling drug smuggling than acting as a body to keep an eye on other special services. The main charge against Yukos would be tax evasion, and it would have been more difficult to prosecute the case if an independent Tax Police still existed, a force that had been infiltrated by Yukos. By the same token, Viktor Zubkov in 2001 was appointed the inaugural head of the Financial Intelligence Agency (FMS, Rosfinmonitoring), and was involved in Putin's early assault against the oligarchs. As head of the FMS he had more information about the movement of legal and illegal funds than anyone else in the country, and as Putin noted, 'the concentration of so much confidential information in one body could have had a negative effect on business, but this did not happen'.[115] Zubkov, however, was aligned with Sechin's politburo, and no doubt furnished the appropriate information.

As we have seen, Yukos was an active lobbyist in the State Duma, and between 2001 and 2003 influenced the legislation on the taxation of energy resources, the indexation of the energy resource tax, export duties on crude oil and petroleum products, and amendments to the PSA law.[116] The skilful use of tax minimization opportunities and legal allowances allowed oil companies to devote up to 50 per cent of their income for investment. Even as Yukos was transforming itself into a well-managed company on Western lines, Yukos resolutely used the whole

[115] Sochi, 14 September 2007, http://president.kremlin.ru/text/appears/2007/09/144011.shtml.
[116] V. Belash, 'Lobbizm s chelovecheskim litsom', *Kommersant-Vlast'*, 21–27 July 2003.

range of tax-minimization schemes. This meant the vigorous use of 'onshore off-shores', the tax havens based in the ethno-federal republics of Mordovia, Kalmykia, Chukotka, and low-tax zones elsewhere. This allowed the company to avoid paying the statutory corporate tax of 24 per cent, and Yukos effectively kept its tax at around 13 per cent.[117] More than this, the Kremlin was clearly irked at the company's lobbying power, and that of its associates, in being able to block the passage of laws in the Duma that would have removed these and other tax loopholes. No sooner was Yukos weakened than these laws were pushed through parliament in late 2003. It is clear that on a whole number of policy issues Yukos was perceived as a threat to the Kremlin's management of the economy. That is why Yukos was chosen as the target as the administration sought to reassert its prerogatives in this area.

Like all companies Yukos sought to minimize its tax burden, but it was probably not the worst.[118] While Yukos paid some $45 a tonne in taxes, Sibneft paid only $28; only TNK-BP paid more taxes than Yukos (cf. Table 5.2).[119] Sibneft, however, was shielded from reprisals. Transfer prices were set deliberately low to reduce liabilities, with profits shifted to offshore trading companies to avoid Russian taxes. Yukos funnelled some of its earnings through various onshore offshores, with the main funds passing through Mordovia, from where in 2003 Nevzlin became a senator. The prosecution would later make great play out of Yukos's alleged abuse of transfer pricing to exploit its production subsidiaries, and in particular the use of the term 'liquid from the wells' (zhidkost' na skvazhine) that was of low value but which once entering the market miraculously became oil, which commanded much greater value kept by the head company. This ignores the usual mark-up for transport, distribution and marketing. The energy ministry found that in 1999 over 90 per cent of oil sold by Russian companies was sold via transfer pricing.[120] This was the peak year for this stratagem, and thereafter declined sharply.

Following an extensive tax audit the tax ministry in April 2003 concluded that Yukos had only a small amount of excess tax to pay for the years 2000 and 2001, a sum which Yukos paid a few months later. In autumn 2003 the ministry issued several certificates confirming that Yukos had no tax liabilities.[121] However, on 8 December 2003 the ministry announced a re-audit, and on 29 December it reported that Yukos had in fact underpaid taxes since 2000 to the tune of R79.6 billion (€2.27 billion). On 14 April an additional tax was imposed for

---

[117] Catherine Belton, '$5Bln Tax Charge Hangs Over Yukos', *Moscow Times*, 3 December 2003, p. 1.

[118] For a detailed discussion of the tax charges against Khodorkovsky and Lebedev, see A. Rodionov, *Nalogovye skhemy, za kotorye posadili Khodorkovskogo* (Moscow, Vershina, 2006). A tendentious but clear account is in Yurii Simonov, *Yukos v kartinkakh* (Moscow, Evropa, 2005), pp. 23–31.

[119] 'On obeshchaet vernutsya: Mikhail Khodorkovskii gotovitsya k politicheskoi deyatel'nosti', *Izvestiya*, 10 September 2004, p. 4.

[120] Reported by Egor Gaidar, who provides details of oil pricing systems, demonstrating that Yukos practices were not at all unusual, *New Times*, 5 March 2007.

[121] On 19 September 2003 a certificate was issued stating that there was no liability on 1 September 2003, on 23 October 2003 for 1 September, and on 17 November for 1 November.

Table 5.2. The official income tax rate and actual taxation
of selected companies (in %)

Company	1999	2000	2001	2002	2003
Official income tax rate	35	35	35	24	24
Lukoil	15	32	31	29	22
Sibneft	3	10	15	12	7
Yukos	25	33	18	20	19*

* First 9 months.

Source: M. B. Olcott, 'Vladimir Putin i neftyanaya politika Rossii' (Moscow,
Carnegie Center, 2005), Working Papers No. 1, p. 18; www.carnegie.ru/
en/pubs/workpapers/WP-2005-01-www.pdf.

assessments since 2000 of R99.4 billion ($3.4 billion), including interest and fines.
At the tax ministry's request the tax court ordered that Yukos pay the sum within
two days, and the next day the court imposed a freezing order forbidding it to
alienate or encumber its property. Yukos was given little time to acquaint itself
with a vast quantity of material presented in a chaotic format, and on 1 June 2004
the tax court confirmed the greater part of the claim against Yukos, and on 29
July the tax appeal court confirmed the full claim of R99.4 billion. On 14 July
the Russian tax bailiff attached the claim regarding the additional tax assessments
to the shares owned by Yukos in YNG, and on 18 November announced that
they would be sold in a public auction (see below). This was not the end of the
matter, and the tax ministry imposed additional assessments for the years 2001
to 2004 totalling R692 billion (€20.1 billion).[122] The state's appetite was certainly
growing with the eating.

According to a fascinating account by Gerashchenko, who headed the Yukos
board for three years, the tax demands had been 'dreamed up' by Sergei Shatalov, a
deputy minister of finances responsible for taxes, 'evidently on orders from above'.
Failing to get a promised meeting with the president, in July 2004 he met with
Putin's aide Igor Shuvalov. After discussing general matters, Shuvalov declared:
'As for Khodorkovsky, we don't trust the man.' Gerashchenko argued that that was
irrelevant, since Khodorkovsky was offering to pay the tax demands and that the
problem could be 'solved lawfully and in a civilised fashion'. Shuvalov reiterated his
view: 'We don't trust Khodorkovsky, he is offering his shares so as to get a lighter
sentence but then he'll start saying that he was unjustly treated, forced to act in
this way, and so on', an allusion to the way Gusinsky had repudiated the alleged
deal with Lesin in 2001. Attempts by Jean Chrétien, the Canadian prime minister
1993–2003, to mediate also came to nothing. In return for Chrétien advancing
Russia's case to become a full member of G8, Yukos should be given two years
to sort out its tax affairs. Chrétien fulfilled his part of the deal, but on 30 August
Yukos was notified that there would be no deferral and instead the government
pressed on with the sale of YNG. Gerashchenko was convinced that Sechin was the

---

[122] Figures compiled from the judgement of the Amsterdam District Court, see Chapter 7.

driving force, exploiting his combination of posts as head of Rosneft's board and a deputy head of the presidential administration. He stressed: 'We know that behind the Kremlin walls there was not so much different approaches to dismembering Yukos as a clash of appetites', with Gazprom under Medvedev also angling for a piece of the pie, although Sechin's Rosneft emerged with the lion's share.[123]

The various hearings before the tax court violated fundamental principles of due process of law, without adequate safeguards or judicial tests about the manner in which the tax assessments were made. Even if the company was guilty of tax avoidance, the state's case is prey to the charge of selectivity. Yukos was doing no more than many other companies were doing; and in some cases was doing it less.[124] At the same time, some oil companies were hardly doing it at all, notably Surgutneftegaz. In 2002 alone Yukos paid $4.5 billion to the state in taxes, and as Table 5.1 shows, it was not the worst payer, an accolade that fell to Sibneft where Berezovsky's habits remained deeply ingrained. Thus the later suggestion that the company had developed a type of internal autarky in which it refused to pay taxes was unfair, although in common with most other energy companies it tried to win as much autonomy in its tax affairs as possible.

When in March 2001 Fradkov had been appointed head of the Federal Tax Service (FNS) he declared a vendetta against tax crimes. Out of 2.7 million registered companies and individuals in the late 1990s, a third made no tax return or paid no tax at all.[125] However, the tax take as a proportion of GDP had been improving: from a miserable 21 per cent in 1995 it remained at roughly that level until 1999 saw a big jump to 31.5 per cent, then reached 33.9 per cent in 2001 before reaching a new peak of 36.2 per cent in 2004, in the wake of the Yukos affair.[126] Table 5.3 vividly demonstrates the sharp rise in the budget contribution of the energy sector from 2005. Taxes as a proportion of the federal budget rose from 73.6 per cent in 1995 to 91.5 per cent in 2004.[127] Fradkov's good work was rewarded on 5 March 2004 when he became prime minister. His successor as premier from September 2007, Victor Zubkov, had from 2001 been the inaugural head of the Financial Intelligence Agency (FMS, Rosfinmonitoring), and must have been involved in Putin's assault against the oligarchs, as no doubt was his successor at the head of the FNS, Anatoly Serdyukov. A Constitutional Court decision of 27 May 2003 resolved that a tax payer commits a criminal offence only if they consciously sought to avoid payment.[128] On this basis Yukos later appealed, but the Court refused to accept the case on 18 January 2005. In another appeal based on the three-year statute of limitations in tax cases (Article 113 of the Tax Code), the Court on 14 July 2005 resolved that Article 113 did not apply when the tax payer had impeded a tax inspection.[129] This meant that any backdated tax charges could be laid against the company, irrespective of how long ago the alleged offences took place.

[123] Gerashchenko, 'I Encountered Total Disregard for the Law'.

[124] For a review, see Fortescue, *Russia's Oil Barons and Metal Magnates*, chapter 6, pp. 112–20.

[125] Rodionov, *Nalogovye skhemy, za kotorye posadili Khodorkovskogo*, p. 244.   [126] Ibid., p. 238.

[127] Ibid., p. 239.   [128] Ibid., pp. 268–77.   [129] Ibid., pp. 278–9.

Table 5.3. Budget revenues from the oil and gas sector

	2000	2001	2002	2003	2004	2005	2006
Enlarged budget revenues (% GDP)	37.3	37.5	37.1	36.5	37.0	40.1	39.7
Including those from oil and gas (% GDP)*	8.6	9.1	8.0	8.2	9.8	13.3	13.7
Share of revenues from oil and gas complex in enlarged budget (%)	23.1	24.2	21.6	22.5	26.6	33.2	34.6

* Production of oil and gas, refining, transport by pipelines.

Source: Igor Y. Yurgens, *Russia's Future Under Medvedev*, English edition edited by Professor Lord Skidelsky (Warwick, Centre for Global Studies, 2008), p. 47; calculated by Economic Expert Group.

The political nature of the case is reflected in the Kremlin's refusal to accept a solution that would have allowed Yukos to pay its tax arrears and remain a viable company. Khodorkovsky on a number of occasions offered his shares in Yukos in attempts to save the company as a whole. On his arrest he understood that he would lose the business: '[B]ut I never thought that this would be done by destroying the company.'[130] Yukos also offered the government its stake in Sibneft, which would have paid most of the arrears, but this and other offers were refused.[131] In July 2004 Khodorkovsky through his lawyers announced that he would be willing to transfer his 44.1 per cent stake in Yukos to the state (worth about $7.7 billion) to resolve the tax issue.[132] It was at this time that Theede offered the state an $8 billion three-year plan to settle outstanding tax issues, but it was clear that the government was not interested in an out-of-court settlement. This was made explicit by finance minister Kudrin, who stressed that 'I'm in favour of letting a court solve this problem'. He also argued that the Yukos case was not an isolated event and that other oligarchs could face prosecution: 'You have to punish stealing, and we will do so even if it happened three to five years ago.'[133] However, no other major oligarch was brought to book. On 19 November 2004 Yukos was hit with another $6 billion tax demand, bringing the total tax bill to $20 billion. By the time Khodorkovsky's trial ended in May 2005 the total bill for alleged tax arrears had risen to $27.5 billion, with the tax bill in some years (2001, 2002), as we have seen, exceeding the total income of the company in that year. The eventual tax bill reached $33 billion. Given time and its enormous revenues Yukos could pay these bills, whether they were justified or not.

The way that the tax bills were handled makes it clear that the case was about far more than legitimate tax recovery but about political expropriation. This is made all the more apparent in the way that tax arrears of other companies were handled. In November 2004, for example, both Sibneft and BP-TNK were asked for back

[130] Mikhail Khodorkovsky: vpervye—intervyu iz tyur'my, 'Tyazhelo, chto sovsem net solntsa', *Newsweek*, 31.01–06.02.2005, p. 16. This interview is discussed in Chapter 6.

[131] Carola Hoyos and Arkady Ostrovsky, 'Politics First', *Financial Times*, 5 August 2004.

[132] Artem Eiskov, 'Khodorkovskii gotov pogasit' dolgi "Yukosa" svoimi aktsiyami', *Izvestiya*, 13 July 2004, p. 1.

[133] Catherine Belton, 'Stock Market Dives Over Yukos Worries', *Moscow Times*, 31 May 2004, p. 1.

taxes, but the sums involved were perfectly reasonable and consistent with fiscal recovery, and payment plans were arranged. Equally, Vimpelcom and the Caspian Pipeline Consortium received large claims for back taxes, all of which came to negotiated settlement. All companies had in the past engaged in extreme tax-minimization schemes, but at the time these loopholes were legal. In an addendum to the Council of Europe (CoE) report on the Yukos affair (see Chapter 6) Sabine Leutheusser-Schnarrenberger, after having been in contact with the head of the FNS Serdyukov and Konstantin Kosachev, the chair of the Russian delegation to the CoE, stated: 'Yukos and its leading executives have indeed been "arbitrarily singled out by the authorities". The cases of other companies were examined, and there was nothing, in her view, exceptional about Yukos except its political salience.[134] The tax behaviour of companies, however, did change: '[T]here is evidence that the Yukos affair has encouraged Russian companies to start paying taxes in full and become more law-abiding.'[135] Ever ready to exploit an emerging market, handbooks were published detailing how tax could be 'optimized' without becoming another Khodorkovsky.[136]

We have noted how Yukos transformed itself into a relatively transparent company, using Western accounting standards and with its accounts up to 2005 audited by PwC. In March 2007, however, PwC itself came under attack, with its offices raided by police officers and investigators in search of evidence relating to Yukos as well as in connection with the possible criminal liability of its Russian managers in a tax evasion case that the firm had lost in 2006. In February 2006 the company was charged with underrating its profit tax base in 2002 by transferring funds to its Dutch branch for services provided by foreign specialists for Russian clients; and in yet another case an investigation was conducted into its licence terms. On 24 June 2007 PwC withdrew all the audits it had carried out for Yukos between 1995 and 2004, arguing that it had lacked adequate information: 'PwC now believes information and representations [that were] provided to PwC by Yukos's former management may not have been accurate.'[137] PwC insisted that its action had nothing to do with the months of harassment at the hands of the Russian authorities,[138] but others considered that they had bowed to political pressure. Temerko was less than impressed: 'They do what they are told—they're scared to lose money.'[139] PwC was found guilty of violating professional standards in conducting Yukos audits from 2002 to 2004, allowing the company to avoid taxes. The company was found guilty of preparing two diverging sets of audits for

---

[134] Parliamentary Assembly of CoE (PACE), 'The Circumstances Surrounding the Arrest and Prosecution of Leading Yukos Executives', Doc 10368 Addendum, 24 January 2005.

[135] Vladimir Erochkine and Pavel Erochkine, *Russia's Oil Industry: Current Problems and Future Trends* (London, Centre for Global Studies, 2006), p. 39.

[136] For example, O. V. Laskov, *Ne stan' Khodorkovskim: Nalogovye skhemy, za kotorye ne posadyat* (St Petersburg, Piter Press, 2007), which noted that taken separately no item in the Yukos tax strategy was an offence, but the enormity of the schemes taken together was fateful, p. 15.

[137] Miriam Elder, 'Echoes of Yukos Surround PwC Case', *Moscow Times*, 10 July 2007.

[138] Editorial, 'Throwing the Books at Them', *Washington Post*, 20 July 2007.

[139] Elder, 'Echoes of Yukos Surround PwC Case'.

Yukos, and fined $715,000 (R16.8 million).[140] In January 2008 PwC lost its appeal against the charge.[141]

Yukos lawyers argued that the attack on PwC was designed to intimidate them into providing evidence to be used in the second trials of Khodorkovsky and Lebedev. The Kremlin, on the other hand, tried to portray the company as the equivalent of the accounting firm Arthur Anderson, which had audited the accounts of Enron before its collapse, and to suggest that Khodorkovsky was the equivalent of Enron's chief executive, Kenneth Lay, whose illegal financial manipulations brought the company to disaster. In an interview Medvedev made the comparison explicit. Asked whether he saw the Yukos affair as an example of factional conflict and an attempt to use state corporations as tools for achieving political objectives, he answered: 'In my view, no. Yukos was, after all, a company that did have some real taxation problems. And they led to very unfortunate consequences for the company. If you insist on seeing something else behind that, why not go all the way and claim that Enron was a victim of intrigues as well?'[142]

The 'Yukos affair' developed in fits and starts, and at various points it could have come to a negotiated solution. According to some estimates, more than seventy offers to the government to settle the debts went unanswered.[143] Given the enormous revenues generated by Yukos at a time when Brent crude had reached over $50 a barrel (although Russia's Urals blend is discounted, at that time at $6.14 a barrel), a repayment plan for the tax arrears could easily have been arranged, and was repeatedly offered by Yukos executives, although liability was not admitted. In July 2000 a deal had been offered to Gusinsky through the mediation of Mikhail Lesin (the minister responsible for the media), but no such arrangement was offered to Khodorkovsky. By freezing the company's bank accounts and setting deadlines that were impossible to meet, the courts and tax authorities ultimately drove the company into bankruptcy. The refusal to accept a negotiated settlement demonstrates that the Kremlin was playing for higher stakes: the elimination of Khodorkovsky as a political actor, the destruction of Yukos as a significant player on the Russian and world scene, and the reorganization of the Russian energy sector.

The 'scam of the year': The sale of Yuganskneftegaz (YNG)

On 20 July 2004 the ministry of justice announced the sale of Yuganskneftegaz, extracting 62 per cent of Yukos's output and in which Yukos had a 76.79 per cent stake, to pay off Yukos's alleged debts. Yuganskneftegaz has reserves of 11.6 billion barrels, 17 per cent of Russia's total, and it accounts for 11 per cent of Russian oil output and one per cent of world output. The announcement on

[140] Alex Nicholson, 'PwC Loses 2nd Appeal on Tax Claim', *Moscow Times*, 15 April 2008, p. 5.
[141] Dmitrii Kazmin, 'Shancy PwC', *Vedemosti*, 16 April 2008, p. 3; Miriam Elder, 'PwC Facing New Investigation', *Moscow Times*, 16 April 2008, p. 7.
[142] Interviewed by Maksim Glikin and Irina Reznik, *Vedemosti*, 5 July 2007.
[143] 'Gosudarstvo raspravilos s Yukosom', *Izvestia*, 30 December 2004.

19 November 2004 of detailed plans to auction YNG to cover the tax arrears was part of a larger pattern of escalating demands and ever more punitive sanctions. The opening bid was set at only $8.65 billion, even though international investment bankers had estimated its value as between $13 billion and $20 billion. Even the Kremlin-friendly Dresdner Kleinwort Wasserstein, the German investment bank hired by the Russian Ministry of Justice to appraise the value of YNG, calculated that a fair price would be in the range of $15.7–18.3 billion.[144] Pumping over a million barrels of oil a day, and with international oil prices at that time around $50 a barrel, the sale price of the company was a manifest undervaluation.

The auction of the Yukos's shares in YNG on 19 December 2004 was apparently designed to allow Gazprom to buy the company at the nominal asking price, and thus at a stroke to become one of the world's major oil producers. However, on the eve of the auction (on 14 December), with its bank accounts frozen, assets arrested, and some of its core shareholders and managers facing charges of fraud and tax evasion, Yukos filed a Chapter 11 bankruptcy petition in a court in Houston, Texas. On 16 December the judge, Letitia Clarke, issued an injunction suspending the auction for ten days. International financial institutions were warned not to assist Gazprom with loans, or other financing to help the company buy YNG. Even though later in December the case was rejected for lack of jurisdiction (a decision confirmed on appeal in March 2005), it was enough to change plans in Russia.[145]

Worried about the possible consequences, on 19 December Gazprom dropped out of the serious bidding. A hitherto unknown company stepped in, the Baikal Finance Group (BFG), registered two weeks earlier to an office above a coffee shop in Tver (café 'London', named after a hotel by the same name that had been located in the building at 126 Novotvorzhskaya Street before the revolution), along with a mobile phone shop and the alcohol shop 'Adonis' (selling forty-four different types of vodka). This was a rather ironic reminder of Menatep's own official headquarters in a post office box in Gibraltar.[146] The founder of BFG, Reforma OAO, was headed by Alexander Konobievsky, Surgutneftegaz's deputy director for industrial supplies. Gazprom put in a bid not a rouble above the asking price, while Baikal offered $500 million more than the entry price of $1.7 billion (the tender bail), with a total bid of $9.35 billion. As noted, this was far below the consensus market valuation of the company at around $15 billion. Baikal was clearly just a name plate company, standing in for some other group and no more than a front for the Kremlin. Being no more than a shell, Timchenko arranged for people from Surgutneftegaz to take on the role of bidder, at the auction

---

[144] 'Yukos Facing New $5.7bn Tax Bill', *Moscow Times*, 1 November 2004.

[145] Giuditta Cordero Moss, 'Between Private and Public International law: Exorbitant Jurisdiction as Illustrated by the *Yukos* Case', *Review of Central and East European Law*, Vol. 32, 2007, pp. 1–17.

[146] In the second auction for Sibneft shares in 1997 Berezovsky had also played the same trick, with the main bidder a hitherto unknown Finance Oil Corporation, to be distinguished from the organizer of the auction in 1995, the Oil Financial Corporation, Khlebnikov, *Krestnyi otets Kremlya Boris Berezovskii*, p. 265.

which was shown live on television.[147] The bidders included Igor Minibaev, the head of organizational matters at Surgutneftegaz and a long-time business partner of Timchenko, as well as Valentina Komarova and Maria Klimovskaya from Surgut's financial department. When Putin in a press conference in Germany on 21 December stated that the founders of BFG were 'private individuals who have been working in the energy sector for many years', he probably had this in mind. In that interview he insisted: 'As far as the possibilities for a state company to acquire these assets are concerned, they have the right to do so, as all other market participants.'[148]

The sale was clearly a holding operation, and within a matter of days, on 22 December, the Baikal group was acquired by Rosneft, giving the government control over YNG and overnight tripling Rosneft's oil output. Various tax claims, however, remained against YNG.[149] The details of the financing arrangements for the purchase of YNG are complex, but the basic story is clear, involving a $6 billion loan from the China National Petroleum Corporation (CNPC).[150] The broad outlines of the purchase of YNG for $9.35 billion were revealed at the time of the IPO (see Chapter 10). Interest-free credits totalling $5.3 billion were drawn from its subsidiaries, who in turn took loans from unknown companies in return for promissory notes for the same sum, which Rosneft purchased in early 2005 with

[147] 'Yukos Assets could pass to Gazprom and the Chinese', *The Times*, 22 December 2004.

[148] http://www.kremlin.ru/text/appears/2004/12/81545.shtml.

[149] On 8 January 2005 the Khanty-Mansi procurator's office announced that it would open a criminal case against YNG for failing to pay R2 billion in taxes, Larisa Kallioma, 'Menedzherov "Yuganskneftegaza" zhdet nakazanie', *Izvestiya*, 13 January 2005, p. 1. Finally, on 10 October 2005 the Moscow Arbitration Court invalidated the tax inspectorate's ruling on the enforcement of about R5.6 billion in taxes and penalties for 1999/2000 on YNG, and legal proceedings regarding the tax claims for 2001–03 were also suspended. 'Yuganskneftegazu prostili 5.6 mlrd nalogovykh pretenzii', News.ru.com, 10 October 2005. The ruling finally allowed Rosneft to take full control of the former Yukos subsidiary.

[150] For a good discussion of the complex financing arrangements that allowed Rosneft to acquire YNG, see *Vedemosti*, 3 June 2005, p. A1; also Gazeta.ru, 25 August 2005, 'Putin lgal'. The basic position is clear: Rosneft provided the funds for the dummy company Baikal Finance Group to purchase Yuganskneftegaz. The fundamental question then focuses on the source of funds used by the highly indebted Rosneft to finance the deal, and here we enter into deeply contentious territory. The relatively straightforward account suggests that Rosneft received $5.3 billion in promissory notes from its subsidiaries, with the latter realizing their assets by selling their bills of exchange to Vneshekonombank (through a company called Trade Express Ltd), which received the money from the finance ministry (apparently from the Stabilization Fund). Rosneft then returned the money to its subsidiaries from a $6 billion loan from the Chinese on account of future oil supplies (N. Semënov, 'Rosneft zalozhila sebya po krupnomu', *Kommersant*, 26 August 2005). According to Irina Aleshina and Nikolai Karadzhich, writing in the same issue of *Kommersant* on 26 August 2005 (and produced in Gazeta.ru on 25 August 2005 and later in Kompromat.ru), the bulk of the money came illicitly from state funds, funnelled through Vneshekonombank and Sberbank, from reserves put aside for the payment of the foreign debt. These transactions and associated ones violated the Budgetary Code, the Law on Joint Stock Companies, and elements of the Civil Code. In fact, according to Temerko, Rosneft borrowed $6 billion from the China National Petroleum Company, secured not against future oil production but pledged against 20 per cent of YNG itself. Alexander Temerko, 'Rosneft Buyer Beware', *Wall Street Journal Europe*, 24 May 2005.

money financed by credits from CNPC and the Chinese Development Bank.[151] The lack of transparency prompted the leading English-language paper in Russia to comment as follows:

Putin's 'dictatorship of the law' grows more hollow with each passing day. As the Yugansk auction so farcically demonstrated, laws are nothing more than tools that the Kremlin uses to neutralize unwanted actors on their stage. The irony of this story is that a rigged auction is exactly what landed Khodorkovsky in jail in the first place and triggered the wider assault on Yukos. With this most recent ersatz auction, we are right back where we started.[152]

Andrei Illarionov, at the time an economic adviser to Putin, was no less scathing:

The sale of the main oil-producing asset of the best Russian oil company ... and its purchase by Rosneft company, 100% owned by the state, has undoubtedly become the scam of the year. ... When the Yukos case began, everybody was asking which will be the rules of the game. ... Now it is clear that there are no rules of the game.[153]

A year after buying YNG, Rosneft bought Yukos liabilities of $437 million at a discount from a syndicate of Western banks, a case we shall return to. The industry and energy minister Viktor Khristenko announced on 30 December 2004 that CNPC might buy up to 20 per cent of YNG.[154] This was clearly a concession to China to offset the sting of the decision announced the day before that the Eastern pipeline would go to Nakhodka rather than to Daqing. Between 2005 and 2010 Rosneft was committed to supplying CNPC with 48.4 million tonnes of oil, at a discounted price (Brent minus $3), in return for the loan that had been used to refinance the purchase of YNG. Sechin's role at Rosneft signalled the advent of a new generation of state officials to top jobs in the economy. Sechin proved most effective in lobbying the interests of Rosneft, ensuring that Yuganskneftegaz went to his company, rather than to Surgutneftegaz (tipped widely as the likely winner of the auction). Sechin was able to drive the case against Yukos forward to the extent that President Putin's own promise that Yukos would not be driven to insolvency was vitiated.

---

[151] Irina Malkova and Elena Mazneva, 'Tsena "Yuganska" ', *Vedemosti*, 29 January 2008, p. 1. See also Chapter 5 on the financing of the YNG purchase.

[152] 'Russia's Latest Auction Farce Eerily Familiar', *Moscow Times*, 21 December 2004.

[153] David Holley, Sergey Loiko, 'A Top Advisor to Putin Calls Oil Takeover the "Scam of the Year" ', *The Los Angeles Times*, 29 December 2004.

[154] 'Khristenko: China May Buy 20% of Yugansk', *Moscow Times*, 31 December 2004.

6

Khodorkovsky Goes to Jail

Democracy may disarm a given oligarchy, a given privileged individual or set of individuals, but it can still crush individuals as mercilessly as any previous ruler.

Isaiah Berlin[1]

The Khodorkovsky and related cases focused on charges of tax avoidance and fraud, but from the outset it was clear that the Yukos affair was about a much larger restructuring of political and economic relationships. The trials themselves were clearly politicized, and judicial impartiality was subordinated to political ends. The Yukos affair represented a political struggle between the state (and subsections of the state), and a powerful business concern in which judicial proceedings were used to advance particular interests. There is much evidence to suggest that the Yukos case was politically motivated and sensitive to changes in the domestic and international political situation. The old security officials shared an 'anti-bourgeois' ideology, and it was this mindset that predisposed the regime to launch the Yukos affair. As for Khodorkovsky himself, he refused to go into exile, which would have effectively meant not only his political annihilation but also the repudiation of his expressed values of civic responsibility.

YUKOS INVESTIGATED

By late 2004 it was clear that the case was moving towards a dénouement. The piling on of extra tax demands increased the pressure on Yukos to breaking point, and in December 2004 the company prepared to file for bankruptcy. Khodorkovsky himself faced a ten-year prison sentence if convicted. It was clear that the exile option, offered to oligarchs in the early period of Putin's rule, was not going to be used in this case. Gusinsky was allowed to leave the country and after a brief sojourn in Spain, when the Russian authorities put in an extradition request but this was refused, he now lives primarily in Israel. Similarly, the most egregiously political of the oligarchs, Boris Berezovsky, sought exile in London and in 2003 was granted asylum by the British government. Khodorkovsky, as we have noted,

---

[1] Berlin, 'Two Concepts of Liberty', in *Four Essays on Liberty*, pp. 118–72, at pp. 163–4.

had plenty of opportunities to stay abroad in 2003, but he repeatedly insisted that he would meet his fate in Russia.

Pre-trial detention

At the GPO's request, the Basmanny court repeatedly extended the length of Khodorkovsky's pre-trial detention.[2] In the end, Khodorkovsky spent nearly two years in block 4 of the Matrosskaya Tishina pre-trial detention centre (SIZO—investigative isolator IZ-99/1) in Moscow. This is a relatively small detention centre for some 100 inmates located on the territory of the general prison but administratively separate, with its own rules including frequent moves from cell to cell. It had previously been under the control of the KGB, and it was here that the members of the junta that had launched the attempted coup in August 1991 were held.

There were numerous attempts to allow Khodorkovsky out on bail, with up to forty Duma deputies ready to stand as guarantors.[3] An international group of defence lawyers called for his release. Karinna Moskalenko, at the appeal against the Basmanny court's ruling denying bail heard in the Moscow City Court on 15 January 2004, argued that none of the points in Article 108 of the Criminal Procedure Code (Ugolovno-protsessual'nyi kodeks, UPK), detailing reasons for refusing bail, applied to her client.[4] Moskalenko is the founder of the International Protection Centre, based in Moscow, specializing in cases to be heard at the European Court of Human Rights (ECtHR) in Strasbourg, to which Russia is legally bound since joining the Council of Europe in 1996. At that hearing Khodorkovsky offered to surrender all of his passports (he apparently had three) and promised that he would not flee, noting that 'I travelled abroad several times during the investigation', and stressed 'that I will not hide from the proceedings'. His request for house arrest was rejected, not only on the grounds that he could escape but that he could use his freedom to 'launder his ill-gotten gains'.[5] Back in 2000 Gusinsky had promised a court that if released he would not try to escape, but in the event he fled, first to Spain, then Greece and Israel. However, Khodorkovsky was a very different character, and he had already demonstrated that he had no intention of taking the exit option.

The procedures associated with pre-trial investigation, when the evidence is examined and collected into a folder which then dominates the trial, reflected Soviet traditions and remain in Russia's new UPK, which came into force in

---

[2] For example, in March 2004 his detention was extended by two months, Dmitrii Simakin, 'Khodorkovskii ostaetsya za reshetkoi', *Nezavisimaya gazeta*, 22 March 2004, p. 7.

[3] Yuliya Mikhailina, 'Sud i tyur'mu soedinili mostom dlya mikhaila khodorkovskogo', *Gazeta*, 12 November 2003, p. 1.

[4] Anastasiya Samotorova, '168 chasov: Khodorkovskii smeyalsya v mosgorsude', *Moskovskie novosti*, 16 January 2004, p. 2

[5] Ol'ga Roshchina, 'Pod strazhei: "Ya ne schitayu vozmozhnym podvesti kollektiv"', *Gazeta*, 16 January 2004, p. 3.

2002. The new system introduced some important innovations, yet ultimately retained its 'neo-inquisitorial' or 'investigatory' character whereby 'the state—objectively and on behalf of everyone concerned, including the accused—actively investigates the circumstances of a crime to determine what happened'.[6] The Russian system is firmly located in the civil law tradition, where the state is considered to be an impartial investigator, and where an early role for defence lawyers or the defence of the procedural rights of the suspect are less prominent than in the Anglo-American adversarial common law tradition, where the trial is everything. The 1993 constitution, however, calls for judicial proceedings to be 'conducted on adversarial principles and equality of the parties' (Article 123.3), which Article 15.1 of the 2001 UPK declares applies to criminal cases.[7] However, there remains considerable scope for the interpretation of what this means in practice.[8]

A later part of the same Article (15.3) asserts: 'The judge is not an agent for criminal prosecution, and sides neither with the prosecution or the defence. The judge creates the necessary conditions for all sides to fulfil their procedural duties and the fulfilment of their rights.' This injunction, to put it mildly, was not always fulfilled in the Yukos case. This prompted appeal to the provisions of Articles 5 and 6 of the European Convention on Human Rights and Fundamental Freedoms (ECHR), which defends the procedural rights of suspects.[9] The long shadow of the pre-trial investigation and apparent pressure by the Russian authorities over the conduct of the trial revealed how much remained to be done to ensure that progressive legislation modified traditional juridical practices.

The conditions in which Khodorkovsky were held were not particularly harsh. The reminiscences of four of his cellmates have been brought out in a small book, which as the author notes, represented Russia in miniature.[10] The number of inmates for much of the time was reduced from the normal four to three, and the whole institution was very small, with only twenty cells each with four people, and rarely eight, and with only two of the six floors occupied by prisoners, and the rest by prison personnel who outnumbered inmates 4:1. The message issued to the criminal world from the first was that Khodorkovsky should be treated well, and he was: 'Which once again only goes to show that the criminal world, big business and high politics are worlds not so alien to each other.'[11] In his first days in prison Khodorkovsky was in a state of shock. He was unable to eat, which in prison could be taken as a hunger strike and alarmed the authorities.[12] The journalist Yulia Latynina apparently passed him a copy of Plutarch, so that 'he did not think that

[6] William Burnham and Jeffrey Kahn, 'Russia's Criminal Procedural Code Five Years Out', *Review of Central and East European Law*, Vol. 33, 2008, pp. 1–2.

[7] *Ugolovno-protsessual'nyi kodeks Rossiiskoi Federatsii*, 12th edition, with all changes up to 1 February 2008 (Moscow, Os'-89, 2008), p. 13.

[8] Burnham and Kahn, 'Russia's Criminal Procedural Code', p. 3.

[9] Council of Europe, *The European Convention on Human Rights*, Rome, 4 November 1950, *and its Five Protocols*, http://www.hri.org/docs/ECHR50.html.

[10] Akhmirova, *Ya sidel s khodorkovskim*, p. 11.   [11] Ibid., p. 16.   [12] Ibid., p. 23.

he was the first person on earth to be persecuted', and to instruct on how to behave when fate turns sour.[13]

Later Khodorkovsky admitted that he had been warned, but all that he had done was put more money in his wife's account so that she could live without him. His cellmates insistently asked whether he regretted not escaping in time, to which he said no.[14] One of his cellmates introduced him to the works of Boris Akunin (the pen name of Grigory Chkhartishvili, an erudite stylist and Japanese translator), and he quickly devoured all of the Erast Fandorin detective mysteries, which he greatly liked.[15] This is hardly surprising, since these novels speak precisely to the concerns of the nascent bourgeoisie, imbued as they are with a spirit of patriotism and individual freedom.[16] Khodorkovsky followed current events on television and daily received a thick package of newspapers and journals, and was very upset when his favourite democrats (Yabloko and SPS) failed to cross the 5 per cent representation threshold in December 2003. He spoke ironically about his business colleagues and politicians, with the exception of the independent liberal Vladimir Ryzhkov, and referred to Putin in polite but sardonic terms as 'Vozhd' (leader), and said he would be willing to make comprises and negotiate with anybody. He noted that running a business and running the country were totally different things, and the highest he had aspired to was to become prime minister.[17] He spent much of his time working at his desk, and when writing 'The Crisis of Liberalism in Russia' (see Chapter 8) he discussed all the main points with his cellmates, and incorporated some of their suggestions.[18] The prisoners joked, as those with any level of consciousness do, that cell number 501 was probably the freest place in Russia.[19]

One of Khodorkovsky's cell companions for a month in 2005 turned out to be retired military intelligence (GRU) colonel Vladimir Kvachkov, accused of the attempted assassination of Chubais on 17 March 2005 by bomb and automatic fire. Kvachkov was arrested that day, and spent his days completing his doctoral (*kandidat*) dissertation, on the subject of special operations by Russia's armed forces, which had to be submitted by 30 March. They discussed the question of liberal socialism in Russia, and agreed that Russia had to be strong, but took differing views on how this should be achieved, with Khodorkovsky questioning the need for an 'iron hand'. Kvachkov denied any involvement in the assassination attempt, and noted later that 'Khodorkovsky is a very intelligent and learned comrade. It was so interesting to discuss things with him that I forgot all about my dissertation.'[20] In June 2008 Kvachkov was cleared of all charges and released, and as in the Yukos affair, the competence of the investigators was

---

[13] Panyushkin, *Mikhail Khodorkovskii*, p. 31.

[14] Akhmirova, *Ya sidel s khodorkovskim*, p. 27.　　[15] Ibid., p. 83.

[16] See Leon Aron, 'A Champion for the Bourgeoisie: Reinventing Virtue and Citizenship in Boris Akunin's Novels', *The National Interest*, Spring 2004, Internet version.

[17] Akhmirova, *Ya sidel s khodorkovskim*, p. 93.　　[18] Ibid., p. 87.　　[19] Ibid., p. 35.

[20] Aleksandr Andryukhin, 'Sideli dva tovarishcha', *Izvestiya*, 25 August 2005, p. 2.

questioned.[21] Another of Khodorkovsky's cellmates, Petr Shchedrov, reported their long conversations on religion, noting that the oligarch considered that the Russian Orthodox Church had much to be guilty about before the people, having accepted subordination to the secular authorities since Peter the Great, and now argued that the Church should be more independent. A high-ranking Orthodox official visited him in jail. They also talked of life on the BAM construction site, and Shchedrov noted how Khodorkovsky tended to keep people at a distance. On several occasions Khodorkovsky called himself a 'public figure', and volunteered the enigmatic formulation: 'Public figures can be neither good nor bad.'[22]

Khodorkovsky was visited on an almost daily basis by a lawyer. His family were allowed to send him up to 30 kilogrammes of supplies a month, and he took mainly fruit and yogurt. He had taken up smoking a few months before his arrest, and continued for a few months in jail, and then gave up.[23] He forbade his children to visit him in the isolator. There were incidents when his lawyers were harassed, as when Olga Artyukhova's notes were confiscated after a visit early on in his incarceration, and attempts were later made to have her disbarred, but the Moscow Bar Chamber headed by Genri Reznik (also a Khodorkovsky lawyer) rejected the justice ministry's request.

As the investigation into the Khodorkovsky case proceeded, various threats were made against other associates, and numerous cases launched. On 23 July 2004 the Basmanny Court issued an arrest warrant against Nevzlin, charging him with organizing a double contract killing and a number of attempted murders.[24] In addition to accusations related to the Pichugin case, which involved allegedly organizing murders on behalf of Yukos, he was charged with tax evasion and fraud. In November 2003 Nevzlin received Israeli citizenship, and Russian extradition requests were twice refused, judgments confirmed by the Israeli Supreme Court in November 2006. From Israel Nevzlin funded Khakamada's presidential campaign in early 2004, about which Khodorkovsky had views as we shall see later. In Israel Nevzlin founded the Leonid Nevzlin Centre for the Study of Russian and East European Judaism at the Hebrew University in Jerusalem, funded by the Foundation for the Support of Israeli Education, established by Nevzlin, Brudno, and Dubov. Dubov as we have seen fled to Israel soon after Khodorkovsky's arrest. He was dropped from the United Russia list in the December 2003 election and expelled from the party, and on 15 January 2004 charges of fraud against him were announced. The Russian government also sought the extradition of a number of other former executives, including Temerko, who had taken over at the head of Yukos after Khodorkovsky's arrest. We will return below to cases against Yukos associates.

---

[21] Maksim Agarkov, 'Sledstvie prikrytiya', *Ekspert*, No. 24, 16–22 June 2008, pp. 74–7.
[22] Vladimir Borsobin, 'Ya byl sokamernikom khodorkovskogo', *Komsomol'skaya Pravda*, 14 July 2005, p. 8.
[23] Panyushkin, *Mikhail Khodorkovskii*, p. 19.
[24] Catherine Belton, 'Nevzlin Faces Murder Charges', *Moscow Times*, 27 July 2004, p. 1.

The case against Khodorkovsky and his associates

The substance of the legal case against Khodorkovsky, Lebedev, and Krainov focused on fraud, tax evasion, and money laundering, while that against Pichugin on criminal matters. Seven charges were levelled against Khodorkovsky personally: major fraudulent embezzlement by an organized group; failure to comply with an enforced court decision; inflicting damage on others' property through fraud; major tax evasion by collusion within a group; avoidance of private income tax and insurance payments to state extra-budgetary funds; repeated forgery of documents; and major embezzlement or laying false claim to others' property within an organized group. The charges were mainly financial, and notably did not include illegal privatization. The proceedings were criticized, *inter alia*, by the special rapporteur to the Council of Europe, to be an infringement of rights according to Article 6 of the European Convention on Human Rights: the public nature of judicial proceedings, protection of the privileged relationship between client and defence lawyer, and the equal standing of the defence and prosecution; and Article 7, that there can be no criminal offence without a valid law at the time of occurrence (*nulla poena sine legem, nullum crimen since lege*), applying in this case in particular to backdated tax claims; and the application of this principle to the protection of private property, as enshrined in the 1st Protocol of the ECHR.

Lebedev had long been one of Khodorkovsky's core business associates, in control of the banking activities from which the whole Yukos empire was born. At the time of his arrest, Lebedev owned 7 per cent of Menatep, giving him a 4.2 per cent stake in Yukos, placing him at number 427 on the Forbes list of the world's richest people with an estimated fortune of $1 billion.[25] He was arrested in connection with fraud charges associated with the privatization of the Apatit fertilizer plant through the Menatep Bank and the Volna subsidiary.

Andrei Krainov is perhaps the most enigmatic of all the main figures in Khodorkovsky's trial. He was the head of Volna, which won the investment competition for Apatit in 1994. Krainov desperately sought to stay out of the limelight. Born on 29 March 1964 in Dushanbe, he studied at the Bauman MGTU. At the head of Volna he won 20 per cent of Apatit's shares, and then sold them on in smaller blocks but failed to invest the promised $283 million in the company. The charge he faced in the Meshchansky court was that Volna was no more than a front company for Khodorkovsky and Lebedev. Krainov admitted as much in court, although as we shall see the situation was rather more complex.

Alexei Pichugin is another of the main victims of the Yukos affair. He considered himself a Don Cossack, and immersed himself in the history of this brotherhood. From school he entered a military academy, from which he was posted to the KGB academy in Novosibirsk, and left the state security service in 1994. He worked in Yukos's economic security service, working under former KGB general Kondaurov, later a Communist member of the State Duma. Pichugin was first called in and asked about the Gorin case on 27 May 2003 but thought little of it

---

[25] Kimmage, 'Putin's Restoration', p. 130.

at the time. In identifying Pichugin as a possible weak link who could incriminate Nevzlin, Khodorkovsky and other senior Yukos managers in criminal matters, the architects of the Yukos affair had clearly misjudged their man. Testimony from friends and relations portray Pichugin as one of 'a dying breed': '[A] military man, raised in the USSR and by no means the worst relic of those times. Patriotic, orderly, true to his word, demanding yet respectful of subordinates, honest, willing to sacrifice his civilian career when the call comes to "Save the Homeland!", and true to his destiny—these are the distinguishing features of the breed.'[26] He had welcomed Putin coming to power, as just the sort of person the country needed to restore order.[27] On 19 June 2003 searches were carried out at his home addresses and office, and on 21 June the Basmanny court issued an arrest warrant even though at that time there was absolutely no evidence against him.[28] On 26 June he was charged with the attempted murder of Kostina and for organizing the murder of the Gorins. Failing to gain a confession or to find any convincing evidence, especially since Nevzlin and Pichugin barely knew each other, they administered a powerful 'truth drug' on 14 July 2003, but since Pichugin evidently knew nothing, he could say nothing of use to the prosecution.[29] Pichugin was held in the FSB detention centre in Lefortovo, which according to commitments Russia signed up to on joining the Council of Europe, should have been transferred to the Ministry of Justice, but in 2004, on the eve of the visit in September by Leutheusser-Schnarrenberger, the PACE rapporteur appointed to investigate the Yukos affair, he was moved to the justice ministry's facility at Matrosskaya Tishina. It was only in 2006 that Lefortovo was transferred to the Ministry of Justice.

CRIMINAL CHARGES

Khodorkovsky was charged with crimes focused on financial matters. There are, however, a whole series of other accusations against him with which he was not initially charged, although they have figured in the trials of some of his associates and are part of the penumbra surrounding the Yukos affair. The story concerning the Avisma company, for example, has been mentioned earlier. They were aired in the media, and thus served to discredit Khodorkovsky.[30] The accusation that

[26] Valerii G. Shiryaev, *Sud mesti: pervaya zhertva dela Yukosa* (Moscow, OGI, 2006), p. 47.
[27] Ibid., p. 39.   [28] Ibid., pp. 65–6.   [29] Ibid., pp. 73–96.
[30] For example, Lev Romanov, 'Zhestokie igry', *Komsomol'skaya pravda*, 20 May 2005. The close links between this paper and the Kremlin are well attested, with the paper carrying some of Vladislav Surkov's most significant interventions. The identity of 'Lev Romanov' is not known, and the article has all the indications of being *'zakazukha'*, or planted material. An attack on Nevzlin soon after, rubbishing his claims that he had evidence of Kremlin corruption and alleging that Abramovich had dismissed these charges, was by the hitherto unknown 'Vadim Yermilov', may also have been *zakazukha*, *Komsomol'skaya pravda*, 21 June 2005. It was this paper that published the open letter backing the verdict in Khodorkovsky's trial, and later the explanations from five of the authors about why they had signed the letter, *Komsomol'skaya pravda*, 2 July 2005. However, a later article argued that Pichugin and Nevzlin were being framed for the murder of the mayor of Nefteyugansk, noting the

Yukos was involved in several killings has been made on several occasions. In particular, Yukos was allegedly implicated in the murder of the mayor of Nefteyugansk in 1998, and an East Petroleum executive in 1998 and 1999. The authorities were at pains to stress that while the opposition may have tried to give the 'Yukos affair' a political colouring, it was in fact a strictly criminal matter. Here we will discuss the main criminal accusations.

The Apatit case

The Apatit case is the *fons et origio* of the whole Yukos affair.[31] The giant Apatit fertilizer and general chemicals company was bought in July 1994 by the Volna company, part of what was to become Yukos, in return for a commitment to invest in the company. The prosecution alleged that all four companies that had tendered for the 20 per cent of Apatit stock had been Khodorkovsky and Lebedev front companies, creating the appearance of competition, as required by law in privatization tenders. The winner, Volna headed by Krainov, was required to invest $280 million in the following year. This was not done, and in response Apatit sued for the return of the 20 per cent stake. In response, Khodorkovsky and his colleagues transferred the appropriate sum to Apatit's account in the Menatep bank, sending the requisite documents to the court, which promptly threw out Apatit's claim. The next day the money was transferred out of Apatit's account and back into Volna's. Volna thereafter sold off its stock in numerous small packets to a number of Khodorkovsky-owned shell companies, many of which were registered offshore. The case was finally settled on 19 November 2002 when Volna paid $15 million to the privatization agency, although by that time it had sold off all its Apatit stock. The prosecution later argued that the $15 million represented a massive undervaluation of the Apatit stock. The reason for this, allegedly, was that Apatit was selling its fertilizer to Khodorkovsky's shell companies at a great discount, hence the low valuation based on minimal profits, whereas these same companies then sold the product at the market price, raking in significant profits. The Russian government argued that because this stake was wrongly valued, the whole peace agreement was rendered invalid.

The case was revived by Novgorod governor Mikhail Prusak, prompted by the Akron Company, which also traded in apatite but which had come into conflict with Apatit. Some other regional leaders in autumn 2002 also demanded a review of Apatit's privatization. We have seen that the head of Akron was Vyacheslav Kantor, who managed to mobilize four governors against Yukos. Kantor was particularly upset that Apatit was selling raw materials to Akron for what he

'abrupt metamorphoses' in the case and 'drastic change' in testimony from witnesses, *Komsomol'skaya pravda*, 9 September 2005. The same issue argued that Khodorkovsky had misled thousands of voters in planning to run for the State Duma by-election in Moscow even though he knew he would not be able to complete the registration formalities.

[31] For a detailed discussion, see Rodionov, *Nalogovye skhemy, za kotorye posadili Khodorkovskogo*, pp. 114–90.

considered an exorbitant price.[32] Thus yet another factor enters the Yukos affair—
business rivalry from competitors. Ordered by Putin on 16 December 2002 to
look into the matter, on 28 April 2003 the prosecutor general, Vladimir Ustinov,
wrote to Putin stating that 'there is no evidence to confirm Prusak's allegations'.[33]
Despite this, Apatit later became the core of the charges against Khodorkovsky
and associates. On 6 June the Duma deputy Vladimir Yudin called on the GPO to
investigate Apatit's privatization. In a separate case in 2005, the Apatit company,
by then a subsidiary of Fosagro and producing 82 per cent of Russian apatite
concentrate (8.8 million tonnes), was charged with tax machinations of the sort
Khodorkovsky was accused of. Khodorkovsky and his associates, part of an 'organized criminal group', had in 2000–2 allegedly used the company to evade taxes
through a transfer pricing scheme which damaged the state, as a 20 per cent
stakeholder in the company and other minority shareholders, for which he was
later convicted. The Murmansk arbitration court in late 2006, however, decided
that the enormous back tax claims against the company, going back to 2001, were
not justified.[34] This was a rare victory for a company against the FNS, but one that
did Khodorkovsky little good.

Pichugin: The Tambov cases and Valentina Korneeva

Investigating a number of horrible crimes in Tambov, the police arrested Igor
Korovnikov, a member of a criminal gang, convicted of eight murders and five
particularly horrible rapes. Under interrogation, he and his colleagues described
a bombing that they had organized. In autumn 1998 they had met 'a man in a
jeep' in Moscow, who ordered them to take a woman called Olga Kostina out of
town and kill her. They were to be paid $15,000 for the job. While preparing to
carry out the murder they found that Kostina was never alone, hence they changed
tack and organized an explosion, which they argued could always be ascribed to
'the Chechens'. This is what happened, and on 28 November 1998 a small bomb
exploded on the landing near to Kostina's parents. Once this evidence came out the
case was immediately transferred to Moscow. As we have seen, Kostina had been
an adviser to Khodorkovsky and deputy head of the Yukos company's analytical
service before moving on to become head of the press service in the Moscow
mayor's office. She later worked for the MVD's press service, and became head
of the 'Soprotivlenie' (Resistance) human rights organization and a member of
the Public Chamber.

 Here they found a lead to Sergei Gorin, Korovnikov's friend from Tambov.
However, they were not able to arrest Gorin, since on the night of 20–21 November
2002 he and his wife Olga disappeared. Masked men forced entry to their house
and took them away. Although their bodies were never found, they are thought to
have been murdered since traces of Sergei Gorin's blood was found in his garage

[32] Tokareva, *Kto podstavil khodorskovskogo*, pp. 163–4.
[33] Shiryaev, *Sud mesti*, pp. 14, 22–3; with the full text of the letter at pp. 251–60.
[34] Irina Malkova, ' "Apatitu" prostili 5 mlrd rub.', *Vedemosti*, 23 November 2006, p. 4.

and also in the car in which their bodies are thought to have been transported.[35] Sergei Gorin was a well-known businessman in Tambov, who in 1993 established the Algoritm financial-construction company. After having attracted major investment in what appears to have been a pyramid scheme, the company went broke in 1997, leaving half of Tambov out of pocket. Later Gorin was employed by the local branch of Menatep, but was soon sacked. In the three years before his disappearance Gorin was unemployed, but had considerable sums of cash at his disposal. He may well have been associated with the St Petersburg Kumarin gang, which dominated criminal life in Tambov at that time. Gorin in his final year tried to lever his Yukos contacts to break into the oil distribution business, but the company by then was so effectively vertically integrated, with a single chain from pumping the crude to petrol sales, that he could find no foothold. The investigation into the Gorin's disappearance went cold, but there is significant evidence to suggest Korovnikov's involvement.

It is in connection with the Kostina case, and in particular the murder of the Gorins, that Pichugin was arrested on 19 June 2003. He was accused of organizing the attack on Kostina and the murder of the Gorins. According to the prosecutors, there was a clear link between the Gorins and Pichugin since the latter was the godfather of the Gorin's youngest son. Pichugin allegedly asked Sergei Gorin to find someone to organize the attack on Kostina. Gorin asked his friend Peshkun to arrange this, who in turn contacted Korovnikov. In a detailed study of the case, Shiryaev argues that Pichugin was the first victim of the Yukos affair and insists that his case is unfairly neglected. Shiryaev notes that the case against him as the alleged mastermind behind the murder of the Gorins is based on flimsy evidence: an alleged conversation with killers three years before the assassinations took place, by people who were never found and in a place which was never established.[36] In the Lefortovo SIZO Korovnikov alleged that not long before his disappearance Sergei Gorin had given him documents that included a photograph of those who had ordered the attack on Kostina. The documents had disappeared, but Korovnikov claimed to recognize Pichugin and Nevzlin. The trial was closed and the defence was unable effectively to challenge what was clearly highly dubious evidence. The stains found by the Gorins' house at first were found not to be their blood type, and only at the second attempt and under considerable pressure were they found to be that of the Gorins.

In pre-trial detention Pichugin was apparently made an offer: in exchange for admitting guilt and that he had acted on the orders of Nevzlin in particular, he would be offered mercy.[37] He refused, and on 14 July 2003 he was administered some psychotropic substance in his coffee to get him to talk. He lost consciousness for some six hours, but even under the influence of the 'truth drug' Pichugin did not incriminate either himself or his Yukos colleagues and the prosecutors had

---

[35] Lev Romanov, 'Zhestokie igry', *Komsomol'skaya pravda*, 20 May 2005. We have noted above that this source may have been influenced by the authorities. At the same time, the bare outline of this case, as with the Nefteyugansk and East Petroleum ones discussed below, coincide with numerous other accounts.

[36] Shiryaev, *Sud mesti*, chapter 4.   [37] Ibid., p. 79.

to look elsewhere to make the case.[38] The substance had long-term health effects, and Pichugin lost weight and developed lumps on his head.[39] The use of such drugs during interrogations clearly violated international law and Russia's treaty obligations. Throughout Pichugin refused to give evidence against his former colleagues or to accept guilt in any way.

In one of the first major trials to be heard by a jury in Russia, Pichugin was found guilty, by a majority of eight votes to four, on all counts: for organizing the murder of the Gorins, organizing the attempted murder of Kostina, and the assault on Victor Kolesov, the managing director of Rosprom. On 30 March 2005 he was sentenced to twenty years in a strict regime colony. No link with Khodorkovsky was established in these cases. Of all the Yukos-related trials this one was presented to the media as being the most clear-cut, based on convictions for criminal offences, but it turns out that this is perhaps the weakest of all, with evidence that may have cleared him ignored.[40] A second person tried in the same case, Alexei Peshkun, received four years. New charges for murder and attempted murder were almost immediately preferred against Pichugin.

In his second trial from March 2006 Pichugin was charged with the attempted murder of Yevgeny Rybin, the managing director of the Austrian company East Petroleum Handels, and the murder of Nefteyugansk mayor Vladimir Petukhov (see below). One of the co-accused was Yevgeny Reshetnikov, who in November 2000 was found guilty of the attack on Rybin. Reshetnikov admitted culpability for the murder of Petukhov as well for an attack (with Gennady Tsigel'nik) on Kolesov, on 5 October 1998. The aim according to the prosecution was to kill Kolesov, since his ambitions had begun to alarm the other Yukos leaders, and they entrusted Pichugin to deal with the matter. Kolesov himself doubted whether Yukos leaders had anything to do with the attack, in which his wallet containing $2,000 was stolen. Reshetnikov accused Nevzlin, Khodorkovsky, and Pichugin of ordering the attacks, although no direct evidence was produced. The case rested on the alleged confessions of Reshetnikov and Tsigel'nik.

Pichugin was also accused of killing the businesswoman Valentina Korneeva on 21 January 1998, after allegedly refusing to sell office space in central Moscow to Menatep. Korneeva had been the director of a shop serving the Western Group of Forces in East Germany, and after the withdrawal of Soviet forces opened a shop in Moscow called Feniks. In summer 2006 the former militia officer Vladimir Shapiro admitted to killing her during Pichugin's second trial and Shapiro was found guilty on 17 August 2006. Her husband, Dmitry Korneev, had been convinced that his wife was killed as part of the conflict with one of the co-founders of Feniks, Valentin Taraktelyuk, who had lost all his money in Mavrodi's MMM pyramid scheme and was thus unable to repay his debts to Korneeva. Instead, the prosecution stressed the alleged conflict with Menatep about the sale of the

---

[38] The incident and its implications are described in detail in Shiryaev, *Sud mesti*, pp. 82–5, with a general discussion of the use of pharmacological substances by the security police on pp. 85–93.

[39] 'Pichugin Denies Murder Accusations', *Moscow Times*, 24 April 2008.

[40] Vera Vasil'eva, *Kak sudili Alekseia Pichugina: Sudebnyi reportazh* (Prague/Moscow, Human Right Publishers, 2007).

'Chai' shop (part of the Feniks group) at 8 Pokrovka Street in Moscow, next door to a Menatep property.[41] She was offered $300,000 for a property worth at least $500,000.[42] Another of the key characters in this case is Mikhail Ovsyannikov, who allegedly drove Vladimir Shapiro, Gennady Tsigel'nik, and Evgenii Reshetnikov to Korneeva's apartment, when Shapiro committed the murder. Dmitry Korneev was acquainted with Sergei Gorin, and according to the prosecution Pichugin ordered Gorin to organize Korneeva's murder; paying the 35-year-old Ovsyannikov and the 41-year-old Shapiro to do the deed.[43] At first Ovsyannikov agreed that the murder had been committed at Yukos's behest, but on 17 July 2006 he withdrew this allegation, stating: 'All the evidence against Khodorkovsky, Nevzlin and Pichugin was given by me under pressure from the investigators.' He also stated that he had only occasionally glimpsed Pichugin, notably when he drove Sergei Gorin to Pichugin's for a wedding; and had barely had contact with Gorin since 1998.

Pichugin and Reshetnikov were found guilty on 17 August 2006, and the latter sentenced to eighteen years in jail while Pichugin was sentenced to a total of twenty-four years for all the crimes, including the two murders for which he was convicted the previous year.[44] In Pichugin's third trial Reshetnikov was now one of the witnesses, testifying against the leaders of Yukos.[45] In that trial Ovsyannikov was brought in as a witness, but refused to testify beyond his statement of July 2006.[46] In the third trial, the inconsistencies in Shapiro's evidence were revealed on 24 May 2007, when he admitted that he had never seen Pichugin or Nevzlin, and that the order to kill Korneeva had come from Sergei Gorin.[47]

Petukhov and the Nefteyugansk case

On 26 June 1998 (Khodorkovsky's birthday; he was 35 that day) the mayor of Nefteyugansk, Vladimir Petukhov, died in a hail of bullets from a machine pistol

---

[41] http://www.alexey-pichugin.ru/index.php?id=253.

[42] Perekrest, 'Za chto sidit Mikhail Khodorkovskii', Part 2, *Izvestiya*, 18 May 2006; Perekrest also describes the case of the artist Svetlana Vragova, who lived not far from Menatep headquarters in Kolpachnyi Pereulok in Moscow. Menatep tried to take over the building, and even though a defence committee against Menatep was created, after considerable pressure, including the death of one of the activists, all the residents agreed to sell up except Vragova. In the end she moved out after they bought her an alternative apartment. Later, when Khodorkovsky met Vragova at a reception he stated: 'I didn't know it was you.' On his arrest, she signed a letter by cultural workers condemning Khodorkovsky, for which she was greatly criticized.

[43] Mariya Rogacheva and Elena Vlasova, 'Alekseya Pichugina budut sudit' vo vtoroi raz', 20 March 2006, http://www.izvestia.ru/investigation/article3091242/index.html.

[44] David Holley, 'Former Yukos Oil Official is Convicted of 2 Murders', *Los Angeles Times*, 18 August 2006.

[45] http://www.alexey-pichugin.ru/index.php?id=264.

[46] http://www.alexey-pichugin.ru/index.php?id=261.

[47] http://www.alexey-pichugin.ru/index.php?id=266.

as he walked to work.[48] Residents immediately blamed Yukos for his death. The company provided 70 per cent of the town's budget, and allegedly sought influence over local affairs commensurate with its tax contribution, whereas the mayor sought to defend the autonomy of the local authorities. Petukhov, moreover, fought tenaciously to get Yukos to pay its debts to the city, including writing open letters to Yeltsin and Prime Minister Kirienko accusing Yukos of failing to pay its taxes to the city and engaging in criminal acts by 'concealing taxes in large quantities from 1996 to 1998'.[49] This stand-off continued for some time, with the mayor's position reinforced by the overwhelming support of the local population. Hence Yukos tried new tactics. This included on 28 May 1998 bringing money, which should have been paid to the town's exchequer, in cash and being paid directly to municipal agencies. On a flying visit to the town on 3 June Khodorkovsky alleged that the tax revenues had been misused by the town authorities. At the same time a national media campaign was launched against the local authorities, accompanied by personal accusations against Petukhov. In response Petukhov declared a hunger strike, and demonstrations attended by up to 25,000 people, the great majority of the able-bodied population, gathered in his support. Petukhov demanded that a criminal case be opened against Yukos for local tax avoidance.

Petukhov was born on 16 December 1949 and in 1978 moved to Nefteyugansk, the headquarters of Yuganskneftegaz, to work on the drills, and later as a technical foreman before joining management. In 1990 he became head of Debet, a company servicing the drilling and capital repairs department of YNG. By 1995 the company had become a major creditor of Yukos, and Debet launched a court case. Yukos responded with counter-charges of financial irregularities, including concealing half of its profits, and at the same time the tax police began to harass Petukhov. To get Yukos to pay him, Petukhov in 1996 ran in the first elections for mayor of Nefteyugansk on an openly anti-Yukos platform. The former mayor had allowed Yukos to pay its local taxes with non-convertible promissory notes, some issued by shady companies, a practice condemned by Petukhov. Riding a wave of anti-Yukos sentiment, Petukhov unexpectedly won the election, setting the stage for a prolonged confrontation. Petukhov demanded that Yukos pay its taxes with money and not promissory notes or property—Yukos had transferred the airport, agricultural installations, and an asphalt plant to the city. With the price of oil halving to $10 in 1998, the company's liquidity problems became even more severe, and it paid even less of a proportion of its local taxes in cash than it had done the previous year, so that the city ran out of money to pay its teachers, doctors, and police.[50]

At the same time, the oil workers of NYG, who for so long had prospered in a successful industry, endured wage cuts and significant wage arrears. In April 1998, with the oil price falling, Yukos announced drastic pay cuts of about two-thirds

---

[48]   As soon as Khodorkovsky heard what happened, and the news came to him early in the morning Moscow time, he cancelled his birthday celebrations.

[49]   Goldman, *Oilopoly*, p. 109; *Moscow Times*, 25 April 2006.

[50]   Satter, *Darkness at Dawn*, p. 108.

accompanied by a restructuring programme that saw 26,000 of the company's 38,000-strong workforce hived off to fifty-one service companies, which were then forced to negotiate directly with the main YNG company. Itself facing liquidity problems, and as the monopoly employer in the town, YNG imposed harsh conditions on the nominally independent companies. In less than a year the oil workers of Nefteyugansk had fallen from relative affluence to poverty, leading to hatred for the company that was held responsible. The best specialists went to work in Surgut and Kogalym, where wages and conditions provided by Surgutneftegaz and Lukoil, respectively, were much better. Surgut, just an hour's drive away over the river Ob, the base for the Kremlin-friendly Surgutneftegaz, 'was an oasis of tranquility and well-being in comparison. Taxes were paid and workers' salaries did not suffer.' Visiting Surgut in early 2003 Putin stressed the difference: 'Surgut and Nefteyugansk are as different as day and night. Here is an example of the businesses' attitudes towards the areas where they work.' He commented that some companies like Surgutneftegaz are good corporate citizens, while others, like Yukos, are irresponsible.[51]

Nefteyugansk is set in a vast marsh, which in the summer releases swamp gas, while the winters are bitterly cold. Yet out of this the Soviet Union since the mid-1960s had created one of the world's largest production fields, and the pioneering Soviet spirit was now affronted by a parvenu entrepreneur who was felt to have no respect for what had been achieved in such difficult conditions. Indeed, according to his wife Farida, Petukhov, a *neftyanik* to his fingertips, had been appalled to discover on Khodorkovsky's first visit to inspect his newly acquired oilfields that he had never 'seen a well and how oil was extracted. This was a real eye-opener for the oilmen here', even though he had occupied ministerial rank in the fuel and energy ministry.[52]

The official trade union as usual collaborated with the employers, so an independent trade union called 'Nefteyugansk Solidarity' was created to defend the workers' interests. On 27 May 1998, the day of the YNG shareholders' meeting, the union staged a massive demonstration in front of the company's headquarters. Addressing the crowd, Petukhov called Yukos 'a criminal organisation that was growing fat on the sale of oil produced by the people of Nefteyugansk'.[53] A second demonstration on 2 June with 25,000 people saw the YNG building blockaded, locking in Muravlenko, who was forced to promise a partial payment of Yukos's debt to the city. Vladimir Dubov, the deputy head of Rosprom-Yukos, then arrived in the city to negotiate with the tax authorities, which announced that Yukos and YNG owed the city about R80 million, whereas the city owed Yukos nearly R228 million! Petukhov now staged an eight-day hunger strike, demanding the dismissal of the heads of the city and *okrug* tax offices. At this point the governor of the Khanty-Mansi autonomous *okrug*, Alexander Filippenko, intervened and established a budget commission to verify the earlier audit. Petukhov had thus

---

[51] Catherine Belton, 'The Oil Town That Won't Forget Yukos', *Moscow Times*, 25 April 2006, p. 1.
[52] Loc cit.   [53] Satter, *Darkness at Dawn*, p. 109.

been able to take the matter to arbitration, and he ended his hunger strike just four days before his murder.

In response to Petukhov's death, on 26 June a crowd of over 30,000 gathered in the central square, at one end of which was the mayor's office and at the other the headquarters of YNG flying the Yukos colours: 'The people in the square had only one explanation for the mayor's death. He had been murdered by Yukos.'[54] The demonstration nearly turned into an assault on the Yukos building; and the passions aroused at the time have still not subsided. Petukhov's funeral on 30 June was attended by 70,000 people, accompanied by a massive outpouring of grief lamenting not only the death of one man but of a whole era. Yukos continued its restructuring and the region on the banks of the Ob, torn from the unforgiving tundra, was forced to adjust to life in the era of neo-liberal capitalism.[55] It should be noted that at least two other credible versions of Petukhov's end are in circulation: the 'family' one, since following his death Petukhov's widow apparently came into over half a million dollars; and the 'Chechen' version, since Petukhov closed the city market dominated by Chechen groups.[56]

The case was later revived as part of the charges against Yukos associates. The weapons were taken with them by the killers, but in the end Tsigel'nik (on 11 July 2006) and Reshetnikov confessed to the murder, accusing Pichugin and Nevzlin of having ordered the killing.[57] Even though eyewitnesses described totally different people as the murderers, the court accepted the confession.[58] The prosecutors in the Pichugin case, Kamil' Kashaev and Kira Gudim, refused to accept any evidence that could prove that Pichugin had nothing to do with the killing. Pichugin's defence, on the other hand, led by Kseniya Kostromina tried to minimize the conflict between Pichugin and Yukos and took the initial tax inspectors' report at face value, and stressed the conflict between Petukhov and the city Duma, charging Petukhov with unsanctioned budgetary expenditures. The defence, however, was on more solid ground when it argued that Petukhov's murder was ultimately not

[54] Satter, *Darkness at Dawn*, p. 107, with more details on p. 110.

[55] The default of 17 August 1998 diverted attention away from Yukos, but Nefteyugansk was heavily represented in a mass demonstration of oil workers outside the White House in October 1998.

[56] Romanov, 'Zhestokie igry'. The Chechen link is possibly deeper, since a delivery of oil intended to pay off a R450 billion non-denominated debt owed to the city from before Menatep took over in 1995 disappeared into the coffers of trading firm Rondo-S, possibly linked to a financier of Chechen rebel groups, Khozh-Akhmed Nukhaev, who is none other than the person suspected of organizing the murder of Paul Khlebnikov in July 2004, Belton, 'The Oil Town That Won't Forget Yukos'. The book by Khlebnikov is called *Razgovor s varvarom: Besedy s chechenskim polevym komandirom Khozh-Akhmedom Nukhaevym o banditizme i islame* (Moscow, DetektivPress, 2003). The main title, *Conversations with a Barbarian*, probably did not go down too well with Nukhaev.

[57] At the same time Tsigel'nik confessed to the attack on the Rosprom director Victor Kolesov, and also to two attacks on the businessman Evgenii Rybin. In Pichugin's third trial Tsigel'nik acted as a prosecution witness.

[58] Two alleged members of the Kamyshinskii criminal gang, Popov and Prikhod'ko, were identified by witnesses as having exactly the features of the murderers, but were nevertheless released on bail and soon after died in mysterious circumstances and the case was closed as a result, http://www.alexey-pichugin.ru/index.php?id=263. Reshetnikov has Caucasian features (in the Russian sense), whereas witnesses described the killers as classically Slavic types.

in Yukos's interest, since it disrupted the work of Filippenko's arbitration efforts, quite apart from inflicting huge reputational damage on the company.[59] Yukos certainly was not popular in the region, especially when other companies were able to pay their workers double what Yukos offered, and few tears were shed when Khodorkovsky was arrested and Yuganskneftegaz once again returned to the state in the form of Rosneft.[60]

The East Petroleum case (Yevgeny Rybin)

Two assassination attempts were made in 1998 and 1999 against Yevgeny Rybin, who had worked for twenty years in the Soviet and then Russian Ministry of Fuel and Energy. In 1994 he joined the management of the Austrian East Petroleum company, and under his leadership the company's Russian activities thrived. However, when in 1997 Yukos took over 60 per cent of VNK as part of the Tomskneft deal, East Petroleum found itself cut off from its oil supplies, and neither its shares or money were returned. Rybin claimed $100 million, but Yukos offered only $25 million. All Rybin's attempts to resolve the conflict with Yukos failed.[61] Finally, in the summer of 1998 East Petroleum applied to the arbitration court in Vienna for compensation against Yukos's aggressive tactics for the sum of $83 million. East Petroleum also referred the case to the International Arbitration and Hague Courts. The first judgment in his favour was soon followed by an attempt on Rybin's life (by our now familiar Yevgeny Reshetnikov) on 24 November 1998, but the bullets passed harmlessly over his head. Despite attempts to sweep away the evidence, a second investigation found a number of bullets. Forensic tests identified them as coming from the same weapon as had been used in Petukhov's murder. A second attempt was made on Rybin's life on 9 March 1999, this time by blowing up his car as it passed over a device laid in the road. The putative killers then fired into the blazing car, killing the driver and bodyguard, and seriously wounding a militia officer. At the last moment Rybin had decided not to travel in the vehicle, having stayed to celebrate a relative's birthday. Rybin was convinced that Yukos was responsible, and declared that Yukos's security service had broken into his apartment and had placed him under observation.[62] In numerous letters to the MVD and the procuracy he argued that Yukos had laundered some $24 billion![63]

All three cases received widespread media attention. The GPO conducted further investigation into Pichugin's activities, and alleged that he was operating on Nevzlin's orders. Nevzlin at the time was a member of the board of directors of Yukos and first deputy director of the Yukos-Moskva board. The allegation was that he ordered Pichugin to kill individuals who in one way or another were

[59] http://www.alexey-pichugin.ru/index.php?id=263.
[60] Arkady Ostrovsky, 'Yukos Workers Shed Few Tears for Jailed Ex-Boss', *Financial Times*, 17 November 2003.
[61] Perekrest, 'Za chto sidit Mikhail Khodorkovskii', Part 2.   [62] Romanov, 'Zhestokie igry'.
[63] Perekrest, 'Za chto sidit Mikhail Khodorkovskii', Part 2.

a hindrance to Yukos. Pichugin's defence, headed by Kostromina, argued that there was no evidence to demonstrate that Rybin's murder would be to Yukos's advantage. The Vienna court had decided 10 per cent in Rybin's favour, and had entirely refused the second appeal. In November 2000 Reshetnikov was found guilty of the murder attempt, and the involvement of Yukos in the case at that time was not even mentioned. In July 2004 Nevzlin, in a letter to prosecutor general Ustinov, accused Rybin of extortion and of colluding with the authorities to provide false evidence against Yukos and in particular against Pichugin, at that time in the Lefortovo isolator. Two days later the Basmanny court issued an arrest warrant against Nevzlin, who by that time was already in Israel. During Pichugin's second trial in July 2006 Reshetnikov suddenly remembered that the assassination attempt against Rybin had indeed been ordered by Pichugin and Nevzlin.[64]

The Mitra and Lesnoi case

The Mitra limited liability company, allegedly a dummy firm, was based in the closed administrative territorial entity (ZATO) of Lesnoi (formerly Sverdlovsk-45), a low-tax city in the Sverdlovsk region in which a number of Yukos enterprises were registered.[65] The city figured prominently in the case against Khodorkovsky and Lebedev, in particular in relation to the Apatit case. The key charge is that the Mitra company, together with some others, was at the heart of the Yukos company's transfer pricing operations. This was a common practice at the time, with oil sold at artificially low prices to a range of intermediaries, and thus depressing the tax liability, but then sold on to final destinations at the full price. Thus the original wins twice, with reduced taxes and full profits from the end sale. In addition to Mitra, other Yukos companies allegedly involved in this practice include Business Oil, Forest Oil, Vald Oil and many more.

In 1999 the Mitra company paid its taxes in the form of promissory notes. In 2003 the promissory notes transferred to the budget of the City of Lesnoi as tax payments in lieu of cash were partially redeemed and partially exchanged for shares in a local petrol station joint venture. The status of these promissory notes is at the heart of the Ivannikov case, and is typical of the Yukos affair as a whole. The case against the long-time mayor of Lesnoi, Alexander Ivannikov, was launched in the immediate aftermath of the sentencing of Khodorkovsky and Lebedev in May 2005. Ivannikov was a popular figure in the town, having first been elected mayor in 1993 and had since been re-elected a number of times. He was accused on the basis of Article 285, Part 3 of the Russian Criminal Code, 'Exceeding the authority of one's position leading to harmful consequences', and Article 286, Part 3, Clause B, 'Exceeding the authority of one's position to cause harmful consequences', and he was explicitly accused of having conspired with Khodorkovsky and Lebedev. Some forty-five volumes of evidence were produced. The four Yukos companies

---

[64] Vera Vasil'evna, 'Nespravedlivo i nekachestvenno', Grani-ru, 17 August 2006; http://www.alexey-pichugin.ru/index.php?id=265.

[65] Rodionov, *Nalogovye skhemy, za kotorye posadili Khodorkovskogo*, pp. 58–93.

registered in the city are accused of tax evasion in 1999 of a sum in the region of R5.4 billion, allegedly abusing the city's 'onshore offshore' tax haven status in collusion with the mayor. In addition, Yukos was accused of paying its 2000 tax bill in promissory notes to the value of R11.9 billion.

The Federal Tax Police began its investigations into the tax affairs of the Mitra company in 2001, but the case was suspended when the investigators were unable to identify a specific individual responsible for any putative wrong-doing. Further investigation into the tax affairs of the Mitra company in 2002 found that there had been no loss to the municipal or federal budgets, hence there had been no tax 'evasion' and no damage had been caused. The investigation also established the important principle that any possible violation of the tax code by the use of promissory notes was a civil rather than a criminal matter.

As with so many cases started in 2003 against Khodorkovsky that had earlier been closed, the Apatit case perhaps being the best known, in July 2003 the deputy prosecutor general Yuri Biryukov (who figures prominently in many Yukos-related cases and was part of the informal 'politburo' that drove forward the Yukos case), ordered investigation by the tax inspectorate to be transferred to Moscow. Biryukov's decree referred 'to the conclusion of legal and economical expert review on the case; there were no losses caused to the federal budget and municipal budget of ZATO Lesnoi town, as a result of granting tax privileges, receiving taxes in the form of OAO NK YUKOS promissory notes and fulfilling the investment programme'. This report was never disclosed to the defence in the Khodorkovsky trial, despite repeated requests for its disclosure by Khodorkovsky's defence lawyers. In the Kartashov extradition request the senior investigator responsible for serious cases in the GPO, Karimov, dwelt at length on the details of the alleged 'criminal episodes' between December 1999 and December 2000 based on the 'Lesnoi town ZATO'.[66] Karimov had been the state prosecutor in the case against Gusinsky's Media-Most in 2000, and in 2002 he led the charge against Berezovsky and the Avtovaz car plant. Neither case came to trial, but the regime had achieved its aim of removing these two troublesome figures.

The trial began on 6 October 2005 and came to an end in March 2006. The prosecution demanded a nine-year sentence, while Ivannikov denied any wrong-doing. Ivannikov on 6 April 2006 was found guilty of exceeding his authority, but he was acquitted of the charge of conspiring with Khodorkovsky and Lebedev, and he received a six-year suspended sentence. The GPO considered this sentence to be too lenient and the Cassation Court partly upheld this complaint. The Court did not change the verdict but disagreed with the sentence, and the case was sent back for re-trial.[67] The prosecution secured the recusal of all the judges working in Lesnoi from the case, because in its view they would not have been impartial during the trial. The case consequently had to be transferred from Lesnoi

[66] 'Information on Circumstances of Crimes Committed by Mr Vladislav N. Kartashov', undated, mimeo.

[67] For Human Rights, *Chronicles of Political Persecution in Present Day Russia*, No. 39, 20 October 2006.

to Kushva.[68] The retrial started on 28 November 2006.[69] On 8 February 2007 Ivannikov was found guilty of abusing his official position and was sentenced to five years in prison.[70]

During the hearings into the Ivannikov case in March 2005 one of the defence witnesses and deputy head of the economic department of Lesnoi administration, Lyubov Myasnikova, argued that cooperation between the city and the four Yukos-affiliated companies had been mutually beneficial and had helped the city to survive at a time when its major employer, a large defence enterprise, had been in crisis. Myasnikova stressed that tax payments had been taken in the form of promissory notes in anticipation that the administration would receive additional profit from the interest on the promissory notes. She insisted that all Yukos promissory notes issued in lieu of taxes had been redeemed and the revenue was received. This evidence was discounted by the prosecutor, Dmitry Shokhin, who led in Khodorkovsky's trial, as being biased since Myasnikova herself could have been part of the alleged conspiracy.[71]

The story with Lesnoi does not end there. In yet another directly related Yukos case, the GPO charged the former Lesnoi tax director, Sergei Karfidov, with having helped the four Yukos subsidiaries (Biznes oil, Forest Oil, Vald Oil, and Mitra) to avoid paying taxes. The case was separated from the main Yukos case on 27 February 2008, and focused on Karfidov's work in Lesnoi between 1994 and 2005. He was alleged to have helped Khodorkovsky, Lebedev, Irina Golub, and others in their alleged conspiracy to get the tax ministry to refund money to the four companies on the basis of promissory notes. Karfidov had been one of the witnesses in the Ivannikov case but at that time there had been no suggestion that he was in any way involved in malfeasance.[72]

KHODORKOVSKY'S TRIAL

The trial of Khodorkovsky and his associates has been described as a 'kangaroo court'.[73] Lawyers conducting the case were subject to searches and other forms of

---

[68] *Regnum.ru*, 28 November 2006.   [69] *Regnum.ru*, 4 December 2006.

[70] *Gazeta.ru*, 8 February 2007; *Kommersant*, 9 February 2007.

[71] Ekaterina Zapodinskaya, 'Promissory Notes are Calculated for the Head of Lesnoy City', *Kommersant*, 29 March 2006. Shokhin also figured in the notorious 'Tri Kita' (Three Whales) furniture smuggling case, having been censured by the first judge Marina Komarova in September 2002, which was lifted at the GPO's request by the Supreme Court; and the case was then returned to the Moscow District Court under a new judge, Olga Kudeshkina. Kudeshkina later complained that she had come under intolerable pressure from Shokhin and the head of the Moscow court, Olga Egorova, to disrupt the case—against highly placed FSB officials, Ekaterina Zapodinskaya, 'Prokurory Yukosa ostalis' bez raboty', *Kommersant*, 20 September 2006.

[72] Igor' Lesovskikh, 'Eks-nalogoviku pred"yavili zloupotrebleniya Yukosa', *Kommersant*, 16 April 2008, p. 5.

[73] Sarah E. Mendelson and Theodore P. Gerber, 'Soviet Nostalgia: An Impediment to Russian Democratization', *The Washington Quarterly*, Vol. 21, No. 1, Spring 2008, p. 92.

harassment that drove them to appeal to legal advocacy organizations to defend their rights. The case was accompanied by repeated breaches of advocacy rules.[74] For example, Anton Drel, the lead lawyer representing Khodorkovsky, was summoned for questioning by the GPO on 17 October 2003, in contravention of Article 8 of the law on the rights and duties of lawyers, which states that a defence attorney cannot be summoned for questioning or to give evidence in a current case, and also Article 56 of the Russian Criminal Code. There were numerous searches of the law offices of companies associated with the Yukos case. On 9 October 2003 Drel's offices were searched and documents connected with the Yukos case confiscated, clearly violating attorney–client privilege. At the time of the search the FSB knew that Drel was at a court hearing representing Lebedev. The investigations were accompanied by improper searches, often executed with a show of force, without proper search warrants, incomplete records of the materials confiscated and without the subjects of the search or their representatives being present, as stipulated by law. The orphanage supported by Yukos was raided by armed men in the presence of the children.

'Basmanny justice'

The trial of Khodorkovsky and Lebedev began on 11 July 2004 and lasted nearly a year. This was the most important trial in the country's post-Soviet history. It took place in the Meshchansky court in Moscow, but the decision on whether bail should be given and other key procedural issues were decided by the Basmanny court. This court specializes in 'political' cases and is closely associated with the procuracy, with the prosecution team working out of the investigative division of the GPO based in the Basmanny district of Moscow, hence the term 'Basmanny justice'. One of the judges who approved Khodorkovsky's arrest, Andrei Rasnovsky, was a former employee of the GPO. We shall discuss criticisms of the trial in Chapter 7, but note here that the two main charges in support of the view that Khodorkovsky and his colleagues did not get a fair trial are that they were kept in pre-trial detention without due cause and that the prosecutors were allowed to confront the defendants without their lawyers being present. A constant criticism is that the defendants had great difficulty communicating freely with their defence lawyers.

While Pichugin was accused of murder and attempted murder, the charges against Khodorkovsky and Lebedev focused on economic crimes, covering eleven charges against seven articles of the Russian Criminal Code.[75] There was no reason to believe that either would attempt to leave the country to avoid trial. In addition, Pichugin was held in the Lefortovo detention centre, run at the time by the FSB in

---

[74] These are listed in *Constitutional and Due Process Violations in the Khodorkovsky/Yukos Case*, A White Paper Prepared by Defense Lawyers on Behalf of Mikhail Khodorkovsky, Platon Lebedev, Alexei Pichugin (Moscow, n.d.), compiled by Robert Amsterdam and Charles Krause.

[75] Details in Mariya Lokotetskaya and Lyudmila Romanova, 'Sud idet: Lebedev i Khodorkovskii ponyali, v chem ikh obvinyayut i ne priznali vinu', *Gazeta*, 16 July 2004, p. 3.

contravention of Russia's Council of Europe commitments. Pichugin was allegedly interrogated with the help of the injection of psychtropic drugs, in an attempt to get evidence that could have turned him into a witness for the prosecution. There are allegations that Lebedev was treated inhumanely while in detention, above all by not being provided with adequate medical assistance. Lebedev suffers from *diabetes mellitus* and a heart condition. Indeed, he was arrested in hospital and taken initially to Lefortovo before being transferred to Matrosskaya Tishina.

The head of Khodorkovsky's legal team, Genrikh Padva, warned his client not to politicize the trial, and in the event, although scandalous, the trial did not become a major political scandal.[76] The opening day of the trial was attended by a moving public demonstration of support outside the courthouse, and for most of the trial small groups picketed the building condemning 'Basmanny justice'. Numerous witnesses were called to give evidence for the prosecution. Among them was Yevgeny Komarov, the governor of Murmansk region at the time of the partial privatization of Apatit. He noted that the Apatit auction had been conducted correctly, but later the investment conditions for the purchase of the 20 per cent stake had not been fulfilled. He conceded that the company's debts for transport and electricity had been repaid, although further investment had not taken place, hence the matter had been referred to the arbitration court.[77] Khodorkovsky vigorously rebutted the charge.[78] On several occasions he attacked the procuracy as a great danger to Russian justice, declaring on 13 January 2005: 'Today's problems in the GPO will be dealt with when genuinely independent courts are established', which the state prosecutor Shokhin interpreted as a threat.[79]

Giving evidence in February 2005 Khodorkovsky declared that he did not consider himself guilty on any of the charges: 'Everything they accuse me of was normal business practice'. Khodorkovsky declared himself proud that for fifteen years he ran a number of successful businesses, 'but I categorically object to the criminal-artistic presentation of normal business practices'. He argued that the prosecution had 'thought up accusations' in matters with which he had no connection: 'Since 1994 I have held over 3,000 meetings and signed over 10,000 documents, so I cannot remember every point and every paper, although I have a good memory'. Khodorkovsky's basic argument was that he was being charged for crimes that did not even exist, about events that were torn out of context.[80] He was not cross-examined by the prosecutor, Shokhin. The judge, Irina Kolesnikova, asked Khodorkovsky to specify precisely what posts he had occupied in his various businesses, so that his personal responsibility could be established.[81] At issue was

---

[76] Panyushkin, *Mikhail Khodorkovskii*, p. 220.

[77] Aleksei Grishin, 'Svideteli s raz"yasneniem', *Vremya novostei*, 25 August 2004, p. 2.

[78] Andrei Skrobot and Roman Ukolov, 'Khodorkovskii sekonomil vremya sudu', *Nezavisimaya gazeta*, 25 August 2004, p. 11.

[79] Anfisa Voronina, 'Khodorkovskii obvinil prokurorov', *Vedemosti*, 13 January 2005.

[80] Dmitrii Simakin, 'Khodorkovskii: "Eto kriminal'no-khudozhestvennoe delo", *Nezavisimaya gazeta*, 28 February 2005, p. 7.

[81] Vladimir Perekrest, 'Mikhail Khodorkovskii: "Vse, v chem menya obvinyayut,—eto normal'naya praktika vedeniya biznesa", *Izvestiya*, 28 February 2005, p. 2.

the freelance consulting work (as a 'predprinimatel' bez obrazovaniya yuridich-eskogo litsa', PBOYuL) that Khodorkovsky had carried out in 1998/9, based on a licence issued on 24 December 1997.[82] Khodorkovsky refused to give the names of companies for which he had provided consulting services, since they had not agreed to their names being given out. For fear of dragging them into the matter, Khodorkovsky pleaded the 51st—the article of the constitution granting the right not to give evidence against oneself.

Khodorkovsky's legal team offered detailed rebuttals of the charges against him. For example, on 5 April 2005 Padva noted that the date at which Khodorkovsky was alleged to have created a 'criminal group' was sometimes stated to have been in 1990, in other documents in 1993, and elsewhere in 1995 or 1997.[83] On 7 April 2005 Padva argued that Menatep had actually saved the situation with the Apatit plant, and he stressed that the company's shareholders had suffered no loss and its directors had been fully aware of the sales plan.[84]

The trial of Khodorkovsky, Lebedev, and Krainov came to a close on 11 April 2005. While the full ten years was asked for the other two, the prosecution recommended a five-and-a-half-year suspended sentence on Krainov because of his 'repentance and partial admission of guilt'.[85] Krainov argued that he had not been able to manage the affairs of Volna in the way that he would have liked because of its complete dependence on the Menatep group. He claimed that when he demanded that the investment conditions in Apatit be fulfilled, he was sacked.[86] He was also involved in the Volgograd case, where the regional authority was allegedly defrauded.[87] Throughout the trial he sat separately on a bench with his lawyers away from the other two in the cage, and his lawyers did not try to coordinate their position with those of Khodorkovsky and Lebedev, and indeed his defence often was at cross-purposes with theirs. In the year-long trial Krainov barely exchanged a word or a glance with the other two defendants.

In his final statement on 11 April Khodorkovsky insisted on his innocence and stated that he would not ask for leniency:

I am a Russian patriot, and therefore I consider the events around Yukos, my partners and myself from the perspective of the interests and values of my country. . . . I behaved the way I did because I love Russia and believe in its future as a strong and legal state. . . . Certain influential people have undertaken the systematic destruction of Yukos so that they can take over a prosperous company, or rather its profits . . . these are mercenary bureaucrats.

---

[82] Vladimir Perekrest, 'Prokuror otkazalsya doprashivat' Khodorkovskogo', *Izvestiya*, 28 February 2005, p. 3.

[83] Dmitrii Simakin, ' "Prestupleniya voobshche ne bylo": genrikh Padva nachal dolguyu rech' v zashchitu Khodorkovskogo', *Nezavisimaya gazeta*, 6 April 2005, p. 1.

[84] Dmitri Simakin, 'V poiskakh zerna istiny', *Nezavisimaya gazeta*, 8 April 2005, p. 7.

[85] Victor Yasmann, 'Khodorkovskii Case is a sign of the Times', RFE/RL, *Russian Political Weekly*, Vol. 5, No. 15, 14 April 2005.

[86] Larisa Kallioma, ' "Ya byl nepravil'nym oligarkhom": Mikhail Khodorkovskii skazal svoe poslednee slovo', *Izvestiya*, 12 April 2005, p. 1.

[87] Rodionov, *Nalogovye skhemy, za kotorye posadili Khodorkovskogo*, pp. 209–26.

The whole country knows why I have been imprisoned, so that I cannot prevent the pillaging of Yukos.... I no longer have major property. In contrast to those modest business men and business-officials who are responsible for the Yukos case and the corresponding actions off the Procuracy, I have no yachts, nor palaces, nor football clubs, or even property abroad.... I was the wrong sort of oligarch, therefore the authorities not only confiscated Yukos but are now holding me in prison for the second year running.

He asserted that he 'did not want to be president', and condemned the damage that the 'home-grown bureaucracy' had inflicted on the country. He was proud of his work over the past fifteen years, creating by 2004 the largest and most transparent oil corporation in Russia, arguing that he had sought to work for the good of the country. On no point had the prosecution been able to prove his guilt. He would not ask for leniency, but would 'strive for justice'.[88] He emotionally thanked his family and wife for their support, movingly speaking of Inna as 'a real comrade-in-arms and Decembrist'.[89] At the end of his thirty-nine-minute speech the court burst into a spontaneous prolonged standing ovation, with the exception of the prosecution team and the judges.

The reading of the verdict was postponed from 27 April to 16 May. In the interim Nevzlin on 3 May made the sensational announcement that he was willing to sell over 60 per cent of Menatep shares in Yukos 'at a discount' in exchange for the cases against himself, Khodorkovsky, and top Yukos managers being dropped. Khodorkovsky reacted sharply, stressing that he did not consider himself guilty and was not willing to buy his freedom; he insisted that he would fight for his freedom through legal means; and he called on others 'not to turn him into the banner of the opposition'[90] or 'to turn me into a political project, the contents of which I do not agree with'.[91] Already in an interview with *Vedemosti* on 17 April Nevzlin threatened to take to court the head of the presidential administration, Medvedev, the finance minister Kudrin, as well as the two deputy heads of the presidential administration Sechin and Surkov, who he declared were responsible for the destruction of Yukos.[92] Once again Nevzlin revealed his lack of judgement, compared to Khodorkovsky's more profound understanding of the dynamics of Russian politics.

The reading of the sentence from 16 May was a long-drawn-out and contentious affair, lasting until 31 May, a fitting culmination of a trial that had continued ten months. By then there were 227 volumes of material associated with the case. Kolesnikova, the lead judge of the three sitting in judgment in the case, read

---

[88] Ekaterina Butorina, 'Nepravil'nyi oligarkh: Mikhail Khodorkovskii skazal sudu poslednee slovo', *Vremya novostei*, 12 April 2005, p. 1; Anfisa Voronina, 'Poslednee slovo', *Vedemosti*, 12 April 2005.

[89] Marina Gridneva and Lina Panchenko, 'Sego dnya: "Ne vinovat, snisokhozhdeniya ne proshu", *Moskovskii komsomolets*, 12 April 2005, p. 3. Later Khodorkovsky was jailed where the Decembrists had been exiled, and Inna could truly reveal her Decembrist qualities.

[90] Yuri Spirin, 'Khodorkovskii zapretil Nevzlinu pokupat' dlya nego svobodu', *Izvestiya*, 6 May 2005, p. 2.

[91] Catherine Belton, 'Khodorkovsky a Cloud Putin Cannot Scare Away', *Moscow Times*, 6 May 2005, p. 5.

[92] Elena Rudneva and Irina Reznik, 'Leonid, ty ne prav', *Vedemosti*, 5 May 2005.

through the verdict, a document 662 pages long summarizing the evidence. In Russia a trial verdict, which is read aloud, is not a straightforward declaration of whether a defendant is guilty but a full summation of prosecution and defence arguments.[93] In the event the verdict consisted of an almost verbatim summary of the prosecution case presented by the lead prosecutor, Shokhin. Outside the court Khodorkovsky's supporters shouted 'Freedom! Freedom!', which turned to cries of 'Shame! Shame!' once the verdict was delivered.[94]

The sentence for fraud, tax evasion, and embezzlement was finally delivered on 31 May 2005. Khodorkovsky was found guilty of nine offences out of the eleven with which he was charged against six articles of the RF Criminal Code, with charges of repeated forgery of documents dropped; and Lebedev on eight charges, also against six articles of the RF Criminal Code. Guilt was found in the following instances:[95]

1. Buying 20 per cent of Apatit shares not at market but at nominal cost, and then failing to fulfil the investment conditions. Because of the statute of limitations the prosecution focused on the failure of the two to fulfil the court order to return shares to the state between 1998 and 2002, and that between 2000 and 2002 they sold the plant's output at low prices to intermediaries, who then doubled the price, making profits of R6 billion.

2. In December 1995 Khodorkovsky and Lebedev bought 44 per cent of the state's shares in the Samoilov Research Institute for Fertilisers and Insecto-fungicides (NIUIF) (through AOZT Walton, run by Khodorkovsky's school friend Usachev), but according to the prosecution once again failed to provide the promised investment but instead were after the land and buildings, located in a desirable Moscow district. The pair were found guilty of failing to fulfil a November 1997 court order to return the shares of NIUIF.[96]

3. Embezzling state funds in 1999–2000, at the time when Khodorkovsky was in charge of Yukos, by claiming refunds in cash based upon false payment of taxes in promissory notes, to the tune of 17 billion, 395 million, and 444,000 roubles.

4. Khodorkovsky transferred, in the form of promissory notes, money from the sale of oil and apatite concentrate to the accounts of the Media-Most bank owned by Vladimir Gusinsky, against which security Gusinsky took out loans. The court found that in this way Khodorkovsky caused material harm to the company of some $100 million.[97]

[93] Larisa Kallioma, 'Sadites' poka', *Izvestiya*, 17 May 2005, p. 1, gives details of the NIIUIF, Apatit and income tax cases.

[94] Lyuba Pronina, '9 Years for Khodorkovsky and Lebedev', *Moscow Times*, 1 June 2005, p. 1.

[95] For a good overview, see Peter Clateman, 'Yukos Affair, Part VII: Review of the Criminal Sentence and Appeal', 29 March 2006, *JRL*, No. 77, 30 March 2006, Item 19; also summed up by Dmitrii Simakin, Mikhail Tolpegin, 'Upryatali', *Nezavisimaya gazeta*, 1 June 2005, p. 1; Yurii Sergeev, 'Iz dos'e "KP"', *Komsomol'skaya Pravda*, 1 June 2005, p. 2.

[96] Rodionov, *Nalogovye skhemy, za kotorye posadili Khodorkovskogo*, pp. 106–13.

[97] Ibid, pp. 191–208.

5. Corporate tax evasion by Yukos through illegally taking advantage of onshore tax havens and paying taxes with promissory notes during 1998/9.
6. Khodorkovsky (in 1998 and 1999) and Lebedev (in 2000 as well) failed to pay the appropriate personal income taxes by diverting company resources to themselves for 'independent entrepreneurial activity' (for alleged consulting services) and thus paid taxes on a lower level. The losses amounted to R54.5 million.[98]

The defence team insisted that the shares in Apatit and NIUIF were bought at a fair price, set by the state itself, and as for the failure to invest, the best evidence was that appropriate investment had been made and both enterprises were flourishing. Khodorkovsky argued that he had never seen the institute's rector until they met in court, when he declared that although the investment terms had been changed, they had been sensible and allowed the institute to make a profit in market conditions. As for the problem of paying local government taxes with promissory notes, the defence team noted that up to 29 December 1999 this had been legal, and the law did not forbid non-monetary forms of payment. In fact, the notes issued by Yukos were interest-bearing, and protected the Lesnoi ZATO budget from inflation. The prosecution had not been able to find any evidence of the transfer of funds to Gusinsky's bank because they had been returned to Yukos, with interest. By signing consulting contracts with various foreign companies, Khodorkovsky allegedly avoided paying a million dollars in personal income tax. According to the prosecution, Khodorkovsky had provided no services. The charge is a bizarre one, since Khodorkovsky had paid millions of his own funds for philanthropic and political purposes, yet allegedly engaged in an extremely complicated scheme to avoid paying $1 million.[99]

Krainov received a five-year suspended sentence. Khodorkovsky received a nine-year sentence to a general-regime penal colony, minus the eighteen months he had served in pre-trial detention. Lebedev, the head of Menatep, received the same term.[100] The sentence was only one year short of that demanded by the prosecution, and its severity took many observers aback. There is little doubt that the sentence was agreed with the Kremlin. Their lawyers immediately announced that they would appeal.

The sentencing of Khodorkovsky and his associates was not the end of the affair, and the issues of transfer pricing and money laundering remained to be dealt with. Even before the sentence was delivered, on 13 May 2005 the prosecutor general announced that further charges could be laid against Khodorkovsky and

[98] Rodionov, *Nalogovye skhemy, za kotorye posadili Khodorkovskogo*, pp. 8–57.

[99] Igor' Smirnov, 'Protsess: Privesti nagovor v ispolnenie', *Moskovskaya Pravda*, 22 April 2005, p. 2.

[100] Dmitrii Simakin and Mikhail Tolpegin, 'Upraytili: Rasprava nad Khodorkovskim i Lebedevym byla ozhidaema, no vse ravno shokirovala svoei zhestokost'yu', *Nezavisimaya gazeta*, 1 June 2005, p. 1. Lebedev's sentence was later reduced on appeal to eight years.

Lebedev, and an international arrest warrant was issued against Temerko.[101] On the day the sentence on Khodorkovsky and his colleagues was delivered, 31 May, the GPO reiterated that there would soon be new charges against Khodorkovsky and Lebedev, probably for money laundering, although no details were given. Appearing on NTV on 6 June 2005, the deputy prosecutor general, Vladimr Kolesnikov, warned that other leading business figures could be in the firing line: 'I can say one thing, [Khodorkovsky's] case will not be the last. We have got plenty of cases in the cartridge clip.'[102] In response to the question why other oligarchs had not been arrested, he stated: 'Unfortunately some managed to run away. We were too humane at that time and they managed to hide.'[103] Possible targets included Nevzlin, and even Chubais and Abramovich, the governor of Chukotka and major shareholder in Sibneft.

Asked whether he understood the ruling, Khodorkovsky from his prison cage in the courtroom stated that '[t]he sentence is clear', and denounced it as a miscarriage of justice and warned that '[i]t is a testament to "Basmanny justice"', using the term that the trial had made famous.[104] In a statement read out after the trial by Drel he declared: 'Judicial power in Russia has turned into a dumb appendage, a blunt instrument of the executive branch of government; and not even the government, but of a few quasi-criminal economic groups.... I do not consider myself guilty and consider my innocence proven.... I know that the verdict in my trial was decided in the Kremlin.'[105] From this perspective, his main crime was not to recognize his own guilt.

Reaction to the trial and verdict

In an interview soon after Khodorkovsky noted that he had expected no less of a sentence, but in due course the sentence 'would not just be reduced but abrogated by the Supreme Court', and he gave it 'some 3–4 years'. In the meantime, he would

---

[101] This is the report of the press conference held on 13 May 2005: 'In the near future the General Prosecutor's office of the Russian Federation will present new charges against ex-head of NK YUKOS, Mikhail Khodorkovsky and head of MFO MENATEP, Platon Lebedev. This was announced to the journalists on Friday by the head of information and PR of General Prosecutor's Office, Natalia Vishnyakova.... The General Prosecutor's Office has declared an international search for Alexander Temerko.... The General Prosecutor's office is seeking the extradition of Ivan Kolesnikov, currently in Cyprus, who is accused of the fraudulent acquisition of the right to shares of OAO "Yeniseinefttegaz". As Natalia Vishnyakova reported on Friday, "the investigation has determined his location and extradition proceedings are under way". She related that Kolesnikov, who was a lawyer-stagiaire at the law firm "ALM-Feldmans", was drawn into committing fraud in 2002 by the member of NK YUKOS board of directors and management, Alexander Temerko.' Reported by Russian agencies; 'Nakanune vyneseniya prigovora prokuratura grozit Khodorkovskomu novym obvineniyami', Newsru.com, 13 May 2005; 'Ukradennye milliardy', *Slovo*, 20 May 2005, p. 11; *Kommersant*, 14 May 2005, pp. 1, 5.

[102] Peter Lavelle, 'The Kremlin's "Cartridge Clip"', *Untimely Thoughts: Analysis*, 7 June 2005.

[103] Nick Paton Walsh, 'Prosecutors Warn Russian Oligarchs', *The Guardian*, 7 June 2005, p. 12.

[104] Catherine Belton, 'Shock and Then Boredom in Court', *Moscow Times*, 1 June 2005, p. 1.

[105] 'Zayavlenie Mikhaila Khodorkovskogo', *Nezavisimaya gazeta*, 1 June 2005, p. 3.

have to sit it out.[106] He insisted that the GPO had worked closely with the Kremlin on the case, and he reserved his sympathy for the judge, Kolesnikova, having to bear the burden of what she had done at the request of the authorities. He warned that the only way to avoid another case like his was to 'create a state based on justice and the law', but he did not think that there would be another Yukos case since one was enough for Putin. Meanwhile, '[p]rivatisation has not been legitimised, and the struggle for big property in our country continues', with the courts, security agencies, and procuracy involved, and with no one guaranteed to be safe: 'The Kremlin is not the only player: those who like the present rules of the game are forced to play by them and at any moment can become their victim.' In response to the question about what some considered the positive aspects of the affair, the end to tax minimization and that 'oligarchs no longer consider themselves masters of the country', he insisted that he had long ago stopped his own personal tax minimization schemes, and that he had never considered himself the country's manager: 'I am convinced that business should be separate from power, but this does not mean that business does not have the right to defend its political interests. This means that business should manage the country, but the authorities should not get involved in business.' He noted that the authorities were no less engaged in individual business affairs than they were in the 1990s.

Asked about the level of support from society, he wryly noted that 'a rich person of Jewish background cannot be too popular in Russia', but he had been struck by the high level of individual support that he had received from all over the country. He repudiated Nevzlin's view that Roman Abramovich had been behind the case, and stated that 'the organiser and motor of the "Yukos affair" was Igor Sechin, one of the competitors in the struggle for influence on Putin'. Here Khodorkovsky recognized the factional nature of Russian politics, and accepted that in this case Putin had been influenced by one of them. He noted that Abramovich had done nothing to help him. Asked about his personal hopes for the future, he stated, first, that he would devote himself to social activity, including his foundation to support Russian art and to help Russian prisoners. 'In this work I am absolutely free of any external obligations and thus full of optimism. Now I know how one feels free, even in jail.' His second hope lay 'with those generations, in a few years, who will have passed through the grey monolithic ranks of bureaucratic incompetence. At that time we will all leave "jail".'

With the opposition lacking a generally recognized leader there was intense pressure for Khodorkovsky to become 'the conscience of the nation'. An article in the Yukos-affiliated *Moscow News* argued that only Khodorkovsky could unite the left and right to become a national leader of the type of that Victor Yushchenko in Ukraine had become, and likened him to Nelson Mandela, who spent 26 years in jail: 'Today Russia needs to change its socio-political climate, it needs freedom. For Khodorkovsky, like for all of us, there will be no easy walk to freedom. But, having

---

[106] 'Ya uveren, chto prigovor budet otmenen', *Vedemosti*, 4 August 2005, p. 5. The date of the interview is not given, but it was published three days after his article 'Left Turn' came out in the same paper, discussed in Chapter 8.

endured the destruction of his company, the loss of friends, imprisonment, he could become the best president in contemporary Russian history.'[107] Once again, this was not something that the Kremlin wanted to hear.

Russian public opinion clearly viewed the case as political. A poll by the Yuri Levada Analytical Centre in late November 2004 found that respondents were of the view that 'civil servants (*chinovniki*) were pursuing their own financial interests' in destroying the country's largest oil company. According to the poll:

41 per cent of Russians believe that the *chinovniki* are deliberately hampering Yukos' tax debt repayment and forcing the company to the verge of bankruptcy, and 69 per cent of respondents were convinced that Yukos' bankruptcy and sale of its assets would be conducted for the benefit of the civil servants and businessmen close to the authorities.

The general view was that the country would only lose from the whole affair, with 48 per cent believing that the authorities pressured court officials to pass a guilty verdict. A remarkably small number (10 per cent) considered that the case was prompted by strictly judicial considerations, while 36 per cent considered the aim was to wrest control of assets owned by Khodorkovsky. Nearly a third, 29 per cent, said the situation was provoked by the authorities' desire to limit Khodorkovsky's political influence, while over half (57 per cent) foresaw similar legal moves against other businessmen in Russia.[108] A film by Vladimir Grechkov called *Reaktsiya* was premiered in November 2005 and dealt with popular reactions to the case. It revealed a deep current of hostility to Khodorkovsky, although this was explained as having nothing to do with Khodorkovsky personally, but was '[a] reaction to all that happened to Russia in the twentieth and even the nineteenth centuries'.[109] The film failed to make it to television or to achieve general release in cinemas.

Reaction to the sentence stressed the political nature of the case. There was a general consensus of opinion abroad that the case and the severe verdict represented the victory of presidential officialdom working with law-enforcement and security agencies over the business tycoons who had come to prominence in the 1990s. A plenary session of the European Parliament (EP) adopted its report on EU–Russian relations on 26 May 2005. An amendment to paragraph 14 of the report proposed by the Greens now read as follows:

The EP expresses its concern about the apparent weakening of Russia's commitment to democracy, market economy and protection of human rights; regrets restrictions on the operation of free and independent media; reiterates its criticism of the use of the judicial system in the apparent pursuit of political goals; notes that these developments affect both the situation of the Russian people and Russia's foreign relations, and that as long as they are not reversed, development of the EU–Russia partnership will be more difficult. Takes

---

[107] Anton Malyavskii, a member of the Moscow city SPS Political Council, 'Tot chelovek', *Moskovskie novosti*, No. 23, 17 June 2005, p. 12.

[108] Mosnews.com, 23 November 2004.

[109] Alla Bossart, 'Ra-by-ne-my', *Novaya gazeta*, 3 November 2005.

the view, in this respect, that the Yukos case represents a fundamental test of Russia's respect for the rule of law, property rights, transparency and a fair and open market for investors.

A press release by Leutheuser-Schnarrenberger, the German MP and Rapporteur for PACE on the proceedings against former Yukos executives, argued:

The enemies of the rule of law and an independent judiciary in Russia have won in the trial against the former Yukos chief executive....The trial was afflicted with numerous shortcomings for the rule of law and the sentence are an implacable act of revenge against a man who dared to stand up openly against the policy of Russia's President Vladimir Putin.... The verdict shows that legal security does not exist in Russia.[110]

Amnesty International was unequivocal in its view that the Yukos case was politically motivated. In a statement not long before the verdict it noted:

Amnesty International takes the view that there is a significant political context to the arrest and prosecution of Mikhail Khodorkovsky, former head of the Yukos company, and other individuals associated with Yukos. The human rights organization recognizes the significance of the case, which has been accompanied by numerous reports of violations of international fair trial standards and health concerns with regard to some of the accused. Amnesty International acknowledges the widespread perception among the defendants' lawyers, Russian human rights organizations and other analysts that the cases are politically motivated and has written to the Ministry of Justice and to the Procurator General of the Russian Federation raising concerns related to the arrest and prosecution and detention of Mikhail Khodorkovsky, Platon Lebedev, his business partner, Aleksei Pichugin, a former security official for Yukos, Svetlana Bakhmina, a senior lawyer for Yukos and Yelena Agranovskaya. Amnesty International has urged the Russian authorities to respect its obligations under international human rights law in these cases, including Article 14 of the UN International Covenant on Civil and Political Rights, and Article 6 of the European Convention for the Protection of Human Rights and Fundamental Freedoms.[111]

Maureen Greenwood, Amnesty International's specialist on Russia, stressed in a news conference launching the organization's 2005 Report on Human Reports the following points:

Amnesty International is concerned that the case against Mr. Khodorkovsky and his colleagues is politically motivated. We are concerned about interference in the lawyer–client process. We are concerned about the closed nature of the procedural issues, about detention and isolation of some of the suspects, about shortcomings in medical care provided to the detainees, and also to the alleged ill-treatment of some of the detainees in detention. We are very closely monitoring the trial so that it meets their trial standards; we are urging medical assistance to those who need it in detention, and we want all to be free from ill treatment and torture.[112]

---

[110] Sabine Leutheuser-Schnarrenberger, Press Release, 31 May 2005, mimeo.

[111] Amnesty International Public Statement, AI Index: EUR 46/012/2005 (public). News Service No: 087, 11 April 2005.

[112] News Conference with William Schulz, Executive Director, Amnesty International. Topic: Amnesty International's 2005 Report on Human Rights (Part 3), 25 May 2005, Federal News Service.

However, Amnesty did not declare Khodorkovsky a political prisoner and its measured condemnation of the trial contrasts with the rather more ideological press release by Freedom House: 'The conviction and sentencing to jail of Russian businessman Mikhail Khodorkovsky underscores the serious erosion of the rule of law and growing intolerance for political dissent in Russia.'[113]

In his reaction to the verdict, Bush stressed that he 'monitored' the Yukos case and would be watching the appeal process. He noted that he had spoken with Putin about his concern that 'it looked like he had been judged guilty prior to having a fair trial'.[114] In a news briefing, Ambassador Richard Boucher, spokesperson for the US Department of State, reiterated his view 'that this case has raised some very serious questions about the rule of law in Russia...about the independence of courts, about the right of due process, about the sanctity of contracts and property rights, lack of a predictable tax regime.... [T]his case and the verdict continue to erode Russia's reputation and public confidence in the Russian legal and judicial institutions.'[115] Lantos, part of a delegation observing the trial, noted that Khodorkovsky was 'being tried for things that others have not been tried for, and could have had a civilized trial rather than being behind bars like an animal'. He stressed that the verdict was political.[116] Together with Congressman Cox and Senator McCain, he called for Russia to be expelled from G-8, or at least for its membership to be temporarily suspended.

In Russia there was no unanimity in response, since clearly oligarch-bashing has a popular constituency. Nevertheless, among serious analysts of Russian politics there was widespread concern. The political aspect was stressed by an editorial in *The Moscow Times*: 'There was never any chance that he [Khodorkovsky] would be allowed to walk free before the 2008 presidential election was safely in the bag.' The paper noted that with time off for good behaviour and barring further convictions, Khodorkovsky could be released in 2009.[117] Thus Khodorkovsky would be well out of the way during the succession crisis of 2007/8. Illarionov weighed in with his view that the attack on Yukos represented a turning point for Russia, warning that Khodorkovsky's conviction 'was only the beginning. The Yukos case is the biggest economic and political event in the country in the past 14 years, since August 1991. As a result, we are seeing fundamental changes in the sphere of business, and in the economic sphere, in economic policy, the political system, the media, ideology, not to mention ethics.' In addition he noted that the court case 'displayed deep incompetence with regard to economics and jurisprudence. I was struck by the low level of competence of those people who represented the state.'[118] The

---

[113] http://www.freedomhouse.org/media/pressrel/053105.htm.

[114] President George W. Bush's Press Conference, The Rose Garden, 31 May 2005; *Vedemosti*, 1 June 2005.

[115] US State Department News Briefing, 31 May 2005, Political Transcripts by Federal Document Clearing House.

[116] Nick Paton Walsh, 'Russian Oligarch Jailed for Nine Years', *The Guardian*, 1 June 2005, p. 15.

[117] *Moscow Times*, 1 June 2005.

[118] Neil Buckley, 'Yukos Oil Affair Has Damaged Russia, Says Putin Adviser', *Financial Times*, 3 June 2005, p. 4.

deterioration in the Russian business climate as a result of the Yukos case was
noted by the OECD, observing that 'The slowdown appears to have resulted from
a policy-driven deterioration in the business climate.'[119]

Appeals

Khodorkovsky's appeal against his sentence was as problematic as the trial itself.
Soon after the publication of Khodorkovsky's open letter *Left Turn 1* (see Chapter
8), challenging Putin to defend the social rights of the population, on 10 August
2005 he was transferred from SIZO 4 to SIZO 1, still in Matrosskaya Tishina. While
No. 4 is a 'special isolator' (it had formerly been under the auspices of the KGB),
No. 1 is 'normal'. Instead of having three to four in a cell, No. 1 had twelve to fifteen, with no refrigerator or television. The physical conditions of Khodorkovsky's
incarceration thus worsened.[120] Fearing for his friend's health, from 19 August he
undertook a hunger strike to protest against Lebedev's seven-day incarceration
in solitary confinement for refusing to go for a walk and allegedly threatening
his guards, only eating again after Lebedev was moved to a general cell on 26
August.[121]

Nevzlin's lack of judgement was once again in evidence that August when he
suggested that Abramovich was the driving force behind the case. For the first
time, Khodorkovsky openly announced his views: 'Roma [*sic*] Abramovich, to
put it mildly, is not St. Peter. But the organizer and the motor behind the Yukos
affair was in fact Igor Sechin, one of his competitors in the fight for influence
over Putin.' Khodorkovsky noted that 'Abramovich of course didn't do anything
to help me, since he is after all Putin's friend and not mine. We never could
count on him.' Khodorkovsky argued that the Yukos case showed that Kremlin
officials were pursuing their own business interests, as they did in the 1990s,
and little had changed: 'On the contrary, the level of cynicism has grown and it
has become clear that the foundation of contemporary Russian capitalism is the
rule of crude force.'[122] He repeated this view in an outspoken interview with a
German paper in September 2005. He insisted that his persecution was a sign not
of the state's strength but of its weakness: 'I was thrown into prison because the
Kremlin is too weak and not willing to lead an open and honest fight with an
independent political opposition.' He was quite open about who was responsible:
'The breaking up of Yukos was initiated by Putin aide Igor Sechin with the help of
Kremlin-loyal business men. The result is known: the discrediting of the Russian
leadership, the Russian state and Putin himself. Putin can thank his vassals for

[119] Rhys Blakely, 'OECD Warns Russia over Yukos Effect', *Times Online*, 24 May 2005.
[120] Mikhail Vinogradov and Vladimir Perekrest, 'Urezannaya paika: Mikhailu Khodorkovskomu
ukhudshili usloviya soderzhaniya—vozmozhno, po politicheskim motivam', *Izvestiya*, 11 August 2005,
p. 1.
[121] Yaroslav Zorin, 'Aktsiya protesta', *Gazeta*, 26 August 2005, p. 8.
[122] *Vedemosti*, 4 August 2005; Catherine Belton, 'Khodorkovsky Says Sechin led Yukos Attack',
5 August 2005, p. 3.

this.' Questioned about the relative lack of Western response to his incarceration, he noted that 'Russia as an independent state with a 1,200-year-old history will resolve its problems by itself' although he stressed the need for 'common values'. As for his future as a politician, he declared: 'I became de facto a politician when the Kremlin put me in prison.'[123]

This now appeared to take concrete form. As with Yeltsin in 1989 when he moved into opposition to Gorbachev's vision of controlled democratization, constituencies lined up to offer Khodorkovsky a political platform and the accompanying immunity. Yabloko and SPS sought to draft Khodorkovsky as a candidate for the Tomsk city Duma,[124] and a number of other initiative groups were formed to advance Khodorkovsky's candidature.[125] In the event, on 31 August 2005 Khodorkovsky announced that he would stand in a by-election in the 201st district (the University constituency) of Moscow for a seat in the State Duma, a traditionally liberal area whose previous incumbent had been Mikhail Zadornov, a close ally of Yabloko. In his 'Appeal to Electors and all Citizens of Russia' on 31 August, Khodorkovsky thanked those who had proposed him as a candidate, and promised that 'as soon as I am released from jail my first trips will be to Tomsk, Novosibirsk, and Ul'yanovsk. Brothers and sisters, thank you. Together we are advancing to victory and together we will win.'[126] An initiative group headed by Ivan Starikov, a member of the SPS council, prepared to fight the election, including collecting the 6,000 signatures (2 per cent of the 298,000 voters) to register him.[127] The deadline for registration was 4 October, and it was this date that determined the date of the appeal hearing. The initiative group included some prominent cultural figures and politicians.[128] The former prime minister, Kasyanov, however, refused to join, and considered running himself if Khodorkovsky's candidature failed.[129] As long as Khodorkovsky's appeal was pending, he had every right to stand in the election, due to be held on 4 December, on the same day as the Moscow City Duma election. Since it usually takes a year for a case to be processed through the appeals

[123] Daniel Brössler, 'Interview with Mikhail Khodorkovsky', *Süddeutsche Zeitung*, 11 September 2005.

[124] Aleksandr Andryukhin, 'Sideli dva tovarishcha', *Izvestiya*, 25 August 2005, p. 2.

[125] Nadezhda Krasilova and Mikhail Belyi, 'Mikhail Khodorkovskii prevratilsya v kandidata "protiv vsekh" ', *Novye izvestiya*, 26 August 2005, p. 2.

[126] Mikhail Khodorkovskii, 'Obrashchenie k izbiratelyam, vsem grazhdanam rossii', *Nezavisimaya gazeta*, 1 September 2005, p. 1.

[127] Aleksandr Kolesnichenko, 'Formal'no zakonno, po suti—proizvol', *Novye izvestiya*, 6 September 2005, p. 2.

[128] Members were the journalists Sergei Dorenko, Andrei Pionkovskii and Vladimir Kara-Murza, the economist Mikhail Delyagin, the writer Eduard Limonov, Aleksei Mel'nikov from the Yabloko party, Boris Nadezhdin and Ivan Starikov of the SPS, and Irina Khakamada from the 'Our Choice' movement. The communists refused to join, noting rather sniffily that 'Khodorkovskii was never close to us' (comment by Oleg Kulikov, secretary of the CC CPRF), Kseniya Veretennikova, 'Ot Dumy i tyurmy ne zarekaisya', *Vremya novostei*, 24 August 2005, p. 2. Nikita Belykh, the leader of SPS, was equally dismissive, noting that 'SPS is a rightwing party, and Khodorkovskii has nothing to do with the right since he is calling for politics to make a left turn', Aleksandr Kolesnichenko, 'Indeks ne tak napisali', *Novye izvestiya*, 23 September 2005, p. 2.

[129] Elena Rudneva, 'Zamena: Kas'yanov', *Vedomosti*, 1 September 2005.

process, Khodorkovsky had plenty of time to fight the election, and as a State Duma member he would have been covered by the normal immunity laws, unless parliament itself decided to lift it, which itself would have caused quite a scandal. Polls predicted that he would win at least a third of the vote,[130] and perhaps more than the 27 per cent won by Zadornov in 2003.[131]

In the event, the appeal was rushed forward to 14 September 2005, but was postponed because of the hospitalization of the only lawyer capable of dealing with the appeal, Padva. Khodorkovsky was unwilling to pass the case to another lawyer since none had been able to familiarize themselves with the 600-page trial record. At the time it appeared that Padva would have to undergo lengthy treatment. The lawyer who had represented Khodorkovsky in the original trial, Anton Drel, was not able to see him since he had not been the lawyer designated to deal with the appeal. Out of thirty volumes of trial material, Khodorkovsky had only been able to read fifteen, and in the four months since the verdict he had prepared a detailed forty-page rebuttal of the charges, but none of this was allowed to delay the accelerated timetable.[132] When finally the appeal was heard on 22 September the verdict was upheld, but the sentence reduced by one year. Most such appeals drag on for months, and thus it was extremely unusual for the matter to be wrapped up in one day. The judge requested the lawyers not to go over the material presented in their written appeal and asked no additional questions. The prosecution simply asserted that the statute of limitations on the key episode had not expired. In the end the final deliberations lasted just eight hours. Khodorkovsky's lawyers insisted that the rushed proceedings represented a travesty of justice, and pledged to take the case to the Russian Supreme Court and Strasbourg. In his detailed rebuttal of the charges Khodorkovsky commented: 'It is not the courts who have found me guilty but a group of bureaucrats who convinced the authorities that I should not fund the opposition.... These people have no honour or conscience. The motherland and its future mean nothing for them.'[133]

Some of these lawyers also became the target of accusations of 'unprofessional conduct' as part of a continuing process of intimidation. The Moscow department of the Federal Registration Service unsuccessfully called for three of Khodorkovsky's ten lawyers, Anton Drel, Denis Dyatlov, and Yelena Levina, to be barred, and then tried to strip the lawyer Yury Schmidt of his licence, a request refused by the St Petersburg Lawyers' Chamber. Schmidt had earlier successfully achieved the acquittal, after a number of trials that revealed the lack of finality in the Russian judicial process, of the ex-submariner and environmental expert, Alexander Nikitin, who since 1998 had faced treason charges for alleged espionage.

[130] A Levada poll gave him no less than 30 per cent, Rustem Falyakhov, 'K urne: Mikhail Khodorkovskii mozhet rasschityvat' na tret' golosov', *Gazeta*, 14 September 2005, p. 3.

[131] Aleksandr Kolesnichenko, 'Kamernaya druzhba', *Novye izvestiya*, 14 September 2005, p. 2.

[132] Lina Panchenko and Marina Gridneva, 'Sego dnya: Otkazatel'nyi protsess', *Moskovskii komsomolets*, 23 September 2005, pp. 1, 2.

[133] M. Khodorkovskii, 'Vinovnym menya priznal ne sud, a gruppa byurokratov', speech of 22 September 2005, http://khodorkovsky.ru/speech/3548.html.

As Schmidt noted: 'Under Yeltsin [in the Nikitin case] we knew that the FSB was placing pressure on the courts...but the president and his administration remained neutral. But today between them there is a touching unity.'[134] These lawyers were now accused of having 'violated Khodorkovsky's rights' by not replacing Padva in the appeal when he fell ill, when in fact none of the other nine lawyers had been legally assigned for that case. Schmidt went on to condemn the precarious state of the rule of law in Russia: 'Even-handed justice doesn't exist in Russia anymore', he insisted. 'If the state has an interest in the case, it is sure to be twisted, infringed and turned upside down. In the Soviet period, prosecution served the ruling party, and it still does. The only difference is that the Communist Party has been replaced by the United Russia [party].'[135] Schmidt was one of the lawyers preparing Khodorkovsky's and Lebedev's appeal to the ECtHR, on the grounds that the prosecutors had violated Article 6 of the ECHR, which guarantees the right to a fair trial. There was also an application to the Chamber of Advocates to have Pichugin's lawyers, Kseniya Kostromina and Mikhail Zhidkov, barred from practice.[136] In the wake of the appeal hearing, moreover, on 23 September the head of the international defence team, Robert Amsterdam, was expelled from Russia.[137]

The rushed verdict on 22 September 2005 put a quick end to Khodorkovsky's chances of standing as an official parliamentary candidate, although informal attempts continued for him to stand as a 'people's candidate'. A further challenge to Putin was Kasyanov's declaration that he would run for the presidency. Already in the wake of Khodorkovsky's sentencing in May 2005, Kasyanov declared: 'Today we live in a different country. The unification of democratic forces is no longer a question of political ambitions; it is a vital necessity for the country.' Kasyanov had not publicly criticized Putin until the Yukos affair began in 2003, when he defended Khodorkovsky and warned that 'the freezing of 44 per cent of Yukos shares was a "new phenomenon" with unpredictable consequences'. He revealed: 'Starting in 2003, various political decisions were taken that I disagreed with and I spoke out against.... The Yukos affair was important, but it was far from the only one.' In particular, he declared that the various policies, including the abolition of gubernatorial elections, announced on 13 September 2004 in the wake of the Beslan tragedy, were 'used for an unconstitutional takeover', and he came out openly in opposition in a press conference in February 2005.[138] There was much speculation that behind Kasyanov's presidential bid was Nevzlin, who would provide the ideology, financing, and the organization of international support.[139]

---

[134] Nikolai Donskov, 'Oni delayut eto bez prikrytiya', *Novaya gazeta*, 14 November 2005.

[135] Galina Stolyarova, 'Chamber Rules On Lawyer In Yukos Case', *St Petersburg Times*, 11 November 2005.

[136] Shiryaev, *Sud mesti*, p. 219.

[137] Tim Wall, 'Canadian Defense Lawyer Expelled', *Moscow Times*, 26 September 2005, p. 1.

[138] Interfax, May 2005; in Alexander Osipovich, 'From Insider to Fighting the Machine', *Moscow Times*, 23 November 2007, p. 1.

[139] 'Posadyat li Kas'yanova?', *Argumenty i fakty*, No. 30, 2005, p. 4.

The judicial process continued, with an appeal against the sentence lodged with Russia's Supreme Court, asking for the sentence to be overturned on the grounds that it was 'illegal and unsubstantiated'. On 3 May 2006 the Moscow City Court upheld the eight-year sentence on Khodorkovsky, insisting that there was no reason to review the verdict.[140] Once the Criminal Collegium of the Supreme Court and the Presidium of the Supreme Court had given their verdicts, all avenues within the country were exhausted and the case could go to Strasbourg. At the same time, as we have noted above, on the very day that sentence was delivered on 31 May 2005, the GPO talked of further charges. The new investigation was opened by the GPO on 6 October 2004 into allegations that Khodorkovsky and Lebedev had illicitly gained and laundered $11 billion. The case was based on materials found by investigators in the 'Trust' bank in June 2003, which serviced Yukos's financial flows. The Yukos Company had allegedly cut a deal with traders to buy oil in Russia at $45 a tonne and to sell it in the West for $150. This transfer pricing meant that the producers lost out, with the proceeds going as dividends to top shareholders, offshore intermediaries, and Yukos's top managers. After all, Khodorkovsky's billions had to come from somewhere. We shall return to the preparations for the second trial in Chapter 7.

IN THE PENAL COLONY

On 9 October 2005 Khodorkovsky undertook the long journey into internal exile. Just before departing he penned a sarcastic birthday message for Putin, regretting that he would not be able to greet him personally 'for reasons that you know', and he commented that Putin was 'an excellent friend and partner: you did not regret ruining your reputation for your colleagues who destroyed Yukos, not long ago the country's biggest oil company'.[141] Khodorkovsky travelled in a 'Stolypin' wagon attached to a normal train, and on 16 October, nearly two years after his arrest, he arrived at his place of incarceration in Chita region. He was defiant, and even though in jail a long way from Moscow, he remained an important political actor. Lebedev also left Matrosskaya Tishina on 9 October to serve his eight-year sentence in Kharp prison colony No. 3 in the Yamal-Nenets autonomous district, 60 kilometres from Salekhard and well into the Arctic Circle. A few days after his arrival Khodorkovsky issued a ringing declaration:

As of October 16, 2005, I have been in the land of the Decembrists, political prisoners subjected to hard labor and uranium mines.... The Kremlin tried to isolate me completely from my country and its people; furthermore—to destroy me physically.... They hope Khodorkovsky will soon be forgotten. They are trying to convince you, my friends, that

---

[140] RIA Novosti, 3 May 2006.
[141] 'Pozdravlenie', *Kommersant*, 7 October 2005; in V. M. Kartashov, *Who is Mr. Hodorkovsky?* (Rostov-na-Donu, Feniks, 2007), p. 6.

the fight is over, that we must resign ourselves to the supremacy of self-serving bureaucrats. That's not true—the fight is just beginning.

The main challenge was 'to formulate Russia's development for the twenty-first century', to '[c]reate from scratch a new breed of officials—those interested in the fate of the country and its people, not their own unbridled personal enrichment', and to 'preserve the Far East and Siberia as part of Russia'. He ended with the rousing exhortation: 'The time of mediocrity is past—the era of heroes dawns.'[142]

The Krasnokamensk prison colony:
From Rokossovsky to Khodorkovsky

The 1996 Russian penal code stipulates that a prisoner serves their sentence in the region where they are convicted unless exempted (women, lifers, and lepers). In the case of Moscow this is often not possible since all the penal establishments in Moscow region are overflowing, hence Ministry of Justice resolution No. 71 of 2004, Article 6, allows a neighbouring region also to be used. Some 12 per cent of the total Russian prison population are serving their sentences outside the prisoner's home or sentencing region.[143] However, there are plenty of prisons in the regions bordering Moscow within the Golden Ring, such as Tver, Vladimir, or Yaroslavl. In the event, the Federal Penitentiary Service (FSIN) sent Khodorkovsky to penal colony YaG14/10 (IK-10) near the town of Krasnokamensk 600 kilometres south-east of Chita, in the trans-Baikal steppe 6,500 kilometres from Moscow and not far from the border with China. It is extremely unusual for Moscow prisoners to be sent to Siberia without their agreement.[144] The colony is located a six-hour flight from Moscow to Chita, followed by a fifteen-hour train journey and then a forty-minute car journey.[145]

Not for the first time in Russia, distance was used as a form of punishment. Despite its latitude being much the same as London's, located in the heart of the Eurasian landmass the climate is typically continental, with temperatures falling below −40°C in winter while in summer temperatures soar above 30°C accompanied by infestation with mosquitoes. Its southerly latitude means that the winters are relatively short by Russian standards, with the snows starting in November and melting by March. Its distance from Moscow made this an ideal location for political exiles, including archpriest Avvakum, the Decembrists, the

---

[142] 'A Statement by Mikhail Khodorkovsky: To Everyone Who Has Supported Me and Continues to Support Me', *Financial Times*, 2 November 2005, p. 9, an advertisement placed with the support of Leonid Nevzlin, Vladimir Dubov, and Mikhail Brudno; An earlier version appeared as M. Khodorkovskii, 'Vse, kto menya podderzhival i podderzhivaet', 27 October 2005, in *Novaya gazeta*, 31 October 2005, which was rather more explicit about the threat from China.

[143] 1999 census of the Russian prison service; thanks to Dominique Moran for the figure.

[144] Vladislav Kulikov, 'Khodorkovskii sekretno pokinul tyur'mu', *Rossiiskaya gazeta*, 11 October 2005, p. 2.

[145] Oleg Kashin, 'Kak doekhat' do Khodorkovskogo', *Izvestiya*, 24 October 2005, p.1, whose account also has rich details about the camp and the region.

Polish insurrectionists of 1830 and 1863, Nikolai Chernyshevsky, the Populists, and even Marshal Konstantin Rokossovsky during Stalin's purge of the Soviet High Command in the late 1930s.[146]

Krasnokamensk was established in its modern form in 1968 as a closed town in connection with the development of uranium mining nearby and the building of the country's leading uranium processing plant in the town, and consists of classic Soviet-style five-storey blocks built in part with prison labour. In earlier years it was considered a high-prestige area, with wages much above the national average, year-round hot water, and Moscow-level supplies, but with the fall of Soviet power and the decline of the mining industry it lost its special status and became an open town. By the mid-2000s it had become a town like thousands of others in Russia, with high underemployment, gently decaying, with many streets still lacking a name (a legacy of its closed status), muddy in wet weather, dusty in the sun, and compacted with snow in winter. Business in the town was controlled by two criminal groups, the 'sportsmen' and the 'criminals', who managed the markets and gaming machines. In the early 1990s they agreed to keep the Chinese out, and despite the proximity of the border the absence of a Chinese presence is remarkable.[147]

The Priargun Mining and Chemical Complex, where uranium is mined and processed, is not far from Krasnokamensk. This is the last of the seven Soviet enterprises of its kind, which together reached maximum output of 16,000 tonnes in 1985. The Priargunskoe complex used to be one of the world's largest, but output declined steeply from the late 1990s as reserves available for strip mining were depleted. All of Russia's nuclear submarines and nuclear power plants use fuel prepared here. Despite fears that the area is highly irradiated, the authorities claim that the radiation levels in the town and in the prison are less than half of permitted norms at 15 micro Roentgen per hour, at most. Radiation levels are constantly monitored by officials, and the area is regularly inspected by independent experts from Moscow, including environmentalists, Greenpeace activists, and others. There are, however, constant fears of accidental releases, and thus residents often carry radiation meters. Local anecdotal evidence suggests a raised incidence of radiation-related illnesses. Prisoners have never been involved in uranium mining here, even in the Soviet period and certainly not now. In an area where jobs are few, local residents seek employment in the uranium mine, where the average wage is above the national average, at R20,000–30,000 a month.

It is still not clear why the FSIN chose precisely this colony out of the 762 prisons in Russia.[148] There is nothing special about it, with most inmates serving three to

---

[146] Vitalii Cherkasov, 'Ot Rokossovskogo do Khodorkovskogo', *Novaya gazeta*, 21 November 2005.

[147] Oleg Kashin, 'Khodorkovskii sprosil o svyashchennike', Izvestiya.ru; http://www.izvestia.ru/russia/article2931095/index.html.

[148] For an interesting study of the life world of contemporary Russian prisons, including the structure of internal order, 'folklore', culture, and customs, see E. S. Efimova, *Sovremennaya tyur'ma: byt, traditsii i fol'klor* (Moscow, OGI, 2004).

five years, 40 per cent for theft, and this could well have been the reason.[149] There is one feature, however, which may well have played a role in Krasnokamensk being chosen as the place to host Khodorkovsky, and that is its lack of 'social status', in criminal jargon. Prisons in Russia are divided into 'red' and 'black', depending on their status in terms of relations between the prison administration and the criminal bosses. In jails where the guards are in control, a prison is known as 'red' (prison guards used to wear red shoulder insignia); but where the criminal elite dominates, the prison is known as 'black', the usual situation in Siberia. As far as normal prisoners are concerned, both are equally undesirable. In 'black' institutions prisoners are forced to live according to the code of the underworld *avtoritety*, having to pay a share of all food parcels and money as a 'tax' to the criminals, and participate in various criminal rituals that establish a whole set of counter-norms that are ignored by an inmate at their peril. In 'red' prisons informing is encouraged, and the regime can often be draconian with solitary confinement imposed for minor infractions. The power of warders is typically unrestrained by criminal organizations, and they then act as oppressors in their own right, stealing wages from prisoners and extorting bribes to allow what should be due by right.

There can be no peace in either the red or the black prisons. Regional and federal penal system officials exert pressure on the administrators of black prisons to reduce the influence of organized criminal groups, while mafia bosses try to increase their influence in red camps. The pressure from one side or the other creates turmoil, with the criminals provoking riots, hunger strikes, labour protests, and escape attempts, while the local authorities are constantly exhorted to tighten discipline. The reason why YaG 14/10 is one of the few prisons in Russia without a colour code is that its management and regional criminal structures had worked out some basic principles on how to live together, and this provided for a degree of stability in the colony. This was facilitated by the regional nature of the colony, with all administrative staff recruited locally, while about a third of its 1,200 inmates are also Krasnokamensk residents, and most of the rest come from the region. About half the prisoners had been found guilty of theft.[150]

Newly arrived prisoners are quarantined for a fortnight, and in that time they decide what sort of work they will do: tailor, carpenter, joiner, metalworker, or welder. Those who wish to work but lack skills are assigned to a special barracks responsible for the upkeep of the prison, to look after its livestock, or to study at a technical school. Detachment 12 is the biggest and is for trusted prisoners serving the last year of their sentence, with their barracks located beyond the guarded perimeter. It is a halfway house, with one foot already in the world beyond the colony. Detachment 11 is for trusties in the colony, recommended by the prison administration and willing to join the prison's Discipline and Order Unit. They

[149] Larisa Kallioma and Vladimir Perekrest, 'Kuda podal'she', Izvestiya.ru; http://www.izvestia.ru/russia/article2911375/index.html.
[150] For a good description of the camp, see Vladislav Kulikov, 'Kandidat tyuremnykh nauk', *Rossiiskaya gazeta*, 27 October 2005, p. 2.

are allowed to miss roll-calls, their quarters are rarely searched, and most are set early release. Detachment 7 is quite the opposite, reserved for hardened criminals who buck the rules, refuse to work, and who do not seek parole—one of the laws of the underworld is that a sentence must be served to the full. There are not many of these in YaG 14/10.

This is not a labour camp in any traditional 'Gulag' sense, hence the correct word to describe it is 'colony'. Conditions in the prison are comparatively comfortable. Inmates are housed in thirteen army-style two-storey barracks. Each block contains between 150 and 200 men, divided into two detachments, one on each floor. The detachments play football or volleyball matches on an almost daily basis, depending on the weather. The diet is also of a relatively high standard, with the food prepared from natural ingredients in the colony, including the use of meat and vegetables grown by the inmates, and the bread is also baked in the colony. In addition, tea, chocolate, condensed milk, and cigarettes are donated to the prison by local companies. Inmates are woken at 6 a.m. for roll-call, donning the black prison uniform with the surname and barrack number, and lights-out is at 10 p.m.[151] In the pre-Gorbachev era prisoners had been sent to a workshop not far from the colony making iron doors and railings, as well as some wooden items. Today prisoners work in a reinforced concrete plant for the mining and building industries, in a timber-working plant, or in a sewing unit making uniforms for the militia.

Life as a prisoner

Khodorkovsky was at first assigned to the fifty-man Detachment 8, designated for inmates who do not question the prison administration but who also respect the laws of the underworld. Khodorkovsky was initially assigned to the sewing unit, the responsibility of Detachment 1, and in the event this is where he stayed, sewing shirts and gloves. While alcohol and drugs are banned, they are smuggled in and are tolerated to the extent that they act as a safety valve for the men's energies. Additional meetings with family members can also be bought, over and above the permitted number. Wealthy inmates can also buy favours for other prisoners, and thus make life rather easier for themselves. As for financial support for prison officials, this is a matter about which all sides keep quiet. With Khodorkovsky's arrival the volume of contributions to the colony increased sharply, with consignments of cigarettes, tea, and canned food arriving regularly.

There had been some confusion at first about notifying Khodorkovsky's wife, Inna, about his whereabouts, and it was three days after he had been allocated to Krasnokamensk that she was informed where he was. The place of incarceration made visiting very difficult. Inna had been able to visit him in Matrosskaya Tishina once a month for forty-five minutes, talking by telephone through a partition made of glass and wire netting. Visiting rights in the Krasnokamensk colony were

[151] Eduard Lomovtsev, 'Podrobnosti: Vybor professii', *Vremya novostei*, 25 October 2005, p. 2.

more extensive, with four three-day visits a year and six visits of three hours each. Having arrived in Chita the hardy traveller negotiates the final 550 kilometres to the colony in one of three ways: a slow passenger train to Krasnokamensk and then a taxi; a minibus along a road that peters out about two hundred kilometres out of Chita, and which starts again not far out of Krasnokamensk; or a taxi. During the longer visits prisoners and their families are accommodated in a small hut with a communal bathroom and kitchen. On arrival in the colony in late 2005 Khodorkovsky forbade his children to visit: his daughter Anastasia was then 14 years old, while their twin boys Ilya and Gleb were 6 years old (his oldest son by his first marriage was by then 20). By June 2008 his mother had visited him eight times, and Anastasia had also been allowed to travel to what had become the Zabaikal region.

After meeting with her husband for the first time in the colony, Inna stressed that his spirit was far from broken, and that Khodorkovsky would dedicate his life to achieving political reform. The meeting came at a time when Khodorkovsky released another in his series of political missives on how to reform Russia (*Left Turn 2*, see Chapter 8), accompanied a week earlier by the full-page advertisements in which Khodorkovsky had called for a new breed of officials. Inna noted after her first three-day visit starting on 26 October, accompanied by his mother: 'He's changed a lot but I recognised the man I knew before his arrest. . . . He is not consumed by anger. Instead he is a man with a clear vision. He is feeling combative. He has no regrets. Nor do I', said Khodorkovskaya. 'Neither of us would have wanted to flee abroad. Russia is our country. They will never break him. He is a man who is going places.'[152] Only in September 2006 did he meet with his daughter, whom he had not seen for a year and half, together with his wife and mother,[153] and another three-day visit followed in December.[154] In a communication with his wife Khodorkovsky described life in his prison colony as an 'anti-world'.[155] He spent much of his time reading religious literature, which Inna noted was analytical: 'He doesn't push faith away, but he has begun to experience it in a new way. If before he approached the subject from a sort of historical point of view, now he feels closer to it.' She noted that they had long feared that the state would attack them, but they had together decided to stay in Russia.[156]

From the first Khodorkovsky was concerned about staying in touch with the world outside, and at his early meeting with the Chita lawyer Natalya Terekhova he asked about access to journals and books.[157] The authorities kept up the pressure on those around Khodorkovsky able to render him support. The case of Father Sergei Taratukhin illustrates the problem. The colony was part of his parish in Krasnokamensk, and he started visiting Khodorkovsky immediately after his arrival. He immediately declared that Khodorkovsky was a political prisoner,

[152] Mark Franchetti, 'Oligarch Plots Political Revenge from Jail', *Sunday Times*, 13 November 2005.
[153] 'Khodorkovskii vestretilsya s dochkoi', *Moskovskii komsomolets*, 13 September 2006, p. 2.
[154] 'Khodorkovskii mnogo pishet', *Moskovskii komsomolets*, 18 December 2006, p. 2.
[155] www.khodorkovsky.ru/bio/5320.html, 6 June 2006.
[156] RFE/RL, *Russian Political Weekly*, Vol. 6, No. 14, 7 August 2006.
[157] Kashin, 'Khodorkovskii sprosil o svyashchennike'.

for which he was sent to a parish deeper in the taiga and then, after repeatedly criticizing the Orthodox Church leadership, in April 2006 he was defrocked by the bishop of Chita and Zabaikalsk. Taratukhin had served four years for 'anti-Soviet activity' in the Perm labour camps between 1974 and 1978, with the well-known human rights activist Sergei Kovalëv, and thus also had a track record as a dissident.[158] Taratukhin openly acknowledged his sympathy for Khodorkovsky: 'We have much in common. We are both against the system. He is not frightened of anyone; he is fighting for freedom.'[159]

On at least four occasions Khodorkovsky was placed in the Krasnokamensk punishment block for minor infractions of prison rules. The first was on 14 December 2005 for unsanctioned movement from his sewing machine when it had jammed, which on 9 February 2006 was judged illegal by Krasnokamensk city court; the second on 24 January 2006 for alleged unsanctioned possession of documents (a copy of prison rules), for which he received five days in solitary confinement; the third was on 17 March 2006 when he was punished for drinking tea in an unsanctioned place, when he missed his supper because he was preparing his appeal to the ECtHR;[160] and the fourth in June 2006 for possession of two unsanctioned lemons.[161] The appeal against the January 2006 incident ended in victory when the Krasnokamensk city court on 18 April 2006 found that his punishment had been illegal.[162]

These punishments exposed Khodorkovsky to new dangers. In the early hours of 14 April 2006 his nose was slashed with a knife by a fellow inmate, the 22-year old Alexander Kuchma.[163] The two had been placed together in a punishment cell; Khodorkovsky for the monstrous offence of eating in an unsanctioned place. The two had initially got on well together but had then fallen out.[164] Khodorkovsky's

---

[158] Sergei Kovalëv, the head of the Moscow Human Rights Institute, met Taratukhin in the camps. While Kovalëv had been sentenced to the Gulag for human rights work, Taratukhin according to one account had been found guilty of distributing leaflets calling for the expulsion of the Buryats from Chita. In the camp Taratukhin openly spoke of his agreement to work with the KGB as an informer, allegedly to ease conditions in the camp, which landed him in the punishment block. He had not been particularly interested in religion at the time, although he did express remorse about his anti-Buryat activities. Paul Goble, 'Window on Eurasia: Three Russian Fates', *JRL*, No. 124, 29 May 2006, 2006, item 15. The full interview with Kovalëv is on the Portal-Credo.Ru site, published 25 May 2006, http://www.portal-credo.ru/site/print.php?act=authority&id=523. It was in the Perm camp that Taratukhin turned to Orthodoxy. He gives a very different reason for his imprisonment: that he had created an anti-Soviet youth organization in his technical college, Kashin, 'Khodorkovskii sprosil o svyashchennike'. See also Oleg Kashin, 'Kak doekhat' do Khodorkovskogo', *Izvestiya*, 24 October 2005, p. 1.

[159] Kashin, 'Khodorkovskii sprosil o svyashchennike'.

[160] 'Reiting pyat' zvezd: Mikhail Khodorkovskii, zaklyuchennyi', *Gazeta*, 20 March 2006, p. 2; Irina Vlasova, 'Khodorkovskii "zaeli" ', *Novye izvestiya*, 7 June 2006, p. 6.

[161] Eduard Lomovtsev, 'Manual'naya terapiya', *Vremya novostei*, 26 October 2007, p. 3.

[162] Andrei Pankov, 'Khodorkovskii pobedil ShIZO', *Novye izvestiya*, 19 April 2006, p. 6.

[163] There are various versions of what happened, with the prison administration asserting that the two got into an argument at 3 a.m., and Kuchma then punched Khodorkovsky in his face. Khodorkovskii later refused to press charges against his assailant, noting that he was 'inadequate', Ivan Sas, 'Shvy na informatsii', *Nezavisimaya gazeta*, 17 April 2006, p. 7.

[164] Andrei Sharov, 'Khodorkovskii popal pod nozh', *Rossiiskaya gazeta*, 17 April 2006, p. 2.

supporters argued that the attack had been ordered from above. As the journalist Anna Politkovskaya put it, on the basis of no evidence: 'It was a well-
planned attack. There had been rumors circulating that something like that could
have happened. The Kremlin is tired of having a convict filing complaints for
every violation committed against him. After this attack, the Kremlin hopes that
[Khodorkovsky] will calm down.' Nevzlin echoed these sentiments though even
more shrilly: 'The Russian regime has stooped to a new low. First, they hold a
show trial. Then, they throw Khodorkovsky in a remote Siberian prison, where he
is being held in appalling conditions. Then, they try to eliminate him physically
by exposing him to danger.'[165] Other sources close to the Kremlin suggest that
Putin had personally ordered that Khodorkovsky be kept safe, and was furious
when he heard of the attack. This certainly makes sense, since as one perceptive
commentator notes: 'The hypothetical possibility of Khodorkovsky's death in the
Krasnokamensk colony would inflict a catastrophic loss of reputation on the
authorities. No one in Russia or in the West would believe that Khodorkovsky's
death was accidental.'[166]

On 20 April Khodorkovsky was placed in a single-person cell by the head of the
FSIN, Yuri Kalinin, 'to end speculation about threats to Khodorkovsky's life', and
he was still there a month after the attack.[167] In an interview on the eve of his visit
to Spain on 7 February 2006 Putin was asked: 'Some people here think that what
is happening with Khodorkovsky is revenge.' The issue was the period of solitary
confinement imposed on Khodorkovsky earlier for possessing a document about
prisoners' rights. Putin answered: 'To be quite honest, I don't know what you are
talking about. I know that Khodorkovsky has been tried, found guilty, and that he
is now in prison....That Khodorkovsky has been sent to solitary confinement, I
can honestly say that the first I hear of it is from you. I have no idea who or what
is meant to be taking revenge.' Told that the incident was written about in the
Russian media, Putin answered: 'It's good, that they write about everything here,
but the thing is, I don't manage to read everything...but I will ask the Ministry
of Justice to look into it since you have raised the issue.' He ended with the stern
words: 'A prison, a colony, is not a corporation, where he was number one and
gave the orders. Here he has to subordinate himself to the rules current in that
institution.'[168]

Khodorkovsky announced that he would work on a doctoral (*kandidat*) dissertation, and he brought two suitcases of material with him to Krasnokamensk. He
cast around for a topic, with the possibilities including a study of the development
of Russia's oil industry, local self-government or the fate of the region in which

---

[165] Valeria Korchagina and Catherine Belton, 'Inmate Slashes Khodorkovsky's Nose', *Moscow Times*,
17 April 2006, p. 1.
[166] Sergei Komarov, 'tri iz vos'mi', *Novye izvestiya*, 25 October 2006, p. 6.
[167] 'Khodorkovskii po-prezhnemu nakhoditsya v odinochnoi kamere, zayavlyayut advokaty',
Izvestiya.ru; http://www.izvestia.ru/news/news106953/index.html; Anton Valer'ev, 'Khodorkovskii
izolirovan ot sokamenikov', *Moskovskie novosti*, 21 April 2006, p. 4.
[168] http://president.kremlin.ru/text/appears/2006/02/101129.shtml.

he found himself, including relations with its neighbours China and Mongolia.[169] In February 2006 he requested the prison administration to allow him to take up scholarly activity instead of working in the sewing shop, planning in the first instance to write an article for the journal *Khimiya i zhizn'* (*Chemistry and Life*). His request could not be satisfied, in the FSIN's view, since academic exchanges would be subject to restrictions, with all letters censored and any meetings with academic colleagues would have to be at the expense of giving up meetings with family and friends. In the end Khodorkovsky gave up on the idea, and continued to work at packing gloves, since he had failed to pass the sewing exams;[170] with two higher education degrees, Khodorkovsky in February 2005 once again tried to improve his professional qualifications.[171] If he had passed the test his wages would have gone up from R27 to R50 a month (just under €2 at the time)— rather less than the millions in which he used to count. The FSIN was faced with numerous sensitive issues in dealing with their illustrious 'guest'. Khodorkovsky had to be seen to be obeying the rules, just as any other prisoner, but at the same time the politically sensitive nature of the case meant that the authorities had to be careful to ensure that Khodorkovsky was looked after and kept safe. As one commentary put it: 'Khodorkovsky the prison inmate poses a greater danger to the authorities than Khodorkovsky the oligarch ever did.'[172]

[169] Interview with Igor' Kovalevskii, 'Advokat Karinna Moskalenko—o visite v koloniyu Krasnokamenske', *Novaya gazeta*, 15 December 2005.
[170] Aleksandr Stepanov, 'Khodorkovskii zaimetsya ukladkoi rukavits', *Izvestiya*, 15 August 2006, p. 3.
[171] Lina Panchenko, 'Khodorkovskii sdaet ekzamen na shveyu-motorista', *Moskovskii komsomolets*, 2 February 2006, pp. 1, 2.
[172] Sergei Dyupin, 'A Soft Landing: A Description of Prison YaG 14/10, the New Home of Mikhail Khodorkovsky', *Kommersant-Dengi*, No. 46 (551), 21–27 November 2005; in *JRL*, No. 9301, 22 November 2005, item 17. Some of the detail above about the camp and the region is drawn from Dyupin's rather sanguine account.

7

There Will Be Blood

I heard about the past, the future, and a lot, a very great deal, about freedom above all: indeed, I can safely say, nowhere does one hear as much about it, it seems, as among prisoners, which naturally makes a lot of sense after all.

Imre Kertész[1]

The 'imposed consensus' of Russia's elite, as Gel'man notes, was achieved through the Kremlin's use of 'selective punishment of some elite sections and selective cooptation of others'.[2] As long as the Kremlin had adequate resources, in material, political capital and authority, to rein in potentially fractious elites, the system could continue, but there was an ever-present threat of defection. It was this system that Khodorkovsky threatened. His actions sought to expand the freedom of actors in the economic sphere and the autonomy of civic association in politics and society. Khodorkovsky's struggle for freedom expanded the freedom of all, while his incarceration commensurately constrained the business elite and other potential independent political actors.

THE BROADER ASSAULT

The high-profile case against Khodorkovsky and his top associates was only the tip of the iceberg, and some forty-five criminal prosecutions were launched against company managers, accountants, lawyers, and others connected with the company. In 2007 alone a total of over three dozen cases were in progress, demonstrating the consistent pattern of the use of law against those associated in any way with Yukos. These subsidiary cases were launched for a variety of reasons: to undermine the financial viability of the defence; to intimidate witnesses into giving evidence against Khodorkovsky and his associates; to weaken the will of defence lawyers; and possibly as a demonstration effect, to warn people not to step forward or even to speak in defence of Khodorkovsky. On occasions courts did not follow the procuracy's line, as when on 30 January 2004 a regional court dismissed the

---

[1] Imre Kertész, *Fatelessness*, translated from the Hungarian by Tim Wilkinson (London, The Harvill Press, 2005), p. 142. The title of this chapter is taken from the film of the same name directed by Paul Thomas Anderson (2007), adapted from the novel *Oil* by Upton Sinclair.

[2] Vladimir Gel'man, 'Political Opposition in Russia: A Dying Species?', *Post-Soviet Affairs*, Vol. 23, No. 3, 2005, p. 242.

charges against the Yukos executive Rafail Zainullin for lack of evidence, but this was an unusual occurrence. We will begin by examining three landmark cases, and then briefly look at some of the others.

The Temerko case

On 13 May 2005 Alexander Temerko was charged with fraud. Temerko at the time was in the United Kingdom and an international arrest warrant was issued against him. Russia's extradition request was heard in Bow Street Magistrates Court, and Judge Timothy Workman refused Russia's extradition request.[3] Prosecutors named lawyer Ivan Kolesnikov an accomplice in this case. Kolesnikov at the time was in Cyprus, and Russia also requested his extradition. Kolesnikov was employed by the Moscow-based law firm of ALM Feldmans from the time of its establishment in 1995. One of the firm's most important clients was the Yukos Group and Khodorkovsky personally, and Lebedev also used the services of the firm. In time, Yukos became the firm's major client. One of the lawyers at the firm, Anton Drel, became Khodorkovsky's personal lawyer. Two other of the firm's lawyers, Elena Agranovskaya (the managing partner) and Pavel Ivlev (the deputy managing partner) feature in the case.

Temerko was one of the most senior Yukos executives to be charged with criminal offences. Temerko and Khodorkovsky got to know each other in the late 1980s when they were both involved in the Moscow Komsomol organization. Khodorkovsky as we have seen used his leadership of the Scientific and Youth Union to transform it into what was later to become Bank Menatep, the base organization on which Yukos was developed. Many of the individuals with whom he worked at the time later took prominent positions in the Menatep/Yukos organization. Temerko's career took a rather different trajectory, although he maintained contact with Khodorkovsky. By 1999/2000 Temerko was president of the Russian Armoury Corporation and then was involved in the creation of Rossvooruzhenie (Russian Arms). On 5 June 2000 Temerko was elected to the board of directors of Yukos as part of the attempt to transform the company into an internationally transparent and vertically integrated company. Temerko was responsible for relations with the Russian government and other oil companies, and he was involved in top-level negotiations with the Chinese government

---

[3] Under Ustinov's leadership Russia was spectacularly unsuccessful in its extradition attempts. The GPO's request to extradite Vladimir Gusinsky was refused by Spain in 2000, Israel in 2001 and Greece in 2003. In July 2003 Bow Street magistrates court refused the extradition of the Chechen leader Akhmed Zakaev, Boris Berezovsky's extradition was refused in September 2003, while a second request in June 2006 accused him of conspiring to seize power in Russia by force. The Yukos-related cases against Dmitry Maruev, Natalia Chernysheva, and Vladimir Temerko failed, and the list also includes the Yukos managers Vladimir Dubov and Mikhail Brudno, accused of gross financial improprieties, as well as Leonid Nevzlin, who in January 2004 were refused extradition by Israel. The extradition of the general director of Apatit-Trade, Alexander Gorbachev, accused of conspiring with Khodorkovsky to sell Apatit's output at inflated prices, was refused in March 2005.

regarding the Daqing pipeline plan. In June 2003 Temerko left the Yukos board, and focused on work with Open Russia.

On 20 October 2003 Temerko was appointed senior vice president of Yukos Moscow, and at this time a management board was created consisting of the more senior vice presidents, and Temerko was one of these. Following Khodorkovsky's arrest on 25 October 2003 Temerko was elected to the board of Yukos-Moskva, with Khodorkovsky's prior agreement, and on 3 November he was elected as chair of the board, a post he held until 15 March 2004, and two months later he was replaced by Gerashchenko. Thus Temerko was responsible for handling the attack, and his prosecution was a way of weakening the ability of Yukos to defend itself. The Temerko case appears connected with Bogdanchikov, who according to Temerko was the driving force behind the whole business.[4] Bogdanchikov had a live interest in neutralizing Temerko, since his defence of Yukos prevented Rosneft from expanding. Temerko as vice-president of Yukos had been involved in the Murmansk project as well as negotiations with the Chinese government, and in particular CNPC, over the planned pipeline to Daqing, and thus was at the heart of the challenge to the Russian government's strategic control of pipelines. The case was accompanied by numerous acts of petty and not-so-petty harassment to encourage him to go into exile. On 6 May 2004 the GPO once again seized documents from Yukos's headquarters in Moscow, in particular from Temerko's office.[5] After Temerko left in November 2004 to live in London, his family in Moscow were subject to a string of complications.

The case against Temerko is deeply entwined with the Vladislav Kolesnikov case. Both can be seen as part of the broader pattern of attacks against Yukos employees and associated legal firms. The offices of ALM Feldmans were raided by the GPO on 9 November 2004,[6] followed on 15 November by the calling in for questioning of its employees. Yukos personnel caught up in the action include Dmitry Gololobov, the former head of Yukos's legal department, with an arrest warrant announced against him on 18 November 2004, and Pavel Ivlev, who was interrogated on 16 November and pressed to provide incriminating evidence against Yukos officials, including Khodorkovsky himself. On 8 December another Yukos lawyer, Elena Agranovskaya, was questioned and then detained, with charges of fraud, money laundering, and tax evasion preferred against her on 17 December, although she was released from pre-trial detention on that day because of poor health. As a Western paper put it: '[T]he arrests and interrogations of Yukos lawyers have fuelled fears that those who defend politically unpopular clients could themselves become targets.'[7]

---

[4] Author's interview, London, 25 October 2005.
[5] Charles Gurin, 'Prosecutors Raid Yukos One More Time', *Eurasia Daily Monitor*, Vol. 1, Issue 5, 7 May 2004.
[6] http://www.yukos.ru/7538.shtml.
[7] http://www.svetlanabakhmina.com/pdf/article_wallstreetjournal.pdf.

The Bakhmina case

The case of Svetlana Bakhmina, deputy head of Yukos's legal department, graphically illustrates failings in the judicial system. In the long list of cases it is worth pausing on this one since it highlights most vividly the human cost of the Yukos affair. On 7 December 2004 she was imprisoned in connection with the Gololobov case, following a series of punitive nocturnal interrogations. Refusing to give the answers sought by the authorities, her status changed from witness to defendant. This was a typical case of the persecution of people associated with Yukos. She was charged with crimes committed seven years earlier, when she was twenty-eight and new to Yukos, and just back from maternity leave.[8] Her arrest in part was designed to increase the pressure on Khodorkovsky himself, to make him feel guilty for the suffering of others. Observers suggest that Bakhmina's prosecution was designed to put pressure on Gololobov, her former boss at Yukos, to return from London.

The case relates back to the time when Yukos launched its bid to take over Tomskneft-VNK, and she was accused of damaging the interests of shareholders by transferring assets out of Tomskneft. The latter resisted, and as was common practice in the late 1990s, claimed to have debts of $440 million to deter the bid. Yukos went ahead anyway and gained control of the company, but refused to pay the debt and instead transferred Tomskneft's assets offshore. When the state, as a minority shareholder in the company, requested Yukos to explain why the transfer was made, Yukos asserted that it was a way of defending itself against the fictitious claimants. Yukos engaged in business in the same aggressive way as was standard at the time. In the event, all the enterprises were returned to Tomskneft a year before Yukos bought out the state's remaining shares in the company.[9] There was thus no crime and no victim. However, in the Bakhmina trial, the temporary transfer was classified as theft, and Bakhmina, the lawyer who carried out the orders of Yukos management, was cited as the mastermind behind the operation.[10] She was refused bail, and in pre-trial detention she was not allowed to talk by telephone with her young children, aged 6 and 3 at the time of her arrest.

Her trial began in October 2005 in Simonovsky court on charges of tax evasion and embezzlement. The prosecutor on 23 March 2006 called for a nine-year sentence to be imposed. The selective nature of the case was reinforced by Tomskneft's insistence that the assets in question had been returned and were still on the company's books. In the event, in April 2006 she received a harsh sentence—seven years in prison—which made her ineligible for amnesty. She received a two-year sentence for large-scale tax evasion, but the main charge, which brought the sentence up to seven years, was conspiracy to commit major fraud against Tomskneft and to transfer the company's financial assets abroad. As noted, Tomskneft had not filed any complaint in relation to any of these charges. In August the Moscow

---

[8] The case is described by Rachel Polonsky, 'Russia in the Dock', *The Spectator*, 2 April 2005.

[9] Mikhail Fishman, 'A Vicious Sentence: The Yukos Case is not Over Yet', *Kommersant-Vlast'*, No. 16, 24 April 2006.

[10] Alexander Shadrin, 'Desire to Press', *Kommersant*, 29 March 2006.

city court overturned the tax evasion conviction, but confirmed the embezzlement charges, and reduced her sentence by only six months. In September her lawyers requested that the court postpone the imposition of her sentence until her younger child turned 14 (at the time only 5), since this lay in the powers of the court. On 2 October 2006 the Simonovsky court rejected the request and she was sent to a women's penal colony in the central part of the country. On 27 December 2006 the Moscow City Court conclusively rejected the request to postpone the sentence.

It is not clear what the government achieved by jailing Bakhmina. Already there had been much commentary in the press, and even by some senior United Russia officials, that Bakhmina had been refused bail and had already spent two years in pre-trial detention, and that this was enough for someone who was no more than a relatively junior Yukos official. What could the state possibly gain by jailing her? A powerful answer is provided by Mikhail Fishman:

> But the state remained adamant, and everyone understands that Bakhmina's sentence is politically motivated. It's an object lesson, precisely due to its excessive severity—intended to show that justice is unconditional, taking no notice of titles or merit. The sentence seems to assert that the Yukos case is nothing personal, and that Khodorkovsky, with his billions, is neither a victim nor a target, but a participant in an extensive crime ring. He has been sent to prison. So has his partner, Lebedev. Alexei Kurtsin, a petty clerk at Yukos, was given 14 years for money-laundering, even though the prosecution actually asked for a lighter sentence (an unprecedented event).
>
> But this isn't just a matter of the state sending the message that everyone is equal before the law. These show trials aren't about legality at all. They're about public morale. Any leniency with regard to Svetlana Bakhmina would have been revealing too, of course. It would have been a signal that the Yukos page has been turned; that's enough, we're through with all that, let's return to a peaceful existence. Not generalized words from meetings and addresses to parliament, but a specific gesture that would have made people breathe a surprised sigh of relief: believe it or not, Bakhmina is free!
>
> But the state has chosen to send a different message. For the repressive justice mindset which has been victorious in the Yukos affair, there is no such thing as a minor, forgivable crime. There are only crimes that haven't been investigated yet.[11]

Vasily Aleksanyan

On 3 April 2006 the Simonovsky court began consideration of the procuracy's request to consider embezzlement and tax evasion charges against Vasily Aleksanyan, a Yukos vice president. He was born into a highly educated family in Moscow in 1971, with his father a physicist and ethnically Armenian, while his mother was Russian. He studied law at Moscow State University and then Harvard, and joined Yukos in 1996, and went on to head Yukos's legal department until 2003. Aleksanyan refused to emigrate; like Khodorkovsky, he considered it part of his 'civil position' to face his persecutors head on. He was known for his sharp legal mind, courage, and loyalty, and having resigned from his corporate

---

[11] Fishman, 'A Vicious Sentence'.

positions in 2003 he worked as a personal lawyer for Khodorkovsky and Lebedev. By early 2006 Yukos's new managing director Steven Theede was in London to avoid a Russian criminal investigation and warning that what was left of Yukos in Moscow was answering to Rosneft rather than to him. Aleksanyan in March 2006 agreed to return to Yukos as an executive vice president to negotiate with the court-appointed bankruptcy manager, Eduard Rebgun. Up to then he had not been caught up in the spirals of conspiracy, but now he was repeatedly called in for questioning by the GPO, and followed by the same four cars. Despite the intimidation, he refused to resign: 'After I said I would not leave Yukos, they told me with a smile that it was the first time they had seen a person voluntarily asking to go to jail.'[12]

He was arrested on 6 April 2006 on charges focusing on dealings with VNK-Tomskneft. He was accused, along with three other Yukos managers, of spiriting $10 billion of assets out of the country through a Dutch-based foundation. He was charged with embezzlement and laundering $433 million and detained in SIZO No. 1, Matrosskaya Tishina. A few months after his incarceration he learned he was HIV-positive, and he began to lose the sight of his one good eye, having become blind in the other in a childhood accident. By 2008, aged 36, he had become gravely ill, contracting tuberculosis in addition to other illnesses. He accused the authorities of trying to blackmail him to testify against Khodorkovsky and Lebedev in exchange for the necessary medical treatment and freedom.[13] The ECtHR from November 2007 four times requested his transfer to a specialist hospital.[14] Khodorkovsky on 30 January 2008 declared a hunger strike to win improved conditions for his former colleague.[15] In his letter to the new prosecutor general, Yuri Chaika, he accused Karimov of acting in concert with Sechin to lay charges against totally innocent people as part of their campaign against Yukos, and noted that a 'direct threat' had been made by Karimov that Aleksanyan would not receive the needed medical help unless he testified against Khodorkovsky. As long as the issue was procedural, Khodorkovsky could play the game, but with a life at stake he was faced by 'an impossible moral choice', and decided to act directly to save his colleague's life.[16]

The government responded with surprising speed, and from 30 January Aleksanyan enjoyed much improved facilities: 'My cell was cleaned. . . . I returned from yesterday's hearing and thought I was in the wrong place.'[17] With the improvement in Aleksanyan's conditions, Khodorkovsky ended his 'dry' hunger

---

[12] Alexander Osipovich, 'From Legal Eagle to Dying in a Cage', *Moscow Times*, 7 February 2008, p. 1.

[13] Statement to the RF Supreme Court, 22 January 2008, www.khodorkovsky.ru/objective/7880.html.

[14] Christian Lowe, 'Ex-Yukos Executive Tells of Blackmail', *Moscow Times*, 17 January 2008, p. 5.

[15] Aleksandr Yakovlev and Roman Ukolov, 'Aleksyanu uluchshili usloviya', *Nezavisimaya gazeta*, 1 February 2008, p. 4; Marina Lepina and Yurii Yudin, 'Milakail Khodorkovskii golodaet za Vasiliya Aleksanyana', *Kommersant*, 31 January 2008, p. 5.

[16] The letter is dated 29 January 2008, http://www.khodorkovsky.ru/speech/7762.html.

[17] Svetlana Osadchuk and Natalya Krainova, 'Aleksanyan Says he is Receiving Care', *Moscow Times*, 1 February 2008, p. 3.

strike and now took liquids, but kept up his refusal to take food.[18] On 1 February 2008, despite having now been publicly identified as suffering from AIDS, which manifested itself as terminal lymphoma, the Simonovsky district court in Moscow, in the person of Judge Irina Oreshkina, ordered Aleksanyan to remain in custody while awaiting trial, even though the head of the detention centre had argued that he needed to be moved.[19] She also refused the defence request for Aleksanyan's case to be joined with that of Nevzlin and Gololobov.[20] Finally, on 8 February Aleksanyan's trial was suspended and on 11 February he was moved to a specialist treatment centre, and Khodorkovsky, after fourteen days, ended his hunger strike, noting: '[W]e have many not indifferent people in the country, the beginnings of civil society. This inspires us with optimism.'[21]

The Bakhmina case and that of Aleksanyan, who had a 6-year-old son, drew the criticism of even the Kremlin's own human rights officials. Ella Pamfilova, head of the Presidential Council for Promoting Civil Society Institutions and Human Rights, called Aleksanyan's situation 'simply monstrous', and called on the author-ities to transfer him to a civilian hospital for treatment, and called on the Supreme Court and the GPO to 'find the means, on the basis of their authority [and] the spirit and letter of the Constitution, to resolve the problems of this person on the basis of the principles of humanism and mercy'.[22] Even the head of the prison had written to the court arguing that Aleksanyan needed to be moved into a special treatment centre. However, Aleksanyan's tribulations continued at Moscow city hospital No. 60, where he was handcuffed to his bed (the authorities deny this), and hindered from taking showers and the like.[23] He was visited in hospital by a special commission created by the Public Chamber to look into his conditions of detention.[24]

Other cases

Some of the more notable of the other cases include the following:[25]

- In January 2004 an arrest warrant was issued for Menatep shareholder Vladimir Dubov, a former State Duma deputy. He was accused of partici-pating in allegedly illegal Yukos transactions intended to avoid tax payments. Dubov currently lives abroad.

[18] Neil Buckley, 'Unbowed in Face of "Absurd" Charges', *Financial Times*, 7 February 2008, p. 9.

[19] Svetlana Osadchuk, 'Aleksanyan Denied release for Illness', *Moscow Times*, 4 February 2008, p. 5.

[20] Marina, Lepina, ' "Kto-to reshil vzyat' menya i unichtozhit" ', *Kommersant*, 1 February 2008, p. 5.

[21] Mikhail Khodorkovsky, writing from SIZO No. 75/1, Chita, on 11 February 2008, http://www.khodorkovsky.ru/speech/7956.html.

[22] Jonas Bernstein, 'Aleksanyan's Plight: A Case of the "Legal Nihilism" Medvedev has vowed to Fight', *Eurasian Daily Monitor*, Vol. 5, No. 21, 4 February 2008.

[23] 'Vasilii Aleksanyan peresel s nar na tsep", *Kommersant-Vlast'*, No. 7, 25 February 2008, p. 22.

[24] Vera Chelishcheva, 'V dush puskaet nadziratel'', *Novaya gazeta*, No. 15, 3 March 2008, p. 15.

[25] This list is based on Robert Coalson, 'All Yukos's Men', RFE/RL, *Russian Political Weekly*, Vol. 5, No. 21, 31 May 2005, but is heavily modified and updated from numerous sources.

- Following his arrest in October 2003 the former Yukos-Moskva CEO Vasily Shakhnovsky was selected by the regional legislature of the Evenk autonomous *okrug* on 27 October to act as their representative in the Federation Council, giving him immunity from prosecution, but the GPO managed to have this rescinded. On 5 February 2004 Moscow's Meshchansky District Court convicted him of tax evasion and sentenced him to a one-year suspended sentence. As we have seen, Shakhnovsky had recanted, hence the light sentence. The court ruled that since Shakhnovsky no longer worked for Yukos, he presented no danger to society, and that he had compensated the government for all losses it had incurred.

- On 11 March 2004 an arrest warrant was issued for Menatep shareholder Mikhail Brudno on tax-evasion charges. On 4 March 2005, an additional warrant for Brudno was issued on charges of fraud and money laundering. Brudno currently lives abroad.

- In September 2004 an arrest warrant issued for former Rosprom executive Natalya Chernysheva and former Yukos deputy financial manager Dmitry Maruev. Prosecutors accused the pair of participating in a criminal organization headed by Khodorkovsky to embezzle R76 billion from the Volgograd regional government and of involvement in the allegedly illegal 1994 privatization of the Apatit fertilizer plant. Russia asked the United Kingdom to extradite Maruev and Chernysheva, a request turned down by senior district judge Timothy Workman at Bow Street Magistrates Court on 18 March 2005.

- On 12 November 2004 an arrest warrant was issued for Yukos lawyer Dmitry Gololobov, living in the United Kingdom. He was accused of fraud in connection with Yukos's takeover of a VNK subsidiary.

- On 18 November 2004 Yukos-Moskva manager Alexei Kurtsin was arrested and charged with large-scale embezzlement and money laundering through alleged charitable donations. On 1 December 2005 he was convicted and sentenced to a fourteen-year term in a hard regime camp. He appealed against this harsh sentence.

- On the day after the arrest of Svetlana Bakhmina, on 8 December another Yukos lawyer, Yelena Agranovskaya, was also arrested in connection Gololobov case. She was released from pre-trial detention on 17 December because of poor health.

- On 10 December 2004 Ratibor General Director Vladimir Malakhovsky was arrested. Prosecutors allege that Ratibor was a shell company created by Yukos to commit fraud and launder money. After a secret trial, on 5 March 2007 the Basmanny District Court convicted Malakhovsky and Vladimir Pereverzin, a former deputy director of Yukos and head of its external debt division who had been arrested on 18 December 2004, of having stolen and laundered $13 billion out of Yukos, and were sentenced to eleven and twelve years, respectively.[26] Many of the charges against Malakhovsky coincided with those in the second case against Khodorkovsky and Lebedev.

---

[26] 'Former Yukos Executives Jailed for 11 and 12 Years', *The Moscow Times*, 6 March 2007, p. 5.

- On 16 December 2004 Yukos personnel manager Anton Zakharov was detained and questioned by prosecutors for two hours in connection with the case against Gololobov, Bakhmina, and Agranovskaya.

- On 28 December, charges in the case were filed against lawyer Pavel Ivlev, but a Moscow court dismissed the case against him on 15 February 2005.

- In January 2005 Rosinkor financial group president Dmitry Velichko was arrested and charged with participating in a criminal group allegedly organized by Khodorkovsky, and with large-scale embezzlement.

- In February 2005 an arrest warrant issued for Yukos-Moskva first vice president Mikhail Trushin on charges of embezzlement in connection with the case against Kurtsin.

- In February 2005 charges were filed against Tomskneft General Director Sergei Shemkevich, who was released on his own recognizance pending trial. He was charged with exceeding his company's production-licence quotas.

- On 25 February 2005 an arrest warrant was issued for Yukos acting president Mikhail Elfimov.

In early 2008 the trial *in absentia* of Nevzlin began, in which he was charged with organizing multiple murders. Although he was in exile in Israel, the court heard a considerable body of evidence. In mid-March Rybin, the director of the Vienna-based East Petroleum Handelgas (whose case we have discussed above) asserted that he believed that Khodorkovsky had been behind the two attempts on his life. On 26 March the widow (Fatima Islamova) of Nefteyugansk mayor Vladimir Petukhov, whose murder in 1998 we also discussed above, testified that Khodorkovsky had been behind her husband's death: 'I can think of no one else but Khodorkovsky who could have done it. There was no one else.'[27] As we have seen, there are a number of other possibilities, although Pichugin was convicted of Petukhov's murder in a rather strange trial. Nevzlin insisted that the trial was politically motivated, and his spokesman Eric Wolf noted that the charges against Nevzlin had been framed in such a way as to allow for the prosecution of other Yukos people, including Khodorkovsky.[28]

THE END OF YUKOS

Following Khodorkovsky's sentencing in 2005, even though bereft of its major production asset, Yukos still owned two major oil producing fields (Tomskneft and Samaraneft), a 23 per cent non-voting stake in YNG worth some $7.5 billion, the 20 per cent stake in what had been Sibneft, five refineries (including Angarsk with a refining capacity of 410,000 barrels a day, and a group of plants in Samara with a total capacity of 300,000 barrels a day) and 1,300 filling stations, worth

[27] Matt Siegel, 'Widow Puts Blame on Khodorkovsky', *Moscow Times*, 28 March 2008, p. 7.
[28] Loc. cit.

between \$15 and \$20 billion, according to Yukos.[29] It was exactly 1,139 days from the beginning of the Yukos saga with the arrest of Alexei Pichugin on 19 June 2003 to the declaration of bankruptcy by the Moscow arbitration court on 1 August 2006. Rosneft eyed Yukos's remaining properties with its typical acquisitive instincts, and wrapping them up into its portfolio would certainly enhance its weight as a global oil company. With its output tripled by the acquisition of YNG, Rosneft lacked refining capacity and hence needed Yukos assets in this area. Putin in June 2004 argued that Russia had 'no interest in the bankruptcy of a company like Yukos', and he appears to have been hesitant about allowing Rosneft to scoop up the remains of Yukos. In the end, however, despite the massive legal and financial complications, Yukos was driven into bankruptcy. The company was sold off piecemeal to pay off \$28 billion (£14.3 billion) in back tax charges.

Bankruptcy

By the time of Khodorkovsky's sentencing on 31 May 2005 the market value of Yukos had fallen to \$1.18 billion, compared to its peak of \$32.54 billion in October 2003. In 2001 Yukos had made a net profit of \$3.156 billion and \$3.058 billion in 2002, and even after it had lost its main production subsidiary YNG in December 2004 it had still managed to pay the tax authorities \$21.3 billion by December 2005, thus reducing its tax bill to \$6.3 billion (a quarter of the total).[30] With sharp rises in the price of oil there is no reason to believe that the company could not have paid off all the penalty charges. Instead the company was driven into bankruptcy in a manner reminiscent of Texaco's bankruptcy in 1987.[31] The struggle to save Yukos, according to Berezovsky, was hampered by tension between Menatep and the new Yukos management, and he argued: 'Khodorkovsky's problem was that he tried to save the company through peaceful negotiations, but the authorities prefer to operate through informal understandings.'[32] The situation did not improve after Khodorkovsky transferred his holdings to Nevzlin, who took a harder line in dealing with the Kremlin.

The fallout over Rosneft's acquisition of YNG continued, with the latter seeking compensation from its former parent company. YNG, now a Rosneft subsidiary,

---

[29] The three main refineries were Achinsk, Syzran, and Strezhevoi with an annual throughput of 30 million tonnes. Yukos also owned VNK (which had the licence to exploit the Yurubcheno-Tokhomeskii field, the core supplier for the ESPO pipeline), the Caspian Oil Company (Kaspiiskaya Neftyanaya Kompaniya), and 20 per cent of Sibneft shares.

[30] *Kommersant*, 3 August 2006.

[31] Texaco in 1987 was valued much the same as Yukos at its peak, \$36 billion, but was bankrupted as a result of a court decision that ordered it to pay \$10 billion in compensation to Pennzoil, which accused Texaco of sabotaging its attempts to acquire Getty Oil. Texaco was quite able to pay the fine but declared a 'technical' bankruptcy, which forced Pennzoil to settle for \$3 billion, and Texaco, after restructuring and merging, lived to fight another day.

[32] Irina Reznik, Yuliya Bushueva, Aleksandr Bekker, and Tat'yana Egorova, 'Khodorkovskii vyshel', *Vedemosti*, 12 January 2005.

sued its former owner, Yukos, for $13 billion in lost revenue as a result of transfer pricing between 1999 and 2003. Once in Rosneft ownership, courts reduced the tax claims against YNG by $3.9 billion.[33] Analysts noted that the forced sale of YNG was not enough to cover Yukos's debts, although Yukos shares continued to be traded, but at an ever-increasing discount, falling to $1 a share by December 2004.[34] Uncertainty over Yukos depressed the Russian share market, with fears that the results of earlier privatizations would be reviewed and with brokers openly asking: 'Who will be next [after Khodorkovsky]?'[35] Despite the sale of its best asset, Yukos in September 2005 still had around $10.4 billion in outstanding back tax obligations to the government. There was also an international context to the confiscation of Yukos assets. The interests of foreign minority shareholders in Yukos had been treated with scant respect, and they launched a major legal suit of their own against the Russian government, as the puppet-master behind the Yukos case. The majority shareholders held some 60 per cent of Yukos stock, while the other 40 per cent was held by minority shareholders, of which 23 per cent was held by three foreign hedge funds, which included the Pentagon's pension fund.[36]

Most of Yukos's top management, led by the American chief executive Steven Theede, who had taken over from Simon Kukes in June 2004, had decamped to London by the end of that year. The ability of Yukos to continue was doubted even by some its senior executives. At a shareholder's meeting on 21 June 2006 Victor Gerashchenko, the chairman of the Yukos board in Moscow, argued that it would make sense to sell what remained of Yukos to Rosneft, rather than to allow the company to become bankrupt and its assets to be sold piecemeal. Already by that time Yukos's fate was being dealt with by a Moscow bankruptcy court.[37] A division in strategy was once again apparent, with Yukos's London-based management arguing that Yukos could emerge triumphant from the bankruptcy proceedings, and asserted that the company was enduring a 'false liquidity crisis' brought on by the 'illegitimate and subjective use of Russian law'. A report by the Deutsche UFG brokerage firm at that time calculated that Yukos's debt exceeded its assets.[38] Theede resigned as Yukos's chief executive on 20 July 2006, calling the bankruptcy proceedings a 'farce'.[39] He noted that he had 'exhausted all possibilities... to either

[33] 'Russian Oil, Going Twice', *The Economist*, 27 May–2 June 2006.
[34] 'Yukos—Brunswick UBS', *Vedemosti*, 1 December 2004.
[35] 'Vektor', *Vedemosti*, 2 December 2004.
[36] Gerashchenko on radio Ekho Moskvy, 27 July 2006, BBC Monitoring, in *JRL*, No. 171, 2006.
[37] The Moscow Arbitration Court from 28 March 2006 examined the claim for R147 billion by nine of Yukos's creditors. In June the temporary manager of Yukos, Eduard Rebgun, successfully asked for a postponement of the hearings to allow the precise claims of the creditors to be assessed. According to Russia's bankruptcy law, once bankruptcy proceedings have begun, it is up to the creditors to decide whether actually to declare the company bankrupt. The main claim against Yukos at that time came from the FNS for back taxes, YNG, and Yukos Capital SARL. Full details in Ol'ga Pleshanova, 'Yukos otpustili na letnie kanikuly', *Kommersant*, 28 June 2006, p. 16.
[38] Andrew E. Kramer, 'Chairman Predicts Bleak Future for Yukos', *New York Times*, 22 June 2006, with the quotations by Clair Davidson, a spokesperson for Yukos's London management.
[39] Tom Parfitt and Terry Macalister, 'The End Comes for Yukos as Oil Firm Declared Bankrupt and Auction Ordered', *The Guardian*, 2 August 2004, p. 22.

preserve or recover value for the company', and he was particularly upset at his inability to stop Rosneft's IPO in London.[40]

Although Putin declared that the government was not interested in bankrupting Yukos, the company now moved towards liquidation, and management attempts to save the company were brushed aside. New obligations appeared out of nowhere, ultimately forcing a fire sale of its assets at below market prices. The main beneficiary was Rosneft, which itself was nearly bankrupted by the burden of debt it assumed to swallow Yukos. Already on 13 May 2005 the Russian arbitration court ordered Yukos to pay $2.2 billion as compensation to Rosneft, for oil that YNG had delivered to Yukos in 2004 but for which Yukos had not paid. The money, Yukos argued, had gone to pay Yukos's tax debts to the state—by May 2005 Yukos had paid some $30 billion in tax recovery charges. Rosneft also sued Yukos for another $10.5 billion: $4.7 billion were tax charges against YNG; and $5.8 billion were Rosneft's alleged losses arising out of transfer pricing.[41] All of Yukos's assets, except its share of Sibneft, were seized to secure these claims. In effect, Yukos was paying its competitors for its own expropriation.

The three main creditors were the Federal Tax Service ($13.1 billion), Rosneft ($4 billion), and various claims by YNG ($2.7 billion), while Tomskneft claimed $460 million and Samaraneftegaz $69 million. The company's creditors on 25 July 2006 voted for bankruptcy, rejecting a rescue plan advanced by Yukos in which the company offered to pay off $18.2 billion in outstanding debts within eighteen months, and thus effectively imposed a death sentence on the company.[42] The Moscow arbitration court announced the company's bankruptcy on 1 August, claiming that Yukos had liabilities of $18.3 billion and assets worth only $17.7 billion, figures that were disputed by Gerashchenko and others, who valued the company at $38 billion, while Timothy Osborne, the director of Gibralter-based GML, Yukos's core shareholder, estimated Yukos's value at $29.5 billion.[43] As late as January 2007 the company's total assets, including share investments (among which was the 20 per cent stake owned by Yukos in Gazprom Neft, formerly known as Sibneft, for which Yukos was asking for $4 billion), property, and dozens of subsidiaries abroad, was assessed by experts as exceeding $22 billion, although GML by then valued the company at $37.2 billion.[44] Eduard Rebgun, the court-appointed liquidation administrator, was tasked with selling the assets as quickly as possible to pay off the debts. Not surprisingly, Rebgun accepted the lower valuation, with a 10–30 per cent discount.

Tim Osborne notes that although he was the designated representative to the creditors' meeting that would decide the fate of the company, Rebgun denied him access to the 'bankruptcy' report, insisting that Osborne went to Moscow

[40] Alex Nicholson, 'Yukos President Announces Resignation', AP, 20 July 2006.

[41] Konończuk, *The 'Yukos Affair'*, p. 48. In the event, on arbitration the tax claim of Rosneft against YNG was reduced to $760 million. Irina Malkova, ' "Apatitu" prostili 5 mlrd rub.', *Vedemosti*, 23 November 2006, p. 4.

[42] Valeria Korchagina, 'Court Declares Yukos Bankrupt', *Moscow Times*, 2 August 2006.

[43] Nicholson, 'Yukos President Announces Resignation'.

[44] Anna Skornyakova, 'Ostatki sladki', *Profil'*, 29 January 2007, p. 42. Yukos's assets included $10.2 billion worth of shares in Gazprom Neft and Rosneft

to see the documentation, but at the same time warning him that his safety in Russia could not be guaranteed. According to Osborne, the rescue plan presented to the meeting would have allowed Yukos to pay its legitimate creditors within eighteen months and to have retained the company as a viable entity. However, with the meeting packed with representatives of state-controlled bodies, the plan was summarily dismissed and the path of bankruptcy chosen.

Russia's bankruptcy law states that when the assets of a company facing liquidation are not enough to cover its debts, the primary debt is paid first, which in Yukos's case was the tax service, and the rest is paid proportionally of what is left. It was assumed that Rosneft and Gazprom would be the primary beneficiaries of Yukos's bankruptcy, but in the event the lion's share went to the former. The greatest losers were the Yukos shareholders, both majority and minority. The Menatep Group was not included on the list of creditors, although it had become the sole beneficiary of the sale on 26 May 2006 of Yukos's 53.7 per cent stake in the Mazeikiu Nafta refinery. The $1.2 billion paid by the Polish company PKN Orlen was to have gone to a Dutch court, to be distributed to Yukos creditors Moravel (itself a Yukos affiliate) and Rosneft. In the event, the money went directly to Yukos International, associated with the owners of Yukos.[45] In a further twist to the story, Rebgun in March 2007 was nominated by Yukos to the nine-member board of Rosneft, to facilitate the disposal of its assets.[46]

At a bankruptcy auction in March 2007 Rosneft bid for 9.44 per cent of its own stock acquired by Yukos earlier. TNK-BP put in an alternative bid to give the appearance of a competitive process (by law at least two companies have to be involved), but it was pitched so low that it allowed Rosneft to acquire the stock for some $7.5 billion. The head of the company, Lord Browne, and his successor Tony Hayward, met Putin on the eve of the auction. The involvement of TNK-BP may well have been a way of currying favour with Putin (as was its participation in Rosneft's London IPO) to avert any attack on the company. In April 2007 ENI bought Artikgas and Urengoil at auction, and in return ENI opened up consumer distribution systems to Gazprom. In May 2007 Rosneft (through its straw-man subsidiary Neft Aktiv) bought half of the oil production unit Tomskneft (producing 240,000 barrels a day in total) and Yukos's other Far Eastern assets for $6.8 billion, and thus became the country's largest crude producer and refiner. In July and August Rosneft scooped up important production licences in the Khanty-Mansi and Evenk oil-producing regions, as well as in Samara.[47] In sum, Rosneft acquired the two remaining Yukos production subsidiaries, Tomskneft and Samaraneftegaz, for $13.2 billion.[48] The takeovers were accompanied by management changes and a review of all management contracts.[49]

[45] Ibid., p. 44.

[46] Anatoly Medetsky, 'Rebgun Nominated for Rosneft Board Post', *Moscow Times*, 2 March 2007, p. 5.

[47] 'Summer: A Time for Auctions', *Rosneft Magazine*, No. 3 (6), July–September 2007, p. 9.

[48] Miriam Elder, 'How the State Got a Grip on Energy', *Moscow Times*, 14 March 2008, p. 1.

[49] For details, see Elena Mazneva, Ekaterina Derbilova, and Vera Surzhenko, ' "Rosneft" menyaet vlast', *Vedemosti*, 15 May 2007, p. B3.

On 11 May 2007 Rosneft purchased Lot 13, which included Yukos's trading house, its Moscow headquarters, and some other assets, for $3.9 billion. The purchase went through a front company called Prana, to protect itself from any possible law suits, a role also played by RN-Razvitie in acquiring Yukos real estate at this time. The Prana deal was described as a record for a real estate sale of this type in Moscow, clearly overvaluing the assets by quadrupling the starting price, as well as being a record deal for its opacity.[50] Temerko argued: 'Every one of these auctions has shown that the whole process is a farce.'[51] Gazprom won only one auction, signing a call option with the Italian companies ENI and ENEL to buy a 20 per cent gas stake for Gazprom Neft on 4 April; otherwise the company, fearing legal action, kept a low profile so as not to sully Medvedev's reputation as he prepared for the presidency.

Former Yukos assets continued to circulate in the market. In December 2007 Gazprom Neft received approval from the Federal Anti-Monopoly Service to buy half of Tomskneft for $3.66 billion. Rosneft had acquired Tomskneft in May 2007, but on 25 June it sold half for the same amount as Prana had bought Lot 13 to the Development Bank (formerly Vneshekonbank) to help service its massive debts, although it remained the operating company in the field. The Development Bank clearly acted as a warehousing transaction, and the ultimate transfer of part of Tomskneft to Gazprom Neft was the first time that Rosneft agreed to share its assets. It had to redeem some $17 billion of short-term debt in 2008 at a time when the volatility of financial markets forced it to postpone a Eurobond issue. The sale reduced Rosneft's output of 2.3 million bpd by about 5 per cent, while Gazprom's oil production increased by 14 per cent to approach the one million bpd threshold.[52] The company's share price fell sharply because of fears that production would fall in Sakhalin-1 and reports that the company was looking for additional funding from the state to help reduce its debt.

In acquiring Yukos assets Rosneft took on their liabilities as well (above all those of Tomskneft and Samaraneftegaz), and financed the purchases through extensive borrowing. The company took out $22 billion in loans in 2007, and had a total debt of $27 billion by the end of that year. It was faced with repayments of $5 billion in February 2008 alone, which entailed extensive refinancing. In addition, the company turned to the state for support, forcing the government to increase its monitoring of private debt transactions by companies and banks with a significant state interest. In 2007 Rosneft had been placed on the list of strategic assets owned by the state, which gave it some sort of shelter from the financial storm that it had brought upon itself.[53]

---

[50] Dmitrii Butrin, 'Neopoznannyi finansovyi ob"ekt', *Kommersant vlast'*, 16 July 2007, pp. 62–3.

[51] Miriam Elder, 'Yukos Auction All Smoke and Mirrors', *Moscow Times*, 15 May 2007, p. 1.

[52] *Moscow Times*, 27 December 2007, p. 5.

[53] Anastasiya Krasinskaya and Tat'yana Frolovskaya, ' "Rosneft" ' prosit deneg u Kremlya', *RBK Daily*, 31 January 2008, p. 1.

Twisting the knife

The destruction of Yukos was accompanied by a range of measures against its public activities. In February 2005 tax inspectors raided the offices of Open Russia, the fourth in three years, looking for evidence that Yukos funds had been laundered through the organization. By order of the Basmanny court in March 2006 its funds were frozen on the grounds that the money in the philanthropic organization's accounts belonged to someone suspected of criminal activities.[54] Between 2001 and 2005 Open Russia had disbursed a total of $60 million through hundreds of regional and national projects.[55] From sixty-seven staff members, the number fell to only twelve by June 2006, with the remaining staff working without pay. The Moscow office closed in August of that year, although all forty-seven of its regional affiliates continued to work, most having found alternative sources of support for their work (for example, its civic education programme was funded by USAID). In particular, the programme of public policy schools, training people in active citizenship, even found support from regional branches of United Russia. In 2005 alone Open Russia had supported over thirty projects, and over the course of its four years of work over 600,000 people had participated in its activities.[56]

In financial terms, the Putin regime won hands down in its struggle with Yukos, although the political and reputational consequences are less easy to calculate. Not only had it managed to squeeze at least $32 billion out of the company in back taxes, it had then been able to buy its assets for roughly half their market valuation. The bulk had gone to Rosneft (with the rest going to Gazprom and ENI), and the company, whose capitalization just four years earlier had been $4 billion, spent $21 billion buying up Yukos assets but saw its capitalization rise to $90 billion in 2007, of which 87 per cent belonged to the state (worth $78 billion).[57] Rosneft rose from eighth place to become Russia's largest oil company.

Another winner was Timchenko's Gunvor Group. By February 2008 it shipped sixteen times more crude than it had done in February 2002, making it the world's fourth largest independent trader after Glencore International AG, Vitol SA, and Tarfigura Behreer BV. With the abolition of the in-house trading arms of Yukos and Sibneft, a large proportion of their former exports went through Gunvor: 'Mr Timchenko's group took everything "virtually overnight", said a former executive of Yukos's now defunct trading arm.'[58] Even after Putin's move from the Kremlin to the White House Timchenko's links with the government remained strong. On 14 May 2008 Putin supported two projects involving Gunvor. He announced that the planned expansion to the Baltic Pipeline System would pass through the

[54] Andrei Kozenko, 'Otkrytata Rossiya zakryvaetsya', *Kommersant*, 21 March 2006, p. 7.
[55] Nabi Abdullaev, 'More Prison Time for Khodorkovsky?', *Moscow Times*, 28 December 2006, p. 3.
[56] http://khodorkovsky.ru/society/actions/5424.html.
[57] 'Igraya s aktivami Yukosa, Kreml' p'et iz dvukh kolodtsev', *Kommersant*, 15 May 2007, p. 12.
[58] Andrew Higgins, Guy Chazan, and Alan Cullison, 'Secretive Associate of Putin Emerges as Czar of Russian Oil Trading', *Wall Street Journal*, 11 June 2008, p. 1.

Kirishi refinery, linked to Timchenko; and that it would terminate at the new Ust-Luga terminal, in which Gunvor was a key stakeholder.[59]

In his final address to the Federal Assembly on 26 April 2007, Putin twisted the knife in the Yukos corpse, and drew a direct connection between the poverty of the many compared to the earlier wealth of a few:

> We need to look the truth in the eyes and recognise that many of our fellow citizens, who have found themselves in very difficult circumstances, are unable to resolve this issue without support from the state....Of course, the question arises, where will the money come from? First, we have the money. Spending decisions are always just a matter of the choice of priorities at federal and regional level. Second, I have a concrete proposal, namely, to allocate considerable additional revenue to these tasks, including revenue obtained through improved tax collection, from the privatisation of state assets and also, perhaps, from the sale of assets belonging to Yukos in payment of its debts to the state.[60]

This may have been Putin's truth, but the situation was rather more complicated and his version was at best partial. Once the assault was launched the powers of the 'prerogative state' were applied intensively against Yukos and its associates. A bill shortly afterwards allocated billions of dollars from the sale of Yukos assets into the Housing Reform Fund and the Russian Nanotechnology Corporation,[61] a rather transparent populist attempt to demonstrate that the liquidation of Yukos had been for the public good.

It is not clear in these circumstances whether Yukos could have defended itself more effectively. The Yukos affair developed incrementally, and indeed, the state's appetite grew with the eating. In late 2003 the aim had been to stymie Khodorkovsky's political ambitions, above all to ensure that he was not able to win a blocking position in the State Duma. Having achieved this, and encountering little coherent opposition from the company, the assault then turned to the economic assets of the company. Without Khodorkovsky at the helm, and with Nevzlin abroad and Lebedev in detention, the company was effectively rudderless. Yukos was hit with repeated tax claims that did not allow it to rise from its knees. Once begun, the process of dismemberment could not be stopped. Then, as bankruptcy loomed the authorities did everything in their power to ensure that the various rescue plans devised by Yukos management were rejected by the company's creditors.

Civil proceedings

Menatep, Yukos, and various oligarchs took full advantage of Swiss banking secrecy laws, introduced in the early 1930s. At Russia's request for legal assistance in August 2003, the Swiss prosecutors in March 2004 froze the assets belonging to Group Menatep, amounting to $4.9 billion in cash and equity investments.

[59] Catherine Belton, 'Gunvor Seeks Oil Asset Investments in Russia', *Financial Times*, 15 May 2008.
[60] http://president.kremlin.ru/text/appears/2007/04/125401.shtml.
[61] Anatoly Medetsky, 'Yukos Tax Going to Housing, Research', *Moscow Times*, 17 May 2007, p. 5.

However, soon after the Swiss authorities came to the view that they had acted 'too speedily', and unblocked most of the accounts except for some $400 million.[62] There were severe recriminations within Switzerland that the request from Moscow may have been made primarily on 'political grounds'.[63]

Yukos shareholders, led by the main stakeholder GML, filed a lawsuit against the Russian government to the International Court for Arbitration in The Hague for compensation for the losses incurred when Yukos was effectively nationalized. The sum in question, around $50 billion, is the largest in the history of commercial arbitration.[64] The group of companies filed the suit on the basis of the Energy Charter Treaty, which Russia signed in 1994. If the court ruled against the Russian state, within the terms of the New York Convention the award, if not settled voluntarily, would be enforceable on any Russian government assets outside the country not covered by sovereign immunity. There was an issue over the exercise of jurisdiction, but the court in all likelihood would declare the case admissible. The Yukos case according to the international lawyer Adnan Amkhan was 'one of the most explosive ever taken to international arbitration'.[65] The Russian government would find itself in the position of the Bolshevik regime after 1917, with its assets in danger of being seized in compensation for illegal expropriation of private property.

In a different case, the Amsterdam District Court on 31 October 2007 resolved that Yukos's bankruptcy was not in conformity with Dutch law, and therefore the decision of Rebgun's temporary administration to liquidate the company's assets were not valid in the Netherlands. This applied to Yukos's daughter company Yukos Finance BV. The specific issue concerned a Yukos debt of $480 million to a consortium of international banks, which Yukos failed to pay in 2004; after which the consortium passed its claim to Rosneft on 13 December 2005; and on 9 March 2006 the Moscow *arbitrazh* court agreed to the consortium's petition to declare Yukos bankrupt. The dismissal of Yukos Finance's former directors Bruce Misamore and David Godfrey on 11 August 2006 by Rebgun on behalf of the creditors, in the wake of the bankruptcy decision a few days earlier, was considered unlawful, and Holland would not register the new owners of the company, since its shares were sold as part of the bankruptcy proceedings which were now declared invalid. The court thus condemned the whole process by which Yukos had been declared bankrupt, and therefore considered that no appeal by Yukos to Russian courts could repair the 'fundamental legal defect attached to the bankruptcy order'; and that 'in the bankruptcy proceedings, no substantive, sufficiently safeguarded, judicial review took place or could have taken place of the manner in

---

[62] 'Swiss Banks Say Attorney is too Quick to Block Accounts', *Bloomberg*, 14 September 2005, mimeo.

[63] Haig Simonian, 'Swiss Banks Voice Fears on Political Interference', *Financial Times*, 15 September 2005.

[64] Yevgeny Kiselëv, 'Worried Over Strasbourg, Scared of The Hague', *The Moscow Times*, 28 March 2007, p. 9.

[65] Adnan Amkhan, paper presented to the University of Kent Energy Analysis Group, Brussels, 21 September 2007.

which the additional tax assessments, as imposed by the Russian tax authorities and determined by the tax court, were determined'.[66] Thus any decisions taken by Rebgun concerning Yukos assets in the Netherlands were nullified.

The case had been lodged by Misamore and Godfrey in 2006 in an attempt to block the sale of Yukos's foreign shares. In August 2006 all of Yukos Finance's shares had been bought by Promneftstroi, a company established by Rosneft but which had been sold for the relatively small sum of $307 million to a company called Monte-Valley, owned by the American Steven Patrick Lynch. Yukos Finance BV had never been directly owned by the main Yukos Company, but it had been controlled through a subsidiary company. Yukos Finance held the 49 per cent of the depository shares of the Slovak company Transpetrol (hence later it would not fall under the Russian bankruptcy proceedings), $1.5bn from the sale of the Mazeikiu refinery, and more. All of this had come into trust in 2006, and Rebgun had unsuccessfully contested the exchange of shares for depository trust accounts.[67]

The Amsterdam District Court struck again on 6 March 2008, when it decided that a group of Yukos shareholders were entitled to compensation. Moravel, a subsidiary of majority shareholder GML, received $850 million on 14 March as repayment for an earlier loan. At issue was money received from the sale in 2006 of Mazeikiu to Poland's PKN Orlen, some of which now went to Yukos International, a Dutch subsidiary of Yukos. The Dutch court at the same time maintained the freeze on another $650 million that remained in a high interest account at Fortis Bank. Yukos International also was unable to dispose of Yukos's 49 per cent stake in Transpetrol. Rosneft had hoped to be able to use the money to help pay off some of its enormous debts. Rosneft had assumed the $480 million Yukos debt to a consortium of international banks, but the court ruled that Rosneft had been adequately compensated through the various Yukos bankruptcy auctions. In one of those auctions Promneftstroi, owned by Lynch, was awarded the right to buy Yukos Finance, the Dutch subsidiary that owned Yukos International, the holder of the company's foreign assets, although in general the Dutch court consistently refused to recognize the legality of Yukos's bankruptcy and the associated auctions.[68]

THE ATTACK CONTINUES

When the verdict was delivered in May 2005 the GPO warned that further charges would follow, and in late 2006 the machine once again creaked into action. With

[66] Tim Osborne, 'How to Steal Legally', *Moscow Times*, 15 February 2008, p. 8.

[67] Elena Mazneva and Vasilii Kashin, 'Yukos Finance ne menyaet khozyaev', *Vedemosti*, 1 November 2007, in section 'Energoresursy'. The full judgement of the civil law division of the District Court of Amsterdam, case number/docket number: 355622/HA ZA 06-3612, of 31 October 2007 is available at http://www.robertamsterdam.com/Dutch%20Yukos%20Decision.pdf.

[68] Anatoly Medetsky, '$550M Released to Yukos Shareholders', *Moscow Times*, 27 March 2008, p. 5.

parliamentary elections due to be held on 2 December 2007 and the presidential elections on 2 March 2008, the regime wanted Khodorkovsky out of the way. A replacement would have to be found for Putin, at the end of the two presidential terms allowed him by the constitution. The electoral cycle was accompanied by factional conflict, in part over the attempt to control the succession as well as over the property settlement of the Putin and Yeltsin years. In the event, in May 2008 Putin moved out of the Kremlin to take up his duties as prime minister in the Russian White House, while Dmitry Medvedev, Putin's nominated successor, moved into the presidential office. The rebalancing of the regime offered an opportunity to put an end to the Yukos affair.

Further charges

In December 2006 Khodorkovsky and Lebedev were moved from their respective camps to the investigative prison (SIZO) in the city of Chita. Although they had been sentenced earlier primarily on charges of tax evasion, the new charges announced on 5 February 2007 focused on embezzlement of over $30 billion through fraud and money laundering between 1998 and 2003.[69] Khodorkovsky and Lebedev faced additional sentences of ten to fifteen years. The money was allegedly laundered through offshore trading companies and philanthropic contributions to Open Russia. Once again the transfer pricing schemes came under scrutiny. The prosecution alleged that between 2000 and 2003 Yukos officials illegally transferred billions in crude sales from its production subsidiaries through two trading companies, Fargoil and Ratibor, registered in tax havens, with the sales from the refined product then transferred back to Yukos, with the profits siphoned off by Khodorkovsky and his associates.[70] In addition, crude oil was allegedly delivered on paper at reduced prices to companies registered in the tax-benefit zones in Mordovia, Evenkia, and other regions, and then sold on at market prices, thus severely reducing tax liabilities. Such tax optimization schemes, according to Ivlev, who had earlier represented Yukos, continued to be practiced by Rosneft.[71] Yuri Schmidt pointed out the absurdity of the new charges, which suggested that Khodorkovsky and Lebedev stole their own oil and then tried to launder the profit of what had been normal cash flows from the sale of a product that was at the core of the company's business.[72]

---

[69] Mariya Lokotetskaya, 'Mikhail Khodorkovskii ostalsya pod strazhei', *Gazeta*, 4 April 2007, p. 10. The new charges were based on Articles 160 and 174 of the RF Criminal Code.

[70] The former head of Fargoil, Antonio Valdes Garcia, fled Moscow in January 2007, just days before he and former Ratibor president Vladimir Malakhovsky were due to be sentenced for this alleged embezzlement scheme, Miriam Elder, 'Bank of New York Sued for $22 Bln', *Moscow Times*, 18 May 2007, p. 1.

[71] Ekaterina Zapodinskaya, 'Khodorkovsky and Lebedev Charged Again', *Kommersant*, 6 February 2007.

[72] Yurii Schmidt, 'Chto dal'she', 25 October 2007, http://www.khodorkovsky.ru/cassation/comments/7430.html.

Khodorkovsky also insisted that the charges were 'absurd' and called the whole trial process a 'farce', based on false evidence provided by 'frightened or fooled false witnesses'. Why the second case was being launched was clear: 'Those people who had invented the "Khodorkovsky affair", to steal one of Russia's most flourishing oil companies, Yukos, are very frightened of seeing me free and want to insure against my release on parole.' Khodorkovsky saw his task in the forthcoming trial to demonstrate 'that in Russia justice is dependent [on the authorities]'. He was not intimidated by a new sentence, since it made little difference to have yet more patently absurd charges preferred against him: 'Platon Lebedev's and my fate will be entirely decided by the fate of our motherland, its features after the change of power in 2008.'[73] Khodorkovsky was given a limited time, by 22 December 2007, to acquaint himself with the seventy volumes of evidence gathered for the second trial.[74] As with the earlier trial, repeated attempt to allow the accused out on bail were refused, and they were held in Chita SIZO No. 1.[75]

Karimov was once again the chief investigator and, as with previous cases, sought to restrict the ability of the accused to prepare an adequate defence. On 29 December 2006 Lebedev filed a motion requesting information about his international travels between 1994 and 2 July 2003, and in particular the dates of his crossing Russia's borders, in order to establish his precise whereabouts and thus to confirm his alibi. On 11 January 2007 Karimov refused this request. On 18 May 2007 the Ingodinsky District Court of the City of Chita severely censured Karimov's decision, arguing that it was incumbent for an investigator to prove 'the time, the venue and other circumstances' in a case. It is worth quoting the relevant part of the judgement in full, since its key charge against Karimov is relevant to the other cases in which he was involved:

[A] suspect has a right to file motions to investigators concerning investigative actions necessary to establish circumstances relevant to the criminal case. Such a motion can be filed at any time throughout proceedings in the case. The fact that a suspect has such a right means that an investigator has the obligation to consider the motion filed and make a decision on it. Making a proper decision includes an obligation to find out, if necessary, what exact circumstances the suspect is asking to be established and whether they are relevant to the case, i.e. to receive an additional explanation from the applicant. The investigator failed to fulfil these requirements, and this led to the premature and groundless decision and violation of P. L. Lebedev's right to defence.[76]

Russian law states that defendants should be tried either in their place of residence or where the crime was allegedly committed. Chita meets neither of these conditions for Khodorkovsky or Lebedev. An appeal on these grounds was supported by the Basmanny District Court in Moscow on 20 March 2007, on the basis of Article

---

[73] 7 February 2007, http://www.khodorkovsky.ru/speech/6273.html.

[74] Ivan Romanov, 'Delo Mikhail Khodorkovskogo stalo srochnym', *Kommersant*, 16 November 2007, p. 6.

[75] Zoya Eroshok, 'Grazhdanin oligarkh', *Novaya gazeta*, 25 October 2007, p. 6.

[76] Judgement of the Ingodinsky District Court of the City of Chita, 18 May 2007 (mimeo). The presiding judge was Ye. M. Mershieva, with the veracity of the document endorsed by assistant judge T. P. Nikitina.

32 of the UPK that the investigation and trial should be held in the place where the alleged offences took place, probably to remove a procedural point that could have supported the appeal to Strasbourg.[77] However, the return of Khodorkovsky and Lebedev to Moscow was appealed by the procuracy, but the decision was upheld by the Moscow City Court on 16 April. The decision should now have been implemented, but the GPO now took the case to 'supervisory review', asking the City Court to change its mind, but on 13 June it refused to do so, and an additional appeal to the chair of the Court was also rejected on 4 July. The GPO still refused to implement the Basmanny Court's decision and now appealed to the Criminal Chamber of the Russian Supreme Court, which asked the City Court at least to entertain the appeal, but on 13 September it once again turned down the appeal. Finally, on 22 November the Criminal Chamber agreed to hear the appeal, and on 25 December it upheld the request by the GPO for the case to be heard in Chita. The incident once again demonstrates the lack of finality in Russian judicial decisions, and the ability of the procuracy to keep appealing until it gets the decision it wants.

With the establishment of the Investigative Committee within but not subordinate to the GPO in September 2007, the case was transferred to the new agency headed by Alexander Bastrykin. Karimov was relieved of responsibility for the case, and a certain Drymanov took over. One of his first acts in office was to refuse to transfer the case to Moscow. This made the work of the defence team much harder since they now had to keep a team in Chita and another in Moscow to research the relevant material and prepare the appropriate documents. Throughout Khodorkovsky insisted that he would continue to seek justice in Russia.[78] Bastrykin, warned against politicizing criminal cases, such as that against Boris Berezovsky,[79] and insisted: 'Khodorkovsky and Lebedev have been brought to justice on the basis of evidence of misappropriating the stock of the subsidiary companies of the OOO (limited liability company) VNK, as well as stealing oil and legalizing stolen property. The preliminary investigation of the case is now complete, and in Chita the defendants and their defence lawyers are familiarizing themselves with the materials of the criminal case.'[80]

In the context of a number of adverse foreign rulings, including six decisions of the Swiss Federal Tribunal in August 2007 that the Swiss authorities would no longer cooperate with Russian prosecutors in Yukos-associated cases, and the uncertainty associated with the succession, the new trial was postponed.

The trials of other former Yukos officials, however, continued. There was no end to the tribulations heaped upon Pichugin. In August 2006 his sentence was extended to twenty-four years, including the twenty-year term imposed earlier. He was now found guilty of organizing Korneeva's murder and of organizing the killing of Nefteyugansk mayor Petukhov in 1998. Pichugin was also convicted of

---

[77] Kiselëv, 'Worried Over Strasbourg, Scared of The Hague'.

[78] Schmidt, 'Chto dal'she', 25 October 2007.

[79] Charged at that time of misappropriating funds from Avtovaz and Aeroflot, illegally exchanging Chechens for captured OMON officers, and laundering criminally acquired finances.

[80] Unattributed interview with Aleksander Bastrykin, *Izvestiya*, 5 October 2007.

organizing attacks against businessman Rybin in 1998 and 1999. In February 2007 the Russian Supreme Court overturned the sentence against Pichugin and ruled that he should face a new trial with a new judge. The retrial would in all likelihood lead to a harsher sentence. The new case against Pichugin implicated Nevzlin, in exile in Israel, and intensified demands for his extradition to Russia, which is probably what the whole trial was about.

In an extensive submission to the Investigative Committee, signed by Khodorkovsky on 22 December 2007, his lawyers provided a forensic and devastating critique of the new case.[81] Despite limited time, the defence team, as well as Khodorkovsky and Lebedev, had finished reading the charges, and they were not impressed. They insisted that the charges were political, 'as part of the deliberate attempt to destroy the Yukos oil company'. In addition to citing the various foreign judgments against Russia in the case, the letter cited the Russian Constitutional Court decision of 22 March 2005 condemning the extension of pre-trial detention without a court hearing, and instead in the Lebedev and other cases this was done by decision of judges, without the relevant lawyers present. A whole range of infringements of the Criminal Procedural Code were cited. They noted that the GPO, and now the Investigative Committee, had ignored court decisions, notably the decision of the Ingodinsky district court of 14 February and 18 May 2007 to allow Lebedev to prove his alibi. The various searches of the defence lawyers' offices, notably of ALM Feldmans on 15 December 2004, without the sanction of a judge, was condemned. The search of Drel's offices on 9 October 2003 was conducted without him being present; and indeed, his absence had been forced. Evidence gathered by illegal means is not admissible. They also criticized the criteria by which the notion of an 'organised criminal group' was applied in the Yukos case. They also went into considerable detail to criticize the charges of money laundering through the various Yukos subsidiaries, notably involving VNK (the case in which Aleksanyan was involved). They concluded by arguing that a whole range of legal guarantees and standards enshrined in Article 6 of the ECHR, as well as procedural violations of a number of other articles. The presumption of innocence had been ignored, and the equality of all parties in a trial had not been respected.[82]

According to Garry Kasparov, the former world chess champion and head of the United Civic Front, a core member of the Other Russia oppositional grouping, Khodorkovsky would have to serve at least three years of his term: 'I think he'll only be free when Putin is no longer where he is now.'[83] A pardon is only technically possible if a prisoner accepts guilt, and can take place three years after arrest. Khodorkovsky and Lebedev consistently proclaimed their innocence. However, once half the term is served they can be released early on the basis of 'conditional-early release' (*uslovno-dosrochnogo osvobozhdeniya*) scheme envisaged by Russian law. However, at the halfway mark of his eight-year incarceration on 25 October

[81] A total of twelve lawyers signed the document, led by Yuri Schmidt and including Elena Liptser.
[82] *Khodataistvuem o prekrashchenii ugolovnovo dela*, 22 December 2007, http://www.khodorkovsky.ru/cassation/petitions/7637.html.
[83] http://www.mbktrial.com/developments/2006Apr11_attack.cfm.

2007 (what in prison jargon is called the 'equator') he was not considered for parole because of a reprimand that he had received over the claimed violation of prison rules.[84] Khodorkovsky allegedly had not had his hands behind his back during a walk on 15 October but down his sides like an ordinary person, but later another inmate, Igor Gnezdilov, who shared a cell with Khodorkovsky for a year, revealed that he had been forced to sign a statement accusing Khodorkovsky of walking in the yard in an unsanctioned manner: 'It wasn't true but I was told that if I didn't sign the statement they would make sure I wasn't released early. So I signed, but later told Khodorkovsky.'[85]

With the infringement logged in his file, when the case for parole came up a few days later, it was refused. For parole to take place the recommendations of the camp administration are taken into account, as well as ensuring compensation for harm caused. In the case of Khodorkovsky and Lebedev, according to the Meshchansky court this came to R17 billion.[86] Over 40 Russian human rights activists and public figures signed an open letter calling for Khodorkovsky's release.[87] The halfway mark of Khodorkovsky's sentence was marked by a demonstration of Yabloko activists in Sverdlovsk region, who gathered (appropriately) at the memorial to the Decembrists, and demanded the release of Khodorkovsky and all political prisoners in Russia. Their banners declared: 'A system which imprisons people for their beliefs is a disgrace for Russia before the civilised world.'[88]

The delay in the second trial was connected not only with technical preparations but also with the succession operation. In the event the Sechin group lost out. The *siloviki*, with no candidate of their own, hoped to force Putin to take up a third term but instead the candidate least sympathetic to the interests of the security establishment was advanced to the presidency. In his first major programmatic speech, delivered to the Civic Forum in Moscow on 22 January 2008, Medvedev's comments reflected his earlier opposition to the attack on Yukos. He stressed that '[w]e shall pursue a firm policy of free development for private enterprise, protecting property rights, and reinforcing the common principles of a market economy', accompanied by the need to turn the struggle against corruption into a national campaign. This was hampered by the fact that

Russia is still suffering from legal nihilism. No European country can boast of this degree of contempt for the law. This phenomenon is rooted in our country's distant past. The state cannot be a law-based state, or a just state, unless the authorities and citizens know and respect its laws, and citizens have sufficient awareness of the law to monitor the actions of state officials effectively.[89]

---

[84] Anatoly Medetsky, 'Khodorkovsky not Eligible for Parole', *Moscow Times*, 26 October 2007, p. 7.

[85] Sergei Dyupin, ' "S Mikhailom Borisovichem ya postupil ne po ponyatiyam" ', *Kommersant-Vlast'*, No. 25, 30 June 2008. Gnezdilov provides much interesting information about Khodorkovsky's time in pre-trial detention in Chita.

[86] http://www.izvestia.ru/incident/article1839552/index.html.

[87] Mariya Rogacheva, 'Srok vyshel', *Gazeta*, 25 October 2007, p. 23.

[88] Marina Lepina, 'Mikhail Khodorkovskii ne mozhet pretendovat' na UDO', *Kommersant*, 26 October 2007, p. 5.

[89] http://www.medvedev2008.ru/english_2008_01_22.htm.

The tone of the speech suggested that the Yukos case would be seen in a very different light under the new presidency.

Despite the vigour with which the second case was being prepared, Schmidt was convinced that Khodorkovsky 'will be released soon. If the courts can at least regain that level of independence that they enjoyed before Putin came to power, we can win the case in Russia.'[90] Asked directly during Chancellor Angela Merkel's visit to Russia to meet with president-elect Dmitry Medvedev on 8 March 2008 about the possibility of an amnesty for Khodorkovsky, Putin left it to his successor: 'The decision to grant an amnesty is one of the powers of the head of state, the president of the Russian Federation.'[91] The option clearly was left open, and was endorsed by Merkel: '[I]f the possibility of amnesty exists, this is something we would welcome.'[92]

Medvedev's accession to the presidency in May 2008 was accompanied by talk of some kind of amnesty (see also Chapter 12), but instead on 1 July 2008 the Investigative Committee brought new charges against Khodorkovsky that threatened to add another fifteen years to his sentence. The charges, however, were essentially a rehash of those preferred in February 2007, accusing Khodorkovsky and Lebedev of embezzling 350 million tonnes of oil and of laundering R487 billion ($20.7 billion) and breaching Articles 160 and 170 of the Criminal Code, the same ones mentioned earlier.[93] It appeared that the reformulated charges were little more than a holding action, designed not to advance the case but to keep it alive while the political authorities decided what to do. Just a few days earlier, on 26 June Khodorkovsky had celebrated his forty-fifth birthday, and his mother, Marina Khodorkovskaya, visiting him at this time feared for his well-being: 'At our last meeting, he looked bad. Some kind of blotches have appeared on his face.'[94]

International appeals and rulings

The appeal to the ECtHR was lodged by Khodorkovsky's lawyer, Karinna Moskalenko, in March 2006 on the grounds that her client's rights under Article 6 of the ECHR (the right to a fair trial), 7 (retrospective imposition of criminal penalty), and 8 (unlawful interference with his private life because of the illegal decision to send him to serve his sentence in Siberia) had been infringed and that the interferences had been politically motivated and were made for 'other purposes' contrary to Article 18 of the Convention. Both the trial and the management of the appeal was the subject of the application. Moskalenko was the head of the International Protection Centre, established in 1995 to help Russian citizens file complaints to the Strasbourg court, to which Russia is legally bound since joining the Council of Europe in 1996. It covered a range of human rights issues, including torture and disappearances in Chechnya, the victims of the

---

[90] Schmidt, 'Chto dal'she', 25 October 2007.
[91] Novo-Ogarëvo, http://www.kremlin.ru/text/appears/2008/03/161952.shtml.   [92] Loc. cit.
[93] Miriam Elder, 'Khodorkovsky faces 15 More Years', *Moscow Times*, 2 July 2008.
[94] Loc. cit.

Dubrovka theatre siege (Nordest), and the imprisonment of political prisoners such as Khodorkovsky.[95] In 2005 this NGO itself came under attack, accused of failing to report grants and other international contributions as ordinary income, and its bank accounts were frozen and staff harassed. In 2004 Moskalenko had established the Centre for International Legal Defence (CILD), which itself was the subject of a punitive tax claim in July 2006, while continuing to work on the Yukos cases. CILD helped victims of human rights violations through international legal mechanisms, above all preparing cases for the ECtHR. However, with a backlog of over 40,000 cases, some 14,000 from Russia, there would be no swift decision on the main case.

Lebedev filed a number of complaints with the ECtHR, and on 25 October 2007 the first, lodged in 2004, was upheld by the Court. It ruled that there had been a number of procedural violations during the investigation into his case and his detention violated rights to freedom and security under Article 5 of the ECHR. These violations included his illegal pre-trial detention between July and August 2003, and March to April 2004, as well as the restrictions placed on Lebedev and his lawyers to attend court hearings. Lebedev was awarded €10,000 in compensation. Three of the court's seven judges voted against the judgement, arguing that Lebedev's rights had not been violated.[96]

In a landmark judgement, on 13 August 2007 the Swiss Federal Tribunal in Lausanne overruled the earlier judgement by the Swiss Federal Public Prosecutor of 21 December 2006 to wind up procedures for a Khodorkovsky account held at UBS Zurich. On 26 January 2007 Khodorkovsky appealed against this order, and called on the Swiss authorities not to engage in judicial cooperation with the Russian authorities, as outlined in the Russian government's request of 15 August 2003 for judicial assistance. This request was now refused, and the decision of 21 December 2006 annulled. Khodorkovsky's claim that the legal proceedings against him were motivated by political and economic reasons was upheld, as was the argument that the Russian prosecutor acted on the orders of the Russian president. The ruling cited the refusal of British and Liechtenstein courts to extradite Yukos officials at the request of the Russian government as well as PACE's view that Khodorkovsky and Lebedev had been 'selected as targets by the authorities in violation of principles of equality',[97] and referred to its citation of the ECtHR decision of 19 May 2004 in the Gusinsky case, which described 'an instrumentalisation of criminal proceedings for purposes of intimidation', and on this basis rejected Russian reassurances that it would respect the ECHR in regards to any person extradited from Switzerland.[98]

---

[95] Bret Stephens, 'On the Right Side of the Law', *Moscow Times*, 16 May 2007, p. 8.

[96] Council of Europe, ECtHR, 'Case of Lebedev v. Russia (application no. 4493/04)', Judgment, Strasbourg, 25 October 2007, mimeo.

[97] PACE Resolution 1523 of 6 October 2006 recalled its prior recommendations and conclusions, and noted with regret that little appeared to have been undertaken by the Russian authorities to remedy the situation.

[98] For more on the judgement of the Swiss Federal Supreme Court, see Knoops and Amsterdam, 'The Duality of State Cooperation', p. 293.

The ruling referred to reports in 2006 by Amnesty International, Human Rights Watch, and the International Federation of Human Rights, which all noted the serious procedural violations in the Khodorkovsky–Lebedev trial and its political motivations. The court insisted that there was no objective justification to incarcerate the two in Siberia, something that was against Russian law. The view was upheld that 'criminal proceedings have indeed been instrumentalised by the power in place, with the goal of bringing to heel the class of rich "oligarchs" and pushing away potential or declared political adversaries'.[99] The judges declared that 'Switzerland would be in breach of its international obligations if it cooperated with a foreign criminal proceeding presenting a risk of treatment of an accused, particularly discriminatory treatment, which is inconsistent with minimal guarantees recognised under international law'. The Tribunal revealed that Russia had provided desultory and inadequate responses to Yukos-related demands for clarification and further details.[100]

Already in July 2007 a Czech court had refused the extradition to Russia of Elena Vybornova, sought in connection with the new charges brought against Khodorkovsky. The court cited numerous instances of the abuse of the Russian judicial system, and concluded that Vybornova stood little chance of a fair trial in Russia. In September 2007 the Lithuanian Prosecutor's Office refused to work with Russia in the Brudno extradition case, concluding: 'Upon analyzing the materials on the Yukos case, we have concluded that this case is politicized and Mikhail Brudno has been persecuted, maybe because of other people involved in the Yukos affair, and we have decided that the charges against him are politically motivated.' In December 2007, as noted, a Dutch court ruled that Russia had illegally pushed through the bankruptcy sale of some Yukos assets in the Netherlands. A number of actions were also being pursued in late 2007 in California and Texas to help Khodorkovsky to prepare his defence, arguing that when prosecutors raided Yukos offices in Moscow before the first trial they were not only collecting evidence but also destroying it, especially any that may have demonstrated Khodorkovsky's innocence.[101] It should be noted that some claims went the other way as well, with the Federal Customs Service in May 2007 filing a lawsuit in Moscow seeking $22.5 billion in damages from BONY for suspected money laundering. The bank was accused of helping Russian businesses (including Menatep) bring money into and out of Russia without paying duties or taxes from 1996 to 1999.[102]

---

[99] *Summary on the Swiss Judgement on Khodorkovsky*, posted on the Robert Amsterdam website, http://www.robertamsterdam.com/2007/08/summary_on_the_swiss_judgment.htm; for the original French judgment 1A.27/2007 /col, Arrêt du 13 août 2007, Ire Cour de droit public, http://www.bger.ch/fr/index/juridiction/jurisdiction-inherit-template/jurisd%3Cbr%20/%3Eiction-recht/jurisdiction-recht-urteile2000.htm.

[100] Robert Amsterdam, 'Khodorkovsky Case Update: Politics Increasingly Transparent', Jurist, http://jurist.law.pitt.edu, 23 January 2008.

[101] Loc. cit.

[102] Miriam Elder, 'Bank of New York Sued for $22 Bln', *Moscow Times*, 18 May 2007, p. 1.

PROBLEMS OF STATE AND LAW

The communist system endowed Russia with an overblown administrative apparatus, which since the fall of the old system has nearly doubled in size. At the same time, officialdom is marked by what Rekosh calls 'a culture of internal political responsibility, with little or no common understanding of responsibility on the basis of professional norms, duty to the general public (taxpayers) or the rule of law'.[103] The public interest takes second place to the corporate interests of the agency itself. Financial incentives (bribes) have to be paid for the citizen to gain what is lawfully theirs. As Vladimir Pastukhov, one of Russia's leading legal experts and a practising legal consultant, notes, it is often 'necessary to pay not to obtain something contrary to the law, but in order to defend one's lawful interests. It is not the violation of the law but its fulfilment that is paid for in Russia.'[104] Both the state and the oligarchs thrived in this anarchic environment, and the methods used by Putin to reconstitute the state in certain respects only exacerbated the problem. According to Gerashchenko, during the time when he headed the Yukos board: 'I encountered lawlessness from the courts and from those enforcing the law... excessively aggravated by—how should I put it?—the forces behind them.'[105]

International commentary

In remarks at Princeton University on 16 November 2004, the American ambassador to Russia at that time, Alexander Vershbow, identified 'a fault line within the Russian government between those policymakers who seek to assert more state control over the economy and those who favor liberal, market-based policies'. He noted that '[t]he arrest of Mikhail Khodorkovsky and the legal case against the oil company Yukos conveyed the strong impression that the Russian government was selectively using the legal system for political aims'.[106] Ella Pamfilova, head of the Presidential Human Rights Commission, argued: 'At meetings with the president, we were the first to raise the problem of Yukos, the issue of restricting interference by law enforcement agencies in financial and economic activities of private enterprises.'[107]

In the autumn of 2004 a letter was published criticizing Putin. It had been inspired by Dick Cheney, and the vice president's office became the clearing house

[103] Edwin Rekosh, 'Remedies to Administrative Abuses; Setting the Stage for Action', *Local Government Brief*, Budapest, Summer 2003, pp. 2–7, at p. 2.
[104] Vladimir Pastukhov, 'Law Under Administrative Pressure in Post-Soviet Russia', *East European Constitutional Review*, Vol. 11, No. 3, Summer 2002, pp. 66–74, at p. 68.
[105] Gerashchenko, 'I Encountered Total Disregard for the Law'.
[106] Alexander Vershbow, 'The United States and Russia: The Next Four Years', *Johnson's Russia List*, 8476/9.
[107] *Moskovskii komsomolets*, 1 December 2004.

for an anti-Russian campaign. Bruce Jackson was also involved, as well as Victoria Newlyn in the vice president's office, who is married to the conservative political commentator Robert Kagan. Bush himself retained a close relationship with Putin, deciding on his own initiative to sign the Beslan condolence book at the Russian embassy on 12 September 2004. At the meeting in Bratislava in February 2005 Bush did not press Putin too hard on human rights issues. The intensely personal nature of the relationship meant that even Putin had to separate himself from his own advisers. It was at this time that Russia began a period of harsh overreaction to the Orange Revolution of late 2004 in Ukraine, including intensified pressure against NGOs. Cheney's virulent speech in Vilnius on 4 May 2005, about which Bush did not know in advance, only worsened the embattled atmosphere of the Russian leadership. This was intensified by Bush's visits to Latvia and Georgia before attending the sixtieth anniversary of the end of the war celebrations in Moscow on 9 May. The Russian side took this as a sign of disrespect, and the two presidents did not meet alone at the Gleneagles G8 summit a few months later and the number of bilateral telephone calls fell sharply. The result in the end was Putin's Munich speech of February 2007 in which he condemned Western 'double-standards'.

Transparency International ranks Russia as one of the most corrupt countries in the world. The Corruption Perception Index score was 90th out of 146 countries in 2004, by 2005 it had fallen to 126th out of 159, and in 2007 Russia was placed 143rd out of 179 countries.[108] Putin in effect has said the same thing in justification for his attempt to strengthen the executive vertical of power. The ability of terrorists to bribe their way to board the two planes brought down by bombs in late August 2004, and for the Beslan terrorists to pass unhindered through various checkpoints is vivid enough evidence of that. The story of Russia's three bankruptcy laws since 1992, with the latest coming into effect in 2002, demonstrates the widespread use of judicial proceedings to achieve commercial advantage. The new law, although probably an improvement on earlier versions, in the opinion of some legal experts appears to contradict a number of other laws, and possibly even the Civil Code.[109]

On 15 March 2004, Leutheuser-Schnarrenberger, a member of the German parliament (FDP) and the former Minister for Justice, was appointed as rapporteur for the Council of Europe (CoE) on the Yukos affair. Her report was presented to the Committee for Human Rights and Legal Affairs of the CoE on 19 November 2004, and adopted by a large majority. It argued that the Yukos case was a serious threat to democracy and the rule of law in Russia. It detailed abuse of legal norms, including delays in transferring Lefortovo prison from the FSB to the Ministry of Justice, the lack of prompt investigation into the administration of a drug to Pichugin, lack of medical treatment for Lebedev (in addition to other ailments, he has chronic hepatitis), obstructions to the work of defence lawyers, and the lack of bail for the defendants, even though they were accused of economic

---

[108] Http://www.transparency.org/policy_research/surveys_indices/cpi.
[109] 'Law Leaves Private Debtors Naked', *Moscow Times*, 8 December 2004, p. 9.

crimes.[110] A resolution adopted by PACE on 25 January 2005 argued that the circumstances surrounding the arrest and prosecution of Khodorkovsky, Pichugin, and Lebedev suggested that they had been 'arbitrarily singled out' by the Russian authorities. The assembly, approving Leutheuser-Schnarrenberger's report, noted that intimidating action by law enforcement agencies and careful preparation of this action in terms of public relations, taken together 'give a picture of a co-ordinated attack by the state'. The prosecutions went beyond the mere pursuit of justice but sought to 'weaken an outspoken political opponent, intimidate other wealthy individuals and regain control of strategic economic assets'. Assembly members noted their concern with human rights problems with the judicial process in Russia revealed by the cases.[111]

In a wide-ranging and balanced assessment of the development of market relations in Russia an OECD report of June 2005 noted significant achievements. However, its section on judicial reform confirmed the concerns raised by PACE and other commentators and was quite clear that in its view Russia still has some way to go before it can be considered to be a rule of law state. We will quote at length from a section that is of particular relevance to the Yukos case:

The involvement of state prosecutors and of the security services in commercial and political disputes remains a problem. The courts are still widely regarded as susceptible to outside pressure and inducements, and a considerable body of circumstantial evidence suggests that this perception is accurate....There is a need for effective arrangements to insulate the judiciary from pressures emanating from *any* level of government, not least the federal authorities themselves.... Establishing the rule of law will require more than just the reform of the judicial system. It will need a strong state, capable of protecting individual rights, of interpreting the law impartially and of enforcing it effectively. But a state strong enough to perform these functions might succumb to the temptation to act arbitrarily itself. So the establishment of the rule of law will require not only a strong state but also strong institutions capable of constraining it..... The weakness of that commitment [to rule-governed behaviour] has been evident in the political and legal campaign against the oil company Yukos since July 2003. However, the Yukos case is unique only in its scale and visibility. The security services, the prosecutors and the police remain highly politicised and have frequently been deployed against businessmen who were in conflict with federal or regional authorities.[112]

These weaknesses have been in evidence in a number of high-profile 'espionage' cases (Igor Sutyagin, Valentin Danilov, and others) in which judicial procedures have delivered the verdict that the authorities clearly wanted. Sergei Pashin, a former Moscow City judge and human rights activist (who was himself sacked as a judge), argues that the judicial reforms launched in the early 1990s had failed.

---

[110] *The Circumstances Surrounding the Arrest and Prosecution of Leading Yukos Executives*, Report for the Committee on Legal Affairs and Human Rights, Parliamentary Assembly of the Council of Europe, 29 November 2004.

[111] http://assembly/coe/int/EMB_NewsViews.asp?ID=592. The sharp Russian reaction is reported in *Gazeta*, 27 January 2005.

[112] *Russia: Building Rules for the Market* (Paris, OECD Reviews of Regulatory Reform, June 2005), pp. 51–2.

He was one of the authors of the measures, but he later argued that while the original intention had been 'to remove the judiciary from the sphere of control of the executive, but now it has once again turned into its appendage'. Despite the introduction of jury trials and many other positive achievements, all of this remained at the formal level, while at the informal level there remain 'shadow technologies' including the falsification of court proceedings.[113] This is a judgement confirmed by the chair of the Constitutional Court, Valeri Zor'kin, who argued that the court reforms rendered judges more corruptible and more dependent on the government.[114] As Pashin put it: 'The sale of services permeates the judicial system. Judicial decisions, and in particular judgements of the arbitration courts, are used by competing industrial-financial groups to strengthen positions gained in the corridors of power.'[115] A different sort of corruption is also in evidence—the inability to achieve the effective separation of powers. The use of office for personal gain is one thing (venal corruption); but the Soviet legacy of what can be called 'meta-corruption' (where the logic of one system, for example governmental power) invades the logic of another (the right to a free and fair trial) is still strong.[116] The Yukos case has been a dramatic example of meta-corruption and of the dual state in action.

Andrew Jack argues that '[t]he Yukos case is important in Putin's Russia not for the details so much as the broader picture it paints of the continued failings in the country's law enforcement system'.[117] Of particular concern to us is the influence that executive authorities exert over the judicial process.[118] The Yukos case, as noted, revealed the power that 'telephone law' (*telefonnoe pravo*) still had over the conduct of cases that are important to the authorities. The term 'Basmanny justice' now entered the lexicon to denote politically arbitrary justice, or justice serving the needs of authorities or powerful persons. Many of those working in the Basmanny court formerly worked with the GPO's investigations department, whose building are adjacent, facilitating the adoption of decisions and their execution. In 2004 a book called *Basmannoe pravosudie* (*Basmanny Justice*) appeared reporting research by Moskalenko's students, who observed trials in the Basmanny district court for a week and analysed the procedural violations that were routine. The last quarter of the book reprints press coverage of the Khodorkovsky detention hearings, which, when compared to the first part, shows how extreme and unusual the procedural violations were in the case.[119]

[113] 'Za chto v Rossii srok dayut', *Moskovskie novosti*, No. 47, 10–16 December 2004, p. 18.
[114] 'Subjugated Court System Stifles Battle With Corruption', *St. Petersburg Times*, 28 December 2004.
[115] *Moskovskie novosti*, No. 47, 10–16 December 2004, p. 18.
[116] See Richard Sakwa, 'Russia: From a Corrupt System to a System with Corruption', in Robert Williams (ed.), *Party Finance and Political Corruption* (Basingstoke and London, Macmillan; New York, St Martin's Press, 2000), pp. 123–61.
[117] Jack, *Inside Putin's Russia*, p. 310.
[118] This is analysed in a recent study, *The Judicial System of the Russian Federation: A System-Crisis of Independence* (London, Russian Axis, 2004).
[119] I am grateful to Peter Solomon for this information.

This is evident in the pressure to achieve convictions. The dismissal of judge Alexander Melikov of the Dorogmilovsky court in December 2004 for what was alleged to be a 'series of strangely soft sentences and other judicial decisions', but in fact for what he claims to be his excessive independence, is a case in point.[120] In Moscow the total number of acquittals is less than one-third of 1 per cent— one acquittal for every 330 convictions. Melikov argued that the chair of the Moscow City Court (Mosgorsud) from January 2001, Olga Yegorova, held weekly meeting with the heads of district courts and required full details of cases and demanded an explanation for every acquittal. Yegorova was urgently appointed to this post by Putin at the time of the hearings in the Gusinksy Media-Most (NTV) case, and she 'is highly influenced by both the executive and prosecutorial authorities'.[121] In her view, every acquittal undermines the work of the prosecutors' office, suggesting that they launched a prosecution with insufficient evidence. Out of the several thousand cases handled by the Meshchansky court in 2007, there were only twenty acquittals.[122] Under Yegorova, the Moscow City Court became known as 'Moscow City Stamp' (Mosgosstamp) because of the eagerness with which it rubber-stamps decisions of the Prosecutor General's office.[123] Under her leadership from 2001 over eighty judges had been forced to leave their jobs.[124]

An earlier case in which Yegorova had forced the dismissal of an independent judge involved Olga Kudeshkina, dismissed from the Moscow City Court in May 2004 accused of 'discrediting the judiciary' when she was involved in the trial of the owners of the Tri Kita furniture store in Moscow.[125] Ironically, Kudeshkina is married to a former KGB officer, and the owners of the furniture store had close links with the security services. The judge in the first Pichugin trial at the Moscow City Court, Natalya Olikhver, had been carefully chosen to ensure loyalty to instructions from above. Although noted for her integrity and firmness of judgement earlier, her Soviet background ensured that she sought to influence the jury in the appropriate way.[126] Despite this, the first jury was dismissed in December 2004, since it was clearly ready to throw out the charges (a procedure that was also applied in the Igor Sutyagin case), and a specially selected second jury finally reached the appropriate verdict on 30 March 2005 after a speedy closed trial.[127] The judicial reforms in the first period of Putin's rule sought to enhance judicial independence through pay increases and the expansion of the jury system, but the Soviet view of judges as officials defending state interests has far from

[120] For a discussion of the Melikov case and the negligible acquittal rate in Russia, see Peter Finn, 'Fear Rules in Russia's Courtrooms: Judges who Acquit Forced Off Bench', *The Washington Post*, 27 February 2005, p. A01. See also 'Judge Says he Lost Job for Being Soft', *Moscow Times*, 10 December 2004, p. 3.
[121] Amsterdam, 'The Dual State Takes Hold in Russia', p. 7.
[122] Il'ya Barabanov, 'Sudeiskie krugi burlyat', *The New Times*, 9 June 2008, pp. 11–13, at p. 13.
[123] *St. Petersburg Times*, 28 December 2004.
[124] Jeremy Page, 'Judges Take Stand Against Putin', *The Times*, 19 March 2005, p. 52.
[125] Loc. cit. [126] Shiryaev, *Sud mesti*, pp. 162–6.
[127] Shiryaev, *Sud mesti*, chapter 9, pp. 180–203.

disappeared. The idea of judges as independent and impartial arbiters has only tenuously taken root.

Law and power

The whole ensemble of procedural and normative violations described above is reminiscent of the grand 'affairs' (such as the 'Leningrad Affair' in the late 1940s), of an earlier era of Soviet history, when one strand led to another, and the snowball effect came to implicate people who were far from the original case. It is in this way that the 'Khodorkovsky Affair' will no doubt be remembered long after the present leadership has passed into history. An open letter in support of Khodorkovsky's and Lebedev's defence team by a number of prominent human rights activists, including Elena Bonner, Ludmila Alexeeva, and Lev Ponamarev, drew comparisons with the great purges of the 1930s, and in particular the way that after a long trial new charges were discovered. They noted:

When arbitrariness rules in the country, when controlled 'justice' is used as a stick to beat people with and law becomes a travesty, every courtroom that hears a political trial turns into a battleground for truth and justice. The battle fought there is very often unequal, so it's all the more important to express solidarity with those who defend victims of political persecution. The new charges in the Yukos case are a gauntlet thrown down to society, a signal that all appearances have been thrown to the four winds. The pressure put on Khodorkovsky and Lebedev's lawyers, aimed at their humiliation, is testament to the fact that the authorities are using all their influence to assist the prosecution.[128]

At the root of the Yukos affair lies a deep paradox: whether the selective application of law can, if only partially, reflect the aspiration to universal justice; or whether the selective application of law is always unjust.[129]

Khodorkovsky's travails in court did not represent a show trial in the classical sense of acting as a warning to others and the world. However, the effect was much the same, acting as a warning for the business community not to overstep the line. The disciplinary effect of the trial was exemplary. The case demonstrated that ultimately there was no defence against the state. The way that the case was pursued, moreover, represented the instrumentalization of law, subordinating it in this case to the power system. The lack of judicial independence was clearly evident. Moskalenko notes that the Yukos case breached fundamental principles not only of due process but also 'of the very idea of justice'. She argues that '[t]his trial demonstrated that the judiciary could ignore rules, human rights, and clear evidence, in its submission to pressure by the executive'. In particular, she insisted that Khodorkovsky's detention was in clear breach of domestic and international norms, and the procuracy decided the trial in which the case would be heard, infringing the rules on court jurisdiction. Moreover, the case against

---

[128] 'Every courtroom that hears a political trial turns into a battleground for truth and justice', 27 February 2007, http://www.khodorkovsky.info/society/documents/134906.html.

[129] *Khodorkovskikh chtenii*, 10 July 2007.

Khodorkovsky was reopened after receiving a letter from Putin, although the letter was not placed in the case file, although the Prosecutors' response is logged: 'It is not understood how President Putin is allowed to instruct the head of the main prosecutorial body on legal questions.' The case also revealed how a dissenting judge could be dismissed from office.[130]

The selective and politically inspired use of law in the Putin era was confirmed by Medvedev's recognition of 'legal nihilism'. On 20 May 2008 Medvedev called for an independent court system when he addressed a meeting with senior judges and legal officials in the Kremlin: '[Unjust] decisions, as we all know, do happen and come as a result of different kinds of pressure, like telephone calls and—it cannot be denied—offers of money.'[131] The Yukos affair graphically illustrated the instrumental use of the law, but with the new leadership in place the struggle was now on to achieve judicial independence.

---

[130] Karinna Moskalenko, 'The Judicial System in Practice', in Jennifer Moll (ed.), *Blueprint for Russia* (London, Foreign Policy Centre, 2005), pp. 41–2.

[131] http://www.kremlin.ru/text/appears/2008/05/201007.shtml.

8

From Oligarch to 'Dissident'

> Why did they not wish to acknowledge that if there is such a thing as fate, then freedom is not possible? ... If there is such a thing as freedom, then there is no fate.
>
> Imre Kertész[1]

On the eve of the new year in December 2004 Khodorkovsky issued a letter in which he stated: 'I, like so many other captives, known and unknown, must say thank you to prison. It has given me months of concentrated thinking, time to rethink many facets of life.' His basic thought was that 'money does not buy happiness'. Not so long earlier he had been one of Russia's richest individuals, and he noted how much effort he had devoted to gaining and defending his property, and had sacrificed much for it, and now he had no regrets about losing it. He promised that 'he would not seek revenge against the authorities and that he placed freedom above property'. He had 'no intention of becoming a Count of Monte Cristo'.[2] Less than a year later he began his eight-year sentence in prison, at first in Krasnokamensk and then in Chita awaiting his second trial, and Khodorkovsky engaged in a spiritual and political odyssey. Even when Khodorkovsky had been a straightforward billionaire, he had been distinguished from other members of Russia's super-wealthy class by awareness of spiritual issues and of debates over Russia's developmental path.[3] Relieved of the burden of running Yukos, he was able to turn his attention to broader questions of public policy and political development. He refused to be trapped into a single identity, as victim of an unjust regime or as fallen oligarch, and asserted his right to find his own solutions to personal and social questions.

In a pattern that is all too familiar in Russian history, a prominent individual falls foul of the power system and suffers exile or incarceration, and from that position of relative freedom is able to comment on the system. Following his arrest in October 2003 Khodorkovsky released a number of missives that had broad relevance on the Russian condition. Like many other 'oligarchs', business appeared to have been thrust upon him, and now Khodorkovsky's other persona was able to emerge—that of a member of the intelligentsia, critical of the current

---

[1] Imre Kertész, *Fatelessness*, translated from the Hungarian by Tim Wilkinson (London, The Harvill Press, 2005), pp. 259–60.

[2] Yurii Sergeev, 'Pis'mo na volyu: Khodorkovskii ne stanet grafom monte-kristo', *Komsomol'skaya Pravda*, 29 December 2004, p. 5.

[3] Maksim Kantor, 'Kazarmennyi kapitalizm', *Moskovskie novosti*, No. 31, 12–18 August 2005, p. 16.

authorities but at the same time willing to offer constructive criticism and support. In the main, Khodorkovsky avoided personal criticism of Putin and limited his comments to the system in the abstract. This was not a case of biting the hand that fed him or caressing the hand that beat him, but a way of maintaining personal dignity and intellectual integrity in adversity. His main argument was that the liberal reforms of the 1990s had given the country freedom but not justice. Khodorkovsky's thinking in this period was deeply paradoxical: while claiming innate rights to freedom and personal development on the personal and collective level, at the same time it remained deeply Soviet, appealing to the principles of social justice and conceptualizing private property not as an inalienable right but as entailing ethical responsibilities. This was a response both to the perceived need to legitimate the property settlement of the 1990s, and to Khodorkovsky's own ambivalence as a capitalist entrepreneur.

BUSINESS AND THE STATE

We will begin with an extended interview with Khodorkovsky given in June 2002, but only published after his sentencing in June 2005.[4] The text was not published at the time since Khodorkovsky considered it too outspoken, and as we shall see, his views on the perilous predicament of business in Russia and the lack of security from a predatory state was certainly hard-hitting. When asked about the risks facing big business in Russia, Khodorkovsky answered: 'There is no doubt that the state can easily destroy us, but this will denote a change in the social structure.' At the time he did not believe that it would be rational for the state to launch such an attack, although he did not discount it. He admitted that at the time when business began it was impossible to observe the law since there were no relevant laws:

So people did what they wanted. These were the conditions under which the original accumulation of capital took place. We did shape some moral requirements to ourselves but those were our moral requirements so we should not even mention them today. They corresponded to the society we lived in. Then gradually the legislative field began taking shape, we continued functioning in its boundaries but it was still quite wide, a situation which remains to this day.

The business ethic of the early oligarchs was one that was to dog the first generation of Russian capitalists. The claim that the laws were weak or non-existent and could thus be flouted with impunity is not one that wins universal adherence. Khodorkovsky however had been able by this time to change his image from rapacious oligarch to benevolent businessman. Yukos had set up various philanthropic foundations, and shortly before the interview Khodorkovsky met the UN general

---

[4] The interview was with special correspondent Natalia Gevorkyan. Khodorkovsky's press service removed the ban following his sentencing, 'Mikhail Khodorkovskii: Rokefelleru bylo namnogo tyazhelee', *Kommersant*, 1 June 2005.

secretary, Koffi Annan. Khodorkovsky admitted that the original accumulation of capital from the late 1980s had been a wild affair, but now insisted that his generation was performing a 'stabilising role'; and that the business atmosphere in Russia was no longer wild, 'otherwise our rating would not be approaching the investment one. If our actions bring Russia back to that epoch the whole society will become poorer.... This is why we are trying to embrace the norms suggested by the Western society.' Asked to be more specific, he answered:

Democracy, transparency, social responsibility of business, corporate citizenship—these are quite clear things. Of course, to some extent our struggle for business ethics is of a mercenary character. Yes, we do profit from that. Yes, this is unprofitable for some our rivals who have failed to break through so far. I will repeat though that in general today all of society benefits from our position.... Someone should be looking further than the others demonstrating with their own example that it is not only possible but even better to live normally.

He was quite explicit about the need to construct a positive image. The interviewer asked him about a recent interview in the West in which Khodorkovsky had mentioned Rockefeller as a role model. Gevorkyan, noted: 'However, Rockefeller "got laundered" only in the third generation—it was only his grandson that became "clean". There were 100 years separating him from his grandfather. And it seems as though you would like to race through these 100 years during your lifetime.'

I sure would. This is an objective requirement in business—the one who is faster will win. You are not surprised by the fact that the path from horse to railway took thousands of years, whereas from a railway to spaceship—only a hundred years. The same applies to the Rockefeller issue. I was in Harvard and heard the director of their business school speak. He said that Khodorkovsky was Rockefeller, Rockefeller's son and Rockefeller's grandson in one person. Rockefeller had it much harder. Back then there were no ready rules. It took a hundred years to create business ethics. It took them three generations. It is easier for us.

In his person Khodorkovsky would be three generations in one, and concertina what had taken a century in America into half a lifetime in Russia. As noted in Chapter 2, by 2002 Yukos was transforming itself into a normal international company. He made the following interesting observation about a similar process taking place in the country as a whole:

During the past year and especially after September 11 they [the West] began perceiving Russia as a normal country. This, incidentally, was the time when I strongly identified with Putin. It does not happen often with me.

However, the country was not quite normal. The next question was 'Do you feel safe in your country?', to which Khodorkovsky responded: 'Of course not. As an individual—absolutely not. I think that the country's present judicial system and the contemporary law-enforcement system fail to protect an individual.' 'How about property?' he was asked: 'No. The present generation is not prepared to treat private property as an absolute basic value.' Nevertheless, Khodorkovsky at this time was not ready to believe that the state would launch an assault against him, as it had done in January 2002 against Nikolai Aksënenko, the 'Yeltsinite' who was dismissed as railways minister and whose affairs were investigated. As the questioner put it, Aksënenko was

[q]uite an oligarch. In power into the bargain, a former candidate for the presidency as well, and he was gone in just a moment. The risk that in just a moment there will be no ... Khodorkovsky? I think that the probability that Khodorkovsky will disappear in just a moment is less than in the case of Aksënenko. The nature of property is different. In that case everything was too simple and clear. The situation has changed, hasn't it? Earlier it was like this (snaps his fingers.—NG) and there was no Yukos. Today (snaps his fingers again.—NG)—and there is no Khodorkovsky is still possible. However, not in regards to Yukos. ... No, it is unlikely. Society has become too pragmatic and understands that the loss of a major business is a big loss for every person. After all it is three percent of the GDP, isn't it?

The fact that a large number of people depended on Yukos, one of the largest companies in the country and a major budget contributor, acted as a type of insurance policy for Khodorkovsky: 'That is why even if he [Putin] does not really like our company he meets with us and inquires what it is that hinders our work.' There was also the foreign insurance policy, as the questioner remarked: 'What about the shaping of your image (in the West as well). Is that also a kind of a safety net for you inside the country?', to which Khodorkovsky responded: 'I would put it differently. This is an additional measure of freedom.'

The discussion then moved on to the events of 1996, the subject that came up later in Khodorkovsky's *Left Turn 1* in August 2005. The questioner noted that Khodorkovsky tried to stay out of politics, with the exception of the 1996 presidential campaign. Khodorkovsky insisted that he would act again as he did in 1996:

I well remember that situation. I was a witness to the conversation between Soros and Berezovsky. In Davos there is a restaurant in the basement. They were sitting at the next table. I turned to them. I actually heard Soros say: 'Many of my friends lost everything— and sometimes their lives—because they did not leave everything behind and depart. You've had a good time, guys, but it's now time to push off. A communist will win.' Zyuganov had a room next to mine, and we talked a lot. And afterwards I said: everything is fine, he represents the outlook of millions of people in the country, my fellow citizens whom I treat with respect as I do Zyuganov, but I do not want him to be in power in the country.

We shall return to this in discussing Khodorkovsky's later missive, in which the effect of these events was still strong. Later in the interview Khodorkovsky admitted funding the SPS and forces advancing a 'liberal economy, democracy and stability'. At the time only 38 years old, he was asked whether he would consider doing something else, 'For example politics?'

You should always do what you are better than others at. I have achieved much in business. I am an effective head of a company and my activity is quite highly evaluated. I will not go into a sphere where the assessment of my activity might be worse. In any case, this is a question of inner conviction. If I sense that I can be up to the mark, for example in international business, I will go for it. The same is true about politics. Why not? Indeed,

I am 38...I still have time. Let alone the fact that I have said that I will withdraw from business at 45.

As for the role of money in his life, Khodorkovsky answered:

Leonid Nevzlin and I once decided: we have enough personal money to keep us happy. From this point of view it plays absolutely no role. And there is money left over for the game, an instrument. This instrument is like ammunition for the military—you barely have time to replenish it.

With broad ambitions and the money to fund them, Khodorkovsky may well indeed have been perceived as a challenge to the regime.

THE CRISIS OF RUSSIAN LIBERALISM

Beginning with the resounding phrase 'Liberalism in Russia is experiencing a crisis—this is now almost indisputable', in a powerful 2,000-word letter from prison called 'The Crisis of Russian Liberalism', published on 29 March 2004, Khodorkovsky developed a powerful critique of the failures of organized Russian liberalism.[5] If before his arrest Khodorkovsky had made arrangements for the management of the company, his incarceration had left the liberal opposition bereft of a major figure. This letter now demonstrated that even from jail Khodorkovsky sought to retain leadership of a restructured liberal perspective on the development of Russian politics.

The provenance of the article caused as much of a stir as its contents.[6] The purpose of the letter was no less contested, with some seeing it as a *mea culpa* before the regime with which he was now suing for peace, while others saw it as a sign of conflict within the Yukos camp.[7] Further confusion is added by

[5] Mikhail Khodorkovsky, 'Krizis liberalizma v Rossii', *Vedemosti*, 29 March 2004; an English version was published as Mikhail Khodorkovsky, 'Liberalism in Crisis: What is to be Done?', *Moscow Times*, 31 March, 1 April 2004. According to the editor of *Vedemosti*, Tatyana Lysova, the article had appeared at the paper without prior consultation. Khodorkovsky's lawyer, Anton Drel, affirmed that his client had been working on the article for three months, Catherine Belton, 'Khodorkovsky Seeks Peace with Putin', *Moscow Times*, 30 March 2004, p. 1.

[6] At the time there was considerable controversy over the authenticity of the letter, with the ubiquitous anti-oligarchic fighter Stanislav Belkovsky allegedly playing his part. It had originally appeared under the title 'Russian Liberalism in the Twentieth Century: Manifesto' on the website Utro.ru on 18 March with the author line 'Initiative Group, Chair Yu. A. Stepanov'. The website stated that it had received the article on 17 March, and about half of it was similar to the version that came out in *Vedemosti* later under Khodorkovsky's name. This was the website where Belkovsky's article on behalf of the National Strategy Council 'The State and Oligarchs' had first appeared in June 2003. For a discussion of the letter's provenance, with much contradictory information, see Irina Nagornykh, Natalya Gevorkyan, and Ilya Bulavinov, 'Oligarkh priznaet liberalizm', *Kommersant*, 30 March 2004. In the same issue Berezovsky questioned the author's motives, and claimed that Khodorkovsky had plagiarized large parts of it, *Kommersant*, 30 March 2004, p. 1.

[7] Belkovsky, who by that time had gained considerable admiration for Khodorkovsky, argued that Nevzlin was trying to discredit Khodorkovsky by leaking his article prematurely to Utro.ru. Not only

Khodorkovsky's studiously ambiguous comments about his authorship, refusing to confirm that he had written it or turned over anything to his lawyers. The deputy justice minister, Yuri Kalinin, announced that in an explanatory note to the prison administration Khodorkovsky declared that he had not written any article or passed anything through his lawyers, but he was 'fully in agreement with its contents'.[8] The aim clearly was to protect the lawyers who had no doubt smuggled the text out of Matrosskaya Tishina. The law demands that all written materials, except complaints and applications relating to the case, have to be censored by the prison administration. The letter was probably smuggled out in fragments and then reconstituted.[9] Earlier, two of Khodorkovsky's lawyers, Olga Artyukhova and Yevgeny Baru, had got into trouble for carrying unsanctioned materials. According to Moskalenko, Khodorkovsky had simply shared his thoughts which had then been written down,[10] while Padva stated that his client 'categorically accepted authorship'.[11] The document as we have it did not pass through the prison administration, and it is interesting to speculate how they would have censored it if it had. The letter was not in the tradition of those by Grigory Zinoviev and Lev Kamenev, who even as they waited to be shot in August 1936 sent Stalin letters of repentance, but of a man convinced of his civic virtue.

Features of the crisis

From his cell in wing 4 of the Matrosskaya Tishina remand centre Khodorkovsky observed the failure of Russia's two main liberal parties, Yabloko and SPS, to cross the 5 per cent Duma representation threshold in the elections of 7 December 2003. He was also less than impressed by Khakamada's performance in the presidential elections of 14 March 2004, when she gained 3.84 per cent of the vote compared to Putin's resounding 71.31 per cent, arguing that 'she did her best to discard her own liberal past', and described Ivan Rybkin's candidature as a 'vulgar farce'.[12] The fundamental problem for him and other liberals in Russia is that liberalism is associated with the failures and hardships of the 1990s, when the country underwent not so much a reform as a socio-political revolution. In a particularly

had they fallen out over support for Khakamada's campaign, but their political views had diverged, and they had fallen out over a number of unspecified 'commercial issues'. Others close to Khdorkovsky and Nevzlin dismissed the view that the two had strained relations, Valeria Korchagina, 'Khodorkovsky Essay Causes Stir', *Moscow Times*, 31 March 2004, p. 5.

[8] Kalinin declared that 'Khodorkovsky did not pass any articles out of jail', and announced that an investigation had been launched to determine 'the circumstances that—if it were really true—allowed the prisoner to prepare an article and pass it to the newspaper', Korchagina, 'Khodorkovsky Essay Causes Stir'.

[9] Aleksei Nikol'skii and Sevast'yan Kozitsyn, 'Po kusochkam', *Vedemosti*, 7 April 2004.

[10] Leonid Berres, 'Khodorkovskii otreksya ot svoei stat'i: Radi advokatov', *Izvestiya*, 7 April 2004, p. 6.

[11] Nikol'skii and Kozitsyn, 'Po kusochkam', *Vedemosti*, 7 April 2004.

[12] Khakamada's campaign was managed by Anatoly Yermolin from Yukos, a former security official, Tokareva, *Kto podstavil khodorskovskogo*, p. 215.

cruel Bolshevik inflexion the ends were once again allowed to justify the means. As Polanyi noted: 'If the immediate effect of a change is deleterious, then, until proof to the contrary, the final effect is deleterious.'[13]

Khodorkovsky argued that 'we are witnessing the surrender of the liberals' in which terms such as 'freedom of speech', 'freedom of thought', and 'freedom of conscience' had become little more than 'parasitic phrases' since everything had become clear: '[T]his is another conflict between the oligarchs and the president, a plague on both your houses.' In addition to the incapacity of the Russian liberals, he lambasted what he termed the 'party of national revenge', who spoke about the 'collapse of liberal ideas; that Russia, our country, does not actually need freedom. The one speaking about freedom is either an oligarch or a rascal (which, on the whole, comes to much the same thing).' He warned against undermining 'the authority' of President Putin and called for large tax impositions on big business.

Caught between the failing liberals and the party of national revenge, he insisted that '[a]gainst this backdrop president Vladimir Putin seems to be Liberal No. 1', far preferable to the 'nationalists' Vladimir Zhirinovsky and Dmitry Rogozin, the latter at the head of the Rodina party that had done exceptionally well in the December 2003 elections, winning 9 per cent of the vote. On this basis he argued: 'Probably Putin is neither a liberal nor a democrat, but he is more liberal and democratic than 70 per cent of the population of our country.' He insisted that 'the cause of the crisis of Russian liberalism is not about ideals of freedom' but the inadequacies of the practitioners of the ideal, accompanied by the failure of the Kremlin to give them special support and the departure of the oligarchs from the lobbying arena, and the 'standard lobbying mechanisms ceased to work'. He placed himself in the ranks of '[s]ocially active people of liberal views' who were 'responsible for keeping Russia on the way to freedom', but, as Khodorkovsky robustly put it: '[I]n Stalin's notorious words of late June 1941, we've f...ed up our cause.' Russian liberals now had to 'analyse our tragic errors and confess our guilt'. The reason was straightforward:

Russian liberalism has suffered a defeat because it tried to ignore, first, some significant national-historic peculiarities of Russia's development, and second, the vital interests of the majority of the Russian people. Above all, it was fatally afraid of telling the truth.

It was not that liberals such as Chubais, Gaidar, and their associates consciously set out to deceive the Russian people, but once in power they 'approached this whole revolution in a supercilious if not outright frivolous manner'. They worked on behalf of the 10 per cent of Russians ready to adapt to the new conditions 'without state paternalism, and forgot about the other 90 per cent', and then 'concealed their failures with deception'. In particular, he condemned the loss of savings, the voucher privatization, and the loans for shares privatization. Since Khodorkovsky was a major beneficiary of the latter, his criticisms must be considered disingenuous at best. At the same time, he criticized the lack of attention in the 1990s to education, healthcare, public utilities, and support for the poor, and in general

[13] Polanyi, *The Great Transformation*, p. 40.

that 'Russian liberals ignored issues of social stability and social peace, which alone could establish the basis for long-term reform and create the foundations of national existence'. Instead, '[a] gulf separated them from the people, into which they pumped rosy liberal views of reality and manipulative technologies with the informational-bureaucratic pump'. He stressed how much effort it had taken in 1996 to get the Russian people to 'vote with their hearts'. He also took issue with liberal arguments that there had been no alternative to the 1998 partial default, in which millions once again lost their savings, when in fact a timely devaluation of the rouble, advocated by Khodorkovsky at the time, could have avoided some of the worst consequences. The attack on the liberals was comprehensive, noting their personal enrichment while the mass of the population sank into poverty, and the much-vaunted liberal 'freedom of speech' was accompanied by 'financial and administrative control over the media so as to use this magical arena for their own purposes'. It was hardly surprising that millions of the old Soviet scientific and technical intelligentsia, which 'in the late 1980s were the main motor of the Soviet liberation movement', now voted for Rodina and the CPRF. The liberal elite, in Khodorkovsky's view, showed nothing but contempt for the Russian people.

This critique of the Bolshevism of the anti-Bolsheviks could have been written by Putin himself, although Putin was never quite so explicit and only hinted at this sort of critique of the social transformation of the 1990s. Putin always feared becoming trapped by a populist attack on 1990s vintage liberals, since it could have provoked an attack on his own liberal economic policies. Within the framework of his remedial approach, Putin sought to ameliorate the consequences of the 1990s, including aspects that Khodorkovsky did not touch upon—above all, the emergence of powerful business leaders like himself who made no secret of their involvement in politics, as Khodorkovsky did in this letter—while building on the foundations established in that era of anarcho-capitalism.

This era was now over: 'The hour of atonement has come. In the 2003 election the people bid its firm and tearless farewell to official liberals.' Even young people refused to vote for Chubais and the SPS. As for big business, it had cast its lot with the liberal rulers and 'helped them to err and lie', and had thus become 'accomplices to their misdeeds and lies', afraid of jeopardizing their own position. They thus were made the scapegoats for what had happened in the country. Attacks on so-called oligarchs obscured, in Khodorkovsky's view, the fact that '[o]ligarchy is the totality of the group that dominates power', and the business sector failed to challenge the rules, or indeed 'the absence of rules', and hence 'nurtured official lawlessness and Basmanny justice'. While big business had created two million jobs and revived whole sectors of industry, it incurred the wrath of society because of its failure to distance itself from the 'party of irresponsibility' and the 'party of deceit'.

The nascent business class failed to defend its distinct class identity and had become little more than a subaltern wing of the liberal reform party. Khodorkovsky condemned the failure of the new entrepreneurial group to become a bourgeoisie in the classical sense of the word, a property-owning class that acts according to the law, while shaping the law to defend its business interests and property rights. Khodorkovsky represented the vanguard of the nascent 'bourgeois' oligarchs, and thus sharply distinguished himself from the 'criminal' oligarchy represented by the likes of Berezovsky. The fundamental problem was that while the defeat of the criminal oligarchs of the Yeltsin era can be justified in terms of overcoming state capture and the end of what the left-nationalist opposition in Russia likes to call 'comprador capitalism', Khodorkovsky represented a different type of capitalism. Even though Khodorkovsky had benefited no less than the criminal oligarchy from the anarcho-capitalism of the 1990s, he now came to represent a new understanding of the social role of big business. The flexing of his political muscles in 2003 can be seen as the attempt by this new bourgeoisie to emerge from the shadows of the state and to exist as an autonomous force in Russian politics. Hence the clipping of the wings of the 'criminal' oligarchs in 2000 was very different from the attack on the consolidation of a bourgeois class three years later. The second event ultimately changed the nature of the post-communist state. The relative liberalism of the first years of Putin's leadership now gave way to a far more *dirigiste* form of neo-patrimonialism. The crisis of liberalism in Russia, from this perspective, was far deeper than the failings of a particular elite group, but reflected a structural shift in the nature of the Russian polity. Reactionary-remedial policies were compatible with genuine pluralism, but the system now began to move beyond this towards a more transformative agenda, accompanied by a more statist developmental model.

Khodorkovsky noted the contradiction between civil society and big business, with the latter seeking maximum profit whereas civil society pursues social goals like environmental and labour protection. Hence business will always find a common language with the state; '[b]usiness does not crave liberal political reforms, nor is it obsessed with freedom'. In addition, 'business can find a home anywhere in the world, and money is not patriotic'. There then comes a remarkable personal statement:

As far as I am concerned, Russia is my motherland. I want to live, work and die here. I want my offspring to be proud of Russia and proud of me as a small part of this country and this unique civilization. Perhaps I was too late in understanding this: I only started my involvement in philanthropy and my support for civic organizations in 2000. . . . That is why I decided to stop working in business, and speak not on behalf of the 'business community' but for myself and on behalf of the liberal part of society and the people I consider my comrades-in-arms. There are among our ranks, of course, major businessmen—the world of genuine freedom and democracy is open to all.

For Khodorkovsky it is not that liberalism is not appropriate for Russia, but that its practitioners—himself included—had not been up to the task, and he now sought to provide his own remedial agenda. By his own example Khodorkovsky tried to draw Russian liberalism out of the deep hole that it had dug itself. Khodorkovsky proposed an alternative form of remedial politics to that offered by Putin, although both in equal measure acted in reaction to the 1990s. By now, however, the regime had begun to move beyond remedialism, and in any case was not open to the proposals of outsiders.

Khodorkovsky argued the need for a programme of constructive work with the regime rather than engaging in futile condemnations of it. To achieve this he outlined a seven-point strategy:

1. Establish a new strategy of interaction with the state: 'The state and the bureaucracy are not synonymous.'

2. 'Learn to seek justice in Russia, not in the West.' He admitted having a high reputation in the West was 'nice', but this was 'no substitute for the respect of compatriots'.

3. 'Abandon senseless attempts to cast the legitimacy of the president in doubt. Whether we like Vladimir Putin or not, it is time to realise that the head of state is not just an individual. The president is an institution that guarantees the integrity and stability of our country. And God forbid that we should live to see that institution collapse. Russia will not survive another February 1917. The country's history demonstrates that bad power is better than none.' He stressed the important role that the state plays in the development of civil society, something that 'is shaped over the course of centuries'.

4. 'Stop lying to ourselves and to society.' Here he criticized Khakamada's presidential campaign, saying that unlike his colleague Nevzlin he refused to sponsor her because 'I saw troubling signs of mendacity in her campaign', namely the allegations she made that Putin was behind the Dubrovka theatre siege in October 2002.[14]

5. 'Legitimate privatisation.' With 90 per cent of the population viewing the privatizations as unjust there will always be a large constituency ready to attack private property. Privatization could only be vindicated if business started to share with the people, primarily through taxation, and it would be best if business initiated this itself rather than waiting for this to be imposed upon them.

6. 'Create real civil society structures' as a way of attracting talented people, and at the same time stopping the brain drain: 'Brains always collect in a favourable medium—civil society.'

7. 'To change the nation, we must change ourselves. To bring freedom back to our country, we need to believe in freedom ourselves.' And it was on this rousing note, reminiscent of Solzhenitsyn's credo, that the letter ended.

The article suggested the interplay of six forces in Russia. *Big business* had taken advantage of the opportunities of the 1990s but had failed to develop its own ethical code, and instead had exploited the weakness of both the state and civil society to enrich itself, even though it was aware that its relationship with Yeltsin 'was a sham'. Some of his criticisms of the business world reflected the original

---

[14] In an interview with *Izvestiya* on 1 April 2004 in the immediate wake of the publication of the letter, Nevzlin stated he would stop funding Khakamada's party, and that since it was impossible to discuss matters with Khodorkovsky in person he was obliged to 'depart the political scene'. Ivan Gordeev, *Vremya novostei*, 5 April 2004, p. 2.

criticisms of the National Strategy Council in May 2003, above all the accusation that the Russian business community had displayed a notable lack of 'patriotism'. The *radical liberals* come in for the harshest criticism, since their idealism had quickly turned to cynicism and contempt for the mass of the people. In effect Khodorkovsky argued that the liberal idea was too important to be left to self-styled liberals. The *state* remained a rather foggy presence in his discourse, but his thought certainly was imbued with elements of the 'democratic statism' that was later to triumph in Surkov's thinking, and given specific form in the idea of sovereign democracy. Paradoxically, echoing Putin, Khodorkovsky's text on a number of occasions stressed the society-forming and leadership role of the state. The letter thus sought to transcend the sterile confrontation between liberalism and the state, and on balance Khodorkovsky veered towards the latter.

He had little to say about the nature of Putin's *regime*, but had some surprisingly positive words to say about Putin himself. As for *civil society*, it would take a long time to develop, and in this Khodorkovsky shared Putin's awareness of temporality, the historical constraints on the actuation of ideals in the present time and the need to take a long-term approach. As he put it, civil society is formed over generations 'and not in [an] instant by the wave of a magic wand'. By the same token, despite the 'complexes and phobias' associated with the development of liberalism in the 1990s, the development of liberalism in Russia since the nineteenth century was highly problematical. This is where the final element comes in, namely the role of the *individual*. Everyone should take personal responsibility for what had happened to Russia after the fall of communism, and be prepared for a long struggle for the achievement of freedom in the country. In this Khodorkovsky's thinking can be placed in the line of dissident critiques of power and the need for personal responsibility and moral consciousness.[15]

Khodorkovsky as political philosopher and commentator

Khodorkovsky's decision to start a debate by sending a letter from prison continues a hallowed Russian tradition. Some of Russia's most powerful political philosophy falls into this genre. Characteristically, the relationship of prisoner to captor, victim to tyrant, is as much of interest as the content of the epistle. In the Russian context, the 'power of the powerless' is typically encapsulated in the romantic notion of the power of the written word to challenge the serried ranks of soldiers and secret policemen; and the power of the martyr to challenge the ease of the throne.

In this case, however, the challenge was notably ambiguous, with some criticizing the 'servile' tone, which appealed to an end to talk of Putin's illegitimacy, while others, like Belkovsky, insisted that Putin should accept Khodorkovsky's repentance. Belkovsky argued that Khodorkovsky challenged 'not Putin and his statehood', but 'his own past and himself'.

---

[15] See Philip Boobbyer, *Conscience, Dissent and Reform in Soviet Russia* (London, Routledge, 2005).

Khodorkovsky has publicly repented for the 1990s and declared that the contemporary crisis of liberalism in Russia is determined not by the intrigues of the semi-mythical 'Petersburg siloviki' but the historical mistakes and miscalculations of the liberals themselves, in power throughout the last decade.

Khodorkovsky, in Belkovsky's view, was the first to recognize 'the full-scale ideological crisis of Russian liberalism', and 'exposed the enduring … myth about the unrestrained freedom of the 1990s. He openly speaks about the illusory nature of that freedom and the price that was paid for this fairytale illusion.' The article's publication, according to Belkovsky, would only reinforce Khodorkovsky's solitude; although there was one person who should use the article as the signal to align himself with Khodorkovsky—Vladimir Putin, and use the document as the 'manifesto of the new Russian elite'.[16]

Khodorkovsky's article was also rather presumptuous, outlining a programme up to 2020 and beyond to be fulfilled, one supposes, by the author himself. The tone of leftist pragmatism also grated on the ears of committed liberals, with the stress on the need to heal the breach between the state and society and recognizing the need to work with the state rather than against it; and arguing that without an end to poverty liberal reforms would run into the sand. In the words of one commentator, 'without restoring a comfortable standard of living to the elites in science, technology and the humanities, there will be no social storehouse for the ideas of freedom'.[17] This was balanced by an insistent patriotic tone that appeared to draw on Dostoevsky-type *pochvennichestvo* (native soilism), which acted as a corrective to the market cosmopolitanism espoused by the liberals in the 1990s. Indeed, there was more than a hint of a great power (*derzhavnik*) mentality in the letter. Equally, the author's attempt to distance himself from all actually existing liberal forces in Russia won him few friends in the liberal camp. His critique of the liberal spectrum of the party system was as devastating as it was accurate, and the failure of liberals to unite contributed to another defeat for them in the 2007 parliamentary elections.

While the article represented a powerful critique of the political practices of the liberals in the 1990s, and their political inadequacies in the 2000s, the work can hardly claim to be major political philosophy. There were major shortcomings in Khodorkovsky's critique of liberalism, notably the failure to discuss Russian liberalism's traditional reliance on an agent of change outside of the liberal dimension itself. This has traditionally been an enlightened bureaucracy or the state, as it was in the 1990s. In the Russian case we are faced with a type of 'disembedded liberalism', with the driver of change external to the liberal process itself. He also had a tendency to treat groups as having coherent and stable sentiments and preferences, whereas a differentiated examination of liberal ideas in Russia would find no such coherence. This was in part a result of the constantly shifting background and context in which liberalism has to operate.[18] Khodorkovsky's views

[16] Stanislav Belkovskii, 'Pokayanie: Odinochestvo Khodorkovskogo', *Vedemosti*, 30 March 2004.
[17] Aleksandr Arkhangelskii, *Izvestiya*, 30 March 2004, p. 2; from which this paragraph draws.
[18] See Kaehne, *Political and Social Thought in Post-Communist Russia*.

had either evolved from a reliance on the ability of spontaneous market forces to generate social order in the 1990s towards a greater emphasis on social justice in the 2000s (on which, more below), or he had always believed in this but only now was free to give expression to this aspect of his character. This intervention in the Russian public sphere at the minimum demonstrated that the maxim of 'once an oligarch, always an oligarch' did not hold in his case. Khodorkovsky had always been ambitious in politics, and now he revealed a different type of ambition: to understand the trajectory of Russian political life. He certainly did not join the Putin camp but sought to salvage something from the liberal opposition and to forge a new understanding of the needs of the country on the basis of 'seeking after truth', a politics of parrhesia that was as welcome as it had been delayed.

As a work of political analysis the article was commended by Ryzhkov, a Duma deputy at the time, as providing at least the start of an explanation for the defeat suffered by the liberals in the 2003/4 electoral cycle, something that the liberals themselves, in his view, had signally failed to do:

> He called things by their proper names. He spoke of the fact that the model of reform that was applied in the 1990s was monstrous. He said openly that it had given rise to immense poverty, immense social stratification, an economic slump and monstrous corruption.... And the model of reform that was proposed to Russia at the time has now been completely discredited in the eyes of the public.

However, Yevgeny Yasin, the former minister of economics, was rather less indulgent, noting that big business and the liberals had allied in 1996 to ensure Yeltsin's re-election, but when in 1997 'it became clear that big capital, which had dubbed itself the oligarchs, really did want to run the country and have a determining say in government decisions, that was when the liberals objected'.[19] Nemtsov, then first deputy prime minister, talked of 'people's capitalism',[20] while Chubais recognized the need to provide a popular social base for the reform project. As Yasin notes, at the time he suspects that Khodorkovsky 'was on the side of the nonliberals'.

The article was variously interpreted. For some it signalled Khodorkovsky's recantation and an attempt to sue for peace in his political struggle for the Kremlin. Such an interpretation is given credibility since just a year earlier Khodorkovsky had challenged Putin over energy and tax policy. The demonstrative attempt to distance himself from 'irreconcilables' such as Nevzlin, who had by then effectively teamed up with Berezovsky to destroy Putin, gives credence to this view. Valeriya Novodvorskaya, the leader of Russia's first post-communist independent political party, the Democratic Union established in May 1998, was typically scathing, condemning Khodorkovsky for 'recanting': 'There are things which are not pardonable even for those held in the prison Matrosskaya Tishina. There can be no forgiveness for betraying one's supporters.' And she sneered at the fact that 'Mikhail Khodorkovsky was desperately defended by the self-same

---

[19] Anatolii Shvedov, *Izvestiya*, 31 March 2004, p. 3.
[20] Jonas Bernstein, 'Liberalism Gets the Blame', *Moscow Times*, 16 January 1998.

liberals whom he smeared with mud'.[21] Gaidar was no less dismissive of the economic basis of Khodorkovsky's arguments, insisting that '[e]ven those who gave it a delighted reception have called attention to the banality of what it says and to the fact that all of it has already been repeated many times over by the opponents of Russia's liberals'. It was only the article's author that was new, not its contents, and Gaidar went on to argue that the structural reforms of the 1990s could only produce a positive effect with a time lag, and that there had been no way of maintaining people's savings in 1990/1, when there had been a massive monetary overhang created by the lack of goods to purchase in the late Soviet years, and in conditions when from autumn 1990 sixteen central banks in the USSR were able to 'create liquidity', that is to print roubles.[22]

At the same time, there was little in the way of personal self-criticism in Khodorkovsky's text. His call was for a collective rethink by the neo-liberal enthusiasts of the 1990s and the current liberal leaders, and while he admitted some oversights on his part, there was little sense of a deeper soul-searching about the way that he had made his fortune. In fact, the article can be seen as very much in line with the pragmatic style that had brought him success in business, a flexibility now adapted, according to his critics, to get him out of the rather deep hole in which he had dug himself. This may be taking an unduly sceptical approach, and while Khodorkovsky condemned Russia's liberals for having degenerated remarkably swiftly from idealism to cynicism and a Bolshevik-style arrogance (although he does not use that phrase), his letter revealed a streak of political romanticism in his character.

It was also clear that he distanced himself from the attempt to defend Yukos, which does not merit a mention in the text. Khodorkovsky had decided to become a political figure, and he left the fight to save Yukos to others. Instead Khodorkovsky declared that he would henceforth devote himself to a life as a social activist, if not as a politician. He began by distancing himself from the liberals and sought to position himself as a national leader, including the leftist forces, to which he appealed in later communications. The letter marked the transformation of Khodorkovsky from a life devoted to the making of money to a life focused on politics. Hence a very different conclusion can be drawn from those who interpreted the letter as Khodorkovsky's attempt to open a dialogue with the regime: with the discrediting of all the old liberal political leaders in Russia a vacuum of leadership of the democratic movement had opened up—and Khodorkovsky was making a bid for the leadership of the democratic forces in the run-up to the 2007/08 electoral season. The letter can be seen as representing a tactical switch but the strategic challenge remained. For the rulers in the Kremlin this potential challenge only reinforced fears that Khodorkovsky represented a major danger to Putin's regime. The fight continued, it appeared, with this 'troublesome priest'.

---

[21] Valeriya Novodvorskaya, 'Grovelling Before the Inquisition', *New Times*, 30 June 2004, p. 21.
[22] Yegor Gaidar, *Vedemosti*, 14 April 2004.

PROPERTY AND FREEDOM

At the end of the year Khodorkovsky once again put his thoughts on paper. By then he had been in custody for over a year, and the destruction of Yukos had ground on. Following the loss of YNG and with the tax bill standing at $27.5 billion, the company's value by the end of 2004 had fallen from around $40 billion to no more than $2 billion. In a broad-ranging open letter from prison he identified a section of the Kremlin bureaucracy as responsible for continuing the affair for their personal benefit, while in his first interview from jail he provided a more political analysis.

Prison and the world: Property and freedom

In a second, rather wistful, open letter from prison at the end of 2004 Khodorkovsky took a philosophical look at what was happening to the country.[23] Entitled 'Prison and the World: Property and Freedom', the letter was published just days after Yuganskneftegaz had been sold to a shady front company for about half of its estimated real value. He noted that six months earlier he had tried to save Yukos, its minority shareholders, and the country by offering to give up his stake as payment of the tax claims, '[b]ut the other side chose a different path: the path of selective application of the law, introducing new provisions and conditions, the public destruction of the first green shoots of business confidence in the arbitration court and government in general'. This in his view was motivated by more than 'political interests alone', and hence the Yukos affair was not so much a conflict between business and the state but an attack by one company on another. He called the culmination of the Yukos case 'the most senseless and economically destructive incident in all of Vladimir Putin's years as president'.

He insisted that loss of his own fortune was not the issue, but the destruction of a company that he and his team had transformed from a loss-making enterprise operating in nine regions producing only 40 million tonnes of oil a year, with a six-months arrears of wages and $3 billion in debts, to one by 2003 employing 150,000 operating in fifty regions and producing 80 million tonnes annually. It had become the country's second largest tax payer after Gazprom, comprising 5 per cent of federal budget revenues. He condemned the 'wild imagination' that had conjured up the back tax claims against the company, in some years exceeding its revenues, and noted: 'It is clear that government officials will stop at nothing in their pursuit of the redistribution of property.' At this point Khodorkovsky's text takes on a philosophical tone:

---

[23] Mikhail Khodorkovskii, 'Tyur'ma i mir: Sobstvennost' i svoboda', *Vedemosti*, 28 December 2004. Note that the word 'mir' can also be translated as 'peace', and the idea that prison had allowed Khodorkovsky to achieve a type of inner peace and reconciliation with his fate is reflected in the text. As he puts it: 'Breathing the spring air, playing with children who study at a normal Moscow school, reading wise books—all these things are more important, pleasant and right than dividing property and settling scores with one's own past.'

It may sound strange to many, but losing my personal wealth is not unbearably painful. Following in the tradition of many prisoners, both known and unknown, I must say thank you to prison. It gave me months for profound thought and time to forge a new outlook on many aspects of life. I now realise that owning property—especially large-scale property— does not make a person free. As part-owner of Yukos I had to make enormous efforts to protect this wealth, and had to set limits on myself so as not to jeopardise this. There were many things that I did not permit myself to say, because speaking openly could have harmed those assets. I had to close my eyes and put up with many things, to preserve and increase my personal wealth. I did not control this wealth: it controlled me. . . . Wealth creates opportunities, but it immobilises a person's creative potential, and to the disintegration of a person's individuality as such. That is what this cruel tyranny demonstrates—the tyranny of wealth. And now I have been reborn. I am now an average upper middle class person, whose purpose is to live and not just to own things. The struggle is not just to acquire property, but to become oneself—for the right to be an individual. . . . This suggests that the only possible and right choice is the choice of freedom.

The logic echoes Vaclav Havel's strictures against the consumer-dominated West,[24] but with the added poignancy that Khodorkovsky was not some isolated intellectual on the fringes of society, but had been one of the richest people in the world, owning a company that could affect the fate of millions. The narrative of prison not so much as a penitentiary but as a retreat allowing a period of self-reflection and self-realization resonates more broadly. There is a tension between penitence, the recognition of wrongdoing and the desire for self-improvement, and self-realization, the attempt by an individual to find their fate. In Khodorkovsky's case, there is no sense that he was in any way guilty in a legal sense, but only that he had been mistaken in an existential sense—and now the burden of defending his property had been lifted, he could realize himself in a new sphere.

From this he moved on to a disquisition on the appropriate form of government for Russia, insisting: 'Russian political tradition is artificial. Russia has always been at the crossroads of civilisations, but for the most part it is a European country. Therefore European political institutions that envisage the separation of powers can be applied in a limited manner to this country'. He then makes the important statement:

However, the other side of the coin should not be ignored. Russian people have traditionally regarded the state as a supreme power that gives them faith and hope. This power cannot be applied until we stop seeing it as supreme. Russian history tells us that the loss of this special, supra-rational respect for the state will inevitably bring the country to chaos, revolt and revolution.

He distinguished between 'authority' and 'governance'. Government was carried out by officials and bureaucrats who were 'merely mortal'. They would not be able to evoke the patriotism of the people: 'No true patriot would give his life for a bunch of bureaucrats who are only interested in feathering their own nests.' In the Yukos affair, the bureaucrats had been let loose and were pursuing policies that

---

[24] Vaclav Havel et al., *The Power of the Powerless: Citizens against the State in Central-Eastern Europe* (London, Hutchinson, 1985).

undermined the sanctity of the state. He was unreserved in his condemnation of 'the bureaucracy':

The destruction of Yukos shows that the unrestrained bureaucrats care nothing for the interests of the state....They only know that the state machinery exists to promote their interests....That is why the Yukos affair is not a conflict between business and government. It is a politically and commercially motivated attack by one company (represented by state officials) on another company. The state, in this particular case, is a hostage to the interests of certain individuals wielding the powers of state officials.

The attempt to manage everything, in his view, was likely to render the country unmanageable because it was 'inconsistent with the traditional rule of authority and the laws of complex systems'. He went further, warning that 'soon the only partner to this omnivorous bureaucracy will be a ferocious, amorphous crowd': 'Then an unmanageable democracy will come into being, with all its innumerable disasters and suffering.' In particular, he pitied those in authority who sincerely believed that the action against Yukos was the right thing to do (no doubt an oblique reference to Putin), and warned 'they will eventually realise that political persecution and forced redistribution of property cannot be combined with modern economic development'.

He stressed the political nature of the case: 'My oppressors know that there isn't any solid evidence at all in the criminal case against me—but that doesn't matter. I could always be charged with setting fire to the Manezh building, or plotting an economic counter-revolution. I have been told that the authorities want to keep me in jail for as long as possible: five years, say, or longer. They fear that I will seek revenge.' He would not act like the Count of Monte Cristo and seek revenge: 'Unlike my persecutors, I have realised that making big money is far from the only goal in a person's life (and probably not that important). The time of big bucks is over for me. Now that I have disposed of the burden of the past, I am going to work for the good of the generations who will rule the country very soon—the generations who will usher in new values and new hopes.'

As in his earlier letter, Khodorkovsky was careful not to attack Putin personally, but his criticism was coming closer to the president. He lambasted elements in the Kremlin for dismantling Yukos, and warned that their bureaucratic attempt to manage society would fail. He continued to disassociate himself from his 'oligarchic' past, and now recast himself as a Soviet-style political exile. Quite how he planned to 'work for the good' of the new generation, he was not specific, but clearly he was setting himself up as the democratic liberal alternative to the existing bureaucracy in power that used patriotic slogans to expropriate property and to enrich themselves.

First interview from jail

Some of the themes addressed in this letter were taken up in his interview published in the Russian version of *Newsweek* at the end of January

2005.[25] In response to the question whether he had anticipated being held in custody for so long, he answered in the affirmative, noting that his incarceration depended not on the courts but on 'a few officials [*chinovniki*] and businessmen close to them', afraid that he would seek revenge for the loss of YNG: 'These are people with a criminal mentality. They judge people by their own standards.'[26] As for why he was arrested, Khodorkovsky argued that Putin had been deceived in late October 2003, having been told that Khodorkovsky was planning to become senator for the Evenk autonomous district, which would have given him immunity from prosecution. In the event, Khodorkovsky supported his colleague Vasily Shakhnovsky to become a representative from the region to the Federation Council.

He agreed that in part the reason for his arrest was his active involvement in politics and his attempt to advance his own people into the Duma, but he went on:

I am personally in favour of a strong state, but consider that the strength of the state lies not in a large number of powerful officials, but in the trust of the people, in the ability to attract and use the best people to resolve tasks, in the competition and mutual accountability of state and social institutions. I supported various political parties and social organisations since I am convinced that our society needs various opinions and views, and our country needs a strong opposition not controlled by the authorities.

He then described quite specifically why he had been arrested:

I am now absolutely convinced that the main reason for the 'Yukos affair' was the desire of a group of four–five physical individuals to take over a large and successful oil company. Politics in general and state policy in particular was used as a excuse to convince the country's leadership to use the full power of the state to redistribute property, ignoring the law. Similar things had happened in the last decade, but never before had the object of attack been such a large corporation. And never before had the instrument been such high-ranking figures.[27]

He admitted that his 'principled and unbending' attitude in regard to the authorities as well as mistakes that he had made in business and social activities were in part the reason for the affair. He went on to say: 'If it was not for my principles I would not be in jail now but abroad or somewhere else, but I did not want to do this and could not do it. Earlier I could, but at a certain moment I felt myself more of a citizen than a businessman.'[28] He noted that in jail he could say less, but he was heard more clearly. 'If I had emigrated, I would have been taken as no more than an oligarch. . . . Today it is hard for me physically, but no one can say that I do not have the moral right to speak.'[29]

The discussion then moved on to Russia's constitutional order in the light of Khodorkovsky's arguments two years earlier that parliament ought

---

[25] 'Mikhail Khodorkovskii: vpervye—intervyu iz tyur'my, "Tyazhelo, chto sovsem net solntsa"', *Newsweek*, 31.01–06.02.2005, pp. 14–17. The questions were passed to Khodorkovsky via his lawyers, and the answers returned in the same way.

[26] Ibid., p. 14.   [27] Ibid., p. 15.   [28] Loc. cit.   [29] Ibid., p. 16.

to have the power not just to appoint but also to dismiss the prime minister. He now argued that 'Russia needs a concept for a new political system', but revisions should be introduced only after much thought. He argued that the president, as 'guarantor of national stability', should remain 'above the political fray', and some presidential powers should be transferred to the parliamentary majority, above all responsibility for forming the cabinet, which should be responsible for the economy. Part of the government would be responsible to parliament, and part to the president, which if Khodorkovsky's ideas were implemented would give the country a unique hybrid, and undoubtedly unworkable, system. It was Khodorkovsky's earlier promotion of the idea of a parliamentary republic that had acted as the trigger for the anti-Yukos campaign. As for the appointment of governors and the like, he argued: 'The authorities are trying to turn all politicians into appointed officials, and thus to "freeze" the ruling class so as not to allow outsiders to enter.... This is a typical stagnation project', comparable to the Soviet system in the early 1980s. Touching on the theme of his earlier letters, he agreed that big business should apologize to the people for what it had done in the 1990s, but he extended the act of repentance to encompass the whole 'ruling corporation, which is responsible for the market reforms of the 1990s being anti-social, as a result of which the people's trust in liberal ideas and values was destroyed'.[30]

Asked what he would say to Putin if given the opportunity, he answered:

Mr president, do not allow power [*vlast'*] to be devalued and profaned. Do not allow it to be transformed into an instrument for the redistribution of property and for the advancement of the private interests of the bureaucracy. This will only multiply the mistakes and problems of the 1990s.[31]

Freedom the Russian way

In response to letters from readers of the *Bolshoi gorod* (*Big City*) magazine, just days before being sentenced in May 2005, Khodorkovsky discussed his understanding of Russian freedom, while explaining why a revolution in Russia would be disastrous.[32] He began with the paradoxical statement: 'I am grateful to prison because it has given me a new understanding of freedom—the freedom that is inside a person.' 'This is a freedom', he argued, '[t]hat is difficult to achieve, but for that equally hard to be taken or lost'. As in his earlier communications, he warned against dependence on the material world: 'If a person is critically dependent on something beyond himself, he is already not free.' For him that had earlier been money, but he now understood '[w]hen you are forced to think about the fate of your capital every waking day, this is dependence, which means slavery.'

He then went on to provide a classical religious understanding of freedom, and one that typified much dissident thinking in the late Soviet period.

[30] Loc. cit.   [31] Ibid., p. 17.
[32] *Bol'shoi gorod*, No. 9 (135), 25 May 2005; http://bg.ru/article?id = 4787.

Freedom in my understanding is first and foremost the opportunity for a person to think without internal limits, and to act according to his ethical code. In that sense, any political institution is merely the striving of mankind towards freedom, but in no way the source of freedom itself. And even in the most undemocratic environment, a person can be much freer than under the conditions of the broadest democracy.... No matter what kind of political system we have had in our country, there was always freedom and free people in Russia.... And that is why freedom cannot be imported the way technology or a natural resource can be.

Thus freedom is not dependent on political institutions but on the inner development and consciousness of the individual. Indeed, for some an authoritarian system, by forcing moral choices, actually enhances the quality of freedom; but faced by legal and administrative arbitrariness, it can only be a partial resolution of the problem.

Khodorkovsky then moved on to the second theme of his article.

Where a Russian revolution is concerned, it has always been—and remains—a dangerous game on the fine line between limitless Russian freedom and equally immense Russian slavery. The Russian is always radical and often marginalised—in both positive and negative ways. And that is why the concept of 'revolution' is sacred for him, even if formally he is a counter-revolutionary. It is no wonder the country is dreaming of revolution, even though right now there are no objective grounds for one to occur. But I don't plan to get involved in this game. A revolution in Russia always involves a lot of bloodshed.

This anti-revolutionary theme is one that Khodorkovsky shared with Putin, and is deeply embedded as part of Russia's post-communist consciousness. This visceral revulsion against Jacobin-Leninism, shared by figures across the political spectrum, suggests that a distinctive lesson of the Soviet experience has been learned: violence begets violence, and in the end the country loses. Khodorkovsky's argument, moreover, represents a rupture with the traditional way of thinking of Russian intellectuals, which too often has been characterized by extremist, utopian or nihilistic analysis. This is a salutary lesson for the Russian intelligentsia, in that their faults were ultimately transcended by someone who was not a member of the intelligentsia in the traditional sense of the word but who had developed a critique from the perspective of the rising bourgeoisie, which itself alienated him from the intelligentsia.

Leninism was a distinct civilization, based on a transnational concept of human liberation focused on the abolition of private property, the instrumentalization of politics, and the subordination of the individual to a larger cause. Khodorkovsky ended by stressing his commitment to what we could call the values of the Russian civilization reflected in the works of the great philosophers of Russia's Silver Age:

I plan, in prison, and with God's help, if I live to my release—to create and develop projects that will cultivate the right understanding of this freedom. The visible and the secret. Where people will get maximum opportunity for genuine creativity, solidarity, and mutual support. However overused the term may be, I call this a civil society.

Thus Khodorkovsky found freedom in jail, while Putin remained imprisoned by the affair, although formally at liberty. The great tragedy for Russia is that two of its most talented people became prisoners of each other: one, in jail in Krasnokamensk and Chita, the other a prisoner of the Kremlin. Khodorkovsky's letter reprised some of the arguments made by revisionist historians of the Soviet Union about the autonomy of society even under the most terrible of authoritarian regimes, and his personal spiritual trajectory reinforced the argument, made by Kertész in the novel from whence the epigraph to this chapter is drawn, that freedom ultimately, even in the most dreadful of circumstances, is a matter of individual conscience and not of fate.

THE LEFT TURN

Khodorkovsky's personal evolution continued while in jail. If the above texts were issued while in remand awaiting trial and sentencing, his next text came out once he knew that a long prison sentence awaited him. In August 2005 he issued his third major missive, 'Left Turn', a review of Russia's post-communist political development and the country's likely future.[33] The key issue was the reconciliation of freedom with justice and the legitimation of privatization. The question of authorship of this article, and the follow-up 'Left Turn 2' issued a few months later, is rather less murky than with 'The Crisis of Russian Liberalism'. One of the contributors to the text was Stanislav Belkovsky, although Khodorkovsky gave his approval to the work.[34] The relationship was similar to that of a speechwriter for a major politician, where the ideas are shaped by the writer but ultimately sanctioned by the person who has to deliver.[35] Belkovsky had been one of the authors of Council of National Strategy report 'The State and Oligarchs' of May 2003, but later the SNS had split and in April 2004 Belkovsky established the National Strategy Institute (Institut Natsional'noi Strategii, INS). By 2005 Belkovsky had moved into opposition to Putin, considering him too much of a neo-liberal, and he was disappointed that the Yukos affair had degenerated into little more than a tawdry struggle over property. Instead, Belkovsky called for a more socialist strategy, and this is reflected in the article. In discussing them, we shall ascribe authorship to Khodorkovsky, although the reader should be aware of the mixed provenance of the works.

---

[33] Mikhail Khodorkovskii, 'Levyi povorot', *Vedemosti*, No. 139, 1 August 2005, p. A5; Mikhail Khodorkovskii, *Levyi povorot 2* (Moscow, Galleya-Print, 2006).

[34] The source for this asked to remain anonymous, but was in an authoritative position to know at first-hand about the writing of these two articles.

[35] In an interview with the present author in Moscow on 3 March 2008 Belkovsky admitted contributing to the text, but denied being the main author.

'Freedom does not bring happiness'

In 'Left Turn', Khodorkovsky began with the striking assertion that '[i]t is generally accepted today that authoritarian trends are returning to the country', but he disagreed with those who associated this with Putin and his group of 'Leningraders'. Instead Khodorkovsky entered into a long discussion of the 1996 presidential election and his role in it, a theme that he had touched on in his earlier missives and which we have discussed in Chapter 2. He noted that in the dreary January of 1996 he, like most other liberals, had been disheartened by the strong showing of Zyuganov's Communists in the parliamentary election held the previous month, and full of foreboding that Zyuganov would win the presidency later that year. With Yeltsin's popularity in single digits and suffering illness and depression it seemed as if, Khodorkovsky argued, the democratic tide of 1990 and 1991 had turned: 'By the mid-1990s it had become evident that the miracle of democracy was not working—freedom did not bring us happiness.' Above all, Khodorkovsky now repudiated the liberal manipulation of the 1996 presidential election, representing the decisive turning point in the erosion of Russian democracy. Honest elections, whatever their outcome, Khodorkovsky suggested, would have prevented the emergence of a gulf between the people and the liberal elite.

By 1999 a whole new set of questions had emerged. He listed these as follows. *Justice*: 'Who should get hold of Soviet socialist property, which three generations had created through blood and sweat.' While people not known for their brains or education made millions, academicians, pilots, and others were plunged into poverty. 'Does that not suggest that Soviet socialism, although thrice blessed and maligned at the same time, was not so bad after all?' Khodorkovsky here reveals, like Putin, a broad streak of neo-Sovietism: not so much for the ideology but for aspects of its social reality. *Sense of national dignity*: 'Why were we respected when we lived in the bad Soviet Union...yet now in the era of freedom we are looked down on as stupid and penniless?' *Morality in politics*: He noted that people had chafed under the rule of communist officialdom, 'but did we deserve rulers who are ten times more cynical and a hundred times more thievish than the party bosses who in comparison look like retired country grandfathers and grandmothers'. *Fear in the face of an uncertain future and unclear goals*: The Russian people had been cast out from their 'dilapidated old Zaporozhets vehicle and had been promised a Mercedes, but instead we were simply tossed out on a muddy road at the end of the world. Where are we? In what corner of the world? And is there some constant source of light for us?'

It seemed at the time, Khodorkovsky argues, that only Zyuganov knew the answers to these questions. It was for this reason that in April 1996 the thirteen businessmen penned the letter 'Get Out of the Impasse', proposing that Yeltsin remain president with Zyuganov as prime minister.[36] Social and economic

---

[36] This was not, as we have seen (Chapter 2) stated explicitly, and it is interesting that Khodorkovsky now revealed what he had in mind.

policy, the letter argued, had to become more leftist because of the inevitable post-election conflicts: 'We needed a left turn so that we could reconcile freedom with justice', where there were a few winners and a great mass who felt they had lost during liberalisation. As we know, this Yeltsin–Zyuganov partnership did not take place, and instead a virulent anti-Communist strategy was adopted: '[M]illions were poured into the machine to manipulate public opinion that would ensure a Yeltsin victory—unquestionably an authoritarian strategy. The values of the late 1990s were formed at that time, and the most important of them was that the end justifies the means.' 'It was at this juncture that journalists changed from being the shapers of public opinion into becoming the servants of their owners, and when independent public institutions became the voice of their sponsors.'

It was impossible, Khodorkovsky argued, 'to prolong the right-liberal Yeltsin regime by democratic means', and this was also the case when it came to 2000, 'when it became clear that the regime could not remain in power without compromises on democracy'. Putin according to Khodorkovsky came to power on the back of a gigantic 'bluff' that questions on the agenda since 1995 were being dealt with when in fact nothing had changed, and political technologies were used to ensure the success of the strategy 'Stability in power and stability in the country'. The contradiction between expectations and reality came to a head in early 2005, with mass demonstrations against the monetization of benefits, with 'the people's desire for justice and to achieve change becoming firmer than ever'. The hard questions of the past had remained unanswered. The people, who had been deceived so often, would not be taken in again, hence the 'successor-2008' project would not be so easy. It was for this reason that 'Kremlin spin doctors know that this state course could only continue by undemocratic means.... They are convinced that the left would win if there were an honest and fair election. The screws are therefore being tightened ... electoral law is being changed so that all parties except those that are 102 per cent controlled by the president's administration.' Despite this, according to Khodorkovsky, opinion polls suggest that the people favour left values, 'state paternalism and democracy, freedom and justice together, all aligned together'. 'This means that the left is bound to win, despite all the tricks.'[37]

The Kremlin could try to block the course of history, but it lacks the resolve to apply full-blooded authoritarian measures, although it can close down papers and 'seize the assets of those who do not toe the line'. In most former socialist bloc countries leftist parties had come to power in the mid-1990s, and they had been able to 'link freedom with justice'. 'As a result the authorities in these countries were able to avoid a severe legitimacy crisis, the crisis that usually marks the start of all revolutions.' The post-Soviet states did not turn to the left in time and engage in real discussions of national priorities, instead they pursued the chimera of 'stability'. This led to the various 'rose', 'orange', and 'tulip' revolutions. In Ukraine the 'orange' authorities were raising the issue of revising privatization: '[I]f the question of the legality of the privatisation process had been raised by the authorities five or six years ago there might not have been an orange revolution.'

[37] He cites a Levada-Centre poll.

Khodorkovsky was at pains to stress that the much-discussed legalization of privatization did not mean 'the nationalisation of the economy in which major enterprises fall under the unlimited control of bureaucrats who are not accountable to anyone'. Instead, Khodorkovsky sought to establish a secure and popularly legitimate system of property rights:

The result of legalising the privatisation process will be to consolidate a class of real owners, who would be seen by the people not as bloodsuckers but as legal owners of legitimate assets. This means that large-scale property owners need to turn leftwards as much as the rest of the people who still see the privatisations of the 1990s as unfair and therefore illegal. Legitimising the process of privatisation will serve to justify property and people's attitude towards ownership, perhaps genuinely for the first time in Russian history.

He asserted that the Communists and Rodina would have to be part of the next administration, and the various liberals would either have to join the 'broad social democratic coalition' or remain 'grumbling on the sidelines'. To meet the popular demand for justice the new authorities would have to deal with 'the problems of legalising privatisation and restoring paternalistic programmes and policies'. Arguing that the coming to power of a left-nationalist government was inevitable, the letter insisted:

A left turn in Russia is as inevitable as it is necessary. Putin does not need to do much to allow the left turn to take place. All that he needs to do is to leave within the constitutional framework of his term and ensure democratic conditions for the conduct of the next elections. Only this will guarantee the prospect of sustained democratic development for the country without upheavals and the risk of disintegration.

Realism or fatalism

How accurate is Khodorkovsky's analysis of the 1990s and later?[38] His attempt in 1996 to broker some sort of deal between the main competitors in the election was doomed to fail, and the idea of the Communists and Yeltsin working together was at best far-fetched. The idea of a government headed by Zyuganov enjoying 'extended powers' being able to coordinate a positive programme with Yeltsin was simply unrealistic; although ahead of the 2003 elections Berezovsky, now in exile in London, returned to the idea and called on the Communists to join forces with the liberals. Khodorkovsky's sense of political tactics appears to be flawed, even though much of his broad strategic analysis may be perceptive. The 1996 letter touches on a theme repeated in latter missives: that it was time 'to put an end to the denigration of the Soviet period of Russian history', but at the same time 'the great ideas of freedom, civility, justice, right and truth' should not be

---

[38] For a discussion of reactions to the letter, see Catherine Belton, 'Khodorkovsky Says a Left Turn is Inevitable', *Moscow Times*, 2 August 2005, p. 1.

The Quality of Freedom

discredited—although the Soviet period did just that.[39] He is indeed right to see the management of the succession to Putin in 1999/2000 as a continuation of the 1996 operation, but there were some major differences. The threat of a 'communist restoration' had passed, and, paradoxically in the light of developments, the issue was the degree to which the privatizations of the 1990s would be investigated by, among others, Primakov and his allies. Again, while no doubt Russians, like people everywhere, wanted extensive welfare, this was a slender basis on which to predict a gathering social revolution.[40] There was very little evidence of a massive wave of social discontent bringing the left to power on its crest. Putin's government in a social sense represented the coming to power of a social democratic left, ensuring the payment of wages, improved living standards that brought millions out of poverty, restraints on the unmitigated power of capital in the political sphere, and a commitment to maintaining the fundamentals of a welfare state. Quite why the 'entrenchment of a class of effective property owners' should help bring about a 'left turn' is unclear; and how the 'left turn' would help legitimize property is no more convincing.

Liberals reacted angrily to the letter. In a considered study some time later Sergei Mitrokhin, the deputy head of Yabloko and in June 2008 Yavlinsky's successor, argued that while coalition politics made some sense in Western countries, in Russian conditions it meant allying with the unreconstructed nationalism and leftism of the CPRF, which had nothing in common with liberalism.[41] Khodorkovsky did not engage with the specific ideas of particular parties. For example, Rodina combined Glaz'ev's idea for a natural rent on big business to restore some sense of social justice with Rogozin's national-chauvinism. It is not clear what aspects of Rodina's programme attracted Khodorkovsky.[42] At the time when the assault against Yukos was launched, in September 2003 Rodina announced that its main theme in the forthcoming parliamentary campaign would be the struggle against the 'oligarchs', with Rogozin stressing the need to suppress the 'oligarchs' rebellion', while Glaz'ev harped on the state taking a cut of the huge natural resource rents made by the oligarchs.[43] Two years later, however, Rogozin was clearly flattered by Khodorkovsky's positive evaluation of Rodina, and was confident that 'left-patriotic forces could well come to power if elections were open and fair', and he argued that Khodorkovsky 'sensibly analysed the

[39] This contradiction is pointed out by an editorial in the same issue in which 'Left Turn' was published, 'Levyi put', *Vedemosti*, 1 August 2005, p. 1.

[40] Dmitrii Polikanov, 'Lodka dlya "sverkh-Putina" ', *Vedemosti*, 8 August 2005, p. A4. The author, director of international links at VTsIOM, demonstrated on the basis of extensive opinion polling that '[t]he idea of the dominance of the left idea in society is greatly exaggerated'.

[41] Sergei Mitrokhin, 'Izobretatel'nost' d'yavola: Ob uchastii demokratov v "pravo-levoi" koalitsii', *Nezavisimaya gazeta*, 20 June 2008, p. 11.

[42] Khodorkovsky's failure to mention United Russia is also enigmatic. Some officials of the latter party accused Rodina of supporting Khodorkovsky, suggesting that mercenary motives were involved. Georgii Il'ichev, ' "Edinaya Rossiya" edet na "Rodinu" ', *Izvestiya*, 8 August 2005, p. 2. See also Syuzanna Farizova, 'Zaklyuchennyi Khodorkovsky zapyatnal "Rodinu" ', *Kommersant*, 6 August 2005, p. 2.

[43] Alexei Titkov, *'Party Number Four'—Rodina: Whence and Why?* (Moscow, Panorama Centre, 2006), p. 16.

situation in the country', although he made no comment about the possibility of an alliance between Rodina and the Communists.[44] Provoked by Khodorkovsky's comments, United Russia launched an assault against Rodina, trying to establish a link between the party and Yukos and in general accusing Rodina of having taken money from oligarchs on the quiet while condemning them in public.[45] More broadly, Rodina has been compared to the new wave of radical right West European parties, led by the likes of Jean-Marie Le Pen, the late Pim Fortuyn (d. 2002) and Jörg Haider (d. 2008), concerned about immigration and the preservation of the nation: 'Russia indeed resembles the old European countries in the sense of being unexpectedly confronted with the problem of preserving its cultural identity and socio-economic stability.'[46]

As for placing any weight of expectation on the CPRF, this revealed a lack of understanding of quite how far the party had degenerated in ideological and organizational terms. Indeed, it was rather far-fetched to compare Zyuganov's Communists with Central European social democrats. Even if the latter encompassed some former communists, the break with the past was irreversible, while this was far from the case in Russia. As the RUIE vice president, Igor Yurgens, put it, he was not yet ready for a 'left turn', if there was not equally an opportunity to turn to the right: 'If there is not such a possibility, then that will be a dead end path.'[47] A left turn at this point would only increase the greed of officialdom. For the broadcaster and CPRF member, Sergei Dorenko, '[t]he left turn has already taken place, the country has long been going leftwards'. He argued that in 2003 the Duma turned left, and in 2004 the president followed: 'The thing is that Putin always proceeds with anti-Putinist slogans. That is his essence, and people like this. Putin is politician number one because of his position, and Khodorkovsky is politician number 2, and not only because he is in jail.'[48]

Khodorkovsky's analysis was mostly pitched at a relatively high level of abstraction, but this was not the case when he discussed liberalism. Here he insists the failure is not that of the ideal but in the practices of its exponents. The attempt to combine a left programme with liberal right values, while unexceptional in principle, is a combination sought by numerous social democratic parties in Russia, with little popular success.[49] Ultimately hard choices have to be made, and although Putin was able to combine elements of both the left and right in his policies, his government was imbued with the principles of the market, rigorous macroeconomic stability, and international integration, although liberal political values were in part sacrificed. It was this missing liberal element that Khodorkovsky sought to provide. However, the character of his own liberalism could be questioned. In 1996 he suggested an alliance of Communists and liberals,

[44] 'Propisnye istiny', *Argumenty i fakty*, No. 32, 2005, p. 11.
[45] Titkov, *'Party Number Four'—Rodina*, pp. 30–1.
[46] Ibid., p. 38
[47] 'Vy gotovy k povorotu nalevo?', *Kommersant-Vlast'*, 8 August 2005, p. 5.   [48] Loc. cit.
[49] For an interesting discussion of the (poor) prospects of the Social Democratic Party of Russia, see Elena Rudneva, Anna Nikolaeva, and Alexei Nikol'skii, 'Gel'man podkhvatil znamya u Gorbacheva', *Vedemosti*, 4 August 2005, p. A2.

and it is not clear whether this entailed the cancellation of the elections. In 2003 he (or his associates) 'invested' in the CPRF, perhaps already having become disillusioned with the 'democrats' and 'liberals' (above all SPS and Yabloko), and in 2005 he fully turned to the left by suggesting that the coming to power of the CPRF and Rodina was inevitable (although it is not clear whether he was actually advocating this).

Khodorkovsky's relationship with leftist organizations was thus deeply paradoxical. His ability to communicate with a leftist electorate could not but be minimal although it was precisely to such an audience that he addressed this missive. He sought to resolve the conundrum in effect by advocating a programme of positive freedom, above all by advancing a socially based concept of justice, recognizing that the negative freedoms unleashed in the 1990s had betrayed deeply ingrained sensibilities. There was no contradiction in his view between freedom and solidarity. In that context, his support for both the left and the right in the 2003 parliamentary election made sense: only a left–right conjuncture could combine aspirations for democracy and social justice. Numerous surveys have confirmed this core combination of the Russian value system. As Lev Gudkov of the Levada polling agency put it, there had been no revolutionary transformation of Russia in the early 1990s; and instead Russia was engaged 'with the slow, very slow, generations-long decay of the Soviet system'.[50]

The very notion of 'justice' in late capitalist society appears anachronistic, although in populist terms it remains an effective slogan; while the idea of 'equality' implies a redistributionist agenda that in Russia would threaten the property rights that Khodorkovsky so eagerly sought to consolidate. The popular constituency for renationalization, the restoration of the full gamut of the social functions of the state, and the return to autarchic economic policies remains strong in Russia. Thus at the heart of Khodorkovsky's programme there lay a contradiction: the leftism that he saw as being able, almost magically, to transmute 'property as theft' into 'property as legitimate right' would unleash forces that would intensify the worst aspects of illiberal modernization while undermining its positive features. The combination of freedom and justice remains elusive.

ANOTHER LEFT TURN

Soon after the original 'Left Turn' article was published, Khodorkovsky through his lawyers apparently issued some of his sharpest criticisms of Putin to date:

The present Kremlin regime has exhausted itself, and its days are numbered. In place of the decayed and disintegrating Putinist system a new generation of leaders must emerge, thinking not of a shameful place at the nomenklatura's trough but of the fate of Russia in the third millennium.[51]

---

[50] *Khodorkovskikh chtenii*, 10 July 2007.   [51] *Kommersant-Vlast'*, 5 September 2005, p. 29.

Khodorkovsky positioned himself as the defender of human rights and social justice and champion of civil society in preparation for what he anticipated would be his election campaign in the by-election for the University Duma seat. Khodorkovsky had hitherto avoided such inflammatory language, providing measured critiques of Russia's situation, but beginning with his interview with a French journal at the beginning of autumn 2005, and again in his return to the themes of his 'Left Turn', the language became noticeably sharper and veered towards personal criticism of Putin.

Civil society and development

While waiting for the outcome of his appeal, the journal *Politique Internationale* conducted a wide-ranging interview with Khodorkovsky.[52] Asked about the development of civil society in Russia, he praised the role that the Russian people had played in history, including in the overthrow of communism in 1991: 'I totally disagree with the idea that Russian citizens are unable to be involved in politics. ... Civil society is just in its formative stages in Russia but it is developing much faster than the Kremlin would like it to do.' He warned, however, that the development of civil society was far from irreversible, and that 'if no infrastructure is created, we run the risk of losing the next generation. The best brains will leave Russia simply because intelligent, talented and ambitious people will not live in a country in which bureaucratic tyranny dominates, as it does today.' He then launched a broadside against the regime:

Putin's system definitely excludes any public development today. The system needs obedient actors, not creative people. Therefore, as long as Russia is under the reign of this regime, no real progress will be possible. ... Today absolutely everything—from railroad troops to days off in prisons—depends on the tastes, mood, complexes and quirks of one person. It is sufficient simply to take a look at those who hold key positions in the government: only people coming from Putin's 'narrow circle', who carry out the decisions of the Kremlin without caring about anything.

Asked about what system he would like to see, Khodorkovsky returned to his idea of a presidential-parliamentary republic. He then introduced a new theme, the development of 'true federalism', which included a return to the election of regional leaders to allow the development of 'new responsible regional elites', and he condemned the bureaucrats 'dropped in by air from Moscow', who only think about 'lining their pockets'.

In response to a question on the condition of opposition parties, he was scathing: 'Russian opposition parties of various tendencies are obviously in deep crisis today.' The main reason is that they were led not by 'political personalities', but what he called 'businessmen from politics': 'These alleged "oppositionists" are themselves part and parcel of the system.' This applied not only to LDPR leader

[52] The questions were posed by Grigory Raiko, *Politique Internationale*, 10 November 2005; http://www.mbktrial.com/about/mbk_11_10_2005.cfm.

Vladimir Zhirinovsky, hence there needed to be a 'modernisation of elites' that encompassed the opposition parties as well. This did not apply to all, he noted, '[b]ut still, it shows that the community of nominal opponents of the head of the Kremlin is as corrupted by cynicism and irresponsibility as the power structure itself'. Asked to specify which groups he would exclude, he made the astonishing claim: 'I think that serious opposition exists only in the political left wing where groups such as the Communist Party or Rodina are being developed. The right wing has disintegrated.' If free elections were held, these parties stood a chance of winning. He warned that 'the post-Putin power structure will be formed by a coalition', what he called 'liberal in the economic sense and left-wing in the social sense'. The coalition would be brought together by '[o]pposition to the corporation of irresponsible bureaucrats. This corporation has paralyzed the Kremlin and the whole political structure of the country. Like a giant parasite, it lives at the expense of the country's natural resources.' He once again asserted the prerequisite for the 'left turn' was the social democratic sympathies of the electorate:

As you know, this necessary turn was about to happen as early as 1996 when the CPRF candidate seemed to be winning the presidential election. Eventually, Boris Yeltsin's regime managed to hold its own, after mobilising all the resources it could. That caused enormous damage to the process of democratisation in the country.

In an interesting reprise of the determinism that paralysed the Second International, Khodorkovsky noted that the government's failures in social policy would stir up dissatisfaction: 'So, in fact, we don't need to do anything to create an influential opposition party—the Kremlin itself will foster its creation through its confused and unpopular policies thereby causing all people of good will, both on the "left" and "right" wings to rise up against it.' He went on to warn that Russia's reliance on natural resources was 'not just "risky", it is suicidal!' It would depress growth rates, inhibit the development of a post-industrial economy, and encourage the 'irresponsible and corrupt officials' in the much-vaunted 'power vertical'. It would ensure that the state administrative system, which was 'just a phantom of what a real administration should be', would continue to dominate, leading to 'stagnation and degeneration'.

On foreign policy Khodorkovsky's views were traditional, and indeed rather Putinite, insisting that 'Russia today does not have the resources necessary to be a world superpower', and while it should concentrate on being a regional power it should also try 'to become the political and intellectual leader of a group of countries that do not want to join the American or the Chinese bloc', a new incarnation of the defunct non-aligned movement. Europe was Russia's 'historical and cultural partner'; but the country should have no illusions about joining the EU soon: 'Russia feels comfortable where it is in the historical role of a natural keeper of the heartland and as a guidepost between Europe and Asia.' Russia should not join NATO but should develop friendly partnership with it, while developing its armed forces. As for the fundamental question about whether 'Western states should be tougher with President Putin', Khodorkovsky gave the wise answer:

Western leaders should deal with Putin while proceeding from the interests of their own countries that invested them with power. As far as Russia is concerned, it should solve its problems itself, mobilizing the creative potential of its people and not asking Western countries to become its sponsors, babysitters, or teachers.

Left Turn 2

The points made in the above article were developed in a second 'turn to the left' article this time written in jail and responding to the discussion elicited by 'Left Turn 1'.[53] The very existence of the article demonstrated that prison would not deter Khodorkovsky from continuing to engage in political debate. However, there is an almost unanimous consensus among even Khodorkovsky's strongest supporters that the article was 'awful and illiterate', allegedly reflecting his isolation from real life in prison.[54]

Khodorkovsky tried to answer the following four questions:

1. Are there effective contemporary opposition forces in Russia today with leftist or left-liberal views?
2. What is the practical economic programme of the 'left turn'?
3. Does the country have adequate human potential to ensure a left turn and the realization of its political and economic program?
4. Prisoner Khodorkovsky and comrades, do you really think that a change of power in Russia will relieve your fate?

He started with the final question, noting that the 2008 succession stimulated many to wish to be leader for what they could get out of Russia, but he insisted that the main question is what they could do for Russia. He admitted that Russia had given him a lot:

In the 1970s and 1980s, it gave me an education I can be proud of. In the 1990s, it made me the richest (according to Forbes) post-Soviet person. In this decade it took away my property and put me in jail where I had the opportunity to receive a second education, this time human and humane. And I can say that the people who are getting ready to run Russia in two and a half or three years must understand that the parasitic approach is no longer working. The country is no longer competitive and the reserves of stability [*prochnost'*] laid down by the Soviet Union have run out.[55]

It was clear that jail had not tempered his sense of irony. He then listed the major problems in Russia that would face Putin's successor in 2008: demographic decline; crisis in the engineering sector; a systemic crisis of the defence industries;

---

[53] Mikhail Khodorkovskii, 'Levyi povorot-2', *Kommersant*, 11 November 2005, p. 8; Mikhail Khodorkovskii, *Levyi povorot 2* (Moscow, Galleya-Print, 2006), p. 3.
[54] For example, Alexei Venediktov, author's interview, 19 June 2008, Moscow; a view shared by Irina Yasina, author's interview, 18 June 2008.
[55] Khodorkovskii, *Levyi povorot 2*, p. 4.

the ageing of the natural science base; the 'effective loss of Moscow's control over the North Caucasus'; 'the collapse of the Russian Armed Forces'; and the 'paralysis of the security system'. To deal with these tasks a new political group needed to come to power, with a long-term view of developmental tasks. This would have to be accompanied by a new, creative, mobilization of the people:

This can be achieved by a qualitative change in state and social policy, a rebirth of democratic methods of governing the country, including state paternalism as an instrument for unifying the state and the people, acknowledging that the state and economy exist for the people.... That is why a left turn is also necessary. To overcome the pathological, existential alienation between elites and the people, the authorities and those they rule. And not, as some theoreticians of 'Putin's stability' suggest, so that the opposition, winning the parliamentary elections, would let Khodorkovsky out of prison. Without overcoming that alienation, no integrated national idea is possible, and without a national idea, there will be no salvation or rebirth of the country. If people don't like the word 'left,' let them find another word. The essence of the turn does not change because of it.[56]

In the event the 2008 succession operation established a new–old leadership, with Medvedev as president and Putin as prime minister. Khodorkovsky once again insisted that a left turn in Russian politics was inevitable, and indeed, had started some time ago. The sooner this 'leftist energy' was incorporated into the system, the better, the more constructive and less dangerous it will be. If the current ruling elite is democratically transformed, we will have a peaceful transfer of power. If they delay it, and all the more so provoke the less responsible part of the elite to pursue an extremist scenario to justify their authoritarianism, the consequences for the country will be disastrous and absolutely unpredictable, and as for stability, post-industrial development and a worthy place in the world, these can be forgotten for a long time to come.[57]

He outlined a twelve-year plan, which he offered as the political and economic programme for the future leaders of Russia. He again talked of the institutional changes required, including the establishment of a presidential-parliamentary republic, the rebirth of genuine federalism, and a new item, the 'creation of genuine local self-government'. He provided details of how to deal with the problems he had listed earlier, including financial incentives to encourage larger families, a measure Putin announced in his state of the nation speech on 10 May 2006, and which the French had long practised, with little discernible effect. The fear of demographic decline was also one that exercised notable figures such as Solzhenitsyn. Khodorkovsky adopted a traditionally sinophobic tone in discussing the need to increase the population of the Russian Far East to prevent the Chinese occupying the territory. In broad terms, he advocated a range of measures that would achieve '[t]he transition from the economy of the oil pipeline to the knowledge economy'. One of the key goals of the programme was to ensure the '[p]reservation and strengthening [of] its present borders', by ensuring that investment was spread across the country. This would involve the reestablishment practically from scratch of the armed forces, and the development of education

[56] Khodorkovskii, *Levyi povorot 2*, p. 6.   [57] Ibid., p. 7.

and basic science. The funds for all this would come from a new tax regime, drawing on the Stabilisation Fund, a compensation tax from earlier privatizations (that would also have a legitimizing function), and increased budgetary revenues from economic growth.

He then once again turned to the question of legitimizing privatization:

It cannot be said that the privatisation of the 1990s was absolutely economically ineffective. Yes, many of the largest enterprises in Russia were sold for symbolic prices. But it should not be forgotten that the main goal of that privatisation was not the rapid filling of the exchequer from the sale of those companies, but the establishment of the institution of effective ownership. This task was completely fulfilled.[58]

He then described at length the changes that he had wrought at Yukos:

I remember what Yukos was like when I joined it in 1996. The company was in relatively satisfactory condition in comparison with other state oil giants. Nonetheless, oil production was falling by 15 per cent a year, debts to contractors amounted to about $3 billion, wages were six months in arrears and employees were either grumbling to themselves or complaining loudly, the stealing at every turn was frightful. When I left Yukos (in 2003), salaries had reached 30,000 roubles per month, there were no delays in pay and tax payments on all levels reached $3.5–4 billion per year, and that was when oil stood at $27–30 per barrel, and not $60 as now. Because of this same privatisation real management was established, which simply did not exist in the era of the 'red directors'.[59]

Although privatization improved corporate management, it was 'ineffective politically and socially', since the great mass of the Russian people considered it unjust. He now came up with a legitimating mechanism that he had not mentioned before, a 'windfall tax' on part of a company's turnover at the time of privatization, which was to be hypothecated for such tasks as stimulating the birth rate. On payment of the tax, the owners were to receive a 'safe conduct pass', and ownership would be considered legal and honest. This would be a 'conscious pact' between the state and owners of big business. As far as business was concerned, Khodorkovsky insisted that it was 'better to give up part today than everything tomorrow', and it would render the legitimization process open and immune to corruption. Khodorkovsky ended with a call for a 'genuine modernisation project', without which Russia would not be able to survive the new century: 'The outline of that project is already visible. There, just beyond the left turn.'

This missive, as with his earlier texts, revealed Khodorkovsky as a traditionally minded Russian patriot, as a man who cared deeply for his country and who was willing to stand up for policies that he felt were right, and who in a tone more of sadness than anger castigated the Putin elite for leading the country into stagnation. The elite in his view was venal and parasitic, but he was careful not to ascribe these qualities to Putin personally. Indeed, one can quite easily envisage Putin making much the same arguments, and in his castigation of the bureaucracy, which from 2005 became ever more severe, Putin echoed many of Khodorkovsky's arguments. This may well have been part of the problem, since in

---

[58] Ibid., p. 11.   [59] Loc. cit.

tone Khodorkovsky's letter appeared remarkably like a presidential manifesto. He considered himself a national policymaker, and with 'the era of big money' behind him, he was transformed from oligarch into new-leftist. Jail was not going to keep him out of politics, although in an attenuated form. The regime could not be sure of Khodorkovsky's intentions; but then, it was not clear that Khodorkovsky did either.

THE WORLD IN 2020

In 2007 an interesting collection of future-oriented essays was published, *The World in 2020*, with Khodorkovsky listed as the editor.[60] Three things are odd about the work. The first is that Khodorkovsky should have been willing to put his name to a book of this sort while in jail. The degree to which he was able to familiarize himself with the articles, or to play any role in shaping the work, is not clear. The second is that while the chapters avoided the catastrophism 'typical of Russian analytical society', as Khodorkovsky put it in his introduction,[61] the texts are imbued with a sense not just of the perils facing humanity, but that the specific peril is identified as neo-liberal globalization and Western neo-imperial hegemonism. For someone who had been so closely identified with the neo-conservative project in America, this was distinctly surprising. The third odd thing is that on the whole there is a very weak sense of Russia's role in the future, and thus the book is strangely without an active subject, and instead Russia is presented as being at the mercy of forces beyond its control.

In his introduction Khodorkovsky notes that on the whole the articles do not see any major changes in the world order: 'The USA will become a bit weaker, China a bit stronger, the struggle between civilisations will intensify, but on the whole the basic organisation of the world will remain much the same.' Khodorkovsky criticized this rather sanguine approach, noting that '[t]he absence of qualitative change in the last 14 years suggests that it is approaching rather than absent in the next 14 years.'[62] He noted that the United States will significantly weaken as the 'market regulator', giving rise to a 'new global balance'. Equally, he criticized the belief that some new technological breakthrough will offset the global decline in reserves of natural resources.[63] Above all, he argued that the very nature of stability would change and assume an ever more dynamic character, which he dubbed 'stable instability'. The key theme in all the chapters was the challenge of creating 'a fairer world order, allowing the majority consistently to improve their living conditions and perspectives'.[64]

Vladislav Inozemtsev, the editor of *Svobodnaya mysl'* (*Free Thought*), also noted the change in understanding the concept of 'manageability' in world affairs,

---

[60] M. B. Khodorkovskii (ed.), *Mir v 2020 godu* (Moscow, Algoritm, 2007).
[61] 'Predislovie nauchnogo redaktora', Khodorkovskii (ed.), *Mir v 2020 godu*, p. 6.
[62] Loc. cit.   [63] Ibid., p. 7.   [64] Ibid., p. 8.

discussing the major geopolitical shifts taking place.[65] We have quoted in Chapter 1 from Neklessa's chapter on the development of a postmodern world, in which America had raised the banner of freedom as the meaning and purpose of its existence. The article raised some thoughtful questions about the role of civilizations in the contemporary world, denoting new forms of social and political community that had been inadequately understood in the discourse of modernity. He pointed to the crisis of the nation state, and the syncretic nature of the notion of the 'dialogue of civilisations'.[66] Although the author recognized the 'transitory nature of all historical situations', the very notion of 'civilisation' suggests something fixed if not primordial. However, the search for a new overarching concept was something shared by those who favour the restoration of the notion of 'empire' to describe contemporary transnational power systems. The article by Tsimbursky was quite explicit about the role of civilizations, and their natural life cycle of rise and decline.[67]

Although Khodorkovsky may have welcomed the relative absence of catastrophism, the final chapters are imbued with a deep pessimism. Mikhail Delyagin presented his characteristic coruscating critique of Russian failings, above all to develop a competitive economy.[68] The next article pointed out the early twenty-first-century 'global chaos', accompanied by the onset of the elements of a new Cold War.[69] Egishyants talked of the world of 2020 as one of 'collapse and division',[70] while the final article in the collection took a highly sceptical view of democratism. Savelova argued that contemporary democracy was a theory of choice predicated on limited choice: 'The secret is that democracy is always managed, and democracy is always managed by someone.'[71] She also condemned the attempt to generalize Western principles as universal.[72] It is not quite clear whether Khodorkovsky subscribed to this view.

FREEDOM, THE MARKET, AND SOVEREIGN DEMOCRACY

A number of themes emerge from Khodorkovsky's various interventions in public debate, while at the same time there is a palpable sense of evolution. The early texts,

[65] Vladislav Inozemtsev, 'What Will Be?', in Khodorkovskii (ed.), *Mir v 2020 godu*, pp. 9–59, at p. 29.

[66] Neklessa, 'Bitva za novuyu zemlyu', pp. 73 and *passim*.

[67] Vadim Tsimburskii, 'Skol'ko tsivilizatsii? S lamanskim, shpenglerom i toinbi nad globusom XXI veka', in Khodorkovskii (ed.), *Mir v 2020 godu*, pp. 142–88.

[68] Mikhail Delyagin, 'Predstoyashchii mir: nekotorye bazovye tendentsii i trebovaniya k rossii', in Khodorkovskii (ed.), *Mir v 2020 godu*, pp. 233–68.

[69] Ruslan Saidov, Anton Surikov, and Valdimir Filin, 'Nachalo XXI veka—epokha global'nogo khaosa', in Khodorkovskii (ed.), *Mir v 2020 godu*, pp. 268–316.

[70] Sergei Egish'yants, 'Mir—2020: Kollaps i razdelenie', in Khodorkovskii (ed.), *Mir v 2020 godu*, pp. 317–26.

[71] Natal'ya Savelova, 'Demokratiya.net', in Khodorkovskii (ed.), *Mir v 2020 godu*, pp. 327–82, at p. 341.

[72] Savelova, 'Demokratiya.net', p. 355.

written before his sentencing, repeat the theme that the oligarchs and the Kremlin liberals in the 1990s were jointly responsible for the crisis of liberalism in Russia, although in different ways. Big business at the minimum had not been able to find the strength to withstand the neo-liberal approach. Quite how it could have done so is a matter that Khodorkovsky does not explore. In 'The Crisis of Russian Liberalism', 'Property and Freedom', and 'Left Turn 1' he stressed the enormous inequalities in wealth that had opened up in Russia, accompanied by his advocacy of a policy of state paternalism. In these he also talked about the need to legitimate the process of privatization, and by doing so to establish the foundations on which a secure private property regime could be established. The mechanism to achieve this legitimation remained rather vague, although he does suggest that a rotation of power and the coming to power of a leftist government would secure the political basis for a permanent settlement of the property question. At the heart of Khodorkovsky's writings is the belief that a new 'social contract' had to be forged between the authorities and the people, based on a paternalistic state run by a selfless and patriotic officialdom. Another part of the contract involved the operation of the market and its associated property rights regime; these had to be 'normalized', digested by the public as the only way to live. Khodorkovsky's focus was on the technical legitimation of the privatizations of the 1990s, but the deeper problem hinted at in his works is his fear that capitalism itself has not yet been accepted as legitimate by Russian public consciousness.

The ambiguities of Russian liberalism

The target of Khodorkovsky's critique was not only the corrupt and self-seeking bureaucracy of the Putin era, or the mistakes made by big business leaders in taking advantage of the weakness of the state in the 1990s, but also the liberals of that period and later. This critique of the right takes two forms. The first is of the economic liberals for the way they shaped the privatization process, and their lack of concern for the social consequences of their programme. The second prong of his critique focused on the inadequacies of the political liberals, the leaders of the various parties who had failed to connect with the people or to offer a viable programme. The partial exception is the Yabloko party. Mitrokin insisted that '[l]iberalism cannot enjoy any success or influence in Russia without recourse to the ideology of social justice', and hence had long ago understood what Khodorkovsky was now saying about 'Russia being a country with very strong left tendencies'.[73] Khodorkovsky, however, paid little attention to them, and instead placed his hopes on leftist forces, although this very much represented the triumph of hope over experience. It is not surprising that Khodorkovsky's interventions were greeted with little greater warmth on the liberal side of the political spectrum than they were by Kremlin functionaries. His position, however, is logical, if

[73] 'Propisnye istiny', *Argumenty i fakty*, No. 32, 2005, p. 11.

one accepts his structural argument about the need for the bourgeois business class to shake itself free not only from the era of criminal oligarchy, but also its subordination to political liberalism.

Khodorkovsky's letters are remarkably similar in tone to various public statements put out by Vladislav Surkov. In his *Delovaya Rossiya* talk on 16 May 2005 Surkov insisted: 'We will not allow a small group of companies to rule the country. As well as this small number of people another 140 million "poor relations" also live here. Their views also need to be taken into account.' In the same speech he insisted that the country needed a 'national elite', thinking not of Monte Carlo but of the country, the basis of a 'national bourgeoisie'. In that speech he insisted that Yukos had represented no threat to the Kremlin leadership, insisting that even if Khodorkovsky had been free the elections results (in December 2003 and March 2004) would have been exactly the same: 'This company represented no political threat', and he went on to report a conversation with Khodorkovsky: 'I told him that power, like love, cannot be bought. It was naïve to think that a few corrupt factions would make someone prime minister. He had some strange ideas.' He insisted that the Yukos affair, 'which was so heavy and unpleasant for us, has no crude political colouring. It was a combination of factors, as happens in life.' When asked about Surkov's speech, Khodorkovsky noted: 'I am in agreement with much of what Slava Surkov said', in particular the passage about 140 million average Russians, and 'I am glad that they have not yet jailed Surkov, and I hope that they won't jail him in the future'. He agreed that numerous factors had provoked the Yukos affair, and one of them was that Yukos had been worth $40 billion and was now burdened by debt: 'Indeed, you cannot buy people's love, but you can serve them. Not everyone achieves this.'[74]

By the time of 'Left Turn 1', however, the thinking begins to diverge significantly and indeed later assumes a directly polemical edge against the Kremlin. If we recall, Surkov spent the early 1990s working with Khodorkovsky, and they came out of a similar milieu. They were remarkably similar in their analysis of Russia's fate in the 1990s, and indeed in their evaluation of contemporary social realities. There were also some similarities in their prescriptions, with the state paternalism advocated by Khodorkovsky not incompatible with Surkov's sovereign democracy. The two could well be combined in some form of democratic sovereign state paternalistic regime. Khodorkovsky's strictures in 'The Crisis of Russian Liberalism' to Russian liberals to 'renounce the cosmopolitan understanding of the world', and that the liberal project in Russia 'can only exist in the context of national interests' echoes some of Surkov's sovereignty themes.

However, fundamental differences emerged when it came to the specific nature of the political system required to lead the country out of crisis. Surkov was unequivocal—the only force capable of doing so was a group of enlightened individuals using the state to achieve its developmental and sovereignty-enhancing goals. While both democracy and sovereignty, Surkov insisted, were important,

[74] 'Ya uveren, chto prigovor budet otmenen', *Vedemosti*, 4 August 2005, p. 5.

his thinking clearly prioritized the latter over the former. In his briefing to foreign journalists on 28 June 2006, on the eve of the G8 summit in St Petersburg, Surkov quoted from the foreign press of 1997 and 1998, describing Russia as riddled by criminality in economic life, cronyism in politics, and that 'Russia is not a democracy'. With Russia facing a barrage of criticism for alleged democratic backsliding, brought to the fore by its chairmanship of the G8, Surkov then made the point: 'This is how you and your colleagues viewed our country in the 1990s. This is what we are backpedalling from and this is what we will continue to backpedal from.' As a close aide to Khodorkovsky in the 1990s, Surkov knew whereof he spoke, and now advocated robust measures to ensure the defence of Russia's national interests and that the country would find its own way to democracy.[75]

Khodorkovsky was less clear about the nature of the desirable political coalition, although he was unequivocal that much of the existing Kremlin leadership had to be changed, and leftist forces brought in. It should be stressed that Khodorkovsky's leftism was more social than socialist, since his writings lack any detailed systemic critique of capitalist society, its class structures and its dynamics of class power, or any valorization of the working class or institutions such as trade unions. Much the same, it may be added, can be said about most of the left parties in Russia. From 'Left Turn 1' it was clear that he had in mind not just the CPRF but also Rodina and its successors. The latter is intriguing, since at the time he was writing Rodina had lost its leftist identity, with the social democratic Glaz'ev wing in the shade, and the Rogozin nationalist theme predominated. The tension between neo-leftist and neo-imperial tendencies is not even noticed in Khodorkovsky's writings.

Commentator on Russian politics

Facing a long prison sentence, Khodorkovsky warned the Kremlin that leftist forces would inevitably come to power—since only with the overthrow of the existing Kremlin establishment did he stand a chance of gaining freedom before the end of his term. Nonetheless, Khodorkovsky throughout was careful to distance himself from the radical anti-Putinists, which included not only Berezovsky, who in 2006 effectively advocated the overthrow of the constitutional order in Russia, but also his former colleague Nevzlin, who if not quite as radical as Berezovsky, was willing to entertain extreme measures to destroy Putin's regime. Khodorkovsky took a more measured approach, arguing that the left would come to power either as a result of elections or a popular revolution demanding social justice. Indeed, on the eve of the December 2007 elections Khodorkovsky condemned those who called for a boycott, arguing that this 'would only encourage the bureaucratic class to greater arbitrariness' and would be taken

---

[75] Natalia Melikova, 'Kreml' skazal vrazheskim SMI svoe tverdoe slovo', *Nezavisimaya gazeta*, 29 June 2006.

as a sign of popular apathy, and called for people to vote for smaller parties 'which did not inspire contempt'.[76] This was a clear call for people to support Yabloko and SPS, but Kasyanov People's Democratic Union, which had tried to stand, condemned Khodorkovsky's call as 'giving legitimacy to the forthcoming theatrical performance' and called for a boycott of the 'farce that are called Duma elections'.[77]

Surkov, as the main architect of the Kremlin's 'power vertical' in relation to social movements, worked assiduously to ensure that neither the communists nor the other leftist forces would come to power through elections, and following Ukraine's orange revolution toiled just as hard to ensure that no 'colour' revolution would take place either. Of course, while he could avert an 'orange-February' revolution, the danger according to irreconcilable opponents of Putin's regime was that Russia's next revolution would be of a 'red-brown-October' hue. The forces on which Khodorkovsky pinned his hopes for a Central European 'turn to the left' were in fact unreconstructed national-communists with a retrograde economic agenda based on neo-imperial yearnings. It is unlikely that if they came to power they would 'legitimate' the privatizations of the 1990s but would possibly start a populist redistributionist crusade. Rather than pinning his hopes on the left, Khodorkovsky could well have paid more attention to the development of an engaged but constrained middle class that in one way or another would be the foundation of liberal democratic values. His work with youth through Open Russia had not come to fruition, hence his turn to the left.

From jail Khodorkovsky released a steady stream of commentary on current affairs, providing a strategic perspective on current events and searching for a real national idea. For example, in an article for *The Economist* in late 2006 he predicted that 2007 would be decisive for the creation of a 'new world order'. The world in his view would be less 'Americocentric' as China emerged as a superpower, and the United States, Europe, and Russia would become 'hostages' to China. 'Sinification', in Khodorkovsky's view, was the main threat for Russia.[78] He returned to this theme in his first face-to-face interview since his arrest in October 2003, held in a courtroom in Chita on 6 February 2008. Facing a second trial, Khodorkovsky remained unbroken. In the ninth day of a hunger strike in support of his former colleague Aleksanyan, Khodorkovsky 'looked gaunt and drawn', but yet remarkable robust. At the time he was wading through some 200 pages of trial documentation a day. He feared that Russia's next president, Medvedev, would be unable to 'undo damage to the rule of law inflicted during the Putin era': 'It will be so difficult for him, I can't even imagine.... Tradition, and the state of people's

---

[76] 'Khodorkovskii prizyvaet golosovat' za malye partii', *Nezavisimaya gazeta*, 8 November 2007, p. 3.

[77] Mariya-Luiza Tirmaste, 'Mikhail Khodorkovskii nachal agitatsiyu', *Kommersant*, 8 November 2007, p. 3.

[78] Boris Popov, 'Iz glubiny sibirskikh rud', *Novye izvestiya*, 27 November 2006, p. 7; 'Mikhail Khodorkovskii—v stat'e dlya zhurnala the economis [sic]', *Moskovskii komsomolets*, 22 November 2006, p. 2.

minds, and the lack of forces able to [support] any movement towards the rule of law, everything's against him. So...may God grant him the strength to do it. All we can do is hope.' Khodorkovsky rejected the extreme views of some of his supporters, and, in the words of the reporter, 'did not share the concerns of some civil society and opposition leaders that democratic freedoms would continue to be eroded in Russia'. As Khodorkovsky put it: 'People can leave freely, the internet works.' It was just 'not possible' for Russia to return to the dark days of the Soviet past.

He argued that China's model of authoritarian modernization was inappropriate for Russia: 'I'm convinced that Russia is a European country, it's a country with democratic conditions which more than once have been broken off during its history, but nonetheless there are traditions.' He dismissed with contempt the charges against Yukos: 'The accusations are not connected with a real crime, but with a desire—the desire to take away people's conscience, the desire to convince a witness to give evidence. It's all about their various, conflicting desires.' He showed no bitterness about the break-up of Yukos, noting: 'I used up all my nerves in 2004, when a company that was working well was seized and handed over to Rosneft....Rosneft today is basically Yukos with a bit added on.' As for the conditions in which he was kept, he called them 'standard'.[79] He noted that he was treated better in Chita than in Moscow: 'Here the word "conscience" has not yet disappeared.' He refused to comment on rumours that he had embraced the Russian Orthodox faith: 'That's a complicated question. I have thought a lot about this. And I'd rather keep it to myself.' Despite the erosion of democracy and the rule of law, he remained optimistic about the country's future: 'It's a question of my personality. I can't provide a lot of arguments for and against but, on the whole, I'm optimistic.'[80] If at some point he changed from political commentator to political leader, this optimism would be invaluable.

Khodorkovsky refused to conform to stereotypes, but the effect of his various missives and other interventions is unclear. They certainly helped him to endure the long years of his imprisonment, and encouraged his associates and the 'dissident' wing of Russian politics, but they had a minimal impact on the shaping of policy. However, imprisonment endowed him with something of the character of a Soviet dissident, and assumed some of the characteristics of a prisoner of conscience, although Amnesty International refused to recognize him as a political prisoner, although it argued that his trial was politically motivated.[81] Like Becket, suffering bestowed him with the martyr's halo, a process encouraged by Khodorkovsky himself in his various interventions from prison. If in the Communist years Havel had argued that even a minor act of resistance could demonstrate 'the power of the powerless', this only applied when the public domain was monopolized by a single coercive authority. In post-communist Russia there was

[79] Neil Buckley, 'Khodorkovsky Still Defiant', *Financial Times*, 7 February 2008, p. 1.
[80] Neil Buckley, 'Unbowed in Face of "Absurd" Charges', *Financial Times*, 7 February 2008, p. 9.
[81] Anna Arutunyan and Oleg Liakhovich, 'Amnesty International: Khodorkovsky Not a Political Prisoner', *Moscow News*, 20 April 2005, p. 3.

a far more tumultuous Babel of discordant opinions, and Khodorkovsky's was a lone, brave but ultimately isolated voice. However, it is fair to say that '[t]he "Khodorkovsky affair" is gradually changing Russia. The longer the former co-owner of Yukos stays in jail, the higher the country holds him in esteem.'[82] It was far from clear whether he would be able to take 'the long walk to freedom' that led Nelson Mandela to the presidency of South Africa, but he had certainly taken the first steps.

[82] Nikolai Smorodin, 'Vtoroi srok khodorkovskogo', *Novye izvestiya*, 11 March 2005, p. 7.

9

Propaganda and Public Opinion

Such sweet release new freedom does beget,
When cherished bonds are shed without regret!
Shakespeare

The Kremlin was convinced that its poor image in the world, and the corresponding attempts to influence Russian domestic affairs by sponsoring 'democracy' through various support programmes, was the result of the distorted view put out by the media. As Putin aide Sergei Yastrzhembsky argued in 2001: 'Russia's outward image is...gloomier and uniformly darker compared with reality. To a great extent, Russia's image in the world is created by foreign journalists who work in our country.' An integral part of this conspiracy view of the world is that

the Western media are excessively influenced by anti-Kremlin oligarchs, such as Vladimir Gusinsky and Mikhail Khodorkovsky, who have spent hundreds of millions of dollars hiring Western public relations and lobbying firms. When former Kremlin Chief of Staff Aleksandr Voloshin was told of the Western media's negative reaction to Khodorkovsky's arrest, he is reported to have said: 'When Yukos' money dries up, so will these reports.'[1]

In response, the Kremlin tried to improve its image abroad by launching a number of initiatives. Khodorkovsky's defenders and the Russian government spent millions to advance their viewpoints. The effort was joined by a number of oligarchs in exile, notably Berezovsky in London, who now used his resources to discredit Putin's regime and to support its opponents.[2] The Yukos affair provided a powerful impetus to the construction of Russophobia abroad, while at home it served as a disciplinary mechanism over the media and political life in general. The casualty of this hubbub was the impartial presentation of facts and the search for unbiased truth. The propaganda struggle associated with the Yukos affair exposed deep problems in the contemporary public sphere, and not just in Russia.

---

[1] Julian Evans, 'Spinning Russia', www.foreign policy.com, posted November 2005; in *JRL* No. 9296, 16 November 2005, item 1.

[2] For a critical view, see E. M. Strigin, *Boris Berezovskii i londonskii shtab* (Moscow, Algoritm, 2006).

THE STRUGGLE FOR HEARTS AND MINDS

The Yukos affair had a powerful effect on the way that the international community viewed Russia, although the tangible effect on the economy and on international affairs is difficult to measure. While Khodorkovsky and Menatep mounted a powerful informational campaign in the West to discredit Putin's government and to garner support in defence of its interests, this on its own would have been far from sufficient to turn Western opinion against Russia. This was achieved by the substantive irregularities in the way that the case was pursued, which placed the spotlight on Russian internal developments. As Yury Rubinsky of the Institute of Europe in Moscow puts it: 'For the West, the start of the Yukos affair in 2003 was a major turning point. From this time on, the West began assessing Russia's domestic policy as unambiguously negative.'[3] Russia's presidency of the G8 in 2006, capped by the summit in St Petersburg in July of that year, was accompanied by siren voices in the West that Russia had no place in what was intended to be a community of leading democratic economic powers.

Media and propaganda

Of Russia's business leaders, Khodorkovsky had long been the one most attuned to developing a positive image in the West. Unlike most other oligarchs, from the first he was oriented towards building links with Western institutions. Menatep launched its first advertising campaign in 1989, and its advertising budget increased tenfold per annum into the 1990s. Surkov, who would be the archpriest of managed democracy in the Putin presidency, was involved in these early campaigns. His philosophy at that time and later was that there is no real freedom in the world, and that all democracies are managed democracies, so the key to success is to influence people, to give them the illusion that they are free whereas in fact they are managed. The only freedom in his book is 'artistic freedom'. Surkov published one of the first Russian texts on the use of political technology, which reflected his admiration for Lenin as a political technologist, and also as someone who in Surkov's view had saved Russia from disintegration, a feat repeated by Putin eight decades later.[4] In the 1990s Surkov worked with those who ruled Russia and he continued to do so in the 2000s, but in the earlier period it was economic elites who shaped the country, whereas in the 2000s the initiative had been regained by the political class.

Business conflicts in the 1990s were accompanied by struggles in the media. In that decade 'they [businesses] got accustomed to using journalists only to fight for profit through the shaping of public opinion'.[5] Already in 1994 Khodorkovsky

[3] Yury Rybinsky, 'Earning a Seat at the GB Table', *Russia Profile*, Vol. 3, Issue 5, June 2006, pp. 18–20, at p. 20.
[4] Author's interview with Dmitry Babich, who had interviewed Surkov in 1992 and on several later occasions, Khanty-Mansiisk, 5 September 2006. For Surkov's own views, see his *Teksty 97-07*.
[5] Panyushkin, *Mikhail Khodorkovskii*, p. 118.

spent millions of dollars on an advertising campaign for Menatep, buying whole pages in the *Wall Street Journal* and the *New York Times*. He hired the accounting company Arthur Andersen to audit the company's accounts, and issued ADRs through BONY.[6] In the early 1990s Nevzlin and Surkov were active in buying journalists.[7] Nevzlin also from an early date was active in ensuring that the activities of Menatep and Yukos were not presented in a dark light, if not daring at that point to think that a positive spin would be credible. To this effect, Nevzlin helped fund the publication of Alexander Korzhakov's memoirs of his association, as head of the presidential guard and earlier, with Yeltsin up to 1996, *From Dawn to Dusk*, and thus ensured that nothing nasty was said about Khodorkovsky and his associates in the book.[8] Nevzlin was responsible for Global Media, a subsidiary of Yukos, which 'bought the media in Siberia: in Tomsk, Krasnoyarsk and a number of other regions where Yukos had ... major business interests and therefore, where they had regularly to brainwash the population'.[9]

According to Golubovich, the precise figure spent by the Khodorkovsky conglomerate on media campaigns, sponsorship, and related activities was kept secret, but he estimated that up to the 1998 crisis it was in the region of $100 million a year. However, as part of the Yukos transformation campaign this increased threefold, with 10–12 per cent of that given as backhanders for those involved in the various campaigns.[10] In the three years up to 2003 Yukos and its associated companies spent between $270 million and $350 million annually on domestic lobbying,[11] and no less on its international campaigns. In his speech at Carnegie in Washington on 9 October 2003 Khodorkovsky was quite open about his strategy: 'Our lobbying activity is open, public and we consider it completely natural. It is far less developed than in the case of American corporations.'[12] He was also open about his vigorous attempts to block unfavourable reports. When the muckraking Kompromat.ru magazine devoted a special ninety-eight-page issue to the company called 'Who is Mr. X', a play on the first letter of Khodorkovsky's name in Cyrillic, the company got an order from the Khamovniki Court, based on an appeal from Kondaurov, to ban its distribution and sale. The journal covered every scandal associated with Yukos's rise, and it appears that Kondaurov sought to buy up the whole issue to prevent its distribution.[13] The issue could well have been another case of *zakazukha* (paid-for material, often masquerading as independent journalism), but whatever its provenance, its distribution would have dredged up dark stories of the past at a time when Khodorkovsky and Yukos were engaged in a remarkably effective PR campaign to clean up their image.

Yukos came late to becoming a press owner, having preferred to work behind the scenes with journalists. Already in 1995 Menatep had been one of the

---

[6] Khlebnikov, *Krestnyi otets Kremlya Boris Berezovskii*, p. 202.

[7] Tokareva, *Kto podstavil khodorskovskogo*, p. 169.   [8] Ibid., p. 38.

[9] Ibid., p. 78.   [10] Perekrest, 'Za chto sidit Mikhail Khodorkovskii', Part 4.

[11] Kononczuk, The *'Yukos Affair'*, p. 39.

[12] Mikhail Khodorkovsky, 'Civil Society and the Role of Business', www.ceip.org/files/events.asp?pr=2US$EventID=649.

[13] Catherine Belton, 'Court Bans Kompromat on Yukos', *Moscow Times*, 30 May 2003, p. 1.

shareholders in Channel 1, and had facilitated Berezovsky's takeover of 49 per cent of its shares in winter 1995, when the channel became ORT (Russian Public Television).[14] Nevzlin was a deputy director of the TASS news agency in 1997/8, and was part sponsor of *Literaturnaya gazeta* to 1997, and up to autumn 1998 remained part of the consortium owning ORT. Khodorkovsky had a 10 per cent stake in the 'Independent Media' publishing house, which owned *The Moscow Times*, *Vedemosti*, and some other periodicals, not all of which were Western-oriented, notably *Literaturnaya gazeta*. These three titles retained a robust independence from both the state and the oligarchs. The company's main effort initially went into developing the website Gazeta.ru, in which it invested up to $1.5 million a year, drawing on the expertise of its trainee journalists in the 'network structure' called 'School of Regional Journalists', one of the projects of Open Russia.[15]

Khodorkovsky followed in the path of Gusinsky and Berezovsky and began to build up a direct interest in the media. The company's main press outlet became the liberal weekly *Moscow News*, bought in 2003 for $2 million and owned by Yukos until mid-2005. The paper had been established in 1930 in English and from 1980 also published a Russian version. Despite promises made when he took over the paper, the veteran reporter and latterly editor, Viktor Loshak, was fired in September 2003 and Khodorkovsky appointed Yevgeny Kiselëv as editor, a refugee from the state's assault against NTV and TVS, where many of the independent journalists from NTV had sought shelter. Nevzlin took over the current management of the paper. Under the editorship of Kiselëv the paper became the main press defender of Yukos, although the quality of its journalism declined. Kiselëv proved a poor editor, provoking conflicts with most of his staff and sacking a number of its long-serving journalists, leading to the mass resignation of its oversight board.[16] The former editor of *Moscow News*, Sergei Roi, is scathing of this period:

I could, of course, outline here in sordid detail the sad story of *Moskovskie novosti*, that flagship of Perestroika, being bought by oligarch Khodorkovsky as part of his drive to buy up the 'commanding heights' of the entire political and media establishment (including, among other things, a majority of the Duma). That was the only time I, as editor of *Moscow News*, was 'stifled'—not by the Kremlin, mark you, but by oligarch Khodorkovsky appointees—and had to leave MN, after ten years of service.[17]

Most of the journalists on the paper were instinctive liberals and would have supported Khodorkovsky and Yukos in any case. Later, Nevzlin sold the paper to the Ukrainian media magnate Vadim Rabinovich, who in turn in October 2005 sold it to the Russian businessman Arkady Gaidamak, who appointed the veteran journalist Vitaly Tret'yakov as editor. From 1 January 2008 the paper changed its profile and became more of a business journal.

[14] Khlebnikov, *Krestnyi otets Kremlya Boris Berezovskii*, p. 159.
[15] Tokareva, *Kto podstavil khodorskovskogo*, p. 139.   [16] *Vedomosti*, 28 June 2005, p. A3.
[17] 'Untimely Thoughts Weekly Russia Experts Panel: How Free is Russia's Media?', introduced by Peter Lavelle, 9 June 2006, in *JRL*, No. 134, 2006, item 6. Roi describes the case in detail in his article 'The Splendor and Misery of the Russian Press', on Intelligent.ru.

Property redistribution was accompanied, in Tokareva's words, by a 'great informational war'. The struggle over Yukos, in her view, was the largest of all the wars, and thus '[f]rom March 2003 the authorities began to undermine Yukos, and Yukos—the authorities', and this was accompanied by the publication of an enormous amount of *zakazukha* in the media.[18] With vast resources available to be spent on various campaigns, the Yukos affair was seldom out of public consciousness. The tone was already set by Khodorkovsky's ability not only to improve the governance of Yukos, but then to sell the undoubted achievement to a wider public as a Damascene conversion. As the assault against Yukos began, Khodorkovsky and his supporters sought to portray the case as a return to Russia's authoritarian traditions, if not the restoration of Soviet totalitarianism; and to this end they played on the fears of the West and of Russian liberals about the dangers of an authoritarian restoration.

Khodorkovsky was a masterful propagandist, able to employ a variety of instruments to ensure that the required message got through. His opponents suggest that much of what was portrayed as philanthropic activity was pursued in a cynical and exploitative manner. For example, funding for the Institute of Applied International Relations was cut even before his arrest, and the argument is made that it had simply been used as an instrument to advance his political ambitions, and dropped brusquely when no longer required.[19] However, media representatives flatter themselves and exaggerate their power when they argue that 'Khodorkovsky as a politician is as much a PR product as Putin was at first'.[20] One reason for the failure to cut a deal with the authorities is the way that Yukos decided to fight the case. As Woodruff stresses, Khodorkovsky 'sought no compromise on the business issues at the root of the conflict', and 'worked tirelessly to turn the Procuracy's campaign into a political issue, presenting it as a battle over the independence of civil society from legal arbitrariness'.[21] From the first Khodorkovsky sought to politicize the conflicts with the Kremlin, and the Kremlin responded in kind. In this battle of the giants, the independence of the courts was left trampled underfoot. As have seen, one aspect of the political struggle was Khodorkovsky's various interventions in public debate.

Public relations

Public relations were handled on behalf of Yukos by Nevzlin, and even after his flight to Israel in late 2003 he continued to wage a fierce anti-Putin campaign. At the turn of the millennium Khodorkovsky hired the public relations company Burson-Marsteller to improve the company's image, but he was soon dissatisfied

---

[18] Tokareva, *Kto podstavil khodorskovskogo*, p. 84.
[19] Author's interview with HE Vadim Lukov, Russian ambassador to Belgium, 20 September 2007, Brussels.
[20] Tokareva, *Kto podstavil khodorskovskogo*, p. 85.
[21] Woodruff, *Khodorkovsky's Gamble*, p. 2.

and tore up the contract with them.[22] Between 1999 and 2004 the Norwegian journalist Hugo Erikssen was head of Yukos's International Information Department.
He became Yukos's public face for the international media, while the management of domestic public relations was handled by Roman Artëmev, but relations
between the two became increasingly difficult.[23] Erikssen was extremely effective
in portraying Yukos as a transparent and open company. One of his methods was
the publication of a glossy English-language corporate journal. The domestic PR
campaign, headed by Artëmev, was on a much lower level and far less successful.

In Chapter 2 we mentioned that Yukos hired APCO Worldwide as its public
relations company. Based in Washington, D.C., and with offices across the world,
APCO is a 'global communications consultancy specializing in building relationships with an organization's key stakeholders', as its website puts it.[24] Its international advisory council contains a roster of former diplomats and politicians.
Those dealing with Russia include William Hartman, a former US ambassador
to the Soviet Union for five years from 1981, the former US Congressperson Don
Bonker, who serves on the board of the Foundation for US–Russia Business Cooperation, and A. Elizabeth Jones, a former assistant secretary for Europe and Eurasia
in the State Department in which she helped shape American policy towards
NATO and European Union countries, Russia, Ukraine, the Caucasus, and Central
Asia. The company advised Norilsk Nickel on its acquisitions strategy in America,
introducing the company to decision-makers in Washington and in the regions. Its
work with Yukos is not listed on its website. APCO is particularly well-networked
with the US Congress, and the latter has held a number of hearings on the Yukos
case. People affiliated with APCO have played a prominent part in shaping the
debates.

Charles Krause, a senior vice president of APCO Worldwide, was closely
involved in the Yukos campaign, and has written material with Robert Amsterdam. His work focused on media relations and strategic communication for governments, international agencies, and corporate clients. Before joining APCO in
2000, Krause was a foreign correspondent, reporting from Latin America, Europe,
Asia, and the Middle East for *The Washington Post*, CBS News, and public television's national news programme, The NewsHour with Jim Lehrer. At the time
of the Yukos affair APCO was handling the company's international PR strategy.
The company opened its Moscow office 1989, and from 2000 'the office has helped
clients communicate more effectively with the news media and the public and has
assisted Russian companies in developing and implementing corporate position-
ing programs in the United States and Europe'.[25] Many of APCO's employees in
Russia were former journalists, and the company was thus particularly adept at

---

[22] Panyushkin, *Mikhail Khodorkovskii*, p. 149. They continue, however, to work with Robert Amsterdam.

[23] Tokareva, *Kto podstavil khodorskovskogo*, pp. 139–41.

[24] http://www.apcoworldwide.com/content/overview/index.cfm.

[25] http://www.apcoworldwide.com/content/locations/emea/russia/index.cfm.

ensuring media coverage and access to decision-makers. It claims to be able to place 150 news mentions of clients a month as well as 100 analytical articles.[26]

Erikssen resigned from Yukos in December 2004, reportedly after disputes with the new management, and after working as a freelancer moved to the Mmd corporate, public affairs, and public relations consultants. Mmd established their office in Moscow in 1999 and under their regional director Stephen Lock in November 2005 won the tender to manage Rosneft's public relations and investor relations activities, and the group successfully placed Rosneft's IPO on the London market in 2006.[27] By 2007 the company had a dedicated Rosneft International Communications department, supported by its Eurasia Strategies Group, with a team of nine people handling all aspects of Rosneft's international communications, including coordinating PR in London and public affairs consultants in Brussels and Washington DC. This division, as its website puts it, 'is led by one of the most experienced professional communicators working in Russia today', none other than Erikssen.[28]

One of the most ardent fighters of the Yukos cause is Robert Amsterdam, a partner of the law firm Amsterdam & Peroff, and international counsel to Khodorkovsky. Amsterdam plays a special role in the Yukos story, if only because of the tenacity with which he brought the Khodorkovsky case to the attention of world public opinion. He engaged in an endless round of meetings with international human rights organizations, academic gatherings, and public sessions to argue the injustice of the Yukos affair. He attended some of the sessions of the Meshchansky court, and thus was able to see first-hand the substance of the case. Ostensibly no more than a lawyer, in fact he was one of the leading activists on behalf of Yukos in its propaganda campaign. He was willing to comment on issues that ranged far from his supposed brief.[29] His blog on Russian affairs became a byword for hostile reporting on Russia, although his own views were nuanced and he has been courageous in the tenacity with which he has fought for justice for the victims of the Yukos affair. Amsterdam took the view that the best form of defence was attack. On 8 November 2007, for example, he wrote: 'Putin is dismantling the cold war settlement. The first was YUKOS. Emboldened by the lack of reaction, he proceeds cautiously with the [CFE] moratorium.'[30] He was particularly exercised by the role played by the former German chancellor, Gerhard Schroeder, as head of the North Stream pipeline consortium, which sought to diversify connections by building a pipeline along the bed of the Baltic from Vyborg to Greifswald in Germany, as well

[26] *Razdvigaya granitsy kommunikatsii* (Moscow, APCO, no date), p. 6; http://www.apcoworldwide.com/content/PDFs/moscow_brochure.pdf.
[27] Yuriy Humber, 'Ex-Yukos Press Chief Switching to Rosneft', *Moscow Times*, 15 November 2005, p. 5.
[28] http://www.mmdcee.com/russia/, last accessed 8 November 2007.
[29] In a letter, for example, he wrote: 'The level of state theft and corruption in Russia is unparalleled in its history. Putin's regime has overseen the destruction of freedom of the press, created a new generation of political prisoners and made a mockery of the rule of law.' He cited a World Bank report 'which placed Russia on par with Zimbabwe in terms of governance standards', *The Guardian*, 22 September 2007, p. 37.
[30] http://www.robertamsterdam.com/.

as the part played by German companies in Russia's development. Deutsche Bank was a leading consultant to Gazprom, while BASF was jointly exploring the giant Yuzhno-Russkoe gas field in Siberia with Gazprom. Schroeder had argued that the Yugansk auction was 'an internal affair', in response to which Amsterdam accused him of ignoring problems in Russia to gain favours from Putin's government: 'Germany is a critical battleground as the German government has sold out its commitment to the rule of law.'[31] Amsterdam tried to portray this activity as capitulationism to authoritarianism, and thus perpetuated Cold War thinking about Russia.

Media and martyrdom

We have noted that after his arrest Khodorkovsky issued a number of reports and epistles from jail. Here we will focus less on their intellectual content than on their political role. On 31 August 2005 his press centre issued an address to the public, a day after the initiative group had been established to advance his candidacy for the by-election in the University district of Moscow. It was clear from this appeal that Khodorkovsky was quite serious about standing as an MP, and he stepped up the struggle against the government: 'The present Kremlin regime has exhausted its potential, and its days are numbered. To replace the decaying and disintegrating *Putinishchina* [Putin system] must come a new generation of leaders, thinking not of their ignominious place in the nomenklatura feeding trough, but of the fate of Russia in the third millennium.'[32] The tone was different from the other letters, which had been philosophically reflective and consensual. Disappointment with the authorities had now turned into contempt and anger.

Soon after Khodorkovsky's arrival in the prison colony in Siberia the Menatep-Yukos media campaign moved into full gear. In a paid article taken out in the *Financial Times* on 2 November 2003, which was widely reported by other media, Khodorkovsky appealed above the head of the Russian government and citizenry to the international community. He noted: 'The Kremlin tried to isolate me completely from the country and people, as well as to destroy me physically. . . . The authorities demonstrated that they are not ready for open and honest argument with me (and in general to direct discussion with the genuine opposition).' In his view: 'The struggle is only beginning.' The subject of this struggle, in his view, was the programme for Russia's development in the twenty-first century. The armed forces and security apparatus needed to be thoroughly reformed, as did the bureaucracy, and the disastrous decline of Russia into a 'raw materials appendage' had to be reversed by development of the knowledge economy. Special attention had to be paid to the Far East and Siberia which 'in only a few years could find

---

[31] Catherine Belton, 'Putin Says He Knows Mystery Buyer', *Moscow Times*, 22 December 2004, p. 1.

[32] Liliya Mukhamed'yarova, 'Khodorkovskii snimaet masku: Vpervye uznik "Matrosskoi Tishiny" otkryto zayavil o namerenii borot'sya s rezhimom, "dni kotorogo sochteny" ', *Nezavisimaya gazeta*, 1 September 2005, p. 1.

itself under China's control'.[33] For the first time Khodorkovsky gave voice to his fears that he could be killed, combined with his characteristic generalization of his condition to comment on the state of Russian politics and world affairs.

At the same time, Khodorkovsky was well aware that he could become a hostage to the frenzy around his name, and thus instead of the media campaign advancing his interests and those of his company, 'brand Khodorkovsky' could become a tool used in the interests of others, notably the hard right in America, and even by his former colleagues, notably Nevzlin. On more than one occasion Khodorkovsky condemned attempts to take his name in vain, and warned Nevzlin in particular not to turn him into 'a flag for political projects'. Asked to comment on Nevzlin's various declarations in early May 2005, Khodorkovsky recognized the right of anyone in a free society to comment, 'but he [Khodorkovsky] retains the right to decide independently whether to comment or not on political events'.[34]

Public opinion

The impact of Khodorkovsky's political interventions was rather less than the effort expended. The target of most of the propaganda work was interested elites in Russia and the West. As for its effect on Russian public opinion, this at best was marginal. One-fifth was aware of Khodorkovsky's comments on Russian liberalism in April 2004, a large proportion in Russian conditions, but two-thirds considered that he used the article to exonerate himself from responsibility.[35]

In the summer of 2003 the *Ekho Moskvy* radio station conducted a virtual presidential contest of its radically inclined listeners, setting Putin against Khodorkovsky: the latter came in with over 70 per cent support.[36] Another poll on the eve of the December elections saw Khodorkovsky win with over 80 per cent of the virtual vote.[37] However, this was a select target audience: the population at large was consistently less forgiving of Khodorkovsky and the reputation of his companies, determined in part by the trauma of the 1990s. As late as 2007, 37 per cent of the population called for the return to the state of assets privatized in that decade while over a third considered that they had lost more than they had gained out of the reforms. These views were not confined, as could have been expected, to the older generation. Asked how they had adapted to current conditions, 29 per cent stated that they had to work non-stop to survive, while a further 22 per cent accepted that they could not maintain former living standards.[38] Against

[33] The article was published on the Khodorkovskii press centre website on 27 October 2005, and discussed in detailed by Liliya Mukhamed'yarova, 'Khodorkovskii obratislya k mirovoi obshchestvennosti', *Nezavisima gazeta*, 3 November 2005, p. 2.

[34] Arkadii Putilin, 'Khodorkovskii Nevzlinu teper' ne tovarishch', *Rossiiskie vesti*, 11 May 2005, p. 3.

[35] Survey conducted by ROMIR 15–20 April 2004, 1,610 respondents in 106 towns and villages, Anfisa Voronina, Vitalii Ivanov, 'Khodorkovskii priblizilsya k narodu', *Vedemosti*, 23 April 2004.

[36] Yur'ev, *rezhim putina*, p. 108.

[37] Dmitrii Yur'ev, 'Oranzhevye polittekhnologii ukrainy: Upravlenie svobodoi', in *Rossiya i 'sanitarnyi kordon'* (Moscow, Evropa, 2005), p. 51.

[38] Polls conducted by Levada Centre, reported by Yulia Mironova, *Izvestiya*, 16 August 2007.

the background of a decile coefficient of 15 (comparing the incomes of the top and bottom 10 per cent), when anything above 10 is usually a sign of a society under strain, these results demonstrate just how deep the refusal to forgive and forget the results of privatization, even though society is now built on precisely this transformation.

From the beginning the Levada Centre tracked views on the Yukos affair. In October 2003, 26 per cent thought it was connected with the financial manipulations of the company's leaders and had nothing to do with politics, while 18 per cent considered it was the outcome of conflict between political clans.[39] Asked about Khodorkovsky's arrest, 5 per cent greeted it with joy, 28 per cent with satisfaction, 19 per cent with bewilderment, and only 6 per cent with concern and 3 per cent with worry, and 1 per cent with terror, while 38 per cent had no views. Actions against Gusinsky in July 2000 were considered by 46 per cent as the restoration of order in the economy and its purging of criminals, while in November 2003, 41 per cent thought the same in relation to Khodorkovsky.[40] Asked earlier why the authorities had picked on Yukos, 40 per cent thought it was because the company was worse than others in terms of financial misdemeanors, while 34 per cent thought it was because the company's leader had upset the authorities.[41] Asked whether the actions leading to Yukos's bankruptcy were legal or arbitrary, in September 2004, 24 per cent considered them legal, while 13 per cent considered them arbitrary, while the plurality (28 per cent) considered the actions legal in form but arbitrary in essence. At that time 33 per cent considered the trials of Khodorkovsky and Lebedev 'fair, objective and impartial', while 30 per cent disagreed, and 37 per cent had no view.[42]

The Kremlin's tightening grip over the economy met with popular approval. Nearly half the population supported increased state control over the economy and business. Some 47 per cent called for greater state interference, while 28 per cent approved of the existing balance. Only 16 per cent favoured greater freedom for business and a free-functioning market economy.[43] As for Khodorkovsky himself, half in October 2005 agreed that Khodorkovsky had not been broken by his tribulations. Asked about the results of the Yukos affair, 16 per cent thought that it had brought order to relations between business and the state, 20 per cent that it had raised Putin's authority and restored the principle of social justice, but 16 thought it had frightened business and damaged the investment climate, and 15 per cent that it had discredited the authorities, who had used the law as an instrument of struggle against an opponent. An astonishing 46 per cent disagreed

[39] Poll conducted 21–24 May 2004, 1,600 respondents, http://www.levada.ru/press/2004052701.html.

[40] Poll conducted 24–28 October 2003, 1,600 respondents in forty regions, http://www.levada.ru/press/2003102901.html.

[41] Poll conducted 21–24 May 2004, 1,600 respondents, http://www.levada.ru/press/2004052701.html.

[42] http://www.levada.ru/press/2004101302.html. The whole range of Levada polls can be found at http://www.khodorkovsky.ru/society/891.html.

[43] VTsIOM poll, 15 November 2005.

with the proposition that the state was right to persecute people and organizations that supported Khodorkovsky, while only 23 per cent favoured such measures.[44] Soon after his arrival in Chita a poll found that 28 per cent considered that such a distant location was chosen to hinder his public activity, while a further 15 per cent thought it was to frighten him. Asked whether people sympathized with him, the same poll found that 57 per cent said no, while 20 per cent tended towards sympathy, while 23 per cent had no view on the question.[45]

RUSSIA'S IMAGE AND FOREIGN POLICY

The Yukos affair revealed some deep behavioural patterns. The Russian authorities undoubtedly dealt with Khodorkovsky and the Yukos company in a high-handed and brutal manner. However, the affair, as we have suggested above, was more than the arbitrary expropriation of one company and the persecution of some its associates. The Yukos affair ultimately helped shape a certain image of Russia abroad that had grave consequences for the conduct of foreign policy, helping shape the policy of others towards Russia, and thus structured international politics in the first years of the twenty-first century. The Yukos affair brought to the surface deep layers of an immanent Russophobia among sections of the Western political elite, and in a distinctive way reprised the late nineteenth-century delegitimation of Russia as a state, reflected in the lack of respect for Russian state interests. The legitimacy of the regime was called into question by Polish insurrectionists following failed uprisings in 1830 and 1863/4, and later by various waves of emigration with unpleasant tales to tell of conditions in Tsarist Russia. In the Soviet era Menshevik émigrés and others also helped shape perceptions, attacking not only Soviet communism but also the alleged deficiencies of the Russian national character that had allowed the Bolsheviks to come to power.

Yukos and orange technologies

In his typically pithy way, Goyal makes a point that is widespread in Russia:

There has been uncontrolled hysteria over the Yukos scandal around the world. Much of it smacks of Russian oil money spent by an enormously rich public-relations machine. Few have asked the pertinent questions: How did Yukos and the rest of the oligarch-run natural-resource behemoths get their start? How did the assets of the Soviet state fall into the hands of a dozen or so men? How have assets been laundered abroad? How, indeed, has Russia been robbed over the last decade? And can this stolen property be allowed to be sold unchecked? This is a story that may have been forgotten by the editorial page of the *Wall*

---

[44] Poll conducted 14–17 October 2005, 1,600 respondents in forty-six regions, http://www.levada.ru/press/2005111002.html.

[45] Poll conducted 21–24 January 2006, 1,600 respondents in forty-six regions, http://www.levada.ru/press/2006020705.html.

Street Journal, but not by the majority of Russians. Oligarchs may be getting sympathy, hurrahs and refuge in the West, but they are loathed at home, living terrified lives and waiting until they can cash out.[46]

He stresses that 'if Khodorkovsky and his fellow oligarchs were to sell large stakes in their natural-resource companies to foreign firms, Russia would be reduced to a colony of Western powers', and he made the paradoxical assertion: 'The Yukos scandal is not about going backwards towards renationalization—it's about how Russia can move forward to build a vibrant, free and fair market economy'; and on the political level the corollary was: 'The actions taken against Yukos are also not an attack on democracy—Putin's government has accrued many such misdeeds in the last three years, but this is not one of them. By no stretch of the imagination does Yukos have anything to do with Russian democracy.'[47]

Sergei Markov, selected to be one of the founding member of the Public Chamber in November 2005 and elected a United Russia MP in December 2007, insisted that the oligarchs 'seeking to take revenge' were funding an orange revolution in Russia, notably Boris Berezovsky who 'while being a British citizen, still remains a Russian politician'. He noted that Mikhail Khodorkovsky, 'who is serving his sentence yet remains an active Russian politician. This is often described as "internal emigration". He has ambitious projects a lot of money, and that works.' He also mentioned Nevzlin as a member of group looking for revenge. Any shift towards a parliamentary republic would find the political parties under oligarch control, as in Ukraine. The new strategy, according to Markov, was to assert the need for justice, as Khodorkovsky had done in his 'Left Turn' missives from jail, and thus an implicit alliance with left forces, above all the Communists, was taking shape. If the regime attempted to impose another reform of the type of the monetization of social benefits, which in early 2005 had provoked widespread protests, 'left forces will destabilize the situation, while oligarchs would employ those "orange" technologies. The scenario is clear.'[48] Fear of an orange alliance of oligarchs and the left in part explains the lack of substantive reform in Putin's second term as well as the regime's obsession with controlling social and political life.

The regime's fears, while exaggerated, were not lacking in substance. There had been at least three major political-propaganda wars in post-communist Russia. The first in 1997 saw Berezovsky and Gusinsky pitted against the 'young reformers', which turned into a struggle over the Svyazinvest auction; the second in 1998 saw the same two fighting Kirienko's government, accompanied by the 'rail war'; and in 1999/2000 the family and Berezovsky turned their guns against Luzhkov, Gusinsky, and Primakov.[49] Even though he was a beneficiary of the latter, Putin's 'equidistancing' policy was quite explicit about its attempt to prevent a recrudescence of such sordid episodes. The idea of an independent public opinion was discounted and instead the regime, as its opponents had done earlier,

---

[46] Goyal, 'Analysis: Sale of a State', p. 11.   [47] Ibid., p. 12.

[48] Press conference with Sergei Markov at *Argumenty i fakty* press centre, 16 November 2005; in *JRL*, No. 9299, 19 November 2005, item 15.

[49] Yur'ev, *rezhim putina*, p. 104.

simply saw a blank space susceptible to manipulation. This tendency became ever stronger as the Putin regime became consolidated, and was given a massive boost by what they considered to be the application of 'colour technologies' in Ukraine in late 2004. Indeed, it is suggested that the 'orange' brand was created by Khodorkovsky's Open Russia in 2002, and was then tested in Georgia in late 2003.[50] The struggle against orangism became an obsession in Putin's second presidential term, against the background of the looming succession in 2007/8.

To interpret Putin's enduring popularity, which seldom fell below 70 per cent throughout his two-term presidency, however, as simply a result of manipulation would be a gross mistake. In 1999/2000 he was able to keep the oligarchs on board while simultaneously presenting himself as the embodiment of popular aspirations because of his appeal to an ideal that transcended both: the aspiration for a period of 'normality', which could be interpreted by all constituencies in a manner that they saw fit.[51] Relations with the oligarchs within this framework could be constructed on the basis of '[h]e who is not against us is with us', whereas Khodorkovsky simply refused to operate within the logic of Putin's normalization agenda, and did not wish even passively to be associated with the regime, and thus the reverse logic of all *dirigiste* systems came into operation: 'Those who are not with us are against us.'[52] Berezovsky and Gusinsky had fallen victim to this logic earlier, but Khodorkovsky's challenge was far more profound. He was not just interested in advancing his business interests by active investment in the political process, but began to set himself up as a source of independent moral authority and the educator of a new generation of citizens. With the support of a skilled media team, he began to shape the terms of debate, dubbing his opponents the 'Putin *siloviki*', while he cast himself as the defender of liberal freedoms. The merger with Sibneft and the transationalization of the joint company as a global player, moreover, would have constrained Russia's foreign policy, setting off alarm bells throughout the Kremlin, which rang with particular intensity when he began to talk of Russia's nuclear disarmament.

Sergei Naryshkin in June 2005 noted that the Yukos affair had broad resonance in the international business community: 'We must acknowledge that the events around Yukos have influenced the Western business community's perceptions on activities in Russia. We want these things to happen as rarely as possible, and I hope this will be the last.'[53] While the Yukos affair was in part a struggle between powerful elite interests, it both revealed and shaped public discourse. In Russia it confirmed the view of many that the Cold War struggle had not ended but only taken new aspects, in particular in the form of information wars. According to one study, geopolitical struggles are largely won or lost in the sphere of 'information wars', and Russia was beginning to undermine Anglo-American hegemony in this

---

[50] Yur'ev, rezhim putina, p. 246, n.   [51] Ibid., p. 130.   [52] Cf. ibid., p. 131.

[53] Sergei Naryshkin, speaking at a Russian–French business event, Paris, 3 June 2005, *Moscow Times*, 26 October 2007, p. 1.

sphere in an arc of territory stretching from Egypt to China, something that could take state form in the creation of 'Eurasian Rus'.[54]

Commenting on the Russian campaign in an interesting discussion chaired by Vladimir Frolov for *Russia Profile*, Eric Kraus, of Nikitsky Russia/CIS Opportunities Fund, noted:

> The attempt to build up Russia's political image among the Atlantic Alliance is doomed in advance. Arrayed against it are all of the media hacks Menatep can buy, a very professionally orchestrated campaign of disinformation centered around Khodorkovsky's lawyer, Robert Amsterdam, and the huge influence and money of the Washington neo-con faction, self-righteously angry at those upstart Russians who dared to question the moral superiority of the superpower.[55]

Russia responded to Western strategies of advancing its interests through various forms of 'soft power' by entering the same competitive struggle for influence and advantage. Soft power is but a milder form of hard power, but exercised within the same competitive logic. Indeed, soft power habituates the powers to operating in manner that prepares the ground for the necessary hard power interventions.

The Kremlin fought back in what it saw as an information war in a number of ways. According to Peter Finn, Russia developed an increasingly sophisticated and well-funded campaign to 'to build and project to the world an image of a country where the economy is booming and democracy is developing'.[56] The idea was to counter what was perceived to be 'unrelenting and unfair Western criticism' of Putin's administration. To this end funds were pumped into various forms of public diplomacy, including new media ventures, foundations to promote Russian culture and language, conferences to air the Russian view of world affairs, and the creation of international NGOs to monitor Western standards of democracy. The Kremlin hired the American public relations firm Ketchum, and in April 2005 established the twenty-four-hour English-language TV station 'Russia Today'. The government only now was catching up with what Khodorkovsky had recommended in 2002, when he had advised the RUIE to create an English-language website and for a major international campaign to improve the country's image.[57] The RIA Novosti information agency, headed since early 2004 by Svetlana Mironyuk, sponsored the publication of the *Russia Profile* journal and the associated news and analysis website, which provided some of the most balanced analysis of Russian affairs. From 2004 a group of Western academics and journalists were invited each year to meet leading Russian politicians and scholars within the framework of the International Valdai Discussion Club.[58] The Russkii Mir foundation was established under the leadership of Vyacheslav

[54] I. N. Panarin, *Informatsionnaya voina i geopolitika* (Moscow, Pokolenie, 2006).
[55] 'Russia Profile Weekly Experts Panel: An Investment of Diminishing Returns?', *Russia Profile*, 14 March 2008; reproduced in *JRL*, No. 57, 2008, item 39.
[56] Peter Finn, 'Russia Pumps Tens of Millions into Burnishing Image Abroad', *Washington Post*, 6 March 2008.
[57] Editorial, 'Missiya Khodorkovskogo', *Vedemosti*, 8 February 2007.
[58] I should declare an interest, having participated in the Club from the beginning.

Nikonov to distribute grants amounting to $20 million a year to unite the scattered Russian communities abroad, what we call 'Russonia' by analogy with the international Polish community, Polonia. In 2008 the Institute for European Democracy was established in Paris, headed by the former Rodina Duma member Natalia Narochnitskaya. It would gather evidence of human rights violations in EU states, and advance the Russian view of sovereignty and democracy. In New York the Institute for Democracy and Cooperation was established to develop civil society and democracy, headed by the political commentator Andranik Migranyan. A National Information Centre was opened in Moscow funded by private donations to provide a forum for foreign and domestic journalists, politicians, and specialists.

Once the struggle against Khodorkovsky began it took both a virtual and real form. Many of the charges against him and his colleagues were patently nonsense, but they served a deeper political purpose. Law was used to advance a specific political agenda. Just as with earlier campaigns in the Soviet era, charges that Lavrenty Beria, for example, was an English spy were believed only by the gullible; but the real nature of the struggle against him (or Kamenev, Zinoviev, and any number of victims of repression earlier) could not be made explicit. Putin's administration had a number of serious charges against Khodorkovsky, but it was not clear how these could be formulated; hence the recourse to law as the substitute for openly political accusations.[59] The corollary was the poor quality of the various trials, with the evidence distorted and moulded to fit preconceived schemas, and the cruel pursuit of peripheral figures to make the case look more substantive.

It is not clear how much influence the money from deposed oligarchs such as Khodorkovsky, Nevzlin, and Berezovsky has been able to buy in the West, above all through the funding of ostensibly independent think tanks.[60] The question, however, is worth asking, since policies affecting the fate of millions are adopted on the basis of information that could be distorted by the lobbying activities of a small group of intensely biased individuals. The aim certainly was to turn Western elites and people against Putin, and to encourage moves to overthrow him. The maximal agenda was not fulfilled, yet Russia's reputation was severely damaged and encouraged talk of a 'new Cold War'.

In the international arena

The Yukos affair provided a powerful impetus to the construction of a new Russophobia. For most of the nineteenth century Russia laboured under a terrible image. Nicholas I's stern and unbending approach helped foster the atmosphere

[59] Cf. Yur'ev, *rezhim putina*, pp. 136–7.
[60] One of the recipients of Yukos-related funding is the EU-Russia Centre, based in Brussels. While on the whole its work strives for academic balance, it sometimes takes the path of easy criticism of Russia.

that prompted France and Britain to fight the Crimean War. Later, with numerous Russian exiles fostering a highly critical perception of Russia, British foreign policy took a resolutely anti-Russian stance, notably in helping to prop up the 'sick man of Europe', the Ottoman empire, and to reverse the gains made by Russia's ally Bulgaria at the Treaty of San Stefano in 1877. Although an Anglo-Russian Convention was signed on 31 August 1907, the foreign secretary, Sir Edward Grey, had quite a job in convincing his colleagues that Russia had legitimate national interests.

In a quite extraordinary way the situation today is remarkably reminiscent of the earlier period. The image of 'liberal' Europe, nowadays couched in terms of democracy, against an 'autocratic' Russia has once again lodged firmly in the popular consciousness, due in no small part to the Yukos affair. It is also due to a number of vigorous advocates of Russian acceptance into the international community only on subaltern terms. We have mentioned Bruce Jackson before (Chapter 4). Jackson's Project on Transitional Democracies was part of the (now defunct) 'Project for a New American Century', a neo-conservative organization devoted to advancing America's hegemony on a global scale. In particular, it advocated the rapid accession of post-communist Eastern Europe into the EU and NATO, goals which it achieved with remarkable ease. Poland, the Czech Republic, and Hungary joined NATO in March 1999, followed by the 'Vilnius round' of expansion that saw Estonia, Latvia, Lithuania, Slovakia, Slovenia, Romania, and Bulgaria join in March 2004. He then turned his attention to the Balkans and the post-Soviet states, chairing the US Committee on NATO (formed in 1996) to promote NATO's eastward enlargement, and in 2002/3 he served as chair of the Committee for the Liberation of Iraq. In the 2008 US election campaign he supported John McCain's bid for the presidency.

Jackson's critics note that much of his advocacy work was combined with employment as vice president for strategy and planning (1999–2002) for Lockheed Martin, the world's largest armaments corporation, which stood to benefit most from NATO enlargement. Having worked with Bush's defence secretary Dick Cheney, Jackson acted as the intermediary between the defence establishment and the neo-conservatives in the Bush administration. Jackson was one of the most vigorous critics of Russia's alleged slide into authoritarianism, and was particularly critical of the country's energy policy. In an interview in 2006 he called the struggle between America and Russia a 'soft war', and he welcomed it: 'There's nothing wrong with a battle of ideas.... It's a soft power competition. It's desirable.' He envisaged three fronts in the new battle of ideas and values between Russia and the West: 'Our institutions versus their Potëmkin institutions, free markets versus their coercive state monopolies, and our democracy versus their managed democracy. What we don't want is militarized competition.'[61] Jackson was one of the most virulent proponents of putting 'democracy' on the agenda,

[61] Ian Traynor, Nick Paton Walsh, and Ewen MacAskill, 'The Russian Bear is Back—and this Time It's Gas-Powered', *Guardian*, 13 May 2006.

condemning Bush after his February 2005 meeting in Bratislava for not having pushed harder on Yukos and Chechnya.[62] He is reputed to have argued that the Yukos affair represented 'the greatest expropriation of a Jew since the Holocaust'.

Lantos was one of the founders of the Congressional Human Rights Caucus (CHRC) in 1983, which became one of the leading lobbying organizations in both houses of Congress on the issue. In 2006 they established the Russian Working Group, which like its parent body regularly held briefings and invited high-profile activists to speak. One of their prominent guests was Thomas O. Melia, the head of Freedom House, who addressed a joint meeting of the CHRC and the Russian Working Group on 13 July 2006. He called for Russia's accession to the WTO to be made contingent on respect for 'human rights and democratic values', and condemned the plans of world leaders to attend the G8 summit in St Petersburg. He stressed that '[t]he deterioration of democracy in Russia—or, perhaps more accurately, the dissolution of that country's democratic potential—has been a serious, deliberate long-term project'. He noted in particular that one symptom of this was part of the effort 'to intimidate business leaders to desist from supporting political parties and candidates they might prefer, through selective prosecution epitomized by the incarceration of Mikhail Khodorkovsky, previously the principal financial backer of several rivals to Vladimir Putin, now languishing in a remote Siberian prison'. He endorsed the visits of the assistant secretaries of state Fried and Lowenkron to the Other Russia meeting that week, which particularly incensed the Russian leadership. In general, he called for continued engagement with Russia, but also the resolute condemnation of infringements of human and civic rights.[63]

In France the political commentator and former Maoist André Glucksmann took up the baton of exploiting human rights issues. His contributions were typically a mix of polemic and passion, in which serious analysis played a very minor role. Nevertheless, he helped shape French public opinion, and this was later reflected in president Nicolas Sarkozy's view of Russia, although trumped by a healthy dose of *Realpolitik* which allowed France to win some important contracts in the late Putin years, notably for Renault to become the main partner in the modernization of Avtovaz, and Total to become a non-equity partner in the exploitation of the Shtokman gas field. In comments to a 'Concert for Human Rights' held in Paris on 29 October 2007 Glucksmann asserted that Khodorkovsky's struggle was akin to that of Andrei Sakharov, insisting that the fight for freedom and conscience in Russia was not idealism, but 'it is a fight for peace, safety for our children because at the borders of the European a kind of rising power exists that is not controlled from the inside and that no one is trying to control from the outside'.[64] In a forceful article in *Le Monde* a few days earlier he compared Moscow to Chicago in the 1930s, and argued that in conditions

---

[62] C. J. Chivers, 'Bush and Putin Mute Differences, Latching on to the Affirmative', *New York Times*, 25 February 2005.

[63] http://www.lantos.house.gov/chrc/index2.php?option=com_content&t.

[64] 'André Glucksmann Speaks on Human Rights in Russia', 29 October 2007, Salle Adyar, Paris, mimeo.

where 50 per cent of the Russian population lived in poverty Yukos offered 'the best working conditions in Russia'. Khodorkovsky, he insisted, had been brought down because he threatened the political and economic 'vertical of power', and challenged the Kremlin's foreign policy plans, which included imposing an energy 'Warsaw Pact' on its neighbours, including through building the North Stream pipeline. He quotes Sakharov's widow, Elena Bonner, who commented on a meeting between Putin and the oligarchs in the Kremlin: 'When Khodorkovsky appeared, I thought this one is too intelligent and too disengaged, courageous and independent—he will pay.'[65]

In this thinking Russia is taken to be the new Soviet Union, and the old and familiar battles are once again rethought. Although the struggle for human and civil rights in Russia is far from over, some of the most prominent fighters for human rights failed to develop an ethics of responsibility, internal limitations that would have allowed them to take a balanced and scholarly approach to what are indeed complex issues. It was much easier simply to place contemporary Russia in the Soviet category, and thus to provide a black and white discourse of the struggle between good and evil. The lumping together of Chechnya and Yukos was typical of this approach, with grave simplifications attending the discussion of both. The upshot was the tendency openly to proclaim that the Russian regime was illegitimate.[66] If this was the case, then any measures taken to overthrow it were logically legitimate, including terror in the North Caucasus and elsewhere. Not surprisingly, the Russian leadership felt ever more embattled, provoking the rise of a pugnacious suspicion of the West. This perhaps is the most dangerous legacy of the Yukos affair.

[65] André Glucksmann, 'Sakharov–Khodorkovski, même combat', *Le Monde*, 25 October 2007.

[66] For example, Sergei Kovalëv, 'Why Putin Wins', translated by Jamey Gambrel, *New York Review of Books*, 22 November 2007, pp. 64–6.

10

Political and Moral Economy

> Uncomplaining acceptance of the reality of society gives man indomitable courage and strength to remove all removable injustice and unfreedom. As long as he is true to his task of creating more abundant freedom for all, he need not fear that either power or planning will turn against him and destroy the freedom he is building by their instrumentality. This is the meaning of freedom in a complex society; it gives us all the certainty that we need.
>
> Karl Polanyi[1]

In his book of interviews published in the first year of his presidency, Putin noted his admiration for Ludwig Erhard.[2] In his annual address to the Federal Assembly in 2004 he described his plans to develop a social state, reminiscent of Erhard's 'social market economy'.[3] However, while the 'Rhineland model' sought to combine democratic freedoms, private property, and market competition while lessening social inequality and building a welfare state, it is not clear that Putin was able to build 'capitalism with a human face' during his leadership. Early in his first term Putin described himself as the 'hired manager' of the 'Russia corporation', appointed by the people, but the meaning only became clear later.[4] The Russian state under his leadership became a type of mega-corporation, expanding both ownership and control over strategic sectors of the economy. The Yukos affair signalled a major shift in the business environment, and raised fears among investors that a new era of deprivatization would begin. The fundamental question is whether the Yukos affair did indeed shift the economy and society on to a new trajectory.

BUILDING NATIONAL CHAMPIONS

The anti-oligarch campaign of 2003/4 was followed by the reinforcement of the *dirigiste* trend in Russian political economy, although 'wrapped in a liberal public

---

[1] Polanyi, *The Great Transformation*, p. 268.

[2] Vladimir Putin, *First Person: An Astonishingly Frank Self-Portrait by Russia's President Vladimir Putin*, with Nataliya Gevorkyan, Natalya Timakova, and Andrei Kolesnikov, translated by Catherine A. Fitzpatrick (London, Hutchinson, 2000), p. 194.

[3] *Rossiiskaya gazeta*, 27 May 2004; http://www.kremlin.ru/eng/text/speeches/2004/05/262021_64906.shtml.

[4] Cited and discussed by Karen Markarian, the director of the Institute of the Global Economy, *Izvestiya*, 26 September 2006.

format'. The 'new course' was signalled as soon as Putin took office, but was now consolidated: 'The logic of contemporary state interventionism is clear: the country is a concern, in which there are numerous nominally independent companies, but they all fulfil a single national project'.[5] Its features were clear: (*a*) the emphasis on large companies with a majority state stake (Gazprom, Transneft, Rosneft), which were to increase their dominance in their respective fields (leading to the merger of Transneft with Transnefteprodukt, dominating the transport of crude and petroleum products); (*b*) The merger of hitherto separate corporations to create market leaders (United Shipbuilding Corporation, United Aircraft Building Corporation, etc.), to act as market leaders; (*c*) an active state investment and innovation programme in these and other cutting-edge sectors, such as nanotechnology; (*d*) energy exports should be accompanied by the development of new technologies, notably LNG, efficient reservoir management, and investment in new fields; and (*e*) the export of 'brand Russia' into new markets abroad, including outward investment in foreign companies. A powerful but dependent distributional coalition formed around the Yukos affair, and was able to feast on the windfall as long as it retained its subaltern status to the Kremlin and demonstratively showed its loyalty. Even for those at the heart of the coalition, however, things did not quite work out as they had hoped.

Rosneft and the turn to statism

Roland notes that '[s]ince the expropriation of Yukos, one sees a clear strategy of takeover of the energy sector by the state'.[6] At an investment conference in Moscow in June 2006 Arkady Dvorkovich, head of the presidential expert board, argued that 'Russia must create national champion companies if it is to develop its economy'. He stressed, however, that state control over such champions would be temporary, and once they had become competitive they would return to private ownership.[7] National champions were created in the form of state corporations in aircraft building, shipbuilding, nanotechnologies, and some other spheres. The idea of national champions allows a company 'with government support, to go straight into the market, allowing them to concentrate on international competition instead of wasting time and resources on competition inside Russia'.[8] There was nothing unusual about Russia's national champion strategy, and the top thirteen oil companies in the world in terms of proven reserves are to some degree also national champions, with state representation on their boards not uncommon. Already in the late Soviet period the energy sector had emerged as the foundation for the rest of the economy, and following the tribulations of the 1990s the state could now restore the sector to its role as the locomotive driving the

[5] Dmitrii Orlov, 'Gosudarstvennaya proryv', *Rossiiskaya gazeta*, 2 June 2005.

[6] Gérard Roland, 'The Russian Economy in the Year 2005', *Post-Soviet Affairs*, Vol. 22, No. 1, January–March 2006, p. 95.

[7] Ivor Crotty, 'The Stereotypical Champion: What Rosneft Says about Russia's Economic Strategy', *Russia Profile*, Vol. 3, No. 8, October 2006, pp. 11–12, at p. 11.

[8] Igor Dines, 'Championing National Industry', *Russia Profile*, Vol. 3, No. 8, October 2006, p. 14.

Russian economy. This of course, as many in the administration realized, was an anachronistic model that tends not to encourage innovation, yet one that others felt had not entirely exhausted its potential.

Already in the late 1990s the lack of a consensus in the Russian elite about the appropriate balance between state and market was noted: 'There is no clear compact among the elites concerning the extent of state regulation and market competition. The wider context of political and economic interests may yet see a revival of state interest.'[9] The Primakov government planned to bring together the three oil companies in which the state retained a majority share, Rosneft (100 per cent), Onako (75 per cent), and Slavneft (75 per cent) and some smaller companies to create a giant national oil company, Gosneft, which would have produced about 10 per cent of national oil production. The idea clearly showed the beginning of a move back towards the reassertion of a particular vision of state interests in the oil industry. The creation of something like Gosneft would have provided cheap fuel for agriculture, the army, and other domestic consumers. However, the plan was opposed by the oil oligarchs such as Khodorkovsky, and was dropped when the Primakov government was dismissed in May 1999. The revival of state involvement in the oil industry, however, was far from over.

The ideology of statism in the 2000s was used to achieve a redistribution of the assets privatized in the Yeltsin era; and these resources were then used for the various political projects of the regime ranging from the development of the United Russia political party to interference in the Ukrainian presidential elections of late 2004.[10] According to one source: 'Gazprom is an instrument of public administration just like the pro-Kremlin United Russia party that commands a majority in the Russian parliament.'[11] The seizure of Yukos's main production asset was commented on by Peter Lavelle as follows:

This has been the Kremlin's plan from the start. Deemed a national security issue, the Kremlin geared up the entire state bureaucracy to employ any means necessary to capture Yukos to serve state interests. As a privately owned company, Yukos was in a position to significantly impact Russia's domestic and international energy policies. After [the sale of YNG], the Kremlin will again be in charge of Russia's energy sector.[12]

In the course of his eight years in office Putin brought over half of Russia's oil industry back into state control, inviting comparisons with the resource nationalism in Venezuela and Bolivia. It is part of the natural cycle of things that when prices are high, governments try to increase their share. The shift began with the break-up of Yukos, and continued with the transfer of Sibneft to Gazprom, and then the buyout of Russneft (see below) by the Kremlin-aligned Oleg Deripaska. Deripaska was a classic example of the Putin-era oligarch, who continued to

---

[9] Dines, 'Championing National Industry', p. 43.

[10] *Ekho Moskvy* radio station, 30 November 2004, quoted in *Eurasia Daily Monitor*, 8 December 2004.

[11] Gazeta.ru, 30 November 2004.

[12] 'Analysis: After Yukos' Funeral', Untimely Thoughts, in www.untimely-thoughts.com, 17 December 2004.

develop their assets but kept out of independent politics, although he adapted to the Kremlin's needs. For example, Deripaska in November 2007 promised to invest $3 billion per annum in developing Russia's infrastructure, an issue that was close to Putin's heart. Deripaska's Basic Element (Basel) holding company owned some eighty companies across the globe, notably the aluminium giant Russian Aluminium (Rusal) and sought a stake in Norilsk Nickel, and in 2006 had revenues of $18 billion and employed 240,000 people.[13] Asset redistribution, however, was accompanied by group struggles, and it took all of Putin's political skills to keep the lid on factional conflict.

As we have seen, Bogdanchikov was one of the crucial figures in the Yukos case, and he aggressively insisted on the acquisition of Yuganskneftegaz, eager to add this asset to Rosneft's oil producing arm. Through the acquisition of YNG by Rosneft, the state became a decisive player in Russia's oil business. The oil from YNG that was once shipped by Yukos-affiliated companies now passed through Gunvor, whose head as we have seen was Timchenko, a member of the 'politburo' which had sponsored the Yukos case in the first place. YNG alone supplied 70 per cent of Rosneft's oil and gas, with the company producing 1.56 million barrels of oil a day from its fields in Western Siberia and the Sakhalin area.[14] Following its acquisition by Rosneft, all the 1,850-strong management staff of YNG kept their jobs, and only five top managers, including the managing director, were replaced.[15] According to YNG's manager, investment had fallen in the immediate aftermath of the Rosneft takeover, but rose rapidly in 2005 to three times the maximum invested in a single year by Yukos. Production had also followed a similar pattern, but by 2005 production was back up to 51.2 million tonnes, with costs of production falling as efficiency improved.[16]

The acquisition of the Vankor oil field in Krasnoyarsk *krai* in 2003, beating off rival bids from Total and Yukos, established Rosneft as the major player in East Siberia, in a region which has direct access to the Northern sea route and thus has the potential of bypassing the Transneft bottleneck. In the Far East its subsidiary Sakhalinmorneftegaz, originally headed by Bogdanchikov, is involved in Sakhalin-1, -3, -4, and -5 projects. Rosneft also has a close relationship with China, since Chinese banks had made possible the acquisition of YNG in December 2004 and they later became shareholders when Rosneft launched its IPO in London. In 2007 Rosneft pumped 102.5 million tonnes of oil, an average of 2.06 million barrels per day, a rise of about a quarter, and without acquisitions oil output rose by 12.9 per cent.[17] In terms of market capitalization, Rosneft at $80 billion became

[13] Catrina Stewart, 'Deripaska's Holding's Tentacles Reach Farther', *Moscow Times*, 28 November 2007, p. 1.

[14] As well as YNG, Rosneft's main production assets included Severnaya Neft, Vankor, and Purneftegaz in West Siberia, East Sugdinskoe and Verkhnechonskoe in the Baikal region, and Sakhalin and West Kamchatsky, as well as refineries in Tuapse on the Black Sea and Komsomolsk in the Far East.

[15] Author's interviews in the Priobskoe oilfield, 6 September 2006.

[16] Speech by Vladimir Kasyanov, head of YNG, in the Priobskoe field, 6 September 2006, personal notes.

[17] *Moscow Times*, 28 November 2007, p. 6.

the world's eighth largest stock-listed company, overshadowing Lukoil in ninth place at $60 billion.[18] Rosneft has larger oil reserves than ExxonMobil. Thus one of the alleged injustices of the 1990s was rectified: from being one of the minnow oil companies of the 1990s as its assets were hived off to competitors, Rosneft was restored as an oil major.[19] Putin certainly did not go so far as many of the world's largest oil states from the 1950s when they nationalized their oil industries, but he did establish a new balance between the state and the private sector.

Gazprom and planned merger with Rosneft

At the same time as the case against Yukos was being pursued, the Kremlin sought to establish a major state-owned integrated energy company of its own. In 2004 the planned merger of Rosneft with Gazprom would have created a major integrated oil and gas company; and it is this company that was intended to become the beneficiary of the sale of undervalued Yukos assets. Gazprom would become, in the words of the minister of trade and economic development German Gref, a 'hyper-monopoly'.[20] This was part of the 'commanding heights' strategy advanced by the Kremlin.[21] After lobbying by Sechin on behalf of Rosneft, Alexei Miller, the head of Gazprom, and Medvedev, then head of the presidential administration and head of the Gazprom board, designated Bogdanchikov head of the planned Gazprom Neft company. This company would have fulfilled the aspirations of those who since the mid-1990s had dreamed of recreating a dominant state role in the oil industry, in a form similar to that mooted earlier of creating a firm called 'Gosneft'.

There was a clear decision in the Putin years to transform Gazprom into a 'national champion', and although this was a political decision, the company acted ever more as a commercial organization and thus it is misleading to see it as 'the political business of the state'. As Mitrova notes: 'The creation of a "champion" means that it has to respect international rules and, more importantly, it has to be profitable, efficient and commercially oriented—otherwise it would never prevail in international competition.'[22] The liberalization of share trading in Gazprom could only take place after removal of the ring fence, imposed by the Gas Law of 1999 which restricted foreigners to 20 per cent of Gazprom shares, and this could only be done after the state's ownership rose above 50 per cent. The initial plan in early 2004 had been to achieve this by Gazprom buying 100 per cent of Rosneft for about $7 billion. By acquiring the 10.74 per cent of its shares and adding them to the 38.57 per cent package already owned by the state, the state's stake in Gazprom

---

[18] Terry Macalister, 'Rosneft Pushes on Towards London', *The Guardian*, 27 June 2006, p. 25.

[19] The argument that Rosneft was intended to be one of the few big oil firms is made, for example, by Yakov Pappe, 'Putin Versus the Oligarchs', *The Economist*, 5 August 2004.

[20] *Kommersant*, 27 October 2004.

[21] Anthony Robinson, 'The Yukos Affair', *Prospect*, April 2005, pp. 36–40, at p. 39.

[22] Mitrova, 'Gazprom's Perspectives on International Markets', p. 6.

would rise above 50 per cent and thus make possible the removal of restrictions on foreign investors.

The Kremlin hoped to use the merger to allow the flotation of Gazprom shares in the international stock market and thus end Gazprom's two-tier share market. By allowing portfolio investors to buy shares in Gazprom, Putin hoped to sweeten the bitter pill of the takeover of Yukos assets. On 14 September 2004, however, the plan was modified, and the project was announced to exchange part of Gazprom and Rosneft shares. The overall aim was to increase Gazprom's market capitalization and thus allow it to secure loans for its plans to build North Stream. Putin was personally committed to this project, and he worked closely with the German Chancellor of the time, Schroeder, to ensure that the project went ahead. A law passed in July 2006 granted Gazprom exclusive rights to export gas from Russia. More broadly, Putin hoped to establish a world-class oil and gas major, a national champion that would dominate the domestic energy market and help advance Russia's state interests in the global economy.[23] Instead of Yukos's assets going to Gazprom to create a single national champion in the energy field, Rosneft hung on to YNG and became a national champion in its own right. YNG remained a separate 100 percent state-owned company and became part of Rosneft's assets separate from Gazprom.

Factional fights between Sechin, representing Rosneft, and Medvedev, taking the Gazprom corner, led to the merger being abandoned: 'Settling the dispute to one or the other's advantage would disturb the balance among the Kremlin factions.'[24] Rosneft as we have seen was the state's main instrument in the dismemberment of Yukos, and this involved, as one commentator puts it, 'all sorts of complicated financial manoeuvring and lawsuits'.[25] Merger with Gazprom was bitterly opposed by the Sechin faction in the Kremlin and by Bogdanchikov, who fought a desperate and ultimately successful battle to keep Rosneft independent. In March 2005 it looked as if Rosneft would be sold to Gazprom.[26] In the event, after intense conflict throughout the first months of 2005, the merger between Gazprom and Rosneft was finally called off in May. Instead, the plan announced in May 2005 was to sell up to 50 per cent of Rosneft shares to buy the 10.74 per cent stake in Gazprom needed to raise the state's ownership to 50 per cent plus one share.[27] The plan confirmed that YNG would be consolidated into Rosneft. This was clearly a victory for Sechin, whose lobbying had successfully defended

[23] The strategy was outlined by Igor Shuvalov, who replaced Andrei Illarionov as sherpa to the G8, *Vedemosti*, 16 February 2005; Peter Lavelle, 'Analysis: Kremlin Explains Itself', Untimely Thoughts: Analysis, 16 February 2005.

[24] Kończuk, The 'Yukos Affair', p. 48; the same view is expressed by Simonov, *Russkaya neft'*, p. 169.

[25] Pavel K. Baev, 'Russia's Shrinking Political Horizons of Economic Planning and Political Plotting', *Eurasia Daily Monitor*, Vol. 2, No. 109, 6 June 2005.

[26] Varvara Aglamish'ian, 'Podeli i vlastvui: "Gazprom" poluchil "Rosneft"', Sergei Bogdanchikov—'Yuganskneftegaz', *Izvestiya*, 3 March 2005, p. 1.

[27] *Financial Times*, editorial, 18 May 2005; *Izvestiya*, 18 May 2005.

the independence of Rosneft. This was an extraordinary display of the power of the Sechin faction.

Sechin and Viktor Ivanov, who had received financial support from Rosneft, were able successfully to resist the absorption of Rosneft into the portfolio of a rival faction.[28] Rosneft was allowed to enjoy its acquisition from Yukos undisturbed, and the absorption of YNG transformed Rosneft into one of Russia's largest oil companies.[29] In September 2005 Rosneftegaz, Rosneft's parent company, took out a loan of $7.5 billion to buy the 10.74 per cent stake in Gazprom, restoring majority ownership in the gas company to the state.[30] Following the absorption of YNG and the end of uncertainty about merger with Gazprom, Rosneft under Bogdanchikov announced ambitious plans to make the company Russia's largest by extraction within two years and in general to make it an international oil major. To achieve its aspirations it was clear that Rosneft would have to take over the remaining Yukos assets (above all Tomskneft and Samaraneftegaz), which as we have seen it achieved. Although majority-owned by the state, it tried to profile itself as an efficient private sector company. It brought in a number of foreign managers, and those from Yukos who were not in jail or exile. The attempt in late 2005 to hire Donald Evans, the former American commerce secretary, sought to seal the company's new respectability, but even though Evans in the end turned down the offer, other independent directors were promised.

Gazprom did not go unrewarded either, and its failure to acquire Rosneft did not mean that it renounced its ambition to diversify heavily into oil. In September 2005 Gazprom bought 72.6 per cent of Sibneft, for $13.1 billion from Roman Abramovich. Gazprom's purchase of Sibneft, against competition from Rosneft, finally gave it a major oil-producing arm, and was in part compensation for not having received YNG. It also allowed factional balance in the regime to be maintained: a victory for Sechin and the *siloviki* was now balanced by allowing Medvedev's Gazprom to expand. The *silovik* interest within Gazprom was sponsored by its deputy chairman, Alexander Ryazanov, who became chief executive of Gazprom Neft after its absorption of Sibneft. Sibneft was one of the largest private oil companies, at the time pumping 22 million tonnes a year, and also owned half of Slavneft. This only reinforced Gazprom's rise to world status, if not to world power.

With majority state ownership achieved, restrictions on trading in Gazprom shares were lifted and from January 2006 foreign investors could access the 49 per cent of Gazprom shares not owned by the state. The market capitalization of Gazprom soared to the point that in 2006 it became the world's second largest company. Matthias Warnig, an old friend of Putin's from Dresden days with a Stasi

---

[28] Ol'ga Kryshtanovkaya and Stephen White, 'Inside the Putin Court: A Research Note', *Europe–Asia Studies*, Vol. 57, No. 7, November 2005, p. 1072.

[29] 'Syrëvvshchiki: promezhutochnie itogi privatizatsii; zachem peresmatrivat to, chto mozhno peredelit', *Novaya gazeta*, 2 December 2004.

[30] Alexander Temerko, 'Rosneft Buyer Beware', *Wall Street Journal Europe*, 24 May 2005.

background, was nominated one of Gazprom's independent directors.[31] Warnig was the head of the Dresdner Bank in Russia, and later went on to become the managing director of North Stream, whose chair was Schroeder. Soon after the acquisition of Sibneft, Gazprom's oil-producing unit was renamed Gazprom Neft. Having failed to take over Rosneft, Gazprom had been compensated with Sibneft and fulfilled its ambitions to become an oil major, to complement its gas business. The purchase of Sibneft allowed Gazprom to strengthen its oil interests, and instead of getting one 'national energy champion', the Kremlin got two. However, rivalry between the two companies exacerbated factional conflict and endowed Russian politics with an added layer of instability, and it also complicated policy-making. While Rosneft, for example, sought direct access to Far Eastern markets for its gas, Gazprom sought to preserve its monopoly. The two companies have been described as 'bitter friends'.[32]

Rosneft goes global

The Initial Public Offering (IPO) in July 2006 of 15 per cent of Rosneft's shares on the London stock exchange valued the company at around $80 billion (£44 billion) and represented the world's fifth-largest IPO. The Russian government sought to raise at least $8.5 billion to cover the $7.5 billion loan it took out to gain the controlling share in Gazprom. The offer brought the ethical question sharply into focus, above all the absence of a middle ground. As the financial correspondent of *The Guardian* put it:

You can take two views of Rosneft's flotation. You can call it a glorified sale of stolen property, in which some of London's leading investment bankers, lawyers and PR folk will pocket about £100m by promoting a firm whose principal asset, Yuganskneftegaz, was acquired in a forced auction controlled by the Russian government. Alternatively, Rosneft's arrival marks a further welcome step by Russian capitalism on to the international stage.[33]

Yukos referred the flotation to the British Financial Services Authority (FSA), providing documentation on the way that its main production field had been forcibly transferred to its rival at a substantial discount. This was a matter, however, not in the FSA's remit, and its main concern was to ensure that the risks associated with the sale had been fully disclosed. There can be little doubt that they had been, with the 'risk factors' chapter of the 500-page flotation document running to 35 pages, covering litigation, arbitration, as well as political risks, including 'instability' in Russia. In advance, moreover, Rosneft brought in an American, Peter

---

[31] *Vremya novostei*, 2 February 2006; Pavel Baev, 'Putin, Gazprom and "the Other Norwegian Company"', *Eurasia Daily Monitor*, Vol. 3, No. 25, 6 February 2006.

[32] Nina Poussenkova, 'All Quiet on the Eastern Front…', *Russian Analytical Digest*, No. 33, 22 January 2008, p. 17.

[33] Nils Pratley, 'Rosneft's Flotation is a Punt on Putin', *The Guardian*, 27 June 2006, p. 23.

O'Brien, as a vice president to advise on the flotation, and thus repeated Yukos's strategy.

Legal challenges were brought before American and Dutch courts by GML, contesting the sale of YNG, as well as by some minority shareholders. The veteran banker George Soros added his voice to the warnings, arguing that Rosneft represented the most egregious use of energy policy for political purposes and argued that 'Rosneft is an instrument of state that will always serve the political objectives of Russia in preference to the interests of the shareholders'.[34] Despite the threat of litigation from various directions, as long as Putin was in power investors in Rosneft could be reasonably confident that their investments were safe. This was certainly Rosneft's view, and there was no discount in the share price to offset the perceived risk. Any slack in take-up by Western investors would be made up by strategic engagement by oil companies in China, India, and other Asian countries.

In the event, the IPO was over-subscribed by a factor of 1.5, with BP, for example, offering $1 billion and CNPC $2.5 billion, and with offers apparently from various oligarchs such as Abramovich and Deripaska, each offering around $1 billion. The 13 per cent block of Rosneft shares raised $10.4 billion, while at the same time ensuring that BP, CNPC (which received a $500 million tranche), and Malaysia's Petronas have a direct stake in the success of the company. At the same time a stock offering was launched in Moscow in which Sberbank, and with it millions of small investors, became shareholders in Rosneft and thus gained a stake in the post-Yukos settlement. A total of 85,000 individual investors bought shares in Rosneft at this time in a sale that in its transparency and broad base was in sharp contrast to the privatizations of the early 1990s. As Gorbachev noted: '[B]y opening the privatisation to the Russian people, the government is crossing an important threshold, giving many more ordinary Russians the opportunity to have a direct stake in the future success of the Russian economy.'[35] The market valuation of the company in the wake of its stock market debut remained at $80 billion, making it second largest in Russia in terms of market capitalization.

Following its successful IPO on the Russian and London stock markets, O'Brien argued: 'Since the IPO, as we've followed through on increasing transparency and profitability, interest and share ownership by leading global institutions has accelerated.'[36] Rosneft on 30 June 2007 held its first general meeting for shareholders after it became a public company, with its 154,000 private shareholders invited to attend. In his first public appearance in eight years as a deputy head of the presidential administration, Sechin outlined the company's strategic direction. These included shifting 'the Company's center of gravity toward oil refining, business diversification, building up the mineral

---

[34] George Soros, 'Rosneft Flotation Would Spur Putin On', *Financial Times*, 26 April 2006. Yukos's former Chief Financial Officer, Bruce K. Misamore, also added his voice to the debate in a letter to the paper, highlighting 'the moral and ethical issues raised by the Rosneft IPO', *Financial Times*, 3 May 2006.

[35] Mikhail Gorbachev, 'Rosneft Will Reinforce Russian Reform', *Financial Times*, 12 July 2006.

[36] Miriam Elder, 'How the State Got a Grip on Energy', *Moscow Times*, 14 March 2008, p. 1.

resource base and optimizing logistics'. He argued that Rosneft's priority was to adhere to international standards of corporate governance, and to achieve this, three independent directors had been appointed to the board of directors, and three board committees created.[37] Bogdanchikov stated that in 2006 the company had produced 80.8 million tonnes of oil and 13.7 bcm of gas, 8.3 per cent and 4.6 per cent more, respectively, than in 2005, with 57.2 million tonnes of oil exported. He noted that the acquisition of various production and refining assets from Yukos though bankruptcy auctions would boost Rosneft oil production in 2007 to over 100 million tonnes. In the first half of 2007 Rosneft had gained five new oil refineries and thus increased its refining capacity from 11 million tonnes per annum to 50 million tonnes. Market capitalization by May 2008 reached $112 billion with an international free float of 15 per cent. One barrel in four of Russian crude was produced by the company,[38] and the company aspired to be become one of the world's ten largest oil and gas companies in terms of market capitalization, and in the long term, one of the top three energy corporations.[39] A new nine-person board of directors was elected, with Sechin once again chair and Sergei Naryshkin (a deputy prime minister) and Gleb Nikitin, the head of the Federal Property Management Agency, as deputy chairs. The legalization of assets seized through administrative pressure would be a challenge for Putin's successors, but a successful Rosneft in part validated the destruction of Yukos.

Rosneft's aggressive acquisition strategy burdened it with debts, which by the end of 2007 reached $26.3 billion. However, as its new assets began to contribute to its income stream and pushed up output, accompanied by high global energy prices, the debt fell to $23.8 billion by the end of March 2008. As Samaraneftegaz and Tomskneft came on stream, Rosnefts's oil output in 2007 rose by 25.8 per cent to 101.7 million tonnes.[40] Output in the first quarter of 2008 rose by 36 per cent to 205.5 million barrels, and the company also doubled production of high-margin refined products to 12.1 million tonnes.[41] Rosneft continued to look for ways to refinance its debt, accompanied by tight cost control.[42] Rosneft's success demonstrated that the state sector, even in Russian conditions, could deliver performance levels that Yukos had claimed was the preserve of private business.

The story of Rosneft's rise is the counterpart of Yukos's fall, and is one of the most dramatic in contemporary history. The company was state-owned in form, but operated essentially as a private company, although the backing of state officials gave it a competitive edge and helped reduce economic risks. The state provided a 'cover' (*krysha*) for Rosneft and used its repressive and juridical apparatus to advance the company's and the state's interests. The quasi-state role

---

[37] 'First Meeting', *Rosneft Magazine*, No. 3 (6), July–September 2007, pp. 2–5, at p. 2.

[38] John Helmer, 'Gunvoracious: Putin Strengthens Oil Concessions for Sechin and Timchenko', http://www.mineweb.com, posted 20 May 2008.

[39] 'First Meeting', pp. 2–3.

[40] Varvara Sokolovskaya, ' "Rosneft" sumela poradovat' rynok', *RBK Daily*, 14 April 2007, p. 11.

[41] 'Rosneft's Earnings Soar on Production Increases', *Wall Street Journal*, 9 April 2008, p. 5.

[42] 'Rosneft Set to Clear $22Bln Yukos Loan', *Moscow Times*, 18 July 2008.

performed by the company was its starkest in Chechnya, where it owned the main production company, Grozneft: 'The state-owned Rosneft behaves in Chechnya as if it is operating in a conquered country, acting as if it can behave with impunity.'[43] Yukos no doubt would take the view that such behaviour was not limited to Chechnya.

The state and the energy sector

Gazprom's purchase of a majority stake in Sibneft brought the state's share of the energy sector to a hegemonic 57.4 per cent. At the same time, the public sector's share of the economy rose from 30 per cent to 35 per cent in 2005. The state's more *dirigiste* approach to managing economic development, however, did not signal a wholesale retreat from market principles. The IPO of Rosneft on the London market was only one of many. Rosneft by now had become Russia's second largest oil company by output and third largest in terms of reserves. However, Rosneft's seizure of YNG led many advisers to warn their clients against involvement with the company. The forlorn fate of minority shareholders in Yukos illustrated the weakness of property rights and the lack of an impartial legal system that could defend these rights in Russia.

The total cost in 2005 of increasing the state's share of Gazprom, and Gazprom's takeover of Sibneft came to $20.21 billion, nearly half of the total of $40.5 billion of mergers and acquisitions (M&A) deals in Russia that year. In 2005 the state was the most active player in the M&A market, using either state-owned companies or companies serving state interests. The idea of enhancing state control over 'strategic' assets spread into non-energy spheres, notably engineering, manufacturing, and banking. The state (via Gazprombank) effectively took over the country's largest heavy engineering company, OMZ, formerly owned by Kakha Bendukidze, and the helicopter company Kamov. In December the state won control of AvtoVAZ, the country's largest motor manufacturer, by appointing officials to dominate its board and through Rosoboronexport's purchase of a controlling stake for $350 million. In 2006 the same company, headed by Sergei Chemezov (Putin's long-time confidant who had served with him in the KGB in Leipzig), took control of the formerly privately owned VSMPO-Avisma company, producing much of the world's titanium for the aircraft industry including Boeing and Airbus.

Gazprom (unlike Rosneft) is renowned for its inefficiency, with its return on total assets—at a time of high energy prices—only 8.9 per cent, compared to the 30 per cent returned by Yukos in its final year of normal business.[44] In 2007 Gazprom managed to wrest control of the Sakhalin-2 project from the international consortium headed by Shell, and TNK-BP was forced to sell its majority stake in the Kovytka gas field. Gazprom became an ever more diversified company,

---

[43] Nathalie Ouvaroff, 'The Oil Factor and War of Clans in Chechnya', *Russian Analytical Digest*, No. 42, 2008, p. 6.
[44] Lucas, *New Cold War*, p. 238.

moving into power generation as well as developing its networks and extraction-supply chain in the CIS while developing new global markets in the Middle East, Latin America, and Asia. Its main market, however, remained Western and Central Europe, although its attempts to buy downstream distribution networks were not always welcome, especially as the EU sought to liberalize its markets. From 2005 the export share increased from what had for a long time been about a third to nearly half of its overall production.[45] Once ensconced as prime minister in May 2008, Putin insisted that Gazprom open up its pipeline network to oil and other companies, in an attempt to reduce flaring;[46] a policy vigorously supported by Sechin, who was confirmed in his post as chair of the Rosneft board in June 2008.

Yukos was bankrupted and its assets transferred to Rosneft at the lowest possible price, thus short-changing the state's exchequer by billions of dollars. At the same time, Gazprom spent $13 billion on acquiring Sibneft at a time when it lacked funds to invest in bringing difficult new gas provinces into production (Yamal, Shtokman) or to achieve the gasification of the country. State officials acted as the champions of these 'national' champions, using administrative levers to advance the business plans of companies that may not always have coincided with the national interest. The independent private sector was forced to coordinate its activities with state interests; while the state-owned sector adapted to market conditions but with all the advantages that insider lobbying could bring. If in the 1990s the government effectively gave some companies a 'licence for corruption', the system now engaged in a type of meta-corruption that eroded both the coherence of the state and the efficacy of the market.

THE ENERGY SECTOR AND RUSSIA'S ECONOMY

According to official statistics, in 2004 the energy sector provided 27 per cent of Russian GDP, and 74 per cent of all investment,[47] and it was the single largest contributor to the budget. Total Russian energy reserves, in oil and gas, are second only to those of Saudi Arabia, and as a major energy exporter Russia benefits from price rises of a commodity that traditionally provides over half of Russian export earnings. Over half of exports (54.7 per cent) are in the petroleum sector, providing just under half of the trade surplus, boosted by the rise in world oil prices, climbing from the low of $10 a barrel in 1998 to $33 a barrel in autumn 2000 to average $61 in 2006, breaking the $100 barrier in December 2007 and then soaring to peak at $147 in July before falling back to under $50 in October 2008. The managers of Russia's oil industry sought to protect their dominance

[45] Andreas Heinrich, 'Gazprom's Expansion Strategy in Europe and the Liberalization of EU Energy Markets', *Russian Analytical Digest*, No. 34, 2008, pp. 8–15.
[46] Anatoly Medetsky, 'Putin Scolds Miller on Pipeline Access', *Moscow Times*, 14 July 2008.
[47] Simonov, *Russkaya neft'*, p. 5.

by excluding external actors, even though well aware of the need for foreign investment to raise the technological level of the Russian oil industry.

The economic consequences of the Yukos affair

Between 1992 and 2004 Russian energy policy was dominated by what Åslund calls a 'liberal-oligarchic model', with the oil sector dominated by powerful independent companies.[48] This period saw the privatization and then the consolidation of the sector into some half dozen successful private companies that benefited from new conditions after 1999, accompanied by a massive growth in output. From 2004, however, a new model emerged, dubbed by Åslund 'state capitalism'. The state insisted on majority control, no less than 51 per cent, and the state monopoly over pipelines and other infrastructure was strengthened, 'undermining the property rights of both domestic and foreign owners'.[49] Khodorkovsky's arrest thus 'marked the end of the liberal model and augured the ascendancy of state capitalism', followed by the 'confiscation of Yukos assets through draconian taxation and biased court judgements reinforcing arbitrary state control over the oil industry'.[50] The new period saw state support for the pre-eminence of 'national champions', primarily Gazprom, Rosneft, and Transneft.

The Yukos affair marked a watershed in the informal rules governing the energy sector, and once the storm had been weathered all those concerned adapted to the new conditions. As a recent study puts it:

[T]hroughout the eight years of Putin's presidency, especially after the Yukos affair in 2003, unwritten rules have been formulated. The essential one is simple: Russia has enormous natural resources and should utilize them effectively to attain the social and economic development of the state. Two more fundamental unwritten rules can be added: first, the state must control the export of its resources; second, foreign investors are welcome only when they are ready to participate in projects that answer principally to Russia's national interests.[51]

Energy companies found new ways of converting their economic power into political influence: the frontal attack of the Yukos type was now a thing of the past. For example, seven of Russia's top 30 banks, accounting for 30–35 per cent of all banking assets, were 'oil banks' working solely for the companies that owned, and continued to engage in lobbying central government while consolidating influence through regional networks.[52] With the establishment of these principles, Russia's energy sector was open for business.

When Putin came to power 92 per cent of Russia's oil production was in private hands. Companies such as Shell and ExxonMobil were running huge projects in

---

[48] Åslund, 'Russia's Energy Policy', p. 323.   [49] Ibid., p. 324.   [50] Ibid., p. 325.

[51] Yoshinori Takeda, 'Russia's New Political Leadership and its Implications for East Siberian Development and Energy Cooperation with North East Asian States', *Russian Analytical Digest*, No. 33, 2008, pp. 5–8, at p. 7.

[52] Anastasia Gnezditskaia, ' "Unidentified Shareholders": The Impact of Oil Companies on the Banking Sector in Russia', *Europe–Asia Studies*, Vol. 57, No. 3, May 2005, pp. 457–80.

Sakhalin on favourable PSA terms, granted in the 1990s to compensate for the fragile rule of law and tenuous property rights. The creation of TNK-BP in 2003, formed among other things to exploit the enormous Kovytka field, appeared to signal an era of international energy cooperation.[53] The private sector powered growth in oil production, with output of the three largest companies rising by 90 per cent between 1998 and 2003. All this changed from 2003. The Yukos affair represented a transfer of assets, not only between companies but also out of the private and into the state sector. The proportion of oil produced by state companies by late 2005 had risen to 30 per cent.[54] The proportion of the Russian oil industry owned by the state rose from 10 per cent in 1999, some 20 per cent in 2004, to reach 42 per cent in 2008.[55] Over the same period the share of GDP in private hands declined from 70 to 65 per cent.[56]

The extension of state management of the economy had both political and economic consequences. At the most basic level, the expansion of state control is seen by many as the application of a less-efficient economic model. Between 1998 and 2004, Shevtsova notes, state-controlled oil companies increased their output by 75 per cent, whereas private companies achieved a 132 per cent rise.[57] According to Illarionov, state interventionism harmed the economy, leading to falls in investment in the oil sector and falling rates of oil production. He noted that since Rosneft had taken over Yukos's main production unit, costs had risen and revenues had fallen. Under Yukos Yuganskneftgaz had increased output by 15–20 per cent annually, was well above world standards, whereas under Rosneft it cut production by 2 per cent in the first year.[58] McFaul and Stoner-Weiss also note that '[r]enationalization has caused declines in the performance of formerly private companies, destroyed value in Russia's most valuable companies, and slowed investment, both foreign and domestic'. The change in particular affected Yukos: 'Before Khodorkovsky's arrest, Yukos was Russia's most successful and transparent company, with a market value of $100 billion in today's terms. The redistribution of Yukos's properties not only reduced the value of these assets by billions of dollars but also dramatically slowed the company's oil production.'[59]

Some of these charges are true. They cite the case of Sibneft, whose value and output levels fell after being acquired by Gazprom. Even YNG registered a small fall in output when it passed out of Yukos's hands, producing 51.8 million tonnes of oil in 2004 and only 51.2 in 2005.[60] Ahrend notes that investment in

[53] Miriam Elder, 'How the State Got a Grip on Energy', *Moscow Times*, 14 March 2008, p. 1.

[54] Iwona Wiśniewska, *The Invisible Hand... of the Kremlin: Capitalism 'à la Russe'* (Warsaw, Centre for Eastern Studies, February 2997), p. 42.

[55] According to UralSib research, cited in Elder, 'How the State Got a Grip on Energy'.

[56] Hanson, 'The Russian Economic Puzzle', p. 877.

[57] Liliya Shevtsova, 'Rossiya pered novym politicheskim tsiklom: Paradoksy stabil'nosti i Petro-State', in Wojciech Konończuk (ed.), *Putin's Empire* (Warsaw, Stefan Batory Foundation, 2007), p. 21.

[58] 'Not a Sycophant', *Russia Profile*, Vol. 3, Issue 1, January–February 2006, pp. 15–18, at p. 15.

[59] Michael McFaul and Kathryn Stoner-Weiss, 'The Myth of the Authoritarian Model: How Putin's Crackdown Holds Russia Back', *Foreign Affairs*, Vol. 87, No. 1, January–February 2008, p. 82.

[60] Wiśniewska, *The Invisible Hand... of the Kremlin*, p. 62, n. 35.

oil extraction decreased by a quarter between January and September 2004, which he attributes directly to the Yukos affair.[61] However, even after the start of the Yukos affair foreign investment in 2004 rose by 50 per cent to $11.7 billion from $8 billion the previous year,[62] although the year as a whole saw a net outflow of $8 billion as individuals and businesses pulled money out of the country in the wake of Khodorkovsky's arrest, although from 2005 there were accelerating net capital inflows.[63] The immediate reaction to the Yukos affair was a fourfold increase in capital flight in 2004 term over the previous year,[64] but this soon levelled off and despite the difficult political conditions Russia became an attractive region in which to invest. The Yukos affair, therefore, had a limited impact on foreign investment in Russia.

The story is similar for its effect on production, although it is difficult to separate the Yukos factor from the general slowdown in growth. Crude oil output increased by 55 per cent from 1998 to 2005, but after 2004 the growth rate levelled off, falling to 2.2 per cent in 2006.[65] Russian oil production and export volume growth fell sharply after 2004. Output growth in 2003 was 11 per cent, but in 2005 it fell to 2.8 per cent and only 2.1 per cent in 2007, compared to an average of 8.5 per cent between 2000 and 2004.[66] By 2008 output growth had moved into negative territory, falling by 0.2 per cent in the first quarter of 2008. No single factor explains the declining growth rates, and as Sagers stresses, political issues were only part of the story. He looks at the mix of political (above all Yukos-related), economic (the rising cost of inputs and rouble appreciation), geological (diminishing returns from Soviet 'legacy' fields in West Siberia and the slow development of new fields), and transport issue (notably distribution bottlenecks) factors involved.[67]

According to Vladimir Milov, the head of the Institute of Energy Policy in Moscow, and colleagues, the slowdown in oil production growth was caused by four main factors:[68] (1) the redistribution of assets and property rights, notably through the Yukos affair; (2) the weakening incentives to produce for export, because of high taxes on oil exports; (3) the relegation of the energy sector as a 'secondary economic sphere that should service and subsidize other sectors';[69] and (4) pipeline capacity bottlenecks, exacerbated by the postponement of the Murmansk oil export project. Interestingly, writing in 2006 they note that even

---

[61] Rudiger Ahrend, 'Russia's Post-Crisis Growth: Its Sources and Prospects for Continuation', *Europe–Asia Studies*, Vol. 58, No. 1, January 2006, pp. 1–24.

[62] Anna Smolchenko, 'OECD: Investment Rises 50% in 2004', *Moscow Times*, 28 June 2005, p. 7.

[63] Shaun Walker, 'A Reverse in Capital Outflow', *Russia Profile*, Vol. 3, No. 3, April 2006, p. 11.

[64] *Izvestiya*, 17 January 2005, p. 1.

[65] Kryukov and Moe, 'Russia's Oil Industry', p. 341.

[66] Philip Hanson, 'How Sustainable is Russia's Energy Power?', *Russian Analytical Digest*, No. 38, 2 April 2008, p. 9.

[67] Matthew J. Sagers, 'The Regional Dimension of Russian Oil Production: Is a Sustained Recovery in Prospect?', *Eurasian Geography and Economics*, Vol. 47, No. 5, 2006, pp. 505–45.

[68] Vladimir Milov, Leonard L. Coburn, and Igor Danchenko, 'Russia's Energy Policy, 1992–2005', *Eurasian Geography and Economics*, Vol. 47, No. 3, 2006, pp. 285–313.

[69] Ibid., p. 286.

after the loss of YNG, Yukos still owned Tomskneft and other producers in Eastern Siberia, and remained reluctant to use its resources for ESPO rather than its pet project to ship oil to Daqing;[70] so from the state's perspective, they had to go all the way to remove the Yukos obstruction for its plans for an oil export pipeline to the Pacific. Milov and his team were highly critical of Russia's energy strategy, arguing that it is 'fragmentary and contradictory', and determined by short-term factors.[71]

The usual charge is that state-owned companies have the poorest performance when it comes to extraction.[72] However, the ownership changes were at most only partially responsible. High taxes on the energy sector were also responsible for the slowdown, with any revenues higher than $27 per barrel being taken by the state (a policy partially reversed in 2007). Kudrin acknowledged that the heavy tax burden inhibited investment in the development of new fields, and in response he proposed a $4.2 billion cut in the oil mineral extraction tax in 2009.[73] The tax threshold rose from $9 to $15 per barrel,[74] and speaking to the Federation Council Putin declared that the tax cuts would save the industry up to $6 billion annually from 2009.[75] The old tax regime discouraged the investment needed to develop new fields, as production in old provinces began to peter out. New fields in Eastern Siberia, however, would only come on stream after 2009 to compensate for the depletion of mature provinces in Western Siberia. The need was clear, since oil production in the first quarter of 2008, as noted, fell by 0.3 per cent, compared to the same period the previous year.

The 'peak oil' debate is as intense in Russia as elsewhere. According to Leonid Fedun, the vice president of Lukoil, 'Russia oil production has peaked and may never return to current levels', running in 2007 at nearly 10 million barrels a day, a level of output that in his view was unsustainable; for him, daily output of 8.5 to 9 million barrels a day was sustainable for the next twenty years.[76] The debate over 'peak oil', the supposed exhaustion of reserves, continues in both Russia and the world, with a whole raft of Russian experts challenging Fedun's forecast, while at the global level the cyclical nature of the oil business has been stressed.[77] There were also constraints on export capacity imposed by bottlenecks in the Transneft pipeline system. The Yukos affair in 2003/4, moreover, gave a shock to the economic system, and it took a few years for business leaders to adjust to the new rules of the game.

The redistribution of property, moreover, diverted funds away from investment. According to Milov: 'Funds are being used to finance these deals and not to

[70] Ibid., p. 297.   [71] Ibid., p. 287.

[72] For example, Wiśniewska, *The Invisible Hand ... of the Kremlin*, p. 55.

[73] 'LUKoil Slashes 2008 Output Forecast', *Moscow Times*, 7 April 2008, p. 6.

[74] Alexei Shapovalov, 'Neftyanoi rost zakonchilsya', *Kommersant*, 16 April 2008, p. 2.

[75] Medetsky, 'Putin Scolds Miller on Pipeline Access'.

[76] Alexander Tutushkin, 'Nalogi ili neft'', *Vedemosti*, 16 April 2008, p. 1; Tat'yana Milacheva, 'Pik proiden', *RBK Daily*, 16 April 2008, p. 1; *Financial Times*, 15 April 2008.

[77] Leonardo Maugeri, *The Age of Oil: The Mythology, History, and the Future of the World's Most Controversial Resource* (Boulder, CO, Praeger, 2007).

develop western and eastern Siberia.' Rosneft alone took on $22 billion in debt to finance its takeover of Yukos. Gazprom's acquisition spending spree was accompanied by a cut in capital expenditure in 2008 by 11 per cent to $12.3 billion, while at the same time raising long-term financial investments to $17.1 billion.[78] The company moved into the electricity sector, taking control of Mosenergo among other spin-off companies from United Energy Systems, as well as in nuclear power, quite apart from muscling in on Sakhalin 2 and Kovytka, the latter in May 2007 when TNK-BP sold its largest project to the company after months of pressure. Gazprom even had plans to take over the country's largest coal producer, SUEK, although this was the subject of an investigation of the Federal Anti-Monopoly Service. The development of gas fields at Shtokman, the Yamal Peninsula, and Sakhalin 1, 3, and 4 were all delayed.

The dual economy

The extension of state control was limited to the energy sector and some strategic parts of defence industries, although there were also some state acquisitions in banking, engineering, and metals. State interventionism was opposed by many liberal technocrats in the government but was sponsored by a coalition between the *silovik* and democratic statists in the presidential administration. As Hanson notes, Surkov's notion of 'sovereign democracy' found its counterpart in the idea of 'a sovereign economy', repudiating the alleged liberal denial of the importance of sovereignty. Hanson stresses that the rationale was nativist rather than statist, stressing the priority of 'national capital' in strategic sectors such as the energy, transport, and pipelines.[79]

Hanson notes the emergence of a dual economy, with different rules applying to each. The logic of enhanced state interventionism had little to do with traditional socialist ideas of the benefits of state control, but was located rather more in traditional patrimonial ideas of the beneficent state accompanied by mercantilist notions about the need to exclude foreigners from strategic sectors to allow national (rather than state) capital to develop. Putinist practices divided the nascent capitalist class into, on the one hand, 'trusted' (*doverennye*) people with a 'patriotic' approach, willing to support various state programmes (for example, to invest in the 'real economy' of manufacturing and production) and, on the other hand, 'offshore aristocrats' and 'cosmopolitans' (*kosmopolity*). It was clear that by 2003 Khodorkovsky was perceived as falling firmly into the latter category. The anti-cosmopolitanism of the Putin years, it must be stressed, had nothing to do with Stalin-type anti-Jewish campaigns, since plenty of Jews fell into the 'patriotic' category.

[78] Catherine Belton, 'Warning on Output Levels', *Financial Times: Investing in Russia* supplement, 2 October 2007, p. 4. *Financial Times*, 2 October 2007,

[79] Hanson, 'The Russian Economic Puzzle', p. 881. He cites Surkov's speech to business leaders on 17 May 2005.

Putin and the government insisted that the Yukos case did not signal a whole-sale revision of the privatizations of the 1990s. The long-awaited review by the Audit Chamber of the sell-offs turned out not to be as explosive as anticipated. A preliminary study in July 2004 found that the undervaluation of assets, the failure to meet investment obligations, and the non- or underpayment by auction winners cost the state just $1.6 billion, much lower than most estimates, especially since it is argued that Yukos alone was undervalued by much the same amount, and the same goes for Sibneft. The Chamber also pointed out that the main goal of privatization, the creation of a new property-owning class, had not been achieved.[80] The full report was finally released in December 2004, giving details of the review of 140 privatizations. The report noted that the loans-for-shares auctions, at which stakes in Yukos, Lukoil, Norilsk Nickel, Surgut-neftegaz, and other large companies were sold had 'every sign of being fraudulent deals'.[81] The rather pusillanimous conclusion was clearly intended to draw a line under the events of the 1990s, and to signal that the existing owners could rest secure in their property, as long as they did not cross the Kremlin. This was reinforced by the reduction of the statute of limitations on privatization cases at this time from ten years to three. Asked at the Sixth Russian Congress of Judges on 30 November 2004 whether 'the state itself depends on oligarchic groups, which use the state in their self-interest', Putin conceded that this was still the case, and he promised to use the judicial system to separate the country's richest people from power.[82] Although there would be no wholesale revision of the 1990s privatizations, the political logic of the Yukos affair was far from exhausted.

The first 2 Sakhalin projects had been shaped in the more liberal Yeltsin era, but in later projects Russian firms dominated, with Rosneft enjoying a majority stake in Sakhalin 3, 4, and 5. In the event, environmental concerns were used to lever renegotiations over the 1994 production-sharing agreement in the Shell-led Sakhalin-2 oil and gas project. In December 2006, a deal was reached whereby Shell's stake fell from 55.5 to 27.5 per cent, while the stakes of Shell's Japanese partners Mitsui and Mitsubishi fell to 12.5 per cent and 10 per cent, respectively, while Gazprom's rose to 51 per cent plus one share. At the same time, Gazprom took over control of the Kovytka gas field from TNK-BP. In both cases the prices paid by Gazprom 'were broadly fair'.[83] Neither Sakhalin-2 nor Kovytka were reprises of the Yukos affair, characterized by levered expropriation of its main assets, but now the Russian government used more civilized methods, although it was certainly robust in its negotiations. PSAs are typically concluded with unde-veloped countries lacking an oil industry of their own, such as Angola and Nigeria, but this certainly did not apply to Russia. Khodorkovsky had long argued that the

---

[80] Lyuba Pronina, 'Chamber says $1.6 Bln Lost in '90s Sell-Offs', *Moscow Times*, 5 July 2004.

[81] Olga Proskurina, Alexander Tutushkin, Andrei Lemeshko, Anna Nikolaeva, 'Oligarkhov ne obidyat', *Vedemosti*, 1 December 2004.

[82] http://www.kremlin.ru/text/appears/2004/11/80381.shtml.

[83] Neil Buckley and Catherine Belton, 'Corruption Complicates an Image Problem', *Financial Times: Investing in Russia* supplement, 2 October 2007, p. 2.

PSAs were unfair and a bad deal for Russia, and that Western companies should work in the country on exactly the same basis as Russian companies, complying with local tax, legal, and environmental regimes—the argument now advanced, ironically, by the Russian government. The PSA system, as noted, was abolished in 2003.

The state became ever more prominent in the energy sector, although this was not renationalization but 'deprivatization'. In the economy as a whole by 2006 privately owned companies represented 80 per cent of all enterprises, while the state's share fell to 4 per cent. In the oil industry, however, the split between state and non-state controlled enterprises was 42:58, which would change to 52:48 if Russneft fell into the state's hands (see below). The state's growing role in the energy sector did cause some concern. The head of Russia's fourth largest oil company, Surgutneftegaz, Vladimir Bogdanov, warned that 'monopolism' by the state could lead to a fall in production, and similar concerns had been voiced earlier by Vagit Alekperov, the head of Lukoil. There were persistent rumours that Surgutneftegaz could itself be the subject of a potential takeover by Rosneft.[84] The appropriation of Yukos assets mirrored the way that they had been gathered in the 1990s, but now instead of insider privatization a process of crony deprivatization was at work.

Continuing consolidation

The case of Mikhail Gutseriev, the head of Russneft, reveals a continuing pattern of state attack against independent business, in particular in the energy sector, and had a number of Yukos-like characteristics. According to Latynina, the distinctive feature of Putin's regime was that 'the Russian businessman has been transformed into game being hunted by people in epaulets'. The first victim was Khodorkovsky, with the hunter in her view being none other than the president, and now '[t]he right to commit crime has become part of official privilege'.[85] Gutseriev headed Slavneft from 2000 under Abramovich's patronage, but in connection with the plan to sell the state's share in the company in 2002 he was deposed. A struggle then ensued, with the Sibneft candidate, Yuri Sukhanov, who was not to the liking of *siloviki*, coming under judicial attack but he resisted and ended up at the head of the company. Not surprisingly, when 75 per cent of Slavneft was sold in December 2002, a consortium of Sibneft and TNK won, and Rosneft was not even allowed to bid.[86] Established in 2002 by Gutseriev on assets acquired from the former state company Slavneft, by 2007 Russneft was one of the country's ten largest oil companies, producing in 2006 17 million tonnes and with reserves estimated at 630 million tonnes. Russneft was partly owned by the Swiss commodity trader Glencore International, the company that had invested heavily in Russia even

---

[84] Catherine Belton, 'Warning on Output Levels', *Financial Times: Investing in Russia* supplement, 2 October 2007, p. 4.

[85] Julia Latynina, 'Open Season: Life in Putin's Russia', *Washington Post*, 22 June 2008.

[86] Simonov, *Russkaya neft'*, pp. 59–60.

after its founder Marc Rich had fled to America to avoid charges of tax evasion, racketeering, and fraud; for which he was pardoned by Bill Clinton in January 2001.

In January 2007 Russneft was presented with punitive tax demands, which led the company to make a loss in 2007 of $521.3 million (R12.25 billion), compared to a net profit of R9.94 billion in 2006.[87] In July 2007 Gutseriev was forced to sell his company to a 'friendly' business, Deripaska's Basic Element for some $3 billion (as well as the settlement of outstanding debts to Sberbank and Glencore of $2.8 billion, as well as settling tax issues), after having been presented with tax charges totalling R3.5 billion. This did not save him, and on 28 August he was served an arrest warrant *in absentia*, since by then he had fled abroad to join the lengthening list of fallen Russian oligarchs in London. He had allegedly breached the terms of his pre-trial investigation. As with Yukos, there was much speculation that Sechin sought Russneft's annexation to Rosneft, and the tax issue was once again used to achieve the effective expropriation of a company. It was not clear whether Deripaska was a willing intermediary in this, or whether he had ambitions of his own to merge Russneft with his own companies. In addition, while Deripaska may have coordinated his actions with the Kremlin administration and Putin personally, there were other interests at stake (led by Sechin) which had their own plans. This suggests that the redivision of property was beginning to take increasingly anarchic forms. Kremlin in-fighting once again demonstrated that the Putin administration was far from united, with the various factions fighting for a share of property.

In an open letter published on 30 July Gutseriev argued that he had refused an invitation to leave the oil industry 'the easy way', and when he refused 'they tightened the screws on the company with unprecedented persecution' by the GPO, as well as by the MVD and the Federal Antimonopoly Service (FAS). He insisted that 'the actions of certain people in the power system are directed against me personally'. He denied all the charges, and alleged that hundreds of Russneft employees as well as members of his own family had been the target of 'night searches and searches lasting hours'. The only way to save Russneft, he argued, was for him to leave.[88] The case has many echoes with that of Yukos earlier. Khodorkovsky's attempts to distance himself from Yukos had not saved the company, and the strategy would not work for Gutseriev either. Unlike Khodorkovsky, however, Gutseriev proved less resilient, and two days later he withdrew all the 'political charges', and argued that it had been a simple shareholder's decision to sell the company.[89] In the event, on 7 August FAS declined Basic Element's plan to buy Russneft, on the grounds of inadequate documentation. The shares in Russneft were frozen, and although an arbitrage court in January 2008 slightly reduced

---

[87] 'Tax Claims Push Russneft Into the Red', *Moscow Times*, 2 April 2008, p. 7.

[88] Mikhail Gutseriev, 'Ya reshil uiti', *Vedemosti*, 30 July 2007, p. 12; see also Anna Firsova, 'Poprobui otkazhis', *Gazeta*, 30 July 2007, p. 5. The letter was soon removed from the company's website, and Gutseriev subsequently disavowed its contents, Miriam Elder, 'Court Orders Arrest of Oil Tycoon', *Moscow Times*, 29 August 2007.

[89] Interfax, 1 August 2007.

the tax demand, the international arrest warrant remained in force. The purchase was put on hold, and by early 2008 even Deripaska's Base Element was being investigated for alleged tax avoidance through the use of subsidiaries in 2003/4.[90]

The whole Russneft case had allegedly been provoked by the Kremlin's anger that in 2005 and 2006 Russneft had bought Yukos assets without its sanction.[91] Russneft had taken advantage of Yukos's bankruptcy to take over, for example, its contract with MOL of Hungary for extraction in the Zapadno-Malobalyk field in Western Siberia,[92] and in February 2006 the company bought a 49 per cent stake in Transpetrol, the issue that may well have caused upset in the Kremlin. Another theory held that Gutseriev's problems had arisen because of his political activity in allegedly funding opposition to the Kremlin-backed president of Ingushetia, Murat Zyazikov. Gutseriev was ethnically Ingush, and he had formerly been a Duma deputy for the LDPR, as well as being a deputy speaker in the Duma.[93] Yet another theory argued that Russneft's acquisition by state-sponsored bodies was just another indication of the state's strategy 'to use oil and gas to transform Russia into a global superpower', and for this all significant energy resources had to be concentrated in the hands of people friendly to the Kremlin.[94] Temerko argues that Gutseriev had been given the all-clear from highly placed Kremlin officials to bid for Yukos assets, but that he had then been caught up 'in a serious conflict of interests among Kremlin officials'.[95] In other words, faction fights in the Kremlin allegedly derailed the smooth distribution of Yukos assets.

More broadly, the Russneft case saw the use of an old Bolshevik law dating to the 1920s that allowed the state to confiscate the proceeds of business deals if their purpose was ruled to be contrary to 'the fundamentals of order and morality'. The law had been rarely used, but after the Yukos affair the law was applied in tax cases, allowing the state to confiscate the assets of companies guilty of evasion.[96] Not surprisingly, magnates in other spheres adjusted their behaviour accordingly. Deripaska, for example, emerged as loyal instrument of Kremlin policies, and he repeatedly affirmed his willingness to do the state's bidding. Indeed, questioned whether he would be willing to give up his main holding, Rusal, if asked by the Kremlin, echoing Khodorkovsky's sentiments earlier, he affirmed his readiness to do so, noting that 'I don't separate myself from the state'.[97]

The dismemberment of Yukos allowed a newcomer into the field in the shape of Imperial Oil, established by the British lawyer Peter Levine in 2004. He man-

[90] Lyudmila Podobedova, ' "RussNeft" ' ne proshla kassatsiyu', *RBK Daily*, 28 January 2008, p. 4; 'Odnodnevnoi dozor', *Kommersant*, 29 January 2008, p. 1.

[91] Irina Reznik, 'Gutseriev otdal neft', *Vedemosti*, 24 July 2007.

[92] Wiśniewska, *The Invisible Hand... of the Kremlin*, p. 60, n. 17.

[93] *Vedemosti*, 13 August 2007.

[94] Yuliya Latynina, 'Billion-Dollar Principles', *Moscow Times*, 1 August 2007, p. 7.

[95] Irina Reznik, ' "On vsegda byl beloi voronoi" ', *Vedemosti*, 21 August 2007.

[96] On 10 April 2008 Russia's highest civil court ruled that the law should not be applied in tax cases but only in criminal violations such as arms or drug smuggling and counterfeiting. Gregory L. White, 'Russian Court Limits Use of Civil Law to Seize Assets', *Wall Street Journal*, 11–13 April 2008, p. 2.

[97] *Financial Times*, 10 July 2007; 'Another Billionaire Ready to Give Everything to the State', RFE/RL, *Newsline*, 2 October 2007, at http://rferl.org/newsline/2007/10/021007.asp#archive.

aged to buy Siberian oil assets through intermediaries in Tomsk and most of its 400 employees formerly worked for Yukos at Tomskneft. By the end of 2007 it produced 10,000 barrels of oil per day, and had ambitious plans to expand. The company clearly was able to negotiate the treacherous waters of Russian business and keep on the right side of the state.[98]

Just how treacherous these waters were came home to Robert Dudley, the head of TNK-BP in 2008, which by then had become Russia's third largest oil company valued at $38 billion, when the status of the non-Russian staff of the company's Moscow headquarters was questioned, and then in June Dudley himself was called in for questioning by the MVD as part of a criminal investigation into alleged large-scale tax evasion, the now familiar Yukos gambit. The four Russian partners, Mikhail Fridman, German Khan, Viktor Vekselberg, and Len Blavatnik (who held their stake through the Alfa-Access-Renova consortium), accused Dudley of 'running the firm as if it were a BP subsidiary' and demanded his resignation.[99] They condemned the use of staff seconded from BP, which the four considered expensive and unnecessary; but above all they wanted to see TNK-BP expand globally, but this could have brought it into conflict with BP's international interests. As far as BP was concerned, this looked like a case of *reiderstvo*, when corporate raiders take over even successful companies. The Yukos link is deeper than the methods employed, since Dudley was questioned about TNK's tax affairs from 2001 to 2003, before the joint company was formed, at the time when Simon Kukes was TNK's president before he went on to take over at Yukos. The link is even deeper, since it still rankled with the government that Alfa-Group and Renova in 1999 had gained 49 per cent of TNK for a mere $90 million.[100]

The attack on Yukos can be considered a massive state-sponsored corporate raid. Corporate raiding has a long pedigree in Russia, and in the 1990s included the use of bankruptcy courts to take over companies for immediate profit, as well as more directly violent methods. Vadim Volkov has described the various stratagems used in what he calls 'violent entrepreneurship'.[101] Contemporary raiding can be seen to represent a step forward towards legality, since it no longer employs the gangster violence of the Yeltsin era, and like the arguments defending equity investment companies in Britain, could improve the performance of the victim companies.[102] However, while a corporate raid in the West usually entails a stronger company using legal means to take over a weaker company and can lead to improved performance, in Russia corrupt government officials and law enforcement officers are often involved using illegal means to seize companies and

---

[98] Miriam Elder, 'A Little Oil Firm Playing a Big Game', *Moscow Times*, 21 December 2007, p. 1.

[99] Luke Harding, 'Chief Executive Grilled in Russian Siege of BP', *The Guardian*, 6 June 2008, p. 30.

[100] Poussenkova, *From Rigs to Riches*, p. 3.

[101] Vadim Volkov, 'Violent Entrepreneurship in Post-Communist Russia', *Europe–Asia Studies*, Vol. 51, No. 5, July 1999, pp. 741–54; Vadim Volkov, *Violent Entrepreneurs: The Use of Force in the Making of Russian Capitalism* (Ithaca, NY, Cornell University Press, 2002).

[102] A. Kireev, 'Reiderstvo na rynke korporativnogo kontrolya: rezultat evolyutsii silovogo predprinimatel'stva', *Voprosy ekonomiki*, No. 8, 2007, pp. 80–92.

assets from their legal owners. In his meeting with business leaders at the Stolypin Club on 30 October 2007 (see below) Surkov noted that raiding had become a major problem in the late 1990s,[103] but as the head of the Higher Arbitration Court, Anton Ivanov, noted, with the onset of the late Putinite stability, raiding had declined.[104] This was probably too sanguine a view.[105]

A NEW MODEL OF POLITICAL ECONOMY

The Yukos affair was used to forge a new model of political economy. The close relationship between business and power was not dissolved but as a result of the Yukos affair it was reconfigured. It is not clear what the new model should be called, with various terms used to describe the strengthening role of state and semi-state companies in the economy. The basic drift is towards the creation of a system in which the state does not renationalize the commanding heights of the economy, but places its representatives in the boardrooms of leading companies, above all in the energy sector. Andrei Ryabov, of the Carnegie Moscow Center, argues that 'state capitalism' is being formed in Russia, accompanied by its increased 'chaebolisation' (the South Korean model).[106] This is a view shared by Soros, who argued that the Yukos case was 'the end of an era, the end of the era of robber capitalism and the beginning of that of state capitalism'.[107] This is probably going too far. The state under Putin did not directly renationalize energy companies, but it asserted a supervisory capacity that can be described as 'deprivatization'. Elements of this have been seen elsewhere, notably when president Chun Doo Hwan in South Korea forced a powerful *chaebol* into bankruptcy for failing to support one of his pet social projects.[108]

Deprivatization

The Yukos case was part of the Kremlin's attempts to introduce a new model of state–business relations in the country. In particular, the leadership under Putin sought to restore for the state a pre-eminent role in the energy sector, above all in the supply and distribution of oil (it already enjoyed an effective monopoly in the gas sector though its stake in Gazprom). On several occasions Putin regretted the

---

[103] Alexander Protopopov, *Ekspert*, No. 41, 5–11 November 2007.

[104] Marina Selina, ' "Kolichestvo sudebnykh sporov rezko vozrastaet ili padaet, kogda v strane proiskhodit ser'eznye potryaseniya": Intervyu s predsedatelem VAS Antonoim Ivanovym', *RBK Daily*, 16 April 2007, p. 13.

[105] 'Corporate Raiders are "Scourge" of Economy', *Moscow Times*, 21 May 2008.

[106] *Gazeta*, 22 November 2004.

[107] RIA Novosti, 18 March 2005, in *Johnson's Russia List*, No. 9096, item 11.

[108] Peter Ferdinand, 'Russia and China: Converging Responses to Globalization', *International Affairs*, Vol. 83, No. 4, 2007, p. 670.

privation of Russia's energy sector in the 1990s, and in power he assiduously built up the Kremlin's energy portfolio to establish what Peter Lavelle, one of the most acute observers of the contemporary Russian political scene, calls 'KremPEC'—the Kremlin Petroleum and Energy Corporation.[109]

In an extraordinarily revealing interview during the 2007 parliamentary campaign, Oleg Shvartsman, the head of the financial-industrial Finansgroup, claimed that his $3.2 billion fund management company handled the financial affairs of 'certain political figures', using a variety of instruments including offshore companies, and had close links with people in the presidential administration, the FSB and the Foreign Intelligence Services (SVR). He claimed that his company had the backing of the state to conduct corporate raids on private companies to force them back into state ownership, what he called the 'velvet reprivatization' of assets initially privatized in the 1990s. Methods included what he termed 'voluntary-coercive instruments', acting as a type of 'collective extortionist' applied with the assistance of the Interior Ministry's (MVD) departments fighting against organized crime and economic crime. He claimed that Sechin, the *éminence grise* of the *siloviki*, was behind the whole exercise. He also revealed Finansgroup's other activities:

We have a political organisation that is called the 'Union of Social Justice of Russia', and I have always been responsible for its economics and finances, and have financed the organisation. This structure was created in 2004, after President Putin said that big business should have a social responsibility to the state. At that time our colleagues from the FSB decided that an organisation must appear that will incline, bend, torment, and lead the various and sundry Khordokovskies toward social activeness.[110]

In other words, the Union of Social Justice would force business to be free and to fulfil its social responsibilities.

The most vivid manifestation of deprivatization is the appointment of senior officials of the presidential administration to key boardroom positions, as the Kremlin imposed direct supervision over Russia's strategic companies. Already in January 1999 Prime Minister Primakov and Chief of Staff Nikolai Bordyuzha had been ordered to increase control over the selection of state representatives to the boards of directors in which the state owned a controlling share, prompted by controversies the previous year over privatization and tax payments with Gazprom, Svyazinvest, and Purneftegaz.[111] If under Yeltsin the appointment of ministers to the boards of state-owned companies had become customary, the practice now changed its form. As well as ministerial officials, now representatives of the presidential administration entered the board room, representing a concentration of power in Putin's inner circle. By mid-2006, eleven members of the presidential administration chaired state companies and had twelve further state directorships; fifteeen senior government officials held six chairmanships and twenty-four other

---

[109] Peter Lavelle, 'Untimely Thoughts: Analysis: The Kremlin's "Energised" 2005', 7 January 2005.
[110] *Kommersant*, 30 November 2007.
[111] 'Kremlin to Increase Control Over State Companies', RFE/RL, *Newsline*, 28 January 1999.

board seats.[112] Russia was unique in allowing serving ministers or senior executive officials to sit on the boards of government companies.

These people did not enjoy operational control and were intended to represent the state's interests, if not the national interest. The appointment of Alexei Miller to Gazprom helped put an end to what had been the grand theft of subsidiaries, and allowed the recovery of at least a $1 billion in assets.[113] Nevertheless, the degree to which officialdom and business had become entwined under Putin is extraordinary. The influence of Soviet appointment practices in post-communist Russia is seen in the continuing interpenetration of political and economic elites.[114] Putin drew on his network of former associates from St Petersburg and the security services not only to staff his administration but also to dominate state-controlled businesses. We have already noted Sechin's appointment as chairman of the board of the Rosneft oil company on 27 July 2004, Surkov became chair of the board at Transnefteprodukt, the carrier of refined oil products, while Sergei Prikhodko, the president's foreign policy adviser, chaired the giant nuclear fuel producer TVEL, which owned the Priargun Complex, one of the world's biggest uranium processing businesses based, as we have seen, near Krasnokamensk. By the end of 2004 just seven board room appointees supervised nine state companies with assets worth $222 billion, or 40 per cent of Russian GDP. This network of Kremlin officials and government ministers represented 'the quasiboard of what might be called Russia Inc, comprising the country's most lucrative assets not just in oil and gas but also nuclear power, diamonds, metals, arms, aviation and transport'.[115]

The regime-centred fusion of economic and political power, accompanied by the dominance of the media, was intended to provide strategic leadership to achieve national goals, but became part of a pattern of self-serving elite reproduction. The logic of struggle against the old perceived oligarchic dominance in a perverse way perpetuated some of the worst features of the old system, including the use of the courts to pursue sectional interests. Soviet practices of the interchange of political and economic officialdom were revived, with inadequate separation of the political sphere from the world of business. Although intended to reduce corruption and to advance the state's developmental goals, the interlocking pattern of appointments provided broad opportunities for personal enrichment in the emerging bureaucratic-faction type system.

The implications of this have been explored by Sergei Peregudov, who argues that the events of summer 2003 represented a revolution in state–business relations in Russia, although the attack on Yukos was only one element of a much larger reorientation. The process of the 'privatization of power' was halted, and

[112] Neil Buckley and Arkady Ostrovsky, 'Back in Business—How Putin's Allies and Turning Russia into a Corporate State', *Financial Times*, 19 June 2006.

[113] Loc. cit.

[114] *Nomenklatura i nomenklaturanya organizatsiya vlast' v Rossii* (Perm, Russian Ministry of Education and Science, together with the Perm State Technical University and the Centre for Elite Studies, 2004).

[115] Buckley and Ostrovsky, 'Back in Business'.

with it the autonomy of big business, the last remaining bearer of independent social and political power. While during the period of 'equidistance' business and the oligarchs were distanced from direct involvement in foreign and defence policy, personnel decisions and the resolution of purely political issues, but their influence on socio-economic questions and the shaping of the socio-economic situation in the country actually grew.[116] Khodorkovsky's plans to support the opposition could have created a genuine alternative to the existing regime, the creation of a parliamentary democracy and the possibility of the rotation of power. Although this programme was not supported by the 'oligarchate' as a whole, it was taken very seriously by the authorities. As Peregudov notes: 'Where Khodorkovsky led, others could follow.'

The authorities were also increasingly concerned by the lobbying activity of corporations, especially those in the energy sector, and their unwillingness to share the windfall with others, including their fellow citizens.[117] Anomalies in distribution and contradictions within the business community explain the weakness of the response to the onset of the Yukos affair. In addition, attempts to reduce the statute of limitations on reviewing property acquired in the 1990s from ten years to three years had not yet succeeded, and hence the state retained a powerful weapon against the narrow and isolated layer of big business.[118] Once the attack began those who were perceived to be on the side of the oligarchs found themselves politically isolated, especially since the 2003 Duma elections were conducted in an atmosphere of populist oligarch-bashing. In Peregudov's view this, and not their failure to unite, explains the severe blow SPS and Yabloko suffered in the December 2003 elections.[119] Their defeat undermined party-political development as a whole and the possibility of effective political opposition, and thus the potential for pluralism. The bureaucratic basis of the regime was intensified, and the strengthening of neo-*dirigiste* policies and the 'power vertical' reduced the scope for independent political initiatives by business. However, this was far from being 'state corporatism', since business retained a degree of autonomy. Big business remained a strong voice in the political process, but the forms of its interventions and lobbying changed.[120] Abramovich was a model for the new system, who while denying any political ambitions deftly exploited political connections and 'administrative resources' to achieve his goals.

The Yukos case thus had a negative element—the reduction of Khodorkovsky's political influence, and also a positive aspect—the creation of a government-supervised economic system to fulfil the strategic objectives set by the administration. The Kremlin sought direct supervision over major revenue streams and senior corporate executives. There was a brutal logic to the case: '[T]he Kremlin learned a simple fact: private owners occasionally have their interests at heart and sometimes—like in the case of the oil company Yukos—go against

---

[116] S. P. Peregudov, 'Biznes i vlast' v rossii: k novoi modeli otnoshenii', in V. G. Ignatov et al. (eds.), *Vlastnye elity sovremennoi Rossii v protsesse politicheskoi transformatsii* (Rostov on Don, Severo-Kavkazkaya akademiya gosudarstvennoi sluzhby, 2004), p. 23.
[117] Ibid., p. 24.   [118] Ibid., p. 25.   [119] Ibid., p. 26.   [120] Ibid., p. 29.

perceived national priorities. In the latter case, the Kremlin resorted to force to uphold its supremacy in economic affairs.'[121] The Yukos affair began as political action, prompted by the fear that even a small part of the resources available to the company could buy political power in the country. The aim was to remove the resources that threatened the autonomy of the state, but soon became a struggle for the redistribution of its assets. The Kremlin feared a rebirth of the oligarchy in a new and perhaps even more dangerous form, and was willing to employ all means to ensure that the business of business was business and not politics.

The assault against Yukos and the way it was conducted sent a signal to the bureaucracy that administrative power was higher than the rule of law, and could be unleashed without fear of redress. The liberal technocrats, however, did not give up, and sought to insulate fallout of the Yukos affair to the energy sector. Gref on many occasions criticized the drift to economic statism, and called for the privatization of Rosneft and the reprivatization of YNG.[122] Equally, finance minister Kudrin noted the damaging effects of the Yukos affair,[123] although he had supported the move to ensure greater tax discipline. The extension of state control over the energy sector in conditions of blurred boundaries between the state and economic life and a weak judiciary put, as Hanson and Teague put it, 'exceptional power over business in the hands of a leader who cares to exert himself to wield it'.[124]

Towards a new embedded capitalism

The Yukos affair was a major disciplinary act to transform oligarchs into business-people. The Kremlin was only partially successful in achieving this goal. Three of the seven magnates identified by Berezovsky in 1997 are still in business, while companies such as Lukoil and Russian Aluminium remain major players on the Russian scene. But two important features have changed. The first is greater insecurity of property and persons. The Yukos affair undermined the sanctity of private property, and indicated that asset ownership was contingent on retaining the good will of the administration. Goyal notes that 'Yukos is a state within a state as much as Gazprom is', and stressed that 'the government has a right, indeed a duty, to interfere'.[125] The alternative to subordination to the political authorities, the ultimate 'trustee' of the state's natural assets, was raids by armed men, the confiscation of documents, the prosecution of executives and support staff, the

[121] Vlad Ivanenko, 'Russian Global Position After 2008', *Russia in Global Affairs*, Vol. 5, No. 4, October–December 2007, p. 147.
[122] *Finansovye izvestiya*, 11 January 2005; cited by Hanson, 'The Russian Economic Puzzle', p. 879, n. 21.
[123] *Moscow Times*, 2 June 2005; cited by Hanson, 'The Russian Economic Puzzle', p. 879, n. 21.
[124] Philip Hanson and Elizabeth Teague, 'Big Business and the State in Russia', *Europe–Asia Studies*, Vol. 57, No. 5, July 2005, p. 675.
[125] Goyal, 'Analysis: Sale of a State', p. 12.

forced bankruptcy of an enterprise, and the confiscation and transfer of property. This atmosphere of arbitrariness gave the green light for lesser bureaucrats to invent their own schemes for extortion and corruption.

Pressure on business was exacerbated by the continued insecurity of life. In 2003, 425 businesspeople were murdered. In July of the following year the murder of Paul Khlebnikov, the editor of the Russian version of *Forbes* magazine, reinforced the generalized sense of insecurity. The Yukos affair also highlighted the factional nature of Kremlin politics. Businesses had to ensure that they retained good connections not just with one faction but with the regime as a whole. We know that Khodorkovsky had good relations with Voloshin and the 'family' faction, but this was not enough to save him as other forces came into the ascendant. Abramovich managed to navigate the treacherous waters of Russian politics by maintaining strong relations with Putin personally, while Deripaska made a point of admitting that he was little more than the 'trustee' of property delegated by the state.

The second change was in the relationship between business and politics. A new category of 'state oligarchs' emerged, accompanied by the establishment of Kremlin control over strategic assets. Daniel Treisman has drawn the analogy between the emergence of what he calls the *silovarchs*, a combination of *siloviki* and oligarchs, in Russia, and the regime-led patterns of industrialization in South Korea in 1961–79 under General Park Chung Hee and in Indonesia in 1965–98 under General Suharto.[126] As he notes: 'Park began by jailing 20 leading Korean oligarchs [who had been accused of enriching themselves through low-priced privatizations], but then struck deals with them, permitting most to keep their property in return for political loyalty and investments in the domestic economy.'[127] Although the economic performance of these two countries is mixed, with Korea devising five-year plans and other Soviet-type instruments within the framework of private property to build an export-oriented economy, in Indonesia the tendency towards 'crony capitalism' in the long run proved dysfunctional. The Golkar party in Suharto's Indonesia acted as a catch-all party to mobilize the vote, but as with United Russia, the regime was hesitant to subordinate itself to this party and firmly kept control of the patronage system and in the end degenerated into a patrimonial dictatorship. The *silovarch* model in Russia proved attractive for foreign investment, rising from $11 billion in 2000 to $54 billion in 2005, and the *silovarch* companies have proved effective in international money markets.[128] However, in countries such as Nigeria various bouts of military rule have proved disastrous, while in Pakistan they have failed to achieve effective state formation.

The development of state corporations intensified the development of a rather more centralized model of national economic management. Already in a book published in 2001 Prokhorov had described 'The Russian Model of Management',

---

[126] Daniel Treisman, 'Putin's *Silovarchs*', *Orbis*, Vol. 51, No. 1, Winter 2007, pp. 147–51.
[127] Ibid., p. 148.   [128] Ibid., p. 149.

entailing centralized administrative management by a distinct managerial class.[129] Catch-up modernization through state activism leads to dubious economic gains but definite political losses, notably the restoration of 'the despotic foundations of state power'.[130] The idea of sovereign democracy entailed not only the affirmation of autonomy in international affairs, the assertion of regime power over political processes internally, but also the imposition of a *dirigiste* economic model that harked back to long-term models of state predominance over the economy. The Yukos affair in that context represented the re-emergence of a statist view of economic management after a brief interregnum of economic laissez-faire in the 1990s, which was a wholly novel experience for Russia. Although in the decade before the First World War a more organic capitalist model was beginning to develop, the state remained the driving force, and thus a Russian model of embedded capitalism remained in force.

Under Putin a new type of embedded capitalism began to emerge. It certainly did not mean the restoration of full-scale state-ownership, but it did tilt the balance towards redirecting the economy towards serving national goals. In his speech to the Russian Academy of Sciences on 8 June 2007 Surkov provided the philosophical foundations for the new approach: 'However much the organisation of the state may change, for all the uncertainty, the basic matrix is preserved of a consciousness [in which] synthesis predominates over analysis, intuition over reason, gathering things together and not dividing them.' The outcome for Surkov is clearly expressed in three fundamental characteristics of the Russian mentality: '[t]he striving for political wholeness and centralised power, the idealisation of goals, and the personification of politics'.[131] Once again Russia was governed by a ruling class with a strong patriotic vision of the country's development, and undoubtedly it drew on the long tradition of national self-affirmation against real and perceived enemies. The exercise of rooting the programme in a philosophical framework was also traditional for Russia. The quality of the political philosophy is not the issue, but what it reveals about the thinking of the regime. It would be going too far to suggest that Surkov had emerged as the court philosopher, undertaking a role like that of Mikhail Suslov in the post-Stalin era in the Soviet Union, or even of that of Konstantin Pobedonostsev under Alexander III and Nicolas II, but his writings did reveal some of the inner discourse of the regime.

With large reserves of petro-dollars the state consolidated its hold over profitable sectors of the economy. Even Medvedev insisted that state ownership and management had 'far from exhausted their potential'.[132] Later, however, he

[129] A. P. Prokhorov, *Russkaya model' upravleniya* (Moscow, Eksmo, 2006). The book is discussed by Stephen Shenfield, JRL Research and Analytical Supplement, issue No. 39, June 2007, in *JRL*, No. 144, 2007.

[130] Ibid., p. 315, quoting V. Krivorotov.

[131] Vladislav Surkov, 'Russkaya politicheskaya kul'tura: Vzglyad iz utopii', in Konstantin Remchukov (ed.), *Russkaya politicheskaya kul'tura: Vzglyad iz utopii. Lektsiya Vladislava Surkova. Materialy obsuzhdeniya v 'Nezavismoi gazete'* (Moscow, Nezavisimaya Gazeta, 2007), p. 8.

[132] Interview in *Ekspert*, 4 April 2005, p. 75.

insisted that the state corporations would be a temporary phenomenon. As his associate Igor Shuvalov put it at the Twelfth International Economic Forum in St Petersburg in June 2008, '[i]n an innovation society too much statism is as dangerous as its absence', and he stressed the need to cut back on 'excessive state intervention in the economy', including the gradual withdrawal of state officials from the boards and their replacement by 'professionals'.[133] A programme to appoint independent directors began.[134]

Meta-corruption, or an economy of rents

The struggle to obtain rents is the natural condition for market agents. Although the term is associated with monopoly, it also applies to a competitive market-place. Andrei Yakovlev distinguishes between innovative and political rent. Market agents in a competitive environment seek to reduce costs and maintain market share through innovation in technology, management practices, and organization. Political rent, 'on the other hand, appears when one market player uses his/her connections in government to influence the regulatory system, artificially limit access for new players, and obtain resources that do not correspond to his perfor-mance'.[135] This describes the position for the latter half of the 1990s, but Putin was able to modify the system to ensure that business needed to pay a political rent to the state to remain in business. At the same time, there was a no less important direct economic rent. Although Putin was lucky to enjoy the commodity price boom of the early twenty-first century, the foundation of his presidency was the state's ability to take the lion's share of the commensurate massive rise in rents. The country saw the return of meta-corruption, when as in the Soviet system corruption is the essence of the political regime, in which corruption is defined as a mechanism for the informal distribution of rents.

Putin's overhaul of the tax system provided the framework for effective collec-tion of energy and other rents later. Some of this was used to pay off external debts, some was invested in the Stabilization Fund and other similar instruments, and some was used to finance current state expenditure, notably in infrastructure, social programmes, and a rearmament plan. However, as Clifford Gaddy argues, total rent is much greater than the part formally collected and distributed by the government. It includes price subsidies on energy for domestic consumers (in par-ticular for gas), as well as forcing energy companies to purchase equipment from domestic manufacturers, even though the quality is often lower than imported

---

[133] Tat'yana Gurova and Ekaterina Shokhina, 'Global'nyi nasos spravedlivosti', *Ekspert*, No. 24, 16–22 June 2008, pp. 19–24, at p. 21. He was later reprimanded by Putin for his outspokenness: 'There are certain things only premiers are supposed to speak about', Putin insisted, *Argumenty nedeli*, No 27, July, 2008, p. 2.

[134] Anna Yukhanova, 'Step Made to Replace State Board Members', *Moscow Times*, 14 July 2008.

[135] Andrei Yakovlev, 'Interest Groups and Economic Reform in Contemporary Russia: Before and After Yukos', in Stephen White (ed.), *Politics and the Ruling Group in Putin's Russia* (London, Palgrave Macmillan, 2008), p. 110.

equivalents. Companies agreed to enter into these informal rent-sharing deals because of the fear of expropriation. Khodorkovsky fell foul of this system. As Gaddy puts it:

> It is very important to recognize the informal rent-sharing. This is the part of the iceberg that lies below the surface. That's the part that is hidden, and the part that tends to be larger. It's the part that can cause shipwrecks. One victim of the hidden iceberg was YUKOS. Khodorkovsky miscalculated. He refused to pay the excess costs. He tried to be a cost-minimizer (profit maximizer) in a system that dictated that he be a cost-maximizer.[136]

Thus in Tomsk, according to Gaddy, the Yukos subsidiary was forced to place orders with 'dinosaur' manufacturers, accompanied by bribes and other corrupt practices. When Khodorkovsky tried to break with this system, he became extremely unpopular.

Gaddy's model renders Putin a 'rent manager', overseeing the system of rent sharing. As we know from the experience of Nigeria and some other countries enjoying windfall energy profits, the mere existence of rent is not enough to improve public welfare. Russia under Putin was able to focus energy rents. As Gaddy puts it: 'First, he has managed the collection of the rent. Second, he has defined priorities for the use of the rent. Third, he has managed the actual process of rent sharing.' The latter was potentially the most difficult, with the various factions and interest groups trying to win control over the process. Even regional governors, as one of the central stakeholders in the distribution of resources, were brought into the system as subaltern 'regional rent managers' on behalf of the central state, dubbed by Gaddy 'Russia, Inc'. The actual ownership of business was less important than the control of rents. Thus we have argued that it is misleading to talk of renationalization under Putin; the notion of deprivatization entails the loss of sovereign company control over its rent, while formally remaining in the private sector. This is why it became so important for business leaders to pay the political rent, called by some 'relational capital', to ensure harmonious relations with the agency (the regime) that stood outside and above normal business transactions.

There remains a considerable debate in the academic literature over the definition of corruption, why it matters, and how to deal with it.[137] The standard response is that corruption increases transaction costs and depresses economic growth. However, Russia by any definition was plagued by both venal and meta-corruption, yet from 1999 it registered strong economic growth. Of course, the growth rate could well have been higher if corruption was higher, as it was in some of Russia's neighbours in the CIS, although it would be hard to argue that corruption was less prevalent in those countries. There are also political

---

[136] Statement of Clifford G. Gaddy, Senior Fellow The Brookings Institution, Committee on House Financial Services Subcommittee on Domestic and International Monetary Policy, Trade and Technology, 17 October 2007, in *JRL*, 219/25, 2007.

[137] For stimulating contributions, see János Kornai and Susan Rose-Ackerman (eds.), *Building a Trustworthy State in Post-Socialist Transition* (New York, Palgrave Macmillan, 2004).

consequences, above all the corrosive effects that corruption can have on democracy. In discussing the 'resource curse' in Chapter 11 we question whether energy rents derail democratic government in Russia.[138]

Russian practice in the 2000s reflects many of the ambiguities of the theoretical literature. Putin's meta-corruption was intended precisely to counter what he considered the earlier meta-corruption of the system. In his acceptance speech to lead the UR party list in the December 2007 elections, on 1 October 2007 Putin recalled the dire state of the country in the 1990s:

It looked at one time as though we would never manage to free ourselves from powerful oligarchs whose influence was based on corruption, violence and information blackmail. We have accomplished a great deal in terms of cleaning out this illegitimate influence from the upper levels of state power, but, as has been said today, we still have much to do in fighting corruption.[139]

After a period of uncertainty as the 'consultative' and 'equidistant' model of state–business relations established in the early 2000s began to unravel, the Yukos affair ended up with 'the complete political defeat of Russian business'.[140] The state under Putin, was able to achieve the 'nationalization of the elites', and the marginalization of what Surkov called the 'offshore aristocracy'.[141] This took the form of the effective deprivatization of the oil industry as well as the decapitation of autonomous elite structures, including the media and regional leaderships, and their subordination to the Kremlin. The process included 'the criminal prosecution of Kremlin opponents, as in the case of Mikhail Khodorkovsky'.[142] A type of service elite emerged.

A moral economy

Grigory Yavlinsky noted his astonishment in the 1990s about how little reformers like Gaidar or Yasin were concerned about the plight of ordinary Russians and talked about them as if they came from another planet.[143] From Polanyi's perspective, this would sooner or later provoke a defensive counter-movement by society, and Putin's leadership placed itself at the head of this. Polanyi was never quite clear how the state would take up the task of creating what Friedrich von Hayek called *taxis* (consciously arranged, instituted, and controlled order; in contrast to *cosmos*, spontaneous order generated by the operation of the invisible hand), but his narrative is permeated by a strong functionalist dynamic whereby objective factors

---

[138] For a comparative analysis, see Balmaceda, *Energy Dependency, Politics and Corruption in the Former Soviet Union.*

[139] http://www.kremlin.ru/text/appears/2007/10/146477.shtml.

[140] S. N. Pshizova, 'Politika kak biznes: rossiiskaya versiya (I)', *Polis*, No. 2, 2007, p. 115.

[141] Ivan Krastev, 'Rossiya kak "drugaya Evropa"', *Rossiya v global'noi politike*, Vol. 5, No. 4, July–August 2007, p. 39.

[142] Loc. cit.

[143] Quoted by Khlebnikov, *Krestnyi otets Kremlya Boris Berezovskii*, p. 103.

would force the hands of government.[144] Certainly, such a functionalist imperative had long been visible in the Russian polity. The argument had earlier been made, for example by Oleg Davydov, the minister for foreign economic relations between 1994 and 1997, that the key strategic sectors of Russian industry, including oil, gas, and metals should have been transformed into state corporations to habituate them to operating in market conditions, and only then gradually privatized.[145] A decade later Putin returned to this idea, but only after most key sectors of the economy had been sold for pitiful sums.[146] In 2000 Khlebnikov noted that the era of Russia's self-destruction was coming to an end, and that Putin would be faced with the need to restore the rule of law and attract foreign investment, but that his first task would be to deal with corruption and 'false-capitalism, whose embodiment was Boris Berezovsky'.[147]

Putin's control of energy rents provided his administration with the ability to achieve his objectives, above all a strengthening of domestic state capacity, its sovereignty abroad, and an improvement in standards of living. Putin's emphasis on 'strategic planning' dates back to his academic work in the 1990s, and now he had the resources to invest in areas considered central for the country's development. He defended his position in an interview when he was declared *Time*'s man of the year in December 2007. Asked about the state's role in regulating Russian industrialists, with a pointed reference to 'some very notable cases where there have been arrests and seizures of companies', Putin answered:

Well, thou shalt not steal. They didn't have difficulties with me. They had difficulties with the people of the country and with the law. When people do not live by the law, and thus get rich, while dozens of millions of Russians at the same time lose their meager lifetime savings, that creates distrust and alienation. My task was, as I've seen it, first of all, to teach everyone to live by the law, abide by the law, regardless of the thickness of their checkbooks. Secondly, to make our business more socially responsible and to remove the wall of alienation between the population and Russian business. We need business to understand its social responsibility, that the main task and objective for a business is not to generate extra income and to become rich and transfer the money abroad, but to look and evaluate what a businessman has done for the country, for the people, on whose account he or she has become so rich. And lastly, we have to do everything to defeat poverty.[148]

Putin's programme of state reconstitution commanded widespread domestic legitimacy, and his high personal ratings suggest also a high degree of support. In his final term as president the theme of morality also figured more prominently. In his

[144] The issue is discussed by Claus Offe, 'After Polanyi', Centre for the Study of Democracy, *CSD Bulletin*, Vol. 5, No. 2, Spring 1998, p. 13.

[145] Khlebnikov, *Krestnyi otets Kremlya Boris Berezovskii*, p. 129.

[146] Khlebnikov notes that Moscow city alone, which resisted the Chubais privatization plan, received more than ten times annually than the Russian government received from the sale of the whole of Russian industry, ibid, p. 149.

[147] Ibid., p. 322.

[148] 'Putin Q & A: Full Transcript', *Time*, 18 December 2007; http://www.time.com/time/specials/2007/personoftheyear/article/0,28804,1690753_1690757_1696150,00.html.

address to the Federal Assembly on 26 April 2007 he talked of 'the moral values that unite us', which are 'as important a factor in development as political and economic stability', and at the end of his speech he argued that the failure of the state to meet popular needs was 'immoral'.[149] Coming from an arch-technocrat, this may appear surprising. Nevertheless, it is a theme to which he returned later in discussing fairness (*spravedlivosti*) and moral values. In the light of the Yukos affair, of course, 'fairness' began to look rather like the redistribution of property and the persecution of independent business. This may well be the case, but the whole problem of what is meant by domestic and international fairness was also one of the central themes in the sovereign democracy discussion advanced by Surkov. At the time of the Medvedev succession the Kremlin appeared to be advancing the idea that the next president would have to deal 'not only with oil and gas, but also the issue of the moral and ethical norms of society'.[150]

In an interview at the time of the 2007/8 succession, Solzhenitsyn asked: 'Should the oligarchy continue to reproduce itself and who will inspire hope in the poor and deprived? Who is responsible for morality: the state or the market?' He criticized the centralization of the state, and stressed his favourite theme, 'the need to develop public initiative through local self government'.[151] Adam Smith insisted than an effective market system required strong social institutions, something notably lacking in post-communist Russia.[152] Ajay Goyal argues that Yukos, like Gazprom, 'is a trustee of the oil finds and reserves that were found during the Soviet years, serviced in part by slave laborers in the Gulag in conditions of imprisonment, illness, cold and misery', and the state had the right to prevent the sale of this 'strategic national reserve' to foreign companies.[153] William Butler develops this idea, noting the positive logic of the Yukos affair, relating to

the efforts of the Putin administration to address the redistribution of wealth concentrations and corruption that have proved to be a major legacy of the privatisation programmes dating from the early 1990s. The Khodorkovsky/Lebedev proceedings, still under appeal, are one, but not the only symptom, of this policy, and the legal system has been a major vehicle and instrument for achieving this end. The roots of these policies, in my view, are not merely that some have more and some less, or an exercise in eliminating a potential political rival. The property that was privatised in Russia actually, as a matter of law, was in the indivisible ownership of all Soviet citizens, so that the eventual massively unequal 'distributions' of that property amounted to not merely what seems to be an unfair

[149] http://president.kremlin.ru/text/appears/2007/04/125401.shtml.
[150] For a discussion of the 'remoralization' of Kremlin discourse, see Svetlana Babaeva, 'Svoboda ot morali: Chto tsenit sovremennaya Rossiya?', *Rossiya v global'noi politike*, Vol. 5, No. 4, July–August 2007, p. 23.
[151] Alexander Solzhenitsyn, 'Chto nam po silam', *Agumenty i fakty*, No. 5, 30 Janaury–5 February 2008, p. 3.
[152] Adam Smith, *The Theory of Moral Sentiments*, edited by D. D. Raphael and A. L. Macfie (Indianapolis, Liberty Fund, 1984).
[153] Goyal, 'Analysis: Sale of a State', p. 11.

accumulation, but the actual deprivation of individuals of their property in which they had a legal interest.[154]

The fundamental question, then, was what sort of market would be built in Russia. The Yukos affair had shown the deep ambivalence in the state and society about the autonomy of market relations, to the point that the head of the SPS in 2007, Nikita Belykh, could argue that '[w]e must rehabilitate capitalism as an idea'.[155]

---

[154] William Butler, 'Law and the Abuse of Power: Some Reflections on Policy for the Putin Administration', in Jennifer Moll (ed.), *Blueprint for Russia* (London, Foreign Policy Centre, 2005), pp. 35–8, at pp. 36–7.

[155] Interviewed by Ekaterina Grigor'eva and Georgii Il'ichev, 'Nam nuzhno reabilitirovat' kapitalzm kak ideyu', *Izvestiya*, 15 May 2007, pp. 1, 5.

11

Polity and Power

This age that believes itself to be the age of 'community' is more individualistic than the Renaissance or the era of the great feudal lords. Everything is happening as if there were a fixed amount of freedom and power in the world that is sometimes divided between millions of people and sometimes between *one single person* and other millions. 'Have my leftovers,' the dictators say.

Irène Némirovsky[1]

Almost any successor to Yeltsin would sooner or later have launched a campaign against the political and other excesses of the oligarchs of the 1990s. Already in the late Yeltsin years the rebalancing of the political system had begun, notably by Sergei Kirienko's government from March to August 1998, and then during Yevgeny Primakov's premiership from September 1998 to May 1999, and this undoubtedly played a major role in the choice of Putin as successor. However, few other than Putin would have acted so decisively and consistently in dealing with the perceived challenge to the political autonomy of the state represented by the oligarchs as a class and by Khodorkovsky individually. The political pretensions of the corporate elite represented an identifiable threat to the political regime, and Putin acted accordingly. However, while at first he distinguished between the 'criminal' and the 'bourgeois' oligarchs, he later unfairly placed Khodorkovsky in the former category. As the Yukos affair rolled on, soaring energy prices encouraged a powerful strain of resource nationalism accompanied by the intensification of factional conflict and the suffocation of public politics. On a personal level Putin appeared trapped by the Khodorkovsky case. The persecution of this independent figure damaged Putin's international reputation, but backing down would erode his prestige. Khodorkovsky retained his composure and, as Pavel Baev notes, has 'gained more respect than any PR-campaign would have brought him. Putin was irritated by his presence on the international arena, too independent and stylish, but now he is wary of his prisoner's shadow.'[2] Paradoxically, in jail Khodorkovsky found freedom, while Putin became ever more a prisoner of forces that he had unleashed but struggled to control.

[1] Irène Némirovsky, *Suite Française*, translated from the French by Sandra Smith (London, Chatto & Windus, 2006), p. 352.
[2] 'The Destruction of Yukos and Putin's Estrangement from the West', *Eurasian Daily Monitor*, Vol. 1, No. 113, 26 October 2004.

POLITICAL CONSEQUENCES

Commentators have often expressed mystification about why the Kremlin did not cut a deal with Yukos at various points in the case, and thus saved itself embarrassment. We argue that the main reason was faction fighting within the Kremlin itself, indicating that Putin did not monopolize power as much as some have suggested. As Ian Bremmer, the president of the Eurasia Group, puts it: '[T]he Kremlin is riven with rivalries that undermine the government's ability to formulate coherent policy approaches to the considerable challenges of the Russian reform process.'[3] This helps explain why pressure was continued against Yukos and its associates even after the first Khodorkovsky trial. According to Belkovsky, the first stage of the Yukos affair was a clear victory for Putin, signalling that the 1990s were over, that money would not determine politics, power was returned to the authorities, and Putin was once again transformed from 'the president of inertia and emptiness into the president of hope'; but in the second phase the whole affair was reduced to 'one lot of rich people stealing from another lot'.[4] From being an exemplary ideological campaign the Yukos affair had been reduced to another tawdry exercise in the redistribution of property.

Resources and power: The oil curse?

The Yukos affair took place in the context when the commodities boom of the 2000s provided a massive injection of energy rents, with both political and economic consequences. When managed effectively by a mature democratic state, the extra revenues can be used for the public good. However, in a whole raft of countries the 'oil curse' has distorted the economy, reduced political accountability, and fostered separatism and domestic conflict. 'The conflicts', according to Michael Ross, 'range in magnitude from low-level secessionist struggles, such as those occurring in the Niger Delta and Southern Thailand, to full-blown civil wars, such as in Algeria, Colombia, Sudan, and of course, Iraq'.[5] Within Russia, the oil-rich regions of Chechnya and Tatarstan were at the head of autonomy struggles, and although many other factors were involved, resource endowment provided local elites with extra confidence to pursue their claims. On becoming prime minister in August 1999 Putin challenged the Chechen insurgency militarily, and used trenchant political mechanisms to restrain Tatarstan's ambitions. He was no less resolute in taming the ambitions of the 'over-mighty subject', Khodorkovsky. The Yukos affair can ultimately be reduced to a struggle between politico-bureaucratic elites for control over the oil sector.

On the economic side, the 'Dutch disease', named after the experience of the Netherlands in the 1970s after it had discovered natural gas in the North

---

[3] 'High Marks on Ratings Can't Hide Russia's Rising Problems', *Financial Times*, 15 November 2004.

[4] Stanislav Belkovskii, 'Poslednie dni Yukosa', APN: Proekt instituta natsional'noi strategii, 1 June 2006; http://www.apn.ru/publications/print1955.htm.

[5] Michael L. Ross, 'Blood Barrels', *Foreign Affairs*, Vol. 87, No. 3, May–June 2008, p. 4.

Sea, describes a situation when revenues from natural resource exports force up the exchange rate, undermining the competitiveness of other sectors of the economy, notably agriculture and manufacturing. This is only one aspect of a broader syndrome identified as the 'resource curse', in which countries with a heavy dependence on the export of primary goods tend to develop comparatively slowly, suffer from various aspects of underdevelopment, and have traditionally failed to develop diversified economies while their democratic development is stymied.[6] The massive influx of gold and silver to Spain in the sixteenth century coincided with the beginning of long-term decline and stagnation. The Middle Eastern countries awash in oil are on the whole not democracies, although the oil-poor countries are not notably more pluralistic.[7] There is also the attendant political 'Nigerian disease', where a large natural resource rent fostered corruption and an insulated political elite who lived off the rich pickings (and sent billions to Swiss bank accounts) while the national infrastructure decayed and the mass of the people fell into poverty.[8] As Shaxson puts it in his study of the 'resource curse' in Africa: 'Mineral dependence turns out to be a curse not just in terms of economic growth, but also in terms of risks of violent conflict, greater inequality, less democracy and more corruption.'[9] Good governance, accountable leadership and social development all suffered. Putin's former economic adviser, Illarionov, has talked of 'Venezuelaisation', where oil revenues expand the state and increase government spending accompanied by economic mismanagement.[10] Auty argues that resource-rich countries encourage factional and predatory states distorted by their pursuit of rents.[11] According to Stephen Fish, large natural rent was one of the main reasons why democracy was 'derailed' in Russia. He argues that resource abundance undermined democracy through corruption and the 'economic policy effect', encouraging economic statism and undermining economic freedom.[12] He identifies a correlation between the openness of markets and political freedom in both developed and industrializing countries.[13]

This may well be the case, but Tompson is correct to inject a note of scepticism and ask the fundamental question: '[D]o we have compelling reasons to believe that Russia's political life would have been substantially healthier—that politics would have been more democratic or governance less corrupt and more

---

[6] For a general discussion, see Terry Lynn Karl, *The Paradox of Plenty: Oil Booms and Petrostates* (Berkeley, University of California Press, 1997).

[7] Michael L. Ross, 'Does Oil Hinder Democracy?', *World Politics*, Vol. 53, No. 3, 2001, pp. 325–61.

[8] It is estimated that of the $400 billion in oil revenues between independence in 1960 and 1999, $380 billion were stolen or wasted, Hiro, *Blood of the Earth*, p. 363.

[9] Nicholas Shaxson, 'Oil, Corruption and the Resource Curse', *International Affairs*, Vol. 83, No. 6, November 2007, p. 1123; see also his *Poisoned Wells: The Dirty Politics of African Oil* (Basingstoke, Palgrave Macmillan, 2007).

[10] Andrei Illarionov, 'A Long-Term Project for Russia', *Russia in Global affairs*, July–September 2005.

[11] R. Auty, 'The Political Economy of Resource-Driven Growth', *European Economic Review*, Vol. 45, No. 4, 2001, pp. 839–46.

[12] M. Steven Fish, *Democracy Derailed in Russia: The Failure of Open Politics* (Cambridge, Cambridge University Press, 2005), chapter 5.

[13] Fish, *Democracy Derailed in Russia*, chapter 6, especially p. 147.

effective—if Russia had begun its market transformation without such large minerals sector?' He answers the question in the negative: '[I]t is difficult to attribute too much significance to Russia's economic structure when explaining the ills that afflict Russia's body politic.'[14] The impact of the resource industries on Russia's socio-political development is far from clear, and there is no unanimity in the literature. Bradshaw sensibly observes that 'it is not the availability of resource rents *per se* that results in underperformance, corruption, and even armed conflict. Rather it is the mechanisms by which that rent is captured and the uses to which it is then put that are the root causes of the problem.'[15] Even mature democracies are not immune to conflicts over the collection and distribution of resource rents. Michael Ellman argues that Russia has largely escaped the 'curse' aspect, and the country in his view plays a far more positive role in global energy issues than the Soviet Union ever did, helping to ensure security of supply for its export partners.[16] Prateek Goorha is rather less sanguine, although he notes that the Russian case is distinctive 'due to its unique transition from an industrialized command economy to a market-based one and from authoritarianism to democracy'.[17] Unlike China, where an authoritarian system gave birth to a distinctive type of economy, in Russia the peculiar nature of Russian development and in particular its highly concentrated resource-based economy fostered the turn towards authoritarianism.

Between 1998 and 2005 the share of fundamental natural resources (FNRs, primarily oil, gas, fuel, and metals) in Russia's exports increased from two-thirds to three-quarters, crowding out other exports. Over the same period the proportion of budget revenue from FNRs increased from 11.4 per cent to 23.8 per cent, although 2005 appears to be the peak year and by 2007 had declined to 20.8 per cent.[18] This point is stressed by Tompson, noting that export duties and resource taxes in 2003 represented about a fifth of revenues, eclipsed by social taxes (22.2 per cent) and taxes on consumption (29.5 per cent), with VAT revenues remaining the single largest tax, accounting for 35.8 per cent of federal revenues in 2004.[19] Although capital stock growth between 1998 and 2002 was negative, this could well have been because of necessary trimming of inefficiently managed companies and was not necessarily a result of oligarchic asset stripping or tunnelling of profits.[20]

Goorha lists some of the key features of FNRs: a tendency towards market concentration and oligopoly; the state takes a special interest in them because

[14] William Tompson, 'The Political Implications of Russia's Resource-Based Economy', *Post-Soviet Affairs*, Vol. 21, No. 4, October–December 2005, p. 336.

[15] Michael Bradshaw, 'Observations on the Geographical Dimensions of Russia's Resource Abundance', *Eurasian Geography and Economics*, Vol. 47, No. 6, 2006, p. 726.

[16] Michael Ellman (ed.), *Russia's Oil and Natural Gas: Bonanza or Curse?* (London, Anthem Press, 2006).

[17] Prateek Goorha, 'The Political Economy of the Resource Curse in Russia', *Demokratizatsiya*, Vol. 14, No. 4, Fall 2006, p. 602.

[18] Ibid., p. 603.

[19] Tompson, 'The Political Implications of Russia's Resource-Based Economy', p. 345.

[20] Goorha, 'The Political Economy of the Resource Curse in Russia', p. 602.

of the high contribution to state coffers; the close business–state nexus in FNRs demarcates this sector from the rest of the economy, undermining the market efficiency of both; focus on the FNR sector impedes the diversification of the rest of the economy; and the fusion of state and economic interests in the FNR sector encourages a conservative mentality, accompanied by an implicit contract between this sector and the rest of the economy based on subsidies and other privileges, in return for acceding to the status quo.[21] The fundamental issue is the large rents to be derived from resource exploitation, but even without that, there is no reason to doubt that Russia's model of economic transition, which demobilized the state, would have been any less characterized by rent-seeking and corruption. In Tompson's words, the 'political pathologies associated with resource-based economies... would appear to be over-determined in the Russian case',[22] and in examining the relationship between resource dependence and poor governance it is not at all clear in which direction the causal arrow runs.[23] The Russian state was too weak in the 1990s to capture a significant proportion of natural resource rents, and instead they were appropriated by oligarchs who used their wealth to capture parts of the state.

Russia had begun the transition with a large state apparatus but 'an exceptionally weak state', although its coercive capacities were greater than its regulatory potential, which permitted agents to enjoy freedom to privatize 'transition rents'.[24] The Yukos affair allowed a renascent state to 'de-privatize' these rents and to use them for state-defined national priorities. It did not put an end to conflicts over resource rents, but it did change the environment in which these conflicts were conducted. Struggles were now primarily conducted within the regime rather than between independent economic actors in society. The extractive capacity of the state was also greatly enhanced as the government learnt how to tax more effectively: 'Quite apart from formal changes in tax legislation, the Yukos affair brought about both a change in the informal rules governing oil companies' tax behaviour and an increase in the state's ability to appropriate oil rents directly as a result of its appropriation of Yukos assets.'[25] The state could not entirely bypass the need to negotiate with society the terms of rent extraction, although it did this in both constitutional and para-constitutional ways.

While the FNR syndrome comprises a number of recognizable phenomena, there is no deterministic relationship in their development. This stricture applies in particular to the notion of the development of a rentier state, defined simply as one in which a large proportion of the budget is derived from a relatively few sources. The state bureaucracy intervenes to husband the market segment that generates the bulk of its income, and this direct relationship bypasses democratic consent and accountability. Ruling elites, moreover, resent claims from society for a greater say in the management of FNR income, and repress threats to their

[21] Ibid., pp. 602, 604; this point is also argued by Karl in *The Paradox of Plenty*.
[22] Tompson, 'The Political Implications of Russia's Resource-Based Economy', p. 336.
[23] Ibid., p. 338.   [24] Ibid., p. 341.   [25] Ibid., p. 345.

control.[26] Resource rents provide a patronage resource to buy off or co-opt potential opposition. This applies to a number of Middle Eastern states, but in Russia
there is the additional factor of the communist legacy of a monopolistic state
running a centralized economy. Fear of economic collapse and social chaos in the
1990s encouraged the state to maintain a 'virtual economy', characterized by wage
arrears and barter which artificially inflated the value added at each stage, and
thus suggested that the Russian economy was much bigger than it actually was.[27]
The FNR sector was crucial in maintaining the virtual economy, with energy and
raw material prices in the domestic market kept artificially low as a subsidy to
the whole society. The distortions engendered by this system allowed ample scope
for insiders, in the state and the economy, to trade corrupt advantages, and were
reluctant to see further reforms jeopardize their current advantages.[28] A semi-
democratic government that could provide at least a modicum of stability was
preferable to a more democratic one that threatened both the accrued privileges
of the winners and the survival strategies of the poor.[29]

Putin's administration in broad terms maintained the 1990s bargain but
changed its terms of operation. The FNR sector continued to subsidize the rest
of the economy while maintaining a strategic alliance with the state. However, the
balance within the state–FNR relationship shifted ever more strongly in favour
of the former. The state gradually moved from a position of dependency to
rough equality by 2003, and with the Yukos affair it gained the upper hand. Not
only was the state the natural monopoly regulator, but with the development
of Gazprom, Rosneft, Transneft, and various para-statal economic corporations
it also intensified its role as an active player. The fundamental question then
becomes whether this was simply a classical manifestation of the pathologies associated with the resource curse, or whether it was the intelligent use of resources
in new circumstances to devise a viable modernization strategy. In other words,
if the bargain with the FNR sector in the 1990s had been a matter of survival, in
the 2000s it became a developmental strategy. The inherent conservatism of the
political regime of a rentier state was transcended, but although developmental,
that aspect of the resource curse which stymies democratic development remained
in place. The partial reform equilibrium noted by Hellman was broken, along
with the extrication of oligarch power from the formal reaches of government,
but the state-centred developmental model generated new pathologies, including
regulatory capture, the threat of internal degeneration and the decline in political

[26] Goorha, 'The Political Economy of the Resource Curse in Russia', p. 604.

[27] Gaddy and Ickes, 'Russia's Virtual Economy'; Clifford G. Gaddy and Barry W. Ickes, 'An Evo-
lutionary Analysis of Russia's Virtual Economy', in M. Cuddy and R. Gekker (eds.), *Institutional
Change in Transition Economies* (Cheltenham, Ashgate, 2002), pp. 72–100; Clifford G. Gaddy and Barry
W. Ickes, *Russia's Virtual Economy* (Washington, D.C., Brookings Institution Press, 2002).

[28] Joel S. Hellman, 'Winners take All: The Politics of Partial Reform in Postcommunist Transitions',
World Politics, Vol. 50, No. 2, January 1998, pp. 203–34.

[29] Andrei Shleifer and Daniel Treisman, *Without a Map: Political Tactics and Economic Reform in
Russia* (Cambridge, MA, MIT Press, 2000).

competitiveness, accompanied by weakening competitive pressures in the economy as a whole.[30]

There is no simple one-way causal relationship between mineral-rich economies and political outcomes. Classical prescriptions to manage resource wealth rely on sound macroeconomic policies, economic diversification, counter-cyclical sterilization of resource rents, combined with transparency and accountability. However, these have been of limited effect and assume a strong functioning state, which for many resource-based economies is far from the case, or state ownership balanced by the need for strong external actors to constrain the state. Domestic private ownership accompanied by the development of strong institutions capable of constraining the state and to encourage investment in institution building are a more viable way of managing resource-strong systems to avoid the authoritarian temptation. Instead of rents going directly to the state, strong corporations act as intermediaries.[31] However, the reliance here is on economic mechanisms, which in the Russian context was liable only to exacerbate the dysfunctional relationship between state and economy that was inherited from the 1990s. The Putin regime pursued classically prescribed macro and other economic policies to manage its resource rents, and thus managed to avoid the Nigerian scenario. The oil industry remained largely in private hands, as did some of the other major resource sectors, with the exception of the gas industry, yet the incentives to build strong independent institutions were not generated by the ownership structure but lie in the political sphere.

The personnel reshuffles in November 2005, and in particular the elevation of Medevdev to become first deputy prime minister while remaining chair of the Gazprom board, together with the appointment of Sergei Sobyanin, formerly governor of Tyumen region, which pumps nearly half of Russia's entire crude oil output, as head of the presidential administration suggested even more focus on the energy sector.[32] The notion of Russia as a petro-state, however, needs to be kept in perspective. While the Soviet Union had become dangerously dependent on natural resource rents, Russia's trajectory is rather different. Russia only produces 3 tonnes of oil per capita, whereas Norway produces 20; less than 2 per cent of the workforce is employed in the oil and gas sector, a lower proportion than are employed on the railways; and oil and gas extraction and processing make few demands on the output of other sectors.[33] A petro-state is a country that 'organises its political, economic and social relations around energy extraction

---

[30] Andrei Yakovlev and Timoti Frai (Timothy Frye), 'Reformy v Rossii glazami biznesa', *Pro et Contra*, Vol. 11, No. 4–5, July–October 2007, pp. 118–34, with survey results on perceived declines in political competition at pp. 123–4.

[31] Erika Weinthal and Pauline Jones Luong, 'Combating the Resource Curse: An Alternative Solution to Managing Mineral Wealth', *Perspectives on Politics*, Vol. 4, No. 1, March 2006, pp. 35–53.

[32] Sergei Blagov, 'Russian Personnel Changes to affect Far East Region', *Eurasia Daily Monitor*, Vol. 2, No. 216, 18 November 2005.

[33] Hanson, 'How Sustainable is Russia's Energy Power?', p. 8.

and suffers from long-term distortions as a result'.[34] Oil accounts for 45 per cent of Norway's exports and 17 per cent of GDP, and yet it has avoided both the Dutch disease and becoming a petro-state, as described here. Norway was able to sterilize much of the resource rent into long-term funds, within the framework of strong property rights, sound macroeconomic policies, and a flexible labour market. The main energy producers, moreover, remain in state hands, whereas in Russia the oil industry was precipitously broken up and privatized with only Rosneft and Gazprom remaining in state hands. The Yukos affair was in part an attempt to rectify this situation.

In the Putin years Russia enjoyed an average 7 per cent economic growth per annum, and the economy remains relatively diversified. The energy rents fed into rising real incomes that significantly raised private consumption and personal credit. There were elements of the Dutch disease, notably the strong appreciation of the rouble and high inflation. Adequate productivity growth would require massive investments, which in turn could foster higher inflation. The Yukos affair in the long run did not deter investment, which by 2007 reached 21 per cent of GDP, although the uncertainty surrounding property rights in the oil industry did lead to a dip in 2004/5. In fact, Khodorkovsky's arrest and imprisonment can be interpreted as having a positive effect, demonstrating that 'the Kremlin is no longer controlled by the oligarchs and can pursue independent macroeconomic policies'.[35] Neither did the Yukos affair put an end to foreign investment. On the very day that Yukos warned of its possible bankruptcy, 22 July 2004, Putin met with James Mulva, CEO of ConocoPhillips, and signalled that the company was welcome to bid for the 7.6 per cent stake in Lukoil that the government planned to sell off.[36] ConocoPhillips quietly built up a stake in Lukoil, which by 2008 had reached 20 per cent, and the American company delegated Kevin Meyers to the Lukoil board.

With the windfall rents from the early 2000s the regime did fall prey to some of the pathologies of resource-based economies, including the temptation to invest in unproductive activities (notably property redistribution and the creation of agglomerative state corporations), as well as the insulation of the regime from society, given the fact that state revenues do not rely on strong state institutions of accountability and consent. However, it is not axiomatic that all 'mineral-rich states inevitably become rentier states', although the rentier syndrome undoubtedly distorts the development of the polity. For Weinthal and Luong, 'Rentier states seek to exert social and political control over their populations by creating and maintaining economic dependencies through their sole authority to allocate and redistribute income obtained from natural resource rents'. [37] As a result, societal opposition is weakened, discretionary spending is funnelled into sustaining

---

[34] Rajan Menon and Alexander J. Motyl, 'The Myth of Russian Resurgence', *The American Interest Online*, March–April 2007; http://the-american-interest-com/.

[35] Pavel Erochkine, 'Russia and Its Oil: Friends or Foes', in Jennifer Moll (ed.), *Blueprint for Russia* (London, Foreign Policy Centre, 2005), pp. 13–34, at p. 27.

[36] Carola Hoyos and Arkady Ostrovsky, 'Politics First', *Financial Times*, 5 August 2004.

[37] Weinthal and Luong, 'Combating the Resource Curse', p. 38.

patronage networks or into buying popular support, and rentier systems are susceptible to state capture and high levels of corruption. Much of this was in evidence in the Gulf states, and in Russia as we have seen the regime was to a degree able to insulate itself from popular accountability while gaining a degree of autonomy from the constraints of the constitutional order.

The differences are also stark, since Russia is one of only four major producer countries where the oil sector is largely in private hands (together with the United Kingdom, the United States, and the Netherlands). Oil revenues do not directly accrue to the state, and the increasing take through strong tax policies have to a degree been sterilized through the Stabilization Fund and other measures, that act to smooth out the business cycle. Russia has been able to do this because it has 'an insulated and autonomous technocracy committed to long-term developmental goals', able to impose 'macroeconomic policies that may be socially and politically unpopular'.[38] It is precisely the role of the corporate intermediary that came into question in the Yukos case. Under Putin there was a degree of policy convergence between the state-owned Gazprom and the private corporate sector. In both the boundary between the main actors, state officials, managers, and political appointees became blurred, although the institutional and property frameworks differed. Russia suffered from major boundary problems, with state and private property aligned along a single axis, although accompanied by major asymmetries in property forms and informational flows. Thus Russia may have become a rentier state, but it was of a distinctive sort in which political rents, in the form of loyalty and donations to the regime, were as important as financial extraction.

The political system and civil society

The Yukos affair was always more than just about economic policy but involved fundamental questions about the ordering of Russian public life. By the same token, for Khodorkovsky Yukos was more than just an oil company but was about self-affirmation and the ability to shape Russian society. As one of the books sponsored by the Open Russia Foundation argued, public life is about choices, and went on to demonstrate the ramification of the choices made in Russian history from 862 and the arrival of the Rurik dynasty in Russia all the way to Yeltsin's choices in the 1990s.[39] For Khodorkovsky the choice now was to institutionalize the public power of the bourgeois class.

The Yukos affair effectively removed a key player from the arena of public politics. The new relationship between big business and the state, in Peregudov's view, differed from the Yeltsin era and the West not so much in its closed nature, but in 'the lack of freedom in the choice of their party political affiliation'. In

---

[38] The example given is Botswana, but it applies equally to Russia, Weinthal and Luong, 'Combating the Resource Curse', p. 39.

[39] I. V. Karatsuba, I. V. Kurukin, and N. P. Sokolov, *Vybiraya svoyu istoriyu: 'razvilki' na puti Rossii— ot ryurikovichei do oligarkhov*, Introd. by A.L. Yurganov (Moscow, KoLibri, 2005).

this context '[t]he "Yukos affair" and the arrest of Mikhail Khodorkovsky was a warning which no big company could ignore or would dare to. This restriction in effect deprives business of the possibility of participating freely in the struggle for political power, to sponsor to high state posts either through their direct representatives or their nominees.'[40] Big business thus became less than a fully fledged actor in civil society and its collective citizenship rights were truncated. This was a conscious response to the exaggerated exercise of influence over political power in the 1990s, and thus became a systemic element of the political system created by Putin. Political decisions were taken independently of big business, although the concerns of the sector were represented by formal organizations (notably the RUIE) and informally by influential magnates close to the Kremlin (above all Abramovich), but this took on a random and voluntary character. One of the major imbalances of the system of the system inherited from Yeltsin was removed, although new imbalances emerged.

The destruction of Khodorkovsky's empire did not mean the end of the powerful business magnates, although their 'class power' was certainly weakened. The country entered a 'post-oligarch' era, where the magnates no longer strove to convert money into power and were ostensibly ready to advance state interests. Three of the big seven remained in business: Mikhail Fridman, Vladimir Potanin, Pyotr Aven; while Mikhail Khodorkovsky, Vladimir Gusinsky, and Boris Berezovsky had fallen foul of the regime and were either in jail or in exile; and Alexander Smolensky had fallen by the wayside. In the period of the Yukos affair alone the combined wealth of the oligarchs, according to *Forbes*, increased from $90 billion in 2005 to $172 billion in 2006. By 2006 soaring stock values endowed Russia with thirty-three dollar millionaires.[41] By 2008 Russia had 110 billionaires, yet their aggregate wealth was still dwarfed by growing Russian GDP, approaching $1.5 trillion by that time. Ownership of Russian industry remained remarkably concentrated in the hands of a few dozen individuals. However, business magnates were unable to exert direct political influence, and their factional representation in the higher echelons of power in the late Putin years was minimal. Individuals such as Abramovich remained close to Putin, while the 'state oligarchs' at the head of state corporations and monopolies, such as the electricity and railway industries, remained major players, but this hardly amounted to political pluralism.

The rise of oligarchical capitalism overshadowed the integrative and aggregative role of political powers; and its downfall did no less damage. In a roundtable on 28 April 2008 the political analyst Andrei Ryabov argued that the funding of liberal parties and movements by the oligarchs was one of the main reasons for their decline. In his view the main threat to democracy in Russia came not from state officials and the bureaucracy, but from those in big business who declared their support for democracy but in practice retarded its development. The turning point in his view was Putin's meeting with business representatives in July 2000,

---

[40] S. P. Peregudov, 'Konvergentsiya po-rossiiskii: "zolotaya seredina" ili ostanovka na polputi', *Polis*, No. 1, 2008, p. 94.

[41] Anna Smolchenko, 'Russia's Richest, Twice as Rich', *Moscow Times*, 13 March 2006, p. 1.

when the new 'social contract' was intended to ensure that business refrained from involvement in political affairs but in fact promised them a preferential political status. Business in broad terms formally abided by the new rules of the game, but continued to enjoy privileged relationship with political leaders and parties. Democracy in Ryabov's view failed to develop as an independent value system separate from political circumstances. The sponsorship of liberal parties only intensified the alienation of liberalism from the mass of the population; and at the same time the liberal parties were being used instrumentally by the oligarchs (notably Khodorkovsky, and also Mikhail Fridman of the Al'fa-Group, also a prominent sponsor of the Yabloko party) for their own political 'insurance' purposes, in Ryabov's words, which had little to do with the public interest but served their purposes in relations with the government and in their international relations. One of the leaders of SPS, Boris Nadezhdin, exclaimed in response: 'We were cynically exploited.'[42] As Panyushkin puts it, '[i]nstead of the opposition winning with Khodorkovsky's money, it was destroyed by it'.[43]

Up to the Yukos affair the argument that democracy was irreversible in Russia could be made with some conviction; afterwards, this was no longer the case: 'It became clear that a reverse is quite possible.'[44] Even before the assault against Yukos observers had noted the trend under Putin towards 'monocentrism', compared to the 'polycentrism' of the Yeltsin years.[45] A recent debate discussed the issue of some fatal 'Russian gene', which turns its history each time towards the reproduction of a patrimonial 'Russian system'. New types of popular 'serfdom' are reproduced because of a distinctive bargain between the political authorities and those with economic resources. Thus '[a]t first glance it appears that the key thing for Russia ... is the socio-economic relation *power—property and redistribution* [italics in original throughout] from the distribution of landed estates in tsarist Russia to the work of Gosplan in the USSR and the restoration of state control over the key resources in the contemporary Russian Federation'. This was only part of the question, and at a more profound level the key issue is the restoration of 'socio-political relations once again in the form of a *vertical contract*, but no longer between the population and the elite, but *between the supreme authorities and the main holders of resources*'. The deal boils down to the political authorities demanding loyalty and a share of the rents in return for oil companies and the like getting on with their business.[46] The whole system depends not only on those with resources but also '*on the behaviour (subjectivity!) of rank and file people*'.[47]

Pastukhov argues that the necessary restoration of statehood in Russia was achieved 'by the corporation that he [Putin] represented. This was fully a

[42] Andrei Kulikov, 'Demokraty nashli vinovnykh', *Nezavisimaya gazeta*, 30 April 2008, p. 4.

[43] Panyushkin, *Mikhail Khodorkovskii*, p. 201.

[44] Gurova and Privalov, 'My teryaem ego!', p. 78.

[45] A. Yu. Zudin, 'Rezhim V. Putina: Kontury novoi politicheskoi sistemy', *Obshchestvennye nauki i sovremennost'*, No. 2, 2003, pp. 67–83.

[46] V. A. Dubovtsev and N. S. Rozov, 'Priroda "russkoi vlasti": Ot metafor—k kontseptsii', *Polis*, No. 3, 2007, pp. 8–23, at p. 19.

[47] Ibid., p. 21.

"corporate matter".[48] The corporation he had in mind were the 'Chekists', whose 'deficiencies were a continuation of their qualities'. They were able to restore some sort of order, but they did this in a Soviet manner: 'The private tyranny (*proizvol*) of the new-born oligarchs was opposed by the tyranny of the reviving state.'[49] And he goes on to make the following comments about the Yukos affair:

For good or ill the task was achieved. The Khodorkovsky affair was the turning point. The latter in a certain sense was the symbol of the license of the period. To neutralise him, the authorities (*vlast'*) had to demonstrate what 'organised' state arbitrariness was capable of. The Khodorkovsky affair was a pyrrhic victory, a victory not only over Khodorkovsky, but over law itself (which does not in any way justify Khodorkovsky). In this way, instead of the decentralised arbitrariness of financial-industrial groups we have the centralised arbitrariness of state power.[50]

Glebova divides Russian society into two parts.

The exit from communism led to yet another socio-cultural split. From common historical roots once again two cultures emerged: the new culture of the authorities (which we call the 'oil and gas [*neftegazovaya*]) elite' and the new mass culture (which we call the culture of the 'reservation'. The first appears (and 'appears' is precisely what it is) to be pro-Western and cosmopolitan and was born in response to the social transformation that changed the face of the country. The second draws on the grass roots, closed sources. The gulf between the two is as wide as that of the eighteenth and nineteenth centuries.[51]

The unique feature of the current situation is that all these metamorphoses, divisions and transformations took place without the usual Russian horrors—bloodshed, civil war, the enslavement and exploitation of all and everyone. On the contrary, freedom is the main attribute of 'post-sovietism'. The authorities [*vlast'*] (both Yeltsinite and Putinist) left the population all their significant freedoms, as well as concern to ensure the possibility of their use.

She goes on to note that the traditional Russian state managed all processes 'from above', 'and thus limited the creation of mechanisms for the self-organization of society', including individual initiative. Today the situation, in her view, is fundamentally different.

The post-Soviet authorities exist above and beyond society. Unable to ensure social integration and development, it does not need enserfed castes, universal compulsory labour, an all-encompassing state sector, the extreme consolidation of the ruling class....The social ineffectiveness of the state is a consequence of the simplification and primitiveness of the self-organisation of Russian society.[52]
'Free' Russia does not show any desire to organise for the common good. It is, rather, inclined to give itself up to 'Russia United', in exchange for a continuation of 'freedoms'.[53]

---

[48] V. B. Pastukhov, 'Temnyi vek: Postkommunizm kak "chernaya dyra" russkoi istorii', *Polis*, No. 3, 2007, p. 34, n. 2.
[49] Ibid., p. 34.   [50] Ibid., p. 35.
[51] I. I. Glebova, 'Politicheskaya kultura sovremennoi Rossii: obliki novoi russkoi vlasti i sotsial'nye raskoly', *Polis*, No. 1, 2006, p. 34.
[52] Ibid., pp. 39–40.   [53] Ibid., p. 40.

The Rodina block fought the 2003 election campaigning for the confiscation of natural resource rents from the 'oligarchs'. In the event, the group won more votes than the liberal parties combined, even in the 'democratic' cities of Moscow and St Petersburg. The government had been able to frame relations between business and the state in terms of 'social justice', but then political entrepreneurs had been able to seize the political initiative and run with the issue, taking it further than the regime had originally intended. In domestic terms, as Nemtsov pointed out, 'conditions have developed in Russia making it extremely dangerous to finance the opposition. For businessmen, the fact became evident after Khodorkovsky's arrest'.[54] As late as the 2007 parliamentary election Putin continued to warn against the return of 'oligarchic rule'. At a rally of his supporters on 21 November 2007 he stressed:

There should be no illusions. All of these people have not left the political arena. You will find their names among candidates and sponsors of several parties. They want to come back, to return to power, to spheres of influence. And gradually restore oligarchic rule based on corruption and lies. There are those who back in the 1990s, while holding high positions, acted to the detriment of the public and state, serving the interests of oligarchies and squandered national resources. They made corruption the main tool of political and economic competition.[55]

The crackdown on business, provoked by some justified concerns of the state, reduced the autonomy of the economic sphere, and the strengthening of vertical relations undermined the development of civil society. As Rutland argues, 'in many respects a true civil society in Russia seems no closer in 2004 than in 1991'.[56]

The debate on freedom in the wake of Khodorkovsky's arrest

There was much talk at this time that Russia was a 'leftist country', but this in turn provoked a powerful debate over the meaning of freedom in the Russian context. An important article in the *Ekspert* journal stressed that already in the early twentieth century the philosopher Ivan Il'in had argued against the view that Russians were by nature collectivist, not concerned with personal initiative and private property. The article quotes Il'in: 'By the beginning of Stolypin's reforms Russia had 12 million peasant households. Of these, 4 million already conducted independent farming, and soon another 6 million declared their willingness to have their own land and full economic independence.'[57] Il'in was frequently quoted by Putin, under whose leadership not only were Il'in's remains brought back to Russia from where he had died in exile, but also in 2006 his library and archives were also repatriated from New York.

[54] *Kommersant*, 1 November 2007.

[55] 'Vladimir Putin: Nasha obshchaya tsel'—pobeda "Edinoi Rossii" na vyborakh v Gosdumu', 21 November 2007, http://www.edinross.ru/print.html?id=125609.

[56] Rutland, 'Business and Civil Society in Russia', p. 91.

[57] Tat'yana Gurova, Aleksandr Privalov, and Valerii Fadeev, 'Nasha malen'kaya svoboda', *Ekspert*, No. 33, 8 September 2003, in *Ekspert: Luchshie materialy*, No. 2, 2007, pp. 68–75, at p. 69.

The article cited above argued that '[a]ll of Russian philosophy from Skovorod to Il'in begins with and conscientiously develops one theme—the freedom of individual choice'. The authors go on to argue that '[i]n its Russian version freedom is a primary value, not subordinated a priori to duty or law or institutions. This is important, since its primacy means that only when there is freedom in Russia can effective, that is accepted by all, norms of law and institutions be defined and created.' They also note Berdyaev's view that freedom is the ability to do good, but in equal measure to do evil. Thus for Berdyaev '[f]reedom is not a moral-juridical or pedagogical category, but has a tragic character. Freedom is the basic requirement for a moral life, for good or evil.' Their fundamental argument was that for Russia freedom is a primary good, and that this should be proclaimed from every wall since Russia as never before enjoyed the possibility of living in freedom. A similar choice had faced the country in the early twentieth century, but the revolution destroyed everything. This was the fundamental question facing the country, since without freedom there will be no meaning to oil, to innovation, democracy, or totalitarianism: 'Russia will simply disappear.'[58]

Several practical consequences arise from this. The first is that the outcome of the privatizations must be accepted. The oligarchs had demonstrated the ability to exercise their freedom in full measure: 'Whether this freedom was for good or ill, let them sort this out themselves, but only through recognizing their right do we take a step, and a very big one, to learning how to live in freedom.' Second, current threats to freedom should be dealt with only when they arise, and thus the preventative approach should be avoided. It was clear that 'there is a great danger that force structures can be used for political or economic purposes. We must put an end to this.' All institutions that 'limit and control freedom' should be developed very carefully, 'since we do not yet know its full measure'.[59]

AN 'ENERGY SUPERPOWER'

The Yukos affair showed the single-mindedness with which Putin's administration was willing to go to achieve its aims, although it also showed how contradictory were these goals. Leaving aside the power and personal aggrandizement issues, in broad terms the state sought to restore its pre-eminent position in energy policy, and in industrial strategy more broadly. As Putin noted at a meeting of the Security Council in 2005, reflecting the views of his mentor Vladimir Litvinenko earlier which he developed in his dissertation: 'Russia cannot dominate in any field other than energy.'[60] This was confirmed by Putin signing on 5 May 2008 the long-awaited law on strategic industries, which brought 'strategic industries, above all oil and gas, back under state control after they were sold off during the

---

[58] Gurova et al., 'Nasha malen'kaya svoboda', p. 69.   [59] Ibid., p. 69.
[60] Wolton, *Le KGB au pouvoir*, p. 194.

privatization of the 1990s'.[61] The law clarified the rules for investing in Russia, and listed forty-two sectors where foreign investment was restricted, such as nuclear energy, natural monopolies, exploration of strategic mineral deposits, aviation, space, and related defence industries. This was one of Putin's last acts in office, and fittingly marked the achievement of his own long-term strategy. The state had long been a monopolist in energy transport, and had now restored elements of state monopoly in energy production as well.

Energy imperialism?

In late 2006 Russia had 6.6 per cent of proven global oil reserves and 26.3 per cent of proven gas reserves.[62] The country benefited greatly from high energy prices, but its energy policy, notably in the Yukos affair, damaged the country's reputation. Although the state now dominated the energy sector (not always through ownership), the role of energy in foreign policy became even more controversial. In May 1995 the Council on Foreign and Defence Policy (SVOP) issued a report developing what Rutland calls the 'Russian bear' model,[63] urging the government to eschew military methods of asserting its interests but to deploy economic instruments.[64] The imbalance between Russia's energy wealth and the energy poverty of its Western and some of its Southern neighbours should be exploited to Russia's benefit, the report urged. As could be anticipated, the argument did not go down well among Russia's neighbours, and added yet more fuel to those who considered Russia a renascent imperial power and accelerated the centrifugal tendencies in the CIS. Already on the eve of the December 2003 parliamentary elections Chubais had talked in terms of a 'liberal empire', in which Russia would bind its neighbours and other willing states to itself in an economic community that could form the basis of a political alliance.[65]

The former defence minister Sergei Ivanov later was even more explicit and referred to Russia as an 'energy superpower', suggesting the instrumental use of energy resources to achieve geopolitical ends.[66] Balmaceda talks of Russia using energy as a 'foreign policy tool' in relations with former Soviet states, exploiting their energy dependency on Russia to impede 'the development of broader relationships with Western institutions',[67] while Zeyno Baran argues that '[u]nder the leadership of Putin, the Kremlin has pursued a strategy whereby Europe's substantial dependence on Russian energy is levered to obtain economic and

---

[61] 'Putin Signs Law on Strategic Sectors', *Moscow Times*, 6 May 2008.

[62] *BP Statistical Review of World Energy*, June 2007, http://www.bp.com/statisticalreview.

[63] Rutland, 'Oil, Politics, and Foreign Policy', in Lane (ed.), *The Political Economy of Russian Oil*, p. 182.

[64] 'Vozroditsya li soyuz?', *Nezavisimaya gazeta*, 23 May 1996.

[65] Anatolii Chubais, 'Missiya Rossii v XXI veke', *Nezavisimaya gazeta*, 1 October 2003.

[66] Sergei Ivanov, 'Triada natsional'nykh tsennostei: Sergei Ivanov o suverennnoi demokratii, sil'noi ekonomike i voennoi moshchi', *Izvestiya*, 13 July 2006.

[67] Balmaceda, *Energy Dependency, Politics and Corruption in the Former Soviet Union*, p. 5.

political gains'.[68] A Russian view argues that the country faced a dilemma: 'either being a democracy—at the cost of giving the West more or less strict control over our raw materials (access to fields, freedom of transit, profits taken out of Russia), or becoming an autocracy, where control over raw materials is an end in itself and a means of survival for the ruling regime'.[69] If that was indeed the choice, then Putin took the latter path.

In response, the former prime minister and now Putin's opponent, Kasyanov, talked in terms of 'petro-dollar sovereignty' and instead called for an 'empire of freedom'.[70] Others were less polite and the *Washington Post* railed against Russia acting as an 'energy bully'.[71] Many of the methods employed in the Putin era, however, had already been applied in the 1990s, and there is a considerable body of evidence demonstrating how energy companies had already become instruments of the state.[72] Between 1998 and 2000 Transneft had cut off supplies nine times to prevent the Lithuanian government selling the Mazeikiu refinery, the single largest industrial installation in the Baltic republics, to Williams. In the event, Williams sold it to Yukos in 2001, but the refinery reverted to Lithuania following Yukos's demise, and they then sold it to PKN Orlen.[73] The sale was followed on 29 July 2006 by the closure for 'technical reasons' of the Druzhba (Friendship) pipeline that supplied it with crude. Delays in repairing the line looked set to become permanent, forcing Lithuania to import oil through the Butinge terminal. Rosneft's hopes of incorporating the refinery into its expanding empire were dashed.

The Yukos affair intensified debates over Russia's reliability as an energy supplier. Russia is locked into mutual interdependency as a supplier to its markets, and is itself a transit country, and claims to be a reliable partner, but there are numerous instances of the 'energy weapon' being used.[74] Peter Rutland in 1999 noted that 'Gazprom has repeatedly pressed the ex-Soviet republics to pay off their gas debts with equity in energy installations', and he notes the 'annual ritual' of conflict over transit and energy charges with Belarus and Ukraine, 'breaking out in January, when the new year's tariff agreements can no longer be delayed'.[75] In the wake of the Yukos affair and the energy cut-off to Ukraine on 1 January 2006 and to Belarus on 1 January 2007, Russia's reliability as an energy supplier was questioned. What was new, however, was that Russia now moved from being perceived as a 'raw materials appendage' of the West to becoming an autonomous

[68] Zeyno Baran, 'EU Energy Security: Time to End Russian Leverage', *The Washington Quarterly*, Vol. 30, No. 4, Autumn 2007, p. 132.
[69] Editorial, 'Soblazn avtoritetizma', *Ekspert*, No. 31, 28 August 2007.
[70] Mikhail Kasyanov, 'Imperiya svobody', *Kommersant*, 29 August 2006.
[71] *Washington Post*, editorial, 23 August 2006.
[72] See, for example, Igor Khripunov and Mary M. Matthews, 'Russia's Oil and Gas Interest Group and its Foreign Policy Agenda', *Problems of Post-Communism*, Vol. 43, No. 3, May–June 1996, pp. 38–48; also Duncan, 'Oligarchs', Business and Russian Foreign Policy, p. 9.
[73] Duncan, 'Oligarchs', Business and Russian Foreign Policy, p. 14.
[74] For a study of the cases, see Robert L. Larsson, *Russia's Energy Policy: Security Dimensions and Russia's Reliability as an Energy Supplier* (Stockholm, Defence Research Institute, 2006); www.foi.se, who lists the various cut-offs.
[75] Rutland, 'Oil, Politics, and Foreign Policy', p. 167.

subject in international economic life. Limits were placed on the participation of foreign companies in the Russian economy, some of the deals forged in the 1990s were revised, and Russia insisted on its voice being heard in the forging of the rules and norms governing the energy and other markets.[76] At the EU-Russia summit in Sochi on 25 May 2006 Putin insisted that Russia would not unilaterally open up its energy transportation system, which he called 'the holy of holies', as required by the Transport Protocol of the Energy Charter Treaty.[77] Energy had indeed become the altar on which everything else was sacrificed.

With energy revenues pouring in and owning enormous strategic reserves of oil and gas, 'Russia's predominant position . . . strengthened Russia's hand in playing the geopolitical game of hydrocarbons'.[78] The cut-off in gas supplies to Ukraine in January 2006 was not the first time that Russia had resorted to such drastic measures, but the manner in which it was done alarmed those affected by the supply interruption further West. The speech of Vice President Dick Cheney at a conference of East European leaders in Vilnius on 4 May 2006 warned Russia against its alleged abuse of the energy instrument: 'No legitimate interest is served when oil and gas become tools of intimidation or blackmail, either by supply manipulation or attempts to monopolize transportation.'[79] His sentiments were somewhat vitiated by having welcomed the president of Azerbaijan, Ilham Aliev, to the White House just before his speech, a country not known for the transparency of its elections but in the Western camp on energy issues; and then flying on to energy-rich Kazakhstan where he expressed 'admiration and friendship' for the president, Sultan Nazarbaev, who in December of that year would win a surprising 95 per cent of the vote for his party in parliamentary elections. Thus we agree with the view of Konstantin Simonov, the head of the National Energy Security Foundation in Moscow, that we are entering an era of 'global energy wars', which will not necessarily take military form but will shape the international politics of the future.[80]

The Yukos affair confirmed the Kremlin's control over energy resources and policy—the question now was what to do with it. The effective nationalization of Yukos meant that the Kremlin now had the strategic leverage over the oil industry that it had long enjoyed over the gas sector. One strategy was to use energy to enhance Russia's international standing, sometimes described as becoming an 'energy superpower'. The term was not adopted by Putin, and was only rarely used by top leaders, with the exception of Sergei Ivanov. The semantic nuances in interpreting this phrase carry potent political weight. If by energy superpower we mean simply that the energy sector was the locomotive for economic development

---

[76] Derek Averre, ' "Sovereign Democracy" and Russia's Relations with the European Union', *Demokratizatsiya*, Vol. 15, No. 2, Spring 2007, p. 176.

[77] 'Press konferentsiya po itogam sammita Rossiya-ES', http://www.kremlin.ru/text/appears/2006/05/106059.shtml.

[78] Hiro, *Blood of the Earth*, p. 245.

[79] Press release of the Office of the Vice President, The White House, 4 May 2006.

[80] Konstantin Simonov, *Global'naya energiticheskaya voina: Tainy sovremennoi politiki* (Moscow, Algoritm, 2007).

and for the country to become a major international economic actor, then this is
no more than would be expected of a country like Russia, which from the first days
of independence considered itself a 'great power', with major energy resources.
However, if the emphasis is placed on 'superpower', then the phrase can be interpreted as the manifesto of the use of energy and its export routes as an instrument
to lever Russia's geopolitical advantage. Economics would become subordinate to
politics, and the instrumentalization of energy policy would inaugurate a new era
international insecurity. Russia would be diverted from the pursuit of a rational
model of modernization and would instead pursue an archaic model of development in which the state and capital would merge to create a single corporation.[81]

Energy policy would become the core of geopolitics. Such a policy would
indeed threaten Russia's neighbours, with energy dependency acting as a threat
to national sovereignty. It would also justify the concern in Russia's major market, the EU, about excessive dependency on Russian energy imports. As Yulia
Tymoshenko, former prime minister of Ukraine, put it at Chatham House on 2
February 2006: 'The gas dispute between Russia and Ukraine has been a wake-up
call for many in Western Europe and Washington, and attracted great attention
to the use of energy as a post-Soviet neo-imperialist weapon.'[82] Most informed
observers would disagree with this evaluation, but Russia's diplomatically inept
pursuit of what may well be justifiable aims certainly damaged its status in world
opinion. The Yukos affair raised fears in Russia's Western neighbours about their
energy dependency, and argued that '[t]he state concerns and private companies
which are controlled by the Kremlin serve as important instruments of pressure
in Russian foreign policy'.[83]

The whole notion of an 'energy superpower' is built on sand, and is little
more than a rhetorical device for its advocates and a useful term of abuse for
its critics. For Milov, the idea would lead to stagnation and the loss of Russian
prestige.[84] He notes in particular that the ratio of population to energy resources
was far lower than in most other energy exporters, hence 'our ability to convert
national hydrocarbon potential into national prosperity is limited'.[85] This is not
to say that energy is not a crucial factor in Russia's rise as a great power and
its greater self-confidence in international affairs. As Rutland notes, the idea is
built on the contradictory logic of a 'superpower', whose dynamic is very different
from that of the 'energy' market. It is extremely difficult to convert energy into
political influence, and attempts to do so can easily backfire.[86] As the Soviet Union
discovered, subsidized energy for its Soviet bloc allies won neither loyalty nor

[81] Włodzimierz Marciniak, 'From Retrospection to a Prognosis: On the Difficulties in Prognosticating the Development of the Political Situation in Russia', in Wojciech Konończuk (ed.), *Putin's Empire*
(Warsaw, Stefan Batory Foundation, 2007), p. 40.

[82] Yulia Tymoshenko, 'Where is Ukraine Going?', official transcript, mimeo.

[83] Wiśniewska, *The Invisible Hand ... of the Kremlin*, p. 39.

[84] Vladimir Milov, 'Anatomiya odnogo zabluzhdeniya', *Kommersant*, 6 September 2006, p. 7.

[85] Vladimir Milov, 'Mozhet li Rossiya stat' neftyanym raem?', *Pro et Contra*, Vol. 10, Nos. 2–3,
March–June 2006, p. 6.

[86] Peter Rutland, 'Russia as an Energy Superpower', *New Political Economy*, Vol. 13, No. 2, June
2008, p. 206.

respect, and similar arrangements worked little better in Russia's relations with an independent Belarus. Used as a stick, energy is a two-edged sword, and is a rather inefficient way of trying to achieve hard power goals with soft power methods. It can also create what Andrew Monaghan has called the 'energy security dilemma', where the insecurities felt by both suppliers and markets (in this case Russia and the EU) provoke anticipatory actions that precisely promote the outcome that the preparations were intended to avoid.[87]

If Russia was in any way an 'energy superpower', its main instrument would be Gazprom. A recent study makes the argument explicit, calling Gazprom the 'new Russian weapon'.[88] With the break-up of the Soviet Union Gazprom lost a third of its pipeline network, a third of its gas fields, and a quarter of its compressor installations. However, as the authors note, unlike the Soviet Union Gazprom continued to operate, and began to recoup some of its losses. In the 1990s Gazprom lost control over many of its assets, including the giant Urengoi field in northwest Siberia, but under Putin and Miller its holdings were reassembled. The company contributed 8 per cent of national tax revenues and had become a central player in national politics while continuing to act as a paternalistic employer to its 330,000 workers. Its monopoly on gas exports was formalized by law in July 2006, and the company owns extensive media assets and Russia's third largest bank. Russia in gas and, after the Yukos affair, in oil as well, was not only a major energy power but one in which the state took the leading role. As Putin stressed on the tenth anniversary of the founding of the company: 'Gazprom, as a strategically important company, should be kept, and has been kept, as a single organism. . . . Gazprom is a powerful political and economic lever of influence over the rest of the world.'[89] Issues of production and distribution thus became matters of state policy, and reflected back on to Russia's international standing.

The Yukos affair changed the terms of trade. If up to 2003 TNK and Yukos led the way for Russian companies to merge into the existing transnational corporate order, after that time Russian energy companies were far more cautious in their global agenda. There would be no more talk of the wholesale purchase of Russian energy companies. While internationalization was acceptable if agreed with the Kremlin, independent transnationalization was no longer an option. Equally, Western companies wishing to do business in Russia realized that the business environment had changed. No sooner was Shell mooted as a possible purchaser of a blocking share of Yukos than the *siloviki* responded through the ministry of natural resources in July 2003 about the possible withdrawal of its licence to exploit the Verkhnesalymsky field.[90] Further evidence of this was demonstrated in the ownership shifts in the various Sakhalin projects and the Kovytka gas field.

---

[87] Andrew Monaghan, 'Dilemma energicheskoi bezopasnosti', *Pro et Contra*, Vol. 10, Nos. 2–3, March–June 2006, pp. 16–31.

[88] Zygar and Panyushkin, *Gazprom: Novoe russkoe oruzhie*.

[89] Cited by Jeronim Perovic and Robert Orttung, 'Russia's Energy Policy: Should Europe Worry?', in Robert Orttung et al. (eds.), *Russia's Energy Sector between Politics and Business*, Working Papers of the Research Centre for East European Studies, Bremen, No. 92, 2008, pp. 7–17, at p. 9.

[90] Simonov, *Russkaya neft'*, p. 211.

Russia's vastness is not matched by access to open sea, and now this historical frustration was reflected in a series of choke points on its access to world energy markets. The attempt to bypass the energy transit countries of Ukraine and Poland encouraged the search for alternative routes. Hence the plans to build the North European Gas Pipeline (North Stream), while the South Stream project sought to transport gas under the Black Sea and then across the Balkans to Southern Europe. The bitter struggles over these routes, and alternatives promoted by the EU, notably the Nabucco project in the South that would bypass Russia, demonstrated that energy security was as much a struggle for geopolitical advantage as it was about getting energy to markets. The Russian foreign minister, Sergei Lavrov, stressed in 2006 that '[e]ven if all the ambitious plans are implemented to save energy, the world's need for energy security will not diminish', and hence he called for 'a new concept of international relations'.[91] No new concept was forthcoming, and instead conflicts over the diversification of pipelines routes were accompanied by a struggle by all sides to diversify suppliers and markets, with commensurate weakening of energy security for all.

Resource nationalism

The issue of the use of energy resources for political purposes became the centre of policy discussions between Russia and its partners. It is also an issue at the heart of the question of the viability of the system of 'sovereign democracy'. The material basis for Russia's 'sovereignty' under Putin was provided by high energy prices and expanding output. Andrei Kokoshin, head of the Duma committee with relations with former Soviet republics, stressed: 'The United States has to deal with an absolutely different Russia today—a Russia that has restored its real sovereignty in many areas and is pursuing a course on the world arena that meets mainly its own national interests.'[92] 'Real sovereignty', in his view, was 'the capacity of a state in reality (and not merely in declaratory fashion) to conduct independently its internal, external and defence policies, to conclude and tear up agreements, enter into strategic partnerships or not', and Russia was one of the handful of countries in this category, along with India and China.[93] In April 2006 Condoleezza Rice noted that '[n]othing has taken me aback more as secretary of state than the way that the politics of energy is—I will use the word "warping"—diplomacy around the world', a rather surprising statement from a leader of a country that had repeatedly engaged in military interventions to safeguard American energy interests, as well as being a former director of Chevron.[94] It was especially remarkable since she must have been aware of the May 2001 policy document issued by the National Energy Policy (NEP) Development Group, bringing together the energy lobby around the White House and chaired by Cheney, which

---

[91] Hiro, *Blood of the Earth*, p. 246.   [92] Ibid., p. 172.

[93] Andrei Kokoshin, *Real'nyi suverenitet v sovremennoi miropoliticheskoi sistemy*, third edition (Moscow, Evropa, 2006).

[94] Ibid., p. 343.

sought to shift energy dependency away from the Middle East to NANI (non-Arab, non-Iranian) states, with Russia prominent among the nine listed.[95]

The relationship between the energy-hungry developed world, the growing energy appetite of developing countries such as China and India, and the supply countries like Russia will shape international politics in the twenty-first century. The unipolarity of the early post-Cold War years will give way to the creation of a more coherent multipolar system in which a second world coalition led by Russia and China will challenge Anglo-American hegemony. A foreign policy founded on hydrocarbons, however, is fragile. In a perceptive study Gaidar, the architect of Russia's neo-liberal reforms in the early 1990s, described how the Soviet Union's dependence on high energy prices provoked its collapse when prices fell sharply after 1985. Saudi Arabia's decision in 1985 to sharply increase production, probably at America's behest, led to a sharp fall in world energy prices, accompanied by a dramatic collapse in Soviet foreign currency earnings. According to Gaidar, it took Gorbachev and his colleagues three years to come to understand the implications of what had happened. The previous Soviet leadership had been massively negligent to have placed the country in such a position of dependency, and to have failed to make contingency plans. With low gold and foreign currency reserves, the reformist Soviet leadership was faced with some hard choices: to raise domestic prices, which would have disrupted the informal 'social contract' between the Soviet regime and the people; to stop subsidizing the East European communist regimes, which would have signalled the end of empire; or to have cut internal investment. All these were tough political choices, but there was no popular forum in which these could have been debated. By 1991 the system had collapsed. The lesson for Gaidar is clear: that economic dependency on energy exports is extremely dangerous, and tough democratic institutions are essential to allow the country to navigate crisis situations and to ensure a reasonable quality of state administration.[96]

While there has been considerable discussion about the dangers for the Russian economy of the 'Dutch' disease, the reassertion of state supervision over the economy was called, as noted, the 'Venezualan' disease by Illarionov. The nationalization of energy resources, however, has a long history, ranging from Iran's attempts from the early 1950s (which led to an Anglo-American-backed coup against Prime Minister Muhammed Mussadiq on 19 August 1953) to Saudia Arabia's staged nationalization of Aramco between 1976 and 1980. President Hugo Chávez brought the main oil company PDVSA under tight state control after coming to power in 1998. Just as with Yukos, PDVSA was considered a state within the state, but the imposition of state controls did not make the company any less corrupt. The Venezualan example is held as a warning that the deprivatization, if not outright nationalization, of natural resources can retard economic growth. At the same time, the resurgence of the populist left in Latin America, evident also in the election of Evo Morales in Bolivia in 2005, reflected deeper problems about

---

[95] Ibid., p. 344.
[96] Egor Gaidar, *Gibel' imperii: uroki dlya sovremmennoi Rossii* (Moscow, Rosspen, 2006).

the role of foreign capital and the limited benefits accruing to the host country: 'In retrospect, it is clear that the view from within Latin America that there was no alternative to neo-liberalism began to unravel in the early 1990s',[97] just at the time when the idea took hold so powerfully in Russia. The attempt to reassert state control over 'strategic' sectors of the economy in both Latin America and Russia reflected concern about the pattern of unequal integration into the world economy, although neither region rejected the logic of international economic integration. Only the reassertion of state power could mitigate the unequal terms of economic exchange. The Anglo-American ideology of globalization, which suggested that opening up to the world economy would on its own improve economic performance and thus national well-being, was challenged.[98] The tide was turning against the neo-liberal hegemony that had dominated since the early 1990s.

Fareed Zakaria notes that Russia could well 'settle into a version of the regimes that dominated Latin America in the 1960s and 1970s: quasi-capitalist, with a permanent governing alliance among the elites'; it would be 'an elected autocracy with more and more of its freedoms secure in theory but violated in practice'.[99] The resurgence of economic nationalism in Russia, however, was accompanied by a continued commitment to the ideology of technocratic necessity, and thus lacked the populist edge that was found in some Latin American countries. For this reason some have talked of developments in Russia as the onset of 'market authoritarianism'.[100] Zakaria suggested that the alliance in Russia would be 'between the oligarchs and the former Communist elite',[101] but the Yukos affair was precisely the repudiation of such an alliance and instead affirmed the autonomy of the political elite buttressed by the development of a large para-statal sector in the economy. In the short term this fostered both venal and meta-corruption, but it did not foreclose the potential for democratic opening. More broadly, Azar Gat argues: 'Authoritarian capitalist states, today exemplified by China and Russia, may represent a viable alternative path to modernity, which in turn suggests that there is nothing inevitable about liberal democracy's ultimate victory—or future dominance.'[102] The alleged failings of this model have attracted considerable attention.[103]

The Yukos affair in 2003 signalled the beginning of a new period in Russian politics. If the first period of Putin's leadership focused on ensuring an attractive investment climate for domestic and foreign capital, this now gave way to the priority of national security. The remedial agenda changed to a transformative

---

[97] Jean Grugel, Pia Riggirozzi, and Ben Thirkell-White, 'Beyond the Washington Consensus? Asia and Latin America in Search of More Autonomous Development', *International Affairs*, Vol. 84, No. 3, May 2008, p. 507; see also Jean Grugel and Pia Riggirozzi, 'The Return of the State in Argentina', *International Affairs*, Vol. 83, No. 1, January 2007, pp. 87–107.

[98] See for example Joseph E. Stiglitz, *Globalization and its Discontents* (New York, W. W. Norton & Co., 2002); see also his *Making Globalization Work* (New York, W. W. Norton & Co., 2007).

[99] Fareed Zakaria, *The Future of Freedom: Illiberal Democracy at Home and Abroad* (New York, W. W. Norton, 2003), p. 92.

[100] Glenny, *McMafia*, p. 83.   [101] Zakaria, *The Future of Freedom*, p. 92.

[102] Gat, 'The Return of Authoritarian Great Powers', p. 60.

[103] e.g. McFaul and Stoner-Weiss, 'The Myth of the Authoritarian Model'.

one. This meant new conditions for business and for most of the elite, with the exception of the *siloviki*; instead of partners, they were reduced to functionaries. As Aleksei Makarkin notes, the Putin coalition of 2000–3, which included the bureaucracy and big business, now gave way to a period where the only partner for the top executive was the bureaucracy, within which the *siloviki* became predominant.[104] Within the new framework the Kremlin was able to resolve a number of tasks that it had not been able to do earlier: to get big business to pay its taxes in full; to launch long-term infrastructural projects such as the ESPO pipeline; and to create state corporations for aircraft, shipbuilding, and many other spheres. However, the new system carried some powerful political risks. Since it was relatively insulated from social forces, tensions over power and policy were concentrated within the regime itself, leading to intensified factional conflict. Putin spent much of his second term managing these conflicts, and tried to find para-institutional answers to para-constitutional problems, as when he created the Investigative Committee. Intensified state involvement in economic management also threatened stable economic development. As in the Soviet period, economic modernization without political modernity was an unstable construct.

---

[104] Nikolai Silaev, 'Modernizatsiya moshchi', *Ekspert*, No. 9, 3–9 March 2008, pp. 21–6, at p. 23.

12

Conclusion: A Question of Interpretation?

> Ill at ease in the tyranny, ill at ease in the republic, in the one I longed for freedom, in the other for the end of corruption.
>
> Czesław Miłosz[1]

Property remains a key factor in the structure of political authority, and to this day there is no satisfactory constitutional alignment between political and economic power. The Yukos case revealed the dangers of the commercialization of the political sphere, but the outcome was the further politicization of the economic sphere. We thus have a triangle of power, freedom, and property accompanied by political as well as economic contradictions. The Yukos affair inhibited the move away from neo-patrimonial approaches to economic life, but it did not resolve the fundamental constitutional question about the proper scope for autonomous economic activity. The Yukos affair came to symbolize both the achievement and failings of Russia's headlong rush to the market. The freedom of the 1990s came at a high price, but the attempt in the 2000s to modify the earlier settlement came with penalties of its own. Sections of the elite used the attack on Khodorkovsky to achieve certain goals of the regime and to enhance the perceived interests of the state. Whether these goals are desirable, laudable, or achievable remain contested. The Yukos affair was not a Tiananmen Square massacre, when in June 1989 the Chinese authorities asserted their power over mass popular demonstrations calling for greater popular inclusion in the political process, but it did mark the moment when the political state in Russia reasserted its predominance over the nascent business class to determine the main contours of domestic and foreign policy. The power of the oligarchs had originally derived from authority delegated from government, and this practical dependency was now turned into political reality.

THE YUKOS CASE: RIGHT AND WRONG?

The profound, but perverse, political logic of the Yukos affair is noted by the commentator Andrei Kolesnikov:

---

[1] Czesław Miłosz, 'To Raja Rao', *Selected Poems* (New York, Ecco Press, 1980), p. 29.

Perhaps the basic reason why Khodorkovsky is being brought to criminal responsibility was, as everyone says, his excessive political activity. But in the time that he spent in jail, the process turned into a trial of the economic logic of privatisation, of the historic mission of the 1990s, which laid the groundwork for today's growth and relative prosperity of the Russian economy.[2]

The Yukos case was part of a much larger struggle in contemporary Russian politics, and its multifaceted and controversial character means that Terence's tag 'Quot homines tot sententiae' ('Many people, many opinions') accurately describes the multiplicity of views about the affair.[3] It was driven by the coincidence of economic, political, and personal factors, but at its heart lie issues of political economy. The Kremlin was intent not so much in reversing the outcome of the privatizations of the 1990s as asserting its prerogatives over a part of the economy (the energy sector) that it considers should never have passed out of state hands. We have called this process 'deprivatization', falling short of full renationalization but infringing on the sovereignty of property rights. The state was able to reassert its strategic management of the energy sector, and at the same time to remould the relationship between business and the state. To be successful in big business one now had first to ensure adequate political cover. The Yukos affair was less a battle with the oligarchs as a class than as a means of ensuring that the right ones were selected to support the aims of the state and thereby not only retain but greatly to multiply their wealth.

The Yukos affair changed the balance of power between the factions and acted as the motor of a redistribution of property in the energy sector. Equally, issues of economic policy were central. The government reasserted its prerogatives as the arbiter in pipeline policy since energy exports are crucial in the Russian government's ambitious aims for economic development. The windfall energy rents fostered a reassertion of great power (*derzhavnik*) aspirations, while the redistribution of property accompanying the Yukos affair reinforced the autonomy of the regime from political control and the constraints of the constitutional state. It would be exaggerated to suggest that oil had replaced ideology, yet it was oil and associated energy rents that helped propel Russia on a new path. It could even be argued that the new political economy set the country on to a post-European model of development, not quite state monopoly capitalism but a different type of modernization dynamic which set it at odds with the prevalent Western ideology.

The broader context was an attempt to impose a state-centred developmental model, and to push through a particular vision of modernization. This was a hybrid model, since it certainly did not return to Soviet-style nationalization and planning but accepted liberal market principles. However, while accepting the framework of market *competition*, the Putinite developmental model sought to constrain and shape the operation of market *forces*. At the heart of Putin's approach to politics and the economy was the idea of *temporality*. By this we mean

---

[2] Gazeta.ru, 12 April 2005.
[3] From the Roman dramatist (190–159 BC) Terence's play *Phormio*.

that while Putin may well have understood the arguments of the liberal members of his team, demonstrated by their strong presence in the government and his patience with advisers such as Illarionov, he also believed that the path to the desirable condition from the actual state of affairs required time and management. Just as democracy in his view was too important to be left to the wilfulness of democrats, so, too, the development of the market could not be left to the operation of market forces.

The tension between ends and means ultimately rendered the Soviet system unviable, and it was now reproduced in new forms in Putinite Russia. While the goals pursued in the Yukos affair—to restore state autonomy, to reduce what was perceived to be excessive business interests in politics, and to allow the state to shape energy policy in particular and economic policy in general—are rational and understandable, the means applied to their achievement undermined the goals. The methods were reminiscent of those used in the 1990s, although now intended to achieve not so much a revision and repudiation of the earlier methods as a redistribution of property and the sources of social initiatives. Yukos could have avoided bankruptcy if allowed to pay off its obligations, but that was not the purpose. The state used the Yukos case to establish a new model of state-economy relations in which a type of *dirigiste* capitalism began to emerge accompanied by elements of a neo-mercantilist approach to natural resources.

The emergence of a dual economy was accompanied by the development of a dual state. In areas where the state's interests were involved, law and due process were suborned. The Yukos case was about the assertion of the prerogatives of the state in the political sphere. Putin's regime would not tolerate the development of an *imperium in imperio*, and moved decisively to remove the challenge to the government's monopoly over the decision-making process. This entailed also the repudiation of the development of a political caste beholden in any way to the Yukos company, in the form of parliamentary deputies, political parties, or social organizations. Instead the 'politburo' advanced an alternative path of development. Although 'personal freedom in most respects has not diminished under President Putin', the political freedoms of Russian citizens were constricted, accompanied by the growing arbitrary powers of security agencies.[4] The *proizvol* (licence) of the oligarchs was now replaced by a different and rather more traditional form of *proizvol*, the selective and despotic use of state power.

Russia's bourgeois revolution without a bourgeoisie at first allowed an 'oligarchy' to emerge, and then the Yukos affair represented a fundamental reassertion of state power. Russia has undergone an involuted bourgeois revolution, where the forms of capitalist development are preserved, but the content and dynamic diverge sharply from classical patterns. Above all, the autonomy and independence of the bourgeoisie was sharply circumscribed, and the state sought

---

[4] Roderic Lyne, Strobe Talbott, and Koji Watanabe, *Engaging With Russia: The Next Phase* (Washington, Paris Tokyo, The Trilateral Commission, 2006), p. 147.

to act as the motor of development with the business class co-opted as a subaltern social formation.[5] In part, this was a way for Putin's Russia to engage with the challenge of globalization. Putin certainly was in favour of Russia's integration into the international economy, demonstrated by his commitment to Russia joining the WTO, but the terms of engagement were distinctive. Internationalization was acceptable, but independent transnationalization was not.

His strategy in part reprised those of earlier 'developmental states', but given the fact that Russia was already a mature industrial society the emphasis was more on becoming a 'competition state',[6] able to hold its own in a world of competing 'trading states'.[7] Competitiveness in the modern economy is typically measured by improved national systems of education and research, and ability to provide a 'flexible labour market' to attract foreign direct investment. Putin's Russia, however, took a rather more traditional view of things. Russia would engage with the world economy, but as a type of transnational corporation, hence its fear that this role would be supplanted by powerful independent corporations like Yukos. As Surkov put it in his speech to United Russia activists on 7 February 2006, 'sovereignty is the political synonym for competitiveness'.[8] Old Soviet ideas of autarchy and mercantilist ideas about protectionism now gave way to a state-supported programme of international competition. While no advanced capitalist state is bereft of this, Russia's rather crude and aggressive version, accompanied by great power claims, alarmed the rest of the world. The internal viability and external efficacy of this model are uncertain.

The claim to be an 'energy superpower', with domestic monopoly structures, both political and economic, came into contradiction with global agendas. This liberal agenda, of course, is set by the strong, and it is this order that is challenged by the G20, and countries such as Venezuela under Chávez and Bolivia under Morales, and even Castro's Cuba. Russia under Putin certainly did not want to become part of this anti-globalization rejectionist front. Neither did it wish to become part of a geopolitical revisionist alliance represented potentially, for example, by the Shanghai Co-operation Organisation (SCO). The SCO, established in June 2001 as a regional multilateral mechanism for security and cooperation, is the antithesis of the liberal universalist principles proclaimed by the leading Western powers, and instead takes a hard-headed realist approach to international politics based on interests rather than 'values'. China's developing economic ties in Central Asia, focusing on energy and pipelines but broadening out into manufacturing, trade, and banking, were accompanied by its strategic goal to minimize

---

[5] For a comparative study, see Graeme Gill, *Bourgeoisie, State and Democracy: Russia, Britain, France, Germany and the USA* (Oxford and New York, Oxford University Press, 2008).

[6] Cf. P. G. Cerny, *The Changing Architecture of Politics: Structure, Agency, and the Future of the State* (London, Sage Publications, 1990).

[7] R. Rosecrance, *The Rise of the Trading State* (New York, Basic Books, 1986).

[8] Vladislav Surkov, 'Suverenitet—politicheskii sinonim konkurentosposobnosti', in *Tektsy*, pp. 125–73.

Western influence in the region.[9] This was a concern shared by Russia, although China's own growing weight in the area could not but worry Moscow.

The assault against Yukos and its employees is bound up with the personal ambitions of some key economic actors (above all Bogdanchikov at the head of Rosneft, allied with Timchenko's Gunvor) and figures in the presidential administration (pre-eminently Sechin), and this helps explain the continuation of the assault against Yukos and those associated with it even after the end of the Khodorkovsky trial in May 2005. Yukos was pushed into bankruptcy, but this was not an outcome that Putin intended. The Yukos affair once again demonstrated the link between oil and power; as Simonov notes: 'They who control oil, control the country.'[10] The change of the presidency and Medvedev's accompanying personnel reshuffles reshaped the 'politburo' and also offered an opportunity for policy change. In particular, the faction headed by Sechin was weakened by his removal from the presidential administration to become one of five deputy prime ministers responsible for civilian shipbuilding and energy. As Åslund notes: 'The scourge of the Putin administration was the Sechin group, which spearheaded the confiscation of Yukos and reinforced repression. It seemed invincible, but now its four top members have been demoted: Sechin, Viktor Ivanov, Patrushev, and Justice Minister Vladimir Ustinov. Apparently, their only support was Putin's presidency.'[11] Although the factions were fragmented and some were dismantled, the reality of factional conflict had not disappeared but only changed its forms.

A system of 'managed democracy' emerged in Russia in which the political elite is relatively insulated from the constitutional norms that it is committed to uphold. Khodorkovsky emerged as an individual who refused to subordinate himself to the new system, and this is a crucial reason why he was chosen for persecution. His funding of political parties, support for civil society, and his potential personal political ambitions all jarred with the Kremlin's aims to manage political processes. Khodorkovsky came to represent political pluralism, and thus emerged as a threat. Just as the war in Chechnya dominated the first part of Putin's presidency, the attack on Yukos was the defining episode of Putin's presidency as a whole. Khodorkovsky represented not so much a systemic challenge to the regime but the possibility of an alternative.

The Yukos case is a forceful example of what we call meta-corruption. The logic of political struggle and the attempt to reforge a new model of political economy undermined the independence of the judiciary. The law was used selectively against Khodorkovsky and his colleagues. Judicial impartiality and the independence of the Russian judicial system became casualties, and thus the opportunity for the key actors to receive free and fair trials was undermined.

---

[9] Hsiu-Ling Wu and Chien-Hsun Chen, 'The Prospects for Regional Economic Integration Between China and the Five Central Asian Countries', *Europe–Asia Studies*, Vol. 56, No. 7, November 2004, pp. 1059–80.

[10] Simonov, *Russkaya neft'*, p. 5.

[11] Anders Aslund, 'Unlike Putin, Medvedev Took Charge Quickly', *Moscow Times*, 21 May 2008.

The case demonstrated the degeneration of the independence of the Russian legal system. Putin's 'dictatorship of law' began to slip into something approaching 'dictatorship by law'. A new atmosphere of intimidation emerged, characterized by the re-emergence of Soviet-style attitudes and practices, including the use of 'telephone' law and threats against the independence of judges. When the state was involved, law was used as an instrument of state policy.

The election of Medvedev as president changed the balance of power, and represented a major defeat of Sechin, Patrushev, and the 'politburo' sub-faction among the *siloviki* and its allies. In his first interview following Medvedev's election as president, Khodorkovsky once again voiced his conviction that Sechin had been responsible: 'He orchestrated the first case against me out of greed and the second out of cowardice.' Khodorkovsky expressed bewilderment:

Exactly how he managed to convince his boss is hard to say. Maybe Putin really thought I was plotting some political coup, which is ridiculous, since at the time I was publicly supporting two opposition parties, which at best could have won 15% in parliamentary elections. More likely they didn't need any reason, just an excuse to raid Yukos, Russia's most successful oil company.

Khodorkovsky voiced cautious optimism about the new presidency, but noted that it would take some time for Medevedv to act independently: 'For a while Medvedev will be held back by his personal obligation to Putin':

The outcome of my case depends on the speed with which reform to the judicial system, which Medvedev has said he wants, will take place. In an independent court only a complete idiot would swallow the kind of case brought against me. Unfortunately reforms don't happen overnight, but some steps taken by Medvedev's team are cause for cautious optimism.[12]

Khodorkovsky continued to read a lot, but admitted that '[t]he years in prison, the isolation, isn't easy but it's bearable....Education and reflection are prison's great bonuses.'[13] Since Medvedev's accession did not entail a change of elites, those who had put him in jail remained in power and therefore Khodorkovsky would continue to have time for reflection.

This appeared confirmed by Putin's comments to *Le Monde* on 31 May that any decision on relaxing the conditions of Khodorkovsky's imprisonment or reducing his term was one that the president would have to make 'on his own'; he stressed that Khodorkovsky had broken the law 'repeatedly and grossly', and that he had been part of a group accused not only of economic crimes but also murders. 'This kind of "competition"', he insisted, 'is not admissible, and we will do our best to stop it.'[14] Medevedev, however, took a rather different tack. In a press conference

[12] Mark Franchetti, 'Jailed Tycoon Mikhail Khodorkovsky "Framed" by Key Putin Aide', *Sunday Times*, 18 May 2008.

[13] Ibid.

[14] *Le Monde*, 1 June 2008, pp. 1, 2; http://www.government.ru/content/governmentactivity/mainnews/archive/2008/05/31/8104212.htm.

with German Chancellor Angela Merkel on 5 June 2008 Medvedev was asked
about the 'pardoning or freeing' of Khodorkovsky. His answer opened the door a
little:

I would like to say that all procedures, including executive and criminal procedures that
exist in our country, must be based on Russian law, and issues of enforcement or issues
of pardon should not be subject to interstate negotiations. It is a matter of national sovereignty.

As for the procedures themselves, they do exist and should be observed in strict
accordance with our rules. There is a procedure for pardoning someone, to which
any citizen convicted of a crime (including Khodorkovsky) can resort, as well as
other procedures that exist in regard to criminal law enforcement. But such issues
cannot be resolved in discussions at the intergovernmental level or by decisions
taken by politicians.[15]

In other words, the possibility of freeing Khodorkovsky existed, but it would
be done at a time of Russia's choosing and in a manner that observed established
procedures.

The prospects of Khodorkovsky's early release increased, although accompanied by two main concerns. First, any amnesty raised the prospect of litigation by
shareholders who had lost out as Yukos stock became devalued, and thus a 'zero-
option' deal would have to be struck: Khodorkovsky's release and the end of associated prosecutions in exchange for a moratorium on economic claims. Second,
Khodorkovsky's release would signal the lack of continuity in the succession from
Putin to Medvedev, so his release would have to take an extremely legalistic form to
occlude its political implications. Any deal would have to include the renunciation
of political activity by Khodorkovsky.

Although in the short term the Yukos affair weakened the position of Yeltsin's
old guard, it did not lead to the full-scale victory of the *siloviki* and neither
did it allow them to dominate the policy process, although their influence was
strengthened. Relations between government and big business did change significantly, with the state adopting a more clear-cut tutelary role over the strategic
management of the economy, and a reduction in the political autonomy of business leaders. The energy sector was reshaped, with a much greater role for state
companies in general and for Rosneft, as the 'national' oil company, in particular.
However, the Yukos affair was never a single planned operation, but evolved incrementally, escalating from individual arrests to the destruction of the country's
second largest oil company. In the same way, with the change of presidency and
staff reshuffles, there was the prospect of a gradual de-escalation. It was unlikely,
however, that there could be a full-scale restitution, with the return, for example,
of YNG to a reconstituted Yukos. Even the most liberal of governments would find
it impossible to restore a goldfish from this particular fish soup. The rehabilitation
of the individuals involved, however, is another matter.

---

[15] http://www.kremlin.ru/text/appears/2008/06/202120.shtml.

CLASS AND STATE POWER

The Yukos affair prompts larger questions about the nature of the social and political order emerging in Russia in the wake of the communist collapse. With the coming together of business and the state, one commentary argued as follows:

A new socio-political system has taken shape in the country, primitive in its construction and with a low creative potential. Is this a tragedy? No. We find ourselves in a natural historical process which we have to endure and devise a strategy. Every revolutionary crisis is followed by a calm, which does not mean a move backwards.[16]

In other words, the Yukos affair was a symptom of a Thermidorean reaction after the storms of the democratic capitalist revolution, allowing the system to consolidate while undermining the revolutionary spirit and dealing with its excesses. More broadly, a recent study suggests that the Yukos affair is part of a broader historical pattern:

Over the last 150 years, Russia has repeatedly fallen victim to the same cycle. The pattern is as follows. First, liberal reforms lead to a rapid economic upturn. Then, different interest groups clash over the distribution of its economic benefits and are tempted to use these benefits for geopolitical ends. Social tension grows as military expenditure rises. The reforms are checked, and conflicts at home and abroad lead to political and social collapse.[17]

The study suggested four possible scenarios: the Rentier model, where Russia's elite lives off rents, above all from energy resources; the Mobilization model, designed to make Russia and energy and raw material 'superpower' accompanied by a military build-up; the Inertia scenario, a tactical response combining populist measures and 'half-hearted reforms'; and finally the Modernization model, requiring a broad modernizing coalition, the 'strengthening of civil society, the reform of public and private institutions, and the enhancement of business efficiency'.[18] In the view of the authors, this was the least likely scenario.

At least four influential narratives combine and compete. The first concerns the move to the market, and the social resistances to that process. Russia's 'black privatization' in the 1990s was an extreme case of the pillaging of state assets by favoured groups. As Khodorkovsky stressed in his various missives, this raised sharp questions about the legitimacy of the market order, the need to reconcile justice with freedom, and the appropriate scope for state action. At the same time, Khodorkovsky's personal role in black privatization entailed a fundamental contradiction in his position. His moral credibility to resolve the issue was questioned; but at the same time, he was perhaps best placed and with the authority to help the country come to terms with the way capitalism had been born. While the liberal

---

[16] Fadeev, 'Opasnost' prostoty', p. 88.

[17] Igor Y. Yurgens, *Russia's Future Under Medvedev*, English edition edited by Professor Lord Skidelsky (Warwick, Centre for Global Studies, 2008), chapter 1, 'How to Break the Vicious Cycle: a History of Russia's Economic Development', pp. 9–11, at p. 9.

[18] Ibid., p. 10; with the four models discussed in more details in chapter 4, pp. 45–56.

architects of the new economic system in the 1990s became the political victims of the process, Khodorkovsky ended up as both a winner and a loser of the new order. His incarceration endowed him the moral authority to speak on behalf of all the constituencies, both those who had gained and those who had lost.

The second problem focuses on the political system that emerged in this period. It was clear that simplified transition narratives are inadequate on their own, although much of the technical analysis of the transitological literature is pertinent to the Russian case. For some, as we have seen, the Yukos affair demonstrated that Russia's democratic transition has failed. There is no doubt that the case provided much material to support the 'failed democratization' camp.[19] The undermining of judicial independence and the almost wilful destruction of a major economic corporation clearly demonstrated the emergence of a power regime in Russia that had achieved dangerous levels of independence, both from the constraints of the constitutional order and the rule of law, and from effective accountability to the representative system, parties, social organizations, and parliament. The Yukos affair illustrated the dangers of the hyper-development of executive power. Thus the Yukos affair is considered 'part of the genetic makeup of Russian history', where in the course of centuries independent figures are cut down either consciously (Ivan the Terrible and Stalin) or spontaneously (the burning of independent farmsteads during the Stolypin reforms): strong individuals and independent classes were periodically destroyed by 'the authoritarian (totalitarian) Russian state'.[20] Patrimonial traditions were restored, with economic assets considered the property of the elites.

However, the material above has demonstrated that a straightforward 'failed democratization' approach does not encompass the complexities and multiple processes at work, and neither does a simple 'genetic' model of the inevitability of Russian authoritarianism. The Yukos affair was far from a straightforward reprise of the repressions of the Stalinist era, although there are undoubtedly some echoes. There were even greater resonances with the post-Stalin epoch, above all in the systematic and generally non-violent repression against dissidents under Brezhnev. The Yukos case is comparable to the trials of Sinyavsky and Daniel in 1965, and some later cases. However, post-communist Russia was not the Stalinist or Brezhnevite Soviet Union, but a society engaged in a complex process of renewal and reconstitution. The openness with which the Yukos affair was discussed, the sharp debates and the soul-searching, all suggest that adherents of the 'democratic evolutionist' approach to post-communist Russia can find some material to support their case. Khodorkovsky's materials were published and became the subject of intense debate, the views of a critic such as Illarionov were widely publicized, and criticisms of the judicial proceedings were aired at even the highest levels.

---

[19] See Richard Sakwa, 'Two Camps? The Struggle to Understand Contemporary Russia', *Comparative Politics*, Vol. 40, No. 4, July 2008, pp. 481–99.

[20] Sergei Gavrov, 'Neobratim li perekhod k avtoritarizmu?', *Svobodnaya mysl'*, No. 1, January 2006, p. 85.

This leads us to the third narrative. Although some of Khodorkovsky's supporters sought to present him as blameless and the Yukos of 2003 as a model of corporate governance, it is clear that this is a simplistic picture. Equally, critics that seek to portray him in the darkest light, as a murderer, systematic tax avoider, and corrupter of the political process is equally flawed and one-dimensional. In practice, the Yukos affair throws up a mirror to Russia, and what emerges about both Yukos and Russia is neither as dark nor as light as various advocates would suggest. In fact, both are part of the same social order, and neither is the fount of all virtue or the source of all wickedness. This comes out particularly strongly when we look at the personalities of Putin and Khodorkovsky, so similar in many ways. It turns out that Putin was the more rebellious in his youth, and Khodorkovsky the more conformist. Both were shaped by the post-totalitarian late Brezhnev era, although Putin, a decade older than Khodorkovsky, imbibed rather more of the spirit of stagnation of the late Brezhnev years. When young they listened to the same semi-rebellious music of Bulat Okudzhava, Vladimir Vysotsky, Alexander Galich, and Mikhai Zhvanetsky and were shaped by the same post-ideological but strongly patriotic culture. Neither was particularly 'Soviet' in their views, but then almost none of their generation believed in the 'indissoluble union' of Soviet peoples and the building of communism, and this is one reason why the USSR collapsed so quickly in 1991. They were Russians first and Soviets second.

We have noted in Chapter 8 how much of what Khodorkovsky wrote could be ascribed to Putin. Khodorkovsky was harshly critical of the failings of the neo-liberals in the 1990s and the liberal opposition in the 2000s, perhaps even more so than Putin. Indeed, Khodorkovsky went further than Putin in supporting the patriotic-left tendency in Russia, while Putin stuck far more firmly to the liberal technocratic approach. Both had a strong sense that the 1990s were a period of disgrace for Russia, and had strong views on the way to overcome Russia's renewed time of troubles. Both were statist, patriotic, and integrationist at the international level. They were also both charismatic leaders, although in different ways, with strong wills and a powerful aura of leadership, and hence in part the Yukos affair was provoked by a clash of powerful personalities. Khodorkovsky was ready to sacrifice his own freedom as well as his property, but in doing so achieved some of what he intended, but not the way that he had planned. As an editorial in *Vedemosti* noted, a new type of corporate social responsibility was imposed on business in the wake of his departure, while tax collection from companies and the population improved: 'Possibly, just as with tax discipline, Khodorkovsky, at the cost of his own freedom, will succeed in improving the state of affairs in the Russian law-enforcement system.'[21]

The stain of the black privatization period could in part be removed by Khodorkovsky's legitimization agenda. However, the problem was deeper than that and brings us to the fourth narrative, the emergence of an independent bourgeoisie and its role in national modernization. Here American modernization theories and the Marxist metaphor about base and superstructure collude to suggest that

[21] 'Ot redaktsiya: Missiya Khodorkovskogo', *Vedemosti*, 8 February 2007.

changes in the economic system will, with an undefined degree of determinacy, lead to changes in the political system, which in our epoch gave rise to discussion of the 'third wave' of democracy.[22] In Eurasia, however, things were always more complicated than that, and Russia's post-communist trajectory has seen a path determined as much by cultural, geopolitical, and political factors as by structural changes in the economy. The emergence of an autonomous business class was inhibited by some fundamental systemic problems inherited from the 1990s. The very word 'oligarch' tainted the whole emerging business elite, although it could be applied in practice to no more than a handful of the very powerful individuals for a short period, notably Berezovsky's 'seven bankers' of 1997. The swagger and arrogance of Berezovsky and his ilk tainted the whole class. The managers of state-owned corporations were by definition in a position of dependence. For a number of reasons the business elite was unable to convert economic power into class power in anything other than the crudest attempt to undermine state autonomy. Putin's first step, through the policy of 'equidistance', was to chase this type of oligarch from the temple of power. This still left the fundamental philosophical question unresolved: what are the boundaries of the legitimate rights of the nascent bourgeoisie; and by the same token, what is the proper scope and necessary limits on state power?

This is a question that did not find a satisfactory answer in Russia's first attempt at capitalist development from the middle of the nineteenth century to 1917, and Russia's second attempt from 1991 stumbled over the same problem. In both cases the development of big business was inscribed in a rather artificial way into a social order that drew its legitimacy from non-market sources. In both cases the transformation of a business class into a bourgeoisie, with a defined legitimate right to participate in governmental affairs, was at best partial. In the first period Russia's big business was considered in some way 'unnatural', as alien to Russia's traditionalist bureaucratic paternalistic traditions accompanied by the large role played by foreign capital; while in contemporary Russia black privatization was seen as theft, conspiracy, and betrayal, as well as being unjust. Just as democracy in post-communist Russia had to create the conditions for its own existence, so Russia was building a capitalist system in which the capitalists themselves were not the outcome of a historical process of development but artificially created by the transition itself. Contrary to much simplistic 'orange' thinking, structural modernization does not automatically lead to a democratic breakthrough, and as the Ukrainian events in late 2004 demonstrate, external forces have a key role to play.[23] Putin spent most of his leadership precisely ensuring that 'external forces' would not be able to shape Russia's internal development, and that was in part the reason for Khodorkovsky's downfall.

---

[22] Samuel P. Huntington, *The Third Wave: Democratization in the Late Twentieth Century* (Norman and London, University of Oklahoma Press, 1991).

[23] Anders Åslund and Michael McFaul (eds.), *Revolution in Orange: The Origins of Ukraine's Democratic Breakthrough* (Washington, D.C., Carnegie Endowment for International Peace, 2006).

Business–state relations under Putin became severely instrumental. As we have seen in our discussion of the RUIE, the Yukos affair nipped in the bud its development as an autonomous peak organization discussing matters of national importance as equals. Indeed, the whole state–business relationship became instrumentalized, with the imposition of de facto social obligations and a peculiarly Soviet-style definition of 'corporate social responsibility'. Business corporations also became instruments in a newly active industrial policy, where the stronger acted as 'patrons' of weaker companies, as in the defence sector taking *sheftstvo* (guidance and support) over motor manufacturing. The instrumentalism extended to foreign policy, in particular in the energy sector where companies such as Gazprom advanced Russian interests in post-Soviet Eurasia, while the 'national champion' Rosneft increasingly took the lead in developments such as the various Sakhalin projects. It was increasingly unclear where the state ended and business began.

While elements in Putin's regime identified Khodorkovsky as part of the problem, he was also part of the solution to Russia's developmental dilemmas. His 'left turn' arguments were more than just about the legitimization of the privatizations of the 1990s, but about ensuring that capitalism in Russia was 'socialized' to overcome popular resentment and mistrust and to ensure that 'capital' did not come into systemic contradiction with the state. In the 'bourgeois revolution' of February 1917 the leading force had certainly not been the capitalist class but a narrow stratum of intellectuals and bureaucrats, and this pattern was repeated in Russia's second 'bourgeois revolution' of 1991. Thus there is a striking similarity between the internal structure of the two bourgeois revolutions, as well as in some of the effects, notably the weakening of the state. The international context, of course, was fundamentally different, and thus Russia's second bourgeois revolution is sustained in part by foreign resources. This had the paradoxical effect of intensifying domestic alienation, and thus Putin was concerned less with 'socializing' capitalism than to 'nativize' it, to inscribe it into the pattern of Russian history, and the instrument to achieve this was state activism. Both Putin and Khodorkovsky are proponents of capitalist development in Russia, but while Khodorkovsky sought to find ways to make the autonomy of the bourgeoisie palatable to the people he failed to make it acceptable for the state, whereas Putin tried to ensure that capitalism's autonomy was constrained 'from above' and thus provided an alternative, and probably more effective, mode of legitimation to that proposed by Khodorkovsky.

Ultimately the Yukos affair was generated by the struggle between two visions of the appropriate model of modernity for Russia. The struggle between the authorities and business in Russia reflects two different types of freedom, although neither appears in anything like a 'pure' form. On the one side, the proponents of 'state capitalism' insisted that the state should retain the strategic initiative in all spheres of economic life, although they favoured de-privatization rather than full-blooded re-nationalization. Against the background of the free-for-all in the 1990s, this *dirigiste* approach, reminiscent of De Gaulle's France of the 1960s, resonated strongly with the Russian public. It resonated even more strongly with

Russia's bureaucratic elite, who in the Soviet period were de facto owners and were accustomed to dealing with state property as their own.[24] On the other hand, Russia's nascent big business class insisted that market autonomy, secure property rights, and freedom for the emerging bourgeoisie were the only way that Russia could avoid falling once again into the statist trap. At a profound level the tension is between proponents of a genuine bourgeois revolution, where the state really is constrained by spheres that are beyond politics, and the bureaucratic-statist model of modernization from above that tends to exclude society as an autonomous actor in the developmental process. Interestingly, both Khodorkovsky and Putin were ambivalent about both approaches, and neither shared fully the vision of one or the other. Undoubtedly Khodorkovsky defended liberal freedoms, but equally Putin never denied their validity. At the same time, Khodorkovsky's 'left turn' arguments suggested a strong role for the state, and in his refusal to accept the left-nationalist agenda, Putin in some ways was more liberal than Khodorkovsky.

Although the Yukos affair can be inserted into a narrative of state reassertion, the case in practice only partially achieved this and in a profound sense demonstrated the opposite. The assault against Yukos did not signal a narrowing of the gap between the rule of law and arbitrary power, but in fact saw the gulf widen. The case did not allow even the regime to consolidate itself, but revealed the degree to which it was factionalized. The laws of factional conflict transcend those of Russia's post-communist regime, and indeed are 'the rules of every society that does not enjoy the rule of law'.[25]

FATE AND FREEDOM

The Yukos affair brought to the fore broader issues concerning the developing of a public subjectivity, and in particular the role of the individual and his or her relationship to state power and authority. Nikolai Gogol, notably in *Taras Bulba*, suggested that, as one commentator puts it: 'Each life is dictated by fate and must be endured and challenged rather than thought through or arranged.' Hence in that story the characters are in a sense little more than emanations of their ascriptive national characteristics, with true Russianness defined as

bold, muscular, nationalistic, and backward-looking.... National characteristics persist: Poles are Catholic, gaudy, effete, and treacherous; Tatars are unknowable; Jews are well-connected ...; Cossacks are real men. But these national characteristics do not necessarily lead to salvation or redemption—in the context of 16th-century Ukraine, they only lead to more complex dilemmas and more gruelling challenges that must be endured.[26]

---

[24] The point is made by Alexander Lebedev, a United Russia deputy in the Fourth Duma, 'Kurs na burzhuaznuyu revolyutsiyu', *Ekspert*, No. 25, 3–9 July 2006, pp. 70–72, at p. 71.

[25] Kimmage, 'Putin's Restoration', p. 142.

[26] Jane Smiley, 'War Not Peace', *Saturday Guardian Review*, 22 April 2006, p. 22.

Khodorkovsky refused to accept a single role for himself, and that in part was the problem. His Soviet inclinations, his Jewishness, his Russianness, his ruthless flair for business, his political aspirations, his citizenship of the world, his media persona, his family life as a *bourgeois gentil'homme*, none of these for him were to determine his fate: the whole story of Khodorkovsky is the assertion that a citizen of free Russia has the freedom to choose their own life path. Life, however, had a different fate in store for him in the form of the Putin regime's insistence that people should understand the limits of what is permissible, and that the acceptance of constraints is also a type of freedom.

The many facets of Khodorkovsky's personality allowed him to act as a type of mirror to a diverse range of views, and at the same time ideas and aspirations were projected on to him. People saw in him what they wanted to see, usually a reflection of their own aspirations. As in Tarkovsky's *Solaris*, immanent dreams were projected as tangible facts. Thus the Yukos affair became an open book, in which each could write their own narrative without concern for how each chapter tied in with the others. This also in part helps explain why in the end Khodorkovsky was unsatisfactory for all, and his refusal to adopt a single persona or political characteristic meant that he could not become the leader of a single movement.

For the ordinary Russian citizen there was not much to choose between Khodorkovsky and other greedy oligarchs of the likes of Berezovsky or Gusinsky, but he could be respected for his civic courage; for liberals Khodorkovsky represented the fulfilment of a century-old dream to see a native bourgeoisie emerge, but if only he had paid his taxes and been rather less arrogant in dealing with the authorities; others considered the whole affair a rather distasteful struggle between political and business elites to grab a larger share of the pie, with no more than a few crumbs coming down to the people; while for sympathetic foreign observers the case demonstrated the fragile nature of the rule of law in Russia and how far the country had to go before it could be considered a genuine constitutional state, but why did Khodorkovsky have to be so critical of the liberals and such a patriot; whereas for those inclined to take a traditionally Russophobic view, the case demonstrated that Russian political culture more or less inevitably tends towards the despotic, and thus the country should be kept in a firmly subaltern position and not treated as a respected equal in international affairs. With so many former KGB operatives on both sides, for some the struggle between Yukos and the state was little more than '[a] conflict between two departments of the Lubyanka'.[27] Khodorkovsky's refusal publicly to renounce his wealth and his past tarred him with the image of an irredeemable oligarch, however much he talked of liberalism and social justice. Jail, however, liberated Khodorkovsky from the burden of property, which itself is a form of freedom today. Khodorkovsky was an individual who had the civic courage to defend greater pluralism in society, while refusing to be trapped into a single definition of self. He was also no doubt

---

[27] Tokareva, *Kto podstavil khodorskovskogo*, p. 138.

intelligent enough to understand that 'freedom is anathema to dreams nurtured in captivity'.[28]

Khodorkovsky's persecution has been compared to the Dreyfus affair, when the Jewish army office Alfred Dreyfus was accused of treason for allegedly having passed information to the Germans. After a massive public campaign in his defence, including Emile Zola's famous open letter *J'accuse*, in 1906 Dreyfus was exonerated. It is immediately striking how little public agitation there was in Russia on Khodorkovsky's behalf. However, there is one similarity, and it is well drawn out in the historian Vincent Duclert's argument for Dreyfus's remains to be transferred to the Panthéon, the mausoleum for the great and the good of France, including Zola himself: 'Although he was a victim of a conspiracy at the heart of state Dreyfus was a heroic fighter for justice. Even after undergoing this terrifying deportation he refused to behave like a condemned man. He behaved like someone who was innocent. He did not see himself as a victim because he was Jewish but a citizen fighting for the truth.'[29]

Freedom for Khodorkovsky entailed an element of personal self-fulfilment. When Pichugin and Lebedev were arrested Khodorkovsky behaved in an extraordinary way, openly challenging the Kremlin, travelling abroad, and thus internationalizing the struggle. Khodorkovsky represented the advancement of an economic class, social pluralism, and personal freedom. Khodorkovsky defended his existential freedom to fulfil his own destiny; anything else could be characterized as bad faith. His revolt in 2003, when he repudiated the framework of the conventions of political behaviour imposed in 2000, was however a personal one, although with broad social ramifications. Neither he nor Putin sought to tie their personal political careers to a transcendent vision for the nation. Cheah has noted the 'organic vitalism' that underlines modern, and in particular postcolonial, nationalism, based on an idea of freedom that incarnates teleological time to allow the fulfilment of the cultural destiny of a nation in some form of organic life and the 'transcendence of finitude'.[30] Rather than transcending finitude, both Khodorkovsky and Putin were concerned with the instantiation of temporality: the conflict was about property and power, and only secondarily about the historical destiny of the Russian nation. In that sense, the Yukos affair showed that Russia had come of age, casting aside classical political conflicts informed by ideological struggles in favour of the brute struggle for superiority between forces firmly rooted in the social forces of contemporary modernity.

Khodorkovsky in prison gave voice to the fears of the business class about its 'ethical vulnerability', the awareness that the mass of the Russian people did not accept the privatizations of the 1990s as lawful or business power as legitimate.[31]

[28] Gary Shteyngart, *Absurdistan* (London, Granta Books, 2006), p. 234.
[29] Kim Willsher, 'Dreyfus Saga Goes on Amid Calls for Reburial with France's Finest', *The Guardian*, 28 June 2006, p. 19.
[30] Pheng Cheah, *Spectral Nationality: Passages of Freedom from Kant to Postcolonial Literatures of Nationality* (New York, Columbia University Pres, 2003); the term 'transcendence of finitude' comes from the review by Angharad Closs, *Nationalities Papers*, Vol. 34, No. 5, November 2006, p. 637.
[31] Vyacheslav Kostikov, *Argumenty i fakty*, No. 47, 22 November 2006.

Some magnates sought a safe haven abroad, while others dealt with their fear of the authorities giving organized expression to popular hostility by demonstrating exaggerated loyalty to the government. It was not that the population resisted privatization on ideological grounds, but for severely practical reasons resented a process that left them marginalized and humiliated.[32] Khodorkovsky gained enormous political capital through his various trials and as a result of his tribulations. However, the great bulk of this capital was in the West. In his homeland there remained an enormous reservoir of hostility to what he was seen as representing, and this in part reflected the intense trauma that the 1990s represented for Russia.

Khodorkovsky conducted himself with great dignity throughout his trial and imprisonment. He had time to think of the fate of the country, although he was in part responsible for having brought the country to the condition where it treated him as it did. His friend the artist Maksim Kantor dismissed the comparison with Andrei Sakharov, insisting that Khodorkovsky was not so much a dissident as a capitalist: 'And it is remarkable that precisely a capitalist took on the role of defender of human rights.' Khodorkovsky was also in a unique position to declare that the type of capitalism established in Russia was a deformed type of 'barracks capitalism'. The slogans of the communist period had been replaced by money, and instead of venal corruption, whole factories, lands, and resource basins were traded behind doors. This was the meta-corruption of which we have spoken earlier. Instead of barracks socialism the country had achieved barracks capitalism, with the old Soviet nomenklatura transformed into a new ruling class where democratic centralism had been transformed into Putin's centralized democracy. The moment of betrayal was, as Khodorkovsky pointed out, 'the farce of 1996', when the intelligentsia took its revenge on the people for its humiliations during the Soviet period.[33]

The rise and fall of Yukos is one of the great dramas of our age. Built on the efforts of the preceding Soviet generation, the company symbolized both the robber baron phase of Russian capitalist development and then its move into the age of corporate capitalism. The development of the free market and secure property rights ran into the rock of the Russian state and a profound cultural prejudice against not so much capitalism as the cultural exigencies that it demands, as so well described by Polanyi. Russia is not America; but then neither is America today the America of the Rockefellers or Carnegies. It is not clear that a man with Khodordovsky's overweening ambition would prosper in any contemporary advanced capitalist democracy; but that, of course, is no justification to send him to Siberia. Aside from the main actors, the Yukos affair drew in a vast cast of villains and heroes, lawyers and journalists, political scientists and interested

---

[32] Cf. Hilary Appel, *A New Capitalist Order: Privatization and Ideology in Russia and Eastern Europe*, Pitt Series in Russian and East European Studies (Pittsburgh, University of Pittsburgh Press, 2004).

[33] Maksim Kantor, 'Kazarmennyi kapitalizm', *Moskovskie novosti*, No. 31, 12–18 August 2005, p. 16.

members of the public. The lives of many were altered as a result. The murder of the mayor of Nefteyugansk, the sordid tales and nasty characters revealed in the Tambov cases, the heartbreak of Svetlana Bakhmina, the lives in exile of various Yukos associates, and the shadow that all this cast on Russia's development as a democracy, are all aspects of the Yukos affair. No study of the country can avoid dealing with it; and the affair is at the heart of our understanding of the complexities of contemporary Russia, which themselves reflect the contradictions of the modern world.

Bibliography

Adachi, Yuko, 'The Ambiguous Effects of Russian Corporate Governance Abuses of the 1990s', *Post-Soviet Affairs*, Vol. 22, No. 1, January–March 2006, pp. 65–89.

Ahrend, Rudiger, 'Can Russia Break the "Resource Curse"?', *Eurasian Geography and Economics*, Vol. XLVI, No. 8, December 2005, pp. 584–609.

—— 'Russia's Post-Crisis Growth: Its Sources and Prospects for Continuation', *Europe–Asia Studies*, Vol. 58, No. 1, January 2006, pp. 1–24.

—— and William Tompson, *Realising the Oil Supply Potential of the CIS: The Impact of Institutions and Policies*, OECD Economics Department Working Paper No. 484, 12 May 2006.

Akhmirova, Rimma, *Ya sidel s Khodorkovskim: otkroveniya sokamernikov znamenitogo uznika Matrosskoi Tishiny* (Moscow, Sobesednik, 2005).

Amirov, A. Kh. et al., *Rossiya Putina: Istorii bolezni* (Moscow, Panorama, 2004).

Appel, Hilary, *A New Capitalist Order: Privatization and Ideology in Russia and Eastern Europe*, Pitt Series in Russian and East European Studies (Pittsburgh, PA, University of Pittsburgh Press, 2004).

Åslund, Anders, 'Russian Resources: Curse or Rents?', *Eurasian Geography and Economics*, Vol. XLVI, No. 8, December 2005, pp. 610–17.

—— 'Russia's Energy Policy: A Framing Comment', *Eurasian Geography and Economics*, Vol. 47, No. 3, 2006, pp. 321–8.

—— and Michael McFaul (eds.), *Revolution in Orange: The Origins of Ukraine's Democratic Breakthrough* (Washington, DC, Carnegie Endowment for International Peace, 2006).

Auty, Richard, 'The Political Economy of Resource-Driven Growth', *European Economic Review*, Vol. 45, No. 4, 2001, pp. 839–46.

Averre, Derek, ' "Sovereign Democracy" and Russia's Relations with the European Union', *Demokratizatsiya*, Vol. 15, No. 2, Spring 2007, pp. 173–90.

Babaeva, Svetlana, 'Svoboda ot morali: Chto tsenit sovremennaya Rossiya?', *Rossiya v global'noi politike*, Vol. 5, No. 4, July–August 2007, pp. 22–32.

Baker, Peter and Susan Glasser, *Kremlin Rising: Vladimir Putin's Russia and the End of Revolution* (New York and London, Scribner, 2005; revised edition 2007).

Balmaceda, Margarita, *Energy Dependency, Politics and Corruption in the Former Soviet Union: Russia's Power, Oligarchs' Profits and Ukraine's Missing Energy Policy, 1995–2006* (London, Routledge, 2008).

Balzer, Harley, 'The Putin Thesis and Russian Energy Policy', *Post-Soviet Affairs*, Vol. 21, No. 3, 2005, pp. 210–25.

—— 'Vladimir Putin's Academic Writings and Russian Natural Resource Policy', *Problems of Post-Communism*, Vol. 53, No. 1, January–February 2006, pp. 48–54.

Baran, Zeyno, 'EU Energy Security: Time to End Russian Leverage', *The Washington Quarterly*, Vol. 30, No. 4, Autumn 2007, pp. 131–44.

Barnes, Andrew, 'Russia's New Business Groups and State Power', *Post-Soviet Affairs*, Vol. 19, No. 2, 2003, pp. 154–86.

—— *Owning Russia: The Struggle over Factories, Farms and Power* (Ithaca, NY, Cornell University Press, 2006).

Barnes, Andrew, 'Extricating the State: The Move to Competitive Capture in Post-Communist Bulgaria', *Europe–Asia Studies*, Vol. 59, No. 1, January 2007, pp. 71–96.

Bauers, Birgit, 'Kazakhstan's Economic Challenges: How to Manage the Oil Boom?', *Transition Studies Review*, Vol. 14, No. 1, 2007, pp. 188–94.

Bay, Christian, *The Structure of Freedom* (Stanford, CA, Stanford University Press, 1958).

Belkovskii, Stanislav and Vladimir Golyshev, *Biznes vladimira putina* (Ekaterinburg, Ul'tra.Kul'tura, 2006).

Benediktov, Kirill, 'Roman s neft'yu: Zek i gubernator', *Smysl*', No. 1(20), January 2008, pp. 28–9.

Benn, Stanley I., *A Theory of Freedom* (Cambridge, Cambridge University Press, 1988).

Berdyaev, Nikolai, *Istoki i smysl russkogo kommunizma* (Paris, YMCA-Press, 1955; reprinted Moscow, Nauka, 1990).

Berlin, Isaiah, *Four Essays on Liberty* (Oxford, Oxford University Press, 1969).

Bessonova, O. E., *Razdatochnya ekonomika Rosii: Evolyutsiya cherez transformatsiyu* (Moscow, Rosspen, 2006).

Bivens, Matt and Jonas Bernstein, 'The Russia You Never Met', *Demokratizatsiya: The Journal of Post-Soviet Democratization*, Vol. 6, Fall 1998, pp. 613–47.

Black, Bernard, Reinier Kraakman, and Anna Tarassavo, 'Russian Privatization and Corporate Governance: What Went Wrong?', *Stanford Law Review*, Vol. 52, 2000, pp. 1731–808.

Boobbyer, Philip, *Conscience, Dissent and Reform in Soviet Russia* (London, Routledge, 2005).

Boyko, Maxim, Andrei Shleifer, and Robert Vishny, *Privatizing Russia* (Cambridge, MA, The MIT Press, 1995).

Bradshaw, Michael, 'Observations on the Geographical Dimensions of Russia's Resource Abundance', *Eurasian Geography and Economics*, Vol. 47, No. 6, 2006, pp. 724–46.

Brady, Rose, *Kapitalizm: Russia's Struggle to Free its Economy* (New Haven, CT, Yale University Press, 1999).

Bryant, Christopher and Edmund Mokrzycki (eds.), *The New Great Transformation?* (London, Routledge, 1994).

Brzezinski, Matthew, *Casino Moscow: A Tale of Greed and Adventure on Capitalism's Wildest Frontier* (New York, Free Press, 2001).

Brzezinski, Zbigniew, 'Putin's Choice', *The Washington Quarterly*, Vol. 31, No. 2, Spring 2008, pp. 95–116.

Bunich, Andrei, *Osen' oligarkhov: Istoriya prikhvatizatsii i budushchee Rossii* (Moscow, Yauza-Eksmo, 2006).

Burnham, William and Jeffrey Kahn, 'Russia's Criminal Procedural Code Five Years Out', *Review of Central and East European Law*, Vol. 33, 2008, pp. 1–93.

Buszynski, Leszek, 'Oil and Territory in Putin's Relations with China and Japan', *The Pacific Review*, Vol. 19, 2006, pp. 287–303.

Cerny, Philip G., *The Changing Architecture of Politics: Structure, Agency, and the Future of the State* (London, Sage Publications, 1990).

Chau, E., 'Rossiiskie truboprovody: Nazad v budushchee?', *Pro et Contra*, No. 3, 2004, pp. 164–73.

Cheah, Pheng, *Spectral Nationality: Passages of Freedom from Kant to Postcolonial Literatures of Nationality* (New York, Columbia University Press, 2003).

Chicherin, B. N., 'Razlichnye vidy liberalizma', in I. E. Diskin (ed.), *Revolyutsiya protiv svobody: Diskussiya o reformakh Aleksandra II i sud'be gosudarstva* (Moscow, Evropa, 2007), pp. 91–103.

Colton, Timothy J., *Yeltsin: A Life* (New York, Basic Books, 2008).

Considine, Jennifer I. and William A. Kerr, *The Russian Oil Economy* (Aldershot, Edward Elgar, 2002).

Cranston, Maurice, *Freedom*, third edition (London, Longmans, Green & Co., 1967).

Crouch, Colin and Wolfgang Streeck (eds.), *Political Economy of Modern Capitalism: Mapping Convergence and Diversity* (London, Sage Publications, 1997).

Danilin, Pavel, Natal'ya Kryshtal', and Dmitrii Polyakov, *Vragi Putina* (Moscow, Evropa, 2007), pp. 157–94 on Khodorkovsky.

Dewey, John, *Freedom and Culture* (New York, Capricorn Books, 1939).

Dubovtsev, V. A. and N. S. Rozov, 'Priroda "russkoi vlasti": Ot metafor—k kontseptsii', *Polis*, No. 3, 2007, pp. 8–23.

Duncan, Peter, *'Oligarchs', Business and Russian Foreign Policy: From El'tsin to Putin* (UCL SSEES, Centre for the Study of Economic and Social Change in Europe, October 2007), Economics Working Paper No. 83.

Economides, Michael J. and Donna Marie D'Aleo, *From Soviet to Putin and Back: The Dominance of Energy in Today's Russia* (London, Energy Tribune Publishing, 2008).

Efimova, E. S., *Sovremennaya tyur'ma: Byt, traditsii i fol'klor* (Moscow, OGI, 2004).

Ellman, Michael (ed.), *Russia's Oil and Natural Gas: Bonanza or Curse?* (London and New York, Anthem Press, 2006).

Energitecheskaya strategiya Rossii na period do 2020 goda, 28 August 2003, www.minprom. gov.ru/docs/strateg/1.

Erochkine, Pavel, 'Russia and Its Oil: Friends or Foes', in Jennifer Moll (ed.), *Blueprint for Russia* (London, Foreign Policy Centre, 2005), pp. 13–34.

Erochkine, Vladimir and Pavel Erochkine, *Russia's Oil Industry: Current Problems and Future Trends* (London, Centre for Global Studies, 2006).

Etzioni, Amitai, *Security First: For a Muscular, Moral Foreign Policy* (New Haven, CT, Yale University Press, 2007).

Evstigneeva, Lyudmila and Ruben Evstigneev, 'Ot uskoreniya k uskoreniyu: Razmyshleniya nad itogami dvadtsatiletiya', *Obshchestvennye nauki i sovremennost*, No. 3, 2005, pp. 17–36.

Eyal, G., Ivan Szelenyi, and E. Townsley, *Making Capitalism Without Capitalists* (London, Verso, 1998).

Ferdinand, Peter, 'Russia and China: Converging Responses to Globalization', *International Affairs*, Vol. 83, No. 4, 2007, pp. 655–80.

—— 'Sunset, Sunrise: China and Russia Construct a New Relationship', *International Affairs*, Vol. 83, No. 5, 2007, pp. 841–67.

Fish, M. Steven, *Democracy Derailed in Russia: The Failure of Open Politics* (Cambridge, Cambridge University Press, 2005).

Fortescue, Stephen, 'Pravit li Rossie oligarkhiya', *Polis*, Vol. 5, No. 8, 2002.

—— *Russia's Oil Barons and Metal Magnates: Oligarchs and State in Transition* (Basingstoke, Palgrave Macmillan, 2006).

Fraenkel, Ernst, *The Dual State: A Contribution to the Theory of Dictatorship*, translated from the German by E. A. Shils, in collaboration with Edith Lowenstein and Klaus Knorr (New York, Oxford University Press, 1941; reprinted by The Lawbook Exchange, Ltd., 2006).

Freeland, Chrystia, *Sale of the Century: Russia's Wild Ride from Communism to Capitalism* (New York, Crown Business, 2000).

Friedman, Milton, *Capitalism and Freedom* (Chicago, IL, University of Chicago Press, 1962).

Frye, Timothy, 'The Perils of Polarization: Economic Performance in the Postcommunist World', *World Politics*, Vol. 54, No. 3, April 2002, pp. 308–37.

—— 'Capture or Exchange? Business Lobbying in Russia', *Europe–Asia Studies*, Vol. 54, No. 7, November 2002, pp. 1017–36.

—— 'Markets, Democracy and New Private Business in Russia', *Post-Soviet Affairs*, Vol. 19, No. 1, 2003, pp. 24–45.

Gaddy, Clifford G., 'Perspectives on the Potential of Russian Oil', *Eurasian Geography and Economics*, Vol. 45, No. 5, 2004, pp. 346–51.

—— and Andrew C. Kuchins, 'Putin's Plan', *The Washington Quarterly*, Vol. 31, No. 2, Spring 2008, pp. 117–29.

—— and Barry W. Ickes, 'Russia's Virtual Economy', *Foreign Affairs*, Vol. 77, No. 5, September–October 1998, pp. 53–67.

—— —— 'An Evolutionary Analysis of Russia's Virtual Economy', in M. Cuddy and R. Gekker (eds.), *Institutional Change in Transition Economies* (Cheltenham, Ashgate, 2002), pp. 72–100.

—— —— *Russia's Virtual Economy* (Washington, D.C., Brookings Institution Press, 2002).

—— —— 'Resource Rents and the Russian Economy', *Eurasian Geography and Economics*, Vol. 46, No. 8, December 2005, pp. 559–83.

Gaidar, Egor, *Gibel' imperii: uroki dlya sovremmennoi Rossii* (Moscow, Rosspen, 2006).

Gaidar, Yegor, *State and Evolution: Russia's Search for a Free Market* (Seattle, WA, University of Washington Press, 2003).

Gat, Azar, 'The Return of the Authoritarian Great Powers', *Foreign Affairs*, Vol. 86, No. 4, July–August 2007, pp. 56–69.

Gavrov, Sergei, 'Neobratim li perekhod k avtoritarizmu?', *Svobodnaya mysl'*, No. 1, January 2006, pp. 80–9.

Gellner, Ernest and Cesar Cansino (eds.), *Liberalism in Modern Times: Essays in Honour of José G. Merquior* (Budapest, Central European University Press, 1996).

Gill, Graeme, *Bourgeoisie, State and Democracy: Russia, Britain, France, Germany and the USA* (Oxford and New York, Oxford University Press, 2008).

Glasman, Maurice, *Unnecessary Suffering: Managing Market Utopia* (London, Verso, 1996).

Glebova, I., 'Politicheskaya kultura sovremennoi Rossii: obliki novoi russkoi vlasti i sotsial'nye raskoly', *Polis*, No. 1, 2006, pp. 33–44.

Glenny, Misha, *McMafia: Crime Without Frontiers* (London, The Bodley Head, 2008).

Gnezditskaia, Anastasia, ' "Unidentified Shareholders": The Impact of Oil Companies on the Banking Sector in Russia', *Europe–Asia Studies*, Vol. 57, No. 3, May 2005, pp. 457–80.

Goldman, Marshall I., *The Piratization of Russia: Russian Reform Goes Awry* (London and New York, Routledge, 2003).

—— 'Putin and the Oligarchs', *Foreign Affairs*, Vol. 83, No. 6, November–December 2004, pp. 33–44.

—— *Oilopoly: Putin, Power, and the Rise of the New Russia* (Oxford, Oneworld Publications, 2008).

Goorha, Prateek, 'The Political Economy of the Resource Curse in Russia', *Demokratizatsiya*, Vol. 14, No. 4, Fall 2006, pp. 601–11.

Goyal, Ajay, 'Analysis: Sale of a State', *The Russia Journal*, 31 October 2003, pp. 10–13.

Grace, John, *Russian Oil Supply: Performance and Prospects* (Oxford, Oxford University Press, 2005).

Graham, Thomas Jr., 'The Fate of the Russian State', *Demokratizatsiya*, Vol. 8, No. 3, 2000, pp. 354–75.

Gray, John, *False Dawn: The Delusions of Global Capitalism* (London, Granta Books, 1998).

Grugel, Jean and Pia Riggirozzi, 'The Return of the State in Argentina', *International Affairs*, Vol. 83, No. 1, January 2007, pp. 87–107.

—— —— and Ben Thirkell-White, 'Beyond the Washington Consensus? Asia and Latin America in Search of More Autonomous Development', *International Affairs*, Vol. 84, No. 3, May 2008, pp. 499–518.

Gustafson, Thane, *Crisis Amid Plenty: The Politics of Soviet Energy under Brezhnev and Gorbachev* (Princeton, NJ, Princeton University Press, 1989).

—— *Capitalism Russian-Style* (Cambridge, Cambridge University Press, 1999).

Hale, Henry E., *Why Not Parties in Russia? Democracy, Federalism and the State* (Cambridge, Cambridge University Press, 2006).

Hanson, Philip, 'Observations on the Economic Costs of the Yukos Affair in Russia', *Eurasian Geography and Economics*, Vol. 46, No. 7, October–November 2005, pp. 481–94.

—— 'The Turn to Statism in Russian Economic Policy', *The International Spectator*, Vol. 42, No. 1, March 2007, pp. 29–42.

—— 'The Russian Economic Puzzle: Going Forwards, Backwards or Sideways?', *International Affairs*, Vol. 83, No. 5, September–October 2007, pp. 869–89.

—— 'How Sustainable is Russia's Energy Power?', *Russian Analytical Digest*, No. 38, 2 April 2008, pp. 8–10.

—— and Elizabeth Teague, 'Big Business and the State in Russia', *Europe–Asia Studies*, Vol. 57, No. 5, July 2005, pp. 657–80.

Hedlund, Stefan, *Russia's 'Market' Economy: A Bad Case of Predatory Capitalism* (London, UCL Press, 1999).

—— 'Vladimir the Great, Grand Prince of Muscovy: Resurrecting the Russian Service State', *Europe–Asia Studies*, Vol. 58, No. 5, July 2006, pp. 775–801.

Hellman, Joel S., 'Winners take All: The Politics of Partial Reform in Postcommunist Transitions', *World Politics*, Vol. 50, No. 2, January 1998, pp. 203–34.

Henderson, Sarah L., *Building Democracy in Contemporary Russia: Western Support for Grassroots Organizations* (Ithaca and London, Cornell University Press, 2003).

Herspring, Dale R. and Jacob Kipp, 'Understanding the Elusive Mr. Putin', *Problems of Post-Communism*, Vol. 48, No. 5, September/October 2001, pp. 3–17.

Hill, Fiona and F. Fee, 'Fuelling the Future: The Prospects for Russian Oil and Gas', *Demokratizatsiya*, Vol. 10, No. 4, 2002, pp. 462–87.

—— and Clifford Gaddy, *The Siberian Curse: How Communist Planners Left Russia Out in the Cold* (Washington, Brookings Institution Press, 2003).

Hiro, Dilip, *Blood of the Earth: The Global Battle for Vanishing Oil Resources* (London, Politico's, 2008).

Hoffman, David E., *The Oligarchs: Wealth and Power in the New Russia* (New York, PublicAffairs, 2002).

Hollingworth, Rogers and Robert Boyer (eds.), *Contemporary Capitalism: The Embeddedness of Institutions* (Cambridge, Cambridge University Press, 1997).

Holmes, Leslie, *Rotten States? Corruption, Post-Communism and Neoliberalism* (Durham and London, Duke University Press, 2006).

Huntington, Samuel P., *The Third Wave: Democratization in the Late Twentieth Century* (Norman and London, University of Oklahoma Press, 1991).

Illarionov, Andrei, 'A Long-Term Project for Russia', *Russia in Global Affairs*, July–September 2005, pp. 49–51.

Itoh, Shoichi, 'Sino-Russian Energy Relations: The Dilemma of Strategic Partnership and Mutual Distrust', in Hiroshi Kimura (ed.), *Russia's Shift Toward Asia* (Tokyo, The Sasakawa Peace Foundation, 2007), Chapter 4, pp. 63–77.

—— 'The Pacific Pipeline at a Crossroads: Dream Project or Pipe Dream?', Research Division, ERINA, working paper, 2007.

Ivanenko, Vlad, 'Russian Global Position After 2008', *Russia in Global Affairs*, Vol. 5, No. 4, October–December 2007, pp. 143–56.

Ivanov, A. I., V. O. Kazantsev, M. B. Karpenko, and M. M. Meier (eds.), *Prioritetnye natsional'nye proekty—ideologiya proryva v budushchee* (Moscow, Evropa, 2007).

Jack, Andrew, *Inside Putin's Russia* (London, Granta Books, 2004).

Johnson, Juliet, 'Russia's emerging Financial-Industrial Groups', *Post-Soviet Affairs*, Vol. 13, No. 4, 1997, pp. 333–65.

The Judicial System of the Russian Federation: A System-Crisis of Independence (London, Russian Axis, 2004).

Kaehne, Axel, *Political and Social Thought in Post-Communist Russia* (London and New York, Routledge, 2007).

Kandiyoti, Rafael, *Pipelines: Flowing Oil and Crude Politics* (London, I. B. Tauris, 2008).

Kapustin, B. G., 'Tri rassuzhdeniya o liberalizme i liberalizmakh', *Polis*, No. 3, 1994, pp. 13–26.

—— 'Nachalo rossiiskogo liberalizma kak problema politicheskoi filosofii', *Polis*, No. 5, 1994, pp. 23–37.

Kapustin, Boris, 'Liberal'naya ideya v Rossii: Prologomeny k kontseptsii sovremennogo rossiiskogo liberalizma', in *Inoe*, Vol. 3 (Moscow, Rossiya kak ideya, 1995), pp. 125–62.

—— ' "Freedom from the State" and "Freedom Through the State" ', *Social Sciences*, No. 3, 1 July 1999; from Boris Kapustin, *Voprosy filosofii*, No. 9, 1998.

Karatsuba, I.V., I. V. Kurukin, and N. P. Sokolov, *Vybiraya svoyu istoriyu: 'razvilki' na puti Rossii—ot ryurikovichei do oligarkhov*, Introd. by A. L. Yurganov (Moscow, KoLibri, 2005).

Karl, Terry Lynn, *The Paradox of Plenty: Oil Booms and Petrostates* (Berkeley, University of California Press, 1997).

Kartashov, V. M., *Who is Mr. Hodorkovsky?* (Rostov-na-Donu, Feniks, 2007).

Kenney, Padraic, *The Burdens of Freedom: Eastern Europe since 1989* (London and New York, Zed Books, 2006).

Khlebnikov, Pavel, *Krestnyi otets Kremlya Boris Berezovskii, ili Istoriya razgrableniya Rossii* (Moscow, DetektivPress, 2001); the book had earlier come out in English as Paul Klebnikov, *Godfather of the Kremlin: Boris Berezovsky and the Looting of Russia* (New York, Harcourt, 2000).

—— *Razgovor s varvarom: Besedy s chechenskim polevym komandirom Khozh-Akhmedom Nukhaevym o banditizme i islame* (Moscow, DetektivPress, 2003).

Khodorkovskii, Mikhail, *Levyi povorot* (Moscow, Galleya-Print, 2006).

—— *Levyi povorot 2* (Moscow, Galleya-Print, 2006).

—— (ed.), *Mir v 2020 godu* (Moscow, Algoritm, 2007).

—— and Leonid Nevzlin, *Chelovek s rublëm* (Moscow, Menatep-Inform, 1992).

Khodorkovskikh chtenii, Konferentsii 'Rossiiskie al'ternativy', 10 July 2007, http://www.polit.ru/dossie/2007/10/05/conf.html

Khodorkovsky, Mikhail B., 'Keynote Address', *Russian Business Watch*, Vol. 11, No. 3, Fall 2003, pp. 2–3.

Khripunov, Igor and Mary M. Matthews, 'Russia's Oil and Gas Interest Group and its Foreign Policy Agenda', *Problems of Post-Communism*, Vol. 43, No. 3, May–June 1996, pp. 38–48.

Kimmage, Daniel, 'Putin's Restoration: Consolidation or Clan Rivalries?', in Geir Flikke (ed.), *The Uncertainties of Putin's Democracy* (Oslo, NUPI, 2004), pp. 129–43.

Kireev, A., 'Reiderstvo na rynke korporativnogo kontrlya: rezultat evolyutsii silovogo predprinimatel'stva', *Voprosy ekonomiki*, No. 8, 2007, pp. 80–92.

Klein, Naomi, *The Shock Doctrine: The Rise of Disaster Capitalism* (London and New York, Allen Lane, 2007).

Klyamkin, Igor' and Lev Timofeev, *Tenevaya Rossiya: Ekonomiko-sotsiologicheskoe issledovanie* (Moscow, RGGU, 2000).

Knoops, Geert-Jan Alexander and Robert R. Amsterdam, 'The Duality of State Cooperation Within International and National Criminal Cases', *Fordham International Law Journal*, Vol. 30, 2007, pp. 260–95.

Kokoshin, Andrei, *Real'nyi suverenitet v sovremennoi miropoliticheskoi sistemy*, third edition (Moscow, Evropa, 2006).

Kolesnikov, Andrei, *Vladimir Putin: Ravnoudalenie oligarkhov* (Moscow, Eksmo, 2005).

——*Anatolii Chubais: Biografiya* (Moscow, AST Moskva, 2008).

Kolodko, Grzegorz W., *From Shock to Therapy: The Political Economy of Post-Socialist Transformation* (Oxford, Oxford University Press, 2002).

Konończuk, Wojciech, '*Sprawa Jukosu': przyczyny i konsekwencje* (The 'Yukos Affair', Its Motives and Implications), *Prace OSW/CES Studies*, No. 25, Centre for Eastern Studies, Warsaw, August 2006, English version pp. 33–60; http://www.osw.waw.pl/files/PRACE_25.pdf.

Kornai, János and Susan Rose-Ackerman (eds.), *Building a Trustworthy State in Post-Socialist Transition* (New York, Palgrave Macmillan, 2004).

Korzhakov, Aleksandr, *Boris Yeltsin: Ot rassveta do zakata* (Moscow, Interbuk, 1997).

——*Boris El'tsin: Ot rassveta do zakata—Posleslovie* (Moscow, Detektiv Press, 2004).

Kosals, Leonid, 'Klanovyi kapitalizm v Rossii', Neprikosnovennyi zapas: Debaty o politike i kul'ture, http://www.nz-online.ru/print.phtml?aid=80019312.

Krastev, Ivan, 'Rossiya kak "drugaya Evropa"', *Rossiya v global'noi politike*, Vol. 5, No. 4, July–August 2007, pp. 33–45.

Kryshtanovkaya, Ol'ga, 'Biznes-elita i oligarkhi: Itogi desyatiletiya', *Mir Rossii*, Vol. 11, No. 4, 2002, pp. 3–60.

——'Rezhim Putina: Liberal'naya militokratiya?', *Pro et Contra*, Vol. 7, No. 4, Autumn 2002, pp. 158–80.

——*Anatomiya rossiiskoi elity* (Moscow, Zakharov, 2005).

——and Stephen White, 'From Soviet Nomenklatura to Russian Elite', *Europe–Asia Studies*, Vol. 48, No. 5, July 1996, pp. 11–33.

——— 'Putin's Militocracy', *Post-Soviet Affairs*, Vol. 19, No. 4, October–December 2003, pp. 289–306.

——— 'The Rise of the Russian Business Elite', *Communist and Post-Communist Studies*, Vol. 38, No. 3, September 2005, pp. 293–307.

——— 'Inside the Putin Court: A Research Note', *Europe–Asia Studies*, Vol. 57, No. 7, November 2005, pp. 1065–75.

Kryukov, Valery and Arild Moe, *The Changing Role of Banks in the Russian Oil Sector* (London, RIIA, 1998).

—————— 'Russia's Oil Industry: Risk Aversion in a Risk-Prone Environment', *Eurasian Geography and Economics*, Vol. 48, No. 3, 2007, pp. 341–57.

Kusznir, Julia and Heiko Pleines, 'The Russian Oil Industry between Foreign Investment and Domestic Interests', in Robert Orttung et al. (eds.), *Russia's Energy Sector between Politics and Business*, Working Papers of the Research Centre for East European Studies, Bremen, No. 92, 2008, pp. 31–5.

Lane, David (ed.), *The Political Economy of Russian Oil* (Lanham, MD, Rowman & Littlefield, 1999).

—— (ed.), *Russian Banking: Evolution, Problems and Prospects* (Cheltenham, Edward Elgar, 2002).

Larsson, Robert L., *Russia's Energy Policy: Security Dimensions and Russia's Reliability as an Energy Supplier* (Stockholm, Swedish Defence Agency (FOI), March 2006).

Laskov, O. V., *Ne stan' Khodorkovskim: Nalogovye skhemy, za kotorye ne posadyat* (St Petersburg, Piter Press, 2007).

Ledeneva, Alena V., *How Russia Really Works: The Informal Practices that Shaped Post-Soviet Politics and Business* (Ithaca, New York, and London, Cornell University Press, 2006).

Lloyd, John, *Rebirth of a Nation: An Anatomy of Russia* (London, Michael Joseph, 1998).

Lucas, Edward, *The New Cold War: How the Kremlin Menaces both Russia and the West* (London, Bloomsbury, 2008).

Lyne, Roderic, Strobe Talbott, and Koji Watanabe, *Engaging With Russia: The Next Phase* (Washington, Paris and Tokyo, The Trilateral Commission, 2006).

Makarenko, Boris, 'Demokraticheskii transit v Rossii', *Mirovaya ekonomika i mezhdunarodnye otnosheniya*, No. 11, 2004, pp. 44–58.

Mandela, Nelson, *A Long Walk to Freedom: The Autobiography of Nelson Mandela* (London, Abacus, 1995).

Makarkin, A., *Politiko-ekonomicheskie klany sovremennoi Rossii* (Moscow, Tsentr politicheskikh tekhnologii, 2003).

Marciniak, Włodzimierz, 'From Retrospection to a Prognosis: On the Difficulties in Prognosticating the Development of the Political Situation in Russia', in Wojciech Konończuk (ed.), *Putin's Empire* (Warsaw, Stefan Batory Foundation, 2007), pp. 29–42.

Maugeri, Leonardo, *The Age of Oil: The Mythology, History, and the Future of the World's Most Controversial Resource* (Boulder, CO, Praeger, 2007).

Mavrodi, Sergei, *Vsya pravda o 'MMM': Istoriya pervoi piramidy. Tyuremnye dnevniki* (Moscow, RIPOL klassik, 2007).

McDaniel, Tim, *The Agony of the Russian Idea* (Princeton, NJ, Princeton University Press, 1996).

McFaul, Michael and Kathryn Stoner-Weiss, 'The Myth of the Authoritarian Model: How Putin's Crackdown Holds Russia Back', *Foreign Affairs*, Vol. 87, No. 1, January–February 2008, pp. 69–84.

Mendelson, Sarah E. and Theodore P. Gerber, 'Soviet Nostalgia: An Impediment to Russian Democratization', *The Washington Quarterly*, Vol. 21, No. 1, Spring 2008, pp. 131–50.

Menon, Rajan and Alexander J. Motyl, 'The Myth of Russian Resurgence', *The American Interest Online*, March–April 2007; http://the-american-interest-com/.

Merkel, Wolfgang, 'Embedded and Defective Democracies', *Democratisation*, Vol. 11, No. 5, December 2004, pp. 33–58.

Midgley, Dominic and Chris Hutchins, *Abramovich: The Billionaire from Nowhere* (London, Harper Collins, 2005).

Milov, Vladimir, 'Mozhet li Rossiya stat' neftyanym raem?', *Pro et Contra*, Vol. 10, Nos. 2–3, March–June 2006, pp. 6–15.

——— Leonard L. Coburn, and Igor Danchenko, 'Russia's Energy Policy, 1992–2005', *Eurasian Geography and Economics*, Vol. 47, No. 3, 2006, pp. 285–313.

Mitrova, Tatiana, 'Gazprom's Perspectives on International Markets', *Russian Analytical Digest*, No. 41, 20 May 2008, pp. 2–6.

Monaghan, Andrew, 'Dilemma energicheskoi bezopasnosti', *Pro et Contra*, Vol. 10, Nos. 2–3, March–June 2006, pp. 16–31.

Moser, Nat and Peter Oppenheimer, 'The Oil Industry: Structural Transformation and Corporate Governance', in Brigitte Granville and Peter Oppenheimer (eds.), *Russia's Post-Communist Economy* (New York, Oxford University Press, 2001).

Moskalenko, Karinna, 'The Judicial System in Practice', in Jennifer Moll (ed.), *Blueprint for Russia* (London, Foreign Policy Centre, 2005), pp. 39–43.

Moss, Giuditta Cordero, 'Between Private and Public International law: Exorbitant Jurisdiction as Illustrated by the *Yukos* Case', *Review of Central and East European Law*, Vol. 32, 2007, pp. 1–17.

Mukhin, A. A., *Novye pravila igry dlya bol'shogo biznesa, prodiktovannye logikoi pravleniya V. V. Putina* (Moscow, Tsentr politicheskoi informatsii, 2002).

Myant, Martin and David Lane (eds.), *Varieties of Capitalism in Post-Communist Countries* (Basingstoke, Palgrave Macmillan, 2006).

Nomenklatura i nomenklaturanya organizatsiya vlast' v Rossii (Perm, Russian Ministry of Education and Science, together with the Perm State Technical University and the Centre for Elite Studies, 2004).

O'Dwyer, Connnor, *Runaway State-Building: Patronage, Politics and Democratic Development* (Baltimore, MD, The Johns Hopkins University Press, 2006).

OECD, *Russia: Building Rules for the Market* (Paris, OECD Reviews of Regulatory Reform, June 2005).

Olson, Mancur, 'Why the Transition from Communism is so Difficult', *Eastern Economic Journal*, Vol. 21, No. 4, 1995, pp. 437–61.

——— *Power and Prosperity: Outgrowing Communist and Capitalist Dictatorships* (Oxford, Oxford University Press, 2000).

Orttung, Robert, Jeronim Perovic, Heiko Pleines, and Hans-Henning Schröder (eds.), *Russia's Energy Sector between Politics and Business*, Working Papers of the Research Centre for East European Studies, Bremen, No. 92, 2008.

Ouvaroff, Nathalie, 'The Oil Factor and War of Clans in Chechnya', *Russian Analytical Digest*, No. 42, 2008, pp. 5–8.

Panyushkin, Valerii, *Mikhail Khodorkovskii: uznik tishiny. Istoriya pro to, kak cheloveku v Rossii stat' svobodnym i chto emu za eto budet* (Moscow, Sekret Firmy, 2006).

Pappe, Ya. Sh., *'Oligarkhi': Ekonomicheskaya khronika 1992–2000* (Moscow, Vysshaya shkola ekonomiki, 2000).

Pastukhov, Vladimir, 'Law Under Administrative Pressure in Post-Soviet Russia', *East European Constitutional Review*, Vol. 11, No. 3, Summer 2002, pp. 66–74.

Pastukhov, V. B., 'Temnyi vek: Postkommunizm kak "chernaya dyra" russkoi istorii', *Polis*, No. 3, 2007, pp. 24–38.

Peregudov, S. P., 'Biznes i vlast' v rossii: k novoi modeli otnoshenii', in V. G. Ignatov, O. V. Gaman-Golutvina, A. V. Ponedelkov, and A. M. Starostin (eds.), *Vlastnye elity sovremennoi Rossii v protsesse politicheskoi transformatsii* (Rostov on Don, Severo-Kavkazkaya akademiya gosudarstvennoi sluzhby, 2004), pp. 22–30.

Peregudov, S. P., 'Konvergentsiya po-rossiiskii: "zolotaya seredina" ili ostanovka na polputi', *Polis*, No. 1, 2008, pp. 91–108.

Perekrest, Vladimir, 'Za chto sidit Mikhail Khodorkovskii', *Izvestiya*, 17, 18 May, 7, 8, 9, 16 June 2006.

Piacentini, Laura, *Surviving Russian Prisons: Punishment, Economy and Politics in Transition* (Cullompton, Willan Publishing, 2004).

Pipes, Richard, *Property and Freedom* (New York, Alfred A. Knopf, 1999).

Pivovarov, Yu. P., 'Istoki i smysl russkoi revolyutsii', *Polis*, No. 5, 2007, pp. 35–55.

Polanyi, Karl, *The Great Transformation: The Political and Economic Origins of Our Time*, Foreword by Joseph E. Stiglitz, Introduction by Fred Block (Boston, MA, Beacon Press, 2001 [first published 1944]).

Poussenkova, Nina, *From Rigs to Riches: Oilmen Vs. Financiers in the Russian Oil Sector* (Rice University, Texas, The James A. Baker III Institute for Public Policy, October 2004).

—— 'Rosneft' kak zerkalo russkoi evolyutsii', *Pro et Contra*, Vol. 10, Nos. 2–3, March–June 2006, pp. 91–104.

—— 'All Quiet on the Eastern Front ...', *Russian Analytical Digest*, No. 33, 22 January 2008, pp. 13–18.

Procaccia, Uriel, *Russian Culture, Property Rights and the Market Economy* (Cambridge, Cambridge University Press, 2007).

Prohorov, A. P., *Russkaya model' upravleniya* (Moscow, Eksmo, 2006).

Prokhorov, A. P., *Russkaya model' upravleniya* (Moscow, Eksmo, 2006).

Putin, Vladimir, *First Person: An Astonishingly Frank Self-Portrait by Russia's President Vladimir Putin*, with Nataliya Gevorkyan, Natalya Timakova, and Andrei Kolesnikov, translated by Catherine A. Fitzpatrick (London, Hutchinson, 2000).

—— 'Mineral Natural Resources in the Strategy for Development of the Russian Economy', *Problems of Post-Communism*, Vol. 53, No. 1, January–February 2006, pp. 49–54.

Pshizova, S. N., 'Politika kak biznes: rossiiskaya versiya', Part I, *Polis*, No. 2, 2007, pp. 109–23; Part II, *Polis*, No. 3, 2007, pp. 65–77.

Rekosh, Edwin, 'Remedies to Administrative Abuses; Setting the Stage for Action', *Local Government Brief*, Budapest, Summer 2003, pp. 2–7.

Robinson, Neil, 'The Myth of Equilibrium: Winner Power, Fiscal Crisis and Russian Economic reform', *Communist and Post-Communist Studies*, Vol. 34, No. 4, December 2001, pp. 423–46.

Rodionov, A., *Nalogovye skhemy, za kotorye posadili Khodorkovskogo* (Moscow, Vershina, 2006).

Roland, Gérard, 'The Russian Economy in the Year 2005', *Post-Soviet Affairs*, Vol. 22, No. 1, January–March 2006, pp. 90–8.

Rose, Richard and Neil Munro, *Elections without Order: Russia's Challenge to Vladimir Putin* (Cambridge, Cambridge University Press, 2002).

—— William Mishler, and Neil Munro, *Russia Transformed: Developing Popular Support for a New Regime* (Cambridge, Cambridge University Press, 2006).

Rosecrance, R., *The Rise of the Trading State* (New York, Basic Books, 1986).

Ross, Michael L., 'Does Oil Hinder Democracy?', *World Politics*, Vol. 53, No. 3, April 2001, pp. 325–61.

—— 'Blood Barrels', *Foreign Affairs*, Vol. 87, No. 3, May–June 2008, pp. 2–9.

Russkaya neft' o kotoroi my tak malo znaem (Moscow, Neftyanaya kompaniya Yukos and izdatel'stvo 'Olimp-Biznes', 2003).

Rutland, Peter, 'Oil, Politics and Foreign Policy', in David Lane (ed.), *The Political Economy of Russian Oil* (Lanham, MD, Rowman & Littlefield, 1999), pp. 163–88.

—— (ed.), *Business and State in Contemporary Russia* (Boulder, CO, Westview, 2001).

—— 'Business and Civil Society in Russia', in Alfred B. Evans Jr, Laura A. Henry, and Lisa McIntosh Sundstrom (eds.), *Russian Civil Society: A Critical Assessment* (Armonk, NY, M. E. Sharpe, 2005), pp. 73–94.

——, 'Russia as an Energy Superpower', *New Political Economy*, Vol. 13, No. 2, June 2008, pp. 203–10.

Sagers, Matthew J., 'The Regional Dimension of Russian Oil Production: Is a Sustained Recovery in Prospect?', *Eurasian Geography and Economics*, Vol. 47, No. 5, 2006, pp. 505–45.

Sakwa, Richard, 'Russia: From a Corrupt System to a System with Corruption', in Robert Williams (ed.), *Party Finance and Political Corruption* (Basingstoke and London, Macmillan; New York, St Martin's Press, 2000), pp. 123–61.

—— 'The Age of Paradox: The Anti-revolutionary Revolutions of 1989–91', in Moira Donald and Tim Rees (eds.), *Reinterpreting Revolution in Twentieth-Century Europe* (London, Macmillan, 2001), pp. 159–76.

—— 'From Revolution To *Krizis*: The Transcending Revolutions of 1989–91', *Comparative Politics*, Vol. 38, No. 4, July 2006, pp. 459–78.

—— *Putin: Russia's Choice*, second edition (London and New York, Routledge, 2008).

—— *Russian Politics and Society*, fourth edition (London and New York, Routledge, 2008).

—— 'Two Camps? The Struggle to Understand Contemporary Russia', *Comparative Politics*, Vol. 40, No. 4, July 2008, pp. 481–99.

—— *The Crisis of Russian Democracy: Factionalism and the Medvedev Succession* (forthcoming).

Satter, David, *Darkness at Dawn: The Rise of the Russian Criminal State* (New Haven, CT, Yale University Press, 2003).

Schneider, Eberhard, 'The Russian Federal Security Service under President Putin', in Stephen White (ed.), *Politics and the Ruling Group in Putin's Russia* (London, Palgrave Macmillan, 2008), pp. 42–62.

Schroder, Hans-Henning, 'El'tsin and the Oligarchs: The Role of Financial Groups in Russian Politics between 1993 and July 1998', *Europe–Asia Studies*, Vol. 51, No. 6, 1999, pp. 957–88.

Schumpeter, Joseph A., *Capitalism, Socialism and Democracy*, fifth edition (London, George Allen & Unwin, 1976).

Sen, Amartya, *Development as Freedom* (New York, Random House, 1999).

Shaxson, Nicholas, *Poisoned Wells: The Dirty Politics of African Oil* (Basingstoke, Palgrave Macmillan, 2007).

—— 'Oil, Corruption and the Resource Curse', *International Affairs*, Vol. 83, No. 6, November 2007, pp. 1123–40.

Shelley, Louise L., 'Crime and Corruption: Enduring Problems of Post-Soviet Development', *Demokratizatsiya*, Vol. 11, No. 1, Winter 2003, pp. 110–14.

Shevtsova, Liliya, 'Rossiya pered novym politicheskim tsiklom: Paradoksy stabil'nosti i Petro-State', in Wojciech Konończuk (ed.), *Putin's Empire* (Warsaw, Stefan Batory Foundation, 2007), pp. 13–28.

Shiryaev, Valerii G., *Sud mesti: pervaya zhertva dela Yukosa* (Moscow, OGI, 2006).

Shleifer, Andrei and Daniel Treisman, *Without a Map: Political Tactics and Economic Reform in Russia* (Cambridge, MA, MIT Press, 2000).

Simonov, Konstantin, *Russkaya neft': Poslednii peredel* (Moscow, Eksmo Algoritm, 2005).

—— *Global'naya energiticheskaya voina: Tainy sovremennoi politiki* (Moscow, Algoritm, 2007).

Simonov, Yurii, *Yukos v kartinkakh* (Moscow, Evropa, 2005).

Skuratov, Yurii, *Variant drakona* (Moscow, Detektiv Press, 2000).

Smith, Adam, *The Theory of Moral Sentiments*, edited by D. D. Raphael and A. L. Macfie (Indianapolis, IN, Liberty Fund, 1984).

Smith, Gordon B., *Reforming the Russian Legal System* (Cambridge, Cambridge University Press, 1996).

Specter, Michael, 'Kremlin, Inc.: Why are Vladimir Putin's Opponents Dying?', *The New Yorker*, 29 January 2007, pp. 50–63.

Stefes, Christoph, H., *Understanding Post-Soviet Transitions: Corruption, Collusion and Clientelism* (Basingstoke, Palgrave Macmillan, 2006).

Stern, Jonathan P., *The Future of Russian Gas and Gazprom* (Oxford, Oxford University Press for the Oxford Institute for Energy Studies, 2005).

Stiglitz, Joseph E., *Globalization and Its Discontents* (New York, W. W. Norton & Co., 2002).

—— *Making Globalization Work* (New York, W. W. Norton & Co., 2007).

Streeck, Wolfgang and Kozo Yamamura (eds.), *The Origins of Nonliberal Capitalism: Germany and Japan in Comparison* (Ithaca, NY, Cornell University Press, 2001).

Strigin, E. M., *Boris Berezovskii i londonskii shtab* (Moscow, Algoritm, 2006).

Surkov, Vladislav, 'Russkaya politicheskaya kul'tura: Vzglyad iz utopii', in Konstantin Remchukov (ed.), *Russkaya politicheskaya kul'tura: Vzglyad iz utopii. Lektsiya Vladislava Surkova. Materialy obsuzhdeniya v 'Nezavismoi gazete'* (Moscow, Nezavisimaya Gazeta, 2007).

—— *Teksty 97–07* (Moscow, Evropa, 2008).

Takeda, Yoshinori, 'Russia's New Political Leadership and Its Implications for East Siberian Development and Energy Cooperation with North East Asian States', *Russian Analytical Digest*, No. 33, 2008, pp. 5–8.

Tokareva, Elena, *Kto podstavil khodorskovskogo* (Moscow, Yauza, 2006).

Tompson, William, 'Putin and the "Oligarchs": A Two-sided Commitment Problem', in Alex Pravda (ed.), *Leading Russia: Putin in Perspective* (Oxford, Oxford University Press, 2005), pp. 179–202.

—— 'Putting Yukos in Perspective', *Post-Soviet Affairs*, Vol. 21, No. 2, April–June 2005, pp. 159–82.

—— 'The Political Implications of Russia's Resource-Based Economy', *Post-Soviet Affairs*, Vol. 21, No. 4, October–December 2005, pp. 335–59.

Tregubova, Elena, *Baiki kremlevshogo diggera* (Moscow, Ad Marginem, 2003).

Treisman, Daniel, 'Putin's Silovarchs', *Orbis*, Vol. 51, No. 1, Winter 2007, pp. 141–53.

Varese, Federico, *The Russian Mafia* (Oxford, Oxford University Press, 2002).

Vasil'eva, Vera, *Kak sudili Alekseya Pichugina: Sudebnyi reportazh* (Prague/Moscow, Human Rights Publishers, 2007).

Volkov, Vadim, 'Violent Entrepreneurship in Post-Communist Russia', *Europe–Asia Studies*, Vol. 51, No. 5, July 1999, pp. 741–54.

—— *Violent Entrepreneurs: The Use of Force in the Making of Russian Capitalism* (Ithaca, NY, Cornell University Press, 2002).

——— 'The Yukos Affair: Terminating the Implicit Contract', *PONARS Policy Memo*, No. 307, November 2003.

——— ' "Delo Standard Oil" i "delo Yukosa" ', *Pro et Contra*, Vol. 9, No. 2, September–October 2005, pp. 66–91.

Way, Lucan A., *Pigs, Wolves and the Evolution of Post-Soviet Competitive Authoritarianism, 1991–2005*, Center on Democracy, Development, and the Rule of Law, Stanford University, working paper, No. 62, June 2006.

Weinthal, Erika and Pauline Jones Luong, 'Combating the Resource Curse: An Alternative Solution to Managing Mineral Wealth', *Perspectives on Politics*, Vol. 4, No. 1, March 2006, pp. 35–53.

White, David, *The Russian Democratic Party Yabloko* (Aldershot, Ashgate, 2006).

Wilson, Andrew, *Virtual Politics: Faking Democracy in the Post-Soviet World* (New Haven, CT, Yale University Press, 2005).

Wiśniewska, Iwona, *The Invisible Hand . . . of the Kremlin: Capitalism 'à la Russe'* (Warsaw, Centre for Eastern Studies, February 2007), Policy Briefs, English version, pp. 39–72.

Wolton, Thierry, *Le KGB au pouvoir: Le système poutine* (Paris, Buchet-Chastel, 2008).

Woodruff, David, *Money Unmade: Barter and the Fate of Russian Capitalism* (Ithaca, NY, Cornell University Press, 1999).

——— *Khodorkovsky's Gamble: From Business to Politics in the YUKOS Conflict*, PONARS Policy Memo 308, November 2003.

Worth, Owen, *Hegemony, International Political Economy and Post-Communist Russia* (Aldershot, Ashgate, 2005).

Wu, Hsiu-Ling and Chien-Hsun Chen, 'The Prospects for Regional Economic Integration Between China and the Five Central Asian Countries', *Europe–Asia Studies*, Vol. 56, No. 7, November 2004, pp. 1059–80.

Yakovlev, Alexander, *Striving for Law in a Lawless Land: Memoirs of a Russian Reformer* (Armonk and London, M. E. Sharpe, 1996).

Yakovlev, Andrei, 'The Evolution of Business-State Interaction in Russia: From State Capture to Business Capture?', *Europe–Asia Studies*, Vol. 58, No. 7, November 2006, pp. 1033–56.

——— 'Interest Groups and Economic Reform in Contemporary Russia: Before and After Yukos', in Stephen White (ed.), *Politics and the Ruling Group in Putin's Russia* (London, Palgrave Macmillan, 2008), pp. 87–119.

——— and Timoti Frai (Timothy Frye), 'Reformy v Rossii glazami biznesa', *Pro et Contra*, Vol. 11, Nos. 4 & 5, July–October 2007, pp. 118–34.

Yeltsin, Boris, *Midnight Diaries* (London, Weidenfeld & Nicolson, 2000).

Yergin, Daniel, *The Prize: The Epic Quest for Oil, Money, and Power* (New York, Simon & Schuster, 1991).

Yudenich, Marina, *Neft'* (Moscow, Popularnaya literature, 2007).

Yur'ev, Dmitrii, *rezhim putina: Postdemokratiya* (Moscow, Evropa, 2005).

——— 'Oranzhevye polittekhnologii ukrainy: Upravlenie svobodoi', in *Rossiya i 'sanitarnyi kordon'* (Moscow, Evropa, 2005), pp. 37–51.

Yurgens, Igor Y., *Russia's Future Under Medvedev*, English edition edited by Professor Lord Skidelsky (Warwick, Centre for Global Studies, 2008).

Zakaria, Fareed, *The Future of Freedom: Illiberal Democracy at Home and Abroad* (New York, W. W. Norton, 2003).

Zudin, Aleksei, 'Neokorporativizism v Rossii', *Pro et Contra*, Vol. 6, No. 4, 2001, pp. 171–98.

Zudin, Aleksei, 'Gosudarstvo i biznes v Rossii: evolyutsiya modeli vzaimootnoshenii',
    Neprikosnovennyi zapas: Debaty o politike i kul'ture, http://www.nz-online.ru/
    print.phtml?aid=80018067
Zudin, Aleksei Yu., 'Oligarchy as a Political Problem of Russian Postcommunism', *Russian
    Social Science Review*, Vol. 41, No. 6, November–December 2000, pp. 4–33.
——'Rezhim V. Putina: Kontury novoi politicheskoi sistemy', *Obshchestvennye nauki i
    sovremennost'*, No. 2, 2003, pp. 67–83.
Zweynart, Joachim, 'Economic Ideas and Institutional Change: Evidence from Soviet Eco-
    nomic Debates 1987–1991', *Europe–Asia Studies*, Vol. 58, No. 2, March 2007, pp. 169–92.
——'Conflicting Patterns of Thought in the Russian Debate on Transition: 1992–2002',
    Europe–Asia Studies, Vol. 59, No. 1, January 2007, pp. 47–69.
Zygar, Mikhail and Valeri Panyushkin, *Gazprom: Novoe russkoe oruzhie* (Moscow, Zakharov,
    2008).

Index

Note: note numbers in brackets indicate the whereabouts on the page of quotations from authors who are not identified in the text. Page references in *italics* refer to tables.

Abramovich, Roman 32, 58, 347, 349
   and aluminium industry 82, 94
   and Berezovsky's removal from Sibneft 83
   and Chelsea Football Club, purchase of 93, 127–8
   in 'Risks and Threats Facing Russia' report 90–1
   and Yukos 130, 173–4
active citizenship: and liberalism 6–8
Adachi, Yuko 46
Adamov, Alexander 103
ADR (American Depository Receipt) 69
Afanas'ev, Yuri 126
Agranovskaya, Elena (Yelena) 232, 233, 238
Ahrend, Rudiger 335–6
AKIB (Commercial Innovation Bank for Scientific and Technical Progress) 34
Akron Company 176, 195
Aksënenko, Nikolai 81, 266–7
Akunin, Boris (Grigory Chkhartishvili) 191
Alekperov, Vagit 41, 58, 60, 82, 340
Aleksanyan, Vasily 235–7
Aleshina, Irina 186 n. 150
Alexeeva, Ludmila 262
Al'fa Bank 44 n. 66, 48–9, 56, 60, 125 n. 82
ALM Feldmans 232, 233
aluminium industry 61, 82, 85, 94
American Depository Receipt (ADR) 69
Amnesty International 216–17, 256
Amoco 61–2
Amsterdam, Robert 15, 221, 309, 310–11
Amsterdam & Peroff 310
Amsterdam District Court 247–8
Angarsk-Daqing pipeline 135, 136–8, 187, 232
Angarsk Petrochemical Company 50
Anisimova, Tatyana 34
Antonova, Galina 116
AO Avisma 37
AOZT Volna 37, 193, 195, 209
Apatit mineral fertilizer company 37–8, 149, 195–6, 208
APCO Worldwide 68, 309–10
Appeal of the Thirteen 53–4

'Appeal to Electors and all Citizens of Russia' (Khodorkovsky) 219
Arkhangelskii, Aleksandr 275 (n. 17)
Artëmev, Roman 309
Artikgaz 50, 66, 134, 243
Artyukhov, Vitalii 172 n. 97
Artyukhova, Olga 192, 269
ASK (public relations company) 150
Åslund, Anders 141, 334, 384
Audit Chamber 85, 338–9
Auty, R. 359
Auzan, Alexander 146
Aven, Pyotr (Petr) 67, 366
Avisma (titanium company) 37, 168, 169–70, 332
Avtovaz 80, 332

Backes, Ernest 169–70
Baev, Pavel 357
Baikal Finance Group (BFG) 44 n. 65, 185, 186
Baker, Peter 117, 121, 147 (n. 170)
Bakhmina, Svetlana 167, 234–5
Balmaceda, Margarita 371
Baltic Pipeline System 245–6
Bank Leu 168, 169–70
Bank Menatep 34, 36, 59, 69, 150, 169–70, 232
Bank of New York (BONY) 51, 165, 169, 256, 306
banking industry 42, 334
   CPSU Central Committee and 35–6
   Menatep 34–40
   and 1998 financial crisis 59
   and oil industry 48–9
   private 33
   and privatization of oil industry 44–5
   semibankirshchina (group of seven bankers) 53–4
   see also *individual banks*
Baran, Zeyno 371–2
Barnes, Andrew 20, 68, 87
Baru, Yevgeny 269
BASF 311

Basic Element (Basel) holding company 325, 341–2
Basmanny Court 62, 158, 189, 207, 260
 convictions 238
 and further charges against Khodorkovsky and Lebedev 250–1
 and Khodorkhovsky's appeal 250-1
 warrant against Nevzlin 192, 204
 warrant against Pichugin 194
 and Yukos 245
Basmanny justice 207, 213, 260
Bastrykin, Alexander 251
Belkovsky, Stanislav 89, 145, 358
 on Khodorkovsky's arrest 158
 on Khodorkovsky's 'The Crisis of Liberalism in Russia' 274–5
 and 'Left Turn 1' 284
 'State and the Oligarchs, The' 75, 89–92, 268 n. 5
 on Yukos case 148
Belykh, Nikita 219 n. 128, 356
Benn, Stanley 11
Berdyaev, Nikolai 17, 370
Berezovsky, Boris 3, 55, 82, 94
 charges of illegal business activity 80–1
 exile 79, 82, 188
 extradition 232 n.
 and Gusinsky 52–3
 Khodorkovsky and 52
 and miners' strikes 57
 and Sibneft 45, 47 n. 80, 58, 83
 and Svyazinvest, sale of 56–7
Berlin, Isaiah 7, 188
Bespalov, Yuri 58
Bessonova, O. E. 29
Biryukov, Yuri 81, 139, 205
Blavatnik, Len 129, 343
Bobkov, Filipp 39 n. 41
Bogdanchikov, Sergei 80, 139, 233, 325
 and Gazprom merger 327
 and Gazpromneft 326
 and Rosneft 58, 327, 331
Bogdanov, Vladimir 44 n. 64, 340
Bond, Peter 169
Bonker, Don 309
Bonner, Elena 262, 321
BONY, *see* Bank of New York
Bortnikov, Alexander 139
Boucher, Richard 217
BP 106, 129, 132, 330: *see also* TNK-BP
Bradley, Bill 124
Bradshaw, Michael 360
Brazauskas, Algirdas 168
Bremmer, Ian 358

Browder, Bill 44 n. 64
Browne, Lord (John Browne, Baron Browne of Madingley) 243
Brudno, Mikhail 69 n. 171 & 172, 168, 192, 238
 extradition 232 n., 256
Brzezinski, Zbigniew xiii
Bugera, Mikhail 149–50
Bukharin, Nikolai 33
Burganov, Ramil 149, 149 n. 5
Burson-Marsteller 308–9
Bush, George W. 4, 131, 154–5, 217, 258
Butler, William 355–6

capitalism 20, 75, 272
 crony 86
 embedded 25, 26, 27, 348–51
 establishment of 3
 robber baron 45–6
 state 163, 334, 344
 varieties of 24–9
Carey, Sarah 68, 175
Carlyle Group 72
Carothers, Thomas 4 n. 8
Caspian Pipeline Consortium 183
Central Bank of Russia (CBR) 174
Centre for Inter-Sectoral Scientific-Technical Programmes (Tsentr mezhotraslevykh nauchno-tekhnicheskikh program) 34
Centre for International Legal Defence (CILD) 255
Cheah, Pheng 394
Chekhov, Anton 108
Chelsea Football Club 93, 127–8
Chemezov, Sergei 332
Cheney, Dick 154, 257–8, 373
Cherkesov, Viktor 178
Chernobyl disaster committee accounts 34–5
Chernomyrdin, Viktor 37, 40, 43
Chernysheva, Natalia 232 n., 238
ChevronTexaco 131–2
Chicherin, Boris 9–10
China 383–4
 and Angarsk-Daqing pipeline 135, 136–8
China National Petroleum Corporation (CNPC) 87, 186–7, 330
Chinese Development Bank 186–7
CHRC (Congressional Human Rights Caucus) 320
Chrétien, Jean 180
Chubais, Anatoly 41, 43, 53, 80, 159, 276, 371
Chun Doo Hwan 344
CILD (Centre for International Legal Defence) 255

citizenship
  active 6–8
  constrained 8–11
civil society
  in 'The Crisis of Liberalism in Russia'
    (Khodorkovsky) 274
  Khodorkovsky on 274, 283, 291
  and political system 365–9
Clarke, Letitia 185
Clearlake 141
Clearstream 169
Cleland, David 97
Clifford Chance law firm 169
Club of Regional Journalists 124
CNPC, *see*, China National Petroleum
  Corporation
Collongues-Popova, Elena 165–6, 167, 168,
  170
Colton, Timothy J. 9
Commercial Innovation Bank for Scientific
  and Technical Progress (AKIB) 34
Communist Party of the Russian Federation
  (CPRF) 8, 10, 113, 288–90
  and Yukos 116–17, 118
Communist Party of the Soviet Union
  (CPSU) 32
  Central Committee and banking
    industry 35–6
  and NTTMs 33
Congressional Human Rights Caucus
  (CHRC) 320
ConocoPhillips 364
Constant, Benjamin 7
constrained citizenship: and
  paternalism 8–11
contracts 20
corporate raiding 343–4, 345
corruption 143
  government action against ('werewolves in
    uniform' campaign) 139–40, 151
Council for Industrial Policy and
  Entrepreneurship 37
Council of National Strategy (Sovet po
  natsional'noi strategii, SNS)
  'The Great Game in Russia' report
    89–90
  'Risks and Threats Facing Russia'
    report 90–1
  'The State and the Oligarchs'
    report 89–92, 268 n. 5
Council on Foreign and Defence Policy
  (SVOP) 371–6
CPRF, *see* Communist Party of the Russian
  Federation

CPSU, *see* Communist Party of the Soviet
  Union
Cranston, Maurice 5
Criminal Procedure Code
  (Ugolovno-protsessual'nyi kodeks,
  UPK) 189–90
'Crisis of Liberalism in Russia, The'
  (Khodorkovsky) 191, 268–77, 298,
  299
crony capitalism 86
Curtis, Stephen 166–7, 174, 175

Dahl, Vladimir 5
D'Aleo, DonnaMarie 65 n. 151
Dart, Kenneth 59–60, 62, 68, 168
Davydov, Oleg 354
Debet 200
Delovaya Rossiya (Business Russia) 76, 159
Delyagin, Mikhail 297
democracy 9
  domain 79
  phoney 52, 111
  Putin and 3, 4
deprivatization 107, 340, 344–8, 361, 377,
  381
  and transnationalization 106
Deripaska, Oleg 82, 93, 94, 177, 324–5, 349:
  see also Basic Element (Basel) holding
  company
Deutsche Bank 311
Development Bank (formerly
  Vneshekonbank) 244
Diskin, Iosif 89
Dobrovolskaya, Elena 70–1
domain democracy 79
Dorenko, Sergei 289
Drel, Anton 207, 220, 232, 268 n. 5
Dresdner Kleinwort Wasserstein 185
Dreyfus, Alfred 394
dual economy 338–40, 382
dual state
  Russia 15–16, 26
  Soviet Union 14
Dubov, Vladimir 34, 38, 86, 113, 192, 201
  accusations against 237
  extradition 232 n.
  flight to Israel 150
Duclert, Vincent 394
Dudley, Robert 343
Dvorkovich, Arkady 323
Dyatlov, Denis 220

East Petroleum case 203–4
East Siberian Oil and Gas Company 50

East Siberian–Pacific Ocean (ESPO)
  pipeline 137, 138
Eastern Oil Company (VNK) 42
ECHR (European Convention on Human
  Rights and Fundamental Freedoms)
  190
economic policy 128–42
  energy strategy 128–9
  merger of Yukos and Sibneft 129–33
  pipelines 133–8
Economides, Michael J. 65 n. 151
economy
  dual economy 338–40, 382
  energy sector and 333–44
  moral 353–6
  1998 financial crash 59, 60, 97
  political 77–8, 344–56
ECtHR, *see* European Court of Human
  Rights
Egishyants, Sergei 297
Eizenstat, Stuart 72
Ekho Moskvy radio station 312
Ekspert (journal) 369–70
Elfimov, Mikhail 239
Ellman, Michael 360
embedded capitalism 25, 26, 27, 348–51
ENEL 244
Energy Charter Treaty 247, 373
energy imperialism 371–6
energy sector
  and economy 333–44
  international cooperation 334–5
  siloviki and 106, 134, 136, 162
  state and 332–3
ENI 243, 244
enlightened despotism 24
Enron 169
equidistance policy (*ravnoudalennost'*) 3,
  78–88
Erhard, Ludwig 322
Erikssen, Hugo 309, 310
espionage cases 259
Etzioni, Amitai 3–4
EU–Russia Centre 318 n. 60
European Convention on Human Rights and
  Fundamental Freedoms (ECHR) 190
European Court of Human Rights
  (ECtHR) 189, 221, 236, 254, 255
European Parliament (EP): report on
  EU–Russian relations 215–16
Evans, Donald 328
extraditions 167, 188, 192, 213 n. 101, 232,
  256
ExxonMobil 131, 132

Fadeev, Valeri 125, 163 (n. 70), 163 (n. 71),
  163 (n. 72), 387 (n. 16)
'family' faction 81, 102, 103
Fargoil 249
Fatherland-All Russia alliance (OVR) 75,
  113
Fatherland (Otechestvo) party 113
Federal Anti-Monopoly Service (FAS) 341
Federal Anti-Narcotics Agency
  (Gosnarkokontrol, FSKN) 178
Federal Penitentiary Service (FSIN) 223, 230
Fëdorov, Boris 38
Fedun, Leonid 337
feudalism 22
Filippenko, Alexander 201
Filippov, Vladimir 126
financial-industrial groups (FIGs) 45, 112
Financial Intelligence Agency (FMS,
  Rosfinmonitoring) 178, 181
Financial Services Authority (FSA) 329
Financial Times 311–12
Finansgroup 345
Finn, Peter 317
Fish, Steven 359
Fishman, Mikhail 235
Fogel'zang, Alexander 32
Foreign Economic Bank
  (Vneshekonbank) 137
Fortescue, Stephen 11, 52
Foundation for the Support of Israeli
  Education 192
Fradkov, Mikhail 138, 162, 181
Fraenkel, Ernst 14
Frank, Sergei 141
freedom xv, 264, 304, 305, 392–6
  active citizenship and liberalism 6–8
  Bush's global freedom agenda 4
  concept of 5–13
  constrained citizenship and
    paternalism 8–11
  debate on 369–70
  Khodorkovsky on 282–3, 284
  liberalism and 27–9
  and moral code 2
  Polanyi on 23, 322
  proizvol (licence) 5, 10, 368, 382
  and property 16–20
  svoboda 5
  volya 5
Fridman, Mikhail 94, 128, 143, 159, 343,
  366
Friedman, Milton 2, 56
Frye, Timothy 94
FSIN (Federal Penitentiary Service) 223, 230

FSKN (Federal Anti-Narcotics Agency, Gosnarkokontrol) 178
fundamental natural resources (FNRs) 360–2
Furman, Dmitry 83

Gaddy, Clifford G. 65, 351–2
Gaidamak, Arkady 307
Gaidar, Yegor 17–18, 26, 38, 277, 377
Gat, Azar 378
GAZ (Gorky Automotive Works) 85
Gazprom 40, 76, 138, 162, 244, 324, 375
  and 1998 financial crisis 60
  and NTV 80, 82
  and Rosneft, merger with 326–9
  and Sibneft 328, 329, 332, 333
  and transnationalism 132–3
  and YNG 185
  Yukos and 134
Gazprom Neft rubric 242, 244, 326, 328, 329
Gel'man, Vladimir 231
General Prosecutor's Office (GPO) 93, 149, 150, 166, 238, 341
  extradition requests 232 n.
  and Ivannikov 205
  and Karfidov 206
  Khodorkovsky on 152, 208, 214
  and Khodorkovsky, further charges against 213, 222, 251
  and Khodorkovsky's trial 189, 207, 252
  and Pichugin 203
  'werewolves in uniform campaign' 139–40, 151
  and Yukos 158, 233, 236
Generalov, Sergei 112
Gerashchenko, Victor 144, 174, 176, 180–1, 241, 257
'Get Out of the Impasse' letter 285–6
Gevorkyan, Natalia 265–8
GKI (Goskomimushchestvo, State Property Commission) 44
Gladkov, Yuri 140
Glasser, Susan 117, 121, 147 (n. 170)
Glaz'ev, Sergei 93, 288
Glebova, I. I. 368
Glencore International 340
Glenny, Misha 170
Global Media 306
Glucksmann, André 320–1
Gnezdilov, Igor 253
Godfrey, David 247, 248
Gofstein, Alexander 167
Gogol, Nikolai 392
Goldman, Marshall I. 31

Gololobov, Dmitry 233, 234, 238
Golos Rossii movement 113
Golubev, Yuri 167
Golubovich, Alexei 34, 110, 165–6, 167, 168, 306
Goorha, Prateek 360–1
Gorbachev, Alexander 232 n.
Gorbachev, Mikhail xii, 330
Gorin, Sergei 196–7, 199
Gorky Automotive Works (GAZ) 85
Goskomimushchestvo (GKI, State Property Commission) 44
Gosnarkokontrol (Federal Anti-Narcotics Agency, FSKN) 178
Gosneft 324
Goyal, Ajay 131, 147, 314–15, 348, 355
GPO, *see* General Prosecutor's Office
Grachev, Ivan 115
Graham, Thomas 55
'Great Game in Russia, The' report 89–90
Grechkov, Vladimir 215
Green, T. H. 7
Greenwood, Maureen 216
Gref, German 106, 114, 326
Grey, Sir Edward 319
Grishankov, Mikhail 116
Gromov, Boris 101
Group Menatep 35, 66, 69, 72, 169, 173, 246
Guardian, The 329
Gudim, Kira 202
Gudkov, Lev 290
Gunvor Energy 140–1
Gunvor Group 245–6
Gunvor International 141
Gupta, Raj Kumar 68, 175
Gurfinkel-Kagalovsky, Natasha 51, 169
Gurova, Tat'yana 163 (n. 70)
Gusinsky, Vladimir 3, 36, 55, 80
  Berezovsky and 52–3
  blackmail allegations against Lesin 83
  exile 79, 188, 189
  extradition 188, 232 n.
  political parties, support for 38 n. 37
  Putin regime, condemnation of 82
  and Svyazinvest, sale of 56–7
  and Yeltsin 100–1
Gustafson, Thane 39
Gutseriev, Mikhail 86–7, 340–2

Hale, Henry E. 112
Hanson, Philip 15, 171 n. 92, 338, 348
Hartman, William 309
Harvey, John xiv

Havel, Vaclav 279, 302
Hay, Jonathan 168
Hayward, Tony 243
Hedlund, Stefan 28
Hellman, Joel 62, 362
Hermitage Capital 44 n. 64
High Temperatures Institute, Academy of
Sciences 33
Housing Reform Fund 246
Hu Jintao 135
Hulley Enterprise Ltd 169
Human Rights Watch 256

IAIR (Institute for Applied International
Relations) 125
Il'in, Ivan 369
Illarionov, Andrei 106, 151, 187, 217, 335,
359
Imperial Oil 342–3
Inkombank 44 n. 66, 59
Inozemtsev, Vladislav 296–7
Institute for Applied International Relations
(IAIR) 125
Institute for Democracy and
Cooperation 318
Institute for European Democracy 318
institutional nihilism 26–7
International Federation of Human
Rights 256
International Protection Centre,
Moscow 189, 254–5
internationalization 383
Iraq war (2003) 121–2
Iraqi oil for food abuse 141
ISC Global 166, 175
Islamova, Fatima 239
Ivanenko, Victor 39
Ivannikov, Alexander 204–6
Ivanov, Anton 344
Ivanov, Sergei 371
Ivanov, Viktor 91, 10, 106, 139, 328, 384
Ivlev, Pavel 232, 233, 239, 249
Izvestiya 82

Jack, Andrew 114–15, 141, 260
Jackson, Bruce 154, 258, 319–20
Japan 25
and Nakhodka pipeline 135, 136, 138, 187
Jefferson, Thomas 10
Jones, A. Elizabeth 309

Kagalovsky, Konstantin 38, 50–1, 116
Kagarlitsky, Boris 116–17
Kalinin, Yuri 229, 269

Kalyuzhny, Victor 61
Kamov 332
Kamyshev, Dmitry 145 (n. 162)
Kantor, Maksim 395
Kantor, Vyacheslav 176–7
Kapustin, Boris 8, 28
Karadzhich, Nikolai 186 n. 150
Karamanov, Alexei 59
Karasëv, Vladimir 127
Karfidov, Sergei 206
Karimov, Salavat K. 106, 158, 205, 236, 250
Kashaev, Kamil' 202
Kasparov, Garry 252
Kasyanov, Mikhail 103, 134–5, 136, 149,
219, 372
on arrests 151, 162
dismissal of 162
and oil industry 137
political ambitions 221
reaction to Khodorkovsky's arrest 159
response to Lebedev's arrest 155
and Slavneft boardroom coup 86–7
Kazakov, Viktor 117
Kertész, Imre 231, 264
Ketchum public relations firm 317
KGB 39, 228
Khakamada, Irina 164, 192, 269
Khan, German 343
Khlebnikov, Pavel (Paul Klebnikov) 54, 71,
165, 167, 354
murder of 202 n. 56, 349
Khloponin, Alexander 113
Khodorkovskaya, Inna 71, 226–7
Khodorkovskaya, Marina Filippovna 31,
254
Khodorkovsky, Boris Moiseevich 31
Khodorkovsky, Mikhail xii, 1, 11, 36, 67, 111
and America 152–4, 156
and Appeal of the Thirteen 53–4
'Appeal to Electors and all Citizens of
Russia' 219
arrest 93, 103, 157–8
arrest: political fallout from 161–4
arrest: reactions to 158–61
arrests: response to 151–7
background 31–2, 35, 70–1
and Berezovsky 52
and Carlyle Group 72
charges against 193, 194
and Chernomyrdin 43
on civil society 274, 283, 291
consulting services 208–9
corruption speech 143
court action against *Novaya gazeta* 62

'Crisis of Liberalism in Russia, The' 191,
    268–77, 298, 299
critique of liberalism 298–300
and exile 156, 188–9
on factionalism 103
final statement (at end of trial) 209–10
Financial Times article 311–12
and foreign policy 121–2
on freedom 6–7, 282–3, 284
further charges against 212–13, 222,
    249–54
Gaidar and 38
Gevorkyan interview 265–8
on government/administrative reform 118
influence of 114–15, 116
and Iraq war (2003) 121
Kuchma and 228–9
and Lebedev case 93
'Left Turn 1' 284–90,
    298
'Left Turn 2' 293–6
letters from prison 11, 19, 60, 264–5,
    299–303, 311–12: see also *individual
    letters*
on lobbying 156, 306
Medvedev on 385–6
and Menatep 34–7, 42
Newsweek interview 280–2
and NTTMs 33–4
and offshore companies 169
open letter in support of 262
Open Russia Foundation 123–5
in penal colony 222–30
personal wealth 71
philanthropic work 123–8
and politics 3, 54–5, 77, 113, 115–18
Politique Internationale interview 291–3
pre-trial detention 189–92
and Primakov 52, 61
'Prison and the World: Property and
    Freedom' 278–84, 298
on privatization 287, 295
on property 19
and public opinion 312–14
and Putin 80, 142–7, 290–1, 385
and Rand US–Russia Business Leader
    Forum 72, 158–9
and religion 303
and reorganization of power 118–21
in 'Risks and Threats Facing Russia'
    report 90–1
on Rosprom 49
on Sechin 218
sentence 212, 213–214

Spiegel, Der interview 120
and SPS 116, 219
trial 206–22
trial: appeals 218–22, 254–6
trial verdict 210–12
trial verdict: appeal against 250-1
trial verdict: reactions to 213–18
and United Russia 117
and US–Russia Business Council 72
World in 2020, The 295, 296–7
and Yabloko 113, 116, 219
and Yeltsin's 1996 election campaign 53
and Yukos 44–5, 60, 63, 69
Khodorkovsky Foundation 124
Khomyakov, Alexei 12
Khristenko, Viktor 187
Kimmage, Daniel 75, 146
Kinex 140
King, William 97
Kinsbourg, Roger 167
Kirienko, Sergei 57
Kiselëv, Yevgeny 307
Kissinger, Henry 124
Klimovskaya, Maria 186
Klyamkin, Igor' 109
Knoops, Geert-Jan Alexander 15
Kokh, Alfred 44
Kokoshin, Andrei 376
Kolesnikov, Andrei 380–1
Kolesnikov, Ivan 213 n. 101, 232
Kolesnikov, Vladimir 213, 233
Kolesnikova, Irina 208, 210–11, 214
Kolesov, Victor 198
Komarov, Yevgeny 208
Komarova, Valentina 186
Komsomol'skaya pravda (newspaper) 194
    n. 30
Konanykhin, A. 36 n. 24
Kondaurov, Alexei 39, 116, 118, 306
Konobievsky, Alexander 185
Konończuk, Wojciech 86, 108
Korneev, Dmitry 198, 199
Korneeva, Valentina 198–9
Korovnikov, Igor 196
Korzhakov, Aleksandr 306
Kosciusko-Morizet, Jacques 68, 175
Kostina, Olga 110, 196
Kostromina, Kseniya 202, 204, 221
Kovalëv, Sergei 228
Kozak, Dmitry 118, 176
Krainov, Andrei 193, 209, 212
Krasnokamensk 223–6
Kraus, Eric 157, 172, 317
Kraus, Margery 68

Krause, Charles 309
Kruchina, N. 35 n. 23
Kuchma, Alexander 228
Kudeshkina, Olga 206 n. 71, 261
Kudrin, Alexei 98, 104, 106, 155–6, 173, 182, 337, 348
Kuibyshevnefteorgsintez 42
Kukes, Simon 173, 175
Kulikov, Anatoly 61
Kurtsin, Alexei 235, 238
Kvachkov, Vladimir 191
Kvaerner 64, 66
Kvitsinsky, Yuly 118

Laguna company 44
Lantos, Tom 154, 217, 320
Latin America 377–8
Latynina, Yulia 22, 110, 190–1, 340
Lavelle, Peter 324, 345
Lavrov, Sergei 376
Lay, Kenneth 169
Lazard Frères bank 42
Lebedev, Platon 35, 36
    arrest of 93, 149, 151
    charges against 150, 193
    and ECtHR 255
    further charges against 212–13, 249–54
    'oligarchs', first reference to 38
    sentence 212
    treatment of in custody 208
    trial: procedural violations 256
Ledeneva, Alena V. 100
Lefortovo prison 194
'Left Turn 1' (Khodorkovsky) 284–90, 298
    authorship of 284
    reactions to 288–9
'Left Turn 2' (Khodorkovsky) 293–6
legal nihilism 12, 253, 263
legal system 257–62
    international reactions to 257–9, 260
    pressure to achieve convictions 261
Leonid Nevzlin Centre for the Study of Russian and East European Judaism, Hebrew University, Jerusalem 192
Lesin, Mikhail 83, 184
Lesnoi (Mitra) case 204–6
Leutheusser-Schnarrenberger, Sabine 183, 194, 216
    report on Yukos case 258–9
Levina, Yelena 220
Levine, Peter 342–3
liberalism 26
    active citizenship and 6–8
    anti-liberalism 25

and freedom 27–9
    Khodorkovsky's critique of 298–300
    and *sobornost* 11–12
Ligachev, Yegor 33
Limarev, Yevgeny 167, 168
Literaturnaya gazeta 307
Litvinenko, Alexander 166, 167
Litvinenko, Vladimir 97
Lloyd, John 38
loans-for-shares auctions 44-5, 90, 93, 339: *see also* shares-for-loans schemes
lobbying 61, 80, 86, 113, 178
    Khodorkovsky on 156, 306
Logovaz 60
Logovaz-United Bank 45
Lopukhin, Vladimir 42
Loshak, Viktor 307
Lotman, Yuri 12
Loze, Bernard 68
Lukoil 41–2
    establishment of 39
    and 1998 financial crisis 60
    privatization of 41, 43, 44
    and United Russia 117
    and Yukos, relationship with 65
Luong, Pauline Jones 364
Luzhkov, Yuri 60–1
Lynch, Patrick 248
Lysova, Tat'yana 268 n. 5

McFaul, Michael 335
Mach, Joe 63–4
Makarenko, Boris 76
Makarkin, Aleksei 379
Malakhovsky, Vladimir 238, 249 n. 70
Mandela, Nelson 13
Mann, Michael 3
Markov, Sergei 315
Maruev, Dmitry 232 n., 238
mass media 76, 79
    and propaganda 304, 305–8
    see also *individual journals, newspapers, radio stations, etc.*
Matrosskaya Tishina detention centre 189, 194, 218
Mavrodi, Sergei 35
Mazeikiu Nafta refinery 66, 243, 248
Mazeikiu scandal 167, 168
MDM 61
Media-Most group 38 n. 37, 80, 82
Medvedev, Dmitry 104, 155, 156, 162, 176, 326
    on Khodorkovsky 159, 385–6
    and legal nihilism 263

on legal system 253–4
on state capitalism 163
on state ownership/management 350–1
Melia, Thomas O. 320
Melikov, Alexander 261
Menatep (Mezhotraslevye i
    nauchno-tekhnicheskie programmy)
    advertising 305–6
    AOZT Volna subsidiary 37
    and Avisma 168, 169–70
    and banking industry 34–40
    and BONY 169, 306
    creditors 59
    and KGB 39
    Khodorkovsky and 34–7, 42
    and media 306–7
    and 1998 financial crisis 60
    Surkov on 38, 96–7
    and Yukos 44, 46–7, 49
Menatep Group 243
Menatep-Moscow 59
Menatep SA (later Group Menatep Ltd, then
    GML) 35, 165
Menatep-St Petersburg 59
Merkel, Angela 254
meta-corruption 112, 260, 351–3, 395
Miller, Alexei 104, 134, 326, 346
Milov, Vladimir 336–7, 374
miners' strikes 57
Minibaev, Igor 186
Miłosz, Czesław 380
Misamore, Bruce K. 69, 174, 176, 247, 248
Mitra case 204–6
Mitrokhin, Sergei 288, 298
Mitrova, Tatiana 326
Mitvol, Oleg 172 n. 97
M*m*d public relations consultants 310
Mogilevich, Semën (Semyon) 51, 170
Monaghan, Andrew 375
Monakhov, Sergei 33
Monblan 46–7, 50
money laundering 3, 51, 256
Monte-Valley 248
moral economy 353–6
Moravel 243, 248
Moscow Times, The 217, 307
Moskalenko, Karinna 189, 254, 255, 262–3,
    269
Most Group 39 n. 41, 60
Muravlenko, Sergei 42, 116, 118, 201
murders 93, 149
    accusations against Yukos 194–5
    Gorins 196–7
    Khlebnikov 202 n. 56, 349

Kostina 196
Petukhov 199–200, 202–3
Myasnikova, Lyubov 206

Nadezhdin, Boris 367
Nakhodka pipeline 135, 136, 138, 187
Narodnaya Volya (People's Will) 5
Naryshkin, Sergei 316, 331
national champions 323–33: *see also*
    Gazprom; Rosneft; Transneft
National Energy Policy (NEP) Development
    Group 376–7
National Information Centre 318
National Security Strategy, USA 4
National Strategy Institute (Institut
    Natsional'noi Strategii, INS) 284
NATO 319
Neft Aktiv 243
Nefteyugansk Solidarity 201
Neklessa, Aleksandr 4 (n. 8), 297
Némirovsky, Irène 357
Nemtsov, Boris 51, 84, 276, 369
neo-patrimonialism 272
Nevzlin, Leonid 33–4, 53–4, 119, 120, 210
    case against 202, 204
    charges against 192
    extradition 192, 232 n.
    and Khodorkovsky 38, 53–4
    and Kostina 110
    on Kuchma's attack on Khodorkovsky
        229
    and Lebedev case 93
    and Litvinenko 166
    and mass media propaganda 306
    and murders 149
    on 19 February 2003 meeting 144
    as rector of Russian State Humanities
        University (RGGU) 126
    and Rybin, assassination attempts
        on 203–4
    and TASS 307
    threat to remove Yeltsin from power 57
    trial *in absentia* 239
    on Yukos-Sibneft merger 130
Newlyn, Victoria 258
Newsweek 280–2
Nezavisimaya gazeta 54
Nicholas I, tsar 318–19
nihilism
    institutional 26–7
    legal 12, 253, 263
Nikitin, Alexander 220–1
Nikitin, Gleb 331
Norilsk Nickel 44, 45, 80, 94, 309

North Stream (North European Gas Pipeline) 133, 321, 327, 376
Novaya gazeta 62
Novodvorskaya, Valeriya 276–7
Noyabrskneftegaz 47 n. 80
NTTMs (Tsentry nauchno-tekhicheskogo tvorchestva molodezhi) 33–4, 35
NTV 80, 82, 83
Nukhaev, Khozh-Akhmed 202 n. 56

O'Brien, Peter 329, 330
OECD 218
Oganesyan, Sergei 162
oil industry 40–2
    American markets 133, 138
    banking industry and 48–9
    budget revenues 182
    mergers 57–8
    privatization of 43–5, 62
    Saudi Arabia 40
    Soviet Union 30, 40
oligarchs 101
    Appeal of the Thirteen 53–4
    attacks on 92–4, 148
    beginnings in politics 52–6
    campaign against 85, 93–4
    feuding amongst 57
    first reference to 38
    and lobbying 80, 113
    and politics 75–8, 113
    and state 78–88
    types of 31
    and Yeltsin's re-election 53–4, 55
    see also *individual oligarchs*
Olikhver, Natalya 261
Olson, Mancur 19
OMZ 332
Onako 324
Oneksimbank 48–9, 59
OPEC (Organisation of Petroleum Exporting Countries) 70
'Open Letter to the Heads of State and Government of the European Union and NATO' 164
Open Russia Foundation 7, 123–5, 127, 245
OPOR (Ob 'edinenie predprinimatel' skikh obshchestv Rossii, United Entrepreneurial Societies of Russia) 76, 159
orangism 315–16
Oreshkina, Judge Irina 237
ORT (Russian Public Television) 307
Osborne, Timothy 242–3
Osovtsov, Alexander 116

OVR (Fatherland-All Russia alliance) 75, 113
Ovsyannikov, Mikhail 199
Owen, David (Lord Owen) 68, 175–6

PACE 258–9
Padva, Genrikh 208, 209, 220, 269
Pamfilova, Ella 237, 257
Panyushkin, Valerii xvi–xvii , 367
Park Chung Hee 349
Parliamentary Assembly of the Council of Europe (PACE) 255
Pashin, Sergei 259–60
Pastukhov, Vladimir 257, 367–8
paternalism: constrained citizenship and 8–11
patrimonialism 18–19
Patrushev, Nikolai 106, 384
Pavlovsky, Gleb 32, 88, 102–3, 151
PDVSA 377
People's Democratic Union 301
Peregudov, Sergei 346–7, 365–6
Perekrest, Vladimir 199 n. 42
perestroika (restructuring) xii
Pereverzin, Vladimir 238
Peshkun, Alexei 197, 198
petro-states 363–4
Petronas 330
Petukhov, Vladimir 199–203
    murder of 199–200, 202–3
phoney democracy 52, 111
Pichugin, Alexei 93, 149, 207–8, 251–2
    case against 193–4, 197–8, 202, 203–4
    trial of 261
Piontovsky, Andrei 109
Piotrovsky, Mikhail 124
pipelines
    Angarsk–Daqing 135, 136–8, 187, 232
    Nakhodka 135, 136, 138, 187
    North Stream 133, 321, 327, 376
    South Stream 376
Pipes, Richard 18–19
Pitertsy 103, 104–5
Pivovarov, Yuri 19
PKN Orlen 243, 248
pluralism 77–8
Polanyi, Karl 17, 21, 22, 23, 270, 322, 353–4
political economy
    models of 77–8
    new model of 344–56
political factions
    'family' 81, 102, 103
    old Muscovites 103, 104, 106
    Pitertsy 103, 104–5

'politburo' 106, 107, 139–40, 162, 176, 177
politicized financial-industrial groups (PFIGs) 112: *see also* Menatep-Yukos
Politique Internationale 291–3
Politkovskaya, Anna 229
Ponamarev, Lev 262
Potanin, Vladimir 43, 45, 55, 93, 161, 366
Biryukov's accusations against 81
and Guggenheim Museum, New York 128
and media 82
and Svyazinvest 56
Prana 244
Priargun Mining and Chemical Complex 224
PricewaterhouseCoopers (PwC) 69, 183–4
Prikhodko, Sergei 346
Primakov, Yevgeny 52, 61, 81, 139
'Prison and the World: Property and Freedom' (Khodorkovsky) 278–84, 298
prison system
conditional early release/parole 252–3
investigative prisons (SIZOs) 189, 197, 218, 249
Krasnokamensk 223–6
Lefortovo prison 194
Matrosskaya Tishina detention centre 189, 194, 218
prison life 226–30
red/black prisons 225
Privalov, Aleksandr 163 (n. 70)
privatization 84–5, 149
Audit Chamber review 338–9
black 31, 387, 390
Khodorkovsky on 287, 295
nomenklatura 41
of oil industry 43–5, 62
of Rosneft 57–8
of Sibneft 44, 49, 58
voucher privatization 35, 43
Procaccia, Uriel 19–20
production-sharing agreements, *see* PSAs
proizvol (freedom/licence) 5, 10, 368, 382
Project for a New American Century 319
Project on Transitional Democracies 319
Prokhanov, Aleksandr 74
Prokhorov, A. P. 349–50
Promneftstroi 248
Promradtekhbank 39
propaganda: mass media and 304, 305–8
property
cultural revolution of 20–4
freedom and 16–20
Prusak, Mikhail 195

PSAs (production-sharing agreements) system 95, 114, 122, 174, 178, 334, 339–40
Pugachëv, Sergei 102
Putin, Vladimir xiii, 11, 139, 164, 246, 322
anti-oligarch campaign 85, 101
and Bush 155
on corruption 353
and democracy 3, 4
doctoral dissertation 97
on economic crime 150
on economic development 97–8
equidistance policy 3, 78–88
Federal Assembly address (25 April 2005) 10
fiscal plans 88
and food for oil scandal 140
on freedom and communism 10
on Gazprom 375
Izvestiya interview (14 July 2000) 83–4
and Khodorkovsky 80, 142–7, 385
Khodorkovsky's criticism of 290–1
meetings with business leaders 84–5, 142–4
and oligarchs 78–9, 353
and ownership 20
and reorganization of power 119–20
'Russia at the Turn of the Millennium' open letter 10
security agencies, reorganization of 178
social contract 79, 85, 92, 93, 100
and state reconstitution 354–5
statism of 74
on Yeltsin 30
on Yukos affair 146, 160
PwC (PricewaterhouseCoopers) 69, 183–4

Rabinovich, Vadim 307
Rand US–Russia Business Leader Forum 72, 158–9
RAO UES (Russian Stock Company United Energy Systems, Edinye Energosistemy), *see* UES
Rasnovsky, Andrei 207
Ratibor 238, 249
Razumovsky, Vadim 125
Reaktsiya (film) 215
Rebgun, Eduard 242–3, 247
Rekosh, Edwin 257
Reshetnikov, Yevgeny 198, 199, 202, 204
resource nationalism 376–9
Reznik, Genri 192
RGGU (Russian State Humanities University) 126–7

Rheinstein, Max 14
RIA Novosti information agency 317
Rice, Condoleezza 154, 376
Rich, Marc 36, 340–1
'Risks and Threats Facing Russia' report 90–1
RN-Razvitie 244
robber-baron capitalism 54–6
Rodina party 93, 270, 288–9, 300
Rogozin, Dmitry 270, 288–9
Roi, Sergei 307
Roland, Gérard 323
Rosfinmonitoring (FMS, Financial
    Intelligence Agency) 178, 181
Rosneft (formerly Rosneftegaz) 41, 42, 44
    n. 65, 76, 80, 142–4, 245, 324, 325–9
  acquisitions 50, 325
  and Baikal group 186
  BP and 330
  in Chechnya 331–2
  and China 137, 325
  flotation of 329–32
  merger with Gazprom 326–9
  Mmd public relations consultants and 310
  privatization of 57–8
  sale of 56, 58
  and Severnaya Neft 50, 142, 143
  and YNG 186–7, 240–1, 325, 327, 335
  and Yukos 139, 240–4, 248
Rosneftegaz (later Rosneft) 41
Rospan 50, 66, 70
Rosprom 37, 39, 45, 49
Ross, Michael 358
Rossiiskii Kredit 44 n. 66
Rosugol' 41
Rosvooruzhenie (arms export monopoly)
    36
Rubinsky, Yury 305
RUIE (Russian Union of Industrialists and
    Entrepreneurs) 76, 85, 87, 102, 149, 159
Russia
  as dual state 15–16, 26
  as energy superpower 370–9, 383
  financial crisis (1998) 59–61
  image 314–21
  inequality in 3
  as petro-state 363–4
'Russia at the Turn of the Millennium' open
    letter (Putin) 10
Russian Aluminium (Rusal) 61, 85
Russian Nanotechnology Corporation 246
Russian Orthodoxy 12
Russian State Humanities University
    (RGGU) 126–7

Russian Union of Industrialists and
    Entrepreneurs, *see* RUIE
Russian Working Group 320
Russia's Choice party 38
Russkie Investory (Russian Investors) 167
Russkii Mir foundation 317–18
Russneft 340–2
Rutland, Peter 77, 92, 369, 371, 372, 374
Ryabov, Andrei 344, 366–7
Ryazanov, Alexander 141, 328
Rybin, Yevgeny 203–4, 239
Rybkin, Ivan 141, 269
Ryzhkov, Vladimir 163, 276

Sagers, Matthew J. 336
Sakhalinmorneftegaz 325
Sakhaneftegaz 50, 174
Sal'e, Marina 140
Samaraneftegaz (SNG) 42, 47, 48, 49, 51,
    243
Satter, David 55
Savelova, Natal'ya 297
Sberbank 330
SBS (Stolichnyi Bank Sberezhenii) 45, 48–9
SBS-Agro 59
Scaramello, Mario 167
Schlumberger 64–5
Schmidt, Yuri 220–1, 249, 254
Schneider, Eberhard 92 n. 56
Schroeder, Gerhard 310, 311, 327
SCO (Shanghai Co-operation
    Organisation) 383
Sechin, Igor 91, 97, 104, 149, 177, 187, 384
  biographical details 105–6
  and Khodorkovsky 158, 162
  and Rosneft 139, 327–8, 330–1
semibankirshchina (group of seven
    bankers) 53–4
Serdyukov, Anatoly 181
Severnaya Neft 50, 142, 143
Shafranik, Yuri 37, 41
Shakespeare, William 304
Shakhnovsky, Vasily 116, 150, 176, 238
Shanghai Co-operation Organisation
    (SCO) 383
Shapiro, Vladimir 198, 199
shares-for-loans schemes 55, 56, 94: *see also*
    loans-for-shares auctions
Shatalov, Sergei 180
Shaxson, Nicholas 359
Shchedrov, Petr 192
Shell 332, 339
Shemkevich, Sergei 239

Shevtsova, Liliya 96, 121, 335
Shiryaev, Valerii G. 197
Shokhin, Alexander 161, 208
Shokhin, Dmitry 206
Shuman, S. I. 14
Shuvalov, Igor 180, 351
Shvartsman, Oleg 345
Sibneft 3, 42, 50
  Berezovsky and 45, 47 n. 80, 58, 83
  charges against 150
  and Gazprom 328, 329, 332, 333
  privatization of 44, 49, 58
  in 'Risks and Threats Facing Russia'
    report 90–1
  and Slavneft 86–7
  tax demands 182–3
  tax minimization schemes 179
  TNK and 87
  transformation of 67
  and Yukos 58, 70, 93, 106, 129–33, 173
Sidanko oil company 39, 42, 44
Silaev, Ivan 36
silovarchs 349
siloviki 75, 102, 104–5
  and energy sector 106, 134, 136, 162
  and Gazprom 328
  'The State and the Oligarchs' report 75
  and state interventionism 338
  and Timchenko 140
  and Yukos 176, 386
Simonov, Konstantin 49, 103, 373, 384
SIZOs (investigative prisons) 189, 197, 218,
  249
Skarga, Dmitry 141, 177–8
Skuratov, Yuri 81
Slavneft 50, 86–7, 324
Smiley, Jane 392 (n. 26)
Smith, Adam 355
Smith, Gordon 14
Smolensky, Alexander 43, 366
SNG, *see* Samaraneftegaz
SNS, *see* Council of National Strategy
sobornost (spiritual communion): liberalism
  and 11–12
Solzhenitsyn, Alexander 10, 355
Sonin, Konstantin 163–4
Soros, George 52, 125, 267, 329–30, 344
Soskovets, Oleg 43
Soublin, Michel 68
South Stream 376
Sovet po natsional'noi strategii (SNS), *see*
  Council of National Strategy
Sovkomflot 177–8

Spiegel, Der 120
SPS (Union of Right Forces) 113, 116, 219
Stanford Law Review 48
Starikov, Ivan 219
'State and the Oligarchs, The' (Belkovsky) 75,
  89–92, 268 n. 5
state capitalism 163, 334, 344
State Committee for Science and
  Technology 34
state power
  inertia scenario 387, 389
  mobilization model 387, 388
  modernization model 387, 389–92
  rentier model 387–8
State Property Commission
  (Goskomimushchestvo, GKI) 44
statism 74, 96–9, 274, 324
Stiglitz, Joseph E. 21
Stolichnyi Bank Sberezhenii (SBS) 45, 48–9
Stoner-Weiss, Kathryn 335
Strebel, André 169–70
Streeck, Wolfgang 25 (n. 94), 26, 27
Stringer journal and website 111, 116
Sukhanov, Yuri 86–7, 340
Surgutneftegaz 39, 41, 43, 44, 140, 174,
  185–6, 201
Surkov, Vladislav 34, 36, 78, 103–4, 112,
  299–300, 383
  on corporate raiding 343–4
  and embedded capitalism 350
  on freedom 1, 305
  and mass media propaganda 306
  on Menatep 38, 96–7
  and Yukos 161, 176
Svetlichnaya, Yulia 166, 167
svoboda (freedom) 5
SVOP (Council on Foreign and Defence
  Policy) 371–6
Svyazinvest 44, 56–7
Swiss bank accounts 246–7
Swiss Federal Tribunal 251, 255

Takeda, Yoshinori 334 (n. 51)
Taraktelyuk, Valentin 198
Taratukhin, Father Sergei 227–8
TASS news agency 307
taxation
  offshore accounts 165, 168–70, 179, 195
  shell companies 50, 59, 70, 150, 165, 169,
    175, 195
  tax minimization 91, 150, 164, 178–9
  Yukos and 114–15, 150, 164–5, 171, 175,
    177, 178–84

Teague, Elizabeth 348
Temerko, Alexander 129, 170, 186 n. 150,
  213, 244, 342
  and Daqing pipeline 232
  extradition 192, 232
  fraud charges 232–3
  on PcW 183
  and Yukos-Moskva 233
Texaco 240
Theede, Steven 174, 182, 236, 241–2
Timchenko, Gennady 139, 140–1, 185–6,
  245–6
Timofeev, Lev 109
TMC Trading International 168–9, 170
TNK (Tyumen Oil Company) 42, 50, 56
  and BP 106, 129, 132
  and Sibneft 87
  and United Russia 117
  and Yukos 70
TNK-BP 243, 332, 334–5, 343
  and tax 179, 182–3
Tokareva, Elena 111, 125 n. 80, 308
Tokobank 42
Tompson, William 99, 359–60, 361
Tomskneft 48, 49, 60 n. 130, 69–70, 234, 243,
  244
Topolánek, Mirek 148
Trade-Industrial Council
  (Torgovo-promyshlennaya plata, TPP)
  76
transnationalism 132–3
transnationalization 95, 106, 375, 383
Transneft 41, 134, 138, 372
Transneftprodukt 41
Transparency International: Corruption
  Perception Index 258
Transpetrol 66, 248
Treisman, Daniel 349
Tret'yakov, Vitaly 307
Trushin, Mikhail 239
Tsigel'nik, Gennady 198, 199, 202
Tsimbursky, Vadim 297
Tymoshenko, Yulia 374
Tyumen Oil Company, *see* TNK

UBS (Swiss bank) 169
UES (United Energy Systems) 41, 85,
  162
Union of Right Forces, *see* SPS
Union of Social Justice 345
United Civic Front 252
United Nations (UN): Paul Volcker
  committee 141

United Russia (UR) party 113, 117,
  289, 324
Unity party 113
UPK (Ugolovno-protsessual'nyi kodeks,
  Criminal Procedure Code)
  189–90
Urengoil 50, 134, 243
US–Russia Business Council 72
Usmanov, Alisher 128 n. 89
Ustinov, Vladimir 106, 139, 158, 196, 384

Vainshtok, Semën 136
Valdai Discussion Club 317
Valdes Garcia, Antonio 249 n. 70
Valmet Group 169
Vasilyev, Sergei 56 n. 117
Vavilov, Andrei 142
Vedemosti 307, 389
Vekselberg, Viktor 128, 161, 343
Velichko, Dmitry 239
Vershbow, Alexander 257
Vickers, Sally xvi
Vimpelcom 183
Vishnyakova, Natalia 213 n. 101
Vneshekonbank (Foreign Economic
  Bank) 137
VNK 50, 57, 69–70, 149 n. 5
Volkov, Vadim 75, 96, 103, 343
Volna, *see* AOZT Volna
Voloshin, Alexander 103–4, 121, 155, 159,
  161–2
Vol'sky, Arkady 85, 102, 152, 159, 161
volya (freedom/will) 5
Volzhsky Pipe Factory 37, 38
voucher privatization 35, 43
Vragova, Svetlana 199 n. 42
Vserossiiskii Birzhevoi Bank 36 n. 24
VSMPO-Avisma 332
Vyakhirev, Rem 40–1, 60, 80
Vybornova, Elena 256

Warnig, Matthias 328–9
Way, Lucan 75
Weinthal, Erika 364
Williams International 168
Wilson, Andrew 92
Wolcott, Don 63–4
Wolf, Eric 239
Woodruff, David 22, 308
Workman, Judge Timothy 232
World Economic Forum (Davos, 1996) 52
World in 2020, The (ed. Khodorkovsky) 295,
  296–7

Yabloko party 38 n. 37, 113, 116, 118, 150,
    219
Yagodin, Gennady 32
Yakovlev, Alexander 28, 126
Yakovlev, Andrei 351
Yakunin, Vladimir 104
Yasin, Yevgeny 146, 276
Yasina, Irina 124
Yastrzhembsky, Sergei 304
Yavlinsky, Grigory 38 n. 37, 113, 116, 353
Yegorova, Olga 261
Yeltsin, Boris 10, 36 n. 24, 285–6
    and Gusinsky 100–1
    and *lichnaya predannost'* (personal
        loyalty) 75
    and oligarchs 53–4, 55, 75, 101
    Putin's assessment of 30
    re-election 53–4, 55
Yeniseinefgaz 50
Yudin, Vladimir 148, 173 n. 102, 196
Yuganskneftegaz (YNG) 42, 44 n. 65, 49,
    201
    and Gazprom 185
    Rosneft and 186–7, 240–1, 325, 327, 335
    sale of 171, 173, 184–7
    tax claims against 186
    Yukos and 47, 48, 51, 173, 335
Yukos 39
    and American Depository Receipt
        (ADR) 69
    assets 239–40
    attack on 170–87
    bankruptcy 185, 240–4, 247
    capitalization *172*
    consolidation of 45–62
    and CPRF 116–17, 118
    creditors 242, 243
    development of 2
    and Duma 114
    and electricity generating business 66
    establishment of 42
    and gas sector 66
    and Gazprom 134
    GPO and 158
    growth of *50*
    influence on legislation 61, 114–15, 178
    Khodorkovsky and 63, 69
    and Kvaerner 66
    and Lukoil 65
    Menatep and 44, 46–7, 49
    Netherlands assets 247–8
    oil production/output 63, 64–5, *64*, 66
    and Open Russia Foundation 123–5
    as para-state 108–12

partners 39
and Petukhov 200
philanthropic work 123–8
politburo ranged against/anti-Yukos
    coalition 139–40
post-Khodorkovsky 171–8
privatization of 43, 44
profits 66
public relations 308–11
in 'Risks and Threats Facing Russia'
    report 90–1
and Rosneft 139, 240–4, 248
security service 110
share price 171
shareholders' lawsuit against
    government 247
and Sibneft 58, 70, 93, 106, 129–33, 173
siloviki and 176, 386
and SNG 51
and subsidiaries 47–9
and taxes 114–15, 150, 164–5, 171, 175,
    177, 178–84
and TNK 70
transfer pricing 47
transformation of 62–73
and transnationalism 132
and United Russia 117
and VNK 57
and YNG 47, 48, 51, 173, 335
Yukos affair 95–107
    dualism of 16
    economic consequences of 334–8
    factional theory 101–7
    influence on politics 2
    Leutheusser-Schnarrenberger report
        on 258–9
    political consequences 358–70
    political theory 99–101
    Putin on 146, 160
    and state power 387–92
    statism, ideology of 96–9
Yukos-EP 46, 68
Yukos Finance BV 247–8
Yukos International Ltd 168, 243, 248
Yukos-Menatep 169
Yukos-Moskva 46, 49, 68, 174, 233
Yukos-RM 46, 68
Yukos Universal 169
Yuksi 58
Yurgens, Igor 159, 289, 387 (n. 17)
Yuri Levada Analytical Centre poll 215
Yusufov, Igor 129, 162

Zagorsky, Andrei 125

Zainullin, Rafail 231–2
Zakaev, Akhmed 232 n.
Zakaria, Fareed 378
Zakharov, Anton 239
Zaostrovtsev, Yuri 106
Zhidkov, Mikhail 221
Zhilsotsbank 34

Zhukov, Alexander 114
Zolotarëv, Boris 113
Zor'kin, Valeri 28, 260
Zubkov, Viktor 178, 181
Zudin, Aleksei Yu. 76, 95 n. 61
Zweynart, Joachim 17, 27 n. 102
Zyuganov, Gennady 53, 117, 267, 285